D1605451

THE ECONOMICS AND ECONOMETRICS OF INNOVATION

The Economics and Econometrics of Innovation

by

David Encaoua

EUREQua,
Université de Paris I, Panthéon-Sorbonne,
France and CNRS

Bronwyn H. Hall

Nuffield College,
Oxford University, U.K. and
University of California, Berkeley,
U.S.A. and NBER

François Laisney

BETA,
Université Louis Pasteur,
France and
ZEW, University of Mannheim, Germany

and

Jacques Mairesse

CREST, Paris, France
and Ecole des Hautes Etudes en
Sciences Sociales, Paris,
France and NBER

KLUWER ACADEMIC PUBLISHERS
BOSTON / DORDRECHT / LONDON

A C.I.P. Catalogue record for this book is available from the Library of Congress.

ISBN 0-7923-7800-8

Published by Kluwer Academic Publishers,
P.O. Box 17, 3300 AA Dordrecht, The Netherlands.

Sold and distributed in North, Central and South America
by Kluwer Academic Publishers,
101 Philip Drive, Norwell, MA 02061, U.S.A.

In all other countries, sold and distributed
by Kluwer Academic Publishers,
P.O. Box 322, 3300 AH Dordrecht, The Netherlands.

Printed on acid-free paper

Printed in the Netherlands.

Contents

THE ECONOMICS AND ECONOMETRICS OF INNOVATION

Overview

David ENCAOUA, Bronwyn H. HALL, François LAISNEY, and Jacques MAIRESSE*

During the past few decades, the interest of economists in the sources of long run economic growth has led an increasing number to focus their attention on the role of innovation in creating that growth. Although some researchers have always been interested in this topic, in the last few years many others have recognized the central role played by innovation in almost all spheres of economic activity. Taking a somewhat U.S.-centric perspective, one can probably date the origins of the mainstream development of this research agenda from Solow's (1957) «discovery» of the importance of the «residual» in aggregate productivity growth and Nelson's (1959) and Arrow's (1962) influential papers on the economics of knowledge creation.

Of course, economic historians had for a long time been well aware of the importance of technical change in explaining economic development (see Rosenberg (1976), *inter alia*), and to some extent, modern research in this area has been more influenced by a historical and institutional approach than economic research in other areas. This is perhaps inevitable and necessary when dealing with a topic like innovation, so much of which seems to involve historical accidents and behavioral influences other than the purely economic. Nevertheless, the specific contribution that economists have made to the study of

* David ENCAOUA:EUREQUA, Université de Paris-I Panthéon-Sorbonne, and CNRS; Bronwyn HALL: Nuffield College, Oxford University; University of California at Berkeley; and NBER; F. LAISNEY: BETA, Université Louis Pasteur, Strasbourg and ZEW, University of Mannheim; J. MAIRESSE: CREST; Ecole des Hautes Etudes en Sciences Sociales, Paris, and NBER.

D. Encaoua et al. (eds.), The Economics and Econometrics of Innovation, 1–29.
© 2000 *Kluwer Academic Publishers. Printed in the Netherlands.*

this topic has been and is to remind us of the importance of economic incentives in shaping and directing innovative activities, both by individuals and firms.

Following on Solow's early work, a few empirical pioneers began the task of measuring and understanding the micro-economic determinants and outcomes of innovative activity, at the same time that theorists began to use the new game theoretic tools to study the behavior and interactions of the firms undertaking innovative activity.[1] The same period saw a large increase both in government supported research and in organized industrial R&D in the United States and elsewhere, which has served to focus the interest of policy-makers on the topic; this last fact has had the welcome effect of increasing both the data sources available to researchers and the demand for their output.[2]

Thus the papers collected in the present volume reflect the enormous increase worldwide in the economics of innovation and technical change that has occurred. They are a selection of the over fifty papers that were first presented at the 10th international ADRES conference which was held at the European Parliament in Strasbourg, June 3-5.[3] This foreword briefly describes the contributions of the twenty-two articles making up this published volume, situating them within the major body of literature which has been built up around this topic during the past several decades.

We have gathered together the contributions to this issue under seven headings, structured by the types of questions addressed rather than by methodological differences such as the traditional distinctions between microeconomic and macroeconomic approaches and between theoretical and econometric approaches. In fact, one of the particular goals of this conference was to bring out the complementary nature of the various approaches to

---

[1] For early empirical work, see Schmookler (1966), Mansfield (1961), and Griliches (1957). Among the first theoretical contributions were Arrow (1962), Kamien and Schwartz (1980), Loury (1979), and Dasgupta and Stiglitz (1980). See Reinganum (1989) for a survey of some of this literature.

[2] For example, several papers in this volume make use of the French version of the new Innovation Surveys that have now been conducted for several European countries as well as for the United States (in a different form). See Duguet and Kabla (this volume) and Barlet, Duguet, Encaoua, and Pradel (this volume) for France and Cohen, Nelson, and Walsh (1996, 1997) for the United States.

[3] The conference was organized in collaboration with the ninth Franco-American CREST-NBER Seminar (the Centre de Recherche en Économie et Statistique and the National Bureau of Economic Research) as part of the European Commission's TSER program on innovation and productivity. In addition to the financial contributions of the organizing institutions (ADRES, CREST, NBER and the European Commission), the conference received assistance from the Alsace-USA Association, the CEPR (Centre for Economic Policy Research, London), the CNRS (Centre National de la Recherche Scientifique, Paris), the Strasbourg City Council, the Bas-Rhin Regional Council, the Ministry of Foreign Affairs (Paris), the University of Paris-I Panthéon-Sorbonne and Strasbourg's Louis Pasteur University. We should like to thank these institutions for making the conference and this volume possible.

innovation, and to make possible in-depth dialogue both between microeconomists and macroeconomists, and between theoreticians and econometricians. As will be seen in the following pages, the dialogue was successful and produced an interesting and challenging juxtaposition of ideas and results. Above and beyond the wealth of information presented in the articles, readers of this volume will also appreciate the value of examining a single question from different angles and using different methods.

The seven general topics that are considered in this special issue are the following: 1) the economy-wide effects of innovation on growth and employment; 2) the organization and assessment of public sector scientific research; 3) the role of intellectual property rights and patents in protecting innovation; 4) the analysis of networks and standardization; 5) the determinants of Research and Development (R&D) investment and its relationship to firm productivity; 6) variation of individual firm innovative performance with respect to uncertainty and international competition; 7) the assessment of knowledge spillovers, in particular between countries, the consequences for competition and technology policy. In the following we discuss each of these topics in turn, highlighting the contributions made by each of the papers to the topics.

1. Macroeconomic Effects of Innovation

Our first topic concerns the analysis of the overall or aggregate **effects of innovation** on economic growth, employment and total factor productivity. These effects are of considerable importance, and much research is currently being devoted to their study. The theories of endogenous growth developed over the last few years have made it possible to bring new analytical methods to bear on the forms of technical progress and on its impact in terms of global performance.[4] Three aspects are analyzed in this issue:

- *the role of innovation in economic business cycles through the medium of collective learning;*

- *the influence of the system of property rights of innovation on the diffusion of knowledge and on the economic growth rate;*

- *technical change and the impact of imperfections in labor market matching mechanisms on unemployment levels in endogenous growth models.*

---

[4]There are a sufficiently large number of recent works presenting full accounts of the various growth theories for us to omit here a synthesis of work being carried out in that field. See particularly the works of Aghion and Howitt (1998), Barro and Sala-i-Martin (1995) and Grossman and Helpman (1991).

The article by Philippe AGHION and Peter HOWITT (*On the Macroeconomic Effects of Major Technological Change*) concerns the question of why an instance of high technological discontinuity, such as the emergence of a major innovation, can initially have the effect of causing a decrease in economic activity before having a beneficial effect on long-term growth. Analysis of the link between innovation and economic activity cycles refers back to the Schumpeterian tradition of the technological origin of fluctuations and to the older literature devoted to Kondratieff's long cycles. An explanation for this link was recently given by Helpman and Trajtenberg (1995). It rests on the idea that the emergence of a major technological innovation - meaning an innovation with potential applications in many sectors of activity - requires a period of adjustment before having beneficial effects.[5] During this period, considerable capital and labor resources are taken away from traditional technologies and allocated to activities relating to the development of the new technology, in which the yield is uncertain and the results less readily appreciable than in traditional activities. In addition, the new technology requires the development of complementary tools, the perfection of which is a precondition for the success of the innovation. How is it possible to explain why the beneficial effects of the innovation only appear late in the second phase of the cycle under these conditions? The originality of Aghion and Howitt's model is to add to the foregoing pattern certain learning-related externalities based on the collective dimension of the process of evaluating the advantages arising from the new technology. The interaction between this process of collective learning, formalized as a circulation process, and that of the creation of additional tools, leads to an effect of sharp macroeconomic deceleration in activity, occurring a certain time after the appearance of the innovation. An obvious contemporary example is information technology, and from this point of view, Aghion and Howitt's analysis might be considered to provide an explanation of the «Solow paradox,» according to which computers may be observed everywhere except in productivity statistics.[6]

More fundamentally, Aghion and Howitt's model constitutes a theoretical basis for the Schumpeterian idea that long-run business cycles originate in technological discontinuity resulting from the emergence of major innovations. At present, there are few empirical tests proving the existence of these long cycles. However, it is likely that Aghion and Howitt's model will serve as a springboard for later empirical work. Furthermore, the model presented makes it possible to analyze the differential effect of three factors that influence the extent of recession and should be taken into account in empirical work: (i) the segmentation of the labor market according to skills; (ii) the existence of imperfections in the labor market, particularly that connected with difficulties in

---

[5]This type of innovation is sometimes designated by the term «General Purpose Technology.» See Bresnahan and Trajtenberg (1995), David (1990), and Rosenberg (1976) for development of these ideas.

[6] For an interesting discussion of this point, see Oliner and Sichel (1992); also David (1990).

matching labor supply and demand; and (iii) the idea - once more Schumpeterian - that technological innovation is marked by a type of intrinsic obsolescence, given that a technological innovation may quickly be replaced by a second innovation inspired by the first.

The article by Philippe MICHEL and Jules NYSSEN (*On Knowledge Diffusion, Patents Lifetime and Innovation-Based Endogenous Growth*) analyses the impact on growth of the institutional constraints of the patent protection system, defined both as right of ownership and as a means of diffusing the knowledge contained within the innovation. During the protection period, a registered patent does not describe all the technological expertise involved, either because this expertise cannot be easily codified, or because the innovator wishes to retain some element of technological secrecy. The knowledge embodied in the innovation thus loses part of its status as public property as long as the patent is in force. For this reason patent policy should take into account not only the traditional balance between the encouragement to innovate and the market allocation inefficiency due to the innovator's monopoly power, but also a new dimension of dynamic balance between, on the one hand, the choice of a path to maximum economic growth obtained by encouraging the diffusion of knowledge through a reduction in the protection period, and on the other hand, the option of extending protection in order to encourage innovation to the detriment of the diffusion of knowledge.

The interest of the article lies in the fact that the authors study the impact of the institutional characteristics of the patent protection system within the framework of a general equilibrium model of endogenous growth, whereas most work related to determining the optimum combination of patent characteristics (legal duration of protection, scope of protected claims, authorized improvements, etc.) approaches the question in terms of partial equilibrium analysis.[7] One of the most striking results of the article is that the patent lifetime that maximizes the economic growth rate does not generally coincide with the lifetime that maximizes consumer welfare. One question the article does not tackle, but which is discussed below, is the fact that the effective lifetime of a patent is generally shorter than the legal lifetime.

The article by Frédérique CERISIER and Fabien POSTEL-VINAY (*Endogenous Growth and the Labor Market*) raises the important question of whether technical progress destroys more employment than it creates, or whether low-skill jobs destroyed in innovative industries are counterbalanced either by skilled jobs created in those same industries or more generally by low-skill jobs in other industries due to the increase in overall demand. This is probably one of the issues to which society is most sensitive. To answer this question using a conceptual analysis, Cerisier and Postel-Vinay develop a multi-sector model of

---

[7]See for example Nordhaus (1969), Klemperer (1990), Green and Scotchmer (1990), Gilbert and Shapiro (1990), and Chou and Shy (1991).

qualitative endogenous growth, combining it with a process of imperfect matching of job supply and demand on the labor market. Growth is generated by the production of new varieties of goods and the improvement of the quality of the existing products. The process of *creative destruction* leads to established firms seeing their market shares decline, leading them gradually to lay off staff, while new firms creating new products take on workers. Recruitment implies frictions which the authors model as a process of matching as in Pissarides (1990): the number of matches per time period depends both on the number of unemployed and the number of vacant posts, and new firms are able to fill all their vacant posts only after a certain lapse of time. Furthermore, the cost of setting up these new firms is positive. In a steady state, there is a positive relation between growth and unemployment, in that the negative effect of the redistribution of labor due to frictions in the matching process prevails over the positive effect due to growth. Innovation thus creates unemployment through the creative destruction process.

Is this, however, a reliable conclusion? It is difficult to answer this question with a high degree of certainty, although it is clear that empirical studies can be highly useful here. For example, Davis and Haltiwanger (1992) show that there is a distinct long-term balance between growth and unemployment in the United States, and that periods of high unemployment are also those in which work mobility is greatest. However, further empirical studies are doubtless necessary, particularly on European data, in order to take into account the specific features of the labor market reallocation processes and the influence of technological bias on the characteristics of labor skill demand in Europe.[8]

2. Public Sector Scientific Research

Our second major topic concerns the upstream part of the innovative process, namely the resources devoted by many governments to basic or fundamental science. Against the present backdrop of budget deficit reduction and the partial privatization of certain major public services that had formerly taken an active part in national research and development efforts, the question of the organization of public sector research is a subject of current debate. This issue examines various aspects of this debate:

- *the problem of assessing academic research and the evaluation of the corresponding knowledge production function using scientific citation measures;*

---

[8]For studies carried out on French data, see Duguet and Greenan (1997) and Goux and Maurin (1997), and for studies using data from a variety of OECD countries, see the special issue of the *Economics of Innovation and New Technology*, volume 6, issue 2/3/4, edited by Hall and Kramarz (1998). In general, a clearcut answer has not yet been obtained to this question.

- *the effects of reputation and competence on the funding and productivity of scientific research;*

- *the organization and localization of public sector research in Europe.*

The article by James ADAMS and Zvi GRILICHES *(Research Productivity in a System of Universities)* in one of the first empirical studies on the productivity of fundamental research in universities, a field which, according to their conclusions, is sure to be a rich research area for many years to come. Academic research accounts for some 50% of fundamental research in the United States and is a major component of national research. Beyond that, it is also an essential factor in innovation and economic development. The authors constructed an original database by matching the R&D expenditure of a wide sample of private and state-run universities with the number of articles published and the number of citations for these articles. Their work covered the 1980s and focused on eight major scientific fields: agriculture, biology, chemistry, computer science, engineering, mathematics and statistics, medicine and physics. A hundred institutions were studied for the first, more general, part of their analysis, and some thirty institutions for the second part, which goes into greater depth. The analysis of this new database, both descriptive and econometric, leads to interesting observations and questions.

Adams and Griliches highlight the significant discrepancy between the yields of research in terms of articles and citations estimated at the aggregate level of the major scientific fields and yields at the individual university level for each scientific field. The returns are constant at the aggregate level, whereas they are decreasing at the individual level (with an average coefficient value of 0.6 to 0.7). The authors suggest two interpretations of this discrepancy. One explanation may be the existence of positive research externalities created by the dissemination of knowledge among universities and among scientific fields (notably through the training of young researchers). Another equally, if not more, probable explanation may be the measurement errors resulting from individual comparison - necessarily difficult and imperfect at this level - between research (and expenditure) and the number of articles (and citations) arising from this research, and the partial, reductive nature of the measurement of scientific production in terms of numbers of articles (even when weighted by the citations). Adams and Griliches also document the absence of significant results of regressions in the «temporal dimension» of the data (the absence of correlation between growth in research expenditure and growth in the number of publications), which is yet another manifestation of a difficulty often encountered in the analysis of panel data when one wants to control for heterogeneity in the form of fixed effects or permanent unobserved differences across units.[9]

---

[9]For discussion of this question in the wider context of identification and estimation of production functions, see Griliches and Mairesse (1999).

The article by Ashish ARORA, Paul DAVID and Alfonso GAMBARDELLA *(Reputation and Competence in Publicly Funded Science: Estimating the Effects on Research Group Productivity)* focuses on the distribution of public funding for research among research teams according to reputation and competence, and on the productivity of these teams according to the allocation of funds they obtain. Like the foregoing article, this is one of the first empirical contributions to the new «economics of science.» The three authors also emphasize that this topic of study is in its infancy and needs to be developed further. They base their study on an original database which they constructed from the archives of the Italian National Research Center's five-year program (1989-1993) in the fields of molecular biology, genetic engineering and bio-instrumentation. They obtained a sample of almost 800 research teams proposing research projects, some 350 of which were selected and received, for five years, annual research budgets of varying amounts (and in varying proportions to the sums requested). For these teams, they compiled their budgets, their publications (numbers and journals) produced during and as a result of their research programs, and publications by the team leaders (that is, the principal investigators), taking into account work they published in the relevant field over the five years preceding the funding request. To analyze their data, Arora, David and Gambardella develop and estimate a model that conforms to the features of the system they are studying, although this model might also be applicable on a more general level.

Like Adams and Griliches, they find that research returns (measured by research budget) in terms of articles (weighted according to the international reputation of the journals in which they are published) estimated at the individual team level are decreasing (0.6 on average). However, they demonstrate that returns in relation to past performance are of the same order, mostly via the indirect effect of past performance that is both is due to the fact that the probability of a team having its project selected is higher if past performance is good, and to the fact that once chosen, the amount of funding allocated is correspondingly higher.[10]

In the first part of their article *(The Impact and Organization of Publicly Funded Research and Development in the European Community)*, Maryann FELDMAN and Frank LICHTENBERG study the important and often controversial question of the complementary nature of public and private research. In the second part, they test the hypothesis that the more decentralized research activities are (both administratively and geographically), the more the knowledge they produce is codified, and conversely, the more they are centralized, the more the knowledge produced is to a large extent tacit (barely codified, or difficult to codify). To perform these analyses, they take advantage of

---

[10]It should be pointed out that these results, like the main results of Adams and Griliches, are based on the analysis of cross-sectional data (as opposed to panel data where it is possible to control for unobserved individual effects and to take account of the dynamics of the relationship).

the rich database CORDIS (Community R&D Information Service) of the European Community, illustrating the usefulness of this resource. Feldman and Lichtenberg observe that private and public research in 16 European countries, from Norway to the United Kingdom, shows a strong tendency to be specialized in the same major scientific fields (26 in their study) in each country. They conclude that this fact gives a clear indication of the great extent to which the two forms of research are complementary, at least in Europe.[11] On the basis of two indicators of the degree of codification (the number of articles published in journals compared to the number of reports, and the proportion of tangible results of research such as prototypes or processes, as opposed to expertise, competence and methods), they also observe that the more these programs are spread over a large number of countries, and the more projects there are per program, the higher the degree of codification of the results.

3. Intellectual Property Rights and Patents

Our third topic concerns problems related to systems that protect the ownership of innovations through intellectual property rights and patents. The patent, which is a right of ownership designed to ensure that the patent holder enjoys legal protection against possible imitation during the patent protection period in return for publication of the protocol defining the innovation, offers both problems and solutions to those studying technical change.

For example, patents are extremely useful to empirical researchers as the only easily and widely available measure of innovation output that carries with it some information about technological field. However, not all innovations are necessarily patented, even among those that do meet the legal requirements of patentability, indicating either that the protection conferred by the patent is not considered as valuable as it might initially appear, or that the legal costs incurred in filing for a patent or by bringing an action for patent infringement are deemed to be too high. Clearly these factors have been changing over time, which limits the ability to use patents as a measure of the fecundability of R&D in the temporal dimension.

In addition, in many economic models, patents are often treated more as a technical instrument than as a strategic instrument, although firms appear to use them strategically in some cases. That is, whether or not a firm applies for a patent or renews a patent may depend on some cases on the behavior of competitors or other factors outside the immediate profit stream expected from

---

[11]More precisely, the greater the number of private research organizations (consultancies, industrial and service organizations) specialized in a given field in a given country, the greater the number of public research organizations (state laboratories, technology transfer centers, universities) specialized in the same field in the same country.

the innovation associated with that particular patent. This could be either for signaling reasons (see the article in this volume by Crampes and Langinier) or because firms wish to have a strong bargaining position in the case of patent litigation threats (see Hall and Ham 1999).

The results of analyzing the functioning of patent and intellectual property systems can also be of considerable policy interest. For example, the documentary purpose of a patent is that it provides information necessary for the improvement of existing innovations. Therefore, if technological development is part of a cumulative process, and more new possibilities for development are offered when accumulated knowledge is greater and more codified, it is clear that the recent drop in the number of patents in Europe, as revealed by statistics, is cause for concern. The production of patented innovations in the countries which now make up the European Union fell from 110 000 a year in 1950 to some 85 000 in 1995, whereas in the other two major trading blocs, the United States and Japan, the annual figures for patents have risen from 55 000 to 140 000 and from 18 000 to 320 000 respectively. Understanding the reasons for the drop and whether it can be expected to slow down the knowledge accumulation process in Europe are thus important for policy makers.

Several patent-related topics are discussed in this issue:

- *the problems raised by the imperfect protection conferred on the patent holder, particularly the potential necessity of litigation to enforce the property right;*

- *the choice of various modes of intellectual property protection;*

- *the strategic dimension of patents;*

- *the relationship between patenting and R&D inputs.*

The article by Jean LANJOUW and Josh LERNER *(The Enforcement of Intellectual Property Rights: A Survey of the Empirical Literature)* is a contribution to the emerging literature on the economic analysis of law.[12] The authors provide an analytical model of litigation concerning intellectual property rights and an overview of the empirical literature studying this litigation. They attempt to answer a number of questions: What is the cost of detecting and taking legal action for patent infringement? What influence does the cost of enforcing patents have on the private value of patent rights? What is the impact of the threat of litigation on the innovation process? Lanjouw and Lerner report figures relating to the United States which show that the cost of patent litigation is substantial, and that the start of a trial leads to a considerable fall in the stock

---

[12]Among available references on the law and economics of intellectual property, the editors recommend Lerner (1994, 1995), and Hughes and Snyder (1995). The legal aspects of intellectual property rights in the EC are covered in Korah (1994, chapters 9 and 10).

market value of the defending company. Furthermore, these costs occasionally lead small companies to renounce their property rights and seek a compromise rather then go to court.

To analyze these facts, they propose a model of a two-stage game with two players, in which the plaintiff is the patent holder and the defendant is the company allegedly having infringed patent rights. In the first stage of the game, the defendant decides whether or not to move into the market for the product in question. If this happens, the plaintiff may either file a suit or suggest a compromise with the defendant. All things being equal, an increase in legal costs or a decrease in the probability of winning the case (or even a drop in the expected returns) can encourage the parties to seek a compromise. Empirically speaking, the studies that they survey confirm these predictions of their mode, demonstrating that small and medium-sized companies often avoid innovating in fields in which large companies are already present, and that in jurisdictions where legislation provides that the legal costs of a trial shall be borne by the losing party innovation is reduced.

Michael WATERSON and Norman IRELAND *(An Auction Model of Intellectual Property Rights: Patents versus Copyright)* seek to determine which of the two methods of protection - patent and copyright - is the more effective, and more precisely, in what types of activity one would be more appropriate than the other. The question is all the more relevant since patents do not cover all inventions: for example, historically computer software could only be protected by copyright.[13] Using the criterion of total private profit for evaluation, Waterson and Ireland demonstrate that different protection systems should be used for different industries, depending on the volume of R&D expenditure, the number of competitors and the number of potential applications for a given discovery. For example, in the pharmaceutical industry - in which considerable sums are invested in R&D, the number of agents pursuing the same research track are few, and technological spillovers linked to the applications of a discovery are low - the patent seems to be the most appropriate protection. On the other hand, in the computer software industry - in which investment is relatively lower, the number of agents is fairly large, and a vast number of potential applications are linked to the development of a program - copyright is preferable. The analysis presented in the article thus yields a useful method for studying the properties of various instruments for the protection of intellectual property and their effects on innovative activity, according to the characteristics of the innovation, the environment in which it is made and the methods by which it is disseminated.

---

[13] This is an evolving area of the law in some countries. For example, in the United States it is now possible to protect certain types of software code and algorithms by patent rather than copyright. Also, code that is embedded in physical microprocessors can by protected using mask work protection (although patenting is preferred where it is feasible).

In their article *(Information Disclosure in the Renewal of Patents)* Claude CRAMPES and Corinne LANGINIER examine the strategic dimension of patents, more precisely that dimension due to asymmetry between the market information held by the innovator and that held by potential competitors. Consider the case in which a patent is taken out by an innovator, and he must decide whether or not to renew it during the legal lifetime of the patent. Under perfect information, the fee will be paid if later profits compensate for the renewal cost.[14] When information is imperfect, another element comes into play. The decision to renew means that the innovator sends out a positive signal concerning the profitability of the market for the innovation, which may encourage a potential competitor to enter this same market. Thus the decision not to renew clearly has a strategic dimension, since it lowers the potential entrant's belief in the profitability of the market.

The model is presented as a signaling game yielding multiple equilibria. In one of these equilibria, if the potential entrant expects *a priori* a low probability of the market being profitable, the innovator will not pay the renewal fee in order to send a negative signal to the competitor. Crampes and Langinier's model thus provides a plausible explanation for the observation that the effective lifetime of a patent is generally much shorter than its legal lifetime, although of course it does not rule out other explanations. A model similar to theirs was presented in Choi (1985), which studied the decision not to announce an intermediate discovery so as to discourage competitors who were also working towards the final innovation. The analysis of strategic behavior when information is imperfect thus makes it possible to explain a number of phenomena in the field of innovation.

In their article *(Appropriation Strategy and the Motivation to Use the Patent System)* Emmanuel DUGUET and Isabelle KABLA examine the determinants at play in the decision to patent an innovation. It is widely known that the patent is not the only appropriation mechanism available. Secrecy, particularly in the case of processes, and, more simply, the technological lead one company has over others may be sufficient to protect its innovations effectively. In the second case, the patent may even harm the innovator if the patented technology can be improved upon. By using the information disclosed by the patent, competitors may improve on any innovation which is sufficiently innovative to be patented, close the technological gap and even leapfrog the initial innovator. However, the patent may still be necessary in order to transfer the technology to another party.

Until recently, the determinants of the decision to apply for a patent have not been the subject of empirical economic studies due to the lack of appropriate data, although many studies of the patent yield in relation to R&D expenditure

---

[14] Unlike that of Pakes (1982), this analysis is performed under certainty. When the future profit stream is uncertain, the patent may be renewed because it has option value even though expected profits might not justify renewal.

have been conducted.[15] The availability of new data from the French Appropriation Survey, carried out in 1992 by the SESSI industrial statistics service, made it possible for Duguet and Kabla to carry out such a study. From this survey, they obtain the percentage of innovations which companies decide to patent and also their views on the main qualities and defects of the patent as a means of appropriating the profit from the innovation. They observe that companies register patents for only one-third of their innovations on average. They also verify that the major factor differentiating companies in terms of the percentage of patented innovations is the extent to which they fear that the information disclosed by the patent will be used by competitors. They find that this factor affects not only the percentage of patented innovations but also their actual numbers, independently of the influence of R&D expenditure levels. Another interesting observation is that the use of patents in technological negotiations is a significant motivation for companies to patent their innovations, whereas patent application and renewal fees are of little significance.

The article by Georg LICHT and Konrad ZOZ *(Patents and R&D: An Econometric Investigation Using Applications for German, European and US Patents by German Companies)* uses data from a European Community survey on innovation in Germany to explore the relation between R&D expenditure and the filing of patents in the German, European and United States patent offices.[16] A descriptive study of the data first demonstrates that the probability that a company invests in R&D or applies for a patent increases with company size. Large companies are also more likely to apply for patents in more than one country, whereas the national patent office is clearly more important to small and medium-sized companies. Econometric count data models are then used to study the relation between R&D spending and the patents filed at the various patent offices. In each case the chosen econometric specification is one which separates the decision to file for patents from the number filed.[17]

The main results of this research are the following: R&D expenditure in companies has a considerable influence on the number of patents obtained, with an elasticity varying between 0.8 and 1.1, depending on the level of R&D expenditure and the location of the patent office. This coefficient was much higher for the United States and lower for Germany. The spillover effect,

---

[15]For a review of the U.S. literature in this area see Griliches, Pakes, and Hall (1987), and for work using French and German data, Crepon and Duguet (1997a,b) and Licht and Zoz (this issue), respectively.

[16]This was the first survey carried out on the MIP (Mannheim Innovation Panel).

[17]This two stage econometric model corresponds to a Type II negative binomial specification combined with a hurdle model (see Cameron and Trivedi 1998 for the econometric details on this kind of model). The negative binomial model itself is an extension of the basic Poisson specification where the patenting propensity parameter is assumed to follow a gamma law chosen so that the ratio of the variance to the expectation is an affine function of the expectation.

estimated by including total industrial R&D expenditure in the model, appeared to be of little significance. However, the size of the company has a significant effect on the tendency to file for patents. A number of explanations may be submitted to explain the behavior of small companies. There may be a lack of information about the patent system, there may be other mechanisms for protecting innovation, it may be due to the more incremental nature of innovations brought about by smaller companies, or it may simply be that there are fixed costs in obtaining patents so that smaller firms find each patent relatively more expensive to obtain.

4. Networks and Standardization

The fourth heading concerns the analysis of decisions for network standardization. There are many links between the economics of innovation and the economics of networks. First, decisions about the compatibility of goods that are complements to a particular innovation (such as peripherals for a personal computer) may themselves be considered product innovations, since they make available new combinations and thus new varieties. Second, the choice of technological standards in a large number of industries is crucial for their survival, and gives rise to stiff competition. Whether it be GSM standards for mobile phones, VHS standards for video-cassettes, standards for high-definition television,[18] the arrangement of typewriters and computer keyboards,[19] or computer operating systems, the choices made for standards often depend more on the historical background and strategies used by the companies in which the innovations originated than the intrinsic technological superiority of the standard adopted. In addition, network externalities leading to the adoption of a standard must themselves be related to the general innovation-generated externalities linked to growth that were described under our first heading.

Two topics that concern standardization are examined using theoretical tools in this volume:

- *the determinants of the decision by competitors to conform to a common standard;*

- *the effects of standardization on output.*

In their article *(Equilibrium Coalition Structures in Markets for Network Goods)* Nicholas ECONOMIDES and Frederick FLYER seek to determine what encourages firms in an oligopolistic industry producing goods exhibiting network externalities to conform to a common standard (compatibility) or to maintain the

---

[18]See Farrell and Shapiro (1992).
[19]See David (1985).

specific features of their products (incompatibility). On the one hand, compatibility increases the number of available varieties, thereby increasing overall demand in the industry. On the other hand, compatibility makes competition more intense among producers of alternative goods. What will be the nature of the outcome between these opposing forces?[20]

To answer this question, Economides and Flyer consider a symmetrical model in which the goods on offer are identical, with the exception of the standards to which they conform. The quality of the product on offer increases with the number of companies conforming to the same standard. Coalitions conforming to the same standard may be formed. The notion of equilibrium is expressed in terms of coalitions. A coalition structure constitutes an equilibrium so long as no single company wishes to leave the coalition to which it belongs and join a parallel coalition. The conclusions are the following: Perfect compatibility, meaning the conformity of all companies to the same standard only constitutes an equilibrium in those industries in which the network externalities are low. However, in those industries in which the network externalities are high, various standards exist in equilibrium. In these industries, it is even possible for total incompatibility to constitute an equilibrium. In addition, the larger the scale of a coalition among companies having chosen the same standard, the more reluctant its members are to allow another company to adhere to it. This effect is even stronger when network externalities are high. These results are interesting in that they help understand why, for network goods, there may remain instances of high asymmetry, with, on one side, one dominant company together with a large number of smaller companies that survive in the shadow of its standard, and on the other side, other groupings of companies choosing their own standards. The personal computer operating systems industry in the 1990s, which is dominated by Microsoft's Windows standard, could be an illustration for this analysis.

In his article *(Does Standardization Really Increase Production?)* Hubert STAHN returns to the result of Katz and Shapiro (1985) according to which, in an industry with network externalities, the level of overall production is higher when firms choose compatible rather than incompatible goods. This result had been established using the hypothesis of a constant marginal production cost. Stahn succeeds in demonstrating that with the hypothesis of a more general cost of production function, the result does not hold. This is significant, as the widespread belief that compatibility generally increases the overall surplus available is called into question by this analysis. Stahn shows, through a counter-example including three products, that the result of Katz and Shapiro does not hold if quadratic or convex cost functions are considered. In this case, the surplus is at its highest when the three products are incompatible. It is therefore necessary

---

[20]This type of question applies to many network activities. For air transport, see Encaoua, Moreaux, and Perrot (1996).

to exercise caution when assessing the effects of compatibility or standardization on social welfare.

5. R&D Investment and Productivity

The fifth heading concerns the analysis of R&D investment expenditure and its productivity. This is far from being a recent problem, however it is clear that investigation into it will never be complete, given the difficulties in terms of concepts, measurement, and estimation methods to say nothing of the varying impact of R&D over time and across countries. Three questions are discussed in the present issue:

- *the measurement of R&D capital and its impact on productivity;*

- *the financing of investments in R&D (and in physical capital).*

These themes have been discussed in a number of earlier studies.[21] The latter has given rise to a particularly vast body of literature regarding physical investment, though it has rarely been applied to the study of R&D investment.[22] The two articles brought together under this heading are highly representative of current investigation into company panel data, while at the same time providing certain interesting variations in approach and modeling.[23]

The article by Tor Jacob KLETTE and Frode JOHANSEN *(Accumulation of R&D Capital and Dynamic Firm Performance: A Not-so-Fixed Effect Model)* takes as its starting point empirical regularities frequently observed in R&D investment and productivity at the firm or establishment level. Using relatively homogeneous samples of establishments or «lines of business» (rather than companies) in four major Norwegian industries, they first verify that R&D activities are persistent in time (individual differences in the intensity of R&D efforts are significant and auto-correlated); then, they determine that the correlation between different levels of productivity and R&D capital intensity are significantly positive in the cross-sectional individual dimension, but that the correlation between variations in productivity and R&D capital intensity in the time series dimension is much weaker, and occasionally not significant.

---

[21]See, for example, the overview of econometric studies on company data by Mairesse and Sassenou (1991) and by Griliches (1995).

[22]For a recent example with some survey results, see Mairesse, Hall, and Mulkay (1999). For examples using R&D investment, see Himmelberg and Petersen (1994) and Hall (1993).

[23]Both use GMM panel data estimation methods, making it possible to take into account the nature – not strictly exogenous, but merely predetermined – of certain explanatory variables and the presence of correlated individual effects.

On the basis of these observations and analytic considerations inspired by Penrose (1959) and Uzawa (1969), the two authors suggest an alternative model of R&D capital accumulation (multiplicative or log-linear) instead of the usual linear model.[24] They show that this pattern leads to a simple dynamic model in which the present level of productivity is a function only of the R&D investments made the previous year (rather than R&D capital) and the productivity level of that same year. The major advantage of this model is that it does not require the construction of the R&D capital stock variable.[25] Klette and Johansen, in estimating this model, find that the R&D capital depreciates rapidly, with a depreciation rate in the region of 18%, and that the rate of return on R&D investments are fairly close to the figure for physical investment.

In his article *(Are There Financing Constraints for R&D and Investment in German Manufacturing Firms?)* Dietmar HARHOFF sets out to assess to what extent R&D and physical (equipment) investment decisions in German manufacturing firms are affected by financing constraints. The principal reason for the existence of such constraints (which result from the imperfections of the capital markets) has been thoroughly analyzed in the theoretical literature, and arises largely from the asymmetry of information between the company and its potential creditors. Many empirical studies have shown the existence of financing constraints influencing the physical investment decisions of companies. For Germany, two types of study can be distinguished. Studies on panel data concerning large companies quoted on the stock exchange have mostly concluded that these constraints are absent. However, cross-sectional studies (where it more difficult to control for unobserved heterogeneity) on smaller companies have regularly concluded that such constraints are present and are of considerable importance. No previous study has assessed the impact of these financing constraints on R&D investment in German companies.

Harhoff uses a new panel of German companies involved in R&D, mostly companies not quoted on the stock exchange (236 companies over the period 1987-1994). For this panel he estimates various equations for R&D expenditure and physical investment, beginning with the simple dynamic specifications suggested by Bond, Elston, Mairesse and Mulkay (1997). For smaller-scale companies, these indicate that R&D and investment are highly sensitive to cash flow. This effect is attenuated, yet does not disappear, if the specification tested

---

[24]The use of this model was first suggested and implemented by Hall and Hayashi (1988); one can show that a firm faced with such an accumulation pattern will tend to smooth its R&D investment relative to that of a firm facing a linear accumulation pattern with no adjustment costs.

[25]The estimated model also posits a «margin-based» behavior pattern in firms, in order to take into account the fact that productivity measured at the individual level is expressed in terms of nominal value rather than in real terms, and that it may therefore reflect differences in the level of prices faced by the firms and changes in their market power over time. On this point, see Klette and Griliches (1996).

includes an error correction mechanism. The interpretation of the relation between cash flow and investment does however pose a problem. It may be considered either to express the link between investment and expected profitability, or to result from the existence of financial rationing (on imperfect capital markets). High cash flow can be an indicator of high profits, and may therefore be correlated with anticipated future profits. Thus Harhoff, in the following part of his study, tests a specification of a more «structural» nature using Euler equations derived from the dynamic program of the firm (inspired by Bond and Meghir (1984)). For physical investment, he finds estimates that are consistent with the absence of financing constraints in large companies, but not in small companies.[26] The Euler equations estimated for R&D are not informative, probably because the necessary differencing of the equation for estimation leaves little real variation in the series to be explained.[27]

6. Profits from Innovation

Obviously innovation is seldom an end in itself, and for a fuller understanding of its effects it is important to assess the relative advantages gained by the innovator. The measurement of individual firm performance is however a delicate matter, and there are few appropriate indicators available.[28] Innovating companies face three types of uncertainty: technological, strategic, and market. Technological uncertainty refers to the fact that companies that have decided to devote R&D resources to the application of a discovery are never sure beforehand that they possess the expertise necessary to transform the discovery into a technically viable industrial project. Strategic uncertainty arises from the fact that a company allocating funds to the development of an industrial project is never sure of being the first to introduce the corresponding innovation onto the market. Market uncertainty refers to the fact that the existence of potential buyers of the innovation is rarely guaranteed at the moment when the company chooses an industrial R&D project. This uncertainty is often the most difficult for companies to overcome, and the commercial performance of the innovation is strongly affected by it.

Three topics related to the measurement of innovative performance are discussed in this issue:

---

[26]Additional survey data reported in the paper does suggest that the sensitivity to cash flow of investment in small companies may reflect true financing constraints, rather than mere problems of an econometric order.

[27] It is well known in the empirical innovation literature that R&D is a rather smooth series at the firm level, probably because it consists primarily of the salaries and other expenses associated with scientists and engineers that are costly (in terms of lost human capital) to hire and fire. See Hall, Griliches, and Hausman (1986) or Lach and Schankerman (1988).

[28]See Kleinknecht (1996)

18

- *the degree of asymmetry or skewness in the ex post distribution of innovation profits;*

- *the effects of trade restrictions on innovative performance;*

- *the impact of different types of innovation on commercial performance.*

In their article *(The Commercial Success of Innovations: An Econometric Analysis at the Firm Level in French Manufacturing)* Corinne BARLET, Emmanuel DUGUET, David ENCAOUA and Jacqueline PRADEL emphasize the observed market uncertainty about the success of innovation using a performance indicator provided by the proportion of total sales of a company accounted for by recent innovative products (i.e. products marketed for less than five years). The use of this indicator of the commercial success of innovations has spread thanks to the increasingly frequent Innovation Surveys (particularly in European countries), in which it is generally available in interval form, not only for the total sales of innovating companies, but also for export sales.

The article is based on the first large-scale survey of innovation in French industry (the 1990 Innovation Survey), and it studies how the commercial performance of innovating companies varies according to the nature of the innovation (process or product, the imitation or improvement of an available variety or the creation of a new variety, brought about by market forces or technological advance, etc.). The article also compares commercial performance in terms of total sales and exports. Because performance figures for innovations were requested and reported in large interval ranges (0-10%, 10-30%, 30-70% and above), the authors use maximum likelihood estimation of an ordered probit model to analyze the data. They find that the proportion of innovative products is lower for exports than for total sales, but that the innovative *content* of exported products is higher. In addition, innovations in the form of product imitation or improvement only perform well commercially in sectors in which the level of technological opportunity is low, whereas completely new products perform better commercially in sectors in which the level of technological opportunity is high. With the diffusion of the Innovation Surveys across countries, this type of study should facilitate international comparisons for the purpose of examining differences among the various measures of the commercial success of innovations, interpreting more effectively the results of such analyses, and testing their reliability.

Celia COSTA CABRAL, Praveen KUJAL and Emmanuel PETRAKIS *(Incentives for Cost Reducing Innovations under Quantitative Import Restraints)* examine the question of whether the existence of import quotas or voluntary export restrictions leads to an increase or reduction of incentives for cost-reducing R&D. They continue the work of Reitzes (1991) by studying the question within the framework of a differentiated product model. They demonstrate that the effect of the quotas varies depending on how restrictive they are relative to unrestricted trade, and on whether one is assessing the effect on a company in the country which fixes the quota (the domestic company) or the effect on a rival company in the country on which the quota is imposed (the foreign company). The main conclusion is that there exists a threshold effect. If quotas are not excessively restrictive, the domestic company reduces its R&D expenditure, whereas the foreign company increases its R&D expenditure. Highly restrictive quotas have the opposite effect. This conclusion weakens the «infant industry» argument on which protectionist commercial policy is based: fixing import quotas does not encourage the protected company to build up a competitive long-term advantage, unless the quotas are very high.

In his article *(The Size Distribution of Profits from Innovation)*, F. M. SCHERER attempts to ascertain the *ex post* distribution function for the profits resulting from technological innovations, and more precisely, to assess the degree of asymmetry in this distribution. The question is important for two reasons. First, on the statistical level, some early data suggested that moments of order one and two of the data generating process may not be finite, and therefore conventional central limit theorem properties may not hold, implying that asymptotic values may not be approximated more closely as larger samples are drawn. For example, this phenomenon would occur if the underlying distribution were Pareto and the estimated slope coefficient of the log cumulative distribution were less than unity in absolute value. Second, from an economic standpoint, the more skewed the distribution, the more difficult it is to form a varied portfolio of research projects or patents with a moderate and predictable variance, which would complicate the financing of innovative activities, since investors might find it difficult to reduce their risk enough through diversification.

To estimate the distribution of innovation outcomes, Scherer uses a variety of sources, including patent portfolios of American universities, profits realized by approved pharmaceutical products, stock market yields for newly established hi-tech companies, and a cohort of German patents that were regularly renewed until expiration. He finds that the Pareto distribution does not typically provide the best fit. The less skewed log normal distribution appears to fit the data better. More skewness is evident for distributions of individual patent values than for whole innovations or firms (both of which may entail multiple patents). Nevertheless, the similarity of the distribution outcomes across different samples and measures of innovative output seems to indicate that analogous stochastic processes underlie the generation of innovation profits. An interesting avenue for future research is opened up by these findings.

7. Spillovers

The final heading grouping together the articles in this issue concerns the **measurement of spillovers** from the dissemination of knowledge, or research and innovation spillovers, which are known to play a crucial role in the analysis of the economics of innovation. The existence of research spillovers implies that there is a difference or wedge between profitability or the private returns on research and the social returns on the research. These spillovers generally being positive (unlike, for example, pollution spillovers), the private returns are lower than the social returns. This may cause an insufficient level of private investment in research from the collective or societal point of view and is the major justification for intervention by public authorities not only through the patent system but also through public research programs, financial assistance and subsidies, tax incentives, and so forth. In principle, the degree of state intervention should be related to the degree of research spillovers and to the insufficiency of appropriation mechanisms for knowledge and innovation. This is particularly true when spillovers cannot be internalized privately within institutions or within the existing economic system. The latter characteristic may especially be the case for fundamental research, and whether it has a purely scientific purpose or is application-based, whether it is original research or an adjunct to already established programs. Such research pursues non-commercial interests (or those which are only partly commercial, more frequently in medium- and long-term projects rather than short-term projects), and the conditions for its success are relatively uncertain.

Understanding these features of scientific research make it easier to understand the economic importance of public management of research spillovers. It is extremely difficult to assess these spillovers, in terms not only of prospective assessment, but also of their retrospective assessment. Econometricians have only been working in this field recently, and their early research has produced results which are still rather fragile on the whole. Among the range of questions concerning spillovers, two recent issues are considered here:

- *the assessment of knowledge spillovers between countries, and comparison with spillovers within given countries;*

- *the analysis of policies toward competition, coordination or cooperation among companies doing R&D in the presence of spillovers.*

In his article *(Looking for International Knowledge Spillovers: A Review of the Literature with Suggestions for New Approaches)* Lee BRANSTETTER provides a critical review of empirical studies assessing international knowledge spillovers. He calls upon the theoretical contributions of Grossman and Helpman (1991), showing the structuring role of spillovers in international exchanges and the possibility for several long-term equilibria. The establishment of these equilibria depends on the initial situations of the countries, though it must be added that spillovers within countries dominate spillovers among countries. He also evokes the important distinction, developed notably by Griliches (1978,

1992), between pecuniary spillovers, linked to the exchange of goods in the marketplace and dependent on the pricing system for such goods, and non-pecuniary spillovers, linked to «intangible» exchanges (the dissemination of knowledge) and independent of the pricing of market goods.[29]

Branstetter then presents the methods and models implemented by econometricians to assess the effective importance of spillovers. The principal model used is the production function model, where production is increased by internal research capital for the company or the sector, and by research capital external to the company or sector. This external research capital can itself be divided into research capital within sectors or within countries, and research capital among sectors or countries. Internal research capital is measured by the cumulative sum of past R&D investments by the company or sector, usually depreciated with a constant depreciation rate (often in the region of 15%). The various components of external capital are measured as the weighted sums of capital of other companies, other sectors, of the country or of other countries. In principle, the weights are chosen to reflect technological proximity between the research fields of other companies and those of the company under consideration, or between those of other sectors and those of the sector under consideration. The closer the technological proximity among companies or sectors, the greater the probability of spillovers. The choice of weighting may also be based on other considerations. For example, for calculating international research capital, levels proportionate to the volume of trade for the sectors and countries under consideration are often chosen. This was done notably by Coe and Helpman (1995) in a frequently quoted article, in which the two authors find a high level of international research spillovers. In the last two parts of his contribution, Branstetter presents this article in detail alongside the criticism it provoked, notably from Keller (1996), and then summarizes his own results concerning research spillovers in the United States, in Japan, and between the two countries. Keller showed that Coe and Helpman's results persist and are even improved by random choice of the weights used to measure international research capital variables, thus casting serious doubt on whether their results are indeed due to direct spillovers.

On the basis of two panels of high-tech companies in the United States and Japan, for which R&D and patent behavior is known, and drawing heavily upon Jaffe (1986), Branstetter obtains estimates showing that spillovers within countries are higher than spillovers among countries. These last spillovers prove not to be statistically significant. The author concludes his review by highlighting

---

[29]Pecuniary spillovers result when the benefits of quality-improving innovations are passed onto buyers in the form of lower prices rather than being captured by the seller. That is, they typically reflect a fairly competitive post-innovation environment in an industry. A good example is the market for peronal computer components such as disk drives, where innovation has lead largely to lower prices for higher densities and speed rather than high margins for the manufacturers.

both the difficulties inherent in econometric studies attempting to evaluate spillovers and the necessity for such studies.

Jeffrey BERNSTEIN (*Factor Intensities, Rates of Return, and International R&D Spillovers: The Case of Canadian and US. Industries*) seeks to estimate private and social returns on R&D in eleven manufacturing industries in Canada and the United States, and research spillovers among industries (in a single country) and among countries (between Canada and the United States for a single industry). He works on aggregate annual data for the eleven industries and the two countries, over the period 1962-1989, and he estimates a system of factor demand equations (four equations for physical capital and research capital, labor and intermediate consumption) rather than a production function. He finds that the social returns to R&D in the two countries are distinctly higher than private returns, due to significant positive spillovers. As expected, domestic spillovers are predominant in the case of the United States, while for Canada, the reverse is true: spillovers originating in their powerful neighbor prevail over home-grown spillovers. One of the conclusions of the study is thus that R&D investment may be too low from a social point of view in both countries. Another is that research coordination and cooperation are of great importance, and that information and knowledge dissemination networks between Canada and the United States possibly ought to be developed beyond mere commercial exchanges and agreements.

Henri CAPRON and Michele CINCERA (*Exploring the Spillover Impact on Productivity of World-Wide Manufacturing Firms*) constructed a panel of 625 major manufacturing firms with substantial research activities for the period 1987-1994. These companies, for the most part American (378), Japanese (133) and European (101), account for some 30-50% of the R&D expenditure in their respective countries, in the United States, in Japan and in Europe.[30] For this sample they obtain estimates of the elasticity of sales with respect to internal research capital that is highly significant and higher than the figures for most previous studies (including for the temporal dimension). Their estimates of the external capital elasticity are comparable to those of several recent studies,

---

[30]Most of these companies engage in multinational activities, and the variables of the study (sales, staffing levels, R&D, etc.) cover all of these activities, not simply domestic operations. For the companies in their sample, the authors also matched data relating to the number of European patents registered by major technological field (there are 50 such fields). On this basis they could construct indicators of technological proximity enabling them to assess external national and international research capital. Following Jaffe (1986), they consider 18 relatively homogeneous technological groupings based on several classification methods, and construct four external research stock packages, introducing a distinction between local (technological sector-specific) stock (national and international) and strictly external (to the technological sector) stock (national and international). The local national stock for a company may, for example, be obtained as the weighted sum of past R&D expenditure of the companies of a given country belonging to a given technological grouping, etc.

notably Jaffe (1986) and Branstetter (in the present issue). Spillovers are deemed to be mostly intra-national for the United States and international for Japan. They appear to be much lower (and not significant) for Europe. However, the authors conclude by emphasizing the fragile nature of their estimates and the difficulties that must be faced when attempting the econometric assessment of spillovers in general.

In their article *(Innovation Spillovers and Technology Policy)*, KATSOULACOS and ULPH undertake to show how knowledge dissemination spillovers affect the levels of research in companies. Unlike most microeconomic work devoted to the subject, this article adopts an approach which considers that these dissemination spillovers are endogenous variables, i.e., variables resulting from strategic choices on the part of the companies rather than exogenous parameters outside their control. Taking as a starting point the model of d'Aspremont and Jacquemin (1985), which gave rise to much research on the ownership of cooperative and non-cooperative research in the presence of spillovers, the authors present two important distinctions. The first emphasizes the differences among three strategies: information sharing, research coordination, and cooperation. In the case of information sharing, companies commit themselves independently to research activities by determining the corresponding investment expenditure and then, according to the results obtained, deciding on the amount of information they wish to share. When research is coordinated, the timing of the decisions is reversed, with the level of spillover being decided before the R&D levels. Finally, cooperation consists in choosing jointly the whole set of variables. The second distinction relates to the nature of the products on which research is carried out. According to whether the products are independent, substitutable or complementary, the motivation for choosing the methods of sharing, coordination or cooperation differ. By adopting the traditional social surplus as a welfare criterion, the authors discuss the relevance of technological subsidy policy for research activities in each of the cases studied. This work is thus both a useful clarification of the many methods of cooperative research in the presence of spillovers and a decision-making tool for state intervention concerning the formation of joint ventures.

* *
*

On perusing this overview of the presentation of recent developments in the economics and econometrics of innovation, and more specifically of the way the articles in this special issue contribute to the field, the reader will perhaps share the twofold feelings of the editors.

The first perception is that the economic analysis of innovation has many facets that are difficult to enumerate, given the degree to which the appropriate methodologies shatter the traditional boundaries of economic analysis and create close interdependence among fields within the discipline that are normally considered separate. The boundaries between microeconomics and

24

macroeconomics are becoming blurred, and substantial links are being established among growth theories, the economics of labor, the economics of science and research, the analysis of methods of apprenticeship through experience, the study of dissemination and diffusion processes, competition analysis, the study of incentives and ownership rights, the management and organization of companies, the financial environment, the legal framework, the social structure, the intervention of state authorities, international trade and many other fields within economics.

The second feeling, a corollary of the first, is that investigative methods have themselves received benefits from this widening of perspective. The economics and econometrics of innovation should no longer be perceived as distinct and separate fields of investigation, but rather as complementary means of analyzing the same issues. While people's specializations naturally make them inclined to choose the approach in which they have, comparatively, the greatest advantage, a dialog has definitely begun. New databases, frequently qualitative, are now available and new empirical investigation methods are being perfected. The economic importance of innovation is such that theoretical and empirical studies come together on many issues. Has it been possible to achieve unified representation? Not yet, and probably never. However, the editors do hope that this volume, while demonstrating the diversity and wealth of a flourishing field, has contributed to the case for integration and dialogue among those engaged in different approaches to the problem.

• References

Aghion, P. and P. Howitt (1998): *Endogenous Growth Theory*, Cambridge, Mass.: The MIT Press.

Arrow, K. (1962): "Economic Welfare and the Allocation of Resources for Invention," in Nelson, R. R. (ed.), *The Rate and Direction of Inventive Activity*, 609-25. Princeton, NJ: Princeton University Press.

Barro, R. J. and X. Sala-i-Martin (1995): *Economic Growth*, New York: McGraw-Hill.

Bond, S., J. A. Elston, J. Mairesse and B. Mulkay (1997): «A Comparison of Empirical Investment Equations Using Company Level Data for France, Germany, Belgium and the UK», NBER Working Paper n° 5900.

Bond, S. and C. Meghir (1994): «Dynamic Investment Models and the Firm's Financial Policy», *Review of Economic Studies*, 61, 197-222.

Bresnahan, T. F. and M. Trajtenberg (1995): «General Purpose Technologies: 'Engines of Growth'»?», *Journal of Econometrics* 65: 83-108.

Cameron, A.C. and P.K. Trivedi (1998): *Regression Analysis of Count Data*, Cambridge: Cambridge University Press.

Choi, J.P. (1991): «Dynamic R&D Competition under 'Hazard Rate' Uncertainty», *Rand Journal of Economics*, 22: 596-610.

Chou, C.F. and O. Shy (1991): «New product development and the optimal duration of patents», *Southern Economic Journal,* 57: 811-821.

Coe, D. and E. Helpman (1995): «International R&D Spillovers», *European Economic Review, 39(5)*.

Cohen, W.M., R.R. Nelson, and J. Walsh (1996): «A First Look at the Results of the 1994 Carnegie-Mellon Survey of Industrial R&D in the United States,» unpublished manuscript, February 28.

Cohen, W.M., R.R. Nelson, and J. Walsh (1997): «Appropriability Conditions and Why Firms Patent and Why They Do Not in the American Manufacturing Sector,» unpublished manuscript, June 24.

Crépon, B. and E. Duguet (1997a): «Research and Development, Competition, and Innovation: Pseudo Maximum Likelihood and Simulated Maximum Likelihood Methods Applied to Count Data Models with Heterogeneity,» *Journal of Econometrics* 79: 355-78.

Crépon, B. and E. Duguet (1997b): «Estimating the Innovation Function from Patent Numbers: GMM on Count Panel Data,» *Journal of Applied Econometrics* 12: 243-63.

Dasgupta, P. and J. Stiglitz (1980): «Industrial Structure and the Nature of Innovative Activity,» *Economic Journal*, 90, 266-293.

D'Aspremont, C. and A. Jacquemin (1985): «Cooperative and Non-Cooperative R&D in a Duopoly with Spillovers, *American Economic Review*, 78: 1133-1137.

David, P. (1990): «The Computer and the Dynamo: An Historical Perspective on the Productivity Paradox», *American Economic Review*, 80: 355-361.

David, P. (1985): «CLIO and the Economics of QWERTY», *American Economic Review, Papers and Proceedings*, 75: 332-337.

Davis, S.J. and J. Haltiwanger (1992): «Gross Job Creation, Gross Job Destruction and Employment Reallocation», *Quarterly Journal of Economics*, 107 : 819-864.

Duguet, E. and N. Greenan (1997): «Le biais technologique : une analyse économétrique sur données individuelles», *Revue Economique*, 48 (5): 1061-1089.

Encaoua, D., M. Moreaux and A. Perrot (1996): «Compatibility and Competition in Airlines», *International Journal of Industrial Organization*, 14: 701-726.

Farrell, J. and C. Shapiro (1992): «Standard Setting in High Definition Television», *Brookings Papers: Microeconomics* 1-93.

Gilbert, R. and C. Shapiro (1990): «Optimal Patent Length and Breadth», *Rand Journal of Economics*, 21 (1): 106-112.

Goux and Maurin (1997): «Le déclin de la demande de travail non qualifié. Une méthode d'analyse empirique et son application au cas de la France», *Revue Economique*, 48 (5): 1091-1114.

Green, J. and S. Scotchmer (1990): «Novelty and Disclosure in Patent Law», *Rand Journal of Economics*, 21 (1): 131-147.

Griliches, Z. (1995): «R&D and Productivity: Econometric Results and Measurement Issues», in *Handbook of the Economics of Innovation and Technical Change*, P. Stoneman (ed.). Basil Blackwell: Oxford.

Griliches, Z. (1957): "Hybrid Corn: An Exploration in the Economics of Technological Change," *Econometrica,* 25, 27-52.

Griliches, Z. and J. Mairesse (1999): «Production Functions: The Search for Identification,» in S. Ström (ed.), *Econometrics and Economic Theory in the 20th Century: The Ragnar Frisch Centennial Symposium*, Cambridge: Cambridge University Press.

Griliches, Z., A. Pakes, and B.H. Hall (1987): «The Value of Patents as Indicators of Economic Activity,» in Dasgupta and Stoneman (eds.), *Economic Policy and Technological Performance*, Cambridge: Cambridge University Press.

Grossman, G.M. and E. Helpman (1991): *Innovation and Growth in the Global Economy*, Cambridge, Mass.: The MIT Press.

Hall, B.H. (1992): «R&D Investment at the Firm Level: Does the Source of Financing Matter?» Cambridge, Mass.: NBER Working Paper No. 4095.

Hall, B.H., Z. Griliches, and J.A. Hausman (1986): "Patents and R&D: Is There a Lag?" *International Economic Review,* 27, 265-83.

Hall, B.H. and R.M. Ham (1999): "The Determinants of Patenting in the U.S. Semiconductor Industry, 1980-1994," Cambridge, Mass.: NBER Working Paper No. 7062 .

Hall, B.H. and F. Hayashi (1989): «Research and Development as an Investment,» Cambridge, Mass.: NBER Working Paper No. 2973.

Hall, B.H. and F. Kramarz (eds.) (1998): *Economics of Innovation and New Technology* 6, Issue 2/3/4, special issue on the effects of innovation on firm performance, employment, and productivity.

Helpman, E. and M. Trajtenberg (1994): «A Time to Sow and a Time to Reap: Growth Based on General Purpose Technologies,» NBER Working Paper No. 4854.

Himmelberg, C. P. and B. C. Petersen (1994): «R&D and Internal Finance: A Panel Study of Small Firms in High-Tech Industries, *Review of Economics and Statistics,* 76: 38-51.

Hugues, J. and E. Snyder (1995): «Litigation and Settlement under the English and American Rules: Theory and Evidence», *The Journal of Law and Economics*, 38: 225-250.

Jaffe, A. (1986): «Technological Opportunity and Spillover of R&D: Evidence from Firms' Patents, Profits,and Market Value», *American Economic Review* 4, 76,:984-1001.

Kamien, M. I. and N. L. Schwartz (1980): *Market Structure and Innovation*, Cambridge: Cambridge University Press.

Katz, M. and C. Shapiro (1985): «Network Externalities, Competition and Compatibility», *American Economic Review*, 75: 424-440.

Keller, W. (1996): «Are International R&D Spillovers Trade-Related: Analyzing Spillovers among Randomly Matched Trade Partners,» NBER Working Paper No. 6065.

Kleinknecht, A. (1996) «New Indicators and Determinants of Innovation: An Introduction», in *Determinants of Innovation, the Message from New Indicators,* edited by Alfred Kleinknecht, London, MacMillan Press.

Klemperer, P. (1990): «How Broad Should the Scope of Patent Protection be?», *The Rand Journal of Economics* , 21 (1): 113-130.

Klette, T. J. and Z. Griliches (1996): «The Inconsistency of Common Scale Estimators when Output Prices are Unobserved and Endogenous», *Journal of Applied Econometrics*, 11: 343-361.

Korah, V. (1994): *An Introductory Guide to EC Competition. Law and Practice*, 5th edition, London: Sweet and Maxwell.

Lach, S. and M. Schankerman (1988): «Dynamics of R\&D and Investment in the Scientific Sector,» *Journal of Political Economy*, 97, 880-904.

Lerner, J. (1994): «The Importance of Patent Scope: An Empirical Analysis», *The Rand Journal of Economics,* 25: 319-333.

Lerner, J. (1995): «Patenting in the Shadow of Competitors», *Journal of Law and Economics*, 38, 463-496.

Loury, G.C. (1979): «Market Structure and Innovation,» *Quarterly Journal of Economics*, 93, 395-410.

Mairesse, J., Hall, B.H. and B. Mulkay (1998): «Firm-Level Investment in France and the United States: An Exploration of What We Have Learned in Twenty Years», *Annales de l'Economie et de la Statistique,*n 55/56, Sept./Dec., p. 27-67.

Mairesse, J. and M. Sassenou (1991): «Recherche-Développement et Productivité: un panorama des études économétriques sur données d'entreprises», *Revue Science - Technologie - Industrie*, Paris, OCDE, 8,. 9-45. [English Version: «R-D and Productivity: a Survey of Econometric Studies at the Firm Level», *Science-Technology Industry Review*, Paris, OECD, 8,. 9-43].

Mansfield, E. (1961): "Technical Change and the Rate of Imitation," *Econometrica,* 29, 741-766.

Mohnen, P. (1996): «R&D Externalities and Productivity Growth», *Science-Technology Industry Review*, Paris, OECD, 13,. 39-66.

Nelson, R. R. (1959): "The Simple Economics of Basic Scientific Research," *Journal of Political Economy,* 51, 297-306.

Nordhaus, W. (1969): «An Economic Theory of Technical Change,» *American Economic Review* 59 (2): 18-28.

Oliner, S. and D. Sichel, (1994): «Computers and Output Growth Revisited: How Big Is the Puzzle?», *Brookings Papers on Economic Activity*, 2, 273-317.

Pakes, A. (1982): «Patents as Options: Some Estimates of the Value of Holding European Patent Stocks,» *Econometrica,* 64, 755-784.

Penrose, E.T. (1959): *The Theory of the Growth of the Firm*. Oxford: Basil Blackwell.

Pissarides, C.A. (1990): *Equilibrium Unemployment Theory*, Oxford: Basil Blackwell.

Reinganum, J.F. (1989): «The Timing of Innovation: Research, Development, and Diffusion,» in R. Schmalansee and R.D. Willig, eds., *Handbook of Industrial Organization,* New York: North-Holland.

Reitzes, J.D. (1991): «The Impact of Quotas and Tariffs on Strategic R&D Behavior», *International Economic Review*, 32 (4): 985-1008.

Rosenberg, N. (1976): «Technological Change in the Machine Tool Industry, 1840-1910,» in *Perspectives in Technology*, Cambridge: Cambridge University Press.

Schmookler, J. (1966): *Invention and Economic Growth,* Cambridge, Mass., Harvard University Press.

Solow, R. M. (1957): "Technical Change and the Aggregate Production Function," *Review of Economics and Statistics,* 39, 312-320.

Uzawa, H. (1969): «Time Preference and the Penrose Effect in a Two-Class Model of Economic Growth», *Journal of Political Economy*, 77, 628-652.

On the Macroeconomic Effects of Major Technological Change

Philippe AGHION, Peter HOWITT *

ABSTRACT. – This paper analyses how a General Purpose Technology (GPT) diffuses throughout the various sectors of an economy. The model outlined in this paper can account for a number of empirical observations: in particular, the existence of delays followed by acceleration phases in the experimentation and implementation of a new GPT, and the occurrence of productivity slow-downs and wage inequality increases during the acceleration phase of the logistic diffusion curve.

* Ph. AGHION: University College London, EBRD, London; P. HOWITT: Ohio State University, CIAR. Special thanks are due to Paul David, for very helpful discussions.

31

1 Introduction

Why is it that the adoption of new (more advanced) technological paradigms often entails *cyclical* growth patterns including long recession periods?

Among various attempts to account for Schumpeterian waves [1], one that appears particularly promising and fruitful is the approach based on the notion of "General Purpose Technologies" (GPTs), that is technologies whose introduction affects the entire economic system. More precisely, whilst each new GPT raises output and productivity in the long-run, it can also cause cyclical fluctuations while the economy adjusts to it. Examples of GPTs include the steam engine, the electric dynamo, the laser and the computer (see DAVID [1990]).

An interesting model of cyclical growth based on GPTs is HELPMAN-TRAJTENBERG [1995]. The basic idea of this model is that GPTs do not come ready to use off the shelf. Instead, each GPT requires an entirely new set of intermediate goods before it can be implemented. The discovery and development of these intermediate goods is a costly activity, and the economy must wait until some critical mass of intermediate components has been accumulated before it is profitable for firms to switch from the previous GPT. During the period between the discovery of a new GPT and its ultimate implementation, national income will fall as resources are taken out of production and put into R&D activities aimed at the discovery of new intermediate input components.

There are two aspects of this theory which may call its empirical relevance into question. The first is the likely *size of the slump* that it might cause. All of the decline in output is attributable to the transfer of labor out of manufacturing and into R&D. But since the total amount of R&D labor on average is only about two and a half percent of the labor force, it is hard to see how this can account for change in aggregate production of more than a fraction of a percent. (The size of the slump would be even smaller if we assumed, as HT do, that some national income is imputed to the R&D

---

1. Precusory contributions include JOVANOVIC and ROB [1990] and CHENG and DINOPOULOS which tried to generate Schumpeterian waves based on the dichotomy between fundamental and secondary innovations, with each fundamental innovation being followed by a sequence of more and more incremental innovations. Of particular interest as a macro-economic model is the CHENG-DINOPOULOS [1992] paper in which Schumpeterian waves obtain as a unique [non steady-state] equilibrium solution, along which the current flow of monopoly profits follows a cyclical evolution. "Because the economy's wealth is equal to the discounted present value of aggregate monopoly profits, fluctuations in profits generate procyclical fluctuations in wealth, the interest factor, consumption (...) and aggregate R&D investments" (CHENG-DINOPOULOS).

workers even before their research pays off in a positive stream of profits in the intermediate sector) [2].

The second questionable aspect of this theory has to do with the *timing* of slow-downs: the HT model implies an *immediate* slump as soon as the GPT arrives. This in turns follows from the assumption that: (i) agents need to see the new GPT before investing in research in order to discover the complementary components, and: (ii) these research activities are sufficiently profitable that they always divert some labor resources away from manufacturing. In fact, as Paul DAVID argues in this [1990] paper on "The Computer and the Dynamo", it may take several decades before major technological innovations can have a significant impact on macroeconomic activity (P. DAVID talks about a pre-paradigm phase of 25 years in the case of the electric dynamo). Then it is hard to believe that labor could be diverted on a large scale into an activity which will pay off only in the very distant future. The fact that so much secondary knowledge has to be accumulated before anyone will know what to do with the new GPT means instead that most firms will choose to ignore it, so treat it as just an academic theoretical discovery with no foreseeable practical significance, and that no significant speed-up R&D activity, and hence no significant slump, will take place for a long time.

The first of these problems is relatively easy to deal with (at least conceptually), as one can think of a number of reasons why the adjustment to a massive and fundamental technological change would cause adjustment and coordination problems resulting in a slump. For example, as ATKESON and KEHOE [1993] analyse, the arrival of a new GPT might induce firms to engage in *risky experimentation* on a large scale with startup firms, not all of which will succeed. The capital sunk into these startup firms will not yield a competitive return right away except by chance; meanwhile national income will drop as a result of that capital not being used in less risky ways using the old GPT. Also, an increase in the pace of innovation aimed at exploiting the new GPT may well result in an increased rate of job turnover, and hence in an increased rate of unemployment (Section 3.4 below). GREENWOOD and YORUKOGLU [1996] present an analysis in which the costs of learning to use equipment embodying the new GPT can account for a prolonged productivity showdown. HOWITT [1996] shows how the arrival of a new GPT can cause output growth to slow down because it accelerates the rate of obsolescence of existing physical and human capital.

---

2. Helpman-Trajtenberg find that a measured slump occurs when the GPT arrives even if the full cost of R&D is as imputed national income. The reason is that the discovery induces workers to leave a sector where their marginal product is higher than the wage (because the intermediate sector is imperfectly competitive and pays according to the marginal revenue product of labour rather than the marginal value product), and to enter a sector – research – where their (imputed) marginal product is just equal to the same wage.

The second problem is more challenging to deal with. The question is, if the exploitation of a new GPT is spread out over a period of many decades why should it not result in simply a slow enhancement in aggregate productivity, as one industry after another learns to use the new technology?

Again, several answers come to mind and we actually think of the following three explanations as being complementary. First are the *measurability* problems: as already stressed by David and others, it may take a while before the new products and services embodying the new GPT can be fully accounted for by the conventional statistics. (This, however, does not explain the possibility of delayed *slumps*). Second, the existence of *strategic complementaries* in the adoption of new GPTs by the various sectors of the economy may generate temporary lock-in effects, of a kind similar to the implementation cycles in SHLEIFER [1986]. It may then take real labor costs or other "exogenous" economic parameters to reach a minimum threshold before a critical number of sectors decide to jump on the bandwagon of the new GPT. A third explanation, which will be the main focus of our analysis in Section 3, lies in the phenomenon of *social learning*. That is, the way most firms learn to use a new technology is not to discover everything on their own but to learn from the experience of other firms in a similar situation: that is, for a firm to learn from other firms for whom the problems that must be solved before the technology can successfully be implemented bear enough resemblance to the problems that must be solved in this firm, that it is worth-while trying to use the procedures of those successful firms as a "template" on which to prepare for adoption in this firm. Thus at first the fact that no one knows how to exploit a new GTP means that almost nothing happens in the aggregate. Only minor improvements in knowledge take place for a long time, because successful implementation in any sector requires firms to make independent discoveries with little guidance from the successful experience of others. But if this activity continues for long enough, a point will eventually be reached when almost everyone can see enough other firms using the new technology to make it worth their while experimenting with it. Thus even though the spread of a new GPT takes places over a long period of time, most of the costly experimentation through which the spread takes place may be concentrated over a relatively short subperiod, during which there will be is a cascade or snowball effect resulting sometimes in a (delayed) aggregate slump.

The paper is organized as follows. In Section 2 we present a simplified version of the Helpman-Trajtenberg model of GPT which fits nicely into the basic Schumpeterian framework developed in AGHION-HOWITT [1992], and which also permits us to endogeneize the long-run growth rate which HT take as given. We then extend this in Section 3 to introduce social learning considerations with a view to addressing the objections concerning the timing of economic slow-downs. Finally in Section 4 we illustrate how the objection concerning the size of slow-down might be addressed by introducing three alternative features into the basic social learning model of Section 3, namely skill-difference, job search and obsolescence.

34

2 A Simplified Presentation of the Helpman-Trajtenberg Model of GPTs

2.1. A Brief Reminder of the Basic Schumpeterian Growth Model

Let us first recall the main features of the basic Schumpeterian growth model as developed in AGHION-HOWITT [1992]. Final output is produced according to the flow production function:

$$y = A \cdot x^{\alpha},$$

where x is the flow of intermediate input and A is a productivity parameter measuring the quality of intermediate input x. [Intermediate input itself is produced with labor according to a one-to-one linear technology, so that x corresponds also to the flow of manufacturing labor]. In this economy where population is constant (equal to L, which is also the total flow of labor supply under the assumption that each individual is endowed with one unit flow of labor per unit of time), growth will entirely result from vertical innovations, that is from quality improvements in A. That is, each innovation will augment current productivity by the multiplicative factor $\gamma > 1$: $A_{t+1} = \gamma A_t$. Innovations in turns are the [random] outcome of research activites, and are assumed to arrive discretely with Poisson rate $\lambda.n$, where n is the current flow of research activities.

In steady-state the allocation of labor between research and manufacturing remains constant over time, and is determined by the arbitrage equation:

(A)
$$\omega = \lambda \gamma v,$$

where the LHS of (A) is the productivity-adjusted wage rate $\omega = \frac{w}{A}$ which a worker earns by working in the manufacturing sector; and $\lambda \cdot \gamma \cdot v$ is the expected reward from investing one unit flow of labor in research. The productivity-adjusted value v of an innovation is determined by the Bellman equation:

$$rv = \pi(\omega) - \lambda n v,$$

where $\pi(\omega)$ denote the productivity-adjusted flow of monopoly profits accruing to a successful innovator and where the term $(-\lambda n v)$ corresponds to the capital loss involved in being replaced by new subsequent innovators.

The above arbitrage equation, which can be reexpressed as:

(A)
$$\omega = \lambda \gamma \frac{\pi(\omega)}{r + \lambda n},$$

together with the labor market clearing equation:

(L)
$$x(\omega) + n = L,$$

where $x(\omega)$ is the manufacturing demand for labor [3], jointly determine the steady-state amount of research n as a function of the parameters $\lambda, \gamma, L, r, \alpha$. Figure 1 below depicts the two curves (A) and (L), and shows the straight-forward comparative statics results: $\frac{dn}{d\lambda} > 0$, $\frac{dn}{d\gamma} > 0$, $\frac{dn}{dL} > 0$, $\frac{dn}{dr} < 0$.)

FIGURE 1

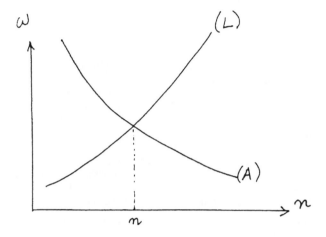

In steady-state the flow of consumption good (or final output) produced between the t-th and the $(t+1)$-th innovation is:

$$y_t = A_t (L - n)^\alpha,$$

which implies that in real time (when we denote by τ), the log of final output will increase by $\ln \gamma$ each time a new innovation occurs. Thus in this *one-sector* economy where each innovation corresponds by definition to a *major* technological change (*i.e.* to the arrival of a new GPT), growth will be *uneven* (see Fig. 2) with the time path of log $y(\tau)$ being a random step function.

The average growth rate will be equal to the size of each step, that is $\ln \gamma$, times the average number of innovations per unit of time, that is λn: *i.e.*, $g = \lambda n \ln \gamma$.

3.
$$x(\omega) = \arg\max_x \underbrace{(\alpha \cdot x^{\alpha-1}}_{p(x)} \cdot x - \omega \cdot x)$$

and
$$\pi(\omega) = \max(\alpha \cdot x^{\alpha-1} \cdot x - \omega \cdot x).$$

36

FIGURE 2

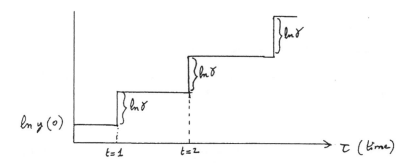

Although it is uneven, the time path of aggregate output as depicted above does not involve any slump. Accounting for the existence of slumps requires an adequate extension of the basic Schumpeterian model, for example of the kind developed by Helpman and Trajtenberg to which we now turn.

2.2. The Helpman-Trajtenberg Model Revisited

As before, there are L workers who can engage either in production of existing intermediate goods or in research aimed at discovering new intermediate goods. But each intermediate good is now linked to a particular GPT. We follow HT in supposing that before any of the intermediate goods associated with GPT can be used profitably in the final goods sector, some minimal number of them must be available. But we lose nothing essential by supposing that this minimal number is one. Once the good has been invented, its discoverer profits from a patent on its exclusive use in production, exactly as in the basic model in 2.1 above.

Thus the difference between this model and our basic model is that now the discovery of a new generation of intermediate goods comes in *two* stages. First a new GPT must come, and then the intermediate good must be invented that implements that GPT. Neither can come before the other. You need to see the GPT before knowing what sort of good will implement it, and people need to see the previous GPT in action before anyone can think of a new one. For simplicity we assume that no one directs R&D towards the discovery of a GPT. Instead, the discovery arrives as a serendipitous byproduct of the collective experience of using the previous one.

Thus the economy will pass through a sequence of cycles, each having two phases, as indicated in Figure 3 below. GPT_i arrives at time T_i. At that time the economy enters phase 1 of the i-th cycle. During phase 1, the amount n of labor is devoted to research. Phase 2 begins at time $T_i + \Delta_i$ when this research discovers an intermediate good to implement GPT_i. During phase 2 all labor is allocated to manufacturing, until GPT_{i+1} arrives, at which time the next cycle begins. Over the cycle output is equal to $A_{i-1} F (L - n)$ during phase 1 and $A_i F (L)$ during phase 2. Thus the drawing of labor out of manufacturing and into research

FIGURE 3

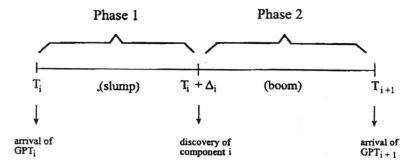

causes output to fall each time a GPT is discovered, by an amount equal to $A_{i-1}[F(L) - F(L - n)]$.

A steady state equilibrium is one in which people choose to do the same amount of research each time the economy is in phase 1, that is where n is constant from one GPT to the next. As before, we can solve for the equilibrium value of n using a research arbitrage equation and a labor market equilibrium curve. Let ω_j be the wage, and v_j the discounted expected net value of profits in the intermediate goods sector in phase j, each divided by the productivity parameter A of the GPT currently in use. In a steady state these productivity-adjusted variables will all be independent of which GPT is currently in use.

Since research is conducted in phase 1 but pays off when the economy enters into phase 2 with a productivity parameter raised by the factor γ, the usual arbitrage condition must hold in order for there to be a positive level of research in the economy:

$$(1) \qquad \omega_1 = \lambda \gamma v_2$$

Suppose that once we are in phase 2, the new GPT is delivered by a Poisson process with a constant arrival rate equal to μ. Then the value of v_2 is determined by the Bellman equation:

$$(2) \qquad r v_2 = \pi(\omega_2) + \mu(v_1 - v_2)$$

By analogous reasoning, we have:

$$(3) \qquad r v_1 = \pi(\omega_1) - \lambda n v_1$$

Combining (1)-(3) yields the research arbitrage equation:

$$(4) \qquad \omega_1 = \lambda \gamma \left[\pi(\omega_2) + \frac{\mu \pi(\omega_1)}{r + \lambda n} \right] / [r + \mu]$$

Since no one does research in phase 2, we know that the value of ω_2 is determined independently of research, by the market clearing condition:

$L = x(\omega_2)$. Thus we can take this value as given and regard equation (4) as determining ω_1 as a function of n. The value of n is determined, as usual, by this equation together with the labor-market equation:

$$(5) \qquad L - n = x(\omega_1)$$

As in the basic model, the level of research n is an increasing function of the productivity of research λ, the size of improvement created by each GPT γ, and the population L; and a decreasing function of the rate of interest r. The arrival rate μ of GPTs, can be shown to have a negative affect on research [4]; intuitively, an increase in μ discourages research by reducing the expected duration of the first of the two phases over which the successful researcher can capitalise the rents from an innovation. The size of the slump $\ln(F(L)) - \ln(F(L-n))$ is an increasing function of n, and hence will tend to be positively correlated with the average growth rate.

The average growth rate will be the frequency of innovations times the size $\ln \gamma$, for exactly the same reason as in the basic model. The frequency, however, is determined a little differently than before because the economy must pass through *two* phases. An innovation is implemented each time a full cycle is completed. The frequency with which this happens is the inverse of the expected length of a complete cycle. This in turn is just the expected length of phase 1 plus the expected length of phase 2:

$$1/\lambda n + 1/\mu = \frac{\mu + \lambda n}{\mu \cdot \lambda n}.$$

Thus we have the growth equation:

$$(6) \qquad Eg = \ln \gamma \cdot \frac{\mu \cdot \lambda n}{\mu + \lambda n}$$

Thus the expected growth rate will be positively affected by anything that raises research, with the possible exception of a fall in μ. In the limit, when μ falls to zero, growth must also fall to zero as the economy will spend an infinitely long time in phase 2, without growing. Thus for small enough value of μ, Eg and n will be affected in opposite directions by a change in μ.

One further property of this cycle worth mentioning is that, as HT point out, the wage rate will rise when the economy goes into a slump. That is, since there is no research in phase 2 the normalized wage must be low

---

4. To show this, it suffices to show that an increase in μ shifts the research arbitrage curve to the left. By applying the implicit function theorem to (4) we see that the sign of this shift is:

$$sgn \, \frac{dn}{d\mu} = -sgn \left(\omega_1 - \frac{\lambda \gamma \pi (\omega_1)}{r + \lambda n} \right).$$

Since no research is done in phase 2, labour market equilibrium requires $\omega_2 < \omega_1$, and hence $\pi(\omega_2) > \pi(\omega_1)$. Applying this to (4) yields:

$$\omega_1 > \frac{\lambda \gamma \pi (\omega_1)}{r + \lambda n} \cdot \frac{r + \lambda n + \mu}{r + \mu} > \frac{\lambda \gamma \pi (\omega_1)}{r + \lambda n}.$$

enough to provide employment for all L workers in the manufacturing sector, whereas with the arrival of the new GPT, the wage must rise to induce manufacturers to release workers into research.

As already discussed in the Introduction, the HT model may not quite fit the empirical and/or anecdotal evidence on the macroeconomic impact of major technological changes, to the extent that it predicts immediate slumps of very small magnitude. Whilst the introduction of social learning considerations in the next section will contribute to explaining the observed *delays* in the macroeconomic response to new GPTs, other considerations such as skill differentials, job search and obsolescence introduced in Section 4 can help account for the macroeconomic *significance* of GPT-driven fluctuations.

3 A Model of Major Technological Change Through Social Learning

3.1. Basic Set-Up

We consider the following dynamic model of the spread of technology, which is similar to the sorts of models used by epidemiologists when studying the spread of disease, which also takes place through a process of social interaction between those who have and those who have not yet been exposed to the new phenomenon. The setting of model is like the model we have just described, with a continuum of sectors, uniformly distributed on the unit interval, except that now each sector must invent its own intermediate good in order to exploit the GPT. We study here the nature of the cycle caused by the arrival of a single GPT, under the assumption that the arrival rate μ is so small that there is insignificant probability that the next GPT will arrive before almost all sectors have adopted the one that has just arrived. In order to simplify the analysis even further we suppose that the amount of research in each sector is given by a fixed endowment of specialized research labor. Thus all the dynamics will result from the effects of social learning on the payoff rate to experimentation. This is the phenomenon that we believe to be at the heart of the timing of the delayed cyclical response to GPTs. Endogenizing the allocation of labor between research and manufacturing would just accentuate the effects we find, as it would draw more labor into research, hence augmenting the intensity of experimentation, just when the informational cascade we focus on is already having the same effect.

Aggregate output at any point in time is produced by labor according to the constant returns technology:

$$(7) \qquad Y = \left\{ \int_0^1 A\,(i)^\alpha\, x\,(i)^\alpha\, di \right\}^{1/\alpha}$$

40

where $A(i) = 1$ in sectors where the old GPT is still used, and $A(i) = \gamma > 1$ in sectors that have successfully innovated, while $x(i)$ is manufacturing labor used to produce the intermediate good in sector i.

We assume now that in each sector an innovation requires *three* breakthroughs rather than the two breakthroughs of the previous model. First, the economy wide GPT must be discovered. Second, a firm in that sector must acquire a "template", on which to base experimentation. Third, the firm must use this template to discover how to implement the GPT in its particular sector. (This third stage is equivalent to the component finding stage in the HT model, whilst the second stage is new). Thus all sectors are in one of three states. In state 0 are those sectors who have not yet acquired a template. In state 1 are those who have a template but have not yet discovered how to implement it. In state 2 are those sectors who have succeeded in making the transition to the new GPT. We let the fraction of sectors in each state be represented by n_0, n_1, n_2, and suppose that initially $n_0 = 1$, $n_1 = n_2 = 0$.

A sector will move from state 0 to state 1 if a firm in that sector either makes an independent discovery of a template or if it discovers one by "imitation" that is by observing at least k "similarly located" firms that have made a successful transition to the new GPT (firms in state 2). The Poisson arrival rate of independent discoveries to such a sector is $\lambda_0 << 1$. The Poisson arrival rate of opportunities to observe m similarly located firms is assumed to equal unity. The probability that such an observation will pay off (in other words the probability that at least k among the m similar firms will have successfully experimented the new GPT) is given by the cumulative Binomial:

$$\varphi(m, k, n_2) = \sum_{j=k}^{m} \binom{m}{k} n_2^j \cdot (1 - n_2)^{m-j}$$

since n_2 is the probability that a randomly selected firm will be in state 2. Thus the flow of sectors from state 0 to state 1 will be n_0 times the flow probability of each sector making the transition: $\lambda_0 + \varphi(m, k, n_2)$.

For a sector to move from state 1 to state 2, the firm with the template must employ at least n units of labor per periods [the equivalent of n in the HT model]. We can think of this labor as being used in formal R&D, informal R&D, or in an experimental starting firm. In any case it is not producing current output. Instead it is allowing the sector access to a Poisson process that will deliver a workable implementation of the new GPT with an arrival rate of λ_1. Thus the flow of sectors from states 1 to 2 will be the number of sectors in state 1, n_1, times the success rate per sector per unit of time λ_1.

We can summarize the discussion to this point by observing that the evolution over time of the two variables n_1, and n_2 is given by the autonomous system of ordinary differential equation:

(S)
$$\dot{n}_1 = [\lambda_0 + \varphi(m, k, n_2)](1 - n_1 - n_2) - \lambda_1 n_1$$
$$\dot{n}_2 = \lambda_1 \cdot n_1$$

with initial condition: $n_1(0) = 0$, $n_2(0) = 0$. (The time path of n_0 is then given automatically by the identity $n_0 \equiv 1 - n_1 - n_2$.)

Figure 4 depicts the solution to the above system (S). Not surprisingly, the timepath of n_2 follows a logistic curve, accelerating at first and slowing down as n_2 approaches 1, with the maximal growth rate occurring somewhere in the middle. Likewise the path of n_1, must peak somewhere in the middle of the transition, since it starts and ends at zero. If the arrival rate λ_0 of independent discoveries is very small then both n_1 and n_2 will remain near zero for a long time. Figure 4 shows the behaviour of n_1 and n_2 in the case where $\lambda_0 = .005$, $\lambda_1 = .3$, $m = 10$ and $k = 3$. The number of sectors engaging in experimentation peaks sharply in year 20 due to social learning.

FIGURE 4

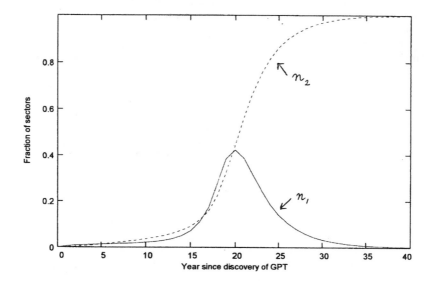

The solution to the system (S) can be used with the aggregate production function (7) and the market clearing condition for labor to determine the time path of aggregate output. Using the symmetry of the production technology (7), which implies that all the sectors using the same GPT (either old or new) will demand the same amount of manufacturing labor, we can reexpress the flow of aggregate output as:

$$(8) \qquad Y = \left\{ \int_0^{1-n_2} x_0 \left(i \right)^\alpha di + \gamma^\alpha \cdot \int_{1-n_2}^1 x_N \left(i \right)^\alpha di \right\}^{1/\alpha}$$

where x_0 (resp. x_N) denotes the flow of labor demand by a sector using the old (resp. the new) GPT.

42

In this Cobb-Douglas world the local monopolists in sectors in state 0 and 1 who use the old technology will demand labor according to the demand function [5]

(9) $$x_0 = (w/\alpha)^{\frac{1}{\alpha-1}} \cdot Y$$

while those in sectors in state 2 will demand according to:

(10) $$x_N = (w/\alpha \cdot \gamma^\alpha)^{\frac{1}{\alpha-1}} \cdot Y$$

where w is the real wage rate.

Now using the market clearing condition:

(L) $$\underbrace{(1 - n_2)\,x_0 + n_2 \cdot x_N}_{\text{manufacturing labor demand}} \underbrace{+\,n_1\,N}_{\text{experimenting labor}} = L,$$

one can solve for the real wage w as a function of Y, n_1 and n_2. Substituting this solution into the above expressions for x_0 and x_N and then substituting the resulting values of x_0 and x_N into (8) yields the following reduced form expression for output:

(11) $$Y = (L - n_1\,N) \cdot (1 - n_2 + n_2\,\gamma^{\frac{\alpha}{1-\alpha}})^{\frac{1-\alpha}{\alpha}}.$$

Figure 5 shows the time path of output, which results from the above dynamics in n_1 and n_2, in the benchmark case where $N = 6$, $L = 10$ and $\alpha = .5$. As expected, output is not much affected by the new GPT for the first decade and half, but then it enters a severe recession precisely when the number of sectors engaging in experimentation increases sharply as a result of social learning: output reaches a trough in year 19, after a 10.5% drop in output. From there output begins to grow, ultimately attaining a value of $\gamma (= 1.5)$ times its original value.

The delay in the slump caused by the GPT could not have occurred without the impact of social learning [6]. That is, suppose that the function $\varphi(m, k, n_2)$ that embodies the effects of social learning were replaced by a constant value, $\varphi_0 = \int_0^1 \varphi(m, k, n_2)\,dn_2$, whose average value was the same but which was not affected by the process of observing other sectors

---

5. This follows from profit-maximization: for any sector i, $x(i) = \arg\max_x \{p_i(x) \cdot x - wx\}$,

where:

$$p_i(x) = \frac{\partial Y}{\partial x} = \alpha x^{\alpha-1} \cdot Y^{1-\alpha} \qquad \text{if sector } i \text{ uses the } old \text{ technology}$$
$$= \alpha \cdot \gamma^\alpha\,x^{\alpha-1} \cdot Y^{1-\alpha} \quad \text{if sector is uses the } new \text{ technology.}$$

The corresponding first-order conditions, respectively for old and new sectors, yield the above equations (9) and (10).

6. GREENWODD and YORUKOGLU [1996] assume a private learning process that also produces diffusion according to a mild logistic curve.

FIGURE 5

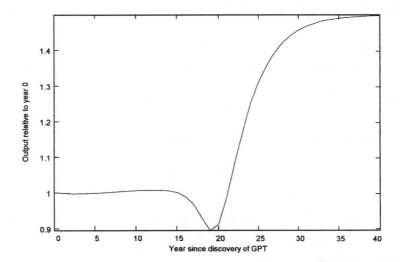

that have succeeded in implementing the new GPT. Then n_2 would still follow a mild logistic curve but the intensity of experimentation n_1 would rise immediately following the arrival of GPT and would fall monotically from then on. Output could go through a slump but the maximal rate of decline would occur immediately at year 0. This benchmark case of no social learning is illustrated in Figure 6.

Intuitively, the reason why the slump cannot be delayed in this case is as follows. In order for output to be falling there must be a positive flow

FIGURE 6

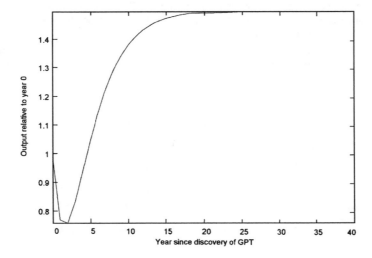

of sectors into state 1, which is drawing workers out of manufacturing. But without social learning this flow must be diminishing whenever a slump is underway, since the rise in the level of n_1 (and in n_2) will be reducing the rate of growth of n_1. (See the above equation $\dot{n}_1$ in (S)). That is, the rise in $n_1 + n_2$ reduces the number of sectors n_0 from which new experimentation can arrive, while the rise in n_1 increases the flow of successful innovators out of the state of experimentation. Thus either the slump starts right away, in which case its intensity will diminish steadily, or it never starts at all [7]. What social learning does is to reverse the effect of n_2 on the rate of growth of n_1; that is, as n_2 rises, the resulting increase in the likelihood of imitation counterbalances the fall in the number of possible imitators, thus causing the cascade at the heart of our analysis.

3.2. **Some Comparative Dynamics**

Table 1 below shows how the time path of aggregate output responds to variations in the basic parameters of the model, namely:

– α, which measures the degree of substitutability across intermediate inputs.

– γ, which measures the size of productivity improvements brought about by the new GPT

– N, the number of workers taken out of manufacturing by each experimenting firm.

– m, the number of sectors potentially "similar" to a given sector.

– k, the required number of observations of successful experimentations in order to acquire a template "by imitation".

– λ_0, the arrival rate of independent ideas for new templates.

– λ_1, the arrival rate of success for experimenting firms.

In all cases the simulation produces either a marked slump, as in Figure 5 above, or a monotonic increase in output. When there is no slump there is an initial period of relatively slow growth followed by a sharp acceleration

---

7. To see this more formally, suppose that the output function (11) can be approximated by its first-order Taylor expansion around $n_1 = n_2 = 0$:

$$Y \simeq L - N \cdot n_1 + \xi \cdot n_2; \; \xi \equiv \frac{1-\alpha}{\alpha} \left(\gamma^{\frac{\alpha}{1-\alpha}} - 1 \right) L > 0.$$

Because $\dot{n}_2$ is always positive, $\dot{n}_1$ must also be positive whenever Y is not rising. Thus: If $Y \leq 0$, then:

$$\dot{Y} \simeq -N \cdot \dot{n}_1 + \xi \dot{n}_2$$
$$\dot{Y} \simeq -N \left[(\lambda_0 + \varphi_0)(1 - n_1 - n_2) - \lambda_1 n_1 \right] + \xi \lambda_1 n_1$$
$$\ddot{Y} \simeq \left[N (\lambda_0 + \varphi_0 + \lambda_1) + \xi \lambda_1 \right] \dot{n}_1 + N (\lambda_0 + \varphi_0) \dot{n}_2$$
$$\ddot{Y} > 0 \; (\text{because } \dot{n}_1 > 0, \; \dot{n}_2 > 0).$$

Hence a delayed slump, with $\dot{Y}$ turning negative or becoming more negative at some date $t > 0$, is impossible.

coming just after the peak in experimentation. When there is a slump it almost always comes after a period of mild growth, which itself is often preceded by a very mild (less than half a percentage point) recession. The size of slump reported in Table 1 is the percentage shortfall from the peak attained at the end of the period of mild growth (or from year 0 if no such period exists) to the trough. From Table 1 we can see:

(a) the magnitude of slumps increases as α decreases; that is when intermediate inputs become less substitutable. This is fairly intuitive: as α decreases, the downsizing of old manufacturing sectors which results from labor being diverted away into experimentation, is less and less substituted for by the new−more productive−intermediate good sectors.

TABLE 1

Parameter	Value	Slump	Size	Peak date	Trough date
Benchmark		yes	11%	12	19
α	0.2	yes	12%	12	19
(0.5)	0.8	yes	8%	15	19
γ	1.1	yes	22%	0	20
(1.5)	3.0	no			
k	1	yes	23%	0	5
(3)	5	yes	4%	37	42
m	3	no			
(10)	30	yes	22%	4	10
N	2	no			
(6)	8	yes	20%	11	19
λ_0	.001	yes	11%	32	40
(.005)	.025	yes	10%	5	10
λ_2	0.1	yes	22%	13	29
(0.3)	1.0	no			

(b) the magnitude of slumps decreases as γ increases, and for sufficiently large γ the slump even disappears. Again, this result is intuitive: the bigger productivity of new sectors compensates for the reduction in output in old sectors caused by experimentation (and by the resulting wage increase), thereby reducing the scope for aggregate slumps.

(c) If m is too small, output grows steadily: indeed the lower m, the lower the scope for social learning and for the resulting snow-ball effects on aggregate output.

(d) An increase in k leads to bigger delays but smaller slumps: as k increases it will take longer for "imitation" and social learning to become operational and by the time it becomes so, a higher number of sectors will

46

have already moved into using the new and more productive GPT, hence the smaller the size of aggregate slumps.

(e) An increase in N leads to larger slumps. This is straightforward: the bigger N, the more labor will be diverted away from manufacturing into experimentation by firms in state 1, and therefore the bigger the size of slumps when social learning causes the fraction of experimenting sectors to sharply increase.

(f) An increase in the arrival rate of independent ideas λ_0 speeds up the macroeconomic response to the new GPT. This is not surprising, for the larger λ_0 the faster the conditions will be created for social learning to operate.

(g) An increase in the success rate of experimentation λ_1 reduces the size of slumps: this is again easy to understand, for the larger λ_1 the faster the emergence of sectors using the new GPT, which compensate for the downsizing of manufacturing activities induced by experimentation activities.

4 Accounting for the Size of Slow-downs

4.1. Skill Differentials

The last five years or so have witnessed an upsurge of empirical papers on skill differentials and wage inequality, and their relationship with technological change (in particular, see JUHN et al. [1993]). It turns out that a straightforward extensions of our GPT model can immediately account for the observed positive correlation between the acceleration of technological progress resulting from the introduction of new GPT, and the increasing skill differential [8]. The same extension can also magnify the slump.

More formally, suppose that the labor force L is now divided into skilled and unskilled workers, and that the implementation of the new GPT requires *skilled* labor whereas old sectors can indifferently use skilled or unskilled workers to manufacture their intermediate inputs. Also, let us assume that the fraction of skilled workers is increasing over time, e.g. as a result of schooling and/or training investments which we do not model here:

$$L_s(t) = L\left(1 - (1-\tau)e^{-\lambda_2 t}\right), \qquad \tau < 1,$$

---

8. Our explanation of both the differential and the slowdown is similar in spirit to that of GREENWOOD and YORUKOGLU [1996] who also emphasize the role of skilled labor in implementing new technologies.

where τ is the initial fraction of skilled workers and λ_2 is a positive number measuring the speed of skill acquisition.

The transition process from the old to the new GPT can then be divided into two subperiods. First, in the early phase of transition (*i.e.* when t is low) the number of sectors using the new GPT is too small to absorb the whole skilled labor force, which in turn implies that a positive fraction of skilled workers will have to be employed by the old sectors at the same wage as their unskilled peers. Thus, during the early phase of transition the labor market will remain "unsegmented", with aggregated output and real wage being determined exactly as before [9].

Second, in the later state of transition, where the fraction of new sectors has grown sufficiently large that it can absorb the whole skilled labor force, the labor market will become segmented, with skilled workers being exclusively employed (at a higher wage) by new sectors whilst the unskilled workers remain in old sectors. Let w_u and w_s denote the real wages respectively paid to unskilled and skilled workers. The demand for manufacturing labor by the old and new sectors are still given by:

$$x_0 = \left(\frac{w_u}{\alpha}\right)^{\frac{1}{\alpha-1}} \cdot Y$$

and

$$x_N = \left(\frac{w_s}{\alpha\gamma^\alpha}\right)^{\frac{1}{\alpha-1}} \cdot Y$$

except that we now have: $w_s > w_u$, where the two real wages are determined by two separate labor market clearing conditions, respectively:

(12) $$L_2 = n_1 N + n_2 \cdot x_N \rightarrow w_s$$

and

(13) $$L_1 = L - L_2 = (1 - n_2) \cdot x_0 \rightarrow w_u.$$

These equations yields:

$$w_s = \gamma^\alpha \alpha \left(\frac{n_2 Y}{L_2 - n_1 N}\right)^{1-\alpha}$$

and

$$w_u = \alpha \left(\frac{(1 - n_2) Y}{L - L_2}\right)^{1-\alpha},$$

which, after substitution for w_s and w_u in the above expressions for x_0 and x_N and after substituting the resulting values of x_0 and x_N in equation (11),

---

9. *i.e.* by equations (L) and (11), which yield:

$$Y = (L - n_1 N)(1 - n_2 + n_2 \gamma^{\frac{1-\alpha}{\alpha}})^{\frac{1-\alpha}{\alpha}}$$

and

$$w = \alpha [1 - n_2 + n_2 \gamma^{\frac{\alpha}{1-\alpha}}]^{\frac{1-\alpha}{\alpha}}.$$

yields the following expression for aggregate output during the segmented phase of transition:

$$Y = [(1 - n_2)^{1-\alpha} (L - L_2)^{\alpha} + n_2^{1-\alpha} \gamma^{\alpha} (L_2 - n_1 N)^{\alpha}]^{\frac{1}{\alpha}}$$

[The cut-off date between the unsegmented and segmented phases of transition to the new GPT is simply determined by:

$$w_s(t_0) = w_u(t_0).]$$

Figure 7a depicts the time-path of real wages and Figure 7b the time-path of aggregate output in the benchmark case of the previous section with $\lambda_2 = .05$ and $\tau = .0.25$. Two interesting conclusions emerge from this simulation:

(a) The skill premium (w_s/w_u) starts increasing sharply in the year $n = 21$ when social learning is accelerating the flow of new sectors in the economy, and then the premium keeps on increasing although more slowly

FIGURE 7

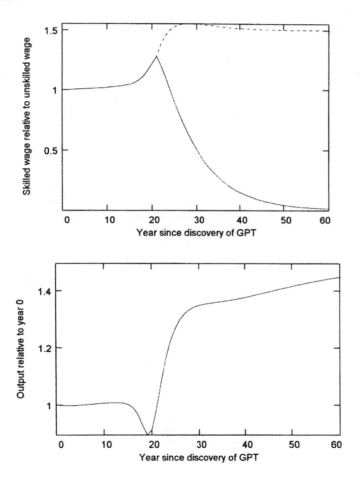

during the remaining part of the transition process [10]. Since everyone ends up earning the same (skilled) wage, standard measures of wage inequality first rise and then fall.

(b) Compared to the benchmark case *without* skill differentials and labor market segmentation, the *magnitude of the slump is* the same (11%) but the recovery is slower: the reason for this is simply that high productivity sectors are "constrained" by the short supply of skilled labor; in simulations with other parameter values we see that the slump is exacerbated by the skill shortage if the market becomes segmented near the peak of experimentation.

4.2. Job Search

Let us now extend the basic set-up in another direction namely by introducing other costly job search which, together with the destruction of jobs by new sectors generates unemployment on the transition path. Unemployment in turn diverts a higher fraction of the labor force out of manufacturing activities, thereby *increasing* the size of slumps relative to the benchmark case simulated in the above Section 3. Indeed slumps can now occur even if the labor N needed to perform experiments is negligible.

More formally, suppose that, the fraction β of workers in each sector that adapts the GPT (and moves in to n_2) go into temporary unemployment, because they are unable to adapt to the new GPT in the sector where they were formally unemployed. Suppose also that the fraction λ_3 of the unemployed per period succeed in finding a new job. Then the evolution of U, the number unemployed, is governed by:

$$\dot{U} = \underbrace{\beta x_0 (w) \lambda_1 n_1}_{\text{job destruction}} - \underbrace{\lambda_3 \cdot U.}_{\text{job creation}}$$

Output and the real wage are determined exactly as in the basic model of Section 3 except with the "effective labor force" $L - U$ instead of L [11]. Putting this real wage into the demand function (9) and substituting for Y yields the equilibrium quantity:

$$x_0 (w) = \frac{L - U - n_1 N}{1 - n_2 + n_2 \gamma^{\frac{\alpha}{1-\alpha}}}$$

Figure 8 depicts the time paths of unemployment and aggregate output with the benchmark parameter set from Section 3 together with $\beta = 0.5$ and $\lambda_3 = 2$. The unemployment rate reaches a sharp peak in year 20, just after

---

10. The acceleration in the premium, with w_s increasing and w_u decreasing sharply at the beginning of the segmented phase, has to do with the high demand for skilled experimentation labor during this time-interval where social learning peaks. The skilled real wage w_s starts tapering off thereafter where most sectors are already in phase 2 and the supply of skilled labor keeps on increasing over time. □.

11. For simplicity, we identify flows into unemployment with flows out of the labor force. This allows us to bypass the technical complications involved in modelling explicitly the bargaining game between new sectors and workers. Taking the latter more traditional modelling route would significantly complicate the algebra without adding much in terms of economic insights. □.

50

FIGURE 8

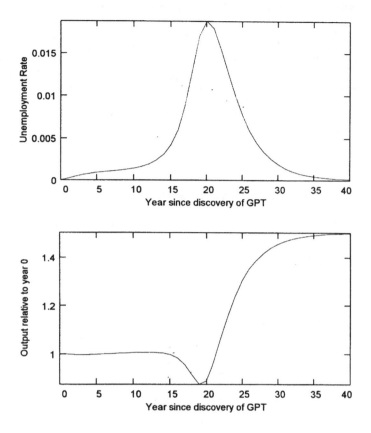

experimentation reaches its peak, with the predictable effect of increasing the size of the slump (from 11% to 13%).

4.3. Obsolescence

Our analysis in the previous section has already discussed various mechanisms that may potentially account for the significant size of macroeconomic fluctuations caused by the arrival of a new GPT: in particular the existence of labor market segmentations; or the occurrence of errors in the experimentation process which, together with labor market frictions, will generate unemployment fluctuations on the transition path to the new GPT. There is however another and maybe more straightforward explanation for the slow-downs or slumps induced by major technological changes, one that should immediately occur to anyone remotely familiar with Schumpeter's ideas: namely, the [capital] obsolescence caused by the new wave of (secondary) innovations initiated by a new GPT.

To capture this idea, we first reinterpret the model of Section 3 by supposing that the factor used in both production and research is not labor but capital, either physical or human. Each time an innovation arrives implementing the GPT in a sector it destroys a fraction δ of the capital that had previously been employed in that sector, because all capital must be tailor made to use a specific technology in a specific sector, and some of the capital is lost when it is converted to use in another sector or with another technology [12]. For simplicity, suppose that people are target savers, that is, they save a constant fraction s per period of the gap between the desired capital stock L and the actual stock K. Then the rate of net accumulation of capital is:

$$\dot{K} = \underbrace{s \cdot (L - K)}_{\text{gross saving}} - \underbrace{\delta x_0\,(w) \cdot \lambda_1\, n_1}_{\text{obsolescence}}.$$

Output and the real wage (that is, the real rate of return to capital) are determined as in the basic model of Section 3, but with L replaced by K. The initial stationary state with $n_1 = 0$ has $K = L$.

It is easy to see that this modification of the basic model of Section 3 is formally equivalent to that of the previous section, with the gap $L - K$ replacing the number unemployed U, the saving rate s replacing the job-finding rate λ_3, and the obsolescence fraction δ replacing the job-destruction fraction β. Thus, for the same reasons as in the previous section, the capital shortfall will peak sharply around the same time as the peak in experimentation, and the slump will be larger than if there were no obsolescence.

● References

AGHION, P., HOWITT, P. (1992). – "A Model of Growth through Creative Destruction", *Econometrica.*

ATKESON, A., KEHOE, P. (1993). – "Industry Evolution and Transition: The Role of Information Capital", *unpublished*, Univ of Pennsylvania.

CHENG, L., DINOPOULOS, E. (1992). – "A Schumpeterian Model of Economic Growth and Fluctuations", *Mimeo,* University of Florida.

DAVID, P. (1990). – "The Dynamo and the Computer: An Historical Perspective on the Productivity Paradox", *American Economic Review,* Vol. 80, 2, pp. 355-361.

GREENWOOD, J., YORUKOGLU, M. (1996). – "1974", *unpublished*, University of Rochester, 1996.

HELPMAN, E., TRAJTENBERG, M. (1994). – "A Time to Sow and a Time to Reap: Growth Based on General Purpose Technologies", *CIAR Working Paper,* No 32.

HOWITT, P. (1996). – "Measurement, Obsolescence, and the Adjustment to a New General Purpose Technology", in preparation for this volume.

---

12. This is the assumption made in HOWITT [1996].

52

JOVANOVIC, B., ROB, R. (1990). – "Long Waves and Short Wave: Growth Through Intensive and Extensive Search", *Econometrica,* 58, pp. 1391-1409.

JUHN, C., MURPHY, K., PIERCE, B. (1993). – "Wage inequality and the Rise in Returns to Skill", *Journal of Political Economy,* 101, No. 3.

SHLEIFER, A. (1986). – "Implementation Cycles", *Journal of Political Economy.*

On Knowledge Diffusion, Patents Lifetime and Innovation Based Endogenous Growth

Philippe MICHEL, Jules NYSSEN *

ABSTRACT. – This paper analyzes the macroeconomic effects of the patents system within the framework of an endogenous growth model with new products development. We assume that patents not only represent a commercial protection for innovators but also entail a partial property right on information. Therefore, increasing the patents lifetime increases the profitability of a given research and development project but also decreases the knowledge spillovers that play a crucial role in the growth process. We then show that when the instantaneous diffusion of knowledge is "low", growth is maximized by a finite patents lifetime while this role is devoted to infinitely lived patents are growth-maximizing when the instantaneous diffusion of knowledge is "high". Furthermore, in the former case, the optimal patents lifetime is also finite and shorter than the growth maximizing one. The design of an optimal patents policy only holds in a second best analysis. When the resource allocation is determined by a central planner maximizing the utility of a representative agent, social welfare is always higher than in the decentralized case.

* P. MICHEL: GREQAM; Université de la Méditerranée; J. NYSSEN: CREUSET, Université Jean Monnet. Thanks are due to Michael Hoy and an anonymous referee for helpful suggestions. All remaining errors are ours.

D. Encaoua et al. (eds.), The Economics and Econometrics of Innovation, 55–81.

1 Introduction

The microeconomics of innovation that underly the growth process is now a strong line of research within the field of endogenous growth theory. The canonical models – AGHION and HOWITT [1992], GROSSMAN and HELPMAN [1991a, b], ROMER [1990], SEGERSTROM et al. [1990] – share a common but never fully justified hypothesis: patents are infinitely lived. In reality, this hypohesis is evidently not verified (the statutory lifetime is 20 years in France, 17 in the US) and it would obviously not be optimal to set patents lifetime to infinity since this would create permanent monopolies with a negative effect on welfare. As an industrial policy tool, patents always result from an arbitrage between maintaining private incentives for innovative investment and limiting the market distortions induced by monopolies. In this paper, we try to understand why this kind of arbitrage never appears in the canonical models, we detail the nature of patents and then we study the impact of their lifetime on growth and welfare.

Actually, the main reason which justifies the "canonical hypothesis" is the fact that for the purpose of modeling, setting an infinite patents lifetime is the most simple way to proceed. Indeed, under finite patents lifetime, two difficulties appear. First, the dynamics of the model are described by non-linear delayed differential equations whose study is far from being completely described by mathematicians and is in many cases, at this time, impossible to conduct. Second, the price vector never reflects the cost structure and the consumers' purchase are not efficiently spread over the different goods. Indeed, households face two kinds of goods: the competitive ones – that are no longer protected by a patent and are priced at marginal cost – and the monopoly ones whose price includes a positive markup over marginal cost. Obviously, infinitely lived patents do not systematically guarantee an optimal sharing out of purchases, but the problem is always simpler when production is devoted to monopolies only. This argument becomes even more obvious for the "expanding variety" models, in the tradition of GROSSMAN and HELPMAN (1991a, ch. 3). Indeed, under infinitely lived patents when (i) the utility function or the final goods' production function is CES – in the way of DIXIT and STIGLITZ [1977] –, uses only differentiated goods as arguments and treats them symmetrically, and when (ii) at the initial state of the model, there does not exist any previously invented good whose production rights are in the public domain, the production of the horizontally differentiated goods is devoted to monopolies only who all adopt the same markup over marginal cost. Under these conditions, the price structure reflects exactly the cost structure and since the positive profits are distributed to the households, the presence of monopolies does not entail any net distortion [1]. The only sub-optimality of the model comes from the public good nature of knowledge and since its diffusion is not affected by variations in the patents lifetime, it is always optimal to set it to infinity.

---

1. See GROSSMAN and HELPMAN [1991a], p. 70f.

56

At this point, we see that in order to reconcile the innovation based endogenous growth literature with reality in terms of patents lifetime, we miss a negative effect of too long a patents lifetime on welfare. Since we cannot expect this negative effect to come from the existence of permanent monopolies, we argue that it may come from the knowledge diffusion process. We believe that the conception of patents, used in canonical models, is in some sense too radical since it makes the level of public knowledge independent of patents lifetime.

Indeed, it is generally admitted that a patent is a contract between an inventor (firm or individual) and the government. This contract is designed in order to ensure a maximal diffusion of knowledge. The government guarantees commercial protection to the inventor in exchange for a detailed diffusion of the corresponding technological information. This information must appear in a form [2] that is made public by the patents bureau within the eighteen months–in the case of France–that follow the date of the patent demand. Thus, taking this idea in a strictly literal fashion, the canonical literature assumes that the whole stock of technological knowledge is public.

But many jurists consider that the information diffused by the patents bureau during the protection period does not represent the whole technological knowledge attached to an invention. In France, it is generally admitted that at most 80% of the technological information appears in the demand form [3]. In order to capture this idea, and following Arrow [1994], we think that despite the fact that knowledge has many of a public good's attributes, all knowledge generated by an economy does not spread instantaneously. Secrecy can be kept on some technological information relative to the private production of a given good. Production experience, learning-by-doing, know-how, are elements that constitute a tacit knowledge, not codified, that does not spread as quickly as technological knowledge in its wide meaning. Furthermore, it is clear that a share of codifiable knowledge may also be kept secret for strategic reasons.

The key point of our analysis is then the assumption that only a share of the knowledge developed through private research and development (R&D) activities diffuses instantaneously, the complementary (private) share diffusing only when the patent protection ends. As long as a prdoucer keeps its monopoly right on the production of a given good, it keeps a given quantity of private knowledge. This is due to two kind of things: first to the fact that a part of this knowledge cannot be codified in a way allowing its use by competitors and secondly to intentional secrecy. But when the patent protection ceases, anybody can produce the good and then has access to the whole knowledge associated with it. Therefore the amount of public knowledge depends on the patents lifetime. Under infinitely lived patents, the amount of public knowledge may be too low to be optimal and it may then become welfare improving–despite the price distortion that will

---

2. The law requires that a patent application form must contain among others: a description of the technical domain, a description of the prior "state of the art", a detailed exposition of the invention, of the technical difficulties, of the technical solutions, a detailed exposition of at least one way to realize the invention, a list of the possible industrial uses, etc.

3. This value is given by the Institut National de la Propriété Industrielle.

appear–to shorten the patents lifetime in order to reduces the share of private knowledge. This will allow us to obtain the negative effect of too long a patents lifetime that canonical models lack. As suggested by DRÈZE [1980], the government can artificially modify knowledge excludability in order to reach a second best optimum [4].

In this paper, in order to study the optimal lifetime of patents, we construct a model based on JUDD [1985] and on GROSSMAN and HELPMAN [1991a]'s expanding variety endogenous growth model. These models are very similar in their basic structure. The main difference is the fact that Judd's model is an exogenous growth model where R&D activities do not produce any knowledge spillover. Innovation is endogenous, but not sustainable when there is no exogenously increasing factor (such as an increasing labor force). The absence of knowledge spillovers can be interpreted as the fact that the knowledge created through the invention of a given variety is product-specific (*i.e.* cannot be used to develop a new variety) and is the private property of the inventor during the patent protection period. This knowledge becomes public when the patent protection ends, but is used only by the competitive producers of the corresponding variety. Thus, Judd's paper does not take into account the effect of horizontal knowledge diffusion. In this framework, given that the nature of knowledge does not entail any sub-optimality, Judd demonstrates that when the initial variety degree is nil, the first best patents policy is to set lifetime to infinity for reasons similar to the ones that make infinittely lived patents the second best solution in GROSSMAN and HELPMAN [1991, ch. 3].

At the opposite extreme, Grossman and Helpman consider that knowledge created through R&D activities is both non rival and non excludable, and can be used in any product line. In short, this means that in the Grossman and Helpman's model, a patent is only a production right that protects against competition (and imitation) but does not preclude the use of knowledge by other agents. This hypothesis, which makes innovation and growth sustainable–as long as the spillover is specified in order to ensures constant returns in the R&D process–explains why, as we have already noted, the patents lifetime has no effect on the diffusion of knowledge.

Our model is closer to Grossman and Helpman's than to Judd's in the sense that it is a model of *endogenous growth* where we have specified the knowledge diffusion process in order to guarantees constant returns to R&D activities.

There does not exist a large macroeconomic literature that studies the incentives and the distortions resulting from a patents system. NORDHAUS [1969] is the first one to study the question in terms of economic policy, but his work is done in a static framework that cannot be used in order to evaluate the dynamic efficiency–*i.e.* the rythm and the rentability of intertemporal investment–of a patents system. A major study, and to date the only one developed in a dynamic general equilibrium framework is JUDD

---

4. Obviously, the design of an optimal patents policy makes sense only if the government canot directly control the allocation of resources. If the government could do so, the aggregate investment would no longer be decided by profit maximizing agents.

[1985] whose main characteristics have just been noted. More recently, CHOU and SHY [1991] studied the consequences of patents lifetime on the equilibrium innovation path using different specifications for the R&D cost function, but their analysis is conducted in a partial equilibrium framework. Finally, GUELLEC and RALLE [1993] modify the Grossman and Helpman's variety model by assuming a finite patents lifetime, but limit the study to an approximation of the innovation rate expressed as a linear increasing function of the patents lifetime when the latter is "relatively short".

The present paper contains three major contributions to the innovation based endogenous growth literature. First, it introduces a new hypothesis that results from a better analysis the role of knowledge as an input of the R&D process. Second, it provides a full characterization of the steady state innovation path in a general equilibrium model of endogenous growth with finite patents lifetime. This characterization allows us to distinguish the situations where the optimal patents lifetime is finite and the ones where it is infinity. Third, it shows that in general, the optimal patents lifetime is not innovation–and growth–maximizing. Furthermore, one can also intepret our model as a generalization of Grossman and Helpman's expanding variety model, the latter then representing a useful benchmark economy with respect to which we can evaluate the effects of restrictions in knowledge diffusion.

The discussion is developed as follows. Section 2 states the basis of the model, section 3 establishes two different specifications of the patents system, section 4 studies the welfare properties of the patents system and section 5 concludes.

2 The Model

There are two kinds of agents: the households that supply inelastically the constant labor force L and the firms who produce a set of horizontally differentiated goods (that we also call "varieties") with labor as the only input. Innovation is modelled as introducing a new variety into the economy. This process is costly since it requires an investment of resources into R&D. The firm that engages such R&D expenses can produce a new variety and is protected from competition for a given length of time T that corresponds to a patents lifetime. The positive profits earned, thanks to this local monopoly position, are used to repay the cost of R&D. Once the patent protection has stopped, the corresponding variety falls into the public domain and is therefore produced by competitive firms. The households have a preference for diversity and growth is measured in terms of utility.

2.1. The Households

The representative (price taker) household maximizes:

(1)
$$U = \int_0^\infty e^{-\rho t} \ln D(t)\, dt$$

where ρ is the subjective discount rate and $D(t)$ is a static utility index inspired from DIXIT and STIGLITZ [1977].

$$(2) \qquad D(t) = \left(\int_0^{n(t)} x(i, t)^\alpha \, di \right)^{\frac{1}{\alpha}}$$

In this equation, $n(t)$ is the "number" of varieties [5] available in t, $x(i, t)$ is the quantity consumed in t of variety i and $\alpha = 1 - \sigma^{-1}$. The parameter $\sigma > 1$ stands for the elasticity of substitution between two varieties. Defining $A(t)$ as private wealth, the intertemporal budget constraint is:

$$(3) \qquad \begin{cases} \dot{A}(t) = r(t)A(t) + w(t)L - \displaystyle\int_0^{n(t)} p(i, t)x(i, t)\, di \\ \lim_{t \to \infty} R(0, t)A(t) \geq 0 \end{cases}$$

where $r(t)$ is the interest rate, $w(t)$ the wage rate, $p(i, t)$ the price of variety i, and

$$R(t_0, t) = \exp\left[-\int_{t_0}^t r(\tau)\, d\tau \right].$$

The representative household's program can be decomposed into a static one—concerning the allocation of consumption among varieties—and a dynamic one—concerning the determination of savings. The resolution of the former leads to the following demand functions [6]

$$(4) \qquad x(i) = \frac{Ep(i)^{-\sigma}}{\int_0^n p(j)^{1-\sigma}\, dj} \qquad i \in [0, n]$$

where E represents consumption expenditures. In order to solve the second program, we define a price index P such that $E = PD$.

$$P = \left(\int_0^n p(i)^{1-\sigma}\, di \right)^{\frac{1}{1-\sigma}}$$

We can then substitute E/P for D in the utility function (1) and E for $\int_0^n p(i)x(i)\, di$ in the budget constraint (3). Given that the representative household is a price taker, his optimal consumption expenditures path is defined by:

$$(5) \qquad \begin{cases} \dot{E}(t) = E(t)[r(t) - \rho] \\ \lim_{t \to \infty} R(0, t)A(t) = 0 \end{cases}$$

---

5. Formally, n is the measure of the continous set of varieties. In the following, for the sake of simplicity, we shall speak of "number" of varieties, just as if they were constituting a discrete set.

6. In the following, we drop the time index and the variety index when they are not strictly necessary for comprehension.

2.2. The Firms

We have two kinds of firms: the competitive ones, acting in branches 0 to n_c, and the monopolist ones, producing varieties n_c to n. They are all characterized by the same production function $x(i) = l(i)$ where $l(i)$ is the amount of labor used in branch i. The monopolistic firms, protected by a patent, maximize their profit $\pi(i) = [p(i) - w] x(i)$, $i \in]n_c, n]$, given the demand function (4). The resulting strategic price and profit are:

$$(6) \qquad\qquad p(i) = \frac{w}{\alpha} = p_m \quad i \in]n_c, n]$$

which implies by (4) $x(i) = x_m$ for $i \in]n_c, n]$, and

$$(7) \qquad\qquad \pi(i) = \frac{1 - \alpha}{\alpha} w x_m = \pi \quad i \in]n_c, n].$$

The competitive firms charge a price equal to marginal cost and earn no profit.

$$(8) \qquad\qquad p(i) = w = p_c \quad i \in [0, n_c]$$

The market value of a monopolistic firm created at date t, $v^e(t)$, is equal to the present value of the flow of profit it will earn until the end of the patent protection.

$$(9) \qquad\qquad v^e(t) = \int_t^{t+T} R(t, z) \pi(z) dz$$

A potential "innovator" accepts to introduce a new variety only if the cost of entry—i.e. the cost of the R&D expenses $v(t)$—is not larger than $v^e(t)$. Since we assume that R&D is a free entry activity, no profit opportunity is left unexploited, so that we always have $v^e \leq v$. When the R&D cost is greater than the market value ($v^e < v$), there is no innovation, and no growth. When $v^e = v$, potential innovators are indifferent between investing or not and the aggregate entry level is determined by the availability of the labor force.

2.3. R&D

We now turn to the important point of this paper: the determination of the R&D cost, $v(t)$. Following GROSSMAN and HELPMAN [1991, ch. 3], we assume that inventing a new variety is an activity that requires labor and public knowledge, and has constant returns with respect to labor (the only "private" input). An invention can be considered as producing knowledge, whose aggregate stock is designated by $n(t)$. As mentioned in the introduction, this knowledge is non rival and, thanks to the patents system, partially excludable. Therefore, the stock of public knowledge at date t—i.e. the stock of knowledge freely available for anybody—is composed of $n_c(t)$, the whole knowledge developed through the invention of varieties that are in the public domain at date t, and a share θ of the knowledge associated with the invention of varieties still protected by a patent at the same date. Thus, defining $\Delta_n(t) = n(t) - n_c(t)$, the stock of public knowledge available at date t is:

$$(10) \qquad k_n(t) = n_c(t) + \theta \Delta_n(t) \quad 0 \leq \theta \leq 1.$$

Public knowledge increases the productivity of the labor force involved in R&D activities. In order to obtain a constant growth rate, we assume that invention $-i.e.$ production of new knowledge $\dot{n}-$is a linear function of the stock of public knowledge (k_n). We can then define the following "production function" for R&D:

$$(11) \qquad \dot{n}(t) = \frac{1}{a} k_n(t) L_n(t)$$

where $a > 0$ is a productivity parameter and L_n is the labor devoted to R&D. Therefore, the cost of developing and introducing a new variety, or equivalently the cost of a patent, can be stated as follows:

$$(12) \qquad v(t) = \frac{aw(t)}{n_c(t) + \theta \Delta_n(t)};$$

When θ, that we call the *diffusion coefficient*, is equal to one$-i.e.$ when knowledge is completely non excludable despite the presence of a patent$-$and when $n_c = 0-i.e.$ when patents are infinitely lived with $n_c(0) = 0-$the specification of the R&D activity is similar to GROSSMAN and HELPMAN's. JUDD [1985]'s specification corresponds to the particular case $k_n = 1$. This hypothesis means that knowledge is always a private good (that disappears when the patent protection ends) and has no effect on the R&D labor productivity. Due to this hypothesis, Judd's model never displays endogenous growth. Indeed, the market value of a monopoly decreases over time with the increase in the number of varieties, and the rentability of R&D investments is therefore also decreasing. As in more usual neoclassical growth models, the growth rate tends to zero if no exogenous force (as an increase in the labor force) is maintaining it. Assuming that the cost of a patent is decreasing with the number of varieties allows for sustained growth. In Grossman and Helpman's model, v is assumed to be a decreasing function of the instantaneous number of varieties. In our model, v decreases proportionally to a lagged number of varieties.

The diffusion coefficient, θ, is exogenous. This means that agents cannot control the part of the knowledge that diffuses instantaneously. In the model, such an hypothesis does not represent any problem since θ determines the sharing-out of something that, in each case, is considered as an externality. In reality, this hypothesis means that agents cannot decide to deliberately maintain secrecy concerning the scientific discoveries that are incorporated into their currently produced goods. This can be considered as a restrictive assumption, but it is necessary to display relatively simple results and it is the only one consistent with the idea of a continuum of innovators/producers.

2.4. **Closing the Model**

The model is closed by a resource constraint that specifies the use of the labor force. Labor demand from R&D, L_n, is given by (11).

$$(13) \qquad L_n = a \frac{\dot{n}}{k_n}$$

Labor demand from the production sector is given by $L_x = n_c x_c + \Delta_n x_m$. Using (4), (6) and (8), we have:

$$(14) \qquad x_c = \frac{E/w}{n_c + \alpha^{\sigma-1} \Delta_n} \qquad \text{and} \qquad x_m = \alpha^\sigma x_c < x_c.$$

The discrepancy between the quantity consumed of competitive varieties and the quantity consumed of monopolistic varieties results from the price distortion due to monopolies. The resource constraint is given by:

$$(15) \qquad L = \frac{E}{w} \left(\frac{n_c + \alpha^\sigma \Delta_n}{n_c + \alpha^{\sigma-1} \Delta_n} \right) + a \frac{\dot{n}}{k_n}$$

In equation (15), the value of the terms between parentheses belongs to $[\alpha, 1]$ and tends to 1 when the share of competitive varieties is large. Since all varieties are produced using the same quantity of labor, everything being equal elsewhere, the less the share of monopolies, the higher the aggregate labor demand from the production sector.

We adopt here the normalization proposed by Grossman and Helpman which consists of setting to one the value of the consumption expenditures. This normalization is useful since it provides a very simple expression for the interest rate. Indeed, with $E(t) \equiv 1$ and (5), the nominal interest rate is just equal to the subjective discount rate: $r(t) = \rho$. It is then variations of the wage rate w that ensure equilibrium on the labor market.

The dynamics of the model are then represented by

$$(16) \qquad \dot{n}(t) = \frac{n_c(t) + \theta \Delta_n(t)}{a} \left[L - \frac{1}{w(t)} \left(\frac{n_c(t) + \alpha^\sigma \Delta_n(t)}{n_c(t) + \alpha^{\sigma-1} \Delta_n(t)} \right) \right]$$

where $n_c(t) = n(t - T)$. Defining

$$(17) \qquad \tilde{w} = \frac{1}{L} \left(\frac{n_c + \alpha^\sigma \Delta_n}{n_c + \alpha^{\sigma-1} \Delta_n} \right)$$

we have

$$(18) \qquad \begin{cases} \text{If } v^e(t) \le \dfrac{a\tilde{w}(t)}{n_c(t) + \theta \Delta_n(t)} & \dot{n}(t) = 0 \text{ and } w(t) = \tilde{w}(t), \\[2ex] \text{If not, } v^e(t) = \dfrac{aw(t)}{n_c(t) + \theta \Delta_n(t)} & \dot{n}(t) > 0 \text{ and } w(t) > \tilde{w}(t) \end{cases}$$

where, by (7) and (14):

$$(19) \qquad v^e(t) = (1-\alpha) \int_t^{t+T} \frac{e^{-\rho(z-t)}}{\alpha^{1-\sigma} n_c(z) + \Delta_n(z)} \, dz$$

In the case $\dot{n} > 0$, the equilibrium value of the wage rate w is determined forwardly and equation (16) is a delayed differential equation depending on $n_c(t)$, with $n_c(t) = n(t-T)$.

We now study the solutions of this model with infinitely lived patents and then with finite patents lifetime.

3 Different Specifications of the Patents System

Innovation based endogenous growth models have the specific property that innovation (and growth) is possible only if the labor supply is high enough to allow both production and R&D activities. The long run equilibrium of the model is represented by a steady state which can be purely static – if the labor supply is too scarce – or can be characterized by a constant and positive growth rate. In the following, we study successively these two possibilities.

3.1. Infinitely Lived Patents

The case with infinitely lived patents corresponds formally to $T = \infty$, $n_c = 0$ and $k_n = \theta n$. This is the simplest case to study since there is no "competitive variety" and therefore no price distortion on the differentiated goods market. The dynamics of the model in this case are described by:

$$(20) \qquad \begin{cases} \text{If } v^e(t) \le \dfrac{a\tilde{w}}{\theta n(t)}, & \dot{n}(t) = 0 \text{ and } w(t) = \tilde{w}, \\[2ex] \text{If not, } v^e(t) = \dfrac{a w(t)}{\theta n(t)}, & \dot{n}(t) = \dfrac{\theta n(t)}{a} \left(L - \dfrac{\alpha}{w(t)} \right), \end{cases}$$

where $\tilde{w} = \alpha/L$ and

$$v^e(t) = (1-\alpha) \int_t^\infty \frac{e^{-\rho(z-t)}}{n(z)} \, dz.$$

Solutions without growth

In this case, the total number of varieties is constant: $n(t) \equiv n_0$. The value of a monopoly is equal to $v^e = (1-\alpha)/(n_0 \rho)$ and must not be greater than the cost of a patent $v = \alpha\, a/(\theta\, n_0\, L)$. Therefore, there is no innovation (and no growth) in this model as long as:

$$(21) \qquad \theta \le \frac{\alpha\, a\rho}{(1-\alpha)\, L} \equiv \theta_1$$

that is as long as the diffusion coefficient is too low relative to the productivity of the r&D process, the subjective discount rate, the elasticity of substitution or the labor supply. Given θ, this case may appear in an economy relatively poor in labor with respect to the R&D productivity, where agents are "impatient" (high ρ) and have a "little" preference for diversity (α near one).

Solutions with sustained growth

In this case, the total number of varieties increases at the exponential rate $g > 0$:

$$(22) \qquad n(t) = n_0\, e^{gt};$$

The value of a monopoly is decreasing with the number of monopolies and given by

$$(23) \qquad v^e(t) = \frac{1-\alpha}{(\rho+g)\, n_0\, e^{gt}}$$

and must be equal to the cost of a patent $v = e^{-gt}\, a w(t)/(n_0\,\theta)$. This determines a constant wage rate

$$w = \frac{(1-\alpha)\,\theta}{a\,(\rho+g)}$$

and, using (20)

$$g = \frac{\dot{n}}{n} = \frac{\theta}{a}\left[L - \frac{\alpha}{w}\right],$$

allows us to establish a first proposition.

> PROPOSITION 1 : Under infinitely lived patents, if $\theta > \theta_1$, there exists an endogenous balanced growth path [7] with a constant and positive rate
>
> $$(24) \qquad g^*_\infty = (1-\alpha)\,\theta\frac{L}{a} - \alpha\rho.$$
>
> If $\theta \le \theta_1$, there is no innovation and no growth.

The rate g^*_∞ depends positively on the labor endowment of the economy, on R&D productivity, on the preference for diversity and on the diffusion coefficient. It depends negatively on the agents' impatience. The degree of

---

7. Note that g is only the growth rate of the number of varieties. As mentioned in section 2, aggregate growth is measured in terms of utility and is just a positive transformation of g. Indeed, it comes from (2) that $D = n^{1/\alpha}\, L_\alpha$ and that in a steady state, $\dot{D}/D = (1/\alpha)\,\dot{n}/n = g/\alpha$.

non excludability of knowledge, as measured by θ, must be greater than the threshold value θ_1 in order for innovation to be possible. If $\theta < \theta_1$, the spillover effect associated with the R&D process is not high enough to allow for sustained growth.

We turn now to the case of finite patents lifetime.

3.2. **Finite Patents Lifetime**

When patents lifetime is finite, the dynamics of the model are defined by equations (16)-(19).

Solutions without growth

When $\dot{n} = 0$ on a steady state, there is no patented variety: $\Delta_n = 0$ and $k_n = n_c = n_0$. The cost of a patent is equal to $v = a\tilde{w}/n_0 = a/(n_0 L)$ and is greater than the value of a monopoly:

$$(25) \qquad v^e = \frac{(1 - \alpha)}{\rho \alpha^{1-\sigma} n_0} (1 - e^{-\rho T}).$$

The equilibrium condition, $v^e \leq v$ can then be written:

$$(26) \qquad 1 - e^{-\rho T} \leq \frac{\rho a}{L(1 - \alpha) \alpha^{\sigma-1}}.$$

Note that the equilibrium condition does not depend on the diffusion coefficient θ contrary to the condition (21) used in the case of infinitely lived patents. The reason for this, in these last case, is the fact that even when $\dot{n} = 0$, there always exist monopolies. Thus a share of total existing knowledge remains private. When patents lifetime is finite, a steady state without growth is characterized by the absence of any patented variety. Therefore, the whole existing knowledge is public and the particular value of θ is not relevant.

When $\rho \geq (1 - \alpha) \alpha^{\sigma-1} L/a$, condition (26) is satisfied for all T. In this case, there exists an equilibrium path without innovation for any patents lifetime. As before, there is no growth when agents are too impatient, have too low a preference for diversity [8] or when the labor endowment relative to the R&D productivity parameter is too low.

On the contrary, under the following hypothesis

H1. $\rho < (1 - \alpha) \alpha^{\sigma-1} L/a$

there exists an equilibrium path without growth only if patents lifetime is short enough. Indeed, in this case, condition (26) is equivalent to $T \leq T_m$ where T_m is defined by:

$$(27) \qquad e^{-\rho T_m} = 1 - \frac{\rho a}{L(1 - \alpha) \alpha^{\sigma-1}};$$

---

8. This comes from the fact that $(1 - \alpha) \alpha^{\sigma-1}$ is a decreasing function of α on $[0, 1]$.

The patents lifetime determines the length of the period during which a monopoly will be able to repay its R&D cost. The shorter is T, the lower is the net rentability of investment. When $T \leq T_m$, investment is never profitable, while it would be so if T were greater than T_m. It is interesting to note that this threshold value increases when L/a decreases or when α increases.

The net effect of ρ on T_m is more difficult to determine. Indeed, it comes from the examination of (25) that ρ has two contrary effects on v^e. On the one hand, a higher ρ-value means that agents are more impatient and are making a lower expectation about the value of a monopoly. Thus, on an equilibrium path without growth, this would allow for higher T_m-values. But on the other hand, ρ measures the weight of the patents lifetime in the valuation of a monopoly. For any given T, the higher is ρ the higher is $(1 - e^{-\rho T})$. Under these conditions, on an equilibrium path without growth, higher ρ-values are consistent with lower T_m-values. Nevertheless, it can be shown that the former effect always dominates [9] and that T_m increases with ρ.

Solutions with sustained growth

We turn now to the most interesting case of our analysis. We determine here the existence condition for a steady state with growth and we analysis how the associated growth rate is affected by the patents lifetime.

On a sustained growth path, the number of varieties is given by (22). The number of competitive varieties is equal to $n_c(t) = n(t - T) = n(t) e^{-gT}$. We can then compute the value of a monopoly

$$(28) \qquad v^e(t) = \frac{(1 - \alpha)\left[1 - e^{-(\rho+g)T}\right]}{n_0\left[1 + (\alpha^{1-\sigma} - 1)e^{-gT}\right](\rho + g)} e^{-gt}$$

which is decreasing at rate g. Given that the value of a monopoly v^e must be equal to the cost of a patent v, equation (12) allows us to write down the equilibrium value of the wage rate, which is a constant.

$$(29) \qquad w = \frac{(1 - \alpha)\left[1 - e^{-(\rho+g)T}\right]\left[\theta + (1 - \theta)e^{-gT}\right]}{a\left[1 + (\alpha^{1-\sigma} - 1)e^{-gT}\right](\rho + g)}$$

The law of motion of n, defined by equation (16) is then equivalent to

$$L\left[\theta + (1 - \theta)e^{-gT}\right] - ag = \frac{\alpha a(\rho + g)\left[1 + (\alpha^{-\sigma} - 1)e^{-gT}\right]}{(1 - \alpha)\left[1 - e^{-(\rho+g)T}\right]};$$

---

9. By differentiating (27) with respect to T_m and ρ, one gets

$$\frac{dT_m}{d\rho} = \frac{a}{\rho L(1 - \alpha)\alpha^{\sigma-1}} e^{\rho T_m} - \frac{T_m}{\rho} = A(T_m) - B(T_m).$$

Since $A(0) > B(0)$ and since, under H1, $A'(T_m) > B'(T_m)$, one has $A(T_m) > B(T_m) \forall T_m > 0$.

and can be rewritten

(30)
$$F(g, T) \equiv A(g, T) - B(g, T) = 0$$

with:

$$A(g, T) = \frac{1-\alpha}{\alpha a} \frac{1 - e^{-(\rho+g)T}}{\rho + g}$$

$$\text{and} \quad B(g, T) = \frac{1 + (\alpha^{-\sigma} - 1) e^{-gT}}{L(\theta + (1-\theta) e^{-gT}) - ag}.$$

We are looking for solutions to (30) where the growth rate is defined as a function of patents lifetime $g = g(T)$. Any solution $g(T) > 0$ satisfies the equilibrium condition $w > \tilde{w}$.

Unfortunately, it is not possible to write down explicitly such solutions. Nevertheless, assuming that assumption H1 is satisfied – *i.e.* that agents are relatively patient – we define

$$\bar{\theta} = \frac{1 - \rho(\alpha^{1-\sigma} - \alpha) a/L}{\alpha^{1-\sigma} + 1 - \alpha}.$$

Under H1, $\theta_1 < \alpha^\sigma < \bar{\theta}$, and since $\sigma = \sigma(\alpha)$ with

$$\lim_{\alpha \to 0} (\alpha^{1-\sigma} - \alpha) = 1$$

we also have $\bar{\theta} < 1$. Thus, we can establish the following results whose formal proof is given in appendix A.

PROPOSITION 2 : [Existence]
If $T > T_m$, there exists a solution $g^*(T) > 0$ which is unique if $\theta \leq \alpha^\sigma$.

PROPOSITION 3 : [Limit of the solution when $T \to \infty$]
Any solution $g^*(T)$ satisfies:

$$\text{if } \theta \leq \theta_1, \quad \lim_{T \to \infty} g^*(T) = 0$$

$$\text{if } \theta > \theta_1, \quad \lim_{T \to \infty} g^*(T) = g^*_\infty$$

PROPOSITION 4 : [Solutions greater than g^*_∞]
For $\theta_1 < \theta < \bar{\theta}$, equation $F(g, T) = 0$ admits a unique solution $g^*(T) > g^*_\infty$ for large enough T-values.
For $\theta \geq \bar{\theta}$, and for any T, $F(g, T)$ admits no solution $g^*(T) > g^*_\infty$.

It comes from the three previous propositions that:

THEOREM 1. [Maximum growth rate]
T1.1. The equilibrium growth rate is maximized by a finite patents lifetime $\hat{T}$ when $\theta < \bar{\theta}$ and by infinitely lived patents when $\theta \geq \bar{\theta}$.
The finite lifetime $\hat{T}$ and the corresponding maximized growth rate $\hat{g}$ are characterized by the system [10]: $F(\hat{g}, \hat{T}) = 0$ and $F'_T(\hat{g}, \hat{T}) = 0$.
T1.2. When the diffusion coefficient θ tends to $\bar{\theta}$, the increasing function $\hat{g}(\theta)$ tends to the limit $g^*_\infty|_{\theta=\bar{\theta}}$ and $\hat{T}$ tends to infinity.

Part 1 of theorem 1 means that when the diffusion coefficient is sufficiently high, the rentability of R&D investments is maximized when innovators are protected forever. If we compare a situation with infinitely lived patents to a situation with finite patents lifetime, the cost of a patent is higher in the former (under infinitely lived patents, a share $1 - \theta$ of knowledge always remains public) but the market value of a monopoly is also higher. The negative effect due to a restriction in the diffusion of knowledge is more than compensated by the length of the commercial exploitation period.

This is no more the case when the diffusion coefficient becomes lower than $\bar{\theta}$. The growth maximizing patents lifetime is then finite. In this case, an economy characterized by $T < \hat{T}$ would be growing slower because the decrease of the commercial exploitation period is not compensated by a sufficient decrease of the cost of a patent. Conversely, an economy with $T > \hat{T}$ would be also growing slower because the increase of the commercial exploitation period is more than compensated by an increase of the cost of a patent.

The diffusion coefficient is always growth promoting when $T = \hat{T}$. Part 2 of theorem 1 show that $\hat{g}$ is an increasing function of θ when $\theta < \bar{\theta}$ and equation (24) show that g^*_∞ is also an increasing function of θ. An increase in θ increases the knowledge spillover effect, and therefore decreases the cost of a patent.

4 Welfare Analysis

Now we have identified the growth-maximizing patents lifetime, we examine what could be the optimal one. By "optimal", we mean the duration that maximizes the utility function (1) taken as a social welfare index. It must be noted that manipulating the patents lifetime allows one only to reach a second-best equilibrium. Indeed, the patent system (when T is finite) induces a price distortion on the differentiated goods market. Furthermore, introducing a new variety induces three different

---

10. The uniqueness of the pair $(\hat{g}, \hat{T})$ is proved in appendix A.

external effects: a rise in the level of public knowledge, a decrease in the instantaneous profit earned by a monopolist and an increase of households' utility. These effects make impossible the coincidence of the competitive equilibrium with the first-best one.

4.1. Optimal Growth Rate

The first-best equilibrium of this model corresponds to a situation where the saving and investment decisions are taken by a social planner. In this case, the patents do not exist and the problem of knowledge diffusion disappears. Indeed, the social planner use the whole knowledge developed through R&D activities and $k_n = n$. The problem to be solved is then very simple and consists of maximizing U with respect to the resource constraint:

$$L = a\frac{\dot{n}}{n} + \int_0^n x(i)\, di.$$

Since (i) the static utility index treats all the varieties symmetrically, (ii) the marginal utility associated with the consumption of each good is decreasing ($\alpha < 1$), and (iii) the production functions are identical, it follows that the optimal static allocation of labor among branches is symmetric. We then have $x(i) = x$ and the first-best equilibrium is the solution of the program

(31)
$$\max_{[x(t)]_0^\infty} U = \int_0^\infty e^{-\rho t}\left[\frac{1}{\alpha}\ln n(t) + \ln x(t)\right] dt$$
$$\text{s.t. } a\frac{\dot{n}(t)}{n(t)} = L - n(t)x(t) \qquad \text{and} \qquad n(t) \geq 0 \forall t \geq 0.$$

The solution corresponds to the growth rate

(32)
$$g^0 = \frac{1}{1-\alpha}\left[(1-\alpha)\frac{L}{a} - \alpha\rho\right] = \frac{g_\infty^*|_{\theta=1}}{1-\alpha}.$$

The socially optimal growth rate g^0 is thus always greater than $g_\infty^*|_{\theta=1}$ which is the highest feasible growth rate in the competitive economy. The latter is thus always characterized by underinvestment with respect to the Pareto-optimal situation.

With this result, one could imagine that every growth increasing factor is also welfare improving. In this case, the optimal patents lifetime would be the growth maximizing one. In a second-best analysis, nonever this is the case, as we show in the next paragraph.

4.2. Optimal Patents Lifetime

In order to determine the optimal patents lifetime, we need to compute the value of the utility function U on a sustained growth path. The representative household's utility is given by

$$U = \int_0^\infty e^{-\rho t} \ln D(t) dt$$

with $n(t) = n_0 e^{gt}$. The static utility index (2) is

$$D = (n_c x_c^\alpha + \Delta_n x_m^\alpha)^{1/\alpha}.$$

where x_c and x_m are given by (14). Thus we have

$$D(t) = \frac{\alpha}{w} [1 + (\alpha^{1-\sigma} - 1) e^{-gT}]^{\frac{1-\alpha}{\alpha}} (n_0 e^{gt})^{\frac{1-\alpha}{\alpha}}$$

which becomes, using the expression (29) of w

$$D(t) = N(g, T) (e^{gt})^{\frac{1-\alpha}{\alpha}}$$

with

$$N(g, T) = \frac{\alpha n_0^{(1/\alpha)-1} a [\rho + g][1 + (\alpha^{1-\sigma} - 1) e^{-gT}]^{1/\alpha}}{(1 - \alpha)[1 - e^{-(\rho+g)T}][\theta + (1 - \theta) e^{-gT}]}.$$

We then deduce the value of intertemporal utility on the equilibrium path characterized by $g = g^*(T)$.

$$(33) \qquad U^*(T) \equiv U[g^*(T), T] = \frac{1}{\rho} \ln N[g^*(T), T] + \frac{1-\alpha}{\alpha} \frac{g^*(T)}{\rho^2}$$

Defining $N^*(T) \equiv N[g^*(T), T]$, the derivative of U^* with respect to the patents lifetime is therefore defined by

$$(34) \qquad \frac{dU^*(T)}{dT} = \frac{1}{\rho N^*(T)} \frac{dN^*(T)}{dT} + \frac{1}{\rho^2} \frac{1-\alpha}{\alpha} \frac{dg^*(T)}{dT}.$$

and its sign is studied in appendix B where we consider a third threshold value for the diffusion coefficient:

$$(35) \qquad \theta_3 = \frac{\alpha}{\alpha^{1-\sigma} - 1 + \alpha}.$$

We now state the following hypothesis:

H.2. $\rho < \dfrac{(1-\alpha)(\alpha^{1-\sigma} - 1 - \alpha)}{(\alpha^{1-\sigma} - \alpha)(\alpha^{1-\sigma} - 1 + \alpha)} \dfrac{L}{a}.$

This hypothesis is more restrictive than H1 – *i.e.*, it imposes a lower value for the subjective discount rate ρ.

> THEOREM 2 : [Optimal patents lifetime]
> If the subjective discount rate satisfies H2, we have $\theta_3 < \bar{\theta}$ and for all $\theta \in [\theta_3, \bar{\theta}]$
> $$\frac{dg^*(T)}{dT} \leq 0 \Rightarrow \frac{dU^*(T)}{dT} < 0.$$
> Thus, the optimal patents lifetime – *i.e.* the patents lifetime that maximizes the representative household's utility – is finite and shorter than the value $\hat{T}$ that maximizes the growth rate.

Unfortunately, we have not been able to conduct a complete algebraic analysis for θ-values belonging to $[0, \bar{\theta}]$ and so we have proceeded with numerical simulations. These simulations, detailed in sub-section 4.3, show that under H2, theorem 2 holds for the whole interval $[0, \bar{\theta}]$.

This theorem means that when the instantaneous diffusion of knowledge is relatively low, the second best patents lifetime is shorter than the growth maximizing one. Although private investment is always too low to be optimal in a first best analysis, we see here that in a second best framework, the resulting effect of the different externalities may induce overinvestment. When the only policy tool is the patents lifetime, the arbitrage between industrial profitability and welfare then entails the choice of legal commercial protection that reduces the incentives for investment faced by private innovators.

4.3. **Numerical Analysis**

The aim of our numerical analysis is to obtain two lists of T-values, given as function of θ, corresponding respectively to the growth maximizing and to the optimal patents lifetime on the interval $[0, \bar{\theta}]$. We restrict the analysis to this interval since it corresponds to the case where growth is maximized by a *finite* patents lifetime. Using theorem 1, we compute $\hat{T}(\theta)$ as the solution of the system $\{F(\hat{g}, \hat{T}) = 0, F'_T(\hat{g}, \hat{T}) = 0\}$, and we repeat this for θ starting at 0 and going to $\bar{\theta}$ by steps of .01. This gives us the plain curve corresponding to the collection of points $\{\theta, \hat{T}(\theta)\}$ that appears in figure 1. We use the same procedure in order to determine the list of T^0-values that maximize social welfare for $\theta \in [0, \bar{\theta}]$. Here, $T^0(\theta)$ is computed as the solution to the system $\{F(g^0, T^0) = 0, U'_T(g^0, T^0) = 0\}$.

The following values have been assigned to the parameters of the model. We have chosen to normalize to one the labor supply L and the productivity parameter a. These two parameters reflect the resource endowment of the economy and play a role mainly on the level of the growth rate. We have fixed to one the value of the initial variety level $n_0 \equiv n(0)$ in order to have always $n(t) = e^{gt}$. The values of ρ and α have been fixed in such a way that assumption H2 – and therefore assumption H1 – is satisfied. More precisely, we have assigned a usual value to the subjective discount rate, which is also the interest rate here, assuming $\rho = .05 = 5\%$. Then, H2 is satisfied for $0 \leq \alpha \leq .7$. This last parameter, that indicates the degree of substitutability between two varieties, is actually the only one (with θ) whose modification could entail qualitative modifications of our results. We have conducted the numerical analysis, described above, for three α-values, namely .1, .5 and .7. In each of these three cases – that correspond to the three graphics in figure 1 –, the main result of theorem 2 is satisfied. Then, as the other parameters, α has only a "level effect" on the equilibrium values of g, U and on the T-values that maximize either g or U. Having tried many different combinations, we can say more generally that the model is qualitatively robust to changes in the parameter values as long as these satisfy assumptions H1 and H2.

Examination of figure 1 confirms the results of theorem 1. The patents lifetime that maximizes the growth rate is finite as long as the diffusion parameter remains lower than $\bar{\theta}$. Furthermore, $\hat{T}$ is an increasing function

FIGURE 1

Numerical simulations for $\theta < \overline{\theta}$. *Results of theorem 2 hold when H2 is satisfied.*

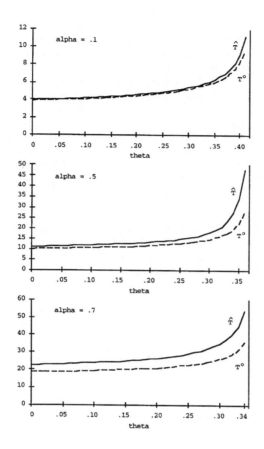

of θ that tends to infinity when θ tends to $\overline{\theta}$. The numerical analysis also extends the result of theorem 2 to a set of θ-values belonging to $[0, \theta_3]$. By theorem 2, we know that the optimal patents lifetime T^0 is lower than the growth maximizing one when $\theta \in [\theta_3, \overline{\theta}]$. Simulations show that this is still the case when $\theta < \theta_3$.

We observe that the collection of points $\{\theta, T^0(\theta)\}$ qualitatively behaves like the collection $\{\theta, \hat{T}(\theta)\}$, that is, $T^0(\theta)$ is increasing with θ. This shows that, if one interprets T as a means for the government to increase or reduce the effective excludability of knowledge, the lower the "natural" degree of non-excludability θ, the higher the "artificial" one T. In other words, the government, in order to reach a second best equilibrium, tends to compensate for the lack of knowledge diffusion by imposing a finite patents lifetime.

Finally, one can see that the lower is α, the smaller the difference between T^0 and $\hat{T}$ and the lower the absolute value of T^0 and $\hat{T}$. This can be explained by the fact that when α tends to 0, the perception of diversity becomes maximal, and therefore so does the profit opportunity for innovators. Thus, everything being equal elsewhere, a decrease in α makes the maximum growth rate consistent with a shorter patents lifetime because a shorter T induces a lower R&D cost. For the same kind of reasons, the optimal patents lifetime can also be reduced. The reduction of the gap between T^0 and $\hat{T}$ when α tends to zero is more difficult to explain but comes from the fact that the weight of the rate of product variety expansion in the utility function becomes higher with respect to the weight of price distortions due to monopolies. These properties are summarized in the following example (table 1) which gives the value of the optimal and growth maximizing patents lifetime when only one third of the knowledge becomes instantaneously public.

TABLE 1

Comparison of the growth maximizing and the optimal patents lifetime when the diffusion parameter is equal to 1/3.

$\theta = 1/3$	$\hat{T}$	T^0
$\alpha = .1$	5.9	5.7 (−4%)
$\alpha = .5$	23.4	17.6 (−24%)
$\alpha = .7$	45.1	31.43 (−30%)

5 Conclusion

We have constructed an innovation based endogenous growth model based on GROSSMAN and HELPMAN [1991a, ch. 3) and on JUDD [1985]. We depart from these two models by assuming that patents are not only a commercial protection for innovators – the only function of a patent in Grossman and Helpman – but also allow innovators to keep private a share of technological information as long as the patent protection lasts – Judd assumes a full property right so that endogenous growth is not possible in his model.

The fact that a patent allows an innovator to keep secrecy on a part of the knowledge he has discovered reduces the knowledge spillover effect that makes growth sustainable. Therefore, the design of the patents policy must take into account not only the usual arbitrage between private profitability and distortions due to the existence of monopolies, but also the diffusion of knowledge that directly influences the pace of growth.

In this framework, we have provided a detailed analysis of the equilibrium growth path. We have shown that growth is maximized by a finite patents lifetime when the property right concerns a large share of knowledge. At the contrary, growth is maximized by infinitely lived patents when this share is low. The same kind of reasoning applies for the optimal patents lifetime. In particular, we show that when growth is maximized by finite patents lifetime, the optimal lifetime is also finite and shorter than the growth maximizing one. The reason for this is quite intuitive. When the "natural" diffusion of knowledge is low, the government can compensate the lack of public knowledge by choosing a lifetime shorter than the one that would have maximized innovators' profitability. Manipulating patents lifetime may then become, in a second best analysis, a means to modify the effective excludability of knowledge.

In this paper, we have treated θ as a parameter. One possible extension would be to consider an endogenous value for the share of public knowledge. This would be more appropriate to the intentional secrecy interpretation of $\theta < 1$. But such a hypothesis would require a very different treatment of the commercial exploitation of an innovation. Here, a patent always ensures full commercial protection; therefore individual innovators have no incentives for manipulating the value of θ. Endogenous determination of firms secrecy policy makes sense only if reducing θ has a direct positive effect on the profitability of an innovation. One way to model this idea may be to take into account the very high costs induced by patent protection and to distinguish innovations according to their degree of knowledge appropriability. Then, innovators must choose between patenting or not, and θ can be reinterpreted as the share of patented innovations. Obviously, this framework is quite different from the one adopted here and its exploration is left to further research.

APPENDIX

A. Proof of Theorem 1

We study here the solution $g^*(T)$ which is implicitly defined by equation (30)

$$F(g, T) \equiv A(g, T) - B(g, T) = 0$$

with:

$$A(g, T) = \frac{1 - \alpha}{\alpha a} \frac{1 - e^{-(\rho + g)T}}{\rho + g}$$

$$\text{and} \quad B(g, T) = \frac{1 + (\alpha^{-\sigma} - 1) e^{-gT}}{L(\theta + (1 - \theta) e^{-gT}) - ag}.$$

First, we proceed with some preliminary results.

I. Any solution g satisfies $M(g, T) \equiv L(\theta + (1 - \theta) e^{-gT}) - ag > 0$. For a given T, $M(g, T)$ is decreasing and positive on the interval $[0, \tilde{g}(T)]$ where $\tilde{g}(T)$, defined by $M[\tilde{g}(T), T] = 0$, is decreasing with T.

II. The sign of the derivative of $A(g, T)$ with respect to g can be deduced from the following computation. For any u, $u > 0$, the derivative of the function $(1 - e^{-u})/u$ is equal to $u^{-2} h(u)$ with $h(u) = ue^{-u} - 1 + e^{-u}$. Since $h'(u) = -ue^{-u} < 0$ for $u > 0$, we have $h(u) < h(0) = 0$. It follows that for any $g \geq 0$ and for a given T, the function $A(g, T)$ is decreasing in g.

III. We now define the sign of the derivative of $B(g, T)$ with respect to g in order to get the sign of $F'_g(g, T)$.

$$B'_g(g, T) = \frac{Te^{-gT} m(g) + a[1 + (\alpha^{-\sigma} - 1) e^{-gT}]}{M(g, T)^2}$$

where

$$m(g) \equiv L(1 - \alpha^{-\sigma} \theta) + (\alpha^{-\sigma} - 1) ag.$$

Note that $m(g)$ is an increasing function of g.

A.1. Existence. When $\theta \leq \alpha^{\sigma}$, $m(g) > 0$, $B'_g > 0$, $F'_g < 0$, and there exists at most one solution.

In the general case, we have

$$F(0, T) = \frac{(1 - \alpha)(1 - e^{-\rho T})}{\alpha a \rho} - \frac{\alpha^{-\sigma}}{L}$$

$F(0, T) > 0$ iff $T > T_m$ and $\lim_{g \to \tilde{g}(T)} F(g, T) = -\infty$. Then, if $T > T_m$, $F(g, T) = 0$ admits a solution. This proves proposition 1.

A.2. Limits of the solution when $T \to \infty$. Consider a sequence $T_n \to \infty$ such that $\lim_{n\to\infty} g^*(T_n) = \overline{g} > 0$. We have then:

$$0 = \lim_{n\to\infty} F\left(g^*(T_n), T_n\right) = \frac{1-\alpha}{\alpha a}\frac{1}{\rho + \overline{g}} - \frac{1}{L\theta - a\overline{g}}$$

which implies: $\theta > \theta_1$ and $\overline{g} = g_\infty^*$.

As a consequence, when $\theta \le \theta_1$, 0 is the unique limit point of $g^*(T)$ and we have:

$$\text{if } \theta \le \theta_1, \quad \lim_{T\to\infty} g^*(T) = 0.$$

This proves proposition 3.

A.3. Solutions greater than g_∞^*. Here, we proceed in two steps.

I. Variations of $F(g, T)$ with respect to T

For given g, $F(g, T)$ is a function of T defined, continuous and differentiable on $[0, \overline{T}(g)[= \{T > 0; \tilde{g}(T) > g\}$ and we have:

$$\overline{T}(g) = +\infty \quad \text{if} \quad g \le L\theta/a$$
$$\overline{T}(g) < +\infty \quad \text{if} \quad L\theta/a < g < L/a.$$

The derivative of F with respect to T verifies:

$$e^{gT} F_T'(g, T) = \frac{1-\alpha}{\alpha a} e^{-\rho T} - \frac{gm(g)}{M(g, T)^2} \equiv \Psi(g, T)$$

$$\Psi_T'(g, T) = -\frac{1-\alpha}{\alpha a}\rho e^{-\rho T} - \frac{g^2 m(g)(1-\theta)e^{-gT}}{M(g, T)^2}$$

• When $m(g) \le 0$, we have $F_T'(g, T) > 0$ and F is an increasing function of T within $[0, \overline{T}(g)[$.

• When $m(g) > 0$, we have $\Psi_T'(g, T) < 0$ and $\lim_{T\to\overline{T}} \Psi(g, T) < 0$.

– If $\Psi(g, T) \le 0$, F is an increasing function of T within $[0, \overline{T}(g)[$.

– If $\Psi(g, T) > 0$, F is first increasing, reaches a maximum at $T = T_0$, and then becomes decreasing.

II. Comparison of $g^*(T)$ and g_∞^*.

We assume $\theta > \theta_1$. We have $\overline{m} \equiv m(g_\infty^*) > 0$ iff

$$\theta < \overline{q} = \frac{1 - \rho(\alpha^{1-\sigma} - \alpha)a/L}{\alpha^{1-\sigma} + 1 - \alpha}.$$

If $\overline{m} > 0$, there exists at most one solution $g^*(T) > g_\infty^*$ because $F_g'(g, T) < 0$ for $g > g_\infty^*$. From **I.**, we have $F_T'(g_\infty^*, T) < 0$ for large enough T and $\lim_{T\to\infty} F(g_\infty^*, T) = 0$. We then deduce that $F(g_\infty^*, T)$ takes positive values and that one unique solution $g^*(T) > g_\infty^*$ necessary exists.

If $\overline{m} \le 0$, then for all g such that $m(g) \le 0$, we have $F_T'(g, T) > 0$ and

$$F(g, +\infty) = \frac{g_\infty^* - g}{\alpha(\rho + g)(L\theta - ag)} \le 0 \quad \text{if } g \ge g_\infty^*.$$

This implies $F(g, T) < 0$ for all T and for all $g \geq g_\infty^*$ such that $m(g) \leq 0$. Let us choose $g_0 \geq g_\infty^*$ such that $m(g_0) = 0$. For $g > g_0$, we have $F_g'(g, T) < 0$ and then

$$F(g, T) < F(g_0, T) < 0.$$

In this case, there does not exist a solution $g^*(T) \geq g_\infty^*$ with a finite T-value. This proves proposition 4.

Proof of Theorem 1.

We are now studying the shape of the implicit function $g^*(T)$. Consider $b \geq 0$ such that $m(b) \geq 0$ and such that there exists only one solution $g^*(T) > b$ to equation $F(g, T) = 0$ for $T \in (T_1, T_2)$. When T belongs to this interval, we have $F_g'[g^*(T), T] < 0$ since $g^*(T) > b \Rightarrow m[g^*(T)] > b > 0 \Rightarrow B_g'[g^*(T), T] > 0$. From the implicit function theorem, it follows that $g^*(T)$ is differentiable and that

$$\frac{dg^*(T)}{dT} = -\frac{F_T'[g^*(T), T]}{F_g'[g^*(T), T]}$$

which has the same sign that $F_T'[g^*(T), T]$.

Lemma 1. If there exists a $\hat{T}$ such that $F_T'[g^*(\hat{T}), \hat{T}] = 0$, then for all $T \in]\hat{T}, T_2[$, we have:

$$F_T'[g^*(T), T] < 0 \qquad \text{and} \qquad \frac{dg^*(T)}{dT} < 0.$$

Proof. We define $X^*(T) = e^{g^*(T)T} F_T'[g^*(T), T]$:

$$X^*(T) = \frac{1-\alpha}{\alpha a} e^{-\rho T} - f[g^*(T), T] \text{ where } f(g, T) = \frac{gm(g)}{M(g, T)^2}$$

Since $M(g, T)$ is decreasing in g and T, $f(g, T)$ verifies $f_g' > 0$ and $f_T' > 0$.

$$\frac{dX^*(T)}{dT} = -\frac{1-\alpha}{\alpha a} \rho e^{-\rho T} - f_T'[g^*(T), T] - f_g'[g^*(T), T]\frac{dg^*(T)}{dT}$$

Then, we have

$$\frac{dX^*(T)}{dT} = -S_1(T) - S_2(T) X^*(T)$$

with

$$S_1(T) = \frac{1-\alpha}{\alpha a} \rho e^{-\rho T} + f_T'[g^*(T), T] > 0$$

$$S_2(T) = \frac{f_g'[g^*(T), T] e^{-g^*(T)T}}{-F_g'[g^*(T), T]} > 0.$$

Near $T = \hat{T}$, $dX^*(T)/dT < 0$. Since for $T = \hat{T}$, $X^*(\hat{T}) = 0$, we have $X^*(T) < 0$ for $T \in]\hat{T}, T_2[$ and $F_T'[g^*(T), T] < 0$, implying:

$$\frac{dg^*(T)}{dT} = -\frac{F_T'[g^*(T), T]}{F_g'[g^*(T), T]} < 0. \quad \square$$

78

Proof of Theorem 1. [Continuation]

Lemma 1 can be used in the case $\theta < \bar{\theta}$ where there exists a unique solution $g^*(T) > 0$ for $T \in]T_m, +\infty[$ if $\theta \leq \alpha^\sigma$ or $g^*(T) > g^*_\infty$ for $T \in]T_1, +\infty[$ if $\alpha^\sigma < \theta < \bar{q}$. The differentiable function $g^*(T)$ reaches its maximum at a point $\hat{T} \in]T_m, +\infty[$ in the first case and at a point $\hat{T} \in]T_1, +\infty[$ in the second, such that $F'_T[g^*(\hat{T}), \hat{T}] = 0$. Thanks to the lemma, we know that no other local extremum exists in $T_l \neq \hat{T}$. By lemma 1, it cannot exist $T_l > \hat{T}$. If it did exist $T_l < \hat{T}$, we should have $F'_T[g^*(T_l), T_l] = 0$ and $dg^*(T)/dT < 0$ for all $T > T_l$.

When $\theta < \bar{\theta}$, the growth rate reaches a maximum $\hat{g} \equiv g^*(\hat{T})$ at $T = \hat{T}$. Let us now study the variations of $\hat{T}$ and $\hat{g}$ with respect to θ. By differentiating $F(\hat{g}, \hat{T}) = 0$, we get:

$$F'_g(\hat{g}, \hat{T}) \, d\hat{g} + F'_T(\hat{g}, \hat{T}) \, d\hat{T} + [1 + (\alpha^{-\sigma} - 1) e^{-\hat{g}\hat{T}}] \frac{(1 - e^{-\hat{g}\hat{T}}) L}{M(\hat{g}, \hat{T})^2} \, d\theta = 0.$$

Since $F'_g(\hat{g}, \hat{T}) < 0$ and $F'_T(\hat{g}, \hat{T}) = 0$, we deduce:

$$\frac{d\hat{g}}{d\theta} > 0.$$

We have $\lim_{\theta \to \bar{\theta}} \hat{g}(\theta) = g^*_\infty|_{\theta = \bar{\theta}}$. At this point:

$$m(g^*_\infty|_{\theta = \bar{\theta}}) = 0.$$

Then:

$$\lim_{\theta \to \bar{\theta}, \, \theta < \bar{\theta}} \hat{T}(\theta) = +\infty.$$

The previous results are synthesized in figure 2 and complete the proof of theorem 1.

FIGURE 2

Summary of the results (appendix A).

0	θ_1	α^σ	$\bar{\theta}$
Unique $g^*(T) > 0$ for $T > T_m$		$\lim_{T \to \infty} g^*(T) = g^*_\infty$	
$\lim_{T \to \infty} g^*(T) = 0$	Unique $g^*(T) > g^*_\infty$ for $T > T_1$		No $g^*(T) > g^*_\infty$
$\frac{d\hat{g}}{d\theta} > 0$, $\lim_{\theta \to \bar{\theta}} \hat{g} = g^*_\infty|_{\theta = \hat{\theta}}$ and $\lim_{\theta \to \bar{\theta}, \, \theta < \bar{\theta}} \hat{T} = +\infty$			Growth is maximized with infinitely lived patents.
It always exists a positive growth rate for large enough T. Growth is maximized by a finite patents lifetime.			

B. Proof of Theorem 2

Our goal here is to study the sign of the derivative defined by (34).

$$\frac{dU^*}{dT} = \frac{1}{\rho \, N\left[g^*\left(T\right), T\right]} \frac{d}{dT} N\left[g^*\left(T\right), T\right] + \frac{1}{\rho^2} \left(\frac{1}{\alpha} - 1\right) \frac{dg^*\left(T\right)}{dt}.$$

We define $Y^*\left(T\right) = e^{-g^*\left(T\right)T}$. Then:

(36)

$$N\left[g^*\left(T\right), T\right] = \frac{\alpha \, n_0^{(1/\alpha)-1} \, a \left[\rho + g^*\left(T\right)\right] \left[1 + \left(\alpha^{1-\sigma} - 1\right) Y^*\left(T\right)\right]^{1/\alpha}}{(1-\alpha)\left[1 - Y^*\left(T\right) e^{-\rho T}\right]\left[\theta + (1-\theta) Y^*\left(T\right)\right]}$$

$$\frac{1}{N\left[g^*\left(T\right), T\right]} \frac{dN\left[g^*\left(T\right), T\right]}{dT} = -\frac{\rho \, Y^*\left(T\right) e^{-\rho T}}{1 - Y^*\left(T\right) e^{-\rho T}}$$

$$+ \frac{1}{\rho + g^*\left(T\right)} \frac{dg^*\left(T\right)}{dT} + P^* \frac{dY^*\left(T\right)}{dT}$$

where

$$P^* = \frac{\left(\alpha^{1-\sigma} - 1 + \alpha\right)\theta - \alpha + \left(\alpha^{1-\sigma} - 1\right)(1-\alpha)(1-\theta) Y^*\left(T\right)}{\alpha \left[1 + \left(\alpha^{1-\sigma} - 1\right) Y^*\left(T\right)\right]\left[\theta + (1-\theta) Y^*\left(T\right)\right]}$$

$$+ \frac{e^{-\rho T}}{1 - Y^*\left(T\right) e^{-\rho T}}$$

A sufficient condition for $P^* > 0$ for all T is $\theta \geq \theta_3$ with:

$$\theta_3 = \frac{\alpha}{\alpha^{1-\sigma} - 1 + \alpha}.$$

This condition is necessary for:

$$\lim_{T \to +\infty} P^* = \frac{\left(\alpha^{1-\sigma} - 1\right)\theta - \alpha}{\alpha\theta} \geq 0.$$

We also have:

$$\frac{dY^*\left(T\right)}{dT} = -e^{-g^*\left(T\right)T} \left(g^*\left(T\right) + T \frac{dg^*\left(T\right)}{dT}\right).$$

Since we have $dg^*\left(T\right)/dT = -F_T'/F_g'$,

$$\left(g^* + T \frac{dg^*}{dT}\right) F_g' = g^* F_g' - T F_T'$$

$$= g^* A_g' - \frac{ag^* \left[1 + \left(\alpha^{1-\sigma} - 1\right) e^{-g^* T}\right]}{M\left(g^*, T\right)^2}$$

$$- T \left(\frac{1-\alpha}{\alpha a}\right) e^{-(\rho+g^*)T}.$$

Then, for all T, $(g^* + T \, dg^*/dT) F_g' < 0$. Since $F_g'(g^*, T) < 0$ when $\theta_1 < \theta < \bar{\theta}$, we deduce that $(g^* + T \, dg^*/dT) > 0$ and that $dY^*/dT < 0$.

80

Lemma 2: If $\theta \geq \theta_3$, then:

$$\frac{dg^*(T)}{dT} \leq 0 \Rightarrow \frac{1}{N[g^*(T), T]} \frac{dN[g^*(T), T]}{dT} < 0.$$

Proof: Indeed, in this case we have $P^* \geq 0$ and the three terms on the RHS of (36) are respectively negative, negative or nil if $dg^*/dT \leq 0$, and negative or nil. $\square$

Under H2, we have $\theta_3 < \overline{\theta}$. Then, by lemma 2 and (34), it comes that when θ belongs to $[\theta_3, \overline{\theta}]$, $dg^*/dT \leq 0 \Rightarrow dU^*/dT < 0$, which proves theorem 2. $\square$

● References

AGHION, P., HOWITT, P. (1992). – "A Model of Growth Through Creative Destruction", *Econometrica*, 60, pp. 323-351.

ARROW, K. J. (1994). – "The Production and Distribution of Knowledge", In Gerald Silvergberg and Luc Soete, eds., *The Economics of Growth and Technical Change*, chapter 2, pp. 9-19. Edward Elgar Publishing Ltd, Hants UK.

CHOU, C.-F., SHY, O. (1991). – "New Product Development and the Optimal Duration of Patents", *Southern Economic Journal*, 57, pp. 811-821.

DIXIT, A. K., STIGLITZ, J. E. (1977). – "Monopolistic Competition and Optimum Product Diversity", *American Economic Review*, 67, pp. 297-308.

DRÈZE, J. H. (1980). – "Public goods with exclusion", *Journal of Public Economics*, 13, pp. 5-24.

GROSSMAN, G. M., HELPMAN, E. (1991a). – *Innovation and Growth in the Global Economy*, MIT Press, Cambridge, MA.

GROSSMAN, G. M., HELPMAN, E. (1991b). – "Quality Ladders in the Theory of Growth", *Review of Economic Studies*, 58, pp. 43-61.

GUELLEC, D., RALLE, P. (1993). – "Innovation, propriété intellectuelle et croissance", *Revue Économique*, 44.

JUDD, K. L. (1985). – "On the Performance of Patents", *Econometrica*, 53, pp. 567-585.

NORDHAUS, W. D. (1969). – Invention, Growth and Welfare, *MIT Press*, Cambridge MA.

ROMER, P. M. (1990). – "Endogenous Technical Change", *Journal of Political Economy*, 94, S71-S102.

SEGERSTROM, P. S., ANANT, T. C. A., DINOPOULOS, E. (1990). – "A Schumpeterian Model of the Product Cycle", *American Economic Review*, 80, pp. 1077-1091.

Endogenous Growth
and the Labor Market

Frédérique CERISIER, Fabien POSTEL-VINAY*

ABSTRACT. – We present a multisectoral model of qualitative endogenous growth with imperfect matching on the labor market. Under these conditions, growth induces unemployment through the Schumpeterian process of creative destruction. We study the long-run link between growth and unemployment. We show that this link structurally depends on the relative importance of the degree of competition in the economy, and that of intertemporal substitutability. Moreover, although the relationship between growth and labor market variables is generally ambiguous, we show that the creative destruction effects are very likely to dominate in this kind of models, thus suggesting that a increase in the growth rate should be accompanied by a rise in long-term unemployment.

* F. CERISIER : MAD, Université de Paris 1; F. POSTEL-VINAY : MAD, Université de Paris 1. We are very much indebted to A. d'Autume, F. Langot, M. Pucci and an anonymous referee for their crucial influence on this paper's late evolution. We also thank J.-F. Jacques and M. Roger for useful comments on earlier versions, as well as Ph. Aghion who was our discussant at the 10th ADRES international conference on the economics of innovation. None of them can be held responsible for any error or shortcoming that would remain herein.

D. Encaoua et al. (eds.), The Economics and Econometrics of Innovation, 83–104.
ⓒ *2000 Kluwer Academic Publishers. Printed in the Netherlands.*

1 Introduction

The analysis of the link between growth and long-run unemployment has recently raised the interest of a rising number of contributors in economic research. Indeed, it appears that models of endogenous growth allow for a common determination of growth and unemployment rates (BEAN and PISSARIDES [1993], AGHION and HOWITT [1994]). In particular, models of growth through technical progress have been exploited for that purpose. In fact, the concern of economists with the effect of technical change on employment appeared, according to the historical survey of PETIT [1993], with the beginning of industrialization in the early nineteenth century. By that time, Classical economists optimistically argued that jobs destroyed in one activity would somehow be replaced in another, by means of an increase in profitability inducing a rise in the level of global demand. This view became known as the "compensation theory". Recent experience as well as recent developments in economic theory highlighted the simplism of this argument and raised a number of related questions. These questions may be roughly classified as follows.

The first issue is much of a microeconomic concern about the influence of technical change on the labor demand at the firm level. Fundamentally, the basic question to be answered here is whether technical change destroys jobs (*e.g.* through substitution of capital for labor), or merely displaces them by changing the structure of labor demand (*e.g.* by making old qualifications obsolete and introducing the need for new ones). The second issue is to study the effects of sustained innovation on the global income, and thus on aggregate demand.

The third issue is the one handled in this article. Innovation, while creating new goods and thus new production opportunities, implies the obsolescence of some production units. This process of creative destruction (primarily introduced by Joseph A. Schumpeter) implies a "recurrent rejuvenation of the productive apparatus" in the words of Schumpeter [1942]. Although Schumpeter remains rather vague on unemployment issues, one can think that the new jobs created by the innovation process are not likely to benefit those workers this process pushed into unemployment. Formally, if matching in the labor market is not frictionless, innovation will induce unemployment.

We develop a model based on the same grounds as the one by AGHION and HOWITT [1994]: to uncover the employment effects of the creative destruction process, we add imperfect matching on the labor market to an innovation-based growth model. However, Aghion and Howitt's original model rested on a somewhat peculiar structure. In the first place, they make the non standard assumption that the renewal of the production sector is due to competition for a scarce input, loosely defined as "human capital". In the second place, their economy is taken unisectoral, which hides the effects arising from imperfect competition. The main purpose of the present contribution is thus to describe the relationship between long run unemployment and growth through the creative destruction phenomenon in a general and tractable model. Our model is multisectoral, and the growth process is close to the standard framework by GROSSMAN and HELPMAN [1991]. It clearly exhibits the conflict between the three competing effects of sustained innovation on labor market variables, namely the direct and indirect creative destruction effects and the capitalization effect (*cf.* AGHION and HOWITT [1994], or d'AUTUME [1995]). An increased rate of innovation first implies higher turnover on the labor market which tends, roughly speaking, to increase altogether unemployment and the number of vacant jobs. This is the direct effect of creative destruction. Furthermore, if newer goods are preferred by consumers, an increased rate of innovation will induce a faster decline in older firms' profitability, which in turn will intensify the flow into unemployment. This is the indirect effect of creative destruction. Finally, those two effects can partially or totally be overshadowed by the positive effect of growth on firms' profitability, namely the capitalization effect. The question of knowing whether or not it will be the case is one of particular interest, which cannot be answered without ambiguity. However, our model uncovers a couple of interesting features that should be kept in mind when trying to move towards such an answer. In particular, we argue that the Schumpeterian view of the growth phenomenon is somewhat biased towards the creative destruction effects.

As a return to the multiple sectors hypothesis, we show that the way the economy looks like in steady states heavily and structurally depends on the relative importance of the degree of competition, and the willingness of private consumers to substitute intertemporally.

The model is made in the spirit of CABALLERO and JAFFE [1993]. Its particular feature is to generate growth through product variety as well as product quality increases. It implies in particular that firms are infinitely lived with heterogeneous employment levels. The creative destruction process is characterized by a continuous decline in the market shares of a given producer, consecutive to the appearance of new goods. Hence, installed producers continuously lay off workers, while a continuous flow of newborn firms hires those workers. This continuity seems relevant and convenient as a "macroeconomic approximation", although it hides the fact that technical progress is likely to have local and discontinuous effects, for an innovation probably leads to the destruction of one particular firm in one particular sector, from time to time, rather than to a smooth and homogenous shrinking of all firms.

Unlike earlier contributions treating problems of resources allocation between production and innovation (see *e.g.* GROSSMAN and HELPMAN [1991], CABALLERO and JAFFE [1993]), we cannot model explicitly the R&D sector, since labor cannot be freely allocated among the production and R&D sectors. In our model, any agent can become an entrepreneur by innovating (creating a new good), and creating a new firm to produce it. An exogenous entry cost must be paid to create a new firm. All firms find themselves in situation of monopolistic competition. The innovation rate, *i.e.* the frequency of firm creations is thus endogenously determined by a condition of free entry on the goods market.

The paper is organized as follows: section 2 presents the model and its intertemporal equilibrium. Steady states are studied and commented in section 3. Section 4 studies some issues of comparative statics. Section 5 concludes.

2 The Model

At any point of time, a continuum of imperfectly substitutable goods indexed by $j \in] - \infty, f_t]$ is produced by monopolistic competitors. At any date, any agent can become an entrepreneur by creating a firm to produce a new good. Creating a new firm implies paying a sunk cost D_t, and getting into a hiring process. To describe this hiring process, we assume as in PISSARIDES [1990] that matching on the labor market is not frictionless. A newborn firm thus has to open a certain number of vacant jobs, and find workers that fit these vacant jobs before it can start production. Hence at some time t there are N_t firms in the economy, while $f_t < N_t$ is the number of firms that did actually start production before date t. A firm that has an index between f_t and N_t is still filling its vacancies, and is not currently producing. More precisely, the sequence of a firm's creation follows four main steps:

1. an agent decides to create a new firm, pays the entry cost and invents a new good;

2. the new firm determines its demand for labor, L^d and opens exactly L^d vacant jobs;

3. vacancies are filled with an imperfect matching technology;

4. once the new firm has completed the filling of its vacancies, and only then, it starts production.

As matching is not costless, there is rent to be shared from successful matches. Wages are thus determined, once production has started, by a continuous bargaining process between entrepreneurs and workers.

We now describe the model in more detail.

2.1. The Production Process

The basic structure of our model borrows from CABALLERO and JAFFE [1993]. Time is continuous. Agents consume the following aggregate of goods in every period:

$$(1) \qquad Y_t = \left[\int_{-\infty}^{f_t} \left(x_t(j) e^j \right)^{1-1/\beta} dj \right]^{\beta/(\beta-1)}, \text{ with } \beta > 1,$$

with $] - \infty, f_t]$ the continuum of available goods in the economy, and $x_t(j)$ the demand for each of these goods. The term e^j in the definition of Y_t

86

reflects the hypothesis that newer goods are preferred by consumers, because of their improved quality relative to older ones [1]. We thus have a model that combines both expanding quality and expanding variety (see CABALLERO and JAFFE [1993]). β is the (static) elasticity of substitution between goods. The assumption $\beta > 1$ means that there is global substitutability. It may be useful to notice that β can be viewed as an indicator of the degree of competition in the economy: the higher β, the more substitutable the goods and hence the tougher competition.

Maximizing aggregate consumption under budget constraint, and using Y_t as numeraire yields the ensuing demand for the good of quality j at time t:

$$(2) \qquad x_t(j) = p_t(j)^{-\beta} \cdot e^{(\beta-1)j} Y_t,$$

and:

$$(3) \qquad \left[\int_{-\infty}^{f_t} \left(p_t(j) e^{-j} \right)^{1-\beta} dj \right]^{1/(1-\beta)} = 1$$

with $p_t(j)$ denoting the current price of good j in terms of the consumption aggregate.

We choose a constant returns production technology, namely $x_t(j) = L_t(j)$, with $L_t(j)$ being the employment level in sector j, and assume that labor is supplied without disutility.

2.2. The Matching Process

A firm created at time t will have to open a certain number of job slots and fill them before it can start production. As previously announced, we assume that the labor market undergoes some frictions in the matching process between firms and job seeking workers. We represent these frictions by assuming that there is a number $m(U_t, V_t)$ of matches per unit time, with m being a standard matching function defined after PISSARIDES [1990]. More precisely, m depends on the number of unemployed, U_t, and on the total number of vacancies, V_t. It is assumed to exhibit constant returns to scale, so that m is homogeneous of degree one.

Due to these frictions, completing a firm's hiring process will take some time. Let d_t be the length of the hiring period. This firm will then start production at date $t + d_t$. Hence we should have $N_t = f_{t+d_t}$. The number of jobs this firm opens at time t depends on the anticipated market situation at time $t + d_t$, and is worth $L_{t+d_t}(N_t)$. We define this number as $V_t(N_t) = L_{t+d_t}(N_t)$.

We then need to ensure that firms get into production by rank of age. For the sake of simplicity, we thus assume that the matching process is

---

1. This term could equivalently appear in the production technology defined below, and thus be viewed as a Harrod-neutral labor augmenting technical progress.

deterministic and that all the matches made at some date t are made in the oldest non-producing firms, *i.e.* the firms created at time τ such that $\tau + d_\tau = t$. The state of the labor market determines the number of such firms that will enter into the productive apparatus, since it sets the total number of their hires. Formally, we have at every date:

$$(4) \qquad m(U_t, V_t) = L_t(f_t) \dot{f}_t.$$

The length of the hiring delay will hence be given by [2]:

$$(5) \qquad \int_t^{t+d_t} m(U_s, V_s)\, ds = V_t.$$

The total stock of vacancies V_t will decrease at every date t by the number of matches, and increase by the number of vacancies opened by newborn firms. Hence, since there are $\dot{N}_t$ new firms arriving per unit time, that stock solves:

$$(6) \qquad \dot{V}_t = -m(U_t, V_t) + \dot{N}_t V_t(N_t).$$

Equilibrium on the labor market then yields:

$$(7) \qquad \bar{L} = L_t + U_t,$$

with $L_t = \int_{-\infty}^{f_t} L_t(j)\, dj$ denoting total employment in the continuum of firms that are actually producing at time t, and $\bar{L}$ being total labor supply.

2.3. **Wage and Price Setting**

The achievement of its hiring process allows any firm to start producing and make profits. These profits have to be shared between entrepreneurs and workers. We assume that this is done through a bargain between the firm and its marginal worker, which takes place at every date once production has started. Let ξ be the relative bargaining power of the worker. The outcome of that bargain is classically supposed to ensure that the global surplus is shared in $(\xi, 1 - \xi)$ proportions, that is:

$$(8) \qquad \mathcal{W}_t^e(j) - \overline{\mathcal{W}}_t^u = \frac{\xi}{1 - \xi} \cdot (\mathcal{V}_t^o(j) - \mathcal{V}_t^v(j))$$

with $\mathcal{W}_t^e(j)$ denoting the wealth of an employed worker in firm j, $\overline{\mathcal{W}}_t^u$ that of an unemployed one [3], $\mathcal{V}_t^o(j)$ the value of firm j's marginal (occupied)

---

2. It could be argued here that, since the opening of a vacant job is costless, it would be in a firm's interest to open a higher (and maybe infinite) number of vacancies in order to accelerate the hiring process. To avoid that, we shall assume that there is some kind of "labor market authority" that forces the firms to commit to opening the "right" number of vacancies, *i.e.* the one derived hereabove.

3. A bar over a variable is used to denote an average value, taken as given by individuals.

88

job, and $\mathcal{V}_t^v(j)$ the value of a job with its worker fired in that firm. The value functions defined above may be derived in the following way: we first assume that a dismissed worker is never replaced [4], so that $\forall(j,t)$, $\mathcal{V}_t^v(j) = 0$. Now let $\lambda_t(j)$ be the instantaneous probability for a job to be destroyed in firm j. Note that this probability *a priori* depends on j. $\mathcal{W}_t^e(j)$ then evolves according to the ensuing asset equation, with r_t denoting the real interest rate:

$$(9) \qquad r_t \mathcal{W}_t^e(j) = w_t(j) + \dot{\mathcal{W}}_t^e(j) - \lambda_t(j)(\mathcal{W}_t^e(j) - \overline{\mathcal{W}}_t^u).$$

Similarly, let $\mu_t = m(U_t, V_t)/U_t$ be the instantaneous probability for an unemployed worker to match a vacant job. As it was assumed zero earnings for the unemployed, one has:

$$(10) \qquad r_t \overline{\mathcal{W}}_t^u = \dot{\overline{\mathcal{W}}}_t^u - \mu_t(\overline{\mathcal{W}}_t^u - \overline{\mathcal{W}}_t^e),$$

with $\overline{\mathcal{W}}_t^e$ denoting the average wealth of an employed worker, thus taken as given by individuals. Finally, the firm's value evolves according to:

$$(11) \qquad r_t \mathcal{V}_t^o(j) = p_t(j) - w_t(j) + \dot{\mathcal{V}}_t^o(j) - \lambda_t(j)\mathcal{V}_t^o(j),$$

Replacing equations (9), (10) and (11) into the bargain outcome (8), one finally gets the wage setting equation for firm j:

$$(12) \qquad w_t(j) = \xi[p_t(j) + \mu_t \overline{\mathcal{V}}_t^o],$$

with $\overline{\mathcal{V}}_t^o$ being the average value of an occupied job.

We now turn to the price setting rule. Firms aim at maximizing their discounted expected value, so that their problem can be written as:

$$(13) \qquad \max_{\{p_s(j), s \geq t\}} \int_t^{+\infty} [p_s(j) - w_s(j)]L_s(j) \cdot e^{-\int_t^s r_u \, du} \, ds,$$

subject to the wage setting equation (12), the demand constraint (2) and their constant returns technology. The latter program is in fact statical, and if one takes the various constraints into account, it can be rewritten statically as:

$$(14) \qquad \max_{p_t(j)} [p_t(j)(1 - \xi) - \xi\mu_t \overline{\mathcal{V}}_t^o] \cdot p_t(j)^{-\beta}.$$

Its first order condition is the price setting equation:

$$(15) \qquad w_t(j) = \left[1 - \frac{1 - \xi}{\beta}\right] \cdot p_t(j).$$

---

4. Which is true at least in the steady state. We return to this assumption below.

This identity together with the wage setting equation has strong implications. The first one is that it makes us able to give the value of the current price $p_t(j)$ (or equivalently, that of the current wage $w_t(j)$) in firm j as a function of exogenous parameters and of the average value of an occupied job. Hence all firms pay the same wage and set the same price. This is important, since all workers are identical so that if the wages were to differ across firms, it could be in the interest of a poorly paid worker to quit his job and search for another match. The fact that all wages are the same, regardless of the firms' ages ensures that workers never quit unless their job is destroyed.

This homogeneity, together with our price normalization (3) yields the current price:

$$(16) \qquad p_t = \left(\frac{1}{\beta-1}\right)^{1/(\beta-1)} e^{f_t}.$$

As the goods market works under monopolistic competition, one can now derive the labor demand of producer j at date t. Indeed, we get this labor demand from equations (2), (16) and the constant returns technology:

$$(17) \qquad L_t(j) = (\beta-1)^{\beta/(\beta-1)} Y_t \cdot \exp\{(\beta-1)j - \beta f_t\}.$$

One sees that this labor demand is decreasing in the number of firms. This reflects the fact that when a firm gets older, it looses market shares because of the consumers' taste for variety and quality. This tends to induce a decline in a given firm's demand for labor over time. However, the relative variation in firm j's labor demand has an overall ambiguous sign, since the growth of global product tends to make it positive, as shown by:

$$(18) \qquad \frac{\dot{L}_t(j)}{L_t(j)} = \frac{\dot{Y}_t}{Y_t} - \beta \dot{f}_t.$$

As it is clear that this relative variation will be of negative sign in a steady state, we have assumed throughout the analysis that we stay close enough to a steady state to be sure it always remains negative. Under this assumption, the probability $\lambda_t(j)$ is given by $\lambda_t(j) = -\dot{Y}_t/Y_t + \beta \dot{f}_t$, and is positive. One sees that this probability is the same for all firms.

Replacing the price setting rule (15) into the wage setting rule (12) one gets:

$$(19) \qquad \frac{1-1/\beta}{\mu_t} = \frac{\xi}{1-\xi} \cdot \frac{\overline{V}_t^o}{p_t},$$

an important equation that will be referred to as (WP) in the remainder. It represents the intersection of the wage setting and the price setting schedules, and links the labor market variables to the growth and interest rates. One can see that it implies a downward sloping relationship between the value of a job (*i.e.* the surplus of an employed worker's welfare over that of an unemployed one) and the probability for an unemployed worker to find a job.

90

2.4. Free Entry and Intertemporal Equilibrium

An agent who wishes to innovate and create a firm must pay an entry cost D_t. Let G_t be the gross expected discounted value of a newborn firm. Remember that a firm gets its first positive profits at $t + d_t$. G_t is defined by the discounted sum of the profit flows accruing to that firm. In our situation, G_t can obviously be written as follows:

$$(20) \qquad G_t = \overline{V}^o_{t+d_t} L_{t+d_t}(N_t) \cdot e^{-\int_t^{t+d_t} r_u \, du}.$$

Free entry on the goods market ensures that this value is equal to the entry cost, namely $G_t = D_t$. To ensure the existence of a balanced growth path, D_t has to grow at the same rate as all nominal variables. Hence we assume $D_t = k \cdot e^{N_t}$, with k being an exogenous constant parameter. This assumption can be viewed as resulting from constant returns in the R&D sector. After some algebra, it is easy to check that this condition can be written:

$$(21) \qquad k \cdot \left(\frac{1}{\beta - 1}\right)^{1 - 1/(\beta - 1)} = \frac{\overline{V}^o_{t+d_t}}{p_{t+d_t}} \cdot L_{t+d_t} \cdot e^{-\int_t^{t+d_t} r_u \, du}.$$

The free entry equation will be referred to as (FE) in the remainder.

The model is completed by writing equilibrium on the goods market. There are in fact two different sources of demand for goods in our model, namely agents' consumption and firms' entry costs. To precise the evolution of consumption, we assume the representative agent to be endowed with a utility function of the CIES type in an aggregate consumption index C_t with intertemporal substitutability σ, so that $U(C_t) = C_t^{1-1/\sigma}/(1 - 1/\sigma)$. He maximizes his discounted sum of utility as of time 0 under intertemporal budget constraint, facing an endogenous interest rate r_t and an exogenous discount factor, ρ. Standard optimal control arguments lead to the following value for the consumption growth rate:

$$(22) \qquad \frac{\dot{C}_t}{C_t} = \sigma(r_t - \rho).$$

As there are $\dot{N}_t$ new firms per unit time, the total income of the economy will be given by $Y_t = C_t + \dot{N}_t \cdot D_t$.

The intertemporal equilibrium in our model is determined by the set of dynamic equations we have written until now. The complete dynamic system is presented in appendix A.

3 Steady State

In a steady state, the rate of innovation is constant. Let g be this rate. Furthermore, the constancy of the labor market variables, and that of the hiring delay imply that $\dot{N}_t = \dot{f}_t = g$. In order to obtain finite present values, we restrain our attention to growth rates such that $g < r$, thus taking account of the usual "transversality condition".

3.1. The Steady State System

The constancy of the number of matches [5] $m(U, V)$ together with the definition of d_t then says that:

$$(23) \qquad d_t \equiv d(V/U) = \frac{V/U}{m(1, V/U)}$$

for all t, by virtue of function m's homogeneity. In the remainder, we shall write $V/U = \theta$. θ is traditionally referred to as the "tightness" parameter of the labor market. It is easy to check that d is an increasing function of θ. We shall assume, in addition, that $\theta \mapsto m(1, \theta)$ satisfies the Inada conditions, so that d bijectively maps $\mathbb{R}_+$ onto itself. One also has $f_t = N_{t-d(\theta)}$.

Stationarity implies that the total flow into unemployment must match the total flow out of unemployment. The total flow out of unemployment is defined as the total number of hires of new firms, as given by equation (4), i.e. the total number of matches per unit time $m(U, V)$. This leads to the well known Beveridge relation [6]:

$$(24) \qquad (\beta - 1)g \cdot L = m(U, V),$$

This equation also reflects the stationarity of V. With the labor market equilibrium $(L = \bar{L} - U)$, it defines a curve in the (U, V) plane that is downward sloping and concave to the origin [7] which will be denoted (BC). The presence of the growth rate in the (BC) equation uncovers a first, direct effect of "creative destruction": faster growth implies faster labor turnover.

---

5. In steady states, time indexes will be omitted when unnecessary.
6. To see this point, just notice that we get from the labor demand (17) the ensuing equality:
$L_t(f_t) = (\beta - 1)L_t$. Also note that this equality imposes $\beta < 2$ to make sense.
7. Differentiating equation (24) with respect to U and V yields:

$$m_1'(U, V)dU + m_2'(U, V)dV = -(\beta - 1)gdU.$$

Since the number of matches is assumed to be increasing with respect to both its arguments, our curve slopes downward. Its convexity can easily be demonstrated from the assumption of nonincreasing returns in the matching technology.

It thus shifts the (BC) curve outwards and tends to increase the stock of unemployed as well as the stock of vacant jobs.

To determine the equilibrium values of U and V, we need two more relationships between these two variables. These relationships will be given by considering equations (WP) and (FE). The first step to study (WP) and (FE) in steady states is to write the stationary value of an occupied job. This is done by writing equation (11) in a steady state:

$$(25) \qquad \frac{\overline{V}_t^o}{p_t} = \frac{(1-\xi)/\beta}{(r-g)+g(\beta-1)}.$$

This expression of the steady state value of $\overline{V}_t^o/p_t$ calls for some comments. Note that the actual discount rate that a firm applies to its flows of profit is $r - g + g(\beta - 1)$. The term $r - g$ corresponds to a "capitalization effect" (PISSARIDES [1990]): $g - r$ can be seen as the net growth rate of a firm's income. The capitalization effect tends to augment the longevity of a job. Indeed, faster growth of aggregate demand is beneficial to all firms and thus implies slower declines in old firms' demand for labor. This is the origin of the $-g$ term in the actual discount rate firms apply to their incomes. The term $g(\beta - 1)$ represents an "indirect creative destruction effect" (AGHION and HOWITT [1994]): it is a measure of the speed at which an installed firm will lose market shares. The indirect creative destruction effect tends to shorten jobs' lifetimes [8]. In conclusion, an opening firm anticipating a rising rate of growth will be willing to open more vacant jobs if the capitalization effect dominates, and less of them if the indirect creative destruction effect dominates.

With these remarks in mind, one can rewrite the (WP) equation in a steady state:

$$(26) \qquad \rho - g[(1 - 1/\sigma) + (1 - \beta)] = \frac{\xi}{\beta - 1} \cdot \frac{\theta}{d(\theta)}.$$

Hence the wage negotiations and the price setting behavior of firms lead to a linear relationship between the rate of growth and the probability $\theta/d(\theta)$ for an unemployed to find a job. The slope of this relationship has the sign of $(\beta - 1) - (1 - 1/\sigma)$.

We now turn to the study of the rentability condition. From equations (21) and (25), we get in a steady state:

$$G_t = \left(\frac{1}{\beta - 1}\right)^{-1+1/(\beta-1)}$$
$$\cdot \frac{\overline{V}_t^o}{p_t} L \cdot \exp\{(g - r)d(\theta) + f_t\} = k e^{N_t}$$

$$(27) \quad \Leftrightarrow G_t e^{-N_t} = \left(\frac{1}{\beta - 1}\right)^{1/(\beta-1)}$$

$$\cdot \frac{(1 - 1/\beta)(1 - \xi)}{\rho - g[(1 - 1/\sigma) + (1 - \beta)]} \cdot L \cdot e^{-rd(\theta)} = k.$$

One thus sees that the (detrended) value of a firm, which free entry imposes equal to the entry cost k, is equal to the sum of constant instantaneous profit flows (this constant being equal to the initial value of the actual flow of profit accruing to the firm), discounted at rate $r - g + g(\beta - 1)$. Those profit flows are proportional to the level of employment, L, as a consequence of our constant returns assumption. Furthermore, profits appear once the firm has waited $d(\theta)$, hence the extra discount term $e^{-rd(\theta)}$. This free entry condition again links the growth rate to the state of the labor market. This link works through three different channels. The first one is the length of the hiring delay which, together with the value of the interest rate, sets the "direct" cost of the labor market frictions. The second channel is the steady state level of employment, which is a measure of the value of the first profit [9] made by a new firm. The third one is the value of the discount rate the firms will apply to their profit streams, $r - g + g(\beta - 1)$, which increase (decreases) with g if $(1 - 1/\sigma) + (1 - \beta) < (>)0$.

We now possess a system of three equations, namely (24), (26), and (27) with three unknown variables, L, g, and θ. We now turn to the study of this system.

3.2. **System Resolution**

Although not difficult, the resolution of the steady state system is a bit tedious. Hence all proofs have been confined in the appendix. Under the assumptions we made about the matching function m, it is straightforward to state the following lemma:

> LEMMA 1 : Equation (26) defines θ as a C^∞ function of g for all values of g such that the left hand side of this equation is positive. Let φ be this function. Then:
> — if $1 - 1/\sigma > \beta - 1$, then $\varphi'(g) < 0$ and $\varphi''(g) > 0$ for all $g \in [0, \rho/(2 - \sigma^{-1} - \beta))$, and:
> — if $1 - 1/\sigma < \beta - 1$, then $\varphi'(g) > 0$ and $\varphi''(g) > 0$ for all $g \in \mathbb{R}_+$.

The proof stems immediately from the implicit functions theorem.

Now solving for L in the system formed by the free entry condition (27) and the Beveridge curve (24), and inserting the solution back into the wage setting/price setting equation (26) yields the following relationship between

---

9. That is, the first positive value taken by the instantaneous flow of profits accruing to that firm: $(p_t - w_t) \cdot x_t(f_t)$.

94

growth and labor market tightness:

$$(28) \quad \left(g + \frac{m(1,\theta)}{\beta - 1}\right) e^{rd(\theta)}$$

$$= \left(\frac{1}{\beta - 1}\right)^{1/(\beta-1)} \cdot \frac{(\beta - 1)(1 - \xi)}{\beta \xi k} \bar{L} = \mathcal{K}(\beta, \xi, \bar{L}, k),$$

in which we introduce $\mathcal{K}(\beta, \xi, \bar{L}, k)$ for the sake of notational brevity [10]. About this last equation, we can state:

> LEMMA 2 : Equation (28) defines θ as a C^{∞} function (say ψ) of g on the interval $[0, \mathcal{K}]$. Function ψ is strictly decreasing on this whole interval, and $\psi(\mathcal{K}) = 0$.

The proof is in the appendix.

With these two lemmas, we have a system of two equations with unknowns (θ, g). Our concern now is to find out whether this system has zero, one or several solutions. This must be done by studying the (virtual, at the present time) intersections of functions φ and ψ within an interval of acceptable values for g (that is $g \in [0, \rho/(1 - \sigma^{-1}))$ if $\sigma > 1$, and $g \in \mathbb{R}_+$ otherwise). Since function ψ is always decreasing, one sees that the "nice" situation will be the one where φ is increasing, *i.e.* the case of low intertemporal substitutability (low σ) and high static substitutability (high β, which can also be interpreted as a situation of tough competition). In the opposite case, although sufficient conditions to ensure the existence of an equilibrium couple (θ^*, g^*) may be given, nothing too precise can be said about the uniqueness of such an equilibrium without further knowledge of the shape of the matching technology. More formally, one can state the following two propositions:

> PROPOSITION 3 [Case of low intertemporal substitutability and hard competition] : Assume $\beta - 1 > 1 - 1/\sigma$. Let:
>
> $$\hat{\theta} = \frac{\beta - 1}{\xi} \cdot \ln \left[\frac{\mathcal{K}\xi}{\rho}\right],$$
>
> and (whenever $\sigma > 1$), $\check{\theta} = \frac{(\beta - 1)^2}{\xi} \cdot \ln \left[\frac{\mathcal{K}\xi}{\rho} \cdot \frac{1 - 1/\sigma}{\xi + \beta - 1}\right]$.
>
> Then:
> — if $\sigma \leq 1$ then a necessary and sufficient condition for the existence and uniqueness of a steady state equilibrium $(L^*, g^*, \theta^*) \in [0, \bar{L}] \times [0, \mathcal{K}] \times \mathbb{R}_+$ is $\varphi(0) < \hat{\theta}$;
> — if $\sigma > 1$ then a necessary and sufficient condition for the existence and uniqueness of a steady state equilibrium $(L^*, g^*, \theta^*) \in [0, \bar{L}] \times [0, \rho/(1 - \sigma^{-1})] \times \mathbb{R}_+$ is $\varphi(0) < \hat{\theta}$ and $\varphi[\rho/(1 - \sigma^{-1})] > \check{\theta}$.

---

10. To avoid uninteresting discussions, we shall additionally assume in the remainder that the total labor force is large enough to ensure $\mathcal{K} \geq \rho/(1 - \sigma^{-1})$ (whenever $\sigma > 1$). This assumption is completely innocuous.

PROPOSITION 4 [Case of high intertemporal substitutability and mild competition] : Assume $\beta - 1 < 1 - 1/\sigma$. Then a sufficient condition for at least one steady state equilibrium $(L^*, g^*, \theta^*) \in [0, \bar{L}] \times [0, \rho/(1 - \sigma^{-1})] \times \mathbb{R}_+$ to exist is either $\varphi(0) > \hat{\theta}$ and $\varphi[1 - \sigma^{-1}] < \check{\theta}$, or $\varphi(0) < \hat{\theta}$ and $\varphi[\rho/(1 - \sigma^{-1})] > \check{\theta}$.
Uniqueness is not ensured by these conditions.

A quick proof for both propositions is contained in the appendix.

Basically, a steady state equilibrium is determined by a pair of equilibrium values θ^* and g^*, given by the (eventual and eventually unique) intersection of the φ and ψ schedules in the (g, θ) plane. Those values determine a position for the Beveridge curve (24) in the (U, V) plane, and a particular point on it defined by the intersection of this curve with the $V = \theta^* U$ line. The point made in propositions 3 and 4 is to give some conditions under which the φ and ψ schedules have one (or more) intersection point(s). More precisely, what they say is that one can be in either one of the situations depicted on figure 1.

FIGURE 1

Steady State Equilibrium.

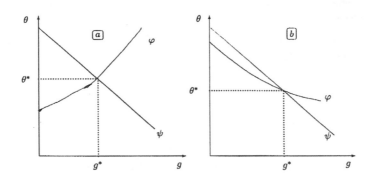

The cases described in proposition 3, which can roughly be gathered under the hypothesis $\beta - 1 \geq 1 - 1/\sigma$, are represented on panel a of figure 1. It is the case in which the indirect creative destruction effect offsets the capitalization effect, which makes the φ schedule slope up. The uniqueness of the steady state equilibrium is therefore always guaranteed. Other cases (one not necessarily unique steady state, proposition 4) occur when the opposite inequality holds – that is, $\beta - 1 < 1 - 1/\sigma$. In that case, the capitalization effect overcomes the indirect creative destruction effect. An example of such a case is depicted on panel b of figure 1 [11].

Hence we see that the relative value of parameters β and σ (static and intertemporal substitutabilities) has crucial consequences on the behavior of endogenous variables. The remainder of the paper is dedicated to the study of that behavior.

4 Comparative Statics

In this section, we turn to some issues of comparative statics. To determine the effects on growth, labor market tightness and employment of shifts in the various exogenous parameters, we note from equations (26) and (28) that the φ schedule shifts upwards in response to positive shocks on ρ and β, and downwards when ξ or σ increase, and that the ψ schedule shifts upwards in response to increases in $\bar{L}$ and σ, and downwards after a rise in ξ, ρ, k, or β [12]. These properties lead to the results of comparative statics for θ^* and g^* that are summarized in the first two lines of table 1 (the labels "case a" and "case b" refer to the same distinction as on figure 1).

TABLE 1

Comparative Statics.

positive shock on...		k	$\bar{L}$	σ	ρ	ξ	β
1. Response of g^*	case a	$-$	$+$	$+$	$-$	?	$-$
	case b	$-$	$+$	$+$	$-$	?	$-$
2. Response of θ^*	case a	$-$	$+$	?	?	$-$	?
	case b	$+$	$-$	$-$	$+$	$-$	$+$
3. Response of u^*	case a	$-$	$+$	$+$	$-$	?	$-$
	case b	$-$	$+$	$+$	$-$	?	$-$

---

11. Of course, the situation depicted there is not the only one possible. Other configurations are studied in detail in a discussion paper version of this article (available on request to the authors). For instance, since when $\beta - 1 < 1 - 1/\sigma$ both schedules slope downwards, one can imagine a situation with the φ schedule being steeper than the ψ schedule. The equilibrium obtained in such a case can be shown to exhibit counterintuitive comparative static properties, which make us term it "undesirable". Moreover, since φ and ψ have the same slope sign, the occurrence of multiple equilibria is quite possible – albeit requiring a rather "pathological" behavior of function ψ. This possibility can be checked in a numerical experiment, also available on request. We choose to focus on the "likely" situations, *i.e.* those depicted on figure 1, the drawing of the omitted cases being left to the fancy of the interested reader.

12. The effect of a rise in β on ψ is *a priori* ambiguous, but it can be shown to be negative for sufficiently small (*i.e.* close enough to one) values of β.

About the comparative statics of employment, notice that substituting the Beveridge relationship into the (WP) equation (26), one gets:

$$(29) \qquad u^* = \frac{\xi}{\xi + \rho/g^* - [(1 - 1/\sigma) + (1 - \beta)]},$$

with u^* denoting the equilibrium unemployment rate. Combining the results of table 1 with this equation yields the results shown in line three of table 1. Those results strongly suggest an inverse relationship between the rate of growth and the long-run level of employment, through a prevalence of the creative destruction effects.

Cutting the entry cost (diminishing k) directly encourages the entry of firms, which raises the equilibrium growth rate and, through creative destruction, augments unemployment. A larger total labor force ($\bar{L}$) raises the growth rate by a standard "scale effect", which again raises unemployment through creative destruction. Variations in σ or ρ have direct straightforward effects on the firms' total discount rate: a rise in σ or a drop of ρ both lower the rate of interest, thus diminishing the firms' discount rate. This encourages entry, and the corresponding rise in the growth rate is transferred to the unemployment rate through the creative destruction channel.

The parameters hitherto considered were basic components of the endogenous growth rate. Hence, a shift in one of those parameters only affects equilibrium employment through the growth rate — that is, through creative destruction. Things are different if one considers shifts in either the workers' bargaining power ξ, or the static elasticity of substitution β, which both affect the growth rate *and* the unemployment rate directly. Indeed, an ambiguity may appear after a rise in ξ. By raising the cost of labor, this directly raises unemployment. But it also makes jobs less profitable, which discourages the entry of firms, thus tending to lower the rate of growth. That in turn attenuates creative destruction, which raises employment and firms' profits. The overall effect on g^* (and therefore, on u^*) is ambiguous. It should be noted, however, that whenever the sign of the change in u^* that follows a rise in ξ is positive, it never results from a prevalence of the capitalization effect. Finally, a rise in the static elasticity of substitution β, which makes the economy more competitive, reinforces the creative destruction effect [13] because it accelerates the loss of market shares incurred by old firms. It also has a direct negative effect on the firms' profits, by reducing their monopoly power and thus the mark-up of prices over wages. Both these effects tend to shorten jobs' lifetimes, thus raising unemployment.

Why does the relationship between growth and unemployment seem so generally positive in this model? A quick answer would be to say that the

---

13. The relationship between growth and the degree of competition in an innovation-based endogenous growth model is studied in great detail in AGHION and HOWITT [1996].

"reallocative" effect of growth when the labor market undergoes frictions always overcomes its effects on profitability. Indeed, remember that the rate of job destruction, λ, is given by $\lambda = \beta \dot{f} - \dot{Y}/Y = (\beta - 1)g$ (see equation (18) and footnote 8). As we already argued, this reflects the creative destruction effects. Faster growth is detrimental to older firms, since it makes newer goods appear faster, those goods being preferred and therefore substituted to theirs by consumers. $(\beta - 1)g$ was therefore viewed as a measure of the speed at which those firms lose market shares: this is the indirect creative destruction effect. Gross substitutability $(\beta > 1)$ implies that the rate of dismissal λ is always positive and proportional to the growth rate [14]. Hence, because of goods substitutability, faster growth always leads to a bigger rate of dismissal, which in turn means faster entry into unemployment. Because of the labor market frictions, this higher turnover rate leads to more unemployment: this is the direct effect of creative destruction. It thus appears that even though the capitalization effect can dominate the indirect effect of creative destruction (that is, even though a rise in g can make in the firms' total discount rate, $r - g + g(\beta - 1)$ drop), the direct effect of creative destruction always raises unemployment. Whether or not the capitalization effect offsets the indirect creative destruction effect is only a matter of knowing whether the steady state real present value of an occupied job, V^o/p, increases or decreases with respect to the growth rate.

The global prevalence of the creative destruction effect of growth on employment is a general feature of exogenous growth models of technological unemployment (MORTENSEN and PISSARIDES [1995], AGHION and HOWITT [1994], although the latter contribution finds a positive relationship between growth and employment at high growth rates). It seems that endogenizing the rate of growth and introducing a "keynesian" ingredient such as imperfect competition into the model does not question that result, and even reinforces it, in some way. We finally stress that the fact that creative destruction effects broadly dominate the capitalization effect in our model does not mean that this latter effect is absent from it. What we argue is that "Schumpeterian" models of growth-induced unemployment are designed to obtain that result, which does not appear as clearly in the available empirical work (see *e.g.* the study by the CEPR [1995]). Whatever the data say, it makes little doubt that creative destruction is a source of unemployment — albeit maybe small —, which is enough for making the schumpeterian models of unemployment interesting, their main purpose being to analyze that particular feature of growth rather than to fit the facts.

---

14. It is clear that this result would be inverted if the goods were gross complements $(\beta < 1)$, for in that case, the appearance of a new good would have a positive effect on the demand for all other goods. Unfortunately, for obvious reasons of concavity of the firms' profits, the model of this article is inadequate for the study of that case.

5 Conclusion

We have developed a model of qualitative endogenous growth with imperfect matching on the labor market. In these conditions, growth induces unemployment through the schumpeterian process of creative destruction. The link between growth and labor market variables remains ambiguous after this study, although it was shown that the negative creative destruction effect of growth on employment was very generally prevalent. We also have exhibited the important structural consequences of a change in the relative value of intertemporal substitutability and static substitutability by showing that the slopes of two among the three fundamental equations of our model (those are the free entry and the wage setting - price setting equations) depended upon the relative value of those elasticities. We have shown that if competition (as measured by static substitutability) is relatively harsh, then the situation is quite clear as there may be zero or one unique steady state equilibrium, depending on the values of some parameters. On the other hand, milder competition may lead to a rather confused picture (with the possible coexistence of multiple equilibria).

Our conclusion that innovation-based growth generally favors frictional unemployment certainly calls for further discussion. Before affirming that growth is definitely bad for employment, it seems fair to acknowledge that schumpeterian models of growth fail to capture a number of positive effects of "technical change" on employment, which might well lead to more optimistic conclusions. Further research should thus focus on the possibility of reinforcing the capitalization effect in that kind of models. An attempt in that direction was already made by MORTENSEN and PISSARIDES [1995], who build a model in which investment is not completely irreversible for firms have access to technological update. Another possibility to foster the positive effects of growth on employment in a multisectoral model would be to posit some complementarity between some of the consumption goods (along these lines, see YOUNG [1993]). In the end, there are two components of the model that would certainly be worth endogenizing. The first one is the research sector (and the cost of innovation). The second one is education and the update of workers' skills during unemployment. Despite its convenience, the assumption of a homogeneous labor force that comes with the matching model is somewhat unsatisfactory from that point of view, for innovation-based unemployment could certainly be thought of as a skill mismatch problem.

100

APPENDIX A

The Dynamics

The unknown variables of our model at some date t are U_t, V_t, L_t, Y_t, r_t, N_t and f_t. The dynamic system ruling the model will thus consist in eight differential-difference equations.

The first one is the Keynes-Ramsey condition (22):

$$(30) \qquad \frac{\dot{C}_t}{C_t} = \sigma(r_t - \rho),$$

together with the value of the GNP $Y_t - k\dot{N}_t e^{N_t} = C_t$. Another one is the law of motion of V_t, namely (6). If one notices that at any date t, $L_t(f_t) = (\beta - 1)L_t$, one can write this law of motion as:

$$(31) \qquad \dot{V}_t = -m(U_t, V_t) + \dot{N}_t \cdot (\beta - 1)L_{t+d_t}.$$

The law of motion of L_t stems from equation (17):

$$(32) \qquad \frac{\dot{L}_t}{L_t} = \frac{\dot{Y}_t}{Y_t} - \beta \dot{f}_t.$$

Moreover, the equilibrium condition on the labor market (7) implies:

$$(33) \qquad \dot{U}_t + \dot{L}_t = 0.$$

The number of firms evolves according to the hiring rule (4):

$$(34) \qquad \dot{f}_t(\beta - 1)L_t = m(U_t, V_t).$$

The definition of d_t (equation (5)) yields [15]:

$$(35) \qquad V_t = \int_t^{t+d_t} m(U_s, V_s)\, ds.$$

The wage setting/price setting schedule yields:

$$(36) \qquad \frac{\beta - 1}{\xi} = \mu_t \cdot \int_t^{+\infty} \frac{Y_s}{Y_t} e^{(f_s - f_t)(1-\beta) - \int_t^{t+d_t} r_u\, du}\, ds.$$

Our last equation is given by the free entry condition (21):

$$(37) \qquad k \cdot \left(\frac{1}{\beta - 1}\right)^{1-1/(\beta-1)} = \frac{\overline{V}^o_{t+d_t}}{p_{t+d_t}} \cdot L_{t+d_t} \cdot e^{-\int_t^{t+d_t} r_u\, du}.$$

---

15. Note that the derivative of this equation together with the previous one leads to the "intuitive" identity: $N_t = f_{t+d_t}$.

APPENDIX B

Proof of lemma 2

For notational simplicity, we shall work with the auxiliary parameters defined below:

$$S = 1 - \frac{1}{\sigma}, \text{and } B = \beta - 1.$$

We can rewrite equation (28) in the following form:

$$\Gamma(g, \theta) = \mathcal{K}(\beta, \xi, \bar{L}, k).$$

Consider a given value of $g \in [0, \mathcal{K})$. Then it stems from our assumptions on function m that the function $\theta \mapsto \Gamma(g, \theta)$ bijectively maps $\mathbb{R}_+$ onto $[g, +\infty)$. Hence, equation (28) will have an unique solution $\theta = \psi(g)$ for any value of $g \in [0, \mathcal{K})$. The remainder of the lemma stems directly from the implicit functions theorem, and the fact that $\Gamma(\mathcal{K}, 0) = \mathcal{K}$ obviously solves equation (28).

APPENDIX C

Proof of propositions 3 & 4

C.1 Proposition 3

We keep the notations S, B, and Γ from the proof of lemma 2 above. Since $B < S$ in this proposition, the φ schedule is increasing. Hence existence of an equilibrium implies its uniqueness. The restrictions on g we derived earlier imply that g must be less than $\mathcal{K}$ (see lemma 2 above), and also that $g < r$, which always holds true when $\sigma \leq 1$, and is equivalent to $g \leq \rho/S$ otherwise. Hence, from the assumption $\mathcal{K} > \rho/S$ if $\sigma > 1$, the binding condition is $g \leq \rho/S$, so that solutions may be studied within such values of g. Then, since φ is increasing, a necessary and sufficient condition for the equilibrium to exist and to be unique is $\varphi(0) < \psi(0)$ and $\varphi(\rho/S) > \psi(\rho/S)$. Since Γ is increasing in both of its arguments, these conditions are respectively equivalent to $\Gamma(0, \varphi(0)) < \mathcal{K}$ and $\Gamma(\rho/S, \varphi(\rho/S)) > \mathcal{K}$. Solving the first inequality for $\varphi(0)$ yields exactly $\varphi(0) < \check{\theta}$. The second is equivalent to $\varphi(\rho/S) > \check{\theta}$. Hence proposition 3.

C.2 Proposition 4

In the case of a decreasing φ schedule, the above conditions still ensure the existence of an equilibrium, but uniqueness is lost. Furthermore, in the decreasing case, existence also holds when φ starts higher and ends lower than ψ. Hence proposition 4.

• References

AGHION, P., HOWITT, P. (1994). – "Growth and Unemployment", *Review of Economic Studies*, 61, pp. 477-94.

AGHION, P., HOWITT, P. (1996). – "A Schumpeterian Perspective on Growth and Competition", in D. Kreps and K. Wallis, editors, *Advances in Economics and Econometrics: Theory and Applications*, Cambridge: Cambridge University Press. Forthcoming.

BEAN, C., PISSARIDES, C. A. (1993). – "Unemployment, Consumption and Growth", *European Economic Review*, 37, pp. 837-59.

CEPR (1995). – *Unemployment: Choices for Europe — Monitoring European Integration 5*, London: CEPR.

d'AUTUME, A. (1995). – "Croissance et Chômage", *mimeo*, MAD, Université de Paris I.

GROSSMAN, G. M., HELPMAN, E. H. (1991). – *Innovation and Growth in the Global Economy*, Cambridge, MA.: The MIT Press.

MORTENSEN, D. T., PISSARIDES, C. A. (1995). – "Technological Progress, Job Creation and Job Destruction", *Discussion Paper 264*, Center for Economic Performance, London School of Economics.

PETIT, P. (1993). – "Employment and Technological Change", in P. Stoneman, editor, *Handbook of the Economics of Innovation and Technological Change*, Oxford: Basil Blackwell.

SCHUMPETER, J. A. (1942). – *Capitalism, Socialism and Democracy*, New York: Harper.

YOUNG, A. (1993). – "Substitution and Complementarity in Endogenous Innovation", *Quarterly Journal of Economics*, 108, pp. 775-807.

104

Research Productivity
in a System of Universities

James D. ADAMS, Zvi GRILICHES *

ABSTRACT. – This paper considers research performance of U.S. universities for eight science fields. At the aggregate level we find that research output follows a constant returns to scale process. However, for individual universities we find evidence of diminishing returns. We offer two explanations for these differing results. First, data errors are more important at the individual level. Second, research spillovers exist between universities and fields that are captured only at the aggregate level.

* J. D. ADAMS: University of Florida, NBER; Z. GRILICHES: Harvard University, NBER. We thank the Mellon Foundation for financial support, and Jian-Mao Wang for excellent research assistance. We thank two referees as well as seminar participants at the University of Florida, the National Bureau of Economic Research, and the Strasbourg Conference for helpful comments.

D. Encaoua et al. (eds.), The Economics and Econometrics of Innovation, 105–140.

1 Introduction

The topic of this paper is the research productivity of a system of universities, where the particular system is a group of leading public and private universities in the United States. Broadly speaking, the measure of productivity that we use is the ratio of the "intermediate" outputs of the research – as measured by papers and citations to those papers – to lagged R&D expenditures. We also explore a multivariate specification of university productivity in a regression system. The two outputs are research and teaching in the form of advanced degrees.

It is important to study trends in university research and teaching productivity because universities account for about fifty percent of basic research in the United States (National Science Board, 1996, Table 4-5) and basic research is one of the mainsprings of industrial innovation. University research takes on additional importance in the United States because it shapes the training of graduate students, many of whom become industrial scientists and engineers. If university research productivity were to decline, then *for a given commitment of resources* to university research, a critical input into industrial research would grow more slowly. As a result new products and processes would tend to appear less frequently [1]. However, it is difficult to study the general relationship between industrial innovation and university research, and more difficult still to value the resulting innovations. Tracing the impact of science is a novelty for economists; we are apprentices in constructing the experiments that would isolate the connections between science and innovation, and a general methodology that reliably values the innovations remains over the horizon [2]. This is especially true given the location of universities in a public sector whose output is notoriously difficult to evaluate (GRILICHES [1994]).

For these reasons we study the more immediate connection between research output and lagged R&D of universities. And yet measuring research productivity even in this way is not a simple exercise. One problem is the unclear boundaries between different sciences and universities, since the results of research may, and hopefully do, show up in an entirely different university and field than their point of origin [3]. A second problem is that R&D statistics are subject to considerable error from the point of view of measuring basic research, and the errors can be of either sign. On the one hand, measured academic R&D underestimates the total value of R&D resources devoted to basic research because of implicitly funded research. On the other hand, measured R&D overstates the total value of resources devoted to basic research because some of the R&D is devoted to

---

1. See EVENSON and KISLEV [1976] for a search-theoretic interpretation of the basic research, industry R&D linkage, and ADAMS (1993) for a cross-industry test of this relationship.
2. But see EVENSON and KISLEV [1975] and HUFFMAN and EVENSON [1993] for the relationship between biological science and agriculture. See STEPHAN [1996] for an excellent survey of the present state of the economics of science.
3. This is a familiar problem in the economics of industrial R&D. See GRILICHES [1979, 1992].

106

infrastructure and contract work rather than basic research. A third problem is that the various deflators for R&D do not agree, so the very definition of real R&D is at issue. Even the measure of what constitutes a scientific paper is an elastic yardstick of scientific achievement. Finally, our citation measurements depend on growth in the scientific professions; indeed they depend on the technology of carrying out the search underlying a citation. Citations are themselves an uncertain metric of the impact of an article, though they are the best measure that we have. We shall see that all of these problems haunt the data, and that some of the problems grow worse as we study the data in more detail.

The remainder of the paper is arranged as follows. Section 2 provides a graphical overview of the research output-research input relationship at the field level during the nineteen eighties in the US. Findings at the more detailed level of individual universities and fields over the same period are presented in Section 3. Section 4 is a summary and conclusion.

Section 2 presents field level graphs for eight broad sciences: agriculture, biology, chemistry, computer science, engineering, mathematics and statistics, medicine, and physics. These fields account for the majority of academic research expenditures, and the 109 universities that form the basis for these graphs account for three quarters of overall academic R&D in the United States. For the majority of sciences we find that papers and citations grow at *very roughly* the same rate as lagged R&D, with computer science and mathematics research being exceptions that grow more slowly than lagged R&D. Nevertheless, at the field level, given the R&D deflator that we use, the data suggest a constant returns to scale production process for research output: the elasticity of papers and citations with respect to lagged real R&D is essentially 1.0.

We report descriptive statistics and regressions based on samples of individual US. universities and fields in Section 3. The descriptive data strongly imply that average costs per citation, interpreted as costs per "quality adjusted" unit of research, are lower in the top ten universities than in universities of lesser rank, and that they are lower in private schools.

A key regression finding is that elasticities of research output with respect to R&D are smaller at the university and field level than for the entire system. The average elasticity is 0.6 for papers and 0.7 for citations at the university and field level, suggesting the possibility of diminishing returns at this level. The evidence at our disposal does not go deep enough to draw a firm conclusion at to why we see the *appearance* of diminishing returns at the level of the individual university but not at the aggregate level. In the course of our research we have been tempted to cite research externalities (R&D spillovers between fields and universities) as the source of this difference in results. According to this story, externalities convert individual diminishing returns to constant returns.

However, such a conclusion would be premature given the ready availability of alternative interpretations for the difference in results at the aggregate and individual levels. The incorrect assignment of R&D to papers and citations is undoubtedly a more important problem at the university level, and it could yield the illusion of diminishing returns at this level. For example, larger research programs may export Ph.D.s, and hence some of their research output, to smaller programs [4]. In general, university departments have rather weak intellectual property rights to the research output they produce.

The result that the citation-R&D elasticity is larger than the papers-R&D elasticity strongly suggests that larger research programs produce more cited, higher quality research. Another finding is that private schools generate more research output per dollar of R&D than public universities. These results in levels disappear when we account for individual school effects by regressing long differences of research outputs on long differences of lagged R&D. There is virtually no connection between growth of research output and growth of R&D input, implying that most of what we find at the university level between research output and input is linked with fixed university effects. To date we have little hold over changes in financial and other circumstances that bring about a change in the stream of a university's research output. Finally we examine the joint determination of research and graduate teaching outputs. We find modest correlations between the error terms in the research and teaching equations. We also show that both lagged R&D expenditures and lagged adanced degrees are factors that increase research output. Finally, in the equation for advanced degrees we find that both undergraduate science enrollments and lagged R&D expenditures in a university and field increase output of advanced degrees. With this summary in mind, we turn now to an examination of the findings.

2 Research Output and R&D at the Field Level

Figures 1 through 16 present graphs at the field level for eight fields of science. The underlying data are based on a constant sample of 109 universities having the largest R&D programs in the US. This set of universities accounts for three fourths of all university R&D; it is larger than the sub-samples of universities employed in Section 3, because of additional data required of the sub-samples. The graphs depict relationships between real R&D lagged two years and papers over the period 1981-1993; and they show the same relationship between real R&D and total citations to papers in the year of publication *and in four succeeding years,* over the period 1981-1989. Underlying data on nominal total and federal R&D derive from the CASPAR database of the National Science Foundation. We convert nominal R&D into constant dollar R&D using the recently constructed university R&D deflator of the Bureau of Economic Analysis (BEA, 1994). The papers and citations are taken from unpublished data of the Institute for Scientific Information (ISI), the source of the *Science Citation Index.*

---

4. The same statement could be true of fields: some sciences could be net contributors to other sciences. However, this problem would afflict the field level results as well as the university and field level results.

The BEA university deflator rises at 6.6 percent per year, almost twice as fast as the R&D deflator for industry, and more rapidly than the increase of 4.1 percent set by the implicit GDP deflator (see ADAMS and GRILICHES [1996]). We are not sure why the university deflator rises this quickly, but it is clear that if we had used the GDP deflator instead then the growth of real R&D would have been greater, and research productivity would have grown more slowly.

For each of the eight science fields we present two pairs of graphs. In each pair, time is on the horizontal axis and research output and lagged R&D are on the vertical axes. Both vertical axes use logarithmic scales. The upper pair of graphs shows the time path of our research output and R&D data in original units. The lower pair expresses all variables as ratios to their 1981 values. The purpose of the ratio specification is to provide a common scale in order to ease comparisons across fields. Left-hand graphs present R&D lagged two years on the left (log) scale and papers on the right (log) scale. Right-hand graphs repeat the curve of R&D lagged two years on the left scale but replace papers with total citations to those papers over a five year period on the right scale. Since vertical axes are in logs, slopes of the curves represent growth rates.

Referring to the *lower* pair of graphs in each field, Figures 1-16 allow us to reach the following conclusions. With the exception of Figures 7 and 8 (computer science) and Figures 11 and 12 (mathematics) most fields show growth in papers and citations that is roughly as fast as, or faster than, growth of lagged R&D. Computer science and mathematics papers and citations are the exception, in that outputs of these fields grow less rapidly than R&D. We are unsure as to the reasons why computer science and mathematics depart from the usual pattern. It is problematic that research output is growing more slowly than R&D dollars in these two fields in the very era when *past* mathematics is more useful than before, owing to its computer applications. This points out a weakness in current university R&D statistics, namely the lack of information on the *purpose* of the R&D. This has special relevance for computer science, given that some of its R&D could be infrastructure-driven research or contract work for industry rather than basic research. In the case of mathematics it is certainly possible that the mathematics of today comes at greater cost and is less useful than in the past; but if the nineteen eighties are an era of increased applications in research as well as industry, then this alone could account for slower growth of mathematics papers and citations, since the results of mathematics would be increasingly intertwined with other fields and more often misclassified. The difficulties of defining field boundaries are especially important for mathematics [5].

---

5. The question is whether ISI omits applications of mathematics from its journal set at an increasing rate over time. We know that *some* applications of mathematics have long been covered by abstracts within mathematics. For example, *Jahrbuch uber die Fortschritte der Mathematik,* the main abstract service until 1940, regularly covered mathematical physics papers in the nineteenth and twentieth centuries. In the present era its successor *Mathematical Reviews* covers technical economics journals like *Econometrica.* See ADAMS [1990].

FIGURE 1

Agriculture

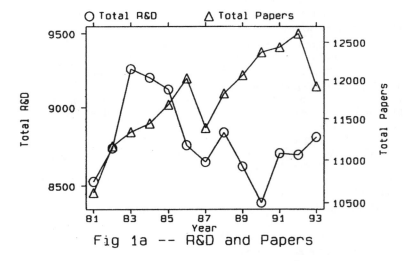

Fig 1a -- R&D and Papers

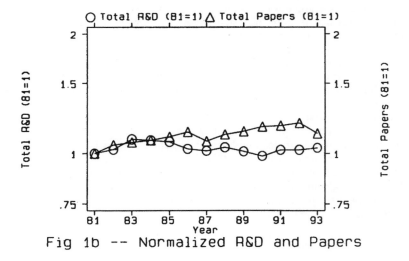

Fig 1b -- Normalized R&D and Papers

110

FIGURE 2

Agriculture

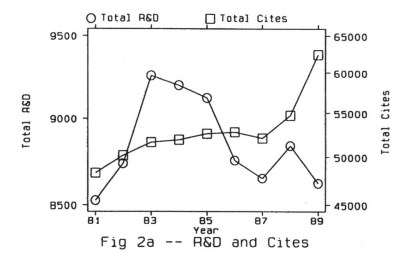

Fig 2a -- R&D and Cites

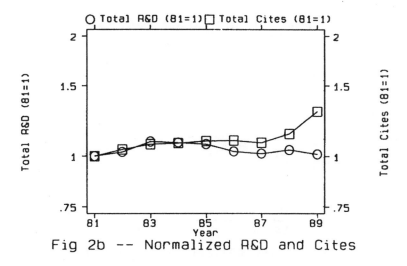

Fig 2b -- Normalized R&D and Cites

FIGURE 3

Biology

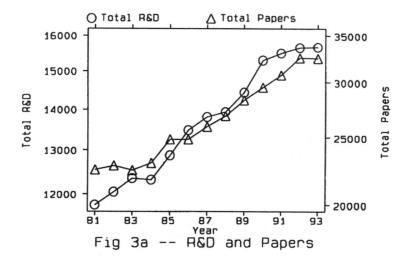

Fig 3a -- R&D and Papers

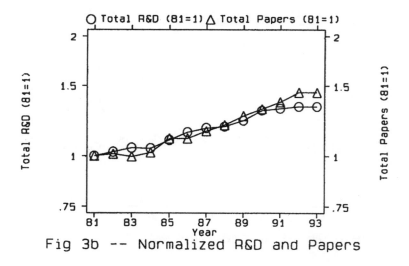

Fig 3b -- Normalized R&D and Papers

112

FIGURE 4

Biology

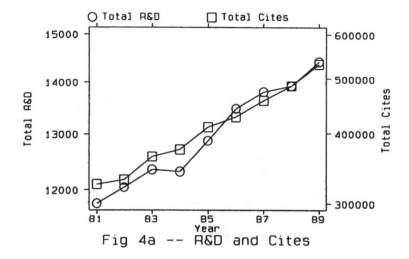

Fig 4a -- R&D and Cites

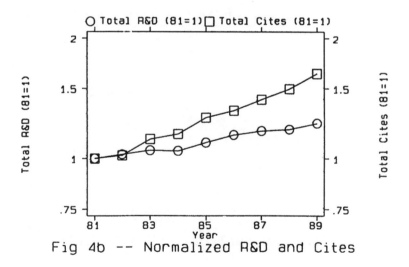

Fig 4b -- Normalized R&D and Cites

FIGURE 5

Chemistry

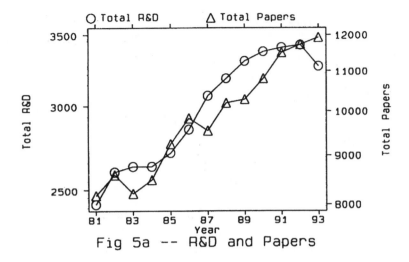

Fig 5a -- R&D and Papers

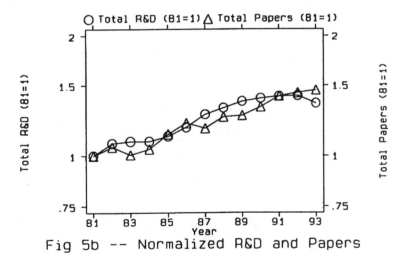

Fig 5b -- Normalized R&D and Papers

FIGURE 6

Chemistry

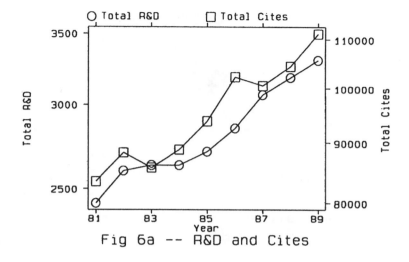

Fig 6a -- R&D and Cites

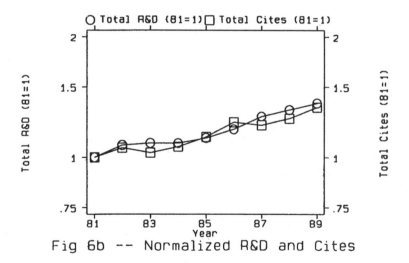

Fig 6b -- Normalized R&D and Cites

FIGURE 7

Computer Science

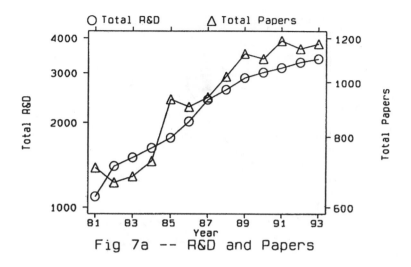

Fig 7a -- R&D and Papers

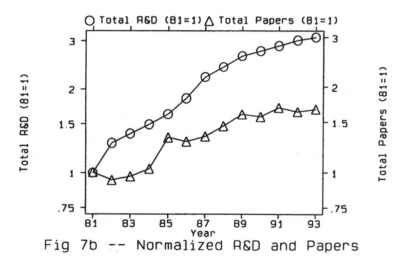

Fig 7b -- Normalized R&D and Papers

116

FIGURE 8

Computer Science

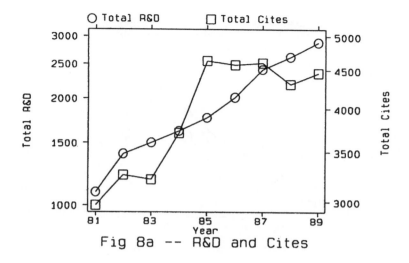

Fig 8a -- R&D and Cites

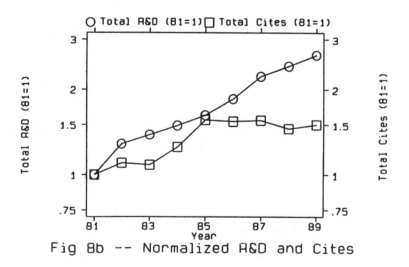

Fig 8b -- Normalized R&D and Cites

RESEARCH PRODUCTIVITY IN A SYSTEM OF UNIVERSITIES   117

FIGURE 9

Engineering

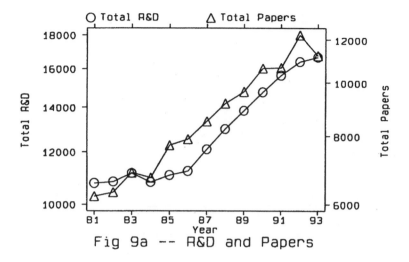

Fig 9a -- R&D and Papers

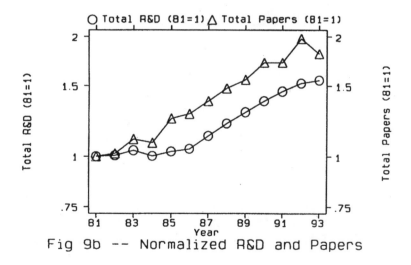

Fig 9b -- Normalized R&D and Papers

118

FIGURE 10

Engineering

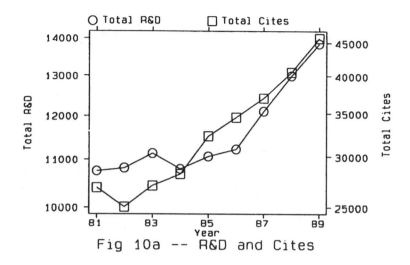

Fig 10a -- R&D and Cites

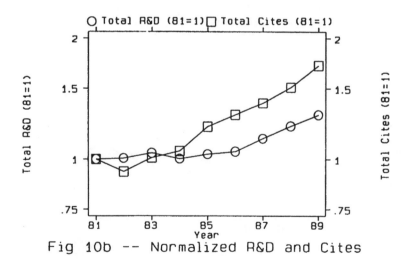

Fig 10b -- Normalized R&D and Cites

FIGURE 11

Mathematics

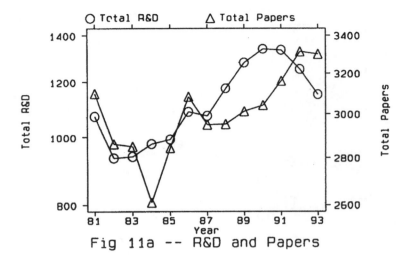

Fig 11a -- R&D and Papers

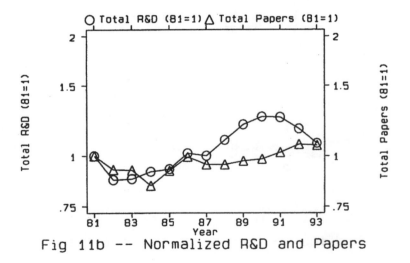

Fig 11b -- Normalized R&D and Papers

120

FIGURE 12

Mathematics

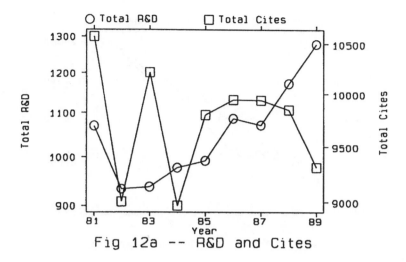

Fig 12a -- R&D and Cites

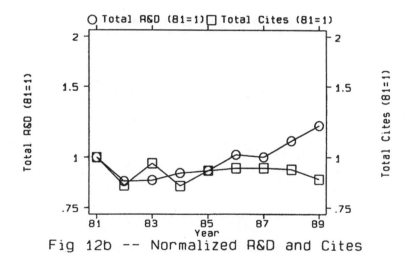

Fig 12b -- Normalized R&D and Cites

FIGURE 13

Medicine

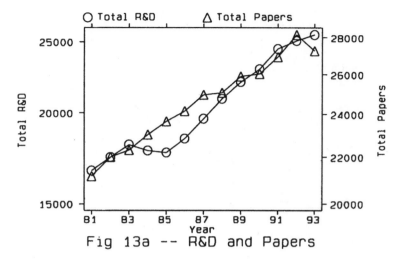

Fig 13a -- R&D and Papers

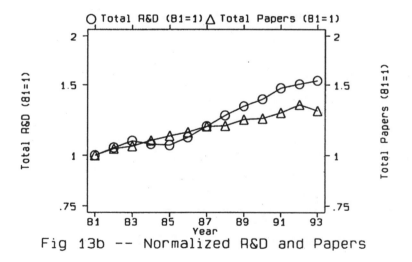

Fig 13b -- Normalized R&D and Papers

122

FIGURE 14

Medicine

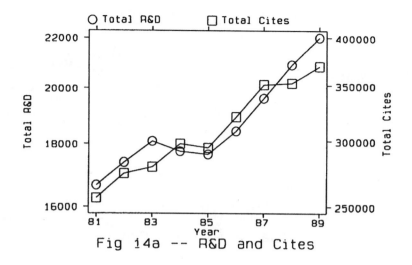

Fig 14a -- R&D and Cites

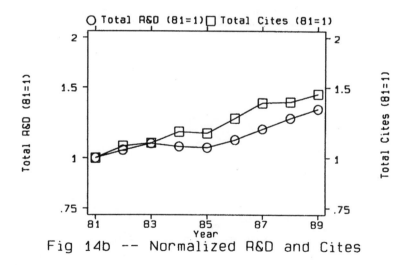

Fig 14b -- Normalized R&D and Cites

FIGURE 15

Physics

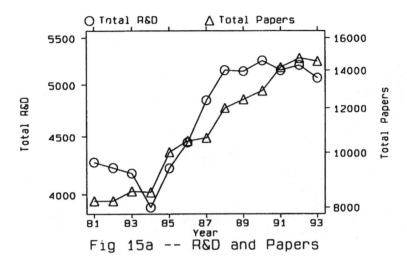

Fig 15a -- R&D and Papers

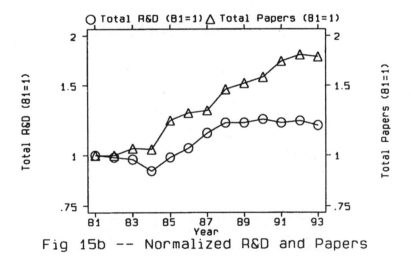

Fig 15b -- Normalized R&D and Papers

FIGURE 16

Physics

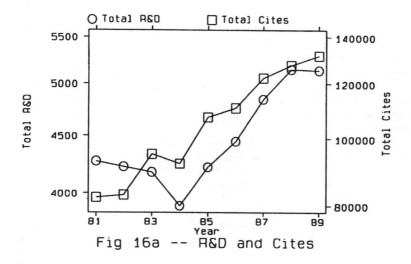

Fig 16a -- R&D and Cites

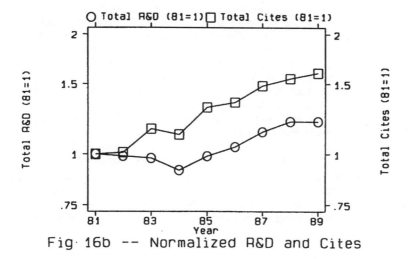

Fig 16b -- Normalized R&D and Cites

RESEARCH PRODUCTIVITY IN A SYSTEM OF UNIVERSITIES   125

3 Findings at the Level of Universities and Fields

We now turn to the behavior of research output at the level of fields and universities. We have reasonably complete data on R&D and other characteristics for about thirty universities over the period 1973-1994, and we have consistent data on research outputs for the same schools over the period 1981-1993 [6]. Note that these samples at the individual university and field level are about one fourth of the 109 university sample on which Figures 1-16 are based.

The greater time span of R&D allows us to lag R&D spending relative to research outputs, although the final data are in fact restricted to the period 1981-1989 by the limited span of research output. Actual numbers of institutions are 24 in agriculture, 39 in biology, 41 in chemistry, 16 in computer science, 37 in engineering, 38 in mathematics, 33 in medicine, and 37 in physics. These numbers reflect the following selection criteria: (i), positive R&D; (ii), an active Ph. D. program (MD in medicine); and (iii), positive research output. We imposed these criteria to obtain consistent R&D data over time as well as samples that link up cleanly with the study of the joint determination of research and graduate teaching towards the end of the paper.

Panel A of Table 1 reports means of key variables. The typical field in a university produces one to two hundred papers per year with one to two thousand citations to those papers over five years. However, there is considerable variability across fields, with the life sciences being the most numerous producers of research and the mathematical sciences (mathematics, statistics, and computer science) the least numerous. The cross field differences arise partly from differences in the size of R&D programs: life sciences lead the group, while mathematics and computer science trail the other fields. Turning to teaching outputs as represented by undergraduate majors and Ph.D./MD degrees, we observe differing patterns by field. Engineering has large undergraduate and graduate programs, while medicine is concentrated at the graduate level. Programs in the mathematical and natural sciences tend to be small at both the graduate and undergraduate levels.

Panel B of Table 1 reports growth rates of research outputs, research funding, and teaching outputs for our regression samples. In most cases growth of research output equals or exceeds growth of research spending, the main exception being mathematics [7]. Turning to teaching outputs within

---

6. We have data on papers and citations over the period 1981-1993. We drop the data for 1990-1993 because we construct five years' worth of citations to papers published in each year, and this is clearly impossible for papers and citations to those papers after 1989.
7. It is important to point out that the samples of Table 1 comprise the upper tail of universities in Figures 1 to 16, and that their behavior is not precisely the same. This is readily seen for computer science, where growth of R&D is much closer to growth in research output in Table 1 than in Figures 7 and 8. Perhaps a larger fraction of computer science research is of a basic science nature in Table 1 than in these two figures.

fields, the pattern varies by discipline and presumably depends on differing market conditions. Life science degrees are flat over the period of the nineteen eighties at both levels, while the natural sciences, mathematical sciences, and engineering seem to shift towards increased focus on graduate education.

Table 2 examines average costs per paper and per citation in subsamples of the university and field level data. The average cost calculations remove scale of research programs from the data, facilitating comparisons across samples. Panel A breaks up the data by top ten research university and below [8]. Costs per paper are nearly the same in the top ten universities as in universities below this rank. Costs per citation are a different matter; on average these are thirty percent less in the top ten institutions [9]. These results suggest that top ten schools have a comparative advantage in producing more highly cited research.

Panel B breaks the data up into samples of private and public institutions. The comparisons exclude agriculture, since public universities dominate the latter field. The public-private comparisons suggest that private universities are more expensive at producing papers, yet cheaper at producing citations; indeed they are twenty percent cheaper [10].

Regression findings are presented in Tables 3 through 7. All the tables use a variant of the specification,

$$(1) \qquad y = \alpha + \beta \cdot W(r) + \gamma \cdot X + u$$

where y is the logarithm of research output, comprised of papers or citations, $W(r)$ is the logarithm of a distributed lag function of real past R&D expenditures, and X is a vector of control variables. X includes year dummies to control for changes in the research production function over time. Sometimes it includes type of school (top ten, public, and so on). Our main interest centers on β, the elasticity of research output with respect to research input, and the measure of returns to scale in research in a field and university. Diminishing (constant or increasing) returns predominate at the university level for a given field when $\beta < 1$ ($\beta \geq 1$). As noted, the calculation of β is beset by multiple problems of measurement having to do with the horizon of the distributed lag, the mismeasurement of the R&D, the boundary of a field, the boundary of what constitutes the research

---

8. The top ten research universities were selected by the Institute for Scientific Information (ISI) on the following basis. First, universities were ranked among the top ten by *citation impact per paper* in each of twenty-one fields of science during the period 1981-1993. Second, those universities that ranked among the top ten most frequently, that is, based on number of appearances across the twenty-one fields, were awarded the title of top ten research university. The list includes the following private universities: Harvard, Yale, Chicago, MIT, Stanford, Princeton, Cornell, and the California Institute of Technology. The two public institutions are Berkeley and the University of Washington. Notice that a number of universities with large and successful research programs are excluded by this criterion, especially the University of Pennsylvania, Northwestern University, and Carnegie Mellon University, but also others.
9. Use the ratio of column means of costs per citation in Panel A: 11.3/16.4 = 0.69. Thus costs per citation are actually thirty-one percent lower in the top ten universities.
10. The ratio of the column means of costs per citation in Panel B is 14.1/17.8 = 0.79.

Table 1

Descriptive Statistics: Research Outputs, Research Funding, and Teaching Outputs of US Universities, 1981-1989.

			Variable			
			Research		Teaching	
Fields of Science	Number of Universities [a] (1.1)	Papers per Year (1.2)	Cites over 5 years [b] (1.3)	5 Year Lagged R&D (1000$) [c] (1.4)	Bacc. Degrees in Field (1.5)	Ph.D./MD Degrees in Field (1.6)
Panel A. Means per University and Field, 1981-1989						
Agriculture	24	286	1223	23082	183	22
Biology	39	322	5759	19139	154	35
Chemistry	41	113	1249	4166	33	18
Computer Science	16	17	91	3882	80	7
Engineering	37	124	563	16223	436	47
Mathematics	38	45	166	1387	54	9
Medicine	33	355	5097	32277	55 [d]	180
Physics	37	148	1645	6887	18	11
Panel B. Annual Rates of Growth, 1981-1989						
Agriculture	24	0.024	0.031	0.006*	−0.093	0.017*
Biology	39	0.034	0.065	0.029	−0.003*	−0.002*
Chemistry	41	0.027	0.038	0.030	−0.034	0.019
Computer Science	16	0.071	0.042	0.061	0.006*	0.034
Engineering	37	0.053	0.067	−0.002*	0.005*	0.064
Mathematics	38	0.002*	0.001*	0.031	0.077	0.036
Medicine	33	0.021	0.046	−0.020	0.022 [d]	−0.013
Physics	37	0.052	0.058	0.010*	0.037	0.028

Notes. Panel A reports means at the university and field level, Panel B reports mean annual rates of growth on data averaged across the set of universities in each row. * *Variable is not significant at the 1% level for a one tailed test.* [d] *Number of schools is the number for which data are available.* [b] *Citations are to papers published in a given year over the current year and the next four years.* [c] *For papers and citations dated in year t, 5 year lagged R&D is the inverted V-lag of deflated R&D over years t − 1 through t − 5, where the weights are 0.111, 0.222, 0.333, 0.222, and 0.111.* [d] *Data on the number of pre-med baccalaureate degrees are available for a smaller number of medical schools than other medical data. Thus the number of observations is 178 here rather than 294.*

community of a university, and the very meaning of R&D expenditures. Likewise the assessment of diminishing return based on the size of β is clouded by exclusion of research externalities between fields and universities (spillovers) that bias our estimates of the *overall* returns to scale towards zero.

Table 3 presents estimates of β, where the type of school (public, private, top ten) is held constant. In this sense the regressions are "within group" estimates. For each measure of research output, papers and citations, we present results for five year distributed lags of R&D. The five year lag uses inverted V weights of 0.111, 0.222, 0.333, 0.222, and 0.111 on R&D dated

Table 2

Mean Research Costs per Unit of Research Output: Subsamples of US Universities, 1981-1989.

	Variable			
Field of Science	Research Dollars in 1000s per Paper	Research Dollars in 1000s per Citation [a]	Research Dollars in 1000s per Paper	Research Dollars in 1000s per Citation [a]
Subsamples of Panel A:	**Universities in the Top Ten** [b]		**Universities Below the Top Ten** [b]	
Agriculture	76.5	13.8	81.6	20.0
Biology	59.1	2.4	60.1	4.2
Chemistry	42.3	3.1	32.9	3.3
Computer Science	217.0	34.9	187.8	43.6
Engineering	163.1	30.1	136.2	35.7
Mathematics	30.9	6.7	28.0	9.0
Medicine	71.6	4.0	91.6	7.4
Physics	67.6	4.8	35.4	3.7
Column Means (All Fields)	**84.3**	**11.3**	**83.1**	**16.4**
Subsamples of Panel B:	**Private**		**Public**	
Biology	61.2	2.9	58.9	4.3
Chemistry	42.1	3.4	31.3	3.2
Computer Science	255.6	42.9	149.8	38.2
Engineering	162.9	31.4	133.7	35.4
Mathematics	34.8	8.2	25.4	8.4
Medicine	87.3	5.6	86.2	7.3
Physics	53.1	4.3	37.2	3.9
Column Means (excluding agriculture)	**99.6**	**14.1**	**74.6**	**17.8**

Notes. Field samples are the same as in Table 1. [a] Citations are to papers published in a given year over the current year and the next four years. [b] The top ten research universities are selected by the Institute for Scientific Information (ISI). The criterion is the university rank among the top ten in terms of frequency of appearance among the top ten schools in 21 individual research fields measured by citation impact in each field.

$t-5$, $t-4$, $t-3$, $t-2$, and $t-1$ relative to research output dated t or later. Five year lags yield a very slightly higher value for the research elasticity than three years lags (not reported here). This could indicate a longer lag in effect or else a fall in measurement error in $W(r)$ as length of lag r increases. The main finding is that research elasticities lie below 1. The difference is almost always significant at the 1% level, with the citation elasticities being about 0.1 higher than the paper elasticities. One interpretation of this finding is that papers "leak" out of the larger research programs as Ph.D. students move to faculty posts in other, usually smaller programs. Thus the R&D that generates these research papers is incorrectly assigned

TABLE 3

Research Output Regressions

	Papers per Year			Citations over 5 Years [a]		
Field of Science	Time Trend of Papers [b] (3.1)	Time Trend of Papers per $ of R&D [c] (3.2)	Coefficient of Lagged Total R&D [d] (3.3)	Time Trend of Citations [b] (3.4)	Time Trend of Citations per $ of R&D [c] (3.5)	Coefficient of Lagged Total R&D [d] (3.6)
Agriculture	0.020	0.018	0.90	0.032	0.031	0.93
Biology	0.015	0.006	0.67	0.041	0.036	0.83
Chemistry	0.011	−0.009	0.44	0.019	0.006	0.64
Computer Science	0.039	0.026	0.54	0.010	0.002	0.71
Engineering	0.050	0.048	0.57	0.059	0.058	0.68
Mathematics	−0.015	−0.037	0.38	−0.020	−0.037	0.53
Medicine	0.031	0.034	0.75	0.058	0.060	0.86
Physics	0.041	0.034	0.53	0.046	0.041	0.65

Notes. Variables and samples are defined in Table 1. Regressions include year dummies, 0-1 dummy variables for top ten research universities, for top ten private universities, and for other private universities. [a] Citations over five years are citations in years t to $t+4$ for papers published in year t. [b] Time trend is the annualized effect of the time dummies. It is the difference between the 1989 year dummy and the 1981 year dummy divided by eight in a regression in which the log of lagged total R&D is a separate variable. [c] Time trend has the same interpretation as in note b, except that the log of papers or citations per dollar of R&D is the dependent variable. This constrains the research output elasticities to be 1.0. [d] Lagged total R&D is the log of total R&D lagged 5 years using an inverted V lag with weights of 0.111, 0.222, 0.333, 0.222, and 0.111 on R&D in years $t-5$, $t-4$, $t-3$, $t-2$, and $t-1$ respectively, for papers in year t and citations in years t and citations in years t through $t+4$.

to different universities. Citations avoid this problem to an extent because research papers of young faculty cite papers in leading programs where their Ph.D. research was carried out. A second interpretation of the higher citation elasticity, by no means mutually exclusive, is that larger research programs focus on more basic research which produces occasionally bigger "hits". This could very well be an implication of the sorting of higher quality faculty to these institutions.

In addition, both the paper and citation elasticities are downward biased because the assignment of the papers and citations to fields is incorrect. Supporting evidence on this point is found in Tables 5 and 6 of ADAMS and GRILICHES [1996]. There it is shown that combining the fields of biology and medicine results in higher papers and citations elasticities than we find in either field separately, while combining the five fields of biology, chemistry, mathematics, medicine, and physics results in higher papers and citations elasticities than are observed for any of the five component fields.

Table 3 consists of regressions controlling for group effects, since the equations include dummies for type of institution. When we remove the dummies and introduce between group effects, research elasticities increase. This effect is important for biology, chemistry, engineering, and

130

Table 4

Eight Year Differences of Research Output: Coefficients of Papers per Year, and Citations over 5 Years, on Eight Year Differences of Lagged R&D

Field of Science	Papers per Year Lagged Total R&D [b] (4.1)	Citations over 5 Years [a] Lagged Total R&D [b] (4.2)
Agriculture	0.08*	0.06*
Biology	0.14*	0.20*
Chemistry	0.17*	0.13*
Computer Science	−0.11*	−0.03*
Engineering	0.02*	0.17*
Mathematics	0.03*	0.06*
Medicine	−0.05*	−0.23*
Physics	0.21	0.31

*Notes. Samples are defined in Table 1. Eight year differences are the difference between 1981 and 1989 of the log of citations and papers regressed on the corresponding difference between 1981 and 1989 of the log of lagged R&D. *Coefficient is not significantly different from zero at the 3% level. [a] Citations over five years are citations in years t to $t + 4$ for papers published in year t. [b] Lagged total R&D is the log of total R&D lagged 5 years using an inverted V lag with weights of 0.111, 0.222, 0.333, 0.222, and 0.111 on R&D in years $t − 5$, $t − 4$, $t − 3$, $t − 2$, and $t − 1$ respectively, for papers in year t and citations in years t through $t + 4$.*

mathematics [11]. Nevertheless, the elasticities remain below unity, indicating as before the *appearance* of diminishing returns to research at the university and field level.

Table 4 estimates eight year, long differences of research output on eight year, long differences of the distributed lag of R&D, thus taking out university and field fixed effects, including quality of university. As is often the case with panel data, the resulting elasticities fall by a large amount and are no longer different from zero. We are unable to control for changes in the financial, personnel, legal and other variables that drive changes in research productivity at this level. More fundamentally, R&D spending is correlated with a host of other factors; R&D spending captures the standing of a university and its faculty and is not therefore, a pure indicator of the effect of lagged research support on research output.

Table 5 departs from the earlier specification in (1) by allowing for separate effects of federal and non-federal R&D. In this case we use the nonlinear specification,

$$(2) \qquad y = \alpha + \beta \cdot \ell n \left[W^* \left(r_f \right) + \delta \cdot W^* \left(r_n \right) \right] + \gamma \cdot X + u,$$

---

11. Taking the five year distributed lag of R&D as a benchmark we find that the within and between group elasticities for papers (citations) are 0.03 (0.08) higher in biology, 0.07 (0.11) higher in chemistry, 0.04 (0.06) higher in engineering, and 0.06 (0.09) higher in mathematics. None of the elasticities were lower than in Table 3.

Table 5

Nonlinear Research Output Regressions: Coefficients of Papers per Year and Citations over 5 Years, on Lagged Federal and Non-federal R&D.

Field of Science	Papers per Year		Citations over 5 Years	
	Coefficient of Lagged Total R&D (β) (5.1)	Coefficient of Lagged Non-Federal R&D (δ) (5.2)	Coefficient of Lagged Total R&D (β) (5.3)	Coefficient of Lagged Non-federal R&D (δ) (5.4)
Agriculture	0.91	0.75 [c]	0.95	0.79 [c]
Biology	0.64	0.07 [b]	0.79	−0.09 [b]
Chemistry	0.44	1.42 [c]	0.63	0.61 [c]
Computer Science	0.56	0.46 [a]	0.75	0.13 [b]
Engineering	0.54	0.11 [b]	0.62	−0.03 [b]
Mathematics	0.41	0.12 [b]	0.57	0.04 [b]
Medicine	0.68	0.20 [a]	0.76	0.10 [b]
Physics	0.54	3.24 [d]	0.66	2.90 [d]

Notes. Variables and samples are defined in Table 1. Estimation method is NLLS. Regressions include 0-1 dummy variables for top ten research universities, for top ten private universities, and for other private universities. Specification of R&D is: log (Federal R&D+δ·NON-FEDERAL R&D). All coefficients are significantly different from zero at the 1% level unless otherwise noted. [a] *Coefficient is significantly greater than zero and less than one at the 1% level.* [b] *Coefficient is not significantly different from zero at the 1% level.* [c] *Coefficient is significantly greater than zero but is not significantly different from one at the 1% level.* [d] *Coefficient is significantly greater than one at the 1% level.*

where ℓn is the natural log, $W^*\left(r_f\right)$ is the *arithmetic* distributed lag of federal R&D and $W^*\left(r_n\right)$ is the *arithmetic* distributed lag of non-federal R&D. Throughout Table 5 we use a five year distributed lag of R&D.

Specification (2) allows the effect of non-federal R&D, δ, to differ from the effect of federal R&D, as given by β. The effect of non-federal R&D is smaller than the federal effect when $\delta < 1$, and at least equal when $\delta \geq 1$. However, we are obliged to point out that (2) is not the experiment we would conduct had we access to more detailed data. We cannot for example, decompose non-federal R&D into state government supported research, much of which could be targeted on service activities rather than publication; into funding by private industry that has an applied focus; and into funding by foundations, some of which may be given over to the most basic science. It is important to also see that any censoring effects on publication that might be due to industry supported R&D are included in the non-federal component of R&D, though we cannot separate industry-supported research from other non-federal sources. Nevertheless, (2) does separate federal R&D from non-federal, and it is the greatest detail of which our R&D data are capable [12].

---

12. Again we wish to emphasize that at the university and field level, non-federal R&D is not broken up into research that is funded by the university itself, by state and local governments, or by private foundations in the CASPAR database.

Columns (5.1) and (5.2) of Table 5 report the β and δ parameters of equation (2) for regressions in which papers are the dependent variable. Columns (5.3) and (5.4) report the β and δ parameters for total citations. Inspection of (5.1) and (5.3) shows that estimates of the effect of federal R&D are very similar to the overall research elasticities in Table 3. To see this, compare column (3.1) in Table 3 with column (5.1) of Table 5 and likewise the two columns labeled (3.3) and (5.3); these are precisely the same specification apart from the nonlinearity of the R&D term in (2) and Table 5.

The surprising result in Table 5 is the wide variation in the effect of non-federal R&D by field in comparison with federal. The non-federal effect, summarized by the parameter δ (see (2) above) is significantly less than the federal effect, summarized by β, in biology, computer science, engineering, mathematics, and medicine. Of the remaining three fields, federal and non-federal R&D have the same effect on research output in agriculture and chemistry, at conventional 1 per cent levels of significance. In the case of physics, non-federal R&D has a significantly greater effect than federal R&D: indeed, the point estimate says that a dollar of non-federal R&D has an effect three times larger than a dollar of federal R&D! Results for chemistry are qualitatively similar to physics, but the point estimate of $\delta = 1.4$ is not estimated with very much precision.

The large amount of variation in the non-federal effect δ that we observe in Table 5 calls for an explanation. Bearing in mind that any explanation must be speculative given the current evidence, there are some obvious candidates for the variation that we observe in δ. For example, the point estimate of the non-federal effect could be larger in chemistry and physics because a sizable part of non-federal R&D is targeted on basic research in these two fields. Nevertheless, the average effect of non-federal R&D across fields is inconsistent with this view: in most cases we observe $\delta < 1$ and a dollar of non-federal R&D is associated with lower observed research productivity compared with a dollar of federal R&D. However, one has to remember that what we call R&D consists of wide-ranging activities. In cases where $\delta < 1$ the non-federal R&D could be more directed towards applied research, even service activities that are less likely to result in publication. Examples are "R&D" funding for participation on public service commissions, consulting and contract research for business firms, and private funding for the construction of university plant and equipment that partly has a teaching function. In reality the results of Table 5 are still more diverse than we have implied. In biology, engineering, and mathematics, non-federal R&D is predicted to have *no* impact on research output. Again, we suspect that in these cases the non-federal component is aimed entirely at objectives other than basic research.

Table 6 stratifies the samples for private and public universities and compares elasticities of research output to lagged R&D in the two samples. In Table 6 alone we drop the dummy variable for top ten schools from the regressions. The reason is that we want to draw a full, "within and between group" comparison between private and public schools. If we control for the greater productivity of top ten schools, then we are making a biased comparison between public and private schools, because the private school sample is more homogeneous within its group. Top ten schools form about half of the private institutions in our private school samples and the remainder are similarly homogeneous within their class. Thus, the "within group" variation is smaller among the private schools than it is for public universities [13].

TABLE 6

Research Output Regressions for Private and Public Universities: Coefficients of Papers per Year and Citations over 5 Years, on Lagged R&D [a].

	Private Universities		Public Universities	
		Citations		Citations
	Papers	over	Papers	over
	per Year	5 Years [c]	per Year	5 Years [c]
Field of Science [b]	(6.1)	(6.2)	(6.3)	(6.4)
Biology	0.77	0.95	0.64	0.90
Chemistry	0.67	0.91	0.37	0.60
Computer Science [d]	0.61	0.65	0.54	0.75
Engineering	0.62	0.72	0.60	0.75
Mathematics	0.46	0.61	0.41	0.64
Medicine	0.82	1.13	0.75	0.87
Physics	0.58	0.78	0.49	0.62

Notes. Variables and samples are defined in Table 1. All coefficients are significantly different from zero at the 1% level. These regressions omit the 0-1 dummies for top ten research universities, for top ten private universities, and for other private universities. [a] Total R&D is lagged 5 years, As in Table 1, this is an inverted V lag with weights of 0.111, 0.222, 0.333, 0.222, and 0.111 on R&D in years $t-5$, $t-4$, $t-3$, $t-2$, and $t-1$ respectively, for papers in year t and citations in years t through $t+4$. [b] Public and private university comparisons are not possible in agriculture, since public universities dominate the field. [c] Citations over five years are citations in years t to $t+4$ for papers published in year t. [d] Samples for computer science are relatively small. The private university sample consists of 5 schools over the 1981-1989 period. The public university sample consists of nearly complete observations on 10 schools over the period 1981-1989.

---

13. The same point can be made more formally as follows. Using standard notation for panel data (see for example BALTAGI [1995]), the within and between group, or total estimator is $\beta_T = (W_{XX} + B_{XX})^{-1} (W_{XY} + B_{XY})$, where W_{ij} and B_{ij} indicate within and between group data matrices. The within group estimator is then $\beta_W = W_{XX}^{-1} W_{XY}$ while the between group estimator is $\beta_B = B_{XX}^{-1} B_{XY}$. It follows that $\beta_T = \phi\beta_W + (1-\phi)\beta_B$, where ϕ is the relative weight on within group variation and $1-\phi$ the weight on the between group variation. Assume, as is correct for out data, that $\beta_W = \alpha\beta_B$, $\alpha < 1$. Now divide the data into two sets 1 and 2 that include both within and between group variation. Using the above relationships the ratio of the total estimators β_T for groups 1 and 2 is related to the ratio of the within estimators β_W by the following formula:
$$\frac{\beta_{T1}}{\beta_{T2}} = \left[\frac{\alpha_2}{\alpha_1} \frac{1-(1-\alpha_1)\phi_1}{1-(1-\alpha_2)\phi_2}\right] \frac{\beta_{W1}}{\beta_{W2}}.$$
Let set 1 be the private schools and set 2 the public schools and assume for simplicity that $\alpha_1 = \alpha_2$. Then the condition that the ratio of the total estimators on the left exceed the ratio of the within estimators on the right is that the bracketed term exceed 1.0, which comes down to $\phi_1 < \phi_2$, or that within group variation is smaller relative to the total variation for set 1, the private institutions.

Columns (6.1) and (6.3) are comparable regressions for private and public universities with papers as the dependent variable. Likewise (6.2) and (6.4) are comparable public-private regressions for citations. Clearly the elasticity of research output is greater in private schools whether we use papers or citations as the measure of output. In fact the private elasticities are about 0.1 higher than the public elasticities. Whether the result is due to smaller errors in the data from private schools or to a genuine difference in the ability to obtain output from given funding is unclear from the evidence, although the question clearly deserves further study, especially from a policy perspective.

So far the regressions we have reported assume that research output can be captured entirely by papers and citations. However, research universities place great emphasis on the production of Ph.D. students whose knowledge reflects recent innovations in research. These students clearly serve a valuable function by transmitting new techniques to researchers in other universities, industry, and government as well as through their own research. In this sense, graduate students comprise a kind of "intergenerational" research output. For all these reasons we conclude our presentation of findings with a table of multivariate results for papers or citations and Ph.D. degrees in a regression system. Our statistical method is Seemingly Unrelated Regression (SUR). As we have noted, the SUR system jointly estimates equations for research output and *graduate* teaching output measured by the logarithm of the number of advanced degrees [14]. In this case the specification consists of two production functions:

$$
\begin{aligned}
y_R &= \alpha_R + \beta_{RR} \cdot W_R(r) + \beta_{RA} \cdot W_A(r) + \gamma_R \cdot X + u_R \\
y_S &= \alpha_S + \beta_{SR} \cdot W_R(r) + \beta_{SU} \cdot W_U(s) + \gamma_S \cdot X + u_S,
\end{aligned}
$$

(3)

where the first equation is the research equation, the second is the graduate degrees equation, and the error terms are assumed to have mean zero, variances σ_{RR} and σ_{SS}, and covariance σ_{RS}.

We add the subscript R to the first equation to indicate research and S to the second to indicate graduate students. $W_R(r)$ is the log of five year lagged R&D, as in earlier tables. $W_A(r)$ is the log of five year lagged advanced degrees: this variable is based on the same inverted V weights as R&D [15]. X is the set of school dummies employed in earlier tables. The second equation expresses graduate student output y_S, the logarithm of the current number of advanced degrees, as a function of lagged R&D, $W_R(r)$, and $W_U(s)$, the log of a distributed *lead* of undergraduate science

---

14. The number of advanced degrees is the number of MD degrees in medicine, the number of Ph.D. degrees in other fields.

15. Thus $W_S(r)$ is the log of the sum of advanced degrees in years $t - 5$ through $t - 1$, with inverted V weights 0.111, 0.222, 0.333, 0.222, and 0.111, just as for R&D.

and engineering degrees in a university. Also included are the same set of controls X consisting of school dummies. The difference between the two equations therefore centers on the variables $W_A(r)$ and $W_U(s)$.

The research equation introduces both the distributed lag of both lagged R&D and lagged graduate students $W_A(r)$ because both research dollars and the pool of graduate students are important inputs into research. But why a distributed *lead* of undergraduate degrees $W_U(s)$ in the graduate degrees equation? We employ this variable since undergraduate degrees proxy for undergraduate teaching in the recent past and because reliable data on undergraduate enrollments are missing [16]. The particular form of the distributed *lead* $W_U(s)$ uses a constant weight of one third on undergraduate science degrees received in periods $t+1$, $t+2$, and $t+3$ relative to doctoral degrees received in period t. The rationale for this form of $W_U(s)$ is that undergraduate students receiving their diplomas in year t took their introductory science courses, in which graduate student teachers are concentrated, in year $t-3$. Likewise, undergraduates graduating in $t+2$ and $t+3$ are likely to have taken their introductory courses in years $t-2$ and $t-1$. In this way we construct a proxy for the introductory science and engineering teaching load over the course of the period t graduate student cohort. Thus, $W_U(s)$ is a demand variable for the services of graduate students in one interpretation, and a source of support, an "input" in another interpretation. The controls that enter the two equations of (3) as before include the year and institutional type dummies that we have already discussed. Of course this system is a reduced form and we do not pretend to have gone very much below the surface to reach the essence of the relationship between research and graduate teaching outputs. If we were to do so we would find that graduate students provide both teaching and research inputs, just as we would find that the services of teachers, including their stock of expertise from past R&D, are key inputs into graduate education. But this structural investigation would require better evidence and modeling of the dynamics of the research-teaching relationship than we have so far undertaken.

Table 7 reports findings for two systems of equations in each of our eight science fields. System A uses log (papers) as the measure of research output, while system B uses log (citations). Both systems use log (advanced degrees) as a proxy for graduate student output; this is the analogue to log (papers) or log (citations) on the research side. We have no readily available measure of quality of graduate degrees to compare with citations. We report regression coefficients of lagged R&D (both research and teaching equations), lagged advanced degrees (research output equation), and the distributed lead of total S&E degrees (teaching output equation). Each system is reported in two columns: the first is the research equation while the second is graduate teaching. For each field we report an estimate of

---

16. CASPAR collects data on undergraduate enrollments by university and field, but the quality of the data is uneven across schools. In addition the data are available over a very short period of time: this makes it impossible to construct meaningful leads of undergraduate enrollments.

136

the cross-equation correlation σ_{RS}. These are usually small, and they are essentially zero in the agriculture and medicine equations.

Since we introduce lagged advanced degrees as well as lagged R&D into the research equation, coefficients on lagged R&D in the research equations in columns (7.1) and (7.4) are less than their counterparts in Table 3, columns (3.1) and (3.3), though they remain statistically significant. For example the coefficient of lagged R&D in the biology papers equation is 0.28 rather than 0.67, and it is 0.18 in the physics equation, rather than 0.53. However, there is a secondary effct of R&D on research output that works through the advanced degrees equation (see (3) above). This is because lagged R&D raises future advanced degrees and thus future research output. We consider this point in the context of a steady state solution of (3) later on. The findings for citations in system B follow a similar pattern: the effects of lagged R&D in Table 3 are to an extent transferred to lagged advanced degrees in Table 7. It is interesting that the effect on research output of graduate students relative to lagged R&D differs so much by science: graduate students are more important in basic

TABLE 7

Systems of Research and Teaching Outputs: SUR Estimates

Field of Science, Variable	System A		System B	
	Equation		Equation	
	Log (papers) (7.1)	Log (Advanced Degs.) [a] (7.2)	Log (Cites over 5 Years) [b] (7.3)	Log (Advanced Degs.) [a] (7.4)
Agriculture				
Lagged R&D [c]	0.68	0.53	0.73	0.52
Lagged Advanced Degrees [d]	0.30		0.27	
Leading Undergraduate				
S&E Degrees [e]		0.48		0.49
σ_{RS}		−0.00		−0.01
Biology				
Lagged R&D [c]	0.28	0.48	0.42	0.48
Lagged Advanced Degrees [d]	0.64		0.67	
Leading Undergraduate				
S&E Degrees [e]		0.59		0.58
σ_{RS}		−0.07		−0.01
Chemistry				
Lagged R&D [c]	0.19	0.65	0.40	0.65
Lagged Advanced Degrees [d]	0.36		0.36	
Leading Undergraduate				
S&E Degrees [e]		0.33		0.33
σ_{RS}		0.04		0.06
Computer Science				
Lagged R&D [c]	0.51	0.43	0.63	0.42
Lagged Advanced Degrees [d]	0.06*		0.13*	
Leading Undergraduate				
S&E Degrees [e]		0.67		0.75
σ_{RS}		0.17		−0.06

TABLE 7 (cont.)

Systems of Research and Teaching Outputs: SUR Estimates

Field of Science, Variable	System A Equation		System B Equation	
	Log (papers) (7.1)	Log (Advanced Degs.) [a] (7.2)	Log (Cites over 5 Years) [b] (7.3)	Log (Advanced Degs.) [a] (7.4)
Engineering				
Lagged R&D [c]	0.08	0.73	0.15	0.73
Lagged Advanced Degrees [d]	0.62		0.67	
Leading Undergraduate S&E Degrees [e]		0.48		0.49
σ_{RS}	**0.10**		**0.11**	
Mathematics				
Lagged R&D [c]	0.27	0.48	0.41	0.49
Lagged Advanced Degrees [d]	0.20		0.22	
Leading Undergraduate S&E Degrees [e]		0.13*		0.10*
σ_{RS}	**0.05**		**0.11**	
Medicine				
Lagged R&D [c]	0.70	0.28	0.81	0.28
Lagged Advanced Degrees [d]	0.16		0.13	
Leading Undergraduate S&E Degrees [e]		0.22		0.22
σ_{RS}	**0.00**		**0.00**	
Physics				
Lagged R&D [c]	0.18	0.59	0.25	0.59
Lagged Advanced Degrees [d]	0.54		0.62	
Leading Undergraduate S&E Degrees [e]		0.53		0.53
σ_{RS}	**0.02**		**0.05**	

*Notes. Samples are slightly smaller than Table 1 due to missing values on new teaching and degree variables. Regressions include 0-1 dummy variables for top ten research universities, for top ten private universities, and for other private universities. σ_{RS} is the SUR estimate of the cross equation correlation between the residuals of the research and graduate teaching equations. * Not significant at the 1% level. [a] Advanced degrees consist of Ph.D. s in all science fields except medicine, and MD s in medicine itself. [b] Citations over five years are citations in years t to $t + 4$ for papers published in year t. [c] Lagged R&D is the log of total R&D lagged 5 years, an inverted V lag with weights of 0.111, 0.222, 0.333, 0.222, and 0.111 on R&D in years $t - 5$, $t - 4$, $t - 3$, $t - 2$, and $t - 1$ respectively, for papers in year t and citations in years t through $t + 4$. [d] Lagged advanced degrees is the log of Ph.D. (MD in medicine) degrees lagged 5 years, an inverted V lag with weights of 0.111, 0.222, 0.333, 0.222, and 0.111 on advanced degrees in years $t - 5$, $t - 4$, $t - 3$, $t - 2$, and $t - 1$ respectively, for papers in year t and citations in years t through $t + 4$. [e] Leading undergraduate S&E degrees is the log of an average of undergraduates degrees in all science fields in a university 1, 2, 3 years in the future.*

sciences like biology, chemistry, mathematics, and physics than in more applied fields like agriculture, computer science, engineering, and medicine.

Now consider the advanced degrees equations, (7.2) and (7.4). We see that lagged R&D is consistently associated with larger outputs of advanced degrees in these equations. Also, leading undergraduate S&E degrees have a positive and generally significant effect on advanced degrees. If we use the "input" interpretation of lagged R&D and leading undergraduate degrees in the advanced degrees equation, then we see that advanced degrees follow a constant returns production process in Table 7. One reason for this contrast with the *appearance* of diminishing returns in the research equation is that errors of measurement are much less for advanced degrees. Students are usually assigned to the schools where they do most of their graduate work. This is not obviously the case for papers and citations.

It is interesting to consider further the relationships between research and graduate teaching that are implied by our results. It is easier to see these relations in a steady state setting, and we attach superscript zeroes to indicate steady state values. In a steady state we can assess the full effect of research on research output by incorporating the indirect effect on advanced degrees using (3) and two facts, that $y_S = W_A^0(s)$ and that $W_R(r) = W_R^0(r)$, to substitute the second equation into the first. This yields

$$(4) \qquad y_R^0 = (\beta_{RR} + \beta_{RA}\,\beta_{SR})\,W_R^0 + Z_R^0,$$

where

$$(5) \qquad Z_R^0 = \alpha_R + \gamma_R \cdot X^0 + \beta_{RA}[\alpha_S + W_U^0 + \gamma_S \cdot X^0].$$

the term Z_R^0 in (5) encompasses steady state effects of variables other than lagged R&D. Equation (4) shows that the steady state, or "full" effect of lagged R&D on research output is $\beta_{RR} + \beta_{RA}\,\beta_{SR}$ rather than β_{RR}, since R&D affects graduate student output and thus indirectly research output, as well as research output directly. In the case of biology papers the full effect of lagged R&D is $\beta_{RR} + \beta_{RA}\,\beta_{SR} = 0.28 + 0.64 \times 0.48 = 0.59$, rather than $\beta_{RR} = 0.28$. For biology citations the full and direct effects are 0.74 and 0.42. In the case of physics papers, full and direct effects are 0.50 and 0.18, while for physics citations these effects are 0.62 and 0.25. Not surprisingly, the full effects are very close to the findings of Table 3, since we have in essence decomposed a nearly steady state effect in Table 3 into direct effects of lagged R&D on research output and lagged, indirect effects that work through the supply of graduate students.

5 Conclusion

The work that we have reported is, in a certain sense, an essay on of the difficulty of drawing distinctions. Many of the difficulties that hinder measurement of research productivity begin with distinctions between fields that are continuously blurred by spillovers and by collaborative ventures, and with distinctions between schools that are connected by the mutual exchange of students and ideas; indeed this is an essential part of the vitality of the university system. The puzzle of the seeming increase in cost of computer science and mathematics research during the nineteen eighties underscores the need to look at interrelationships of scientific research. In a different way, the close connection between fundamental biology and medicine points to a similar intertwining of research interests.

The same quandary shows up in yet another form. At the field level our typical finding *very roughly* approximates constant returns to scale, in contrast with our finding at the university and field level, which is one of diminishing returns. It is clear that both the research and the Ph.D. outputs are interdependent across institutions and time. The dynamics of these interrelationships are surely worthy of further exploration.

Our finding that there are differences between top ten and other universities, and between private and public universities, also deserves another look. It suggests at the very least, careful accounting for real R&D expenditures. Once having achieved that, the resulting evidence would call for a welfare analysis of the distribution of R&D among universities. The economics of universities promises to be a fertile ground for study for a long time to come.

● References

ADAMS, James D. (1990). – "Fundamental Stocks of Knowledge and Productivity Growth", *Journal of Political Economy,* 98, pp. 673-702.

ADAMS, James D. (1993). – "Science, R&D, and Invention Potential Recharge: US. Evidence", *American Economic Review, Papers and Proceedings*, 83, pp. 458-462.

ADAMS, James D., GRILICHES, Z. (1996). – "Measuring the Outputs of Science", *Proceedings of the National Academy of Sciences,* 93, pp. 12664-12670.

BALTAGI, Badi H. (1995). – *Econometric Analysis of Panel Data*, New York: John Wiley and Sons.

Bureau of Economic Analysis, US. Department of Commerce (1994). – "A Satellite Account for Research and Development", *Survey of Current Business* 74, pp. 37-71.

EVENSON, R. E., KISLEV, Y. (1976). – "A Stochastic Model of Applied Research", *Journal of Political Economy*, 84, pp. 265-282.

EVENSON, R. E., KISLEV, Y., *Agricultural Research and Productivity* (1975). – New Haven, Connecticut, Yale University Press.

GRILICHES, Zvi (1979). – "Issues in Assessing the Contribution of R&D to Productivity Growth", *The Bell Journal of Economics,* 10, pp. 92-116.

GRILICHES, Zvi (1991). – "The Search for R&D Spillovers", *Scandinavian Journal of Economics,* 94, pp. 29-47.

GRILICHES, Zvi (1994). – "Productivity, R&D, and the Data Constraint", *American Economic Review,* 84, pp. 1-23.

HUFFMAN, Wallace E., EVENSON, Robert E. (1993). – *Science for Agriculture,* Ames, Iowa: Iowa State University Press.

National Science Board (1996). – *Science and Engineering Indicators 1996.* Washington, DC, National Science Foundation.

STEPHAN, PAULA (1996). – "The Economics of Sciences", *Journal of Economic Literature,* 34, pp. 1199-1235.

140

Reputation and Competence in Publicly Funded Science: Estimating the Effects on Research Group Productivity

Ashish ARORA, Paul A. DAVID, Alfonso GAMBARDELLA *

ABSTRACT. – This paper estimates the "production function" for scientific research publications in the field of biotechnology. It utilises an exceptionally rich and comprehensive data set pertaining to the universe of research groups that applied to a 1989-1993 research programme in biotechnology and bio-instrumentation, sponsored by the Italian National Research Council, CNR. A structural model of the resource allocation process in scientific research guides the selection of instruments in the econometric analysis, and controls for selectivity bias effects on estimates based on the performance of funded research units. The average elasticity of research output with respect to the research budget is estimated to be 0.6; but, for a small fraction of groups led by highly prestigious PIs this elasticity approaches 1. These estimates imply, conditional on the distribution of observed productivity, that a more unequal distribution of research funds would increase research output in the short-run. Past research publication performance is found to have an important effect on expected levels of grant funding, and hence on the unit's current productivity in terms of (quality adjusted) publications. The results show that the productivity of aggregate resource expenditures supporting scientific research is critically dependent on the institutional mechanisms and criteria employed in the allocation of such resources.

* A. ARORA: Heinz School, Carnegie Mellon University; P. A. DAVID: Oxford University; A. GAMBARDELLA: University of Urbino. We thank the Director of the CNR Programme "Biotechnology and Bio-instrumentation", Professor Antonio De Flora, for his co-operation. Previous versions of this paper were presented to seminars at Carnegie Mellon University, the London School of Economics (STICERD), the NBER Summer Workhops in Industrial Organization (Cambridge), and the University of Pittsburgh. We have benefited particularly from the comments provided by Zvi Griliches, Bronwyn Hall, and Steve Nickell, and from Jacques Mairesse's encouragement in preparing this version of the paper for publication. We also acknowledge the financial support we received for various stages of this research from the International Centre for Economic Research (ICER) in Torino, the University of Urbino (MURST 60%), the EC Human Capital Mobility Programme (Contract N.ERBCHRXCT920002), the Renaissance Trust (UK), and MERIT, University of Limburg. Fabrizio Cesaroni, Marco Cioppi, and Aldo Geuna provided competent research assistance.

D. Encaoua et al. (eds.), The Economics and Econometrics of Innovation, 141–176.
© 2000 *Kluwer Academic Publishers. Printed in the Netherlands.*

1 Introduction

The complex and multi-dimensional links between technological progress and scientific research have been recognised for a long time by economists as well as by science administrators and business managers. (See, e.g., DAVID [1993] for an overview.) Moreover, several recent quantitative studies have shown that there is a significant correlation between scientific research and technical change in industry (NELSON [1986], JAFFE [1989], MANSFIELD [1991], NARIN and OLIVASTRO [1992]).

Given this recognition, it is surprising how little attention economists have paid to the determinants of the productivity in scientific research. We know little about how increases in inputs affect the output of the research process, or how shifting marginal research expenditures across research groups with different characteristics would affect total research output. At a time when public support for scientific research is being questioned, and national research budgets are being subjected to retrenchment and restructuring in many countries, empirically-grounded answers to these and related questions are especially important for the sensible conduct of science policy.

Our approach to this problem is to develop a structural model of the process by which research units apply for and receive funds, and estimate the corresponding production function of scientific output, gauged in terms of (journal quality-weighted) publications. In implementing this approach we use an exceptionally complete and comprehensive data set from a pioneering Italian research programme in "Biotechnology and Bio-instrumentation" that was in effect during 1989-1993 under the auspices of the Centro Nazionale delle Ricerche (CNR), the Italian equivalent of the U.S. National Science Foundation (NSF).

We begin by discussing the general institutional context within which public resource allocation for scientific research takes place, and the implications for our modeling strategy. Section 3 describes the specific features of the CNR biotechnology data set, and motivates the development of the formal model in section 4. Section 5 presents the empirical estimates of the parameters of the model. Section 6 examines how changing the distribution of resources would affect the average productivity of research budgets in the short run, taking the characteristics of the population of research units as given. We also compute the estimated direct and indirect effects of past performance, in order to assess the potential way in which budget allocations affecting a unit's publication rate would impinge upon the reputational standing of its principal investigators (PI's), and so affect their expected future levels of public finding support from similarly organised public programmes. Section 7 summarises the findings and concludes the paper.

2 The Institutional Context

2.1. The Institutions of Scientific Research

In this paper we must move beyond the view of science as the pursuit of solitary researchers linked in "invisible colleges". Research in the natural and life sciences has become a collaborative enterprise, carried on by very visible teams that are organised around increasingly expensive physical facilities and instruments. Yet, even the recent careful econometric studies by LEVIN and STEPHAN [1991], and STEPHAN and LEVIN [1992] continue the traditional individualistic focus of sociologists and historians of science, by investigating the life cycle productivity of individual academic scientists in the U.S. Their research seeks to estimate the effects of ageing through analysis of panel data, using fixed effects type procedures to control for unobserved differences. Such an approach could be justified as warranted by the emphasis that American public research programmes have placed upon grants to individual investigators, and the comparatively high degree of inter-institutional mobility that characterises university researchers' careers in the U.S. Such a rationale is not uniformly appropriate across research areas, however, and it is considerably less apposite when applied to the western European institutional context. Moreover, although establishing individual life cycle profiles in productivity allows one to assess the implications for aggregate research productivity of changes in the demographic structure of the scientific community, the immediate policy relevance of such relationships is not so obvious. Policy options for manipulating the demographic composition, essentially those affecting age-specific rates of entry and exit from particular areas of scientific research, are likely to involve indirect and lagged effects that are both costly and difficult to control. By contrast, policy instruments targeting resource allocation and reward are likely to impinge more immediately on research productivity.

The mechanism for resource allocation in the world of open, academic science is different from that of the private sector in which business corporations set R&D budgets and manage the activities of employed scientists; and the situation of the non-profit research organization, whether that of a free-standing institute or department or research unit within a university, differs also from that of the individual scientist [1]. Scientific research groups obtain the bulk of their resources from public programmes in which government agencies offer research grants and contracts to competing applicants. Resources are allocated to selected groups according to the nature of the programme objectives and the scientific reputation that the team or of the unit has established in that area over an extended period of time – a reputation that often is linked with the unit's leadership by one or a few senior scientists.

---

1. DAVID [1994], DASGUPTA and DAVID [1994] examine the efficiency implications of the institutional structures and reward systems characterising academic science. See also DASGUPTA and DAVID [1987].

If some of these group characteristics are only observed and taken into account by the funding agency (and possibly by the groups themselves), but cannot be seen by the econometrician studying the outcomes, and if some among those same characteristics also affect the production of observable scientific results by the group, then the research budgets allocated to the groups cannot be treated as an exogenous factor in the research production function. The "endogeneity" of this input implies that, in the absence of appropriate controls, there will be a bias in the estimated elasticity of research outputs with respect to the associated budget allocations. Therefore, in fitting a cross-section "production function", one needs a model of how resources are allocated among the groups, in order to choose meaningful econometric instruments and properly interpret the estimation results.

A model of the resource allocation process is also helpful in sorting out the different ways in which past performance, by affecting the scientific competence and professional reputation of the researchers associated with a particular unit, will be related to future performance. In addition to a direct competence-based effect, past performance may have two "indirect effects" on research output. First, units with better past records are more likely to be successful in getting research grants. Second, knowing this, they will invest in applying for larger grants. Both effects imply higher expected research budgets for these units, which (stochastically) raises their publication output rates. The model presented in this paper enables us to identify and separately estimate the direct and indirect effects of past performance upon group productivity.

The indirect effects of past performance deserve attention because they may underlie what has been referred to by ROBERT K. MERTON [1968], as the "Matthew Effect in Science" [2]. It is widely observed in studies of scientific productivity that a small fraction of the individuals accounts for the preponderant part of the body of published work (LOTKA [1926], PRICE [1963, 1976] ALLISON et al. [1976]). While differences in talent and ability may be part of the explanation for the pronounced left-skew that characterises distributions of individual research productivities in many specific fields of science, something further must be working to produce the phenomenon (also observed) of temporally increasing skewness of such distributions over the life of given cohorts of scientists. Institutional resource allocation mechanisms that would tend to differentially channel funding towards those who already have established a "track record" of research successes, is a likely candidate for this role in creating a dynamic "cumulative advantage" process. In other words, productive disparities also reflect the outcome of stochastic processes that cumulate advantage by

---

2. By allusion to the passages of the New Testament according to St. Matthew: "For unto everyone that hath shall be given, and he shall have abundance; but... from him that hath not shall be taken away even that which he hath". (Matthew 13:12 and 25:39.) In his original formulation of the Matthew Effect, Merton emphasised the disproportionately greater credit received for their contributions by scientists who had obtained a measure of eminence, but in subsequent work the original formulation was generalised by proposing that self-reinforcing processes affected productivity as well as recognition in science. See DAVID [1994: pp. 77-80] for further discussion.

amplifying the effects of initial heterogeneities in the productivity-related attributes of individuals, or research groups [3].

In this paper, we estimate a static model using cross-section data, and therefore cannot directly identify how initial advantage may cumulate over time. Nonetheless, a model such as ours would be a first step towards specifying the appropriate dynamic structure. In other areas of empirical economies, researchers typically have collected and analyzed cross-section data before proceeding to work with panel data, and we see our present analysis as a similar first step in the empirical research programme of the "new economics of science". But, more immediately, there are other issues of intrinsic economic interest and potential policy relevance that can be addressed directly through the analysis of cross-section data of the form that we have at our disposal, such as the impact of increased funding on research output in a given field of scientific inquiry.

2.2. Biotech Research in Italy

Biotechnology and Bio-instrumentation (henceforth B&B) was the first major public research programme in biotechnology in Italy, and virtually every Italian research group in molecular biology and genetic engineering, more than 800 in all, applied to it. We have been able to obtain information on the characteristics of both the units that were selected for funding, and those that were rejected. Thus, not only can we relate inputs to scientific output, but we can also correct for selection effects.

Unlike the US or UK, Italy is not considered a scientific powerhouse. Between 1989-1991, US based scientists accounted for about 40% of the publications in biomedical research, while Italian based scientists accounted for a little over 2.7%. By comparison, the corresponding figures for Germany, France and the UK are 6.2%, 5.2% and 7.8% respectively [4]. One may be tempted by this to suppose that a study of the Italian academic research sector is therefore of limited value for understanding the economics of modern scientific research in biotechnology, let alone as a basis for broader generalisations. We believe such a view to be mistaken. For one thing, certain structural features of national (and international) research processes are preserved when scale changes. An instance of this, which we will show below in greater detail, is that the distribution of publications for Italian scientists looks no different from that observed in other countries – it is highly skewed, with a small fraction of the researchers accounting for a large fraction of the total publications generated by the population as a whole [5].

---

3. ALLISON *et al.* [1982] surveys the sociological literature in cumulative advantage processes. For economists' view on this subject, see the discussions in DAVID [1994], STEPHAN [1996], and ARORA and GAMBARDELLA [1997].

4. See *The European Report on Science & Technology Indicators* [1994].

5. See figure 2b below. Recall that our sample is close to the relevant universe. The equivalent sample for the US would not be simply the leading research labs but any research lab working in molecular biology or genetic engineering in the country.

Moreover, the relatively small size of the Italian molecular biology sector conveys at least one significant advantage for the purposes of this study. It allows us to neglect the constraint on aggregate output that arises from the fixed number of scientific journals. Put differently, since US scientists author a large fraction of the publications in international journals, their aggregate publication output is constrained by the growth rate of the number of existing journals.

Estimates of the marginal product of research inputs based on US data may be subject to a downward bias on this account. This problem is much less severe in the case of Italy.

Another source of potential doubts about the value of relying upon empirical findings about the scientific research process based upon the Italian CNR experience is the casual supposition that non-scientific, political considerations may intrude into the details of the funding agency's decision process to a degree that is not present in the peer review processes through which resources are allocated in, say, Britain or the US. We believe that in the particular CNR programme we have studied here such a suspicion is unwarranted, and the processing of proposals for funding was conducted in a way that conformed with the norms of scientific peer review. Moreover, our measures of scientific "output" are publications weighted by the quality of the publishing journal, using the so-called "impact factors" of journals based upon the computations of the *Science Citation Index*. Hence, the productivity of the Italian biotechnology research units is being evaluated by the same standards that are used to measure the publication outputs of any other international scientific community [6]. Furthermore, this is not a matter that is left for conjecture; we shall explicitly model the selection process, as well as the setting of the research budgets that the selected units receive, and thereby allow the data themselves to reveal the extent to which the programme from which the data used here have been drawn was broadly conformable with our priors based on information about corresponding institutional arrangments and procedures in the Anglo-Saxon world.

3 Data Description

3.1. Variables Used in the Analysis

B&B is a five-year programme (1989-1993) for research in molecular biology and genetic engineering issued by the Italian CNR in 1987. The programme was divided into seven sub-programmes. The first six

---

6. We may point out again that the small relative size of the Italian research community is a virtue in this respect, since their proportionate contributions to the aggregate citations of journal article, like their proportionate contributions to the international journals' contents, are so small that they cannot be thought capable of influencing the relative impact factors of those journals.

were concerned with various sub-disciplines of molecular biology and genetic engineering. Sub-Programme 7, Bio-Instrumentation, focused on development and experimentation of scientific instrument prototypes. A total of 858 research laboratories applied to B&B, with universities and CNR in-house laboratories accounting for about 62% and 15% respectively. The rest of the applications were from other non-profit research institutions such as foundations and hospital research labs, as well as some commercial firms. The research groups that applied to the programme are well-defined units of scientific production. They are teams of scientists, researchers, technicians and other personnel within established institutions, which are stable over time. They were not formed to carry out just this project. Of the original 858 units, CNR selected 360 for funding. Due to missing data, our final sample is composed of 797 units, of which 347 were selected for funding.

Table 1 defines all the variables used in our empirical analysis. We collected most of our data from the application forms. B&B had an explicit goal of encouraging industrial "transferability" of research. Applicants had to indicate whether the project had potential industrial uses, and if so, who the potential users were. We summarised this information in a dummy variable, *TRANSF,* which takes the value 1 if the applicant declared that his project had potential practical uses, and indicated the name of one or more firms that could use those results. These are projects that signal concrete opportunities of application as the units were able to indicate precise names of industry users. CNR programmes typically have as one of their policy objectives the encouragement of research in the less advanced regions of the country, and particularly in the "Mezzogiorno" or the southern part of Italy. The dummy variable, *DSOUTH,* takes the value 1 for units located in the "Mezzogiorno". The variable, *DPRO7,* is a dummy variable for bio-instrumentation related proposals. We also created dummies *DCNR* and *DUNI* for CNR and university labs. Other characteristics of the units are:

TABLE 1

Definition of Variables Used in the Analysis.

I	Index for selection – dummy equal to 1 if the unit was granted a positive budget
B_A	Total 1989-1991 budget asked by the units (in millions Italian Lire)
B_G	Total 1989-1991 budget granted (in millions Lire)
PUB	Quality-adjusted number of publications of the units that acknowledged contribution of this Programme
DPRO7	Dummy for units in sub-Programme 7 (Bio-Instrumentation)
DCNR	Dummy for CNR laboratories
DUNI	Dummy for university laboratories
DSOUTH	Dummy for units located in the South
TRANSF	Dummy for industrial "transferability" of the project
SIZE	Size of the group (number of people)
K	Quality-adjusted 1983-1987 publications of the PI listed in the application form
COLLAB	Number of research collaborations with foreign non-profit institutions listed in the application form
NUIST	Number of units from the same institution of the applicant that applied to the programme (e.g. University of Rome, CNR of Naples)
PROV_POP	Total 1987 population in the province of the unit (thousands)
AGEPI	Age of the PI (years)

the size of the research unit (*SIZE*) measured by the number of researchers and technicians in the unit; *AGEPI*, the age of the PI, *NUIST*, the number of units from the same institution (e.g. University of Rome, CNR of Naples) that applied to the programme; and *PROV_POP*, the population of the province wherein the unit is located.

CNR supplied us with the list of units that were selected, and the total budget granted to each in each of the five years of the programme. From the CNR we also obtained data on the total number of publications produced by the selected units. These are all the publications available in 1994 that explicitly acknowledged the financial support of this programme. As B&B actually ended in late 1994, the CNR warned us that some of its results were yet to be published, and these publications referred mostly to activities conducted in the first three years of the programme (1989-1991). Accordingly, we define our budget requested and budget granted variables as the amounts pertaining to the first three years of the programme. Since annual budgets tended to be constant over time, this involved little more than simply scaling the variables by three fifths.

To weight publications so as to measure output in comparable units of "quality", we employ the 1987 impact factor (as computed by the *Science Citation Index,* SCI) for the respective journals in which the units' publications appeared [7]. Using the number of citations to the papers is an alternative way to weight for quality. However, because the papers produced in the programme were all relatively recent at the time of data collection, citation measures were likely to be biased. Instead, we define $PUB = \Sigma_j (s_{ij} w_j)$, where s_{ij} is the number of publications of the i-th unit in the j-th journal, and w_j is a linear function of the impact factor of the j-th journal. We experimented with a variety of specifications for w_j. Here we report results using $w_j = 0.5 + IF_{ij}$ [8].

As a measure of past performance of the group, we used the 1983-1987 publications of the PI listed in the application form (K) [9]. These were adjusted for quality in the same way as the publication output. Even though these publications are "older", and the citations are therefore more complete, we have chosen to be consistent with the quality measure used for the units' publication output [10]. We used the research collaborations (*COLLAB*) of the unit with foreign non-profit institutions as another measure of quality. One can think of the past publications of the PI as a measure of the quality of

---

7. The IF is the ratio between the number of citations of the journal by other journals, and its number of citations to other journals. A high value of the IF thus indicates a journal that is cited more frequently than it cites. In our data, IF for journals ranged from close to 0 to about 15. *Nature* for instance had a 1987 IF of 14.77. Articles in books and working papers have a nominal IF of 0.

8. We experimented with $1 + IF_{ij}$ as a weight, as well as simply IF_{ij}. These correspond to giving a high weight to working papers and journal articles to giving no weight to these. After some casual search, we settled on the specification noted above. In all cases, the results were substantially unchanged.

9. Along with other information, the units had to list all relevant publications (to this programme or in related areas) of the PI and of other members of the unit in the previous five years (1983-1987).

10. Note that the research output is of the entire research unit, rather than just the PI.

148

the unit, while *COLLAB* measures the quality of the project, although the two overlap. As with other self reported variables, we assume that research collaborations are exogenously given, at least in the short run.

3.2. Correlations & Reduced Form Regressions

Table 2 presents descriptive statistics for out data. Figures 1 and 2 show the distributions of budget asked (B_A), budget granted (B_G), publication output (PUB), and past publications of the PI (K). All four distributions are skewed, especially the two distributions of publications. The log-normal distribution appears to be a good approximation to these distributions, and is the one specified in our structural model.

Tables 3 and 4 show reduced form regressions of B_A, B_G and PUB, for all 797 units as well as for the 347 units that were selected for funding. We also present the publication equations with and without the budget among the regressors. Table 3 shows that both expected budget asked and budget granted are positively related to transferability, past publications, foreign collaborations and the size of the unit. However, while budget asked by research units from the South was 116 million Lire more than the average, the expected budget given to them conditional on selection is actually lower than the corresponding average. As we show below, this behaviour can be motivated by a higher than average probability of selection, as well as a lower per unit effort cost of preparing larger research proposals.

As Table 4 shows, past publications has a large impact on publication output even after we add budget granted amongst the regressors. Together with the results from Table 3, this suggests and past performance may have

TABLE 2

Descriptive Statistics (797 observations).

	Mean	Std Dev	Minimum	Maximum
I	0.435	0.496	0	1
B_A (*)	350.244	275.743	25	4224
B_G (*) (+)	105.035	62.147	3	519
PUB (+)	17.468	22.442	0	199.19
(non quality-adj. number)	(6.761)	(6.065)	(0)	(50)
DPRO7	0.107	0.309	0	1
DCNR	0.154	0.361	0	1
DUNI	0.645	0.479	0	1
DSOUTH	0.189	0.392	0	1
TRANSF	0.375	0.484	0	1
PROV_POP (§)	195.260	126.290	100	3477
COLLAB	4.018	3.323	0	25
K	31.672	43.556	0	636.79
(non quality-adj. number)	(13.065)	(17.020)	(0)	(226)
SIZE	12.055	6.221	2	99
NUIST	25.152	18.377	1	63
AGEPI	52.287	8.490	34	85

(*) Millions Italian Lire; (+) 347 observations for $I = 1$; (§) thousands.

FIGURE 1

Budget asked, Budget granted.
(Frequency distributions, 797 observations).

a) Budget Asked – B_A.

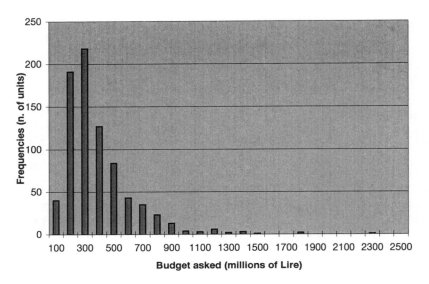

b) Budget Granted – B_G.

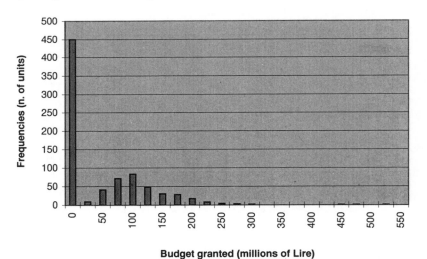

FIGURE 2

Publication Output, Past Publications
(Frequency distributions, 797 observations).

a) Publication Output – PUB.

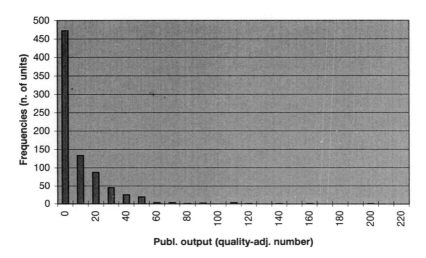

b) Past Publications – K.

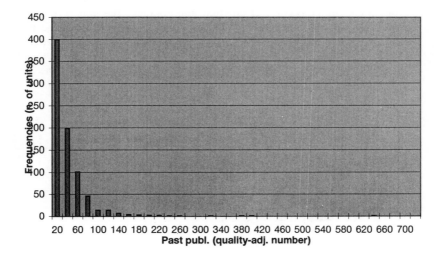

TABLE 3

OLS Estimates: (Budget asked, Budget granted).

	$\ln B_A$	$\ln B_A$ $(I = 1)$	$\ln B_G$	$\ln B_G$ $(I = 1)$
Const	3.497	3.691	−3.294	3.742
	(0.530)	(0.722)	(2.009)	(0.782)
DPRO7	0.165	0.141	0.577	0.413
	(0.079)	(0.106)	(0.253)	(0.121)
DCNR	−0.060	0.033	0.763	0.244
	(0.067)	(0.093)	(0.257)	(0.111)
DUNI	−0.038	0.045	0.380	0.050
	(0.057)	(0.092)	(0.212)	(0.115)
DSOUTH	0.274	0.231	0.100	−0.127
	(0.051)	(0.077)	(0.185)	(0.078)
TRANSF	0.122	0.109	0.587	0.095
	(0.040)	(0.054)	(0.159)	(0.061)
ln(SIZE)	0.547	0.543	0.426	0.177
	(0.059)	(0.093)	(0.167)	(0.074)
ln(K)	0.065	0.105	0.646	0.092
	(0.021)	(0.027)	(0.077)	(0.033)
ln(COLLAB)	0.102	0.118	0.359	0.042
	(0.030)	(0.039)	(0.123)	(0.043)
ln(NUIST)	−0.066	0.006	−0.074	−0.017
	(0.026)	(0.037)	(0.086)	(0.042)
ln(PROV_POP)	0.041	−0.001	0.294	0.031
	(0.027)	(0.039)	(0.096)	(0.046)
ln(AGEPI)	0.101	0.037	−0.130	−0.089
	(0.129)	(0.160)	(0.461)	(0.199)
No of obs	797	347	797	347
Adj.R^2	0.242	0.308	0.174	0.089

Heteroskedastic consistent standard errors in parenthesis.

a direct and an indirect effect on publication output. The impact of budget given varies considerably between the full sample and the restricted sample. This problem arises because both, selection and the amount of funding, are potentially correlated with unobserved variables that also affect output. The structural model set out in the following section attempts to address both issues: selection and endogeneity of budget.

4 The Model and the Estimated Equations

4.1. Two Caveats

• **Knowledge vs. reputation capital:** As remarkable as the available data set is, it does not permit us to distinguish empirically between a

TABLE 4

OLS Estimates: PUB (Publication Output).

	$\ln B_A$	$\ln B_A$ $(I=1)$	$\ln B_G$	$\ln B_G$ $(I=1)$
Const	−1.688	3.302	−0.128	2.239
	(1.194)	(1.577)	(0.733)	(1.591)
$\ln(B_G)$ (*)	−	−	0.474	0.284
			(0.014)	(0.100)
DPRO7	−0.108	−0.720	−0.382	−0.837
	(0.117)	(0.196)	(0.091)	(0.194)
DCNR	0.193	−0.019	−0.168	−0.089
	(0.155)	(0.179)	(0.095)	(0.177)
DUNI	0.149	−0.041	−0.031	−0.055
	(0.140)	(0.179)	(0.079)	(0.174)
DSOUTH	−0.178	−0.570	−0.225	−0.534
	(0.110)	(0.160)	(0.080)	(0.160)
TRANSF	0.184	−0.106	−0.094	−0.133
	(0.096)	(0.114)	(0.062)	(0.113)
$\ln$(SIZE)	0.163	0.105	−0.039	0.054
	(0.099)	(0.132)	(0.071)	(0.132)
$\ln(K)$	0.498	0.435	0.192	0.409
	(0.052)	(0.065)	(0.035)	(0.065)
$\ln$(COLLAB)	0.270	0.220	0.100	0.208
	(0.165)	(0.078)	(0.044)	(0.077)
$\ln$(NUIST)	−0.091	−0.003	−0.055	0.002
	(0.049)	(0.062)	(0.033)	(0.061)
$\ln$(PROV_POP)	0.156	−0.075	0.017	−0.084
	(0.056)	(0.079)	(0.035)	(0.077)
$\ln$(AGEPI)	−0.086	−0.519	−0.024	−0.493
	(0.273)	(0.365)	(0.167)	(0.356)
No of obs	797	347	797	347
Adj.R^2	0.202	0.239	0.683	0.256

Heteroskedastic consistent standard errors in parenthesis. (*) For $I = 0$, $\ln(B_G)$ set equal to 0.

measure of researchers' knowledge capital or "competence", and a measure of their scientific "reputation" capital. Past performance may be related to future performance both because the two reflect some inherent (fixed) attribute of the researchers that affects their productivity, and because superior performance enhances reputation, and thereby results in access to more generous funding. This open up the possibility that past performance may reflect not just inherent differences among researchers' capabilities, but also small idiosyncratic factors of personality, or extraneous circumstances unrelated to talent but nonetheless affecting early funding success. When initial success is rewarded with greater funding, then this increases the likelihood of future success as well. If funding agencies estimate future productivity based on past publication performance without taking into account past levels of funding, this gives rise to state dependence in the production process. Were one to allow for learning effects, gained through the experience of carrying out funded projects, the state dependent nature of the process would become even more marked [11]. Using cross-section data, as we do, one cannot separate state dependence from unobserved heterogeneity. What we seek to do in this paper is to separate the direct effects from the indirect effects of "knowledge capital" on the likelihood of units receiving funding – a reflection of the working of the external institutional mechanisms rather than the internal production capabilities of the group.

• **Marginal** *vs.* **total inputs and outputs.** In a given year, a unit may choose to work on more than one project. Unfortunately, we do not observe the inputs (funding) received by the units for other projects. This is potentially a source of bias if the projects are inter-dependent in either inputs or output. The intuition is straight forward. Suppose each unit can work on two projects. One of these is the CNR project and the other is an alternative project (possibly less attractive). The productivity, per unit of research effort, in the latter may fall if the research unit also works on the CNR project. This implies that merely looking at the inputs and output of the CNR project alone would lead to an over-estimate of the marginal product of research effort. Similarly, the selected units may indicate as an ouptut of the programme publications supported by other funds, leading to "double counting" and an over-estimate. Conversely, if there are positive spillovers across projects, one will end up with an under-estimate.

Since we do not observe the funding for any of the unit's projects other than the one studied here, we will formally assume that the CNR project is independent of its other activities. As a practical matter, this is a reasonable approximation. The average funding for selected project in our sample is 105 million Lire over a period of three years, which is equal to about $65,000 (see Table 2). We do not have a firm benchmark to compare but this clearly is a small enough number to imply that this particular CNR programme was not intended as the major funding source for most of the units. Similarly, based on data from the *Science Citation Index* (provided to us by the ISI), we estimate that the average PI among the selected units in our sample produced about 4.7 publications (unweighted) per year in the five year period prior to the programme [12]. By comparison, for this programme, the annual publication output for an entire research unit was only 1.3 during 1989-1991. Note also that during this time interval, total publications in the area of bio-medical were growing at over 2% per annum, implying that the programme-related publication output of the unit as a whole is less than a fourth of the publication output credited to the typical PI.

Moreover, in the foregoing, the precise meaning of 'independent' should be understood as applying to the "direct cost" aspects of the CNR project. What we assume here is that research outputs that have been directly financed from other sources are not attributed by the unit to its project in the CNR's B&B programme; and, likewise, that funds obtained from the latter programme are not diverted to support research and publications that

---

11. Indeed, if either or both sources of positive feedback are sufficiently strong, the microlevel dynamics of the stochastic process governing publication output and reputational status will become non-ergodic and path dependent. See DAVID [1994: pp. 80-84] for further discussion.

12. The PIs of the selected units produced 8197 publications during the period 1983-1987. The total publication from the programme between 1989-1991 was 1367.

fall outside that programme's (and hence would not be reported among the CNR project outputs). Our assumptions here recognise the possibility that there are elements of "joint-production" in the research unit's operations. The latter are, indeed, quite likely in the case of the larger units which hold a number of grants and/or contracts; the costs of indivisible elements of the "infrastructure" (both staff and facilities) may be met through a policy of levying what are in effect "internal overhead" charges on all concurrently running projects in the unit.

4.2. The Model

Our objective here is to derive three equations that can be estimated. The first two are the equations for budget requested and budget granted. The third equation is the production function of publication output.

• **Research Units.** We assume that the research units maximise their expected research output. They have two choice variables – the size of the project, which we measure by the budget asked, and the amount of research effort (unobserved by us), also reckoned in monetary units. We assume that increasing the size of the project is costly, and these costs are borne by the research unit. Furthermore, actual research effort will differ from the *ex ante* research effort because the units cannot fully predict their actual research budget. In a fully specified model, the units would have to satisfy an inter-temporal budget constraint. Since we only have a cross-section, and since it is possible that units may have other sources of research support, we specify in (3) and (3a) below an *ad hoc* rule linking expected budgets, and the *ex ante* and actual research effort. By substituting in this rule, the unit's decision problem effectively reduces to the choosing the optimal size of the research project, B_A.

• **CNR Decision Making Process.** The CNR is assumed to follow a two-step decision procedure. The first is a dichotomous decision, whereby projects are either selected for funding, or rejected. In the next step, the actual funding levels for the projects selected in the first step is decided. We assume that the budget requested for the project is not included as a criterion in the first step. Although we have chosen this representation for modeling convenience, we believe that this is a fairly accurate representation of the actual decision making procedures followed by public research agencies. Although excluding the budget requested from the first step may appear to be a very strong restriction because projects with very large (or very small) budget requests may be deselected at the first stage, in practice there is informal communication between agencies like the CNR and the research units. In this way, otherwise worthy projects may be modified to fit into any budget criterion that the agency may have implicitly imposed. Note that if this informal (and unobserved) communication takes place, the situation is difficult to distinguish empirically from one where no budget criterion exists.

In a fully specified model, one would also derive the CNR's decision rule as an optimal response to the decision rules followed by the units. That, however, would entail the introduction of a great deal more structure, which presently we lack the necessary data to identify econometrically.

This approach must therefore be deferred for future research based on a still more extensive data set.

Figure 3 shows the sequence of actions from the launch of the programme to production of publications. When the programme is started, the agency sets a rule for selecting projects and for allocating budgets. This amounts to defining the two-step procedure characterised by (1) and (2) below. Given these rules, each unit chooses the optimal size of the research project so as to maximise its utility. The CNR then selects from amongst the projects,

FIGURE 3

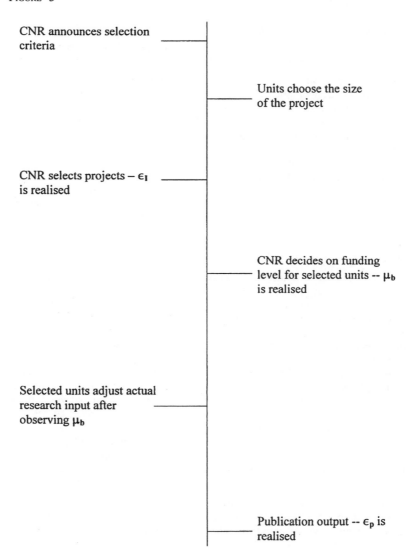

CNR announces selection criteria

Units choose the size of the project

CNR selects projects – ϵ_I is realised

CNR decides on funding level for selected units -- μ_b is realised

Selected units adjust actual research input after observing μ_b

Publication output -- ϵ_p is realised

156

and allocates budget. These decisions depend in part upon characteristics of the unit and project observed only by the CNR (ε_I and μ_b), in part upon characteristics observed by the CNR and the research unit (ε_k), and in part upon publicly observed characteristics of the unit and the project, denoted by $\mathbf{X}$. While we assume that μ_b is distributed independently of ε_I, we allow for ε_k to be correlated with ε_I. Units observe the actual budget, and adjust their planned research effort according to (3). Finally, ε_p is realized, and publication output is determined according to (4). We allow ε_p to be correlated with ε_I, as well as with ε_k.

4.3. Notation

Let:

R	research effort of unit
R^*	"planned" research effort
B_G	budget granted by the agency
B_A	budget requested by units
I^*	latent selection variable
I	index with $\mathbf{I} = 1 \leftrightarrow \mathbf{I^*} > 0$
X, Y, Z	other characteristics of unit and project
$C(A, Z)$	application and set-up costs of a project of size A
P	publication output
K	past publication output
H	other characteristics of the units that influence the production of publications

We also define the following expressions.

• **Selection equation**

$$(1) \qquad I^* = \pi \ln Y + \varepsilon_I$$

where $\varepsilon_I \sim N(0, 1)$. Define ϕ, Φ to be the standard normal and the standard cumulative normal such that $\Phi = \text{Prob}(I = 1)$.

• **Budget granted equation**

$$(2) \qquad \begin{cases} B_G = B_A^\lambda \, X^\theta \, e^{\varepsilon_k + \mu_b} & I = 1 \\ B_G = 0 & I = 0 \end{cases}$$

where $\varepsilon_k \sim N(0, \sigma_k)$ is a measure of quality, observed by the units and the CNR and not by the econometrician. The other term, $\mu_b \sim N(0, \sigma_b)$, is independent of ε_k and ε_I, and represents the uncertainty, from the viewpoint of the research unit, in the actual budget granted. It captures any unobserved

CNR preferences that are not directly related to the publication performance of the research units [13].

- **Research effort**

$$(3) \qquad \begin{cases} R = R^* e^{\delta \mu_b} & I = 1 \\ R = 0 & I = 0 \end{cases}$$

where R^* is "planned" research, defined as

$$(3a) \qquad R^* = E_{\mu_b} (B_G - C|I = 1, \, \varepsilon_k)$$

Note that this implies that research effort is not simply proportional to the allocated budget. Instead, the relationship between research effort and the budget depends, indirectly, also upon the costs, and other characteristics of the research unit.

- **Production Function of Publications**

$$(4) \qquad \begin{cases} \ln (PUB) = \alpha \cdot \ln R + \gamma \cdot \ln H + \varepsilon_p & I = 1 \\ \ln (PUB) = 0 & I = 0 \end{cases}$$

where $\varepsilon_p \sim N(0, \sigma_p)$ accounts for stochastic factors in the production of publications. Note that we allow α, the elasticity of output with respect to research effort, to vary with quality of the unit.

- **Cost equation**

$$(5) \qquad C(A, Z) \equiv c(Z) \cdot A \equiv Z^{-\eta} \cdot A$$

4.4. Optimal Project Size

We assume that units choose B_A to

$$\text{Max } E_I \, E_{\mu_b, \varepsilon_p} (\ln PUB|\varepsilon_k) \equiv \Phi \, E_{\mu_b, \varepsilon_p} (\ln PUB|I = 1, \, \varepsilon_k)$$

Notice that $E_{\mu_b, \varepsilon_p} (\ln PUB|I = 1, \, \varepsilon_k) \equiv \alpha \ln R^* + \gamma \ln H + E_{\mu_B, \varepsilon_p} (\alpha \delta \mu_b + \varepsilon_p|I = 1, \, \varepsilon_k)$. Since B_A does not affect selection, Φ and $E_{\mu_B, \varepsilon_p} (\alpha \delta \mu_b + \varepsilon_p|I = 1, \, \varepsilon_k)$ are also independent of B_A. Thus the problem of the units boils down to

$$\text{Max } R^* \equiv E_{\mu_b} (B_G - C|I = 1, \, \varepsilon_k) = B_A^\lambda \, X^\theta \, e^{\varepsilon_k} \, E_{\mu_b} (e^{\mu_b}) - Z^{-\eta} \, B_A$$

The first order condition of this problem yields

$$(6) \qquad C(\cdot) = \lambda \, E_{\mu_b} (B_G|I = 1, \, \varepsilon_k)$$

---

13. We use the conventon that ε's denote errors whose expected value depends upon I, and μ's errors whose expected value does not depend on I.

4.5. The Estimated Equations

We now derive our three equations to be estimated for selected units [14]. To derive the budget requested and budget granted equations, substitute for B_A from (6) in the expression (2) for B_G, conditional on $I = 1$. This gives

$$(7) \quad \ln B_A = (1 - \lambda)^{-1} \left(\ln \lambda + \sigma_b^2/2 + \frac{\theta}{1 - \lambda} x + \eta \cdot z + \sigma_{IK} \frac{\phi}{\Phi} + \mu_k \right)$$

$$(8) \quad \ln B_G = (1 - \lambda)^{-1}$$
$$\left(\lambda \cdot \ln \lambda + \lambda \cdot \sigma_b^2/2 + \frac{\theta}{1 - \lambda} x + \lambda \cdot \eta \cdot z + \sigma_{IK} \frac{\phi}{\Phi} + \mu_k \right) + \mu_b$$

where σ_{IK} is the covariance between ε_1 and ε_k, and $\mu_k \equiv \varepsilon_k - \sigma_{IK} \frac{\phi}{\Phi}$ [15]. Combining this with (3), (3a), and (6), we can write

$$(9) \quad \ln PUB = \alpha \left[\ln (1 - \lambda) + b_e^* \right]$$
$$+ \gamma \cdot \ln H + \sigma_{IP} \frac{\phi}{\Phi} + \alpha (K) \left(\frac{\mu_k}{(1 - \lambda)} + \delta \mu_b \right) + \mu_p$$

where σ_{IP} is the covariance between ε_p and ε_I, $\mu_p \equiv \varepsilon_p - \sigma_{IP} \frac{\phi}{\Phi}$, and $b_e^* \equiv \ln E_{\mu_B, \varepsilon_k} (B_G | I = 1) = \hat{b} + \frac{\sigma_b^2}{2} + \frac{\sigma_{IK}}{1-\lambda} \frac{\phi}{\Phi}$, where $\hat{b}$ stands for the first four terms of equation (8).

Equation (9) is the production function of publications that we estimate. Note that our model enabled us to transform the production function defined by equation (4), which depended on the unobserved research effort of the units, into an expression that depends on a variable b_e^*, the expected budget conditional on selection and a parameter λ which can be retrieved from the estimated parameters of equations (7) and (8). In addition, equation (9) enables us to estimate the elasticity with respect to the budget (or research effort) after specifying a functional form for $\alpha (K)$.

5 Estimation and Results

5.1. Estimation Strategy, Regressors, and Identification

We first estimate the selection equation (1) as a probit, using all observations. This produces estimates of ϕ and Φ evaluated at $\hat{\pi} y$, where

---

14. This procedure implies that information from the non funded units is only used to estimate the selection equation.

15. Note that by accounting for the covariance between ε_I and ε_k, we are following what amounts to the standard Heckman-Mills procedure for correcting sample selection. In our case, selection correction has to be done in the budget equations as well as the publication equations.

$\hat{\pi}$ is the estimated value of π. We then estimate (7), (8), and (9) for observations $I = 1$ after substituting the estimated ϕ and Φ. This two-step, Heckman-Mills correction procedure was chosen because it is convenient and robust. Using conventional terms, selection correction has to be applied both in the budget equations, as well as in the publication equation.

We next estimate (7) and (8) jointly by GLS. We use the estimated values of λ, $\hat{b}$, σ_b^2, and σ_{IK} to compute $\ln(1 - \lambda) + b_e^*$ which we substitute in (9), and estimate (9) as a Tobit using a variety of specifications for $\alpha(K)$ [16]. Since the data are distributed as log-normal, we use the log-log specification throughout [17]. We also estimated specifications in levels but the fit to the data was poorer, although the point estimates of elasticities were remarkably similar to those reported here.

• **Regressors.** As discussed earlier, we use all exogenous variables (vector **Y** below) except size and budget asked to predict selection. We also exclude *DPRO7* because CNR did not commit *ex ante* to select given percentages of applicants from each sub-programme, but examined the projects altogether and selected them according to characteristics such as quality, and transferability. We impose this restriction primarily to preserve degrees of freedom; it is not critical for identification and a formal test of the restriction implies that the restriction is not rejected.

Recall that the variables in **Z** affect the cost of preparing a project of "size" B_A; the variables in **X** account for factors that affect the fraction of B_A granted; the vector **H** accounts for exogenous variables that affect the productivity of publications. We used the following specification for **Z**, **X**, and **H** (corresponding θ, η, and γ parameters in parenthesis):

Z-regressors	X-regressors	H-regressors
• const (η_0)	• const (θ_0)	• const (γ_0)
• DPRO7 (η_7)	• DPRO7 (θ_7)	• DPRO7 (γ_7)
• DCNR (η_{CNR})	• DCNR (θ_{CNR})	• DSOUTH (γ_S)
• DUNI (η_{UNI})	• DUNI (θ_{UNI})	• TRANSF (γ_T)
• DSOUTH (η_S)	• DSOUTH (θ_S)	• ln(N) (γ_N)
• TRANSF (η_T)	• TRANSF (θ_T)	• ln(K) (γ_K)
• ln(K) (η_K)	• ln(K) (θ_K)	• ln(RCF) (γ_C)
• ln(RCF) (η_C)	• ln(RCF) (θ_C)	• ln(NUIST) (γ_U)
• ln(NUIST) (η_U)	• ln(NUIST) (θ_U)	• ln(PROV_POP) (γ_P)
• ln(PROV_POP) (η_P)	• ln(PROV_POP) (θ_P)	• ln(AGEPI) (γ_A)
• ln(AGEPI) (η_A)	• ln(AGEPI) (θ_A)	
• ln(SIZE) (η_N)		

The **Z**- and **X**-regressors include all the variables used for selection. Unlike **Y**, **X** and **Z** include *DPRO7*. Bio-instrumentation projects are more costly to prepare. To present a "credible" proposal in this area, units have to show that they will be able to utilize expensive equipment or facilities

---

16. We estimate (9) separately by Tobit because more than 10% of the selected units produced zero publications.
17. For variable that take on a value of zero, we added one to that variable when taking logs.

to carry out development and testing activities. Thus, the organization of the proposal may require, to a greater extent than projects in the other more "scientific" sub-programs, time and resource consuming steps like arranging for the use of such equipment or even for their rental or purchase. Finally, we included the size of the team in **Z**. Larger teams can write larger grants because of greater specialisation amongst its members, or because *SIZE* proxies for other resources available to the group. We assume that conditional on the budget asked and other covariates, *SIZE* does not affect the fraction of the budget granted. In the production function of publications (vector **H**) we include all exogenous variables except *DCNR* and *DUNI*. We also include *DSOUTH* in **H** to account for any disadvantages that units in Southern Italy may face.

• **Identification.** Note that we identify our parameters through some key exclusion restrictions. First, we exclude the budget asked and the size of the unit from the selection equation. As discussed above, the exclusion of budget asked is justified if there is informal communication between the units and CNR prior to the formal application process. The exclusion of the size of the unit is also a plausible restriction because given budgets and other characteristics of the units, size does not affect output. Therefore, it is rational for the CNR not to consider size in selection [18].

Second, we assume that the size of the team does not affect the fraction of budget granted. This is a plausible restriction, inasmuch as the fraction of the budget granted is hypothesised to depend upon measures of quality and transferability. Third, we identify the elasticity with respect to the budget in the publication equation by assuming that differences in institutional types, *DCNR* and *DUNI* do not directly influence the productivity of publications, whereas they do influence the fraction of budget granted. University based units and CNR units may face greater costs of writing large grants because they are subject to a variety of constraints on hiring of temporary personnel. These units also are more likely to obtain larger fractions of budget asked. Typically there are formal and informal relationships between a public funding agency like CNR and other public research institutions. This implies that CNR is better informed about the activities and reputation of these groups and their projects. Such groups may, of course, have been in a better position to "lobby" for their projects. Once other factors are controlled for, however, there is no obvious reason why the productivity of research groups should differ according to institutional type. A likelihood ratio test implies that the restriction cannot be rejected [19].

Finally, we identify the budget asked equation by assuming that the cost of writing a proposal is linear in B_A. Identification through functional form is clearly not very attractive. However, it is difficult to conceive of observable variables that would affect outcomes such as selection and publication output but would not affect budget requested. Indeed, although our exclusion restrictions are very plausible, our sample is small and our

---

18. As discussed earlier, DPRO7 is also excluded. However, this exclusion is not critical for identification but for preserving degrees of freedom.
19. The value of the chi-square statistic is 2.98 with two degrees of freedom, so that the exclusion restriction we impose cannot be rejected.

estimates may therefore be sensitive to the interaction between the exclusion restrictions and functional form. Accordingly, for each estimated equation (except the selection equation) we tested for robustness by estimating a linear specification as well. The results do not change much, although the log-log specification fits the data somewhat better. Table A1 in the appendix shows the reduced form estimates using levels. By comparing them to Table 3 and 4, one can see that the log specification is a better fit, but that the qualitative properties of the empirical model are not driven by the specification.

5.2. Results: Selection, Budget Asked, Budget Granted

Table 5 shows the results of the probit estimates. Note that the selection estimates strongly support the notion that selecton is driven by the objectives of the programme. These objectives in turn do not appear to be substantively different from those of comparable public research programmes in the US. Thus, variables correlated with scientific merit (*K, COLLAB*) are quantitatively and statistically significant. Likewise, "industrial transferability" increases the probability of selection. Interestingly enough, units from the South of Italy do not appear to be particularly advantaged, even though

TABLE 5

Selection_Equation (PROBIT).

Dependent variable: $I = 1$ if unit is funded by CNR

Parameter	Estimate
Const	−2.813
	(1.302)
DCNR	0.466
	(0.168)
DUNI	0.293
	(0.143)
DSOUTH	0.090
	(0.128)
TRANSF	0.378
	(0.098)
ln(COLLAB)	0.224
	(0.075)
ln(K)	0.398
	(0.052)
ln(NUIST)	−0.034
	(0.055)
ln(PROV_POP)	0.169
	(0.063)
ln(AGEPI)	−0.065
	(0.303)
Log Likelihood	−475.4
N.obs	797
(of which positive)	(347)

Heteroskedastic consistent standard errors in parenthesis.

162

providing such a preference is an explicit announced aim in many CNR programmes.

Table 6 reports the results of joint-estimation of (7) and (8). Note that the estimates are similar to the reduced form estimates. Larger research groups have lower marginal costs in applying for grants (η_N), but they gain no advantage from being part of larger institutions (η_U) or from being in more populated areas (η_P). Externalities amongst research groups in the same institution or in the same city are not pronounced. CNR acts consistently and puts no weight on NUIST or PROV_POP in the funding decision (θ_U and θ_P). Instrument development projects are more expensive to set up (η_7), and CNR grants them a larger fraction of budget (θ_7). Transferability and past publications increase the fraction of the budget granted (θ_T and θ_K). CNR units also obtain a larger fraction of expected budget (θ_{CNR}). Unobserved characteristics of the units matter as well, although the statistical significance of σ_{ik} is not high. The estimated value of λ suggests that non research (indirect) costs are of the order of 32% of the expected budget conditional upon selection. The coefficients of *DSOUTH*, η_S and θ_S, are

TABLE 6

GLS Estimation of **Budget Requested** *and* **Budget Granted** *equations (Equations (7) and (8)).*

Dependent variables: $\ln(B_A)$ and $\ln(B_G)$. No of obs. $= 347$, $I = 1$.
Log of likelihood function $= -522.6$.

Parameters	Estimates	Parameters	Estimates
Const (η_0)	-0.051	Const (θ_0)	1.769
	(0.887)		(1.252)
DCNR (n_{CNR})	-0.210	DCNR (θ_{CNR})	0.322
	(0.115)		(0.146)
DUNI (η_{UNI})	-0.004	DUNI (θ_{UNI})	0.097
	(0.116)		(0.132)
DSOUTH (η_S)	0.358	DSOUTH (θ_S)	-0.185
	(0.103)		(0.088)
DPRO7 (η_7)	-0.272	DPRO7 (θ_7)	0.369
	(0.156)		(0.125)
TRANSF (η_T)	0.014	TRANSF (θ_T)	0.130
	(0.073)		(0.107)
$\ln(K)$ (η_K)	0.013	$\ln(K)$ (θ_K)	0.136
	(0.038)		(0.107)
$\ln$(COLLAB) (η_C)	0.076	$\ln$(COLLAB) (θ_C)	0.049
	(0.053)		(0.078)
$\ln$(NUIST) (η_U)	0.023	$\ln$(NUIST) (θ_U)	-0.026
	(0.045)		(0.041)
$\ln$(PROV_POP) (η_P)	-0.033	$\ln$(PROV_POP) (θ_P)	0.065
	(0.052)		(0.061)
$\ln$(AGEPI) (η_A)	0.126	LN(AGEPI) (θ_A)	-0.115
	(0.218)		(0.191)
LN(SIZE) (η_N)	0.366	σ_{1K}	0.315
	(0.120)		(0.389)
$\ln(A)$ (λ)	0.319		
	(0.151)		

Heteroskedastic consistent standard errors in parenthesis.

respectively 0.36 and −0.19, and they are well measured. These estimates clarify the reasons for the pattern revealed by the reduced form estimates in Table 3. However, the positive sign of η_S suggests that units in the South prepare larger projects for one reason. All else constant, they have a lower cost of writing larger grants.

5.3. Results: Production Function of Publications

We experimented with different specifications for $\alpha(K)$ in estimating (9). In the end, we settled on a logistic specification, $\alpha(K) = \frac{\alpha_0}{1+e^{-\beta(1+K)}}$, where α_0 and β are parameters to be estimated. The logistic fit the data better than either a constant elasticity $\alpha(K) = \alpha_0$, or a linear specification with interaction, $\alpha(K) = \alpha_0 + \beta \ln(1 + K)$. In each case, the point estimates of the elasticity are almost the same as those reported here [20]. The logistic specification also has the appealing property that it allows the elasticity to vary but within bounds, namely that with $\beta > 0$, α_0 is an upper bound of the elasticity of budget.

For the logistic specification reported in Table 7, the estimated value of α_0 of 1.01 implies that the elasticity of research budgets has an upper bound of about 1. More interestingly, the statistical significance of β indicates that the elasticity of research budget does increase with the stock of past publications K of the PI [21]. In turn, this means that the distribution of the elasticity of research budgets ought to mimic the skewed distribution of past performance. Indeed, as Figure 4 shows, the distribution of our logistic $\alpha(K)$ evaluated at the estimated parameters, α_0 and β, is skewed towards the left. Although the estimated $\alpha(K)$ for our sample ranges between 0.51 and 1.01, its value at the median K of the population of 347 selected units is 0.58. Moreover, about 90% of these units have an output elasticity with respect to research budget that lies in the range below 0.8 [22].

This estimated elasticity is consistent with a characterisation of the scientific enterprise as a "star" system. While the productivity of the large majority of our research groups falls within a limited range around the median of the distribution, a small fraction of the research groups displays higher productivities. The skewed distribution of $\alpha(K)$ suggests that the marginal product of total budget in a given research programme may vary substantially with changes in the resource allocations among research units. Thus, as we show in the next section, changes in resource allocation schemes can change aggregate output.

---

20. Table A2 in the appendix reports our estimated production function of publications using the constant and log-linear elasticities.
21. Note that estimate of β is statistically significant even though $\ln(K)$ appears as a separate regressor.
22. We also estimated (9) by using the actual levels of research budgets instead of instrumenting for it. This amounted to using actual values of $\ln B$ instead of the expression for b_e^* in (9). We found that in this case α_0 is 0.67 and β is 0.007, and they are both statistically significant. Our model then predicts higher elasticities of research budget (and a distribution with greater spread) than if one did not instrument for research grants.

Table 7

Publication Equation – Logistic $\alpha(K)$ *(Equation (9) – TOBIT).*

Dependent variable: $\ln(PUB)$ N obs. $= 347$, for $I = 1$.

	$\alpha(K) = \alpha_0/(1 + e^{-\beta(1+K)})$
const	1.841
	(2.393)
α_0	1.013
	(0.255)
β	0.009
	(0.004)
DPRO7 (γ_7)	−0.990
	(0.231)
DSOUTH (γ_S)	−0.564
	(0.179)
TRANSF (γ_T)	−0.198
	(0.180)
ln(SIZE) (γ_N)	−0.002
	(0.140)
ln(K) (γ_K)	0.082
	(0.221)
ln(COLLAB) (γ_C)	0.257
	(0.122)
ln(NUIST) (γ_U)	−0.001
	(0.057)
ln(PROV_POP) (γ_P)	−0.057
	(0.098)
ln(AGEPI) (γ_A)	−0.515
	(0.380)
σ_{IP}	0.146
	(0.621)
LogLik	−515.75

Heteroskedastic consistent standard errors in parenthesis.

As far as the other parameters of the production function are concerned, Table 7 shows that bio-instrumentation projects and southern units have lower output (*DPRO7* and *DSOUTH*), whereas collaborations with foreign institutions increases output (*COLLAB*). Consistent with our identifying assumptions, the size of the team does not affect productivity. To the extent that *SIZE* proxies for other resources available to the units, this effect manifests itself largely through the size of the project, budget asked, rather than directly affecting research output. This results is also consistent with our earlier assumption that these are "small" projects. We also found that externalities within the same institution or from being part of large metropolitan areas do not play a significant role (*NUIST* and *PROV_POP*).

It was noted, at the end of Section 4.1, that the marginal product of the budgetary resources provided by comparatively small grants from the CNR would tend to be raised when the research unit in question was able to maintain more "infrastructure" by spreading its costs over projects funded from other sources. It should be clear that *SIZE* alone would not serve as a proxy for the capacity to obtain the margins of funding above direct

FIGURE 4

Alpha(K) (Frequency distribution, 347 observations for I=1)

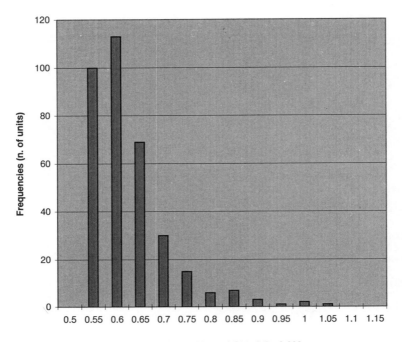

Intervals -- Mean=0.601; S.D.=0.082

research costs that would be required for such purposes; the same factors that affect the probability of receiving a grant, and the magnitude of the project budget, would most likely be just as relevant in obtaining funding from other sources. Among those factors we have found the "knowledge capital" of the unit, K, to be significant in the case of the CNR project. By symmetry, this would imply that some part of the estimated direct effect of K on the unit's productivity in using CNR programme-provided resources may, in some part, be reflecting the positive role of past research performance in furnishing the unit with a better physical and human "infrastructure". Of course, without the necessary data on other sources of research support held by the units, this must remain a conjectural interpretation and the hypothesised "infrastructure effect" of the unit's accumulated knowledge capital cannot be identified separately within the direct production effect of K.

Finally, although their statistical significance is not high, the point estimates of *TRANSF* and *AGEPI* are negative and large in magnitude. The negative impact of the age of the PI may reflect not just life cycle effects, but also selection effects at the tails of the age distribution. More

166

reputed and productive researchers are likely to become PIs at younger ages. Thus, compared with the median age, at lower ages, the expected quality of PIs is likely to be higher. No further interpretation can be given to this coefficient in a cross section data set such as ours. The point estimate coefficient of *TRANSF* suggests that, other things being equal, there is a trade-off between industrial transferability and publications: projects aimed at industrial applications produce about 20% fewer publications.

6 Optimal Resource Allocation and Returns to Past Performance

6.1. Optimal Allocation of Resources and the Aggregate Productivity of Research Budgets

As has already been noticed, the skewed distribution of $\alpha(K)$ suggests that the average productivity of research budgets at the aggregate level may vary considerably with the distribution of research grant allocations, even when the total size of the research budget does not change. Given our estimated parameters, in this section we ask which allocation of resources would equalise the selected units' respective marginal productivities – reckoned in terms of expected quality adjusted-publications [23].

It should be understood at the outset that this is a very short-run allocative criterion, and that qualification must be borne in mind when interpreting our references to the magnitude of the actual CNR allocations' departure from "optimality". Maximising conditional expected aggregate output in this way would not take into consideration the effects upon the research units' subsequent capabilities, their future access to funding (from all sources) and the expected future trajectory of their productivity. Nor does it allow for generalised training effects, and possible long-run spillovers that depend upon the presence of groups pursuing a diversity of approaches, including approaches that have yet to show payoffs in terms of past publication performance measures. It is by no means obvious that the dynamic effects would run in the same direction as the first round consequences of a reallocation that equalised marginal (expected) outputs across the population of funded units; shifting funding towards the presently most productive units might have deleterious effects upon the development of others whose future productivity potential is far higher – even were it to be suitably discounted. Nevertheless, obtaining a sense of the magnitude of the short-run reallocation effects remains an important starting point in any attempt at a more complete dynamic analysis.

---

23. We perform this experiment only for the units that were funded by the CNR. This amounts to taking the actual selection decision of CNR as given, and looking for the allocation of resources that maximise the expected total publications of the programme.

To "re-allocate" resources amongst our selected units we obtained an estimate of their marginal product of publications, MP. Since $\ln E\left(B_G\right) = E\left(\ln B_G\right) + \sigma_b^2/2 - u_b$, one can use the following expression as an estimate of the marginal product of budget

(10)
$$\hat{MP}\left(B, K\right) = \alpha\left(K\right)\exp\left(E\left(\ln PUB | I = 1, B_G\right) \equiv \alpha\left(K\right)\Psi B_G^{\alpha(K)-1}$$

where $\Psi = \exp\left\{\alpha \cdot \left(K\right)\left[\ln\left(1 - \lambda\right) + \frac{\sigma_b^2}{2}\right] + \gamma \cdot h + \sigma_{IP}\frac{\phi}{\Phi}\right\}$

Note that the marginal product of publications depends on all characteristics of the units, not simply B_G and $\alpha\left(K\right)$. Hence, even though $\alpha\left(K\right)$ increases in K, the marginal product need not.

We proceed by ranking our selected units according to K, and comparing the units located at the mid point of each quartile. The total budget received by those units was then reallocated so that their estimated marginal products were equalised. Table 8 shows that to maximise aggregate publications in this way, 85% of total budget should be allocated to the top quartile. In the resulting, short-run "re-optimised" allocation, a very large share of the total available budget would be given to a small percentage of highly productive teams. Also, as shown by Table 8, the efficient allocation to the top unit is roughly of the same magnitude of the amount of budget asked by that unit (496 vs. 477 million Lire). These "optimal" short-run allocations are thus of reasonable size, and do not entail grant awards in excess of the (self-assessed) "absorptive capacities" of the units [24].

We also compared the output produced by the "re-optimized" allocation with the benchmark case of equal allocations. Given the total budget actually allocated to our four units, Table 8 reports what their expected total publications would have been, had they obtained identical shares of that those funds. Rather surprisingly, it turns out that this "egalitarian" distribution of funding would yield the same expected publications output as that obtained with the actual CNR allocations; in effect it "remedies" the disproportionately large budget that was allocated to a relatively low marginal product unit. But, from Table 8 one may also see that the "re-optimized" allocation produces about 19% more total publications (in quality-adjusted units) than both the actual and "egalitarian" allocations.

Needless to say, the foregoing calculations are intended merely to illustrate what our econometric results imply, and are not presented in support of any policy prescriptions. As the introductory caveats in this section have indicated, maximising the existing research community's output of publications is unlikely to be the sole objective of a sensible national science

---

24. We experimented with many different observations around the mid-point of each quartile, and the results discussed here are robust.

policy [25]. What our analysis shows is that by making use of data generated in the management of the public funding process, it is possible to quantify the trade-off between various goals in terms of foregone production of scientific publications.

6.2. Total Returns to Past Performance

Our second experiment is to compute the total returns to past performance K. As discussed in the introduction, the indirect effect of past performance through budget can amplify differences in scientific productivity. The magnitude of this effect may then be suggestive of the extent to which the observed skewed distribution of publications in the scientific enterprise is influenced by the institutional mechanisms of resource allocation in this sector.

The elasticity of output with respect to past performance is

$$(11) \qquad \rho_k \equiv \frac{\partial E\left(\ln PUB\right)}{\partial \ln K} = \Phi \left\{ \frac{\partial \alpha\left(K\right)}{\partial \ln K} \left[\ln\left(1-\lambda\right) + b^* + \delta\mu_b\right] + \gamma_k \right\}$$
$$+ \phi\pi_k\, p + \Phi\alpha\left(K\right)\frac{\partial b^*}{\partial \ln K}$$

where π_k is the elasticity of K in the selection equation, and $b^* = \ln E\left(B_G | I = 1, \varepsilon_k\right)$. Since we do not observe b^* (because we do not observe ε_k), and we do not observe μ_b and ε_p, we cannot compute ρ_k directly. However, we can estimate it by taking the expectation of (11) over ε_k, μ_b, and ε_p, given $I = 1$. Using b_e^* to denote the expected value of the budget conditional upon selection (but not upon ε_k), the estimated elasticity is

$$(11a) \qquad \hat{\rho}_k = \Phi \left\{ \frac{\partial \alpha\left(K\right)}{\partial k} \left[\ln\left(1-\lambda\right) + b_e^*\right] + \gamma_k \right\}$$
$$+ \phi\pi_k \left\{ \alpha\left(K\right)\left[\ln\left(1-\lambda\right) + b_e^*\right] + \gamma\, h + \sigma_{IP}\,\frac{\phi}{\Phi} \right\}$$
$$+ \Phi\alpha\left(K\right)\frac{\theta_k}{1-\lambda}$$

In (11a), the first term measures the direct effect of past performance given the budget, the second term measure the indirect effect through increases in

---

25. One can list a number of reasons. Papers produced by different PIs, even though of the same quality, may not be perfect substitutes. One may wish to encourage certain fields rather than others. In our particular programme we saw that the agency also wanted to encourage industrial transferability of scientific research, and our estimates of the production function of publications suggest that industrial transferability has a negative impact on publication output. Second, one may wish to have a diversified portfolio to minimize risk. Third, one may wish to encourage young talent, even at the cost of a short run reduction in output. This could be either if there is learning-by-doing in research, or if by funding young scientists, the public agency can get a signal about their true productivity, and hence, can make more informed funding decisions in the future. (See for instance ARORA and GAMBARDELLA [1997].)

TABLE 8

Effects of Alternative Reallocations of Research Budget Resources (347 selected units ranked by past publications K, mid-points of each quartile: positions 43, 130, 207, 304).

Marginal product MP (*)	$\alpha(K)$	Actual allocation B_G (+)	Efficient allocation B'_G (+)	Marginal product of efficient allocation $MP(B')$	Expected #pubs. using actual allocation $EPUB(B_G)$	Expected# pubs. Using efficient allocation $EPUB(B'_G)$	Equal share allocation B''_G (+)	Expected #pubs. using equal share allocation $EP(B''_G)$	Past publ. $K(^)$	Budget asked B_A (+)
0.109	0.677	156	496	0.0875	29.3	64.2	145.75	28.0	74.0	477
0.006	0.604	100	23.5	0.0875	8.2	3.4	145.75	10.3	41.0	620
0.189	0.561	120	38.5	0.0875	11.4	6.0	145.75	12.7	22.8	126.2
0.049	0.531	207	25	0.0875	12.6	4.1	145.75	10.5	10.3	562
		Total: 583	Total: 583		Total: 61.5	Total: 77.7	Total: 583	Total: 61.5		

(*) Computed as $\alpha(K) \cdot PUB/B_G$ using actual values of PUB and B_G and estimated $\alpha(K)$, logistic.

(+) Millions of Italian LIre.

(^) Quality-adjusted number.

probability of selection (given expected budget conditional upon selection) and the third term measures the indirect effect through the increase in expected budget conditional upon selection.

Figure 5a shows the distribution of $\hat{\rho}_k$ for our sample of selected units. Table 9 presents descriptive statistics of $\hat{\rho}_k$, and of its three components. The average value of the total elasticity of publication output with respect to past publication performance is 0.64. This value is determined largely by the direct effect $\hat{\rho}_{k1}$, whose sample mean is 0.27, and the indirect effect through selection $\hat{\rho}_{k2}$, whose sample average is 0.31. The indirect effect through budget given selection, $\hat{\rho}_{k3}$, is smaller; its average value in the sample is 0.07.

TABLE 9

Descriptive Statistics for Elasticity with Respect to Past Performance (347 observations for $I = 1$).

	Mean	Std Dev	Minimum	Maximum
$\hat{\rho}_{k1}$ (direct effect)	0.272	0.223	0.011	0.993
$\hat{\rho}_{k2}$ (indirect effect selecton)	0.305	0.096	0.067	0.549
$\hat{\rho}_{k3}$ (indirect effect budget)	0.066	0.030	0.011	0.161
$\hat{\rho}_k$ (total effect)	0.643	0.304	0.109	1.466

This suggests that there are important reinforcing effects of past performance in the scientific sector, operating primarily by increasing the chances of selection. The relative insensitivity of the expected budget conditional upon selection may reflect a measurement issue – it is difficult to find variables that affect the budget conditional upon selection, but not selection itself. Even so, we believe that our results point to the importance of the selection process, where reputation and quality of the research unit appear to play a very prominent role.

Although our cross-sectional data do not allow us to take dynamic considerations into account, the indirect effects seem to be serious enough to be capable of generating increasing returns to past performance. Consider the following suggestive piece of evidence: the total elasticity of publication output with respect to past publications in our sample is greater than unity for 47 of the 347 selected units, and, as shown by Figure 5b, these values are associated with higher K. Since the estimated direct effect is well below one, the institutional mechanisms for resource allocation in the scientific enterprise may be critical in creating the appearance of increasing research returns to the accumulation of knowledge capital at the level of the individual research unit. The marked skewness in the distribution of publication outputs of individual scientists, and of research groups, thus may be due in large part to the way in which academic-style scientific activities are funded. In turn, this points to the importance of controlling for funding levels and for selection in estimating the "competences" of research organizations and the research "abilities" of individual scientists. Failure to do so will produce greatly exaggerated estimates of the dispersion in the underlying distribution of innate research capabilities.

FIGURE 5

Distribution of Rho(K), and plot on past publ.
(347 observations for I=1).

a) Distribution of Rho(K).

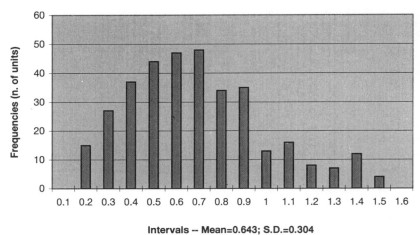

Intervals -- Mean=0.643; S.D.=0.304

b) Plot of Rho(K) on past publications.

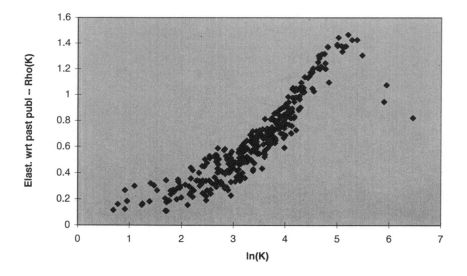

7 Conclusions

Empirical studies of resource allocation in the Republic of Science are still in their infancy. While economists have ignored it, quantitative sociologists of science have largely been concerned with the determinants of the scientific productivity of individuals and their career paths. In the natural sciences and engineering, research is increasingly a group activity, one whose continuity depends upon success in mobilizing not just human resources but costly instruments, materials, and facilities as well.

This paper has examined the determinants of the publication performance of publicly funded scientific research groups. We modeled the process of resource allocation and production of scientific research output. Our analysis allows for unobserved differences across research units and corrects for "funding selection biases", which have been found to be quantitatively quite important.

We estimate that for a large fraction of the research groups in our sample the elasticity of quality-adjusted publications with respect to the budget given is about 0.6. However, for a small fraction of researchers, with high values of quality-adjusted past publications, this elasticity is higher, and it approaches unity. This implies that the aggregate publication output may vary with the distribution of research grants.

This relatively high responsiveness of output to research budgets points to an important indirect route through which past performance influences future performance. Superior performance on the part of the group's leader in the past increase the probability of the research proposal being selected. This indirect effect turned out to be substantial. While the combined elasticity of publication output with respect to past publications is on average 0.64, the indirect component accounts for almost 60% of this figure. Moreover, the elasticity varies across research units; for a small fraction of our applicant units, it is greater than 1.

The nature of the analysis carried out here is not normative, either in its intent or its conclusions. We most certainly would not advance it as suggesting that the institutional mechanisms for funding scientific research are inefficient, or that using past performance to estimate productivity is incorrect. Neither do we claim that the characteristic skewness of the distribution of scientific publications is socially undesirable. Absent systematic micro-level time series data on inputs (funding levels), and research performance in various scientific fields, questions of that kind simply cannot be answered. Our objective in this paper has been to demonstrate the possibilities of quantitatively describing the relationships that proximately govern productivity in scientific research groups. In doing so, we have made a start towards fully uncovering how competence (both innate and acquired), reputation, and the institutional mechanisms for the funding of academic research interact in the production of scientific knowledge.

Results for Alternate Specifications

Reduced Form Equations: OLS Budget Granted and Publication

	B_G	B_G $(I = 1)$	PUB	PUB $(I = 1)$	PUB
Const	9.90	93.14	−0.14	15.42	−0.80
	(14.66)	(21.33)	(3.56)	(7.50)	(3.32)
DPRO7	27.39	54.79	−1.47	−6.21	−3.37
	(10.17)	(16.54)	(0.80)	(1.54)	(1.01)
DCNR	30.55	26.18	−1.32	−3.84	−3.34
	(10.90)	(13.44)	(1.42)	(2.94)	(1.39)
DUNI	9.72	−2.16	0.18	−0.68	−0.46
	(5.717)	(10.34)	(1.44)	(3.52)	(1.33)
DSOUTH	−0.20	−8.70	−2.65	−6.64	−2.64
	(5.65)	(8.96)	(0.90)	(1.87)	(0.87)
TRANSF	17.15	6.12	0.58	−0.46	−0.55
	(4.65)	(6.30)	(0.97)	(1.74)	(0.93)
SIZE	1.32	1.07	0.05	0.00	−0.03
	(0.34)	(0.40)	(0.07)	(0..09)	(0.06)
K	0.32	0.08	0.23	0.25	0.21
	(0.08)	(0.06)	(0.04)	(0.04)	(0.04)
COLLAB	4.38	1.27	0.70	0.66	0.41
	(1.32)	(1.43)	(0.29)	(0.42)	(0.28)
NUIST	0.01	0.35	−0.06	−0.09	−0.06
	(0.18)	(0.28)	(0.03)	(0.07)	(0.03)
PROV_POP*	4.29	−0.86	0.55	0.06	0.25
	(2.45)	(4.21)	(0.44)	(0.95)	(0.41)
AGEPI	−0.46	−0.49	0.00	−0.12	0.03
	(0.26)	(0.40)	(0.05)	(0.12)	(0.05)
B_G					0.07
					(0.01)
No of obs	797	347	797	347	7.97
Adj. R^2	0.14	0.13	0.35	0.42	0.42

(*) Measured in hundreds of thousands.
Heteroskedastic consistent standard errors in parenthesis.

Publication equation – Constant and logarithmic $\alpha(K)$ specification (TOBIT).

Dependent variable: $\ln(PUB)$. No of obs. $= 347$, for $I = 1$.

	$\alpha(K) = \alpha_0$	$\alpha(K) = \alpha_0 + \beta \ln(K)$
const	−0.593	5.816
	(5.879)	(11.10)
α_0	0.611	−0.690
	(0.988)	(2.101)
β	–	0.293
		(0.390)
DPRO7 (γ_7)	−1.014	−0.812
	(0.482)	(0.583)
DSOUTH (γ_S)	−0.504	−0.578
	(0.234)	(0.257)
TRANSF (γ_T)	−0.047	−0.120
	(0.182)	(0.204)
$\ln$(SIZE) (γ_N)	0.20	0.062
	(0.214)	(0.223)
$\ln(K)$ (γ_K)	0.563	−0.766
	(0.176)	(1.798)
$\ln$(COLLAB) (γ_C)	0.301	0.266
	(0.131)	(0.143)
$\ln$(NUIST) (γ_U)	−0.002	−0.014
	(0.062)	(0.064)
$\ln$(PROV_POP) (γ_P)	−0.029	−0.049
	(0.099)	(0.105)
$\ln$(AGEPI) (γ_A)	−0.517	−0.558
	(0.400)	(0.413)
σ_{IP}	0.671	0.284
	(0.921)	(1.096)
Log of Likelihood	−520.11	−519.81

Heteroskedastic consistent standard errors in parenthesis.

• References

ALLISON, P., PRICE, SOLLA, D. J. de, GRIFFITH, B., MORAVCSIK, M., STEWART, J. (1976). – "Lotka's Law: A Problem in its Interpretation and Application", *Social Studies of Sciences*, Vol. 6, pp. 269-276.

ALLISON, P., LONG, S., KRAUSE, T. (1982). – "Cumulative Advantage and Inequality in Science", *American Sociological Review*, Vol. 47(5), pp. 615-625.

ARORA, A., GAMBARDELLA, A. (1997). – "Public Policy Towards Science: Picking Stars or Spreading the Wealth?", *Revue d'Économie Industrielle*, N. 79, pp. 63-75.

DASGUPTA, P., DAVID, P. A. (1987). – "Information Disclosure and the Economics of Science and Technology", in FEIWEL, G. (ed.), *Arrow and the Ascent of Modern Economic Theory*, New York University Press, New York, pp. 519-542.

DASGUPTA, P., DAVID, P. A. (1994). – "Towards a New Economics of Science", *Research Policy,* Vol. 23, pp. 487-521.

DAVID, P. A. (1993). – "Knowledge, Property and the System Dynamics of Technological Change", in *Proceedings of the World Bank Annual Conference on Development Economics: 1992,* Summers, L. and Shah, S. (ed.), Washington DC, March.

DAVID, P. A. (1994). – "Positive Feedbacks and Research Productivity in Science: Reopening Another Black Box", in GRANSTRAND, O. (ed.) *Economics of Technology,* North-Holland, Amsterdam and London.

European Report on Science and Technology Indicators (The) (1994), European Commission, DG XII, EUR 15897 EN, Luxembourg.

JAFFE, A. (1989). – "Real Effects of Academic Research", *American Economic Review,* Vol. 79, (5), pp. 957-970.

LEVIN, S., STEPHAN, P. (1991). – "Research Productivity over the Life Cycle: Evidence for Academic Scientists", *American Economic Review,* Vol. 81, (1), pp. 114-132.

LOKA, A. (1926). – "The Frequency Distribution of Scientific Productivity", *Journal of the Washington Academy of Sciences,* Vol. 16, (12), pp. 317-323.

MANSFIELD, E. (1991). – "Academic Research and Industrial Innovation", *Research Policy,* Vol. 20, (1), pp. 1-12.

MERTON, R. (1968). – "The Matthew Effect in Science", *Science,* Vol. 159, (3810), pp. 56-63.

NARIN, F., OLIVASTRO, D. (1992). – "Status Report - Linkage between Technology and Science", *Research Policy,* Vol. 21, (3), pp. 237-249.

NELSON, R. (1986). – "Institutions Supporting Technical Advance in Industry", *American Economic Review Proceedings,* Vol. 76, (2), pp. 186-189.

OECD (1994). – *Main Science and Technology Indicators,* OECD, Paris.

PRICE, D. J. de Solla (1963). – *Little Science, Big Science,* Columbia University Press, New York.

PRICE, D. J. de Solla (1976). – "A General Theory of Bibliometric and Other Cumulative Advantage Processes", *Journal of the American Society for Information Sciences,* Vol. 27, (5/6), pp. 292-306.

STEPHAN, P., LEVIN, S. (1992). – *Striking the Mother Lode in Science: The Importance of Age, Place and Time,* Oxford University Press, New York.

STEPHAN, P. (1996). – "The Economics of Science", *Journal of Economic Literature,* Vol. XXXIV, pp. 1199-1235.

The Impact
and Organization
of Publicly-Funded
Research and Development
in the European Community

Maryann P. FELDMAN, Frank R. LICHTENBERG *

ABSTRACT. – This paper examines R&D activities in the European Community using several Community R&D Information Service (CORDIS) databases. We find that a country's private companies tend to be specialized in the same scientific fields as its universities and public organizations. In addition, we construct indicators of the degree of R&D tacitness and find that greater expected ability to communicate research outcomes encourages less centralized R&D programs. Programs that yield tangible results are less geographically and administratively centralized. The more that research leads to codifiable knowledge, the less centralized R&D activity needs to be.

* M. P. FELDMAN: Institute for Policy Studies, Johns Hopkins University; F. R. LICHTENBERG: Columbia University, National Bureau of Economic Research. Lichtenberg is grateful for support from the National Science Foundation under award no. 9408915. We benefitted from the comments of two anonymous referees on a previous draft of this paper. We are responsible for any errors.

D. Encaoua et al. (eds.), The Economics and Econometrics of Innovation, 177–200.

1 Introduction

Innovation, rather than the result of the efforts of an individual inventor, is most likely predicated on the orchestration of different and complementary streams of knowledge. A substantial share of this knowledge is the product of publicly-funded research and development (R&D). For example, the fraction of R&D expenditure that is governement-funded is 32% in the United Kingdom, 37% in Germany, and about 45% in both France and Italy [1]. In recent years, a significant amount of publicly-funded R&D in Europe has been coordinated by the Commission of the European Community (CEC). For example, the CEC created the Community R&D Information Service (CORDIS), to "assist interactions and cooperation among individual ...participants; and help promote co-ordination with similar RTD [research and technological development] activities in Member States". A principal objective of publically funded R&D is the overall "advancement of knowledge"; "industrial development" is an important secondary objective [2].

In this paper we examine some important aspects of the impact and organization of publicly-supported R&D activities in the European Community, using several of the large and rich CORDIS databases. We analyze the relationship between public and private R&D-performing organizations, and test the hypothesis of *complementarity* of the research efforts of these two sectors [3]. In particular, we determine whether a country's private organizations tend to be specialized in the same technologies as its public organizations.

We also propose and test a theory of the (geographic and administrative) *organization* of R&D programs. A number of recent studies have suggested that R&D investment has a strong geographic component [4]. Organizations that use similar knowledge tend to locate near one another, presumably because the cost of transmitting and acquiring knowledge increases with distance. (Language differences and political boundaries also further increase these costs). We hypothesize that the extent of geographic and administrative decentralization of R&D activities is greater, the less tacit (or more codifiable) the knowledge generated by the R&D is expected to

---

1. Source: Science and Engineering Indicators 1996, Appendix Table 4-35.
2. The fraction of government R&D budget appropriations devoted to the "socioeconomic objective" of "advancement of knowledge" ranges from 22% in the U.K. to 51% in Germany. In contrast, only 4% of U.S. public R&D is devoted to this objective. (In the U.S., defense and health account for 55% and 17% of public R&D, respectively.) The fraction of European public R&D devoted to industrial development ranges from 7% in France to 16% in Italy; less than 1% of U.S. public R&D is devoted to this objective. (Source: Science and Engineering Indicators 1996, Appendix Table 4-32.)
3. In previous research, LICHTENBERG [1984, 1987, 1988] investigated the issue of complementary (or its opposite, "crowding out") between privately- and government-funded (defense) R&D expenditure in the U.S.
4. See, for example, ACS, AUDRETSCH and FELDMAN [1992, 1994], ZUCKER, L., DARBY, M. and ARMSTRONG, J. [1994], FELDMAN and FLORIDA [1994], JAFFE [1989], and PORTER [1990].

be. We construct several indicators of the degree of R&D decentralization and tacitness of European Community RTD programs from data contained in the CORDIS databases to test this hypothesis.

The remainder of this paper is organized as follows. In the next section, we provide some descriptive statistics about R&D activity in the European Community as reflected in the CORDIS data, including distributions of organizations by type, country, and technological field. Since we can determine, for example, the number of German manufacturing firms and universities engaged in R&D in the area of genetic engineering, we can identify each country's areas of technological specialization. In Section 3, we analyze the relationship between the extent of R&D activity by universities and other public organizations within a given region and field of science and the extent of R&D undertaken by private firms in the same region and scientific field. In Section 4, we advance and test the hypothesis that research programs that produce more tacit results are more geographically concentrated than programs that produce more articulable results. Section 5 concludes.

2 The Degree of Specialization in Country Knowledge Resources

Just as countries specialize in the production of physical goods and services we expect that there will be specialization in the production of knowledge. The data contained in the CORDIS RTD-Partners database – in particular, the technology and industry classification codes-allow us to construct the distribution of each country's knowledge base by scientific field and type of organization [5]. Table 1 provides an accounting of the types of organizations represented in the data. The most prominent type of organization lised is universities and educational organizations (4413). Manufacturers accounted for 2692 organizations [6]. Public, non-university research centers, such as the Commissariat a l'Énergie Atomique (France), Fraunhofer-Institut fuer Materialfluss und Logistik (Germany), and Institutop de Linguistica Teorica e Caomputacional (ILTEC) (Portugal), accounted for

---

5. The RTD-Partners database includes information about all organizations that have registered with the Community R&D Information Service in order to try to establish R&D partnerships with other organizations in the European Community. (International partnership is a necessary but far from sufficient condition to be eligible for EC support.) "Organizations" may be university *departments* or *divisions* of companies. These organizations have not necessarily received any public R&D funding-most probably have not. This reduces the probability that this sample misrepresents the aggregate distribution of private-sector research. The other CORDIS databases (RTD-Programmes, -Projects, and -Results) analyzed later in this paper describe R&D activities that have received some public support.

6. Some private firms may be university spin-offs, but these are not systematically identified in the database.

TABLE 1

Number of Organizations, by Type.

Organization Type	Number of Organizations
Universities and Educational Organizations	4413
Manufacturer	2692
Public Research Center (Non-University)	2167
Service Company	2001
Consultancy	1725
Public Organization (National)	423
Technology Transfer Organization	859

2167 organizations. Technology transfer organizations, such as Zentrum Mikroelektronik Dresden (Germany), Transcend Technology LTD (United Kingdom), Impetus Consultants (Greece) accounted for 859 entries. National public organizations, such as Technicatome (France), Empresa Nacional Adaro (Spain), Ente per le Nuove Tecnologie (Italy), accounted for 423 of the organizations.

The distribution of organizations, by country, is shown in Table 2 [7]. For example, there were 3054 R&D organizations in the United Kingdom and 2502 located in Germany. The relative ranking among countries is consistent with ARCHIBUGI and PIANTA's [1992] analysis based on patent registration and bibliometric indicators. To normalize for population, the last column of Table 2 presents the number of organizations per 1 million population. While the United Kingdom and Germany have the greatest number of R&D organizations, Ireland, with a small population and a high degree of foreign investment, has the highest number of R&D organizations on a per capita basis.

All of the R&D organizations in the CORDIS database report the technological fields in which they are currently working. Since organizations typically work with different technologies, each organization may report up to five unique fields of technological expertise [8]. There are 400 distinct technological fields and the 15,491 organizations report 42,862 fields of technological expertise. Table 3 provides a listing of the most prominent scientific disciplines, which are more aggregate groupings of technological

---

7. This table does not provide data for those countries with fewer than 100 organizations reporting. Other countries and their number of organizations include Luxembourg (39 organizations), Romania (29), Slovenia (20), Czech republic (18), Latvia (18), Poland (17), Israel (14), Estonia (8), and Croatia (3).

8. The mean number of technological fields per organization is 2.77, and the modal number is the maximum number allowed, 5. This suggests that there may be a significant amount of truncation in the reporting of technological fields.

180

TABLE 2

Number of Organizations, by Country.

Country	Number of Organizations	Population	Organizations per million population
United Kingdom	3054	58,295,119	52.4
Germany	2502	81,337,541	30.8
Italy	2205	58,261,971	37.8
France	1740	58,109,160	29.9
Spain	1163	39,404,348	29.5
Greece	911	10,647,511	85.6
Belgium	859	10,081,880	85.2
Netherlands	831	15,452,903	53.8
Ireland	511	3,550,448	143.9
Denmark	395	5,199,437	76.0
Portugal	355	10,562,388	33.6
Finland	278	5,085,206	54.7
Sweden	251	8,821,759	28.5
Austria	165	7,986,664	20.7
Switzerland	146	7,084,984	2.06
Norway	125	4,330,951	28.9

Source for population data: http://www.odci.gov/cia/publication/95fact

fields [9]. For example, there were 3995 organizations engaged in computer science, the most prominent of the disciplines. This represented 9.32% of all the capabilities mentioned by the organizations.

The assessment of national capabilities and performance in technological fields is important from a policy perspective for both government and private firms. Table 4 identifies the scientific disciplines in which countries have a specialization or weakness relative to that country's overall R&D activity. To test for the degree of specialization we use a non-parametric

---

9. The technological fields are hierarchically organized within scientific domains. The data presented in Table 2 and Table 3 are for scientific domains that are the larger categories of expertise. For example, all of the medical subfields and specialities are aggregated in the scientific domain of medicine.

TABLE 3

Number of Organizations, by Scientific Discipline.

Scientific Discipline	Organizations Reporting	Share of all Technologies (%)
Computer science	3995	9.32
Material technology	3546	8.27
Construction technology	3538	8.25
Biochemistry	2475	5.77
Chemistry	2409	5.62
Environmental engineering	2244	5.24
Electronics and related fields	1953	4.56
Mechanical engineering	1880	4.39
Production technology	1873	4.37
Medicine	1784	4.16
Transportation technology	1629	3.80
Physics	1495	3.49
Telecommunications	1065	2.48
Geology	956	2.23
Composite materials and related fields	920	2.15
Biomedical and related sciences	878	2.05
Coatings and surface materials engineering	848	1.98
Electrical engineering	683	1.59
Energy research	662	1.54
Ceramic materials and related fields	628	1.47
Nuclear engineering	524	1.22
Ecology	432	1.01
Microelectronics	417	0.97
Laser technology	366	0.85
Zoology	355	0.83
Thermal engineering	246	0.57

182

TABLE 4

Country Specialization in Scientific Disciplines: Countries and Scientific Fields with "Unexpectedly" High or Low Numbers of Organizations.

Technology	Country	Count	Percent	Chi-Sq
Computer Science	Germany	682	16.98	23.68
Electronics	Italy	52	−62.50	12.50
	United Kingdom	216	24.86	17.77
Material Technology	Spain	150	−75.53	48.75
	Greece	147	−74.22	46.48
	Germany	618	18.67	26.50
	Italy	619	29.13	74.10
Construction Technology	Ireland	60	−81.67	22.03
	United Kingdom	746	−12.68	10.65
	Netherlands	237	19.83	11.63
	Denmark	155	31.74	22.88
	Bulgaria	12	86.67	67.60
Biochemistry	Germany	67	−85.67	26.49
	France	116	28.19	12.84
	Spain	100	34.80	18.57
	Sweden	25	49.60	12.20
	Portugal	51	58.04	40.94
Chemistry	Italy	185	−61.08	42.85
	Denmark	108	33.24	17.88
	Sweden	54	36.11	11.02
Environmental Engineering	Germany	173	−102.78	90.12
	United Kingdom	472	−24.60	22.92
	Italy	566	45.90	220.43
Electronics and Related Fields	Italy	146	−65.48	37.83
	France	150	23.53	10.86
	Austria	59	56.95	44.45
	Luxembourg	14	85.71	72.00
	Solvenia	14	88.57	96.10

TABLE 4 (continued)

Technology	Country	Count	Percent	Chi-Sq
Mechanical Engineering	Greece	39	− 103.08	20.40
	Italy	92	− 47.39	14.02
	Germany	253	38.62	61.46
Production Technology	United Kingdom	283	− 57.10	58.74
	Greece	90	− 50.11	15.06
	Germany	324	18.15	13.04
	Italy	438	47.15	184.20
Medicine	Germany	122	−107.30	67.75
	Italy	115	− 91.91	50.62
	Netherlands	60	− 59.67	13.38
	Belgium	120	29.42	14.71
	France	286	40.84	80.63
	Spain	249	46.79	102.43
Transport Technology	Portugal	16	− 148.13	14.15
	United Kingdom	522	25.84	47.01
Physics	Italy	77	− 140.13	62.97
	Netherlands	46	− 74.57	14.65
	United Kingdom	422	15.83	12.56
	Germany	261	18.81	11.38
	Austria	34	42.94	10.99
Telecommunication	Italy	93	− 41.72	11.42
	Spain	81	32.84	13.01
	Finland	50	53.20	30.24
Geology	Belgium	14	− 224.29	21.72
Biomedical Sciences	Netherlands	39	42.82	12.51
Coatings and Surface	Spain	29	− 117.24	18.35
	Greece	31	− 97.74	14.98
	Italy	60	− 74.83	19.22

184

TABLE **4** (continued)

Technology	Country	Count	Percent	Chi-Sq
Coatings and Surface (cont.)	Germany	199	39.60	51.66
Electrical Engineering	Italy	97	30.83	13.32
Energy Research	Greece	79	39.49	20.36
	Denmark	35	43.43	11.67
	Switzerland	20	64.00	22.76
Laser Technology	Germany	104	50.10	52.30
Electronics	Italy	101	30.10	13.09
	Finland	34	63.24	36.98
Ceramic Materials	Italy	42	−85.00	16.40
Nuclear Engineering	Italy	31	−109.03	17.63
	United Kingdom	183	31.97	27.49
	France	91	45.39	34.32
Microelectronics	Germany	88	32.84	14.13
Zoology	Germany	22	−128.64	15.92
	Spain	54	51.11	28.85
Thermal Engineering	Portugal	14	57.14	10.67

chi-square test of association based on the share of all organizations with the various scientific expertise for a given country relative to the European total [10] . Within each country we identify those scientific disciplines which make a statistically significant contribution to the overall chi-squared value. Column 3 provides the total number of organizations in a country involved with a scientific discipline. Column 4 presents the percentage by which

---

10. The data for all countries are pooled to perform the test. The following simple example illustrates the test procedure. Suppose that there are only two countries and two fields. The following table represents the number of organizations in each country and field

	Country 1	Country 2
Field 1	N_{11}	N_{12}
Field 2	N_{21}	N_{22}

The test we performed is simply a standard chi-square test of the independence of field and country. (The CORDIS data contain a few R&D organizations that are non-European; these were excluded from our sample.)

the actual number of organizations is different than the expected number of organizations under the null hypothesis of no national technological specialization. This provides evidence on the extent to which a scientific discipline is over- or under-represented in a given country. A negative number indicates that the actual number of organizations is less than the expected number of organizations for that country. Column 5 provides the country-discipline contribution to the chi-square and provides an index of the degree of scientific specialization of each country [11]. If a country has no scientific specialization, that is, the same percentage distribution in a scientific discipline as the rest of the European Community, the chi-squared value would be zero. The larger the absolute value of the chi-square, the greater the evidence of scientific strength or weakness.

There is evidence of a high degree of specialization in scientific disciplines among countries. The highest degree of specialization observed is for Environmental Engineering in Italy. There are 566 organizations in this scientific discipline in Italy; this was 45.9% greater than expected. Based on the overall chi-square value, we conclude that the observed patterns of distribution of scientific disciplines among countries are not random. The configuration of knowledge among industries and countries appear to represent distinct competencies.

Table 5 provides the distribution of organizations among a representative sample of the different technological fields. On average, for all fields, universities accounted for 32.2 percent of all organizations. The highest percentage of universities and educational organizations, 65.8%, were reported for technologies involving condensed matter. As this table demonstrates, there is a great degree of heterogeneity in the prominence of different organizational types among technological fields.

3 Complementary Between Public and Private Technological Orientation

Previous studies have suggested that public and private R&D organizations may complement one another. For example, Part 3 of LEVIN *et al*'s [1987, 790] survey of 650 American R&D managers explored the links between an industry's technology and other sources of scientific expertise. The survey asked about the importance of scientific research in general and university-based research in particular, and found a strong association between private firm R&D and external sources of knowledge. Other research has found a strong geographic association between university research and private firm R&D (JAFFE [1989]; ACS, AUDRETSCH and FELDMAN [1992] and MANSFIELD

---

11. A value greater than 10.5 is statistically significant at the 5% level.

186

TABLE 5

How Important are Different Organizations for Each Technology?

Technology (Ranked by University Share of all Organizations)	Number of Organizations	Percent of Organizations Reported as					
		University	Manufacturer	Public Research Center	Service Company	Consultancy	Tech Transfer
Condensed Matter, Electronic Structure	237	65.8	5.1	12.7	4.2	4.6	4.6
Physical Chemistry	157	59.2	4.5	20.4	4.5	6.4	5.1
Semiconductors Physics	108	56.5	8.3	7.4	4.6	13.0	8.3
Condensed Matter Physics	243	56.4	3.7	22.2	4.9	2.9	6.2
Mathematics	186	52.7	6.5	10.2	13.4	10.8	3.2
Hydrobiology, Marine Biology	509	52.3	4.9	11.2	2.9	15.9	2.8
Aquaculture, Pisciculture	518	51.2	5.6	9.5	3.7	16.4	4.1
General Biomedical Sciences	119	50.4	9.2	15.1	8.4	9.2	7.6
Statistics, Operations Research	329	44.1	2.4	8.5	17.0	21.6	4.6
Chemistry	889	42.4	10.8	19.6	16.9	5.2	2.9
Proteins, Enzymology	250	41.2	8.8	28.8	7.6	6.0	5.2
Microbiology, Bacteriology, Virology	388	36.3	8.2	30.9	6.7	9.5	4.9
Mechanical Engineering	1096	36.2	20.3	12.5	14.2	9.2	5.1
Material Technology	3549	34.9	24.9	14.5	12.2	6.4	5.7
Computer Science	1027	34.9	9.9	10.0	19.4	17.8	6.0
Analytical Chemistry	294	34.7	2.7	36.4	6.8	7.5	6.5
Ceramic Materials and Powders	628	34.6	15.1	21.5	9.6	8.3	8.8
Biochemistry	253	34.4	5.5	32.0	11.5	5.5	7.5

TABLE 5 (continued)

Technology (Ranked by University Share of all Organizations)	Number of Organizations	Percent of Organizations Reported as					
		University	Manufacturer	Public Research Center	Service Company	Consultancy	Tech Transfer
Composite Materials	920	34.3	18.2	18.7	11.3	7.7	7.7
Artificial Intelligence	386	33.7	8.0	10.1	15.3	21.8	9.8
Coatings and Surface Treatment	848	32.9	16.3	20.3	11.9	8.5	8.4
Soil Science, Agricultural Hydrology	208	32.7	3.8	28.8	12.0	10.1	5.8
ALL FIELDS	42862	32.3	16.0	16.6	13.2	11.9	6.8
Zootechnics, Animal Husbandry, Breeding	134	32.1	6.7	32.1	3.7	8.2	9.7
Laser Technology	366	32.0	13.9	19.7	10.4	9.3	10.7
Thermal Engineering, Thermodynamics	248	31.9	8.9	12.1	13.3	20.2	10.9
Environmental Chemistry	1277	31.6	7.0	24.5	18.2	9.7	5.2
Air Transport Technology	274	31.4	19.7	13.9	10.6	14.2	7.3
Medical Technology	366	29.5	22.4	11.2	13.9	11.5	9.0
Horticulture	296	29.1	7.8	35.1	5.4	7.8	8.1
Civil Engineering	514	29.0	14.4	11.9	16.5	20.2	5.6
Informatics, Systems Theory	477	27.7	7.3	10.5	18.0	24.9	10.1
Environmental Technology	2138	27.5	10.9	17.9	18.3	14.8	7.1
Imaging, Image Processing	744	26.7	16.0	15.2	15.5	14.9	9.1
Instrumentation Technology	773	26.4	21.0	18.0	14.2	8.7	8.3

188

TABLE 5 (continued)

Technology (Ranked by University Share of all Organizations)	Number of Organizations	Percent of Organizations Reported as					
		University	Manufacturer	Public Research Center	Service Company	Consultancy	Tech Transfer
Computer Systems Technology	2018	26.1	14.5	10.5	22.1	17.8	7.3
Electronics & Electrical Technology	472	26.1	24.6	10.8	16.7	10.0	8.9
Electrical Engineering	393	25.7	34.1	6.6	13.0	12.2	6.1
Metrology, Physical Instrumentation	228	25.4	14.9	23.7	11.0	9.6	7.9
Automation & Robotics	1585	24.9	23.2	11.9	16.0	11.9	9.0
Energy Research	664	24.8	11.3	18.5	13.1	17.8	10.8
Road Transport Technology	438	23.3	20.3	11.6	13.5	21.0	7.5
Microelectronics	418	22.5	27.3	12.4	10.3	12.7	11.2
Production Technology	1873	22.4	34.9	10.4	14.1	9.3	7.6
Transport Technology	498	20.5	18.1	14.5	17.9	21.7	6.0
Telecommunication Engineering	628	19.6	16.7	9.9	19.6	21.5	9.6

[1995]). Similarly, ADAMS [1990] used the distribution of an industry's scientists by academic discipline (e.g., physics, chemistry) to examine the relationship between fundamental stocks of knowledge and industry productivity growth. Public organizations other than universities, such as technology-transfer agencies, may also contribute to knowledge accumulation in private enterprises. Indeed, their RTD activities may have a stronger or more immediate effect on private knowledge than those of university research, which is more basic in nature.

In this section we explore the relationship between private and public knowledge within the same country, by estimating regressions of the number of consultancies, manufacturers, and service companies—which are predominantly private-sector organizations—on the number of public organizations—public research centers, technology transfer organizations, and universities—which are predominantly public-sector organizations—by

country and scientific field. The distribution of organizations by type
and sector (private vs. public) is shown in Table 6. Table 7 reports the
mean number of fields of science, by organization type, and indicates that
there is significant heterogeneity in the degree of scientific specialization.
In general, private sector organizations – consultancies, manufacturers and

TABLE 6

Number of Organizations, by Type* and Sector**.

	Private	Public	Total
Consultancy	55	4	194
Manufacturer	65	12	290
R&D Organization	136	254	80
Service Company	44	7	155
Technology Transfer Organization	3	4	10
University	2	687	1129
Total	254	948	

Source: RTD-Results database. * An organization could be classified as more than one type.
** Sector was not reported for many organizations.

TABLE 7

Mean Number of Fields, by Organization Type.

Organization Type	Mean	Standard Deviation	t-statistic for testing H_0: difference from mean for other org. types $= 0$
Consultancy	2.96	1.62	7.37*
Manufacturer	2.55	1.30	29.32*
Public Organization (National)	3.22	1.37	0.0
Public Research Center (Non-University)	3.28	1.32	−2.09*
Service Company	2.68	1.46	18.81*
Technology Transfer Organization	3.42	1.52	−3.90*
University and Educational Organizations	3.14	1.30	4.75*

* Statistically significant at the 5% level.

190

service companies – are involved in fewer fields of science. The t-statistics for testing the null hypothesis of equality of means across the different types of organizations are shown in the last column of Table 7. The only organizational type for which the mean number of technologies is not statistically significantly different from the others is national laboratories.

The regressions include complete sets of technology field and country dummies, so the coefficients indicate the degree of complementarity between different pairs of public and private organizational types. The country dummies control for all country characteristics that do not vary across fields, such as country size, national R&D budget, public sector employment, and engineering school graduation rates. The regressions are of the form

$$
(1) \qquad \begin{aligned} \text{N\_PRIV}_{ij} &= \beta_1\, \text{N\_PubOrg}_{ij} + \beta_2\, \text{N\_PubRes}_{ij} \\ &\quad + \beta_3\, \text{N\_TechTrans}_{ij} + \beta_4\, \text{N\_Univers}_{ij} + \delta_i + \gamma_j + u_{ij} \end{aligned}
$$

where N_PRIV_{ij} denotes the number of private organizations (consultancies, manufacturers, or service companies) in country i ($i = 1, ..., 38$) active in scientific field j ($j = 1, ..., 198$); N_PubOrg is the number of national public organizations; N_PubRes is the number of public research centers; N_TechTrans is the number of technology transfer organizations; and N_Univers is the number of universities. Significant positive β_k ($k = 1, 2, 3, 4$) coefficients indicate that if a country has an unexpectedly large number of public organizations active in a scientific field (given the size of the country and the field), it also tends to have an unexpectedly large number of private organizations in the field. Stated differently, positive coefficients signify that a country's private organizations tend to be concentrated (specialized) in the same scientific fields as its public organizations. Within each field, private and public organizations tend to be distributed across countries in similar ways.

Some of the coefficients are likely to be biased upwards due to the fact that multiple organization types are reported for some organizations. For example, 40 organizations described themselves as both consultancies and public organizations; one-sixth of public organizations also described themselves as consultancies. When we calculated the number of organizations by country, type, and field to compute the regressions, we "double-counted" organizations: an organization that was listed as both a consultancy and a public organization would be counted twice (in a given field), once as each type. Consultancy and Technology Transfer Organization are the two organization types most frequently involved when there are mutliple organization types, so the β_3 coefficient in the number-of-consultancies regression is most likely to be biased upwards. In contrast, manufacturers, service companies, public organizations, and universities are very infrequently "double counted", so we expect little, if any, bias in the corresponding coefficients.

Estimates of the parameters of eq. (1) are shown in Table 8. The coefficients on public organizations and universities in the manufacturers and service companies regressions are all positive and statistically significant. This indicates that a country's manufacturers and service companies tend to be specialized in the same scientific fields as its universities and public organizations. For example, if few or none of a nation's universities are active in a particular field of science, few or none of its firms are also likely to be active in that field.

TABLE 8

Complementarity Model – Regression Results.

Independent Variables	Dependent Variables		
	Consultancies	Manufacturers	Service Companies
Public Organizations	.093 (1.81)	.873 (3.79)	.333 (4.04)
Public Research Centers	−.046 (3.21)	.122 (1.90)	.220 (9.59)
Technology Transfer Organizations	1.21 (47.5)	1.23 (10.8)	.930 (22.7)
Universities	.071 (10.2)	.058 (1.85)	.050 (4.43)
R-squared	0.8320	0.3660	0.7030

Note: t-statistics in parentheses. All regressions include 198 technical field dummies and 38 country dummies and are based on a sample of 2401 observations.

The coefficients on public organizations are much larger than the coefficients on universities. This might mean that private-sector technological activity is more sensitive to activity in other public organizations than it is to university activity, which is expected to be more basic in orientation. On the other hand, the number of public organizations may be determined, in part, by the number of firms in the same country and scientific field. The might indicate that governments may be inclined to establish public organizations in technical fields in which their private sectors are already specialized. This argument could also apply, albeit perhaps not as strongly, to the establishment of university departments. Thus the data are highly consistent with the hypothesis of complementarity between a country's public and private technological orientation, but the causal mechanism underlying this is difficult to determine. Also, we would like to be able to test whether countries that have the "best matched" input combinations (*i.e.*, in which the distributions of public and private R&D across fields are most similar) are the most productive in terms of innovation. Data limitations make this infeasible, however: although we have indicators of innovative output (numbers of publications and research results), by country, we lack the corresponding country-level data on research inputs or expenditure necessary to make productivity comparisons.

192

4 Codifiability of R&D Outcomes and the Organization of R&D Programs

The endeavor to create useful knowledge is often uncertain and there are questions about how to best organize research programs to best advance scientific and commercial interests. Knowledge, rather than being a homogenous good, appears to vary in terms of tacitness or codifiability across different technologies and this affects the organization of the R&D program (Von Hipple [1994]). Knowledge with a low degree of tacitness may be easily standardized and codified and such knowledge may be easily transmitted via journal articles, project reports and prototypes and other tangible mediums. In contrast, tacit knowledge has a higher degree of uncertainty and the precise meaning is more interpretative and is not easily conveyed in a standardized medium. As a consequence, when the knowledge used in an R&D program is more tacit in nature, face to face interaction and communication are important, and we may expect that R&D programs are likely to be centralized both in terms of their administrative and geographic organization. That is, the more easily codified and articulated the knowledge is expected to be, the greater the degree of decentralization both in administrative and geographic organization.

Previous authors have argued that geographic centralization or localization facilitates the communication of knowledge in the invention process. Henderson [1994] suggested that centralized multi-disciplinary teams are an efficient means for individual companies to organize R&D programs when technology is not standardized. Jaffe, Henderson and Trajtenberg [1993] find that patent citations are more frequently attributed to the state where the patent originated. Similarly, Audretsch and Feldman [1994] find a higher propensity for innovation to cluster geographically in industries where new knowledge plays a more important role. Zucker, Darby and Armstrong [1994] reported that biotechnology firms tend to locate near the "star" researchers that generate new and rapidly evolving commercially relevant knowledge. The consensus is that tacit knowledge that is not codified and easily transferable creates incentives for organizations to locate near one another. Indeed, if knowledge is published or easily licensed it may be disseminated at great distance. In contrast, the more tacit the knowledge produced by R&D programs, the greater the tendency for geographic concentration.

Although previous investigators have hypothesized that tacitness encourages geographic and administrative concentration, there have been few attempts in the literature to measure tacitness. Fortunately, several indicators of the degree of tacitness of European Community RTD programs can be derived from the CORDIS databases. Some projects result in prototypes that might be easily transferred while others result in know-how that is novel and less able to be transmitted. Other outcomes, such as technical reports or new processes, move along the tacitness continuum by being more easily transferred but still requiring some face-to-face collaboration before the results may be adopted.

In this section, we characterize technologies as to their degree of codifiability and then analyze the relationship of this attribute to the degree of administrative and geographic centralization. We expect that programs that rely on tacit knowledge will be more administratively centralized and encompass fewer unique and separate projects. We also expect that, the more difficult knowledge is to codify, the greater the degree of geographic concentration.

It may be worth emphasizing that the unit of observation that we will analyze below—an R&D *program* (which is pursued in a number of coordinated but distinct R&D *projects*, often conducted in a number of *countries*)—is not the same as the unit of observation in the preceding analysis (e.g., a particular field of science in a particular country). In principle, it might be desirable to include scientific "field effects" in the models of R&D program decentralization that we estimate below. There may be much greater scale economies (e.g., due to indivisibilities of research equipment) in certain fields of research (nuclear engineering) than in other fields (artificial intelligence), encouraging more centralized research in the former. Unfortunately, the number of programs for which we have sufficient data is small relative to the number of scientific fields, rendering inclusion of field effects impractical [12]. However, provided that research scale economies (or other unobserved determinants of centralization) are uncorrelated with our measures of tacitness, which does not seem unreasonable, the absence of field effects does not undermine the validity of our hypothesis tests.

To test the effect of the articulability of research outcomes on the organization of R&D programs, we will use data from several related (European) Community Research and Development Information Service (CORDIS) databases: the RTD-Programmes, -Projects, -Publications, and -Results databases. Below we describe key aspects of these databases and the measures that we constructed from them.

The RTD-Programmes Database is fundamental to the CORDIS service and to our analysis. The program is the major instrument through which the European Commission pursues and finances Community policy on Research and Technological Development, fulfilling the objectives of the Single European Act. (The term "program" is used in a broad sense to designate Community initiatives and actions under which individual projects or activities are carried out, usually through contractual agreements placed with outside organizations.)

This database provides a starting point to relate information from the other databases. It contains details of Community RTD-Programmes and provides references to additional sources where the user can obtain further information if required. Each record includes various descriptive fields that

---

12. It is also infeasible to perform the analysis with the *project* as the unit of analysis, since we cannot construct meaningful measures of either decentralization or tacitness at the project level.

give the program objectives, its internal structure and key references. Much of this information is derived from the Official Journal of the European Communities.

We obtained information on two program attributes from the RTD-Programs database: Program Funding (in millions of European Currency Units (ECUs)), and Number of Projects—the number of projects under the program listed in the RTD-Projects Database (described below). Using these two variables (denoted FUND and N_PROJ, respectively), we can judge how administratively decentralized an R&D program is: holding program funding constant, the greater the number of projects, the more decentralized the program. Average funding per project is an inverse indicator of the degree of decentralization.

The data contained in the RTD-Projects Database also enable us to determine how geographically decentralized each program is. This database contains details of individual RTD projects financed wholly or partly from the budget of the European Communities. These projects are normally implemented through contractual agreements placed by the European Commission with commercial organizations, research institutes, universities, or other bodies. Such projects operate within the structure of a specific Commission programme, details of which are contained in the RTD-Programmes Database. The record for each project contains a country code for the prime contractor's country. For each program, we calculated the distribution of projects, by country. We computed two summary indicators of program decentralization from this distribution: the number of countries in which (any) prime contractors were located, and an inverse Herfindahl index (INV_HERF) of geographic concentration. INV_HERF was constructed as follows:

$$(2) \qquad \mathrm{INV\_HERF}_j = [\Sigma_i \, (N_{ij}/N_{.j})^2]^{-1}$$

where N_{ij} = the number of program j's projects located in country i and $N_{.j} = \Sigma_i N_{ij}$ = the total number of projects in program j. The more geographically decentralized a program, the larger the value for both of these indicators.

The last two databases provide information about published or announced outcomes of R&D programs. We use these data to derive indicators of the degree of articulability of the knowledge the program yielded. The RTD-Publications Database provides references containing bibliographic details and abstracts of publications and other documents resulting from EC RTD. Cited publications are: (1) EUR reports, which include: scientific and technical studies; monographs; proceedings of conferences; workshops and contractors' meetings organized by the European Commission; and various reports resulting from the research; (2) other reports and documents produced by the Commission relating to Community RTD activities; and (3) articles and conference papers relevant to the Commission's research activities. If the publication exists in more than one Community language, the citation is usually given for the English language version. The availability of the publication in other Community languages is also indicated. The database contains records dating from 1962. From 1990 onwards, record contents are consistent with other CORDIS databases. Entries made after 1990 enable a publication to be related to a given program via the program acronym. We calculated the number of publications (N_PUB) associated with each program.

The RTD-Results Database contains information about the results of R&D in science, technology and medicine. The information comes from public and private sector organizations, regardless of the funding sources. Entries in this database are comprehensive, providing information about the research result, the contributing organization, type of collaboration sought, the availability of a prototype, the commercial potential, the contact point information, and other details. Records can be identified by program acronym, the type and location of the contributing organization and other details. Each result is classified into one of the following two type categories: (1) process, prototype; or (2) methodology, skill, know-how. For each program we calculated the number of type-1 (process, prototype) results (N_RSLT1), the number of type-2 (methodology, skill, know-how) results (N_RSLT2), the total number of results (N_RSLT=N_RSLT1+N_RSLT2). We also calculate the share of type-1 results in total results (SHR_RSLT1=N_RSLT1/N_RSLT).

We believe that the number of publications and the number and type of announced results of a program are reasonable indicators of the degree of articulability of the knowledge it generated. Holding constant program funding, the greater the number of publications or the number of announced results, the greater the degree of articulability of the knowledge. Since we hypothesize that programs that are expected to generate knowledge that is easier to articulate and communicate will be more decentralized (geographically and administratively), this suggests that, holding funding constant, programs that yield more publications or announced results will be more decentralized. We can test this by estimating models of the form

$$(3) \qquad \ln Y = \Pi_0 + \Pi_1 \ln \text{FUND} + \Pi_2 \ln X + \varepsilon$$

where Y is a measure of program decentralization (N_CTY,INV_HERF, or N_PROJ), X is the number of results or the number of publications, and ε is a disturbance. Positive and statistically significant estimates of Π_2 would be consistent with our hypothesis.

We believe that, conditional on funding, a larger number of results signals that the knowledge generated by a program is more articulable, but certain types of results may indicate more articulability than others. In particular, we hypothesize that type-1 results, which announce the existence of a process or prototype, indicate a higher degree of articulability than type-2 results, which merely announce the acquisition of "skill, methodology, or know-how". We can test for this by generalizing the above model as follows:

$$(4) \quad \ln Y = \Pi_0 + \Pi_1 \ln \text{FUND} + \Pi_2 \ln \left[(1+\theta) \, \text{N\_RSLT1} + \text{N\_RSLT2} \right] + \varepsilon$$

This model allows changes in N_RSLT1 and N_RSLT2 to have different marginal effects on Y. Positive and significant estimates of θ would be consistent with the hypothesis that type-1 results indicate a higher degree of articulability. (In the preceding model, θ was implicitly constrained to

196

equal zero.) This equation is nonlinear in the parameters, but it can be approximated by the linear equation

$$(5) \quad \ln Y = \Pi_0 + \Pi_1 \ln FUND + \Pi_2 \ln N\_RSLT + (\theta \Pi_2) SHR\_RSLT1 + \varepsilon$$
$$= \Pi_0 + \Pi_1 \ln FUND + \Pi_2 \ln N\_RSLT + \theta' SHR\_RSLT1 + \varepsilon$$

where $\theta' = (\theta \Pi_2)$. We expect program decentralization to be increasing with respect to both the total number of announced results and the fraction of those results that are type-1 results, controlling for funding.

An equivalent way of expressing the last equation is

$$(6) \quad \ln Y = \Pi_0 + (\Pi_1 + \Pi_2) \ln FUND + \Pi_2 \ln (N\_RSLT/FUND)$$
$$+ \theta' SHR\_RSLT1 + \varepsilon$$

Only the coefficient on ln FUND is affected by this transformation, not the coefficients on the other regressors, which are of primary interest. The coefficient on ln FUND captures the "pure" effect (if any) of program "scale" on decentralization, since FUND and N_RSLT may be regarded as alternative possible measures of program scale. The other coefficients capture the effects of articulability on decentralization, given scale. We estimate equations of this form.

Estimates of eq. (6) are presented in Table 9. In the regression shown in the first column, the measure of decentralization (the dependent variable) is the log of the number of countries in which prime contractors are located. The coefficients on both indicators of articulability – the log of the number of announced results per unit of funding and the fraction of those results that were type-1 results – are positive and significantly different from zero. The coefficient on the program scale variable, the log of funding, is positive but only marginally significant. R&D programs that generated above-average numbers of results per unit of funding tended to be more geographically decentralized; this is consistent with our hypothesis that greater (expected) ability to communicate research outcomes encourages less centralized R&D programs. We can obtain a point estimate of the "excess" impact on decentralization of type-1 results relative to type-2 results by dividing the coefficient on SHR_RSLT1 ($\theta' = \theta \Pi_2$) by the coefficient on ln (N_RSLT/FUND) (Π_2). This implies that $\theta = .554/.124 = 4.47$, and $(1 + \theta) = 5.47$: one additional type-1 result is associated with 5.5 times as great an increase in decentralization as one additional type-2 result. Programs that yield processes and prototypes are much less centralized than programs that yield the less-well articulated "methodology, skill, and know-how".

Col. (2) presents estimates of an equation with the same regressors but with our alternative measure of geographic decentralization – the inverse Herfindahl index – as the dependent variable. The estimates are somewhat smaller in magnitude and somewhat less significant, but qualitatively very similar.

Col. (3) presents estimates where we replace one of the measures of the degree of knowledge articulation – results reported in the RTD-Results

TABLE 9

Tacitness Model Regression Results (t-statistics in parentheses).

Dependent Variable:	*In* N_CTY	*In* (Inv-Herf)	*In* (Inv-Herf)	*In* N_PROJ
$In \dfrac{(N\_RSLTS)}{(FUND)}$	0.124 (3.54)	0.093 (3.23)		0.174 (2.35)
$In \dfrac{(N\_PUBS)}{(FUND)}$			0.81 (2.39)	
Shr (Results 1)	0.554 (2.66)	0.313 (1.83)	0.405 (2.14)	0.662 (1.50)
In (FUND)	0.090 (1.65)	0.061 (1.37)	0.038 (0.83)	0.488 (4.24)
Intercept	1.806 (7.87)	1.450 (7.65)	1.470 (7.33)	2.515 (5.21)
N	77	77	73	79
R^2	.2075	.1545	.1088	.2302

Note: t-statistics in parentheses.

database per unit of funding – with an alternative measure: publications reported in the RTD-Publications database per unit of funding. The coefficients of the publications variable and the result-share variable are both positive and significant, again consistent with the notion that articulability promotes geographic decentralization.

The dependent variable in the last equation, shown in col. 4, is the log of the number of projects comprising the program, which we have argued is an indicator of the degree of administrative decentralization. Like the geographic decentralization measures, it is highly positively correlated with log (N_RSLT/FUND); unlike them, it is also highly correlated with program funding, and its partial correlation with the results share variable is only marginally significant.

5 Summary and Conclusion

Some previous studies have suggested that public and private R&D organizations may complement one another. We explored the relationship between private and public research investment within the same country and technological areas, by estimating regressions of the number of consultancies, manufacturers, and service companies (which are predominantly private-sector organizations) on the number of public research centers, technology transfer organizations, and universities, by country and scientific field. The estimates indicate that a country's manufacturers and service companies tend to be specialized in the same scientific fields as its universities and public organizations. The data are also consistent with the hypothesis that private-sector technological activity is more sensitive to activity in non-university public organizations than it is to university activity. The causal mechanism underlying the observed correlations between public and private research is, however, difficult to determine.

Previous investigators have hypothesized that the extent of geographic and administrative decentralization of R&D activities is greater, the less tacit (or more codifiable) the knowledge generated by the R&D is expected to be. But this hypothesis has not been tested formally due to inability to measure tacitness (or codifiability). We constructed several indicators of the degree of R&D decentralization and tacitness of European Community RTD programs from data contained in the CORDIS databases. The number of countries in which an R&D program is conducted – controlling for total program funding – is an indicator of geographic decentralization, and the number of distinct projects into which a program is subdivided is an indicator of administrative decentralization. The number of publications and the number and type of announced results of a program – again controlling for program funding – are reasonable indicators of the degree of codifiability (or articulability) of the knowledge it generated. The estimates are consistent with the hypothesis that greater (expected) ability to communicate research outcomes encourages less centralized R&D programs. R&D programs that generated above-average numbers of results per unit of funding tended to be more geographically decentralized. Moreover, programs that yield (relatively tangible) processes and prototypes are much less centralized than programs that yield the less-well articulated "methodology, skill, and know-how".

● References

ACS, ZOLTAN J., DAVID B. AUDRETSCH, MARYANN P. FELDMAN (1992). – "Real Effects of Academic Research: Comment", *American Economic Review*, 82(1), pp. 363-367.

ACS, ZOLTAN J., DAVID B. AUDRETSCH, MARYANN P. FELDMAN (1994). – "R&D Spillovers and Recipient Firm Size", *Review of Economics and Statistics*, 76, (2), pp. 336-340.

ADAMS, J. (1990). – "Fundamental Stocks of Knowledge and Productivity Growth", *Journal of Political Economy*, 98, pp. 673-702.

ADAMS, James, GRILICHES, Z. (1996). – "Measuring Science: An Exploration", *Working Paper #5478, National Bureau of Economic Research*.

ARCHIBUGI, D., PIANTA, M. (1992). – "The Technological Specialization of Advanced Countries", Boston: Kluwer Academic Publishers.

AUDRETSCH, D. B., FELDMAN, M. P. (1996). – "R&D Spillovers and the Geography of Innovation and Production", *American Economic Review*, 86, pp. 630-640.

COHEN, W., FLORIDA, R., GOE, W. R. (1994). – "University-Industry Research Centers", Pittsburgh: Carnegie Mellon University.

FELDMAN, M. P., FLORIDA, R. (1994). – "The Geographic Sources of Innovation: Technological Infrastructure and Product Innovation in the United States", *Annals of the Association of American Geographers*, 84, pp. 210-229.

HENDERSON, REBECCA (1994). – "Managing Innovation in the Information Age", *Harvard Business Review*, 72, pp. 100-5.

JAFFE, Adam B. (1989). – "Real Effects of Academic Research", *American Economic Review*, 79, (5), pp. 957-970.

JAFFE, Adam B., TAJTENBERG, M., HENDERSON, R. (1993). – "Geographic Localization of Knowledge Spillovers as Evidenced by Patent Citations", *Quarterly Journal of Economics*, 63, (3), pp. 577-598.

LEVIN, R. C., KLEVORICK, A. K., NELSON, R. R., WINTER, S. G. (1987). – "Appropriating the Returns from Industrial Research and Development", *Brookings Papers on Economic Activity*, pp. 783-820.

LICHTENBERG, F. (1988). – "The Private R&D Investment Response to Federal Design and Technical Competitions", *American Economic Review*, 78, (3), pp. 550-9.

LICHTENBERG, F. (1987). – "The Effect of Government Funding on Private Industrial Research and Development: A Re-Assessment", *Journal of Industrial Economics*, 36, (1).

LICHTENBERG, F. (1984). – "The Relationship Between Federal Contract R&D and Company R&D", *American Economic Review*, 74, (2).

MANSFIELD, E. (1995). – "Academic Research Underlying Industrial Innovations: Sources, Characteristics, and Financing", *The Review of Economics and Statistics*, 77, pp. 55-65.

National Science Board (1996). – *Science and Engineering Indicators*, Washington, D.C.: Government Printing Office.

PORTER, M. (1990). – *The Competitive Advantage of Nations*, New York: Free Press.

Von HIPPLE, E. (1994). – "Sticky Information and the Locus of Problem Solving: Implications for Innovation", *Management Science*, 40, pp. 429-439.

ZUCKER, L., DARBY, M., ARMSTRONG, J. (1994). – "Intellectual Capital and the Firm: The Technology of Geographically Localized Knowledge Spillovers", *Working Paper #4946*, National Bureau of Economic Research, Cambridge, MA.

200

The Enforcement of Intellectual Property Rights: A Survey of the Empirical Literature

Jean O. LANJOUW, Josh LERNER*

ABSTRACT. – This paper examines several recent avenues of empirical research into the enforcement of intellectual property rights. To frame these issues, we start with a stylized model of the patent litigation process. The bulk of the paper is devoted to linking the empirical literature on patent litigation to the parameters of this model. The four major areas we consider are (i) how the propensity to litigate patents varies with the expected benefits of litigation, (ii) the ways in which the cost of litigation affects the willingness to enforce patents, (iii) how the cost of enforcing patents changes the private value of patent rights, and (iv) the impact of intellectual property litigation on the innovation process itself.

* J.O. LANJOUW: Yale University, NBER. J. LERNER: Havard Business School, NBER. We would like to thank Joel WALDFOGEL and an anonymous referee for useful comments on an earlier draft.

D. Encaoua et al. (eds.), The Economics and Econometrics of Innovation, 201–224.

1 Introduction

The enforcement of intellectual property rights (IPRs) – and the threat of enforcement – are of primary importance to those engaged in innovative activities. Understanding enforcement issues is thus crucial to the design of patent law. Only recently, however, has the legal environment entered into analyses of the patent system and of the relationship between IPRs and economic decisions regarding levels of research and development (R&D) spending, trade, foreign direct investment, and so on. This paper surveys the currently available empirical literature on patent litigation.

Patent owners often turn to the courts to resolve disputes. LANJOUW and SCHANKERMAN [1997] estimate that U.S. patents from the early 1980's will, by the time they expire, generate more than one suit for every hundred patents. The legal costs incurred by patentees in defending their rights through the courts appear to be substantial and increasing. Indicative are the several new financial products that seek to address patent litigation costs. Refac Corporation (New York, New York) and the Intellectual Property Reserve Corporation (Lexington, Kentucky), for instance, allow investors to buy part-ownership in patents solely for the purpose of litigating them. There is also a nascent patent enforcement insurance market (HOFMANN, [1995]). These markets to date, however, have not been well developed. It is likely that their development is handicapped by the severe information asymmetries (and consequent moral hazard problems) that characterize intellectual property: the party that develops the patent is likely to have far greater knowledge of the relevant prior art than the firm that purchases a part-interest in the patent or sells an insurance policy.

This is an important set of issues. As we discuss below, the need to defend patents through costly litigation can have a significant impact on their value. For firms whose primary assets are their intangible knowledge capital, the shift in value can be substantial. Perhaps the most direct evidence is from event studies of the change in firm value upon the filing of litigation. BHAGAT, BRICKLEY, and COLES [1994] examine the market reaction to the filing of 20 patent infringement suits reported in *The Wall Street Journal* during the 1981-1983 period. They find that in the two-day window ending on the day the story appeared in the *Journal*, the combined market-adjusted value of the firms fell by an average of −3.1% (significant at the 0.01 level). LERNER [1995a], using data on 26 patent suits between biotechnology firms, finds an average fall of −2.0% (again significant at the 0.01 level). This represents a median loss of shareholder wealth of $20 million. There is also evidence that the cost of litigation falls most heavily on small firms. If a defendant is unable to raise capital to finance the litigation through the external capital markets, he may be forced to settle the dispute, no matter what the ultimate merits of his case. This asymmetry is particularly troublesome in the context of patent litigation, where studies suggest that small firms are disproportionately innovative (ACS and AUDRETSCH, [1988]).

A rapidly growing theoretical literature in law and economics examines the process of dispute resolution through the courts. This literature highlights several features as affecting the probability of litigation. Among these are: the size of, and asymmetries in, the returns to the parties from litigation, or the 'stakes'; uncertainty, or asymmetric information, about case quality; and the costs of litigation and settlement. In order to give a framework to our discussion of the empirical studies, we begin in Section 2 by outlining a simple model based on this literature and then extend it to capture features specific to patent litigation. In Section 3, we discuss the empirical studies of patent litigation and link the results of these studies to the model parameters. Section 4 presents empirical simulation results, which show the size of the effect of various legal policy reforms on the incentives generated by the patent system. In Section 5 we look at evidence of how patent enforcement concerns shape R&D and foreign investment decisions. Section 6 concludes.

2 The Dispute Process

We begin by outlining a very stylized model, which allows us to characterize those filed cases which will settle and those which will go to trial. We then consider a potential plaintiff's decision whether to file a suit and the potential defendant's decision of whether to avoid harm. The purpose of this modelling is to bring together the various empirical results in a unified way.

Consider a situation where a plaintiff claims to have been damaged by a defendant and has filed a suit to obtain compensation. Whether the parties end up in court depends on the returns that they expect from litigating (the trial value of the game) relative to those they can obtain from cooperation. We specify each in turn. The plaintiff's threat point in pre-trial bargaining is his expected payoff should he go to trial. This is composed of his expected returns, which are equal to the income he can attain given the damage he has incurred, Y, plus the value of the court-awarded judgment, J, times his expectation of winning the case, W[1]. It is net of the legal costs associated with a trial, L[2]:

$$(1) \qquad\qquad Y + WJ - L.$$

(Throughout, plaintiff values shall be denoted by uppercase letters, defendant values by lowercase letters.) The threat point for the defendant is similarly the payoff that he expects should he be taken to trial. It is determined

---

1. Expected income may represent net profit, if the party is a firm, or, if the party is an individual, personal income. More generally it is the expected utility of the party in monetary units.
2. Throughout, we assume that legal costs are exogenous. In a richer model, the choice of investment in legal services by each party would be determined in a final stage of the game. The levels chosen would depend on the function mapping expenditures by each party to court rulings (see Cooter and Rubinfeld, [1989]).

by the level of income he expects given the harm that he has imposed on the plaintiff, y, minus the amount that he expects to pay if the plaintiff wins, j, times the defendant's expectation of paying, w, and again net of legal costs, l:

$$(2) \qquad y - wj - l.$$

The sum of these two threat values represents the trial (non-cooperative) value of the game.

We assume that the costs associated with settlement are negligible. Suppose first that all that is at issue in the dispute is the amount of a transfer to be given by the defendant to the plaintiff (the stakes in the case are symmetric, $J = j$). The settlement (cooperative) value of the game is simply $Y + y$ plus the size of the net transfer, which here is zero. The perceived surplus available from settling rather than going to court is then:

$$(3) \qquad -j(W - w) + (L + l).$$

If the parties reach a settlement whenever the surplus is positive, it follows that they settle whenever

$$(4) \qquad j(W - w) \le (L + l).$$

Equation (4) highlights the importance of similarity in the views that the parties hold regarding likely court outcomes. In particular, if the subjective assessments of the probability that the plaintiff will win coincide, as they would with perfect information, parties will *always* settle. It follows that one explanation for trials is that parties sometimes have divergent views about the quality of the case being brought and, in particular, the plaintiff may view his case more favorably than the defendant does, i.e., $W > w$. If the plaintiff is sufficiently more optimistic about his chances, the cooperative surplus will disappear and the parties will go to the court[3]. Equation (4) also highlights the importance of the size of the stakes and the size of legal costs in determining litigation. As stakes increase, and costs fall, the likelihood of litigation increases.

Trials may also arise because the stakes in the case are not symmetric (a feature discussed further below). Suppose that $J = \alpha j$. The parties will settle then if:

$$(5) \qquad j(\alpha W - w) \le (L + l).$$

---

3. There is a long tradition in the law and economics literature exploring selection in dispute resolution, beginning with PRIEST and KLEIN [1984]. In their model, imperfect assessments of case quality by both parties lead to divergent expectations about win probabilities and, as a result, trials occur (see below).

If α is sufficiently greater than one, so that the plaintiff views the returns to winning a trial as very high relative to the judgment paid by the defendant, the cooperative surplus may disappear even when the parties agree about the quality of the case (i.e., when $w = W$)[4].

When the parties have asymmetric information, equilibrium strategies may entail positive probabilities of trial even where the cooperative surplus is positive. For example, BEBCHUK [1984] and PNG [1983] show that, when there is asymmetric information, the parties may make unacceptable settlement offers with positive probability as a signalling device, and this probability (and thus the likelihood of trial) rises with the degree of asymmetry. SPIER and SPULBER [1993] show that when the plaintiff has private information about case quality and the defendant about damages, the likelihood of trial falls in the accuracy of information.

Finally, there may not be a cooperative surplus in patent disputes for a reason more specific to intellectual property. The purpose of patent protection is to restrict output in order to generate (monopoly) profits, say V_1, to reward inventors. An important feature of patent litigation is that the subject of the dispute, industry profits, changes value depending on whether the parties settle, and, if they go to trial, on what the outcome is (this point is noted in MEURER, [1989]). Licensing limitations (because of antitrust policy or transactions costs) may prevent the patentee plaintiff and the infringer from restricting output in a settlement agreement to the monopoly level. Thus industry profits with a settlement, V_s, may be less than V_1. Litigation often involves attempts on the part of the infringing firm to have the patent sharply narrowed or revoked entirely. If successful, both firms may use the innovation without restraint and total profits fall to the duopoly level, V_2, again less than V_1.

To see how this special feature of patent litigation affects the decision to file cases and to litigate, we consider the threat points of the parties (equations 1 and 2) and the cooperative surplus (3) in this more specific setting. We make the following set of restrictive assumptions to more easily illustrate the point. A trial takes one year and the disputed patent remains valuable for m years after the trial if the patentee wins. Further, assume that if both parties use the innovation in the absence of a settlement, they each obtain $(1/2)V_2$. Let $W = w$ and assume that the discount rate is zero. j is the damage payment from the infringer to the patentee if the patentee wins the suit. Then the threat points may be written:

(6) $$(1/2)V_2 + m[wV_1 + (1 - w)(1/2)V_2] + wj - L$$

for the patentee and

(7) $$(1/2)V_2 + (1 - w)m(1/2)V_2 - wj - l.$$

---

4. α may be less than one. This means that the defendant is "paying" more than the plaintiff receives. This may be in actual costs if there is a third party to the transfer. It may also be because the defendant is more sensitive than the plaintiff to reputational concerns (see below).

for the infringer. The first two terms in (6) and (7) are expected income, Y and y, respectively. They are the parties' profits during the year of the trial plus expected returns over the m years after the trial. The sum of (6) and (7) is the non-cooperative value of the game.

The cooperative (settlement) value to the two parties is simply $(1 + m)V_2$. Thus the cooperative surplus, the difference between the value with settlement and that with trial, is:

$$(8) \qquad (V_s + V_2) + m\{V_s - [(1 - w)V_2 + wV_1]\} + (L + l).$$

The first term is the benefit of cooperation during the year of trial and it is always non-negative, as is the savings in legal costs. The second term, however, may be negative. If monopoly profits are substantially greater than those which may be obtained through licensing, and, in particular, if there is a long future, patentees may go to trial in order to maintain output restrictions.

To complete the story, we return to a general setting and move back a step in the dispute process, extending the model to consider when a *potential* plaintiff will decide to file a suit, and, moving back even further, the extent to which *potential* defendants will invest in avoiding harm in the first place. Suppose that if a suit is filed and a settlement is reached, the share of the cooperative surplus obtained by the plaintiff is θ and that obtained by the defendant, $1-\theta$[5]. Then the payoff that the potential plaintiff expects from filing a claim is:

$$(9) \qquad (Y + W\alpha j - L) + \text{Max}\{0, \theta[(L + l) - j(W\alpha - w)]\}.$$

If the cooperative surplus (the term in square brackets) is negative, the case will go to trial and the plaintiff expects a threat point payoff (the first term only). If the cooperative surplus is positive, the case will settle and he receives, in addition, a share of the surplus[6]. Similarly, the expected payoff to the defendant if a claim is filed is:

$$(10) \qquad (y - wj - l) + \text{Max}\{0, (1 - \theta)[(L + l) - j(W\alpha - w)]\}$$

These equations determine the extent to which the potential defendant will expend resources to avoid harm. If the plaintiff's return to filing a suit (equation 9) is negative, then the defendant can act without fear of being taken to court. If the plaintiff will respond to being harmed, the defendant

---

5. For example, with a Nash bargaining solution $\theta = 1/2$. If one of the parties can make a take-it-or-leave-it settlement offer, that party obtains the full cooperative surplus ($\theta = 1$ or 0), leaving the other with a threat point payoff.

6. Settlement may occur before a case is actually filed.

must balance his expected payoff if he harms the plaintiff (equation 10) with his payoff if he avoids conflict, including the costs of care[7].

3 Empirical Evidence

This section brings together empirical evidence from patent litigation regarding the various features of dispute resolution highlighted above. The first set of studies gives some insights into the magnitude of parameters that affect the expected benefits of litigation. The second set is concerned primarily with the economic effects of litigation costs, in particular, the fact that large legal costs may be an obstacle to the success of small, high-tech companies.

• Evidence Regarding the Expected Benefits of Litigation

Following PRIEST and KLEIN [1984], SIEGELMAN and WALDFOGEL [1996] model the subjective win probabilities, W and w, as follows (see also WALDFOGEL, [1995]). Consider first the plaintiff. He has an assessment of the quality of his case, say q, which is equal to the true quality of the case, q^*, plus a normally distributed, mean zero, error term: $q = q^* + \varepsilon$. The case will win at trial if the true case quality is greater than some threshold decision standard, D. Thus,

$$W = \text{Prob}(q^* > D|q)$$

or

(11) $$W = \Phi[(q - D)/\sigma_\varepsilon],$$

where $\Phi[]$ represents a cumulative standard normal distribution. w is determined analogously. To estimate the model, they assume, first, that legal fees are a constant proportion of the size of the case: $[(L + l)/j] = (1/3)$; second, that true case qualities are normally distributed $\phi(0, 1)$; and, finally, that the assessment errors, ε, of the plaintiff and defendant are independent. The value of a case, j, plays no role in explaining trials in this model because the first assumption ensures that differences in legal costs exactly offset any differences in value.

---

7. In the case of patent disputes, the cost of avoiding harm would include maintaining an awareness of patenting activity by others and tailoring production or research activities to prevent conflicts (see below). ORDOVER [1978], PNG [1987], and HYLTON [1990] are some of the studies of deterrence and the costs of care in other settings.

They estimate the model using data on cases initiated in the District Court for the Southern District of New York after 1979 and resolved by 1989. The estimation is done separately for six types of civil cases: IPRs (which includes patent, trademarks, copyright), civil rights, contracts, labor, prisoner, and torts. They find that IPR cases have the lowest uncertainty parameter, σ_ε. That is, the parties in IPR cases have a relatively precise assessment of the quality of their cases. There are a number of reasons to expect such a finding. Compared to other types of cases, IPR disputes are fairly homogeneous. Patent cases are tried by a specialized bar. In addition, in 1982 a new U.S. Court of Appeals for the Federal Circuit, CAFC, was established to hear all patent appeals precisely in order to make rulings in these complex cases more consistent and predictable.

Although uncertainty seems to be lower in patent disputes than in other types of civil disputes, more detailed data suggests that there is variation among types of patents. One might expect more uncertainty about case quality in new technology areas where there is little precedence to guide assessments of infringement and patent validity. Comparing the litigation rate for patents protecting innovations in the relatively new area of biotechnology with the litigation rates for patents in other areas of technology, the results are consistent with the idea that uncertainty impedes settlement. Based on a sample of 530 new biotechnology firms, LERNER [1995b] estimates that as many as six cases will be generated per hundred U.S. corporate biotechnology patents. This figure was obtained by dividing the number of patent suits in which the sampled firms were involved in Massachusetts during January 1990-June 1994 by the number of patents they were awarded during that period. In constrast, as noted in the introduction, LANJOUW and SCHANKERMAN [1997] estimate that there will be about one case generated per hundred U.S. patents from the early 1980's. By technology group, their litigation rates varied from a low of 0.5 cases per hundred for chemical patents to a high of two cases per hundred for drug and health patents. These estimates are based on comprehensive data on Federal Court filings available from the Inter-university Consortium for Political and Social Research (Federal Judicial Center, 1991) matched to patent data using the Patent History CD-ROM produced by Derwent. The estimate is calculated using actual case filings for the cohorts in question. Even allowing for differences in data and in the estimation method across the two studies, the litigation rate appears to be substantially higher in the area of biotechnology, an area with relatively little prior litigation to help guide expectations.

Turning to the decision standard, D, SIEGELMAN and WALDFOGEL [1996] find that IPR cases are subject to the second lowest decision standard among their six types of civil suits, higher only than contracts. Their estimate of $D = 0.38$ implies a relatively high win probability of 35% for the plaintiff in filed cases. Their estimate is for the entire period, 1979 through 1989. Anecdotal evidence, however, suggests also that the decision standard fell over the past decade. With the establishment of the specialized federal appeals court, courts have become more "pro-patent," enforcing the statutory presumption that "a patent is born valid and remains valid until

208

a challenger proves it was stillborn or had birth defects" (Judge Markey, *Roper Corp.* vs. *Litton Systems, Inc.*, 757 F2d 1266 Federal Circuit 1993)[8].

The model outlined above implies that, if there was, in fact, a fall in the stringency of the decision standard, D, applied in patent cases, there should be a larger proportion of filed cases going to trial and a higher observed win rate in later years[9]. Further, given a dispute, patentees should have become increasingly likely to file cases because of an increase in their expected probability of winning, W (equations 9 and 11). These predictions seem to have been borne out. Plaintiff win rates at trial increased from an average of 61% in the years just before the establishment of the new court to 75% by 1987 (in conjunction with a 50% increase in the number of cases tried). Between 1953 and 1978, circuit courts affirmed 62% of district court decisions holding patents to be valid and infringed, and reversed 12% of the decisions holding patents to be invalid or not infringed (KOENIG, [1980]). In the years 1982-1990, the CAFC affirmed 90% of district court decisions holding patents to be valid and infringed, and reversed 28% of the judgments of invalidity or non-infringement (MERGES, [1992]). Aggregate evidence regarding the proportion of patent disputes leading to filed cases is not available[10]. Again, however, anecdotal evidence suggests that filings are becoming more frequent. For example, several firms have begun aggressively litigating patents awarded in the late 1970s, filing cases for infringement disputes that the patent-holders previously did not consider worth the time and costs of prosecution. Several companies, including Texas Instruments, Intel, Wang Laboratories, and Digital Equipment, have established groups that approach rivals to demand royalties on old patent awards. In many cases, they have been successful in extracting license agreements and/or past royalties. Texas Instruments, for instance, is estimated to have netted $257 million in 1991 from patent licenses and settlements because of its general counsel's aggressive enforcement policy (ROSEN, [1992]).

It should be emphasized that the probability that the patentee will prevail in 35% of the IPR cases, implied by the estimate of $D = 0.38$, is *unconditional* on the case going to trial but conditional on filing. WALDFOGEL [1996] presents empirical evidence using data on U.S. patent litigation which suggests that the probability of plaintiff success unconditional on filing is substantially higher. He makes use of the idea that win proportions will more closely reflect the underlying win probability if there is a great deal of uncertainty and approach 50% as uncertainty is resolved (PRIEST and KLEIN,

---

8. Other important policy changes include instituting renewal fees for patents in 1982 and, as a result of the TRIPs agreement of GATT, a lengthening of the average statutory patent term from 17 years following the date of issue to 20 years from the date of filing.

9. The trial rate increases until $D = 0$. It decreases as D falls further.

10. Certainly, patent applications and awards to U.S. applicants have increased dramatically. For an analysis, see KORTUM and LERNER [1997].

[1984]). He finds that when adjudication occurs within three months, the win proportion in favor of the patentee is 84%, whereas it is only 61% for cases completed after more than a year[11]. If the timing of adjudication is exogenous and parties gain information over time, the outcomes of cases adjudicated early more closely reflect the average probability of plaintiff success among all patent disputes.

Another finding in the study by SIEGELMAN and WALDFOGEL [1996] is that IPR cases are characterized by a substantial degree of stake asymmetry. Their estimate of the asymmetry parameter is $\alpha = 1.77$. What are the possible sources of systematically higher stakes for the plaintiff? One explanation is that disputes are not one-off events. Either party may anticipate other potential conflicts. Winning a case may generate reputational benefits in addition to net current payments. If plaintiffs are more likely than defendants to be repeat players, their stakes will be higher. Siegelman and Waldfogel present two indicators of the extent to which reputation might be important to the plaintiff. The first is the ratio of the percentage of cases with an institutional (non-individual) plaintiff to the percentage with an institutional defendant. Since most IPR cases involve firms, the ratio is close to one. Only contract cases have a higher representation of institutional plaintiffs. LANJOUW and LERNER [1996] find a similar ratio, 0.92, in data from a later period (see below). The second indicator is the average number of previous cases that the plaintiff had been involved in relative to the average number of cases for the defendant. They find plaintiffs involved on average in 50% more cases. For both indicators IPR ranks at the top, suggesting that stake asymmetry, and hence trials, may be more closely associated with reputational concerns in patent disputes.

The statistics above reflect the relative importance of the reputations of the agents. In the case of patent litigation one can also consider reputation with respect to an individual patent. Patents vary in terms of their breadth. Some protect narrowly defined innovations with specific uses. Others protect broadly defined innovations with many possible applications. In the latter case, the patentee is likely to be licensing in multiple markets and therefore generating more potential disputes. In these situations, winning a trial against one infringer has the additional benefit of dissuading infringers in other markets.

Not only may a patent which is broad in scope be more likely to create a situation where the plaintiff has a greater stake than the defendant in the outcome of the trial, evidence suggests that broad patents are also likely to be more valuable (see below). For both reasons – greater α and greater j – one would expect broader patents to go to trial more often.

This hypothesis is explored in LERNER [1994]. He constructs a proxy for patent scope based on the International Patent Classification (IPC). While the best way to measure patent scope might be through subjective assessments, this approach is a practical way to develop a sample of sufficient size for an empirical analysis. His proxy for patent scope is the number of subclasses

---

11. Adjudication includes decisions made on pre-trial motions.

into which the U.S. Patent and Trademark Office assigns a patent. Patent classifications are determined carefully, and extensively cross-checked by patent office officials. Patent examiners simultaneously assign firms to U.S. and IPC subclasses. The IPC system, which had its origin in the Council of Europe's 1954 European Convention, has several advantages which make it preferable for these purposes, including its nested structure. He uses the first four digits only: e.g., a patent assigned to classes C12M 1/12, C12N 1/14, and C12N 9/60 is counted as falling into two classes, C12M and C12N.

Lerner examines patenting by firms in biotechnology, an industry that relies heavily on patents to protect discoveries. He first explores the economic value of patent scope by examining the relationship between the stock of intellectual property and the valuation of firms. Because many factors other than the stock of intellectual property may affect the valuation of a biotechnology firm, particularly as the company's product approaches the marketplace and the strength of the firm's marketing and distribution arrangements become apparent, he focuses on valuations during the venture capital investment process. Venture capitalists typically invest in privately held firms. In each financing round, the venture capitalists and the entrepreneur negotiate a valuation of the firm. Intellectual property is a young biotechnology company's most valuable asset, so if a relationship between intellectual property and valuation exists, this is a natural place to observe it. He identifies the dates of venture financings through the records of two database providers, Venture Economics and Recombinant Capital, as well as other sources. The final sample consists of 962 financing rounds at 350 firms between 1978 and September 1992; for 535 financing rounds at 173 firms, he identifies the valuation of the firm at the time of the investment.

The results suggest that patent scope has an economically and statistically significant impact on the valuation of firms. A one standard deviation increase in average patent scope at the mean of the independent variables translates into a 21% increase in value. This implies that the stakes, j, are greater in disputes over broader patents.

Lerner then investigates the effect of scope on the likelihood that a patent is litigated. To do this, he examines whether firms were more likely to resolve disputes involving broader patents through the costly and time- consuming process of litigation. Using data on 1678 patents awarded between 1973 and September 1992 to independent venture-backed biotechnology firms, he estimates the following probit regression. The dependent variable, LIT, equals one if the patent was involved in any litigation through the end of May 1993:

$$(12) \quad \begin{array}{cccc} LIT = & 2.90 & + & 0.10 \text{ YEARS} & + & 0.17 \text{ SCOPE,} \\ & (0.23) & & (0.02) & & (0.08) \end{array}$$
$$\text{Log likelihood} = -136.36; \chi^2 - \text{statistic} = 20.18.$$

where YEARS is the number of years from the grant of the patent to May 31, 1993, and is included as a control for truncation (standard errors in parentheses). These results imply that, at the mean of the independent variables, a one standard deviation increase in patent scope increases the probability of litigation by 41% (from 1.3% to 1.8%). Again, this is consistent with the hypothesis that patent disputes where both the stakes

(j) and the *asymmetry* of these stakes (α) are high will be more likely to end up in the courts[12].

Further evidence of the importance of the size of stakes in determining litigation activity is presented in LANJOUW and SCHANKERMAN [1997]. Using U.S. data on patents in all technology areas, they investigate the relationship between a range of measures of patent breadth and value and the likelihood of litigation. One measure of the value of a patent is the number of times that it is cited by future patentees as an important antecedent invention. Revolutionary new technologies with commercial value spawn further innovative efforts in the same area and hence the related patents are often cited. Lanjouw and Schankerman find that the number of citations to a patent is very strongly correlated with the probability of an infringement suit being filed.

• Evidence Regarding the Expected Costs of Litigation

The amount of legal costs is another important consideration affecting both the decision whether to risk causing harm and, in the event of a dispute, the payoffs obtained when the court is used to resolve the dispute. It is clear from equations (3) and (8) that the probability of having a cooperative surplus, and therefore the proportion of filed cases which are settled, depends only on the *total* legal costs associated with going to trial ($L + l$). On the other hand, for each party, own costs have a greater (negative) effect on threat points than their (positive) effect on the shared cooperative surplus. The changes in payoffs are $-(1 - \theta)\mathrm{d}L$ and $-\theta\mathrm{d}l$ for the plaintiff and defendant, respectively (equations 9 and 10). Thus, an increase in L makes a potential plaintiff less likely to file a claim when harm occurs, and an increase in l induces a potential defendant to invest more in avoiding harm. The payoffs to either party from a dispute are increasing in the other party's legal costs.

One implication is that it is in the interests of each party to increase the legal costs of the other when a case has been filed. This point is explored in LANJOUW and LERNER [1996] in a study of the use of preliminary injunctive relief in patent litigation. (The grant of a preliminary injunction prevents an infringing firm from using the innovation during the period of the trial.) They investigate the hypothesis that financially strong firms use this mechanism to prey upon weaker firms. The threat of higher legal costs and the possibility of a cessation of operations may lead defendants to settle on less favorable terms.

Lanjouw and Lerner extend the model presented in Section 2 to a two-stage game. In the first stage, the patentee may settle or proceed directly

---

12. Interestingly, the role of patent scope (as measured by the number of 4-digit IPC sub-classifications of a patent) in contributing to litigation is not confirmed in multivariate probits using comprehensive U.S. patent data. In fact, in regressions which control for the value of the patent using other indicators, as well as controlling for the type of technology and ownership, LANJOUW and SCHANKERMAN [1997] find that scope *reduces* the likelihood of litigation.

212

to trial, as above. In addition, however, he now has the option to request a preliminary injunction. If a preliminary injunction hearing is held, then there is a second stage where, again, the patentee may decide whether to continue to trial or to settle.

The primary implications of allowing patentees to request preliminary injunctions are best seen by examining the new threat point of the infringer if a preliminary injunction is certain to be granted:

$$(13) \qquad (l-w)m(1/2)V_2 + (l-w)j^* - [k(l-\lambda) + \delta\lambda]l,$$

and comparing it to the threat point of the infringer without this mechanism (equation 7). Note that it is now the infringer that bears the damages during the trial and obtains compensation, j^*, if the patentee is unsuccessful. The last term indicates that legal costs are increased by a preliminary injunction proceeding in two ways. The share of legal services required for the preliminary injunction proceeding, $1 - \lambda$, is more costly by a factor $k \geq 1$ because it must be financed quickly. The remaining share of legal services required for a trial, λ, is also more costly by a factor $\delta \geq 1$ because the injunction may constrain the infringer's production.

A comparison highlights several reasons to expect small infringing firms to be worse off when faced with an injunction. First, it is likely that a financially weak infringing firm would not be able, or asked, to fully compensate the patentee for damage inflicted during a trial ($j \ll V_1 - 1/2V_2$). A preliminary injunction removes this advantage, lowers the small firms' threat point (13) relative to (7) and weakens their bargaining position. Second, evidence suggests that financing constraints are more of a concern to smaller firms. Empirical studies of capital constraints suggest that an inability to obtain external financing limits many forms of business investment (see HUBBARD, [1996], for a review). Studies by HIMMELBERG and PETERSEN [1994] and HALL [1992] show that capital constraints appear to limit R&D expenditures, especially in smaller firms. These financial burdens are exacerbated by legal limits on the ability of firms to raise external funds to finance litigation. Many states have adopted champerty prohibitions from the common law, which prevent uninvolved third parties from investing in a lawsuit in return for compensation if it is successful. This restriction is particularly important in the context of patent litigation, where the large costs of litigation often preclude financing suits through contingency fee arrangements with attorneys. Because financing considerations relate to size, the model predicts that preliminary injunctions will be used primarily by large firms and, in particular, those with cases filed against smaller firms. As discussed in the introduction, this is of particular concern because it exacerbates the disadvantage that financially constrained firms already face in using the court system for dispute resolution.

Lanjouw and Lerner explore the predation hypothesis empirically, using data on 252 patent lawsuits filed between January 1990 and June 1991 in six Federal districts. Bringing together data from multiple sources, they obtain the characteristics of each legal suit, in particular whether a preliminary injunction was requested by the plaintiff, as well as two measures of the resources of each party: sales and employment[13]. Since uncertainty about how the court will rule in a case may play a role in decisions about use of the court (equation 11, parameter σ_ε), they use three measures of uncertainty as controls: previous litigation of the patent, reexaminations of the patent in the patent office, and the number of total patents granted in the subclass.

The regressions examine in probit regressions whether the plaintiff requested a preliminary injunction. The regressions use the level of the size variable, sales or employment, averaged across co-litigants if there is more than one, as well as the log of the size variable for the largest of the co-litigants. In both cases, the results are similar. Plaintiff size has a positive and significant effect on the likelihood that the plaintiff will request a preliminary injunction. Using the first set of estimates, at the mean of the independent variables, a one standard deviation increase in the plaintiff's sales increases the predicted probability of a preliminary injunction request from 15% to 24%. Defendant size has a negative but insignificant effect. In other regressions, the *difference* between plaintiff and defendant size was found to have a positive and significant effect. These results are consistent with the hypothesis that financially strong firms use preliminary injunctive relief to prey upon weaker firms by driving up their costs.

Other data on enforcement suggests that large and small firms make different use of the IPR system. LERNER [1995b] analyzes the patent and trade secret litigation of a sample of 530 manufacturing firms. His data includes all the litigation in which the sampled firms were involved in the federal and state judicial districts encompassing their headquarters over a four-and-a-half year period. He finds that trade secret disputes are commonplace, representing 43% of the intellectual property litigation. Cases litigated by smaller firms disproportionately involved trade secrets, suggesting that this source of intellectual property protection is more critical to these companies. This result is consistent with the view that less established firms employ trade secrecy because their direct and indirect costs of patenting are relatively high.

Finally, direct survey evidence also supports the statistical results of studies of IPR litigation. In their 1994 survey of 1,478 managers of U.S. R&D units, COHEN, NELSON, and WALSH [1996] asked respondents to indicate the most important reasons, out of five possibilities, for *not* having

---

13. Their primary source for lawsuits was the PACER databases compiled by the various Federal district courts which provide a detailed listing of the litigating parties and an item-by-item catalog of the docket entries. The Federal Judicial Center's Integrated Database was used to identify patent cases. They used four sources to identify the patents involved in these cases. At the time a patent suit is filed, the Clerk of the Court is required to submit a form to the Commissioner of the U.S. Patent and Trademark Office (USPTO) which indicates the district in which the suit was filed, the docket number, and the patent(s) in dispute. This information is printed in the USPTO's *Official Gazette* and compiled in the "LIT/REEX" field in LEXIS's PATENTS database. They also used two other databases from: Research Publications, which prepares an annual listing of patent litigation based on the information provided by the clerks to the USPTO and on the firm's independent searches of activity in the district courts and the Intellectual Property Reserve Corporation, a provider of patent litigation insurance, which has compiled its own proprietary database of patent suits that the firm employs when designing policies. Finally, information was collected from the docket files.

patented a recent innovation: difficulty in demonstrating novelty, disclosure, ease of inventing around a patent, the cost of application, and the cost of enforcement. While enforcement costs are not rated highly overall as a concern, the breakdown of responses by firm size is suggestive. They report that none of the first three reasons for not patenting is correlated with firm size. However the Spearman correlation coefficient between firm size and whether enforcement cost is listed as a concern is –0.23 and that between size and application cost is –0.15 (both significant at the .01 level). Related results come from a smaller 1990 study of 376 U.S. firms (KOEN, [1991]). This survey finds that the time and expense of intellectual property litigation was a major factor in deciding to pursue an innovation for 55% of the enterprises with fewer than 500 employees, but only for 33% of larger businesses. In general, small firms believed that their patents were infringed more frequently, but were considerably less likely to litigate these perceived infringements.

4 Costs of Enforcement and the Value of Patents

The previous section surveyed the empirical evidence regarding the size of the various parameters that determine whether patent disputes will be litigated or settled. Various characteristics may affect the value of bringing suit, including the expectation of winning, W, and the size of the case, J. The empirical evidence – based primarily on differences in behavior across firms of varying size – also suggests that the legal costs associated with enforcement are an important aspect of the IPR system. LANJOUW [1996] presents simulation estimates of the size of the effect of recent changes to U.S. intellectual property law and legal policy on the average (private) value of patent protection received by inventors. She also considers a legal reform being discussed in the U.S. Congress: a move from the American Rule system of legal fee allocation to the British Rule, where the loser pays the legal costs of both parties[14]. Under the latter system, the expected legal costs for the patentee are $(1 - w)(L + l)$,, while those for the infringing firm are $w(L + l)$.

As noted in the introduction, the legal costs actually incurred by firms resolving patent disputes in the courts have been increasing. However, direct legal costs are only part of the story. Legal policy changes also influence

---

14. The relative merits of the American and British rules, and variants, has been studied extensively in the theoretical literature (see MEURER [1989], CHOI [1994] and AOKI and HU [1996], for patents; see SHAVELL [1982], REINGANUM and WILDE [1986], and HYLTON [1993], for examples in general civil litigation settings). However, empirical investigations of these alternatives are few (but see HUGHES and SNYDER [1995]).

the value of patents that are *not* litigated. When the expected benefit of recourse to the courts is low, infringement will be tolerated (equation 9). If, for example, the expected costs of litigation rise, the level of infringement tolerated increases and the value of patent protection is correspondingly diminished. Consequently, patents will be kept in force (through payment of renewal, or maintenance, fees) for a shorter period of time, and some inventors will not find it worthwhile to patent their innovations in the first place.

LANJOUW [1996] presents estimates of some of these less visible effects of legal reforms. The estimation joins two different lines of research by embedding an infringement/litigation game in a behavioral model of patent renewal (see LANJOUW, [1998], for details). The renewal model estimates are used to calculate the value of patent protection, and policy changes are simulated by altering the relevant legal policy variables. Although the choice of simulations relates to U.S. policy, the analysis is done using German data because the recent introduction of renewal fees in the United States precludes, for a few more years, this type of analysis for that country. However, the results regarding the relative magnitude of effects apply more generally.

The data set contains more than 20,000 German patents in four technology groups, randomly sampled from those which were applied for or in force during the period 1955-1988[15]. The size and distribution of patent value implied by the parameter estimates for computers are found in the first column of Table 1, under the heading "Base." The mean value of a computer patent is 24,329 1975 deutschemarks (DM); 6.5% of computer patents never generate any positive returns. The distribution of value is very skewed, with the bulk of the value of protection going to a small share of patentees.

The simulations are presented in columns (2)-(7), with the feature being changed highlighted in bold at the top of the columns. The bottom two rows of the table show the value generated by the patent system as a percentage of its value before the policy change, and the elasticity of value with respect to changes in the indicated policy parameter[16].

Columns (2) and (3) demonstrate the effect on patent value of moving from the German system of fee allocation (British Rule) and the 20-year statutory term limit to the U.S. system (American Rule) and the 17-year term limit in place there until last year[17]. These policy differences have a very substantial effect on the incentives generated by the patent system.

---

15. This data set was constructed by sampling from granted patents published in volumes of the *Patenteblatte* to obtain patent numbers and IPC classifications. Then renewal information for the early cohorts was obtained from cardfiles and, for the later cohorts, from a computerized database, both located at the German Patent Office, Munich.

16. Note that all distributions were calculated with the *same* simulated patents. This means that the standard errors for the mean and percentile estimates found in column (1) do not indicate anything about the significance of the differences across columns.

17. The filing and granting dates are treated as simultaneous which overstates the difference in systems somewhat. The effective terms of a U.S. patent is, typically, longer than 17 years because the granting period is additional.

216

TABLE 1

Simulated Value Distributions for West German Computer Patents.

Simulation	(Base)	(2)	(3)	(4)	(5)	(6)	(7)
Variables (Bold are changes from base case)							
Fee-shifting rule	BR	**AR**	**AR**	**AR**	**AR**	BR	BR
Patent life (years)	20	20	**17**	**17**	**17**	20	20
Win probability (W)	.91	.91	.91	**.94**	.91	**.94**	.91
Legal fees (L)	Base	Base	Base	Base	**1.25* Base**	Base	**1.25* Base**
Value Distributions							
Mean	24,329 DM (2,147)	20,503 DM	15,011 DM	15,326 DM	13,338 DM	25,292 DM	24,210 DM
Percentile:							
50% (median)	13,922 DM (1,295)	5,980 DM	5,096 DM	5,096 DM	5,096 DM	15,039 DM	13,802 DM
75	32,686 (2,881)	27,682	11,296	11,399	10,778	33,192	32,651
99.9	239,868 (19,944)	237,037	232,285	232,285	227,687	239,868	239,868
Percentage of Base							
Value	100%	84%	62%	63%	55%	104%	100%
Elasticity	—	—	—	0.64	-0.45	1.20	-.02

Note: The analysis looks at the distribution of values of computer industry patents under alternative litigation environments. "Base" refers to parameter values estimated from the renewal model and other data. The other cases are selected changes. Values, in 1975 DM, are net of annual renewal and administration fees, as well as application, examination and publication costs. Calculations use 10000 simulation draws. Estimated standard errors for the value (vper) estimates calculated using a Taylor approximation:
$$vper(\omega) \approx vper(\omega_0) + \Gamma'(\omega_0)'(\omega - \omega_0). \text{ Gradient matrices } \Gamma(\omega_0) \text{ are approximated with central finite difference gradients calculated at } \omega.$$

Moving from the British Rule to the American Rule cuts on average about 4,000 DM from the value of a patent, or 16%. This is *before* any actual increase in legal fees paid by patentees under the American Rule is netted out. The reason for the large effect is that patentees have a high expected probability of winning at trial and therefore benefit greatly from the British rule which says that losers pay costs. This expectation in turn means that they are slower to drop their patents simply because of an unwillingness to go to court. Moving from a 20- to a 17-year term limit has an even greater negative effect on the value of patents (column 3), causing an additional 22% loss of value.

Columns (4) and (6) demonstrate the impact of a favorable shift in the court's attitude toward patentees, under the U.S. system and the German system, respectively. This shift in attitude is reflected in an increase in patentees' expectation of winning at trial, W. The size of the increase used in the simulations corresponds to the actual change in W which occurred in the United States in the 1980s following the introduction of the new Federal Court of Appeals[18]. To explore the concurrent increase in legal costs, L, columns (5) and (7) indicate the magnitude of response to a 25% increase in statutory legal fees, with the associated elasticities.

Under the U.S. system, the higher likelihood of a favorable ruling at trial increases the average value per patent by 300 DM, with an elasticity of response of 0.64 (column 4). Increasing legal fees work in the opposite direction, bringing down the value of protection. The elasticity of response to legal costs is somewhat less than the response to changes in the probability of winning (−0.45 versus 0.64). Turning to the results of the same set of simulations under the German system, we see that the elasticity of response to these policy changes is, with one exception, considerably lower. However, the relative importance across the two rules of changes in W and in legal costs is as expected. Under the British Rule, when W is high, as it is here, changes in legal costs have relatively little bite since patentees do not expect to pay them. Similarly, changes in W are relatively important because being liable for both parties' costs makes losses more painful. This relationship can be seen by noting that [column(4)/column(5)] < [column(6)/column(7)].

To put these changes in patent value in perspective it should be emphasized again that these effects are felt by all patents, whether litigated or not, so that even fairly small changes can represent substantial sums in the aggregate. For example, there were 21,515 patents granted in Germany in 1975 for all technology areas. The implicit subsidy to R&D generated by the system, calculated as the total value of protection relative to the R&D expenditure related to the underlying innovations, was on the order of 10% to 15% (LANJOUW, [1998]). The simulation results show that moving from the German system of fee allocation and 20-year term to the U.S. system leads

---

18. Its value was calculated as follows. As noted in Section 2, U.S. patentee's *observed* win proportion was 61% in 1978-1980 and increased to 75% by 1987. In other words, the probability of the infringer prevailing $(1 - W)$ fell by 36% over the period. We take this latter figure and apply it to the estimated unconditional (on filing) win probability, W. This results in $(1 - W)$ falling from 0.09 to 0.06 with a new W of 0.94.

218

to a fall in the mean value per patent of about 10,000 DM, *even if no patents are ever actually prosecuted*. Taking the sampled technology groups as representative, for Germany this difference would be equivalent to a loss of 200 million DM *per year* in the value received by inventors from the patent system (and a fall in the implicit subsidy to R&D investment to 6% to 10%). The change in the value of U.S. intellectual property from these policy changes would be considerably larger, both because of the greater number of patents involved and because U.S. patents offer protection in a much larger market.

5 Intellectual Property Litigation and Innovation

The previous section indicated how the value of patent protection is shaped by the legal environment and the threat of litigation. Changes in the implicit subsidy rate will affect, in turn, the level of investment in R&D by firms and the innovation rate. There is evidence which suggests, however, that enforcement concerns affect not only the level of resources invested in innovation, but also the location and type of research undertaken.

As noted in Section 2, as the costs of becoming involved in a suit rise, the expenditure that potential defendants are willing to incur to avoid harm in the first place increases (equation 10). In the context of patents, one way of avoiding disputes with other patentees is to avoid innovating and producing in areas where others are present. In particular, if the threat of litigation is an important concern, one would expect that small firms would tailor their R&D programs so as to avoid conflict, especially with large firms that have lower legal costs and that would be likely to actively pursue infringements.

These hypotheses are explored in LERNER [1995a] using data on the U.S. patenting behavior of 419 new biotechnology firms. As discussed in Section 3, all patents are classified in one of the more than 120,000 U.S. patent subclasses. Since virtually all biotechnology discoveries are patented, the patent subclass designations are a good indicator of the areas within biotechnology that are the focus of each firm's research efforts. The costs of litigation for each firm are proxied by the firm's previous experience in patent litigation and by its paid-in capital.

Lerner finds that there are two respects in which the patenting behavior of firms varies with litigation costs. First, firms with high litigation costs are less likely to patent in subclasses with many previous awards by rival biotechnology firms. The results indicate that firms with the highest litigation costs are twice as likely as others to patent in subclasses with no rival awards. When high-litigation-cost firms do patent in subclasses in which rival biotechnology firms have already patented, they tend to choose less crowded subclasses. Breaking the sample into high- and low-cost firms, when a patent is granted to a high-litigation-cost firm, the preceding award of a patent to a rival is, on average, 303 days earlier. For low-cost firms, an average interval of only 164 days separates the patent from the most recent, previous rival award. These results are summarized in Table 2.

TABLE 2

Location of New Biotechnology Firm Patents, by Characteristics of Patentee.

	% of patents with no rival in subclass	Days since last patent in subclass
Panel A: Patentees divided by the number of patent lawsuits prior to award		
Patentee involved in no previous patent suits	31.4	270.5
Patentee involved in 1-5 previous patent suits	14.9	182.9
Patentee involved in 6-10 previous patent suits	9.1	153.6
Patentee involved in 11 or more previous patent suits	6.6	192.2
Panel B: Patentees divided by paid-in capital at end of year prior to award		
Patentee's paid-in capital is in bottom quartile	40.6	302.5
Patentee's paid-in capital is in third quartile	25.6	251.6
Patentee's paid-in capital is in second quartile	19.7	216.4
Patentee's paid-in capital is in top quartile	11.0	164.1

Note: The sample consists of 2048 patent awards awarded to 419 new biotechnology firms between 1973 and 1992. Each subclass of these patents is used as a separate observation (a total of 14885 observations). The first column indicates the percentage of the firm's patents that are in subclasses with no earlier patents by rivals. The second column indicates, for those patents that are in subclasses where a rival has patented previously, the mean number of days since the previous award by a rival. Patentees are divided by two proxies for litigation costs at the time of the award, the number of previous patent lawsuits and paid-in capital (in millions of current dollars).

Second, firms with high litigation costs are less likely to patent in subclasses where firms with low litigation costs have previously patented. In his data, a patent awarded to a firm with low litigation costs is followed by an award to a firm with high litigation costs 11% of the time; awards to other firms are followed by a patent to a firm with high litigation costs 21% of the time. The results are robust to controls for a variety of sample selection biases, such as the changing mixture of firms over time and the different technological focuses of various vintages of firms.

At a more macro level, differences across countries in legal enforcement are just beginning to be incorporated in studies of the relationship between IPR incentives and trade, foreign direct investment, technology diffusion, and growth. MANSFIELD [1994] provides survey evidence of the importance of the strength of IPR systems in shaping the foreign investment decisions of firms. The study is based on a random sample of U.S. manufacturing firms in six industries. Each firm was asked the importance of strong intellectual property protection in various investment decisions. Twenty percent of firms reported that the strength of IPRs was a major consideration in decisions to invest in rudimentary production facilities, but about 80% deemed it

220

important for locating R&D facilities. Interestingly, interviewees gave three areas of concern in assessing the strength of IPRs in a country: the laws, the legal infrastructure, and the willingness of government to actively enforce patent rights.

Various non-survey indicators of IPR protection have been used in cross-country analyses. For example, dummy variables indicating whether certain features of patent laws exist in a country have been included as explanatory variables (see FERRANTINO, [1993]). RAPP and ROZEK [1990] and GOULD and GRUBEN [1996] construct an aggregate index of the ''strength'' of IPR protection, again based on laws and procedures. Countries differ widely, however, in the ways in which they enforce their IPR laws. GINARTE and PARK [1997] extend this approach to incorporate patent enforcement issues. In constructing their aggregate indicator, in addition to features of the law, they add measures of the availability of three enforcement mechanisms: preliminary injunctive relief (see Section 2), contributory infringement pleadings; and burden of proof reversals (accused must prove that he is not infringing a process patent). Given the wide range in the effectiveness of legal enforcement across countries, further development in this direction should make IPR indicators more useful in studies of trade and development.

6 Conclusion

This paper has examined several recent avenues of empirical research in the enforcement of intellectual property rights. To frame these issues, we initially presented a stylized model of the patent litigation process. The bulk of the paper was devoted to linking the empirical literature on patent litigation to the parameters of this model.

We summarized four distinct avenues of research. First, we examined studies of how the propensity to litigate patents varies with the expected benefits of litigation. We then considered how the cost of litigation affects the willingness to enforce patents, particularly for young capital-constrained firms. The forth section also analyzed the cost of enforcing patents, but focused on how these costs affected the private value of patent rights. Finally, we considered studies of the impact of intellectual property litigation on the innovation process itself.

This area appears to be one that is ripe for further empirical exploration. Studying intellectual property litigation – and the impact of changes in system on firm behavior – may help address some of the most difficult questions in the economics of technological change. For instance, the extent to which intellectual property protection has a real impact on R&D spending and the rate and direction of technological progress is still largely unclear. The recent strengthening of patent holders' rights in the U.S. courts and elsewhere may help illuminate this issue.

Second, patent litigation is an interesting arena for examining more general models of litigation and settlement. The patent system, with its detailed classification scheme, allows researchers to assess firm behavior even in cases where suits have not been filed. A problem with the examination of filed suits is that, in many cases, the disputants engage in extensive bargaining prior to the filing of a suit. If a potential plaintiff can credibly threaten to sue, many disputes should be settled before a formal filing. Any analysis of suits will consequently face selection biases, whose effects are difficult to predict. Because patents provide a detailed mapping of firm behavior, they should be a useful arena for researching the impact of litigation – and the threat of litigation – on firm behavior.

• References

Acs, Zoltan J., Audretsch David B. (1988). – "Innovation in Small and Large Firms: An Empirical Analysis," *American Economic Review.* Vol. 78, pp. 678-690.

Aoki, R., Hu, Jin-Li (1996). – "A Cooperative Game Approach to Patent Litigation, Settlement, and the Allocation of Legal Costs," *Unpublished working paper*, State University of New York, Stony Brook.

Bebchuk, L. (1984). – "Litigation and Settlement under Imperfect Information," *RAND Journal of Economics.* Vol. 15, pp. 404-415.

Bhagat, S., Brickley, James A., Coles Jeffrey L. (1994). – "The Costs of Inefficient Bargaining and Financial Distress: Evidence from Corporate Lawsuits," *Journal of Financial Economics.* Vol. 35, pp. 221-247.

Choi, Jay P. (1994). – "Patent Litigation as an Information Transmission Mechanism," *Discussion Paper no. 703*, Columbia University.

Cohen, Wesley, Nelson Richard R., Walsh J. (1996). – "Appropriability Conditions and Why Firms Patent and Why They Do Not in the American Manufacturing Sector," *Unpublished working paper*, Carnegie-Mellon University.

Cooter, R., Rubinfeld, D. (1989). – "Economic Analysis of Legal Disputes and Their Resolution," *Journal of Economic Literature.* Vol. 27, pp. 1067-1097.

Federal Judicial Center, *Federal Court Cases: Integrated Data Base, 1970-89.* Ann Arbor, MI: Inter-university Consortium for Political and Social Research. Tapes updated to 1991.

Ferrantino, M. (1993). – "The Effect of Intellectual Property Rights on International Trade and Investment," *Weltwirtschaftliches Archiv.* Vol. 29, pp. 300-331.

Ginarte, Juan C., Park, Walter G. (1997). – "Determinants of Intellectual Property Rights: A Cross-National Study," *Research Policy.* Vol. 26, pp. 283-302.

Gould, David M., Gruben, William C. (1996). – "The Role of Intellectual Property Rights in Economic Growth," *Journal of Development Economics.* Vol. 48, pp. 323-350.

Hall, Bronwyn H. (1992). – "Investment and Research and Development: Does the Source of Financing Matter?," *Working Paper No. 92-194*, Department of Economics, University of California at Berkeley.

Himmelberg, Charles P., Petersen, Bruce C. (1994). – "R&D and Internal Finance: A Panel Study of Small Firms in High-Tech Industries," *Review of Economics and Statistics.* Vol. 76, pp. 38-51.

Hofmann, Mark A. (1995). – "Patent Coverage Lags Well Behind Infringement Suits," *Business Insurance.* 29 (January 15), pp. 3-7.

HUBBARD, R. Glenn (1996). – "Capital-Market Imperfections and Investment," *Journal of Economic Literature*. Forthcoming.

HUGHES, James, SNYDER, E. (1995). – "Litigation and Settlement under the English and American Rules: Theory and Evidence," *The Journal of Law and Economics*. Vol. 38, pp. 225-250.

HYLTON, K. (1990). – "The Influence of Litigation Costs on Deterrence Under Strict Liability and Under Negligence," *International Review of Law and Economics*. Vol. 10, pp. 161-171.

HYLTON, K. (1993). – "Litigation Cost Allocation Rules and Compliance with the Negligence Standard," *Journal of Legal Studies*. Vol. 22, pp. 457-476.

KOEN, Mary S. (1991). – *Survey of Small Business Use of Intellectual Property Protection: Report of a Survey of Conducted by MO-SCI Corporation for the Small Business Administration*. Washington, Small Business Administration.

KOENIG, Gloria K. (1980). – *Patent Invalidity: A Statistical and Substantive Analysis*. New York: Clark Boardman.

KORTUM, S., LERNER, J. (1997). – "Stronger Protection or Technological Revolution: What is Behind the Recent Surge in Patenting?," *Carnegie-Rochester Conference Series on Public Policy*.

LANJOUW, Jean O. (1998). – "Patent Protection in the Shadow of Infringement: Simulation Estimations of Patent Value" *Review of Economic Studies*. Forthcoming.

LANJOUW, Jean O. (1996). – "Beyond Lawyers' Fees: Measuring the Indirect Effects of U.S. Intellectual Property Reforms," *Unpublished working paper*, Yale University.

LANJOUW, Jean O., LERNER, J. (1996). – "Preliminary Injunctive Relief: Theory and Evidence from Patent Litigation," *Working paper no. 5689*, National Bureau of Economic Research.

LANJOUW, Jean O., SCHANKERMAN, M. (1997). – "Stylized Facts of Patent Litigation: Scope, Value and Ownership," Working paper no. 6297, National Bureau of Economic Research.

LERNER, J. (1994). – "The Importance of Patent Scope: An Empirical Analysis," *The RAND Journal of Economics*. Vol. 25, pp. 319-333.

LERNER, J. (1995a). – "Patenting in the Shadow of Competitors," *Journal of Law and Economics*. Vol. 38, pp. 463-496.

LERNER, J. (1995b). – "The Importance of Trade Secrecy: Evidence from Civil Litigation," *Unpublished working paper*, Harvard University.

MANSFIELD, E. (1994). – "Intellectual Property Protection, Foreign Direct Investment, and Technology Transfer," *IFC Discussion Paper Number 19*, World Bank.

MERGES, R. P. (1992). – *Patent Law and Policy*. Charlottesville, Michie Company.

MEURER, M. (1989). – "The Settlement of Patent Litigation," *The RAND Journal of Economics*. Vol. 20, pp. 77-91.

ORDOVER, Janusz A. (1978). – "Costly Litigation in the Model of Single Activity Accidents," *Journal of Legal Studies*. Vol. 7, pp. 243-261.

PNG, I.P.L. (1983). – "Strategic Behavior in Suit, Settlement and Trial," *Bell Journal of Economics*, Vol. 14, pp. 539-550.

PNG, I.P.L. (1987). – "Litigation, Liability, and Incentives for Care," *Journal of Public Economics*. Vol. 34, pp. 61-85.

PRIEST, G., KLEIN, B. (1984). – "The Selection of Disputes for Litigation," *Journal of Legal Studies*. Vol. 8, pp. 1-56.

RAPP, Richard T., ROZEK, Richard P. (1990). – "Benefits and Costs of Intellectual Property Protection in Developing Counties," *Journal of World Trade*. Vol. 24, pp. 75-102.

REINGANUM, Jennifer F., WILDE, Louis L. (1986). – "Settlement, Litigation, and the Allocation of Litigation Costs," *The RAND Journal of Economics.* Vol. 17, pp. 557-566.

ROSEN, M. (1992). – "Texas Instruments's $250 Million-a-Year Profit Center," *American Lawyer.* Vol. 14 (March), pp. 56-63.

SCHWEIZER, Urs (1989). – "Litigation and Settlement under Two-Sided Incomplete Information," *The Review of Economic Studies.* Vol. 56, pp. 163-178.

SHAVELL, S. (1982). – "Suit, Settlement, and Trial: A Theoretical Analysis Under Alternative Methods for the Allocation of Legal Costs," *Journal of Legal Studies.* Vol. 11, pp. 55-81.

SIEGELMAN, P., WALDFOGEL, J. (1996). – "A Taxonomy of Disputes: New Evidence through the Prism of the Priest and Klein Model," *Unpublished working paper*, Yale University.

SPIER, K., SPULBER, D. (1993). – "Pretrial Bargaining under Asymmetric Information: The Mechanism Design Approach," *Unpublished working paper*, Northwestern University.

WALDFOGEL, J. (1995). – "The Selection Hypothesis and the Relationship between Trial and Plaintiff Victory," *Journal of Political Economy.* Vol. 103, pp. 229-260.

WALDFOGEL, J. (1996). – "Reconciling Asymmetric Information and Divergent Expectations Theories of Litigation," *Unpublished working paper*, Yale University.

224

An Auction Model of Intellectual Property Protection: Patent Versus Copyright

Michael WATERSON, Norman IRELAND *

ABSTRACT. – In this paper several firms compete for the right to obtain intellectual property protection for a basic idea which has subsequent potential applications. The modelling employs an auction analogy, taking the context to be an n-player all-pay auction, with a reserve. We find that, even taking only firms' own utilities into account, welfare has no interior maximum, so that either maximal, or minimal, protection is optimal. Through examining a simple version of this game, we suggest that software is socially better protected by means of copyright rather than patent.

* M. WATERSON: University of Warwick; N. IRELAND: University of Warwick. We should like to thank several participants at the 10th International ADRES conference, Strasbourg, June 1996, at the WZB Conference on Advances in Industrial organisation, Berlin October 1996, and an Economics of Law Study Group, Leicester, June 1997 (particularly Clive Fraser), also Marcel Canoy, Paul Dobson, Tuomas Takalo and two anonymous referees for helpful comments and suggestions.

225

D. Encaoua et al. (eds.), The Economics and Econometrics of Innovation, 225–241.
© 2000 *Kluwer Academic Publishers. Printed in the Netherlands.*

1 Introduction

There is a very considerable literature on the social welfare effects of patents. Traditionally, following Nordhaus's [1969] pioneering work, it was concerned with determining the optimal length of a patent. More recently, it has become concerned with patent breadth and patent height. Important contributions on patent breadth include KLEMPERER [1990] and GILBERT and SHAPIRO [1990]. Some authors refer to patent height as breadth, though VAN DIJK [1996] for example is strongly of the view that they are different dimensions. Essentially, height is concerned with the standard of novelty for an incremental development. Apart from van DIJK, examples include SCOTCHMER and GREEN [1990] and FERRANDO [1992]. A related concern voiced more recently is that later discoveries may affect the incentive to invest in enabling innovations, and patents on these might curtail activity on further developments – GREEN and SCOTCHMER [1995] and CHANG [1995] are relevant here. Our paper is concerned in part with novelty requirements. However our major focus is on the optimal extent of coverage to be afforded by intellectual property protection.

In practice, intellectual property protection to enable the appropriation of the results of inventive activities takes a variety of forms. Besides patents the other major rights are copyright and trademarks. One rather important distinction may be made between patents and copyright. Arguably patents are capable of providing rather extensive protection whereas copyright provides a much weaker form of protection, since the thing that is copyrighted is normally not proof against, for example, similar ideas expressed in different ways. It is the form, not the thing itself. PHILLIPS and FIRTH [1995] define an "Absolute Monopoly" as "The right of an intellectual property holder to prevent all other persons from using that property within the market place governed by the law which protects it. An example of the absolute monopoly can be found in the rights enjoyed by the holder of a patent for an invention." (p. 13). By contrast "copyright monopoly is only a limited, qualified sort of monopoly..." (p. 129) where "qualified monopoly" is defined as "absolute monopoly subject to one major qualification: [the owner] cannot stop another party 'stripping down' his creation and thus effectively using it as the basis for his own creation" (p. 14). Clearly, the latter allows significant spillowers from a development to accrue to other firms, whereas the former does not.

Thus we may ask whether it is desirable that some inventive activities receive extensive protection via patents whilst others do not, because only copyright is available. Remarkably, it transpires that having such polar alternatives is socially optimal. Hence the major issue becomes one of determining for which sectors of industry particular types of protection are appropriate.

One of the problems in evaluating existing contributions to the literature is that social welfare losses arise from many sources, whereas of course individual papers include only a subset. The early literature incorporated a tradeoff between monopoly power and incentives, but there are other factors.

For example in KLEMPERER [1990], as well as people paying high prices for the patented good, there are losses to those who buy some related, cheaper but less-desired alternative. A second broad problem, more serious from the viewpoint of implementing actionable policy changes, is that the policy implications are often too subtle. A good example (though by no means unique), is the following proposal from Chang: "Courts should provide the broadest protection to two distinct classes of basic inventions: not only those that are very valuable relative to possible improvements – but also those that have very little value relative to the improvement that one would expect to follow..." (1995 p. 48). It would be difficult to imagine a practical version of this. In our paper, we aim to avoid the second problem by focussing policy discussion on the much less subtle issue of whether copyright or patent protection is the more desirable for particular industries. But at the same time we will not be able to avoid the first problem – there will definitely be relevant considerations not encountered within the model.

The approach in our paper is to develop a model in which there are a number of potential innovators, each engaged in research programmes, only one (at most) of which will be rewarded with intellectual property protection. However it is envisaged there is the possibility that some of these competitors will develop a subsequent stage product. If the initial protection extends to partial coverage of the subsequent developments, the reward will be dependent upon the expected number of such developments and the degree of coverage afforded by intellectual property protection. This will in turn feed back into the effort expended on research and on gaining the initial key patent or other protection. But the size of inventive step required (relative to the likelihood of success), which if large will dissuade some potential innovators from participating, will also be an important factor. The model focuses inter alia on an element which has arguably received too little attention – the expenditure used in attempts to gain the intellectual property right. The modelling procedure draws extensively on the auctions literature in order to obtain results. Section three develops the auctions framework in the particular desired directions, whilst section four draws some implications. Before that, we locate what we do relative to particular previous contributions.

2 Modelling Multi-Player Research Competition

Research and development activity leading to an innovation can be thought of as a tournament, along the lines of the patent race literature (HARRIS and VICKERS, 1995, and others). Those models are relatively simplistic in their industry structure (commonly being limited to two players) but focus on timing. Instead of the emphasis on timing, we wish to focus on industry structure and so it makes sense to think of a number of players all aiming for a new "basic idea".

The paper closest to that we develop below is due to DENICOLO [1996]. It is one of the few to develop the n-firm patent race concept within a context in which questions about patent policy can be addressed, and it also usefully brings out points from a number of previous contributions. In Denicolo's model, there is explicitly only one stage, in which n firms race for a patent, but losers as well as winners make a return. The incentive to innovate is implicitly a function $I(\theta)$ of the degree θ to which technical knowledge is disseminated ($\theta = 1$ implies complete dissemination) as a result of the narrowness of the patent. Patent breadth, $1 - \theta$, will determine the winner's relative return. Similarly the deadweight loss D created by monopoly pricing of the patented product is also a function of θ. In fact if W is social welfare

$$D(\theta) = W(1) - W(\theta)$$

Therefore the trick is to socially optimise patent breadth by

$$\min \psi(\theta) \equiv D(\theta)/I(\theta)$$

As illustrated by the earlier contributions of GILBERT and SHAPIRO [1990], and KLEMPERER [1990], the outcome is extremely sensitive to the underlying assumptions. Prime amongst these, unfortunately, is the nature of behaviour within the industry. For example if competition is Bertrand, minimum breadth is optimal. However it is difficult to imagine how intellectual protection policy can be made conditional on the form of competition which may be presumed to operate in an industry, since we normally consider the patent is awarded first and only afterwards will pricing policy be determined.

Actually, although Denicolo's model incorporates a clear advance in terms of including n potential patentees, an advance we wish to incorporate, it is potentially problematic in its equilibrium conception (who wants to be a loser?) as a result of the high degree of symmetry. This is something our auction analogy can help relax. It would also appear not to take full account of a new source of private and social loss, (new in the sense of something which did not arise in the earlier cited models). This is the "useless" expenditure of those players who do not win the competition.

In our model, at any one time there are a number of players all approaching a similar question or target, perhaps from different directions or with different skills or different expectations concerning the valuation of the prize for being nearest the target based upon their specific experience. Yet once the prize is achieved by one, the other players are excluded by the prize from benefiting directly, though they may perhaps obtain indirect benefits. Therefore there are a number of players each with independent valuations of the prize, each committing expenditure in an attempt to win. In this scenario, it makes sense to draw upon the results of auction theory in analysing the outcome. (This is not an original suggestion; Leininger, 1991, previously made use of it, though in a very different way). For brevity, we will often describe the prize (intellectual property protection) as a patent, but this is not necessarily the outcome, indeed it is the question of policy choice on which we focus later.

228

3 An Auction Model of Patent Competition

3.1. General Considerations

Consider the following scenario. There are n potential players in an *all-pay* auction with a reserve. (Clearly the all-pay framework is approprriate). Each has an *identical* independent distribution from which their valuation v of the patent is drawn. We think of this as a case where each player has their own specialism, but the development is capable of being applied in a variety of alternative areas. The valuation can include a view on royalties to be obtained, so long as it is still independent. Each player has first to decide whether to put in a bid (research programme) in an attempt to capture the prize, and then, if a bid is to be made, how much to spend, given information on its own valuation, while not knowing other firms' v's, only their distribution. The technology of research is assumed to be the following. A bid below a certain value $\underline{b}$ stands no chance of achieving any return – research of less than a certain amount would leave the player out of the race. Thus there are $m \le n$ active players. This minimum value $\underline{b}$ is in large part technologically determined – research in some areas is inherently more costly than in others – although potentially it may be influenced by the novelty requirement demanded by the patent authorities. Beyond that minimum level, the highest bid wins the prize. We assume, for ease of obtaining results, that each v is distributed uniformly on $[0, 1]$.

Assumptions about competition in our model are more aptly described as "standing on the shoulders of your peers" than on the shoulders of the giants depicted in SCOTCHMER [1991] and GREEN and SCOTCHMER [1995]. As we see it, there is a general view about a particular development being feasible and valuable. A set of players competes for the basic patent rather than it being the result of a blinding flash of inspiration on the part of a particular player. Nevertheless, taking part in the competition is (in general) a pre-requisite for being able to compete at later stages. From their model we take the lesson that it is important to pay some attention to what comes after the initial patent. Such considerations are ignored in most papers although the history of the development of, say, the textile industry is replete with examples of improvement patents enabling the spinning and weaving processes to operate more effectively. Therefore the more participants there are at the first stage the more players can take part in the later opportunities.

We take the view that an observer reading a patent description cannot immediately infer how it can be copied; know-how is necessary in addition. (Perhaps, if nothing else, this is because the skilled patent writer has an incentive to keep the description as opaque as possible subject to satisfying the patent examiners). The patent fills in the gaps in knowledge of a player who has kept up technologically in the particular area. More significantly, in this model it cannot be the case that the original inventor of necessity deserves all the reward from the innovation plus any and every development of it, since the patent holder may have 'won' only by a relatively narrow margin. Nor need such a reward be socially desirable.

We assume the private return to consist of a direct element plus a potential gain from spillovers coming from the developments of other players in the active group. Social returns are treated very simply as the sum of potential players' private returns.

3.2. **The Model**

The expected utility of a participating firm of type v, making a bid $b \geq \underline{b}$ which implies a probability of winning of $p(b)$ is composed of two elements: a main prize on winning plus a spillover prize gained whether winning or losing the auction. The former component is $(1 - \theta)v$, where θ is a measure of the imperfection of the intellectual property right, $0 \leq \theta \leq 1$. This main prize is obtained with probability $p(b)$. The "spillover" prize is always obtained. It is composed of a coefficient formed from the property right imperfection (θ) and a spillover parameter α, $0 \leq \alpha < 1$, (the extent to which you benefit from others' work), multiplied into an expression for the v-type's expectation of the winning type: $\theta\alpha(vp(b) + v^*(1 - p(b)))$. Here v^* is some other firm's type (most obviously but not necessarily the highest type among other bidding firms). Note that v^* is independent of v. To check this, recognise that two different v-type firms, *making the same bid* would have the same probabilities of losing and would have no effect on other bidding firms' types.

Putting the two parts together and subtracting the bid b yields

(1) $$U(v) = (1 - \theta)vp(b) + \theta\alpha(vp(b) + z(b)) - b$$
$$\text{where} \quad z(b) \equiv (1 - p(b))Ev^*$$

The conceptual distinction between θ and α will be important in what follows; θ is a policy parameter whilst α is a property of the industry, determined by its technical character. Finally, expected utility of a non-participating firm is scaled to zero.

We make the natural assumptions (which will be confirmed in the equilibrium that we derive) that bids are a monotonic increasing function of valuations, and that the auction is efficient in that only the player with the highest valuation will win. To derive the bidding function, note that since $U(v)$ is maximised by the bidding strategy $(p(b), b)$, (1) yields:

$$\frac{dU(v)}{dv} = \frac{\partial U(v)}{\partial v} = (1 - \theta)p + \alpha\theta p$$

Given the assumptions of efficiency and uniform distributions, the probability of winning is the probability of no other player having a higher valuation, *i.e.*

(2) $$p = v^{n-1}$$

Hence:

$$\frac{dU(v)}{dv} = (1 - \theta(1 - \alpha))v^{n-1}$$

that is, as v increases by dv, so utility increases by $(1 - \theta(1 - \alpha)) := A$ (the marginal coefficient) times the probability of winning.

Therefore, by integration

(3i) $U(v) = U(0) + Av^n/n$ if $U(0) \geq 0$ (everyone participates)

(3ii) $= A(v^n - \underline{v}^n)/n$ if $U(\underline{v}) = 0$ for $\underline{v} > 0$, *i.e.* $U(0) < 0$.

where $\underline{v}$ is the lowest participating type.

> LEMMA 1 : All firms will participate if $\underline{b} \leq \alpha\theta\frac{n-1}{n}$ (case (i)) because the spillover dominates the entry price. Otherwise there will be some non-participants (case (ii)).

Proof: When another firm is bound to win, a $v = 0$-type firm has utility:

$$U(0) = \max(0, \alpha\theta z - \underline{b}) = \max\left(0, \alpha\theta\int_0^1 s(n-1)s^{(n-2)}\,ds - \underline{b}\right)$$

(note again the use of the uniform distribution assumption).

Therefore:

(4i) $U(0) = \alpha\theta\dfrac{n-1}{n} - \underline{b}$ if $\underline{b} \leq \alpha\theta\dfrac{n-1}{n}$

(4ii) $= 0$ if $\underline{b} > \alpha\theta\dfrac{n-1}{n}$.

Clearly, everyone will participate if

$$\underline{b} \leq \alpha\theta\frac{n-1}{n},$$

which completes the proof.

We are now in a position to describe participants' actual bidding behaviour relating to the two alternative possibilities. We assume that v^* in (1) is the highest other type, and confirm this later in Lemma 2.

(i) If $\underline{b} \leq \alpha\theta\frac{n-1}{n}$, equating (1) (using (2) and the definition of z) with (3i):

$$U(0) + Av^n/n = Av^n + \alpha\theta\int_v^1 s(n-1)s^{n-2}\cdot ds - b$$

Solving for $b(v)$

$$b(v) = Av^n\frac{(n-1)}{n} - \alpha\theta\frac{n-1}{n} + \underline{b} + \alpha\theta(1 - v^n)\frac{n-1}{n}$$

(5i) $= (1 - \theta)\cdot\dfrac{n-1}{n}\cdot v^n + \underline{b}$

recalling the definition of A.

(ii) If $\underline{b} > \alpha\theta \frac{n-1}{n}$, so that $U(0) < 0$, from (1) and (3ii) we obtain:

$$A(v^n - \underline{v}^n)/n = Av^n + \alpha\theta(1 - v^n)\frac{n-1}{n} - b$$

Again solving:

$$b(v) = (1 - \theta)\frac{n-1}{n} \cdot v^n + A\underline{v}^n/n + \alpha\theta\frac{n-1}{n}$$

For the lowest valuation participant:

$$\underline{b} = \underline{v}^n \left[\frac{(1-\theta)n + \alpha\theta}{n}\right] + \alpha\theta\frac{n-1}{n}$$

(6)
$$\text{hence}: \quad \underline{v}^n = \frac{\underline{b} - \alpha\theta(n-1)/n}{1 - \theta + \alpha\theta/n}$$

Finally therefore:

(5ii) $\quad b(v) = (1 - \theta)\frac{n-1}{n}v^n + \frac{A}{n}\left[\frac{\underline{b} - \alpha\theta(n-1)/n}{1 - \theta + \alpha\theta/n}\right] + \alpha\theta\frac{n-1}{n}$

Thus we can state

LEMMA 2 : The bidding function defined by (5i) and (5ii) is continuous above $\underline{b}$, and increasing in v – so that the highest participating v – type will win the patent.

Proof: Direct from (5i) and (5ii).

Lemma 2 confirms the assumption that $p = v^{n-1}$ is indeed the probability of a v-type participating firm winning the auction and inter alia justifies interpreting v^* in (1) as the highest type among other bidding firms.

3.3. Social Welfare

Let us consider the most straightforward possible social welfare function,

$$W = \underset{v}{E}\{nU(v)\}$$

which in effect assumes that the intellectual property protection system is run entirely in the (assumed risk neutral) firms' interests, ignoring consumers.

LEMMA 3 : If welfare is defined as $W = \underset{v}{E}\{nU(v)\}$ then there are again two possible cases as defined in Lemma 1 and, given the regularity of the bidding equilibrium demonstrated in Lemma 2

(7i) $\quad W = n\left[\alpha\theta(n-1)/n - \underline{b}\right] + \dfrac{A}{n+1} \qquad$ if $\underline{b} \leq \alpha\theta(n-1)/n$

(7ii) $\quad W = A\left[\dfrac{1}{n+1} + \dfrac{n}{n+1}\underline{v}^{n+1} - \underline{v}^n\right] \qquad$ if $\underline{b} > \alpha\theta(n-1)/n$.

where $\underline{v}^n$ is as given in (6).

Proof: Equation (7i) is obtained from (3i) and (4i) directly. Equations (3ii) and (4ii) yield:

$$W = A \int_{v}^{1} (v^n - \underline{v}^n)\, dv$$

from which (7ii) is obtained by integration.

Of the parameters in the model, we will assume that n, the number of *potential* participants, is fixed (a feature of the industry) and α, the degree of "spillover", is also an industry-specific value. However the size of the minimum investment, ($\underline{b}$), and the degree of protection afforded (θ), are potential policy parameters, although the former is given at least in part by the nature of the technology. In what follows, we shall focus upon θ, asking whether social welfare, as defined above, can be optimised, or at least influenced, by changes in θ, leaving discussion of policy regarding $\underline{b}$ to future work.

We first state

LEMMA 4 : If $\underline{b} > \alpha(n-1)/n$ so that case (ii) in Lemma 1 exists, and welfare is given by (7ii) in Lemma 3, then

(8)
$$\frac{d^2 W}{d\theta^2} = A\, y^{(1-n)/n}\, (dy/d\theta)^2 /n$$
$$+ 2\,(y^{1/n} - 1)\,\alpha\,(1 - 1/n)\,(dy/d\theta)/(1 - \theta + \alpha\theta/n)$$

where $y \equiv \underline{v}^n$ defined in (6).

Proof: See Appendix

Now we can state our proposition

PROPOSITION: For the model and assumptions described, the welfare-maximising value of θ is either 0 or 1. Furthermore if θ is technologically-bounded between $\underline{\theta}$ and $\overline{\theta}$ where $0 < \underline{\theta} < \overline{\theta} < 1$ then the welfare-maximising value of θ is either $\underline{\theta}$ or $\overline{\theta}$.

Proof: a) Consider first that $\underline{b} > \alpha(n-1)/n$ so that only case (ii) exists.

(9)
$$\text{Write } W = \frac{1 - \theta(1 - \alpha)}{n + 1}\,(1 + ny^{\frac{n+1}{n}} - (n+1)\,y)$$

(10)
$$\text{Now } \frac{dW}{d\theta} = -\frac{(1 - \alpha)}{n + 1}\,(1 + ny^{\frac{n+1}{n}} - y) + \frac{1 - \theta(1 - \alpha)}{n + 1}\,(n + 1)\,(y^{\frac{1}{n}} - 1)\,\frac{dy}{d\theta}$$

Note that for a stationary value of W, $\frac{dy}{d\theta}$ has to be negative since

$$(1 + ny^{\frac{n+1}{n}} - y) > 0 \qquad \text{and} \qquad y^{\frac{1}{n}} - 1 < 0 \text{ since } y < 1.$$

If $\frac{dy}{d\theta} < 0$ then $\frac{d^2 W}{d\theta^2} > 0$ (see Lemma 4) and so any stationary value of W is a local minimum. Hence the maximum value of W can only be attained at an extreme value of θ (0 or 1).

b) Now consider that $\underline{b} \le \alpha(n-1)/n$ and both cases in Lemma 1 exist.

For $\theta \geq \frac{b}{\alpha}\frac{n}{(n-1)}$ we have

(11)
$$W = n\left(\alpha\theta\left(n-1\right)/n - \underline{b}\right) + \frac{1-\theta\left(1-\alpha\right)}{n+1}$$

and

(12)
$$\frac{dW}{d\theta} = \alpha\left(n-1\right) - \frac{1-\alpha}{n+1}$$

so that W is linear, with the result that the optimal θ in $(\frac{bn}{\alpha(n-1)}, 1]$ yields no higher value of W that one of the extreme values $(\frac{bn}{\alpha(n-1)}$ if $\alpha < \frac{1}{n^2}$, else 1).

Now at $\theta^* = \frac{bn}{\alpha(n-1)}$, y is zero and the slope of the left-hand derivative of W in (10) at θ^*, $y = 0$ is

(13)
$$\frac{dW}{d\theta} = -\frac{1-\alpha}{n+1} - \left(1 - \theta^*\left(1-\alpha\right)\right)\frac{dy}{d\theta^*}$$
$$= -\frac{1-\alpha}{n+1} + \frac{\alpha\left(n-1\right)\left(1 - \theta^*\left(1-\alpha\right)\right)}{n\left(1 - \theta^* + \theta^*\alpha/n\right)}$$

because at $y = 0$,
$$\frac{dy}{d\theta} = -\frac{\alpha\left(n-1\right)}{n\left[1 - \alpha + \theta\alpha/n\right]}.$$

Now since
$$\frac{\alpha\left(n-1\right)\left(1 - \theta\left(1-\alpha\right)\right)}{n\left(1 - \theta + \theta\alpha/n\right)} < \alpha\left(n-1\right) \quad \text{for all} \quad \theta\varepsilon\left(0, 1\right)$$

we have that at θ^* the left-hand derivative (13) of W with respect to θ is smaller (is more negative) than the right-hand derivative (12). The kink is therefore convex, so that if θ^* is better than points to the right, there exist points to the left of θ^* which dominate θ^*.

Finally, directly from the argument used in (a) we know that there is no interior maximum for $\underline{b} > \alpha\theta\left(n-1\right)/n$.

For the second part of the Proposition, simply note that the above proof shows the absence of any interior local maximum in (0, 1) and hence there can be no value of θ, $\underline{\theta} < \theta < \overline{\theta}$ which yields higher welfare than both $\underline{\theta}$ and $\overline{\theta}$.

COROLLARY : If $\underline{b} \leq \alpha\left(n-1\right)/n$, the welfare maximising value of θ is 0 if and only if
$$\alpha \geq \left(1 + n\underline{b}^{(n+1)/n} + \left(n^2 - 1\right)\underline{b}\right)/n^2$$
and unity otherwise.

Proof: We need only consider θ as $=0$ or 1. Thus directly from (7i) and (7ii), given lemma 3, evaluating (7i) at $\theta = 1$ and (7ii) at $\theta = 0$ and

234

substituting to find when the latter yields more welfare, yields the required condition.

More generally, possible values of θ may be constrained by enforcement technologies or alternative laws. Also comparative statistics are ambiguous in some cases. For this reason we investigate some simulations of welfare as a function of θ for various parameter values in Figures 1 and 2. These plot social welfare values obtained using (7i) and (7ii) for the range of values of the parameter θ for various cases. Figure 1 concentrates on the effect of varying α for $n = 2$ and $\underline{b} = 0.2$. For low α, welfare declines uniformly as θ increases [−indeed this can be shown analytically for $\alpha < 1/n^2$ so

FIGURE 1

Varying α.

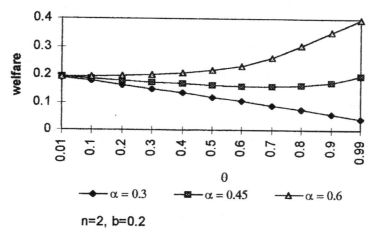

n=2, b=0.2

FIGURE 2

Varying n *and* b.

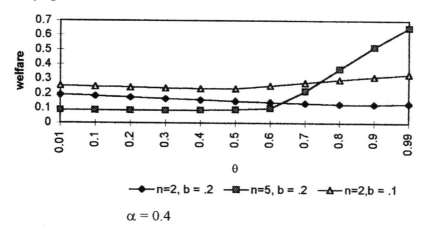

$\alpha = 0.4$

long as all firms participate— see (12)]. However for higher α values, eg $\alpha = 0.6$, welfare rises as θ increases. Figure 2 keeps α fixed at 0.4 but varies n and $\underline{b}$. As n increases it becomes more likely that welfare rises as θ reaches high values. Decreases in $\underline{b}$ also have this effect.

3.4. Discussion

Our Proposition relates to the results on the absence of internal maxima with respect to θ. It might be thought that our welfare function would be likely to yield a policy prescription of extensive protection. However, dependent upon the relevant values, it is optimal either for θ to be very low (zero if possible), that is for protection provided to be very extensive, or for θ to be very high (one if possible). In this sense, our results have something in common with the existing "parent breadth" literature, which tends either to suggest very broad (but short life) or very narrow (but long life) patents.

What, specifically, are the major factors influencing the choice between full and very little protection? Clearly, the higher is α, the extent of spillovers, the more likely is it that very little protection should be provided. Also, examining Figure 2, the greater the number of potential players, n, the more likely it is that little protection should be provided. Finally, the lower the minimum feasible bid, $\underline{b}$, the more likely that little protection should be provided. There is also some indication (though caution is needed here) that the result of getting things wrong in the sense of welfare differences is greater in magnitude if extensive protection is chosen.

Let us consider the intuition underlying these outcomes. A naive (or first glance) view might be that welfare as defined here will fall as θ increases. From (1), partial differentiation gives this result. Reducing the degree of protection reduces the direct benefits from winning but enhances the indirect benefits from participating. However the latter are on average smaller than the former, so reducing protection reduces the expected pay-off. We call this the direct effect, and it would argue for extensive protection.

This reasoning is incomplete in two, possibly opposing, respects, both relating to aggregation. The analysis above ignores the effect of differing numbers of active participants. We know that everyone participates so long as $\underline{b} \le \alpha\theta (n - 1)/n$, a locus which may be sketched on Figure 1 as an inverse relationship between α and θ. The greater is n, the more individual expected utilities there are to be aggregated, and the more likely therefore that the welfare locus rises due to spillovers. The other major factor is the expected number of active participants when not everyone participates. This is directly influenced by $\underline{v}$, namely the higher is $\underline{v}$, the smaller the expected fraction of firms which will participate. In turn $\underline{v}$ is influenced by the underlying parameters through equation (6). Straightforward differentiation reveals that for $\underline{v} > 0$

(14) $$\partial\underline{v}/\partial\theta \gtrless 0 \quad \text{as} \quad \alpha \lessgtr n\underline{b}/(b + n - 1)$$

If the upper inequality is true, the "aggregation effect" goes in the same direction as the naive effect, and welfare will fall as θ rises. In the other case there are offsetting factors. As a result of the "aggregation effect" there

236

is a greater expected number of participants as θ rises, leading to welfare increases, whilst the direct effect leads to welfare falling.

Seen in the light of these two offsetting factors, the detail of the results is readily understood. An increase in α both lessens the impact of reduced protection and makes it more likely that α exceeds $n\underline{b}/(\underline{b} + n - 1)$, increasing expected participation. Thus the higher is α, the more likely that no protection becomes the optimum. Increasing the number of potential participants magnifies the impact of falls in $\underline{v}$ as θ increases, again making it more likely that no protection is best. Reducing $\underline{b}$ again increases the expected number of active participants, so magnifying the aggregation effect. An interior optimum is unlikely, because the aggregation effect increases in intensity as high θ values are increased, so if it is opposing in direction to the direct effect it becomes more likely to outweigh the direct effect as θ increases. (The *sign* of $\partial \underline{v}/\partial \theta$ does not depend on θ, although its magnitude does.)

Clearly, the detail of our results is specific to the particular assumptions, which include the uniform distribution assumption which has allowed us to generate explicit results. However the effects which this particular assumption has allowed us to demonstrate would seem to emanate from much more general forces. The direct effect is clearly general. But so too should be the aggregation effect. Whatever the underlying distribution, the minimum participation valuation, $\underline{v}$, will be influenced by the degree of spillover, α. Therefore we can expect that opposing forces will exist much more broadly, leading to the likelihood of optima at one or other extremes for any particular case.

4 Implications and Conclusions

In practical terms, fine tuning of the intellectual property system largely occurs through moving particular categories of things from being not protected to being covered by patents or covered by designs or copyright legislation, or vice versa. An example is provided by plant varieties and seeds, which first received some protection in the UK as a result of an eponymous act of 1964. It is in making such decisions about categorisation, rather than in modifying patent protection itself, that we feel our approach has most to add.

If this interpretation be accepted, a rationale is provided for the continuing existence of alternative schemes for protecting intellectual property. More significantly, the model suggests that there should be very specific reasons for moving particular new ideas from copyright to patent, rather than it being seen as a tidying up exercise, or, indeed, a matter for gradual case-law development.

In the context of our framework, an industry like pharmaceuticals seems an obvious candidate for tight intellectual property protection. The investment required to develop a new drug (boosted of course by government requirements regarding testing) is measured in tens of millions of dollars (GRABOWSKI and VERNON [1994]). Thus $\underline{b}$ is clearly large. In part as a result, the number of potential players in the pharmaceutical industry is small, even on a worldwide basis. In addition it is likely that spillovers (α) are low. Thus the industry would appear to be a classic example of one suited to patent protection, based upon our model, since the optimal θ is likely to be zero.

At the other end of the spectrum, computer software is an industry where $\underline{b}$ is low. Industry estimates of the investment required to produce a significant development range as low as two person-years and also reflect a rather modest equipment requirement, measured at most in tens of thousands of dollars (see eg MMC 1995). There are large numbers of potential players in many application areas. Additionally, spillovers from developing a particular procedure are likely to find a wide range of applications, and the chances of independently rediscovering something another investigator has already discovered are relatively high. This appears a classic case for copyright protection, based upon the results of our model. If the argument is accepted, moves to change the status of protection of software towards patents (as has happened in the US in some instances) should be resisted.

We should recall that our social welfare function is simply the aggregate of the potential players' expected utilities. This raises two additional issues. The first is that we should consider (static) consumer welfare. From previous work (eg DENICOLO [1996]) it is likely that this would be a factor arguing against strong intellectual property protection, because of the monopoly welfare losses incurred. The fact that we have found arguments in some cases against strong protection without recourse to consumer welfare considerations is noteworthy.

The second issue is that, since we have employed expected n-firm utility as our welfare function in the body of the analysis, might it be the case that the players can reach such an optimum themselves, unaided? This would seem to be more likely when firms find themselves in a symmetric position. A firm with a major development is hardly likely to give up the chance of strong patent protection if it is available even if all other firms in the group want to share it! But in an environment of weak protection, where each player fully recognises mutual benefits from spillovers, there is unlikely to be much pressure to strengthen intellectual property protection. On the other hand, where there is a group view that property rights need to be strengthened, ex ante they can speak with one voice. (This happened in the case of plant breeders' rights in the UK, see PHILLIPS and FIRTH, 1995, ch 25). It is interesting to note that in this case, the breeders wanted protection but argued as a group against such extensive protection as would be allowed by a patent system, (ibid. p. 14). This indicates a bias in the pressures for change. Those cases where strong protection exists may be reluctant to accept change even if it is in the interests of the group as a whole, whereas there will be no individual/group conflict regarding a possible strengthening of property rights.

Moving further outside the model, there is at least one other issue worthy of consideration, namely the question of compatibility or diversity. An important source of welfare in using particular innovating developments is their compatibility (or, to put it another way, a source of annoyance is their lack of compatibility). A strong patents system will tend to encourage diversity (WATERSON [1990]). In some respects this is welfare enhancing, but where compatibility is important, it is welfare reducing. The point is that the context is of considerable relevance in determining an appropriate system. If compatibility is important then a system which encourages developments to have a similar look and feel is desirable – this would not easily be provided by a framework of broad-based protection but might be better promoted by narrow protection. Arguably copyright fits this bill more closely.

APPENDIX

Proof of Lemma 4: Consider (7ii) in Lemma 3, and write this as

$$W = \frac{A}{n+1} z$$

where $z = 1 + ny^{(n+1)/n} - (n+1)y$ and $y \equiv \underline{v}^n$.
Calculate

(A1)
$$\frac{dz}{dy} = (n+1)(y^{1/n} - 1) < 0$$

(A2)
$$\frac{d^2 z}{dy^2} = \frac{n+1}{n} y^{(1-n)/n} > 0$$

Now

(A3)
$$\frac{dW}{d\theta} = -\frac{(1-\alpha)}{n+1} z + \frac{A}{n+1} \frac{dz}{dy} \frac{dy}{d\theta}$$

$$\frac{d^2 W}{d\theta^2} = -\frac{2(1-\alpha)}{n+1} \frac{dz}{dy} \frac{dy}{d\theta} + \frac{A}{n+1} \left(\frac{d^2 z}{dy^2} \left(\frac{dy}{d\theta} \right)^2 + \frac{dz}{dy} \frac{d^2 y}{d\theta^2} \right)$$

From (6)

(A4)
$$\frac{d^2 y}{d\theta^2} = \frac{2(1-\alpha/n)}{(1-\theta+\alpha\theta/n)} \frac{dy}{d\theta}$$

Substitution of A1, A2 and A4 into A3 yields:

$$\frac{d^2 W}{d\theta^2} = Ay^{(1-n)/n} (dy/d\theta)^2/n + 2(y^{1/n} - 1) B (dy/d\theta)$$

where

$$B = -(1-\alpha) + (1-\alpha/n)(1 - \theta(1-\alpha))/(1 - \theta + \alpha\theta/n)$$

which then simplifies to (8).

• References

CHANG, H. F. (1995). – "Patent Scope, Antitrust Policy, and Cumulative Innovation", *Rand Journal of Economics,* 26, pp. 34-57.

DENICOLO (1996). – "Patent Races and Optimal Patent Breadth and Length", *Journal of Industrial Economics,* 44, pp. 249-265.

FERRANDO, A. (1992). – "Patent Policy and Vertical Product Differentiation", *Richerche Economiche,* 46, pp. 221-242.

GILBERT, R., SHAPIRO, C. (1990). – "Optimal Patent Length and Breadth", *Rand Journal of Economics,* 21, pp. 106-112.

GRABOWSKI, H. G., VERNON, J. M. (1994). – "Returns to R&D on New Drug Introductions in the 1980's", *Journal of Health Economics,* 13, pp. 383-406.

GREEN, J. R., SCOTCHMER, S. (1995). – "On the Division of Profit in Sequential Innovation", *Rand Journal of Economics,* 26, 20-33.

HARRIS C., VICKERS, J. (1985). – "Perfect Equilibrium in a Model of a Race", *Review of Economic Studies,* 52, pp. 193-209.

KLEMPERER, P. (1990). – "How Broad Should the Scope of Patent Protection Be?", *Rand Journal of Economics,* 21, pp. 113-130.

LEININGER, W. (1991). – "Patent Competition, Rent Dissipation and the Persistence of Monopoly: the Role of Research Budgets", *Journal of Economic Theory,* 53, pp. 146-172.

Monopolies and Mergers Commission (1995). – *Video Games,* Cm 2781, London: HMSO.

NORDHAUS, W. D. (1989). – *Invention, Growth and Welfare,* Cambridge MA: MIT press.

PHILLIPS, J., FIRTH, A. (1995). – *Introduction to Intellectual Property Law,* (3rd Ed), London: Butterworths.

SCOTCHMER, S. (1991). – "Standing on the Shoulders of Giants: Cumulative Research and Patent Law", *Journal of Economic Perspectives,* 5, pp. 29-41.

SCOTCHMER, S., GREEN, J. (1990). – "Novelty and Disclosure in Patent Law", *Rand Journal of Economics,* 21, pp. 131-146.

VAN DIJK, T. (1996). – "Patent Height and Competition in Product Improvements", *Journal of Industrial Economics,* 44, pp. 151-167.

WATERSON, M. (1990). – "The Economics of Product Patents", *American Economic Review,* 80, pp. 860-869.

Information Disclosure in the Renewal of Patents

Claude CRAMPES, Corinne LANGINIER*

ABSTRACT. – This paper presents a patent choice model allowing strategic decisions in a sequential game with two agents: a patentholder, who knows the characteristics of the market, and a potential entrant who has imperfect information about the value of demand.

We study several Perfect Bayesian Equilibria. We find equilibria where the incumbent prefers not to pay the renewal fee for the patent hoping that it will be interpreted by the challenger as a signal of low market profitability.

* C. CRAMPES : IDEI, GREMAQ; C. LANGINIER : GREMAQ. We would like to thank T. van Dijk, J. Donze, J. Gabszewicz, P. Mahenc, R. Renault and the participants at the 10th ADRES Congress in Strasbourg, the ESEM 96 meeting in Istanbul, the 23rd annual EARIE conference in Vienna and two referees of "Les Annales" for their comments. All errors are naturally ours.

D. Encaoua et al. (eds.), The Economics and Econometrics of Innovation, 243–266.
© 2000 *Kluwer Academic Publishers. Printed in the Netherlands.*

1 Introduction

Patents are one institutional tool to promote research and development by giving innovative firms the possibility to appropriate the gains from their R&D efforts. But, it is widely recognized that many firms use the patent system inefficiently or, in some industries, that they even do not use it at all. Also, in countries where the holder of a patent has to pay a renewal fee in order to keep it in force (as it is the case in most European countries), empirical studies have shown that very few patented inventions are protected for the entire legal duration of 20 years. How can these observations be explained and what kind of lessons can they convey for the political economy of promoting innovation?

The first theoretical contribution to the solution of these questions has been to construct models to analyze how private firms design the scope of their patents (length, height and breadth) within the constraints enforced by national or international laws, and, knowing this behavior, how public authorities accommodate these dimensions in order to maximize social welfare [1]. In these works, all economic agents are supposed to share the same set of information on demand and technology or, if one firm has an informational advantage, the others are not able to infer anything on this information by observing its behavior [2]. On the contrary, many contemporary economic models suppose that there exist strong information asymmetries between economic agents and that they use them strategically.

In the present paper, we adopt this viewpoint in analyzing a patenting decision. We focus on the strategic use of private information by the innovator and show how it can justify a weak incentive to protect an innovation. The situation we study is the following: a patentholder, who perfectly knows the characteristics of the market, is facing the possibility of entry by a challenger with poor market information. We consider the case where the patentholder has to pay an annual fee to keep his patent in force. But the decision to pay or not to pay the renewal fee conveys information about the profitability of the market to the challenger. Our purpose is to show how the patentholder can be induced not to pay the renewal fee of his patent in order not to reveal the truth about the market profitability [3].

Patents are presented as property rights allowing the holder to operate markets in a monopolistic way. We focus on their partial endogeneity by showing how the breadth of the protection they convey is influenced by private or public decisions. But patents are also important signals on

---

1. On the optimal duration of patents and the trade-off between duration and breadth, see KLEMPERER (1990), GILBERT and SHAPIRO (1990).

2. An exception is HORSTMANN, MACDONALD and SLIVINSKI (1985).

3. A similar strategy behavior using advertising expenditures can be found in BAGWELL and RAMEY (1990). The analysis by HORSTMANN and *alii* (1985) is the closest to ours; the main difference is that they do not make explicit the post-entry game and the subsequent profits for both firms.

the inside and outside activity of firms. This second essential feature is included in our model through the asymmetric information on the market value between the patentholder and his challenger.

In section 2, we present some factual and legal motivation for the theoretical model presented in the following sections. In section 3 we develop the hypothesis and timing of the game. As it is a two-period game, we begin by the analysis of the second period equilibrium, namely the investment and production equilibrium, in section 4. The investment is realized by the entrant in order to differentiate its product to respect the breadth of the incumbent's patent. Then, in section 5 we study the first period equilibrium under symmetric information: at this stage the patentholder must decide to keep or not to keep his patent in force by paying the renewal fee and, knowing this decision the challenger must decide to enter or not to enter the market. Section 6 is devoted to the same problem as in section 5, but assuming that the challenger has probabilistic prior beliefs on the state of the market while the incumbent is perfectly informed. In this framework, we study several Perfect Bayesian Equilibria where the incumbent prefers not to pay the renewal fee. The holder expects that patent renunciation will be interpreted by the challenger as a signal of low market profitability and will prevent its entry.

2 The Signalling Value of Patents

Patents are property rights created to stimulate the R&D activity of firms. They allow to control the entry of competitors in markets where the innovators can develop their sales without the pressure of a fierce competition. With such an obvious (private) quality, one could expect that most innovators would apply for a patent. Actually, it is not the case. In some industries, for instance pulp and paper, cosmetics, motors and generators, computers, semiconductors, aircraft etc..., the high-level R&D managers give patents bad marks when compared with alternative means of protecting the competitive advantages of new or improved processes and product [4]. Also, in the countries where a necessary condition for patents to remain valid is that the holder pays a yearly renewal fee, for instance in France, a large number of patents are abandoned long before the end of the maximal legal duration of 20 years [5]. We can infer from these observations

---

4. LEVIN and alii (1987).

5. For a recent survey on the use of patent data see LANJOUW, PAKES and PUTNAM (1996).

that the innovators have objections to the patent system [6]. The dissemination of technical information is the most recognized failure. Innovators can prefer not to patent because of the legal obligation to disclose the details of their innovation and the consequent risks of imitation by informed competitors. But even if the legal conditions of entry are respected by the challengers, patents can have the adverse effect of signalling the profitability of markets for which they are claimed. This is the point of our model.

In order to motivate the foregoing analysis, we begin by presenting a simple model enlightening the advantages and drawbacks of the legal protection conferred by a patent. Consider a firm which hesitates to patent an innovation while a challenger is likely to enter the market. Let Π_{ce} denote the innovator's gross profit when he is protected by a patent (subscript c) and the challenger is in (subscript e). Denoting by subscript $\bar{e}$ the situation where the challenger does not enter and by $\bar{c}$ the case where the innovator has no patent protection, it is clear that

$$(1) \qquad \Pi_{c\bar{e}} = \Pi_{\bar{c}\bar{e}} \geq \Pi_{ce} > \Pi_{\bar{c}e}.$$

Indeed if there is no entry, gross profits are the same for the incumbent with or without a patent, which explains the equality in (1). But profits are decreased by the entry of a competitor. The decrease is weak, and possibly null, if a patent has been granted, while without any legal protection the incumbent suffers a large loss, which explains the ordering of the inequalities in (1). Now, let ρ_c be the probability that an entry occurs when the innovation is patented and $\rho_{\bar{c}}$ when there is no legal protection. Finally the parameter a stands for the cost of patenting.

We want to make explicit the arguments *against* patenting. Clearly, the innovator is better off without a patent iff

$$(2) \qquad (1 - \rho_c)\Pi_{c\bar{e}} + \rho_c\Pi_{ce} - a < (1 - \rho_{\bar{c}})\Pi_{\bar{c}\bar{e}} + \rho_{\bar{c}}\Pi_{\bar{c}e}.$$

Using (1), we can rewrite this inequality as

$$(3) \qquad \rho_{\bar{c}}(\Pi_{ce} - \Pi_{\bar{c}e}) < a + (\Pi_{c\bar{e}} - \Pi_{ce})(\rho_c - \rho_{\bar{c}}).$$

---

6. However, note that from the social viewpoint private inconveniences can turn out to be advantages. If the innovator decides not to patent and keeps his innovation secret, clearly it is a bad social decision. But, if the innovator enters the market without any protection (neither patent nor secrecy) or if he does not pay the renewal fee of a European patent, this is good for society since the innovation can be used for free by anyone.

Without any signalling effect of the patent, we have $\rho_{\bar{c}} = \rho_c = \rho$. Then, (3) is a simple cost-benefit decision rule that compares the expected gain and the cost of the patent:

$$\rho(\Pi_{ce} - \Pi_{\bar{c}e}) < a.$$

Consequently, if we consider that a patent has no *ex ante* effect, in the sense that it does not change the entry decision of challengers, the explanation for the low success of the patent system is a large cost a and/or a low expected gain $\rho(\Pi_{ce} - \Pi_{\bar{c}e})$. For example, the low expected gain argument is the one kept by Schankerman and Pakes [1985] to explain the very short life of a large majority of French patents because the renewal fee a is very low [7].

But on the right hand side of condition (3) appears an additional term measuring the pre-entry effect of the patent. Most arguments used by lawyers to promote patents are reflected by the following hypothesis which is standard in the economics of R&D [8]: patent is a good dissuasion against entry so that $\rho_{\bar{c}} > \rho_c$. Suppose this assertion is true. Then the second term on the right-hand side of (3) is negative, which means that it decreases the advantages of no patenting. Consequently, it cannot be an argument to explain why patents are considered a poor solution to the protection of inventions in many industries.

On the contrary, many practicians argue that the deposit of a patent has the adverse effect of stimulating entry so that

$$(4) \qquad\qquad \rho_{\bar{c}} < \rho_c.$$

If this is the case, the right hand side is clearly increased, which strengthen the no-patenting solution. The classic explanation of (4) is that the applicant to a patent is constrained by law to give a detailed description of his innovation. Then, potential competitors benefit from this information on the process or product technology and this help them to enter the market, maybe illegally.

A complementary argument against deposit is that patenting transmits an information on the profitability of the market(s) claimed by the holder [9]. Indeed, when a firm learns about a deposit, it can rationally infer that the holder prices the market above the cost to enforce the patent. Rather than transmitting this information, the innovator can prefer not to patent.

---

7. "... a large fraction of patents are without any economic value since most of them are abandoned despite very low cost." Schankerman and Pakes (1985), p. 928. Actually the cost of maintaining a patent is much higher than the mere renewal fee because "... there are two aspects to intellectual property...: one is to get patents ... the other thing is to enforce them". Warshofsky (1994), p. 117.

8. Most economic models adopt the naive assumption that $\rho_c = 0$, which means that the patent is a perfect protection against any form of imitation.

9. On the contrary, when challengers have a better information than the patentholder about the market, it can be in the interest of the patentee to propose them a licence on the patent. In this case, the game is no longer a signal game but an adverse selection game. See Macho-Stadler and Pérez-Castrillo (1991).

Such a strategic no-patenting is obviously hard to prove because there is generally a mix of reasons to explain why something does not happen. In some patent cases this desire of no signalling seems to be strongly at work. But of course, the success of a patent or of a no-patent decision is the result of the combined action of all the departments of the firm [10]. The marketing dimension we will stress on from now is only one among the technical, legal, financial and organizational aspects.

The objective of the paper is to present a model explaining why two rational firms can behave in a way that results in (3) and (4). It can be the story of an initial patenting decision like the Kodak and Polaroïd case cited in footnote (10): in this case the trade-off for the innovator is between to reveal explicitly technical information or to keep it secret while the innovator's information on the market is not necessarily better than the challenger's information. But the complexity of a model dealing with a double asymmetry of information, one on the technology and one on the market would be too high. To keep things simple, we assume here that there is only one asymmetry, that is on the demand function. Moreover, we want to focus on the signalling dimension of patents which means that the informational advantage is to be in favor of the patentee. It results that the model described hereafter fits more the renewal decision problem attached to European patents than to initial patenting decisions: both the patentee and his challenger know the technology since it was publicly disclosed and the patentee has a better knowledge of the market since he is already managing it.

3 The Model

There are two firms. Firm H holds a patent that gives him a perfect protection on the market [11]. The second firm denoted E is a potential

---

10. In WARSHOFSKY (1994) one can find a large spectrum of case studies on the strategic use of patents. Several suggest the importance of their signalling drawback. For instance, in the war between Polaroïd and Kodak for the instant photography market, "... [Kodak management] decided [in 1964] that the instant business was not worth a significant effort", p. 71. But in 1968, "... the forerunner of the [Polaroïd] SX-70 film opened Kodak's eyes to the power of Polaroïd's research.... Kodak embarked on an instant program of its own", p. 75. "Whether it was indeed their owe at the brilliance of the Polaroïd research or simply a desire to share in what promised to be a rich market, Kodak's top brass decided to take another look at the instant photography market. What they saw was enticing. Polaroïd sales were booming...", p. 76. "In April 1976, Kodak entered the market", p. 79.
To be complete, we must add that Polaroïd immediately reacted by attacking Kodak for infringing 12 of its patents and that in 1986 Kodak was condemned. "Its losses on the ill-fated adventure were about $100 million" (ibid. p. 86). But the quotations clearly show that the patent decision by Polaroïd had generated a revision of Kodak's beliefs resulting in (4).
11. This means that H is able to detect and to bring an action against any infringer. Entry remains possible as long as the entrant respects the patentee's claims.

competitor. The conditions of its entry are determined by the patent law. According to most patent laws in Europe, we assume that the holder must pay each year a renewal fee in order to keep his patent in force. If he does not pay it, the patent is permanently cancelled and E can enter the market without any constraint [12].

In section 6, the main feature of our model is an information asymmetry on the demand value. We assume that firm H knows whether the market is profitable or not before he pays the renewal fee. The challenger only knows the probability distribution of demand but it can observe the renewal decision by the incumbent. For this reason the incumbent may be induced not to renew his patent despite a high market profitability in order to hide the true value of demand to the challenger.

When the patent is kept in force, entry is not prevented. It is just restricted in the following sense. We assume that the new product has to be sufficiently differentiated from the incumbent's output in order to allow the former innovator to recoup his R&D expenditures. The investment in product differentiation must be paid by the entrant: this is a way to model the so-called breadth of patents. This requirement is justified in terms of R&D incentive. For the incumbent, R&D expenditures belong to the history of the game, so they should not be taken into account in the present public decisions. But if the incumbent cannot recoup these expenditures, future research will be reduced since present innovators anticipate that they will face the same kind of situation in the future.

Both firms have the same production cost function but they differ in their "entry" costs. For the incumbent, the "entry" cost is the renewal fee if he decides to pay it. For the challenger, entry costs are to be paid to install the plant and to advertise the product and additionally, the entrant will have to pay to differentiate its product. We assume that the challenger's entry cost is high enough to prevent it from entering the market when demand is low.

The model is described in a two period game:

- in the first period, the patentholder H decides whether to pay the renewal fee (C) or to give his patent up ($\overline{C}$). The challenger E observes this decision and decides to enter (e) or not to enter ($\overline{e}$). At the time of these decisions in the asymmetric model of section 6, the incumbent knows whether demand is high (demand intercept α_h) or low (α_ℓ), where $\alpha_h > \alpha_\ell$, while the entrant only has priors about the States of Nature: ρ denotes the probability that demand is high,

- the second period is an investment and production game where both firms have the same information. If the challenger did not enter, the incumbent has a monopoly position to choose his output. When entry occurs, since the challenger knows the demand, the subgame is a

---

12. We do not consider the case where E files a patent for its own product or process. This patent would be useless because it cannot prevent H from using his innovation and there is no other candidate for entry.

perfect information game where first the entrant chooses its investment in differentiation and second both firms compete in quantities.

In figure 1, we have depicted the first period game. The gains at the bottom of the tree are those resulting from the investment and production decisions of the second period game. They will be determined explicitly in the next section.

FIGURE 1

Tree of the First Period Game.

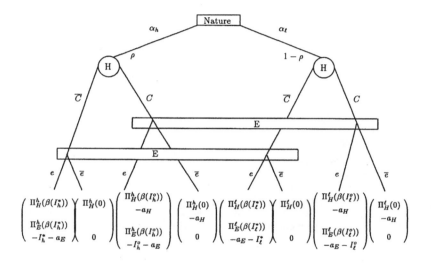

Using the classical backward induction argument, we first determine the Cournot equilibrium and the investment of the post-entry subgame. Then, we characterize the Perfect Equilibria (section 5) and Perfect Bayesian Equilibria (section 6) of the complete game restricted by the differentiation imposed by the government to protect innovations.

4 Production Subgame

We compute the equilibrium quantities sold by the firms when they both have perfect information about the market profitability. Three alternative market situations are possible:

- if the challenger does not enter, the incumbent is a monopolist,

250

- if the challenger enters and the patent is no longer in force, the market is a duopoly with differentiated products. The differentiation level is determined by the entrant without any restriction before firms produce and it is known by both,

- finally, if the patent is still in force and the challenger enters the market, it has to respect the patent law, which means not to infringe the incumbent's rights. It is forced to invest in differentiation at least an amount determined by the government. Knowing this differentiation level, both firms then compete in quantities.

4.1. Choice of Quantities

The demand for product from each firm $i = H, E$ is represented by:

$$(5) \qquad p_i(q_i, q_j) = \alpha - q_i - \beta q_j \qquad j \neq i$$

where $\alpha \in \{\alpha_\ell, \alpha_h\}$ is an index of market profitability and β is a differentiation parameter, $\beta \in [0, 1]$.

$\beta = 0$ means that the challenger has entered a market disjointed from the incumbent's market: we have two juxtaposed monopolies [13].

$\beta = 1$ indicates perfect substitutes.

The inverse demand function (5) can be interpreted as the marginal utility of product i. The utility function of the representative consumer is

$$(6) \qquad u(q_E, q_H) = \alpha(q_E + q_H) - \frac{1}{2}(q_E^2 + q_H^2) - \beta q_E q_H.$$

Finally, we assume that E and H have the same production cost function: let c denote the constant unit cost of production, with $c < \alpha_\ell$.

We first determine the socially optimal quantities. Since differentiation has a social value $(\partial u / \partial \beta < 0)$ and since the firms have the same production cost, it is Pareto superior to have both firms producing positive quantities.

These quantities are determined by the solution of

$$\max_{q_E, q_H} u(q_E, q_H) - c(q_E + q_H)$$

and their values are

$$q_i^0 = \frac{\alpha - c}{1 + \beta} \qquad i = E, H.$$

Putting these quantities into the social welfare function, we get the maximal social welfare

$$(7) \qquad V(q_E^0, q_H^0) = \frac{(\alpha - c)^2}{1 + \beta} \overset{\text{def}}{=} V(\beta).$$

---

13. But even in this case we assume that the private information of the incumbent on α is useful for the challenger in the pre-entry game for evaluating its own market.

Second, we consider the case of a private monopoly, which corresponds either to the situation where the challenger decides not to enter or to the situation where the challenger enters but chooses to differentiate its product perfectly ($\beta = 0$).

The incumbent problem is then

$$\max_{q_H}(\alpha - q_H - c)q_H.$$

So, he produces $q_H^M = (\alpha - c)/2$ and his equilibrium profit is

$$(8) \qquad \Pi_H^M = \frac{(\alpha - c)^2}{4}.$$

As a third case, consider the duopoly structure with differentiated demands (5). Recall that there is perfect information about α. Firm $i = E, H$ solves

$$\max_{q_i}(\alpha - q_i - \beta q_j^* - c)q_i \qquad j \neq i.$$

It is straightforward to calculate the equilibrium quantities

$$q_i^* = \frac{\alpha - c}{2 + \beta} \qquad i = H, E$$

and the equilibrium profits are

$$(9) \qquad \Pi_i^* = \left(\frac{\alpha - c}{2 + \beta}\right)^2 \overset{\text{def}}{=} \Pi_i(\beta).$$

From (7) and (9) it is easy to check that social welfare as well as private payoffs can be increased by decreasing product homogeneity.

4.2. Choice of the Differentiation Level

4.2.1. The Private Choice

We now assume that the challenger can modify the differentiation parameter by its investment I. The investment level is chosen after the entry. Let denote $\beta(I)$ with $\beta'(I) < 0$ this relation.

When the incumbent has not paid the renewal fee, the entrant is free to choose I to maximize its net profit

$$\max_{I \geq 0} \Pi_E(\beta(I)) - I.$$

In order to keep our analysis as simple as possible, we assume that

$$(10) \qquad \beta''(I) \leq 0,$$

so that the differentiation investment will necessarily be a corner solution. Either the entrant invests zero so that only the "natural differentiation" $\beta(0)$

will distinguish the products, or, on the contrary, it chooses to differentiate totally [14] so that $\beta(I) = 0$. We define

$$I_{max} = \beta^{-1}(0).$$

Let us denote I^* the investment chosen by the entrant. It is defined by

(11) $$I^* = \begin{cases} 0 & \text{if } I_{max} > \Pi_E(0) - \Pi_E(\beta(0)) \\ I_{max} & \text{otherwise} \end{cases}$$

4.2.2. The Breadth Requirement

Without any entry condition, competition from the challenger can result in a bankruptcy for the innovator. On static grounds, this can be welfare-improving if the entrants' profits are higher than the incumbent's profits and/or if the utility of consumers is increased. But this free entry is dangerous for the future since the candidates to new innovations will be dissuaded to invest by the bankruptcy of the incumbent. Consequently, the patent system is designed to promote current research by protecting old researchers. In order not to complicate our model, we assume that this concern is materialized in a constraint to compensate the incumbent for his past research expenditures [15]. The solution we choose is to enforce a sufficient width to the incumbent's patent, that is a low substitutability parameter β through a minimal investment in differentiation imposed to the challenger. Denote by D the portion of R&D expenditures the incumbent has not yet recouped [16]. Using (9), the constraint will be written:

(12) $$\Pi_H(\beta(I)) - D \geq 0.$$

Suppose that $\Pi_H(0) \geq D \geq \Pi_H(\beta(0))$ [17].

Let I^S denote the value of I such that (12) is satisfied as an equality. Since $\Pi'(\beta) < 0$ and $\beta'(I) < 0$, inequality (12) can be rewritten

(13) $$I \geq I^S.$$

---

14. There is perfect differentiation for example when the challenger enters a country on which the patentholder has no claim.
15. "The ability of the innovator to capture the surplus generated by his innovation, benefits competition in the long run by encouraging others to innovate as well", Competition Policy and Intellectual Property Rights (OECD, 1989).
16. It can look curious that the public authority in charge of the patents tailors a specific width for each patentholder. Actually, this is what occurs when patent examiners define *ex ante* the claims of applicants and when the courts examine the suits for infringement.
17. $\Pi_H(0) = \Pi_H(\beta(I_{max})) \geq D$ means that the initial R&D choice by the incumbent was at least balanced in a monopoly framework. On the contrary, $D \geq \Pi_H(\beta(0))$ means that the innovator would lose money if he was facing a competitor selling a perfect substitute. This is the rationale for a differentiation requirement: the patentholder needs to be protected and the government will not allow the challenger to enter if it does not respect a minimal breadth from the incumbent. An alternative way to write these two hypothesis is $0 \leq I^S \leq I_{max}$.

The constrained investment maximizes the social utility of the agents living at one date subject to constraint (13):

$$\max_I V(\beta(I)) - I$$

$$s/c \ I \geq I^S$$

It is easy to check that under the hypothesis (10) the objective function is convex. So, the solution is a corner solution defined by

(14) $\qquad I^o = \begin{cases} I^S & \text{if } V(\beta(I^S)) - I^S \geq V(0) - I_{max} \\ I_{max} & \text{otherwise} \end{cases}$

The comparison between the private investment and the constrained optimal one permits to state the following proposition:

PROPOSITION 1 : $I^o > I^*$ for $I_{max} > \Pi_E(0) - \Pi_E(\beta(0))$ and $I^o = I^*$ otherwise.

The proof is presented in appendix 1.

Actually, if the investment needed for a perfect differentiation I_{max} is low, the private choice of the challenger is the same as the constrained choice. But, for high values of I_{max}, the private choice is strictly below the social one.

5 Final Payoffs and Equilibria under Complete Information

We can now justify the payoffs at the bottom of the tree in figure 1. The payoffs of the patentholder (resp. the challenger) are on the first (resp. second) line.

For each case where the challenger does not enter $(\bar{e})$, its payoff is 0 and the incumbent is a monopolist (which is equivalent to facing a completely differentiated competitor: $\beta = 0$) either on a good (h) or on a bad (ℓ) market. On the contrary, the decision to enter (e) results in a duopoly situation where both firms earn the same gross profit: $\Pi_i^h(.) = \Pi^h(.)$ for $i = H, E$ if the state of the market is high, and $\Pi_i^\ell(.) = \Pi^\ell(.)$ if the state of the market is low. The value of this gross profit is determined by the level of the investment in differentiation payed by the challenger. When the incumbent has not paid the patent renewal fee $(\overline{C})$, the investment is the one that maximizes the private profit of the challenger, I_h^* or I_ℓ^*. When the patent remains in force (C) the investment is I^o described in (14). Note that if $I^o = I^S$ determined by the equality in (12), its value is contingent on the

254

state of the market since by (9) and (12) the profit needed by the incumbent to recoup his R&D cost is a function of the profitability of the market α [18].

Finally, we have to subtract from the gross profits the renewal fee a_H for the incumbent when he decides to keep his patent in force, the entry cost a_E and the differentiation expenses I for the challenger when it decides to enter.

Knowing these net profits, let us review the possible equilibria under complete information.

First we assume that

$$(15) \qquad \Pi_E^\ell(\beta(I_\ell^*)) - I_\ell^* < a_E < \Pi_E^h(\beta(I_h^o)) - I_h^o.$$

Because of the first inequality in (15), the challenger will never enter when the market is bad: the low market profitability is such that even if the challenger can freely choose its investment I_ℓ^*, the resulting profit is not sufficient to pay the entry cost a_E. Conversely, as shown by the second inequality, entry is profitable when the market is profitable even if the patent is still active and the investment is determined by legal constraints.

Then, under (15), the challenger enters when $\alpha = \alpha_h$ and he does not enter when $\alpha = \alpha_l$, whichever the decision of the patentholder. Taking into account this behavior of the challenger, what does the incumbent decide? Facing a low profitability market, he will obviously give the patent up. Paying a_H in order to renew the patent would bring no advantage, since the entrant does not enter in this case.

The case with $\alpha = \alpha_h$ is more interesting. Anticipating that E will enter, we see in figure 1 that the best decision for the incumbent is to continue iff

$$(16) \qquad \Pi_H^h(\beta(I_h^o)) - \Pi_H^h(\beta(I_h^*)) \geq a_H$$

and to abandon otherwise.

As an illustration, because $a_H \geq 0$ the equality $I_h^o = I_h^*$ is a sufficient (but not necessary) condition for the incumbent to abandon. An alternative way to write $I_h^o = I_h^*$ is [19]:

$$(17) \qquad I_{max} < \Pi_E^h(0) - \Pi_E^h(\beta(0)).$$

Particularly we see that if $\beta(0)$ is small, the best choice for the incumbent will be to give up. The reason is that with a "natural" strong level of differentiation, the challenger is not a threat for the incumbent even if it enters the market without any additional expense in differentiation. Consequently, it would be useless to pay a renewal fee just to obtain a very small increase in differentiation by the entrant.

---

18. Moreover, one can think that D itself is a function of α. If during preceding periods, the incumbent was facing the same State of Nature as in the current period, residual R&D expenditures depend on this State of Nature. But we assume here that D is a given constant.

19. See figure 2 in appendix 1 and recall that $\Pi_E^j(.) = \Pi_H^j(.)$ for $j = h, l$.

To sum up, we can establish the following proposition:

PROPOSITION 2 : The Perfect Equilibrium of the patent-entry game is:

- if $\alpha = \alpha_\ell$, the challenger does not enter in any case and the incumbent does not pay for renewing his patent,

- if $\alpha = \alpha_h$, the challenger enters in any case and the incumbent pays the renewal fee when (16) is satisfied and does not pay otherwise.

We now turn to the case where the true value of α is unknown by the challenger.

6 Perfect Bayesian Equilibria

It is well known that in a sequential game where the follower possesses less information than the leader, the decisions taken by the leader can convey some information valuable to the follower if it can interpret the observations of these decisions. In our model, the decision by the incumbent to pay or not to pay the renewal fee can, under certain circumstances, be interpreted as a signal about the market profitability.

The essential trade-off faced by the incumbent is the following:

- to pay the renewal fee has a "profit effect" which is positive or negative depending on the competition intensity if the challenger enters and on the value of the fee a_H (see rule (16)).

- to pay the renewal fee has a "probability effect" which is potentially negative since the observation of the payment will never suggest the challenger that the market is bad. Then, observing that the patent is kept in force can only increase the attractiveness of the market. Consequently, paying increases the probability that H will face a competitor.

So, when the "profit effect" is negative, both effects work in the same direction: the incumbent is better off without the patent independently of the state of the market and we have a pooling equilibrium (see below 6.1). When the "profit effect" is positive, it works against the "probability effect" and the incumbent has some incentives to pay when the market is profitable and not to pay when the market is bad. But, as shown in paragraph 6.2, this incentive is not sufficient to generate separating equilibria. Consequently, in paragraph 6.3, we analyze the characteristics of semi-separating equilibria.

As the analysis shows, there exist a large number of different equilibria for alternative values of the parameters. It is out of the scope of the present paper to give a complete description of all these equilibria. As we are essentially interested in the behavior of an incumbent trying to blockade the entry of a competitor, we will focus on the equilibria where the patentholder

256

while knowing that the market is highly profitable prefers not to pay the renewal fee.

6.1. The Pooling Equilibria

In a pooling equilibrium, the incumbent chooses the same strategy independently of the State of Nature. So the challenger cannot update its beliefs and it has to take its decision on the basis of the priors. The value of the priors is essential for the existence of a pooling equilibrium since if the challenger initially thinks that the market is profitable, it will be difficult to make it change its mind by a simple decision of no-patenting. Define [20]

(18)
$$\rho^* \stackrel{\text{def}}{=} \frac{I_\ell^* + a_E - \Pi_E^\ell(\beta(I_\ell^*))}{\Pi_E^h(\beta(I_h^*)) - I_h^* - \Pi_E^\ell(\beta(I_\ell^*)) + I_\ell^*},$$

and denote $d_H(\alpha)$ the decision by the patentholder, and $d_E(d_H)$ the decision by the challenger.

> PROPOSITION 3 : For $\rho \leq \rho^*$, there exists a pooling equilibrium defined by
> $$d_H(\alpha) = \overline{C} \quad \forall \alpha,$$
> $$d_E(\overline{C}) = \overline{e}, \ d_E(C) = e$$
> $$Prob\{\alpha = \alpha_h / d_H = C\} = 1$$

The intuition behind this proposition is the following [21]. When ρ is small, the chances that the challenger enters are weak. To pay the renewal fee will be a good protection if entry occurs ("profit effect") but it will also increase the incentive to enter. Consequently, the incumbent is better off without renewing in any case. The challenger cannot revise its priors and, since $\rho \leq \rho^*$, its expected profits are negative. So, when observing $d_H = \overline{C}$, it cannot infer the true value of α and it decides not to enter. Now, what occurs if it observes the out-of-equilibrium decision $d_H = C$, that is a decision to pay the fee by the patentholder? To keep $(\overline{C}, \overline{e})$ as the equilibrium path, we must define a revision rule of the prior such that it cannot be in the interest of the holder to deviate. With the proposed rule $Prob\{\alpha = \alpha_h / d_H = C\} = 1$, any deviation by the incumbent induce an entry $(d_E(C) = e)$ which is clearly bad for him.

---

20. ρ^* is the value of the prior such that the entrant has a zero expected profit when entering a non protected market.
21. For formal proofs, see Appendix 2.

PROPOSITION 4 : For $\rho > \rho^*$ and

(19) $a_H > max\{\Pi_H^h(\beta(I_h^o)) - \Pi_H^h(\beta(I_h^*)), \ \Pi_H^h(0) - \Pi_H^h(\beta(I_h^*))\}$

there exists a pooling equilibrium where

$$d_H(\alpha) = \overline{C} \qquad\qquad \forall \alpha,$$
$$d_E(d_H) = e \qquad\qquad \forall d_H$$
$$Prob\{\alpha = \alpha_h/d_H = C\} = 1$$

In this case, it would be too costly for the incumbent to prevent the challenger from entering. The renewal fee a_H is so high, or equivalently the natural differentiation is so strong ($\beta(0)$ close to 0) that the patentholder prefers not to pay [22]. On the basis of the priors, the challenger enters in any case and any revision of the prior beliefs on the basis of an out-of-equilibrium observation would be without any effect on the holder's gains but would cost him a_H. So the patentholder does not deviate.

There exist other pooling equilibria, those where the incumbent pays the renewal fee for any value of the market profitability. In this type of equilibrium, an incumbent who knows that the market is bad mimics the behavior of a firm selling on a rich market. This can only increase the chances to attract a challenger. Actually, it is essentially justified by a low renewal fee a_H as compared to the high profits expected from the protection. As we saw with the observations of SCHANKERMAN and PAKES [1985], few innovators are concerned by such a non contingent behavior. A more precise analysis of this behavior would need a clear description of the out-of-equilibrium decisions, particularly the rationale for infringements and legal attack [23].

6.2. The Non Existence of a Separating Equilibrium

A separating equilibrium requires that the challenger can interpret unambiguously the actions it observed from the patentholder. In particular, the non payment of the renewal fee should clearly mean that the market is non profitable. But if the patentholder knows that the follower will interpret the no-renewal as a signal of low profitability and consequently will decide not to enter, it is in his interest not to pay when the market is of type α_h. Then, he will never choose to renew his patent, so that there cannot exist a separating equilibrium.

---

22. When $\beta(0)$ is close to 0, $\beta(I_h^o)$ and $\beta(I_h^*)$ are close to 0 so that the differences in the right hand side of (19) are very small.

23. The Polaroïd vs. Kodak case presented in footnote (10) is a good example of such a situation: entry is "forbidden", nevertheless there is an entry, then the patentholder goes to trial.

6.3. The Semi-Separating Equilibria

The preceding development suggests that we can find semi-separating equilibria, i.e. equilibria in which the incumbent will not take the same decision irrespective of the market characteristics (there is no complete pooling) but nevertheless the challenger cannot discover for sure the missing information by observing the incumbent (there is no complete separation).

Several semi-separating equilibria are possible. We just consider the following one, where π_H is the probability that the holder abandons his patent and π_E is the probability that the challenger enters.

> PROPOSITION 5 : For $\rho > \rho^*$ and
>
> (20) $\qquad a_H < \Pi_H^h(\beta(I_h^o)) - \Pi_H^h(\beta(I_h^*))$
>
> there exists a semi-separating equilibrium where
>
> $$d_H(\alpha) = \begin{cases} (\overline{C}, C; \ 1, 0) & \text{if } \alpha = \alpha_\ell \\ (\overline{C}, C; \ \pi_H, 1 - \pi_H) & \text{if } \alpha = \alpha_h \end{cases}$$
>
> $$d_E(d_H) = \begin{cases} (e, \overline{e}; \ 1, 0) & \text{if } d_H = C \\ (e, \overline{e}; \ \pi_E, 1 - \pi_E) & \text{if } d_H = \overline{C} \end{cases}$$
>
> $$Prob\{\alpha = \alpha_h / d_H = C\} = 1$$
>
> $$Prob\{\alpha = \alpha_h / d_H = \overline{C}\} = \frac{\rho \pi_H}{\rho \pi_H + (1 - \rho)}.$$

When the market is low-valued, the incumbent decides not to pay the fee. But this can also occur when the market is good. Consequently, when it observes a no-renewal, the challenger cannot be quite sure that the market is bad. It can just perform a bayesian revision of its priors. It is only when the challenger observes the payment of the fee that it can be sure that the market has a high value and that it decides to enter with probability 1.

When the incumbent knows that the market type is α_h, he plays a mixed strategy: he decides to give up the patent with a probability

(21) $\qquad \pi_H \overset{\text{def}}{=} Prob\{\overline{C}/\alpha_h\} = \dfrac{1 - \rho}{\rho} \dfrac{a_E + I_\ell^* - \Pi_E^\ell(\beta(I_\ell^*))}{\Pi_E^h(\beta(I_h^*)) - I_h^* - a_E}.$

The challenger who observes that the patent is no longer active decides to enter with probability

(22) $\qquad \pi_E \overset{\text{def}}{=} Prob\{e/\overline{C}\} = \dfrac{\Pi_H^h(0) - \Pi_H^h(\beta(I_h^o)) + a_H}{\Pi_H^h(0) - \Pi_H^h(\beta(I_h^*))}.$

Given (21), the challenger is indifferent between entry and no entry when it observes that the patent is no longer in force. Given (22) the patentholder is indifferent between paying or not paying the fee when the market is good.

The bayesian rule to revise the prior when observing that the patent is abandoned is

$$Prob\{\alpha_h/\overline{C}\} = \frac{Prob\{\overline{C}/\alpha_h\}\rho}{Prob\{\overline{C}/\alpha_h\}\rho + Prob\{\overline{C}/\alpha_\ell\}(1-\rho)}$$
$$= \frac{\rho\pi_H}{\rho\pi_H + (1-\rho)}$$

since the incumbent plays $\overline{C}$ with probability one when he observes α_ℓ.

As compared with the equilibrium in proposition 3, we see that this one needs a high value of the prior beliefs ρ. Consequently, here a complete pooling to try to restrict any entry is not possible since the challenger thinks that the market is good with a high probability.

As compared with the equilibrium in proposition 4, we see that the renewal fee is to be low and/or $\beta(.)$ is to be high which means a weak natural differentiation level. This explains that the incumbent has some interest in keeping the patent in force even if that gives the challenger a reason for entering.

7 Conclusion

When a patentholder possesses private information about the value of demand, he knows that his behavior may affect the entry decision of the challenger. Thus, the decision to pay the renewal fee to maintain the patent active can be used by the holder as a strategic instrument.

In a non strategic framework, not to pay the renewal fee simply means that the expected benefits from the patent (monopoly profit minus duopoly profit) are less than the expected value of its costs. These costs are larger than the mere administrative fees because they include the expected expenditures for monitoring the markets and suing for the infringements. For rational agents, the (publicly observed) payment of the fee should be interpreted as a commitment to sue firms who infringe. Conversely, the non payment should mean that the patent is not worth all the (partially unobserved) incurred costs. But, because of its incomplete information on demand and of the lack of observability of some incumbent's expenditures, the challenger can never be sure of the reason why the patentholder abandons his exclusive right. Thus, the strategic signalling effect consists in abandoning a profitable patent in order to convince the challenger that the market is bad. Because of information acquisition on the markets, such a strategic behavior is more likely at the very beginning of the patent life: the innovator applies for a patent and when he gets it (usually two years later), he does not keep it in force, which could mean that the market studies eventually revealed an unprofitable activity.

The trade-off is between the profit advantages of the patent that obliges any entrant to differentiate its product and the risk to attract a challenger by signalling a highly profitable market. There exist numerous equilibria among which we have considered some. In particular, we have found that when the challenger has low beliefs on the market profitability, the incumbent can prefer not to pay the renewal fee even if the market is favorable, in order to send a bad "signal" to the challenger.

In mixed strategies, the patentholder decides not to pay the renewal fee when the market is bad and to randomize his decision when the market is good. When the challenger observes that the incumbent pays the renewal fee, it knows that the market is good and decides to enter. But, when it observes that the incumbent gave his patent up, it decides to enter or not the market on the basis of revised probabilities.

One can conclude that this signalling feature of the renewal decision is an incentive to shorten the actual duration of patents. This can be a piece of explanation for the surprising short life observed for most patents, despite the very low value of fees at the beginning of their life.

The Breadth Requirement

Proof of proposition 1

We have to show that $I^o \geq I^*$.

First, we determine the "static optimum", which is the investment that maximizes the social utility of the agents living at one date without any constraint

$$\max_{I \geq 0} V(\beta(I)) - I.$$

This is a convex objective function and the solution is a corner solution:

$$(23) \qquad I^{so} = \begin{cases} 0 & \text{if } I_{max} > V(0) - V(\beta(0)) \\ I_{max} & \text{otherwise} \end{cases}$$

I^o is the solution to the same problem but with the additional constraint (13): $I \geq I^S$. Clearly, the exact value of I^o cannot be known and compared with I^{so} without expliciting the functional shape of the $V(.)$ and $\beta(.)$ functions. But because of the constraint (13) it is evident that I^o is generically greater than I^o. On the other hand, from $V(0) - V(\beta(0)) > \Pi_E(0) - \Pi_E(\beta(0))$ it is evident that $I^o \geq I^*$. Consequently, we obtain $I^o \geq I^*$.

We illustrate this result in figure 2 where the levels of optimal private investment I^* and of constrained investment I^o are drawn as a function of I_{max}.

FIGURE 2

Private and Social Values of the Investment in Differentiation.

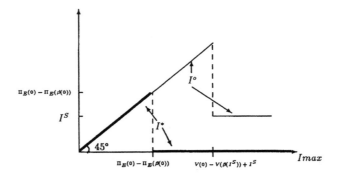

Perfect Bayesian Equilibria

Proof of propositions 3, 4 and 5

• Pooling Equilibria

We determine the pooling equilibrium when the incumbent decides not to pay the renewal fee whatever the value of the market.

The challenger observes nothing and then its posterior belief is equal to its prior $\mu = \rho$. In order to keep the proof as simple as possible, we simplify the notation: $\Pi^j_E(.) = \Pi^j_H(.) = \Pi^j(.)$ with $j = h, l$.

It decides not to enter the market if:

$$\rho[\Pi^h(\beta(I^*_h)) - a_E - I^*_h] + (1 - \rho)[\Pi^\ell(\beta(I^*_\ell)) - I^*_\ell - a_E] < 0$$

$$\Leftrightarrow \rho < \frac{I^*_\ell + a_E - \Pi^\ell(\beta(I^*_\ell))}{\Pi^h(\beta(I^*_h)) - I^*_h - [\Pi^\ell(\beta(I^*_\ell)) - I^*_\ell]} = \rho^*.$$

Then, with an out-of-equilibrium belief $prob\{\alpha = \alpha_h/d_H = C\} = 1$, the incumbent will not deviate because $\Pi^h(0) > \Pi^h(0) - a_H$ and $\Pi^h(0) > \Pi^h(\beta(I^o_h)) - a_H$.

We can conclude that for values of $\rho \leq \rho^*$, there exists a pooling equilibrium for an out-of-equilibrium belief $prob\{\alpha = \alpha_h/d_H = C\} = 1$ (proposition 3).

The challenger decides to enter the market if $\rho > \rho^*$.

And the incumbent will deviate if

(24) $$\Pi^h(\beta(I^*_h)) < \Pi^h(\beta(I^o_h)) - a_H$$

(25) $$\text{or } \Pi^h(\beta(I^*_h)) < \Pi^h(0) - a_H$$

Then, if (24) or (25) is satisfied, there is no equilibrium; whereas if (24) and (25) are not satisfied, (i.e. $a_T > max\{\Pi^h(\beta(I^o_h)) - \Pi^h(\beta(I^*_h)), \Pi^h(0) - \Pi^h(\beta(I^*_h))\}$) there is a pooling equilibrium for an out-of-equilibrium belief $prob\{\alpha = \alpha_h/d_H = C\} = 1$ (Proposition 4).

• Separating Equilibria

If the firm H decides to pay the renewal fee when the market is favorable and not to pay the renewal fee otherwise, the challenger knows the value of demand from the mere observation of the action undertaken by H. Its posterior μ (on good value demand) is equal to one. Then, if the firm E observes that the incumbent pays the renewal fee, it decides to enter the market (because the market is favorable) and if E observes that H gives his patent up, it doesn't enter.

But, when the market is favorable, and the firm E decides to enter, the patentholder will deviate because

$$\Pi^h(\beta(I_h^o)) - a_H < \Pi^h(0).$$

Then, it is not a separating equilibrium.

Conversely, if the patentholder decides to give his patent up when the market is favorable, and to pay the renewal fee otherwise, the challenger discovers the market value. It decides to enter the market when H abandons his patent, and not to enter otherwise. But, the firm H will deviate when the challenger doesn't enter because:

$$\Pi^h(0) - a_H < \Pi^h(0).$$

Thus, we find that there is no separating equilibrium.

• Semi-Separating Equilibria

In mixed strategies, we can calculate some semi-separating equilibria. Among all the equilibria, we determine the semi-separating equilibrium that seems most appealing on economic grounds. If the market is bad, the incumbent always gives his patent up, whereas, when the market is favorable, he decides to randomize his renewal decision. He keeps his patent in force with probability $(1 - \pi_H)$, and he doesn't pay the renewal fee with the complementary probability π_H.

If the strategy "keep the patent in force" (C) is observed, the value of the market is good. Then, the entrant decides to enter the market. When the market is bad the incumbent must be indifferent between "give his patent up" $(\overline{C})$ or "keep his patent in force" (C). It exists a probability $\pi_E \stackrel{\text{def}}{=} Prob\{e/\overline{C}\}$ such that:

$$\pi_E[\Pi^h(\beta(I_h^*))] + (1 - \pi_E)\Pi^h(0) = \Pi^h(\beta(I_h^o)) - a_H$$

$$\Leftrightarrow \pi_E = \frac{\Pi^h(0) - \Pi^h(\beta(I_h^o)) + a_H}{\Pi^h(0) - \Pi^h(\beta(I_h^*))}.$$

This probability exists and belong to $[0, 1]$ if:

$$\Pi^h(\beta(I_h^*)) < \Pi^h(\beta(I_h^o)) - a_H.$$

The profit of the firm E if it enters (e) after observing that the incumbent abandoned his patent $(\overline{C})$ is:

$$\mu(\alpha_h/\overline{C})[\Pi^h(\beta(I_h^*)) - I_h^* - a_E] + [1 - \mu(\alpha_h/\overline{C})][\Pi^\ell(\beta(I_\ell^*)) - I_\ell^* - a_E]$$

whereas the profit of the entrant if it decides not to enter $(\overline{e})$, when it observes that H has gave his patent up is zero.

264

The challenger must be indifferent between the decision of entry or no entry:

(26)
$$\mu(\alpha_h/\overline{C})[\Pi^h(\beta(I_h^*)) - I_h^* - a_E]$$
$$+ (1 - \mu(\alpha_h/\overline{C}))(\Pi^\ell(\beta(I_\ell^*)) - I_\ell^* - a_E) = 0$$
$$\mu(\alpha_h/\overline{C}) = \frac{a_E + I_\ell^* - \Pi^\ell(\beta(I_\ell^*))}{\Pi^h(\beta(I_h^*)) - I_h^* - (\Pi^\ell(\beta(I_\ell^*)) - I_\ell^*)}.$$

By definition

(27)
$$\mu(\alpha_h/\overline{C}) = \frac{\pi_H(\overline{C}/\alpha_h)\rho}{\pi_H(\overline{C}/\alpha_h)\rho + \pi_H(\overline{C}/\alpha_\ell)(1 - \rho)}$$
$$= \frac{\rho\pi_H}{\rho\pi_H + (1 - \rho)}.$$

We can substitute (26) in (27) and then:

$$\frac{\rho\pi_H}{\rho\pi_H + (1 - \rho)} = \frac{a_E + I_\ell^* - \Pi^\ell(\beta(I_\ell^*))}{\Pi^h(\beta(I_h^*)) - I_h^* - [\Pi^\ell(\beta(I_\ell^*)) - I_\ell^*]}$$
$$\Leftrightarrow \pi_H = \frac{1 - \rho}{\rho} \frac{a_E + I_\ell^* - \Pi^\ell(\beta(I_\ell^*))}{\Pi^h(\beta(I_h^*)) - I_h^* - a_H}.$$

As $\rho \in]0, 1[$ and π_H must be smaller than 1 we obtain

$$\pi_H < 1 \Leftrightarrow (1 - \rho)(a_E + I_\ell^* - \Pi^\ell(\beta(I_\ell^*))) < \rho[\Pi^h(\beta(I_h^*)) - I_h^* - a_E]$$

$$\Leftrightarrow \rho > \rho^*.$$

We have demonstrated that for $\rho > \rho^*$, and if $\Pi^h(\beta(I_h^*)) < \Pi^h(\beta(I^o)) - a_H$, there exists a semi-separating equilibrium which is, for the incumbent, to give his patent up when the market is not favorable, and to randomize his renewal decision when the market is favorable.

The challenger decides to enter the market if it observes that the incumbent keeps his patent in force, because it knows that the market is good. But, when it observes that the patentholder doesn't pay the renewal fee, it randomizes its entry decision, because it cannot infer any information.

We can find another semi-separating equilibrium with a similar proof: when the demand is good, the incumbent always gives his patent up, whereas when the demand is bad, he randomizes his decision to pay for $\rho < \rho^*$ and if $\Pi^\ell(\beta(I_\ell^*)) < \Pi^\ell(0) - a_H$. This equilibrium has not a strong economic meaning.

With the same proof, we can show that some semi-separating equilibria cannot exist:

→ if the incumbent decides to pay the renewal fee when the market is not favorable, and chooses to pay or not with some probability when the market is favorable, we find that $Prob\{e/C\} > 1$. It is impossible to reach an equilibrium.

→ if the incumbent decides to pay the renewal fee when the market is favorable and to pay or not with some probability when the market is not favorable, we find that $Prob\{e/C\} < 0$. Such a result is also impossible.

● References

BAGWELL, K., RAMEY, G. (1990). – "Advertising and Pricing to Deter or Accomodate Entry when Demand is Unknown", *IJIO*, 81, pp. 93-113.

van DIJK, T. (1995). – "Innovation Incentives Through Third Degree Price Discrimination in a Model of Patent Breadth", *Economic letters*, 47, pp. 431-435.

FUDENBERG, D., TIROLE, J. (1986). – "Noncooperative Game Theory for Industrial Organization: an Introduction and Overview", in *Handbook of Industrial Organization*, ed. Schmalensee et R. Willig.

GALLINI, N. (1991). – "Patent Policy and Costly Imitation", *Rand Journal of Economics*, 23, pp. 52-63.

GILBERT, R., SHAPIRO, C. (1990). – "Optimal Patent Length and Breadth", *Rand Journal of Economics*, 21, pp. 106-112.

HORSTMANN, I., MACDONALD, G. M., SLIVINSKI, A. (1985). – "Patent as Information Transfer Mechanisms: To Patent or (maybe) not to Patent", *Journal of Political Economy*, 93, pp. 837-858.

KLEMPERER, P. (1990). – "How Broad should the Scope of Patent Protection Be?", *Rand Journal of Economics*, 21, pp. 113-130.

LANJOUW, J., PAKES, A., PUTNAM, J. (1996). – "How to Count Patents and Value Intellectual Property: Uses of Patent Renewal and Application Data", *Working paper 5741*.

LEVIN, R. C., KLEVORICK, A. K., NELSON, R. R., WINTER, S. G. (1987). – "Appropriating the Returns from Industrial Research and Development", *Brookings papers on economic activity*, 3, pp. 783-831.

MACHO-STADLER, I., PÉREZ-CASTRILLO, D. (1991). – "Contrats de licences et asymétrie d'information", *Annales d'Economie et Statistique*, 24, pp. 189-208.

PAKES, A. (1985). – "On Patent, R&D and the Stock Market Rate of Return", *Journal of Political Economy*, 93, pp. 390-409.

SCHANKERMAN, M., PAKES, A. (1985). – "Valeur et Obsolescence des brevets", *Revue Economique*, 36, pp. 917-941.

SCOTCHMER, S., GREEN, J. (1990). – "Novelty and Disclosure in Patent Law", *RAND Journal of Economics*, 21, pp. 131-146.

WARSHOFSKY, F. (1994). – *The Patent Wars. The battle to own the world's technology*, John Wiley, Sons, Inc., New York.

Appropriation Strategy and the Motivations to use the Patent System: an Econometric Analysis at the Firm Level in French Manufacturing

Emmanuel DUGUET
Isabelle KABLA*

ABSTRACT. – This paper studies the determinants of both the percentage of innovations that are patented and the number of European patent applications by industrial firms, using data from the French survey on appropriation (EFAT). We build a two equations model including count and interval dependent variables and estimate it by asymptotic least squares. Controlling for the traditional determinants of innovation, like research and development expenditures, we find that patent disclosure is the main reason why firms do not patent all their innovations. Moreover, once we control for the differences in the propensity to patent, patent disclosure also reduces the number of patents applications. On the other hand, the will of firms to acquire a stronger position in technology negotiations and to avoid trials increases the number of patent applications.

* E. DUGUET: CEME, Université de Paris I et INSEE-DMSE; I. KABLA: INSEE. We thank A. ARUNDEL, B. CRÉPON, W. COHEN and an anonymous referee for helpful suggestions and comments. We also thank the participants at the Xth ADRES *Conference on the Economics and Econometrics of Innovation* (Strasbourg, June 1996) as well as the participants at the *Econometric Society European Meeting* (Istanbul, August 1996).

D. Encaoua et al. (eds.), The Economics and Econometrics of Innovation, 267–305.
© 2000 *Kluwer Academic Publishers. Printed in the Netherlands.*

1 Introduction

The patent system helps inventors to benefit from their research efforts, thanks to the temporary monopoly it provides on the patented inventions. In addition to the private incentives to undertake research that this legal device aims to provide, the patent system has also a positive effect from the social viewpoint: the disclosure of technological knowledge to other firms. In order to patent an invention, firms have to provide the patent office with a detailed technical description of the invention, which is published. This description must be comprehensive enough to allow a 'man of the art' to reproduce it. Thus, by examining patents, any firm working in the same field is able to learn from the technical advances that the patent applicant has made and to use this knowledge to reproduce the invention at the expiry of the patent or to improve on the invention. These features of the patent system seek to avoid the needless duplication of research expenditures and to promote technical progress. Globally, the patent system has a controversial effect on the social welfare due mostly to the trade-off between appropriation and diffusion. On the one hand, the patent system creates or increases the incentives to innovate. On the other hand, it temporarily distorts competition since it grants monopoly rights to the applicants. A vast literature that can be traced back to ARROW [1962] has explored the optimal level of protection that patent should confer and the optimal structure of the protection according to presumably available instruments: patent duration, patent scope or royalties in a compulsory license system (see for instance NORDHAUS, [1969]; KAMIEN and SCHWARTZ, [1974]; TANDON, [1982]; DEBROCK, [1985]; BECK, [1986]; GILBERT and SHAPIRO, [1990]; KLEMPERER, [1990]; GALLINI, [1992]).

Most articles make the assumption that inventions are patented. Less attention has been paid to firms' incentives to patent and to the implication of non-patenting strategies on social welfare. However, several surveys showed that the innovative firms do not always apply for patents and that when they do, they patent only a part of their inventions (LEVIN *et al.* [1987]; BUSSY *et al.* [1994]; ARUNDEL *et al.* [1995]; COHEN, NELSON and WALSH [1997]). One alleged reason is that the monopoly conferred by patent laws is limited in comparison to what an innovator could yield without patenting. In an analysis of the first Yale survey results on the issue of appropriation mechanisms in the United-States, LEVIN *et al.* [1987] found that patent was considered by firms to be neither the only way to appropriate innovation benefits nor as the most efficient one. Firms declared that the most important drawback of patenting was its failure to prevent competitors from inventing around the patented inventions. Moreover, they asserted that methods other than patents, like secret and lead time, could be used to protect against imitation, at least temporarily. The ability of patents to prevent imitation also appears to be limited. MANSFIELD *et al.* [1981] in a survey conducted in the United States, found that the average time required to imitate 48 new products was 70% of the time necessary to innovate and that the imitation cost was 65% of the innovation cost. Moreover, the imitation lag and costs were only moderately increased by patent protection.

268

Another possible reason to decide not to patent is disclosure. This appeared as an important deficiency of patent protection in the analysis of the Yale survey results by LEVIN et al. [1987]. The ability of a patent to provide incentives to innovate should be inversely related to the amount of useful information that leaks out to competitors, particularly when the information is difficult to obtain otherwise.

The failure of the patent system to prevent imitation, in comparison with other means of protection, and the role of patent disclosure are also the principal factors that are considered in the theoretical papers that explore or include the propensity to patent in their analyses (CRAMPES, [1986]; GALLINI, [1982]; SCOTCHMER and GREEN, [1990]; VAN DIJK, [1994]; KABLA, [1997]). The role of a patent as a signal has also been studied by HORSTMANN et al. [1985]). Only a few comprehensive welfare analyses have been conducted regarding the consequences of non-patenting strategies. SCOTCHMER and GREEN [1990] and KABLA [1997] both examine the question in respect to the diffusion of technologies [1].

While some innovations may remain unpatented, other inventions can lead to several patents. Therefore, the number of patents per patented innovation depends on the nature of each innovation and on the firms' patent strategy. On the one hand, a single innovation could be based upon a complex association of several inventions. On the other hand, when different and competing industrial applications of the same innovation are possible, the innovation results from a choice between them. In chemicals for instance, a whole family of molecules could produce similar desirable effects. Industrial usage will often be limited to only one of them but the innovator needs to obtain patents for the whole family in order to be adequately protected against imitation. Firms could even patent less efficient processes than the method that they intend to use, or less performing products than the one they will market, in order to increase their competitive advantage. In short, both the number of inventions behind a single innovation and the need to patent a cluster of similar inventions can result in a profusion of patent applications for a single innovation. "Over" patenting is also a strategy that can be used to increase bargaining power in negotiations with competitors, especially when overlapping technologies are involved. The stronger the patent portfolio, the stronger the position of a firm in convincing competitors that negotiation is preferable to litigation. This phenomenon also increases the risk of technology cartels, where incumbents could block entry trough the threat of a lawsuit.

Finally, patent applications can be made at different stages in the innovation process. Patenting at an early stage of the innovation could be required if the technological competition is fierce, for example when a competitor might patent a similar innovation first. Conversely, early patenting could be dangerous when a perfectible technology is involved.

---

1. The article of SCOTCHMER and GREEN is primarily devoted to the determination of the optimal patent scope in a two-stage patent race. The choice of the first inventor of an intermediate invention wether to patent or not is shown to generally diminish the advantage of a weak protection. KABLA is mostly interested in how the patent disclosure and the level of diffusion of technical knowledge by other means influence the optimal patent scope.

Since information leaks out to competitors through patent documents, they could catch-up and eventually leap-frog the initial inventor. The profitability aspects and the difficulty of the research process can also play a role in the optimal strategy. Early patenting could eventually result in more patent applications than the inverse strategy, if the firm also patents improved versions of its invention.

The paper examines which factors influence significantly the patenting behavior of firms. We are particularly interested in showing the relevance of dividing the analysis of patenting into two aspects: the percentage of innovations that involve patent applications (henceforth, the propensity to patent) and the number of patent applications per innovation. This work was possible to conduct because new data is available in a recent French survey on the use of the patent system and the appropriation of innovation benefits (EFAT survey). The survey provides the share of innovations that are patented at the firm level. The availability of both this measure and the number of patent applications at the firm level allows us, though with some limitations, to split the analysis into the two aspects mentioned above.

The paper is organized as follows. The data are presented in section 2. In section 3 we describe our model and the econometric methods. The results are presented and commented upon in section 4, while section 5 provides a few conclusions.

2 The Data

2.1. Sample Construction

The sample results from matching five data sets. Three of these data sets convey information on the innovative activity of industrial firms, while the last two provide accounting information.

The first data set is the "Enquête Appropriation" (French technological appropriation survey, known as EFAT), where all the variables are measured at the overall firm level. This survey is a part of an international project on the study of technological appropriation and was conducted in the United States, Japan and Europe. The questionnaires vary slightly depending on the country. The French survey was addressed in 1993 by the SESSI [2] to a representative sample of more than two thousand firms of at least 50 people in manufacturing. One of its purposes was to collect information on innovation and the use of the patent system. The survey was conducted at the firm level. It was sent to the R&D manager of the firm. The response rate was approximately 70%. Half of the respondents declared that their firm had conducted innovative activities, which represents 996 firms. We first

---

2. Statistics Department of the Ministry of Industry.

extracted from this sample all firms that had introduced product innovations between 1990 and 1992 and applied for at least one patent during this period. Patent applications could have been made in any patent system, including in France. The reason why the sample is limited to patent applicants is that only these firms were asked to answer questions on the patent system. This limitation reduced the sample to 546 firms.

The responses to questions in the Appropriation survey provide most of the exogenous variables used in the econometric analysis. They include the reasons for patenting and an evaluation of the deficiencies of the patent system. They also include a question on the postponement of patent applications. The questions are not related to any specific national or regional patent system. All qualitative questions on the evaluation of the patent system were asked for in absolute terms, and are not compared to an industry norm. This survey also provides information on the share of product innovations for which a patent application was made. Notice that the question refers to patent applications and not to patents granted.

The second data set is the "Enquête Recherche" (Research survey) which is an annual survey that collects information on the R&D inputs of firms with at least one full-time employee in research activities. We selected all firms that declared an internal R&D activity at least once over 1990-1992. For each we computed the deflated average R&D expenditures over the available years.

The third data set is the EPAT (European PATent) data set. It includes information on all patent applications since the creation of the European Patent system in 1978. We used this data set to compute the firm-level number of European patent applications during the period 1990-1992. This variable is the second endogenous variable in the model. We concentrate on patent applications – and not on patent grants – because the second endogenous variable, the percentage of innovations that are patented, is defined on patent applications.

The other two data sets provide accounting information. The fourth data set is the "Enquête Annuelle d'Entreprises" (EAE, Industry census) from which we extracted sales in 1992 and the primary industry of the firm. The fifth data set is the line-of-business industry census (EAE "fractions") which gives the decomposition of sales between different industry lines for diversified firms. As in a previous study, we computed the domestic average market share of the firm, the Herfindahl index of industrial concentration and a diversification index at the firm level (CRÉPON, DUGUET, KABLA, [1996]). The definitions are given in appendix 3.

The final data set includes 299 firms. Since there is a strong selection, we computed the share of total industry sales due to the firms in the sample. The sample is mostly representative of 6 industries : transportation equipment (49%), basic metals (45%), computer and electronics (36%), chemical products (24%), instruments (24%) and non electrical machinery (15%). These figures are high if we consider that our sample represents a

---

3. The detailed industry classification is given in appendix 1.

little more than 1% of the number of firms in manufacturing [4]. Then, the conclusions in this study apply to relatively large R&D performers.

2.2. Sample Statistics

Table 1 shows the distribution of the propensity to patent. About half of the sample applied for patents for less than a fifth of their product innovations. Although the degree of novelty of each innovation plays an important role in these figures, it is not the only one, essentially because the French patent system is not very restrictive. Each firm assessment of the relative advantages and disadvantages of patenting certainly plays an important role in this outcome.

Table 2 gives the distribution of the number of European patent applications. Almost 40% of the firms in the sample did not apply for a European patent during the period under study, while almost 20% of them applied for at least 10 patents. This is a standard profile among R&D performers in French manufacturing (CRÉPON and DUGUET, [1997b]). All the firms in the sample declared that they had applied for at least one patent during the period 1990-92, but some of the firms have applied in the French system only. Another reason why we observe many firms with a small number of patents is that part of them patent only a small fraction of their innovations. One important aim of our work is to disentangle the determinants of the propensity to patent from the factors that influence the number of patents.

Table 3 gives, for each decile of R&D expenditures, the average number of patents, the number of patents per million French francs (FRF) spent on R&D, and the percentage of patented innovations for each R&D decile [5]. The average number of patents strongly increases with R&D, from 0.6 patents in the first decile to 80 patents in the last one. This confirms the positive relationship between R&D and the number of patents often identified in the literature (GRILICHES, [1990]). The second column shows a decrease in the number of patents per million FRF spent on R&D, which does not mean that patent output decreases with R&D but rather that the value of a patent differs among firms with different R&D budgets [6]. The percentage of patented innovations shows less variation with R&D than the number of patents, remaining around 20% over the entire sample, except for the last two R&D deciles where about half of all innovations are patented.

---

4. There are about 25000 firms of at least 20 people in French manufacturing.

5. In order to compute the average propensity to patent, we set the propensity to patent of a firm equal to the center of its interval (see Table 1, only intervals are available in the Appropriation survey). We do not make this assumption in the regressions.

6. In a companion paper (DUGUET and IUNG, [1997]), based on European patent renewals, we show that firms with a bigger R&D budget support longer patent lives than other firms, once controlled for size, sector, diversification and market share differences. This suggests that the value of their patents is higher, following the model by PAKES and SCHANKERMAN [1986].

Most of the R&D is undertaken in three sectors (see Table 4): computers and electronics (38%), ships aircraft and rail (33%), and motor vehicles (14%), followed by drugs (5%) and chemicals (4%). Table 5 gives the industry averages [7] for the propensity to patent, patents per million R&D, the R&D to sales ratio and diversification. The propensity to patent is higher (between 34 and 38%) in the most innovative sectors, which possibly reflects the novelty requirements. The number of patents per million R&D is the highest in motor vehicles, which is likely to reflect an ability to patent components more easily than in other sectors. But these figures may also reflect differences in the patenting propensity across sectors. The R&D to sales ratio is the highest in ships, aircraft and rail (11%) followed by computers and electronics (10%) and drugs (7%). Finally, we also provide a diversification index. We find that the most diversified firms are in chemicals (2.33), rubber and plastics (1.98), instruments (1.65) and drugs (1.64). At the other end, motor vehicles and non metallic products (both 1.3) are the least diversified sectors.

How do these innovative firms use the patent system? What are the reasons why these firms patent? What deficiencies of the patent system do they fear the most? What are the main differences between industries in the assessment of the patent system? Tables 6 and 7 contain descriptive statistics of the reasons for patenting and patent deficiencies for each industry [8].

The most frequent motivation for patenting is to prevent imitation, which is cited by 92% of the firms. Avoiding litigation initiated by competitors and using patents in technology negotiations are rated second (62% of the respondents). The other reasons are noted by half as many firms: earning license revenue, using patents to enter foreign markets where licensing to a domestic firm is required, and rewarding or evaluating researchers. Some differences appear between industries. Preventing imitation is strong in all sectors, but it is not the case of the two other important motivations for patenting. Avoiding litigation initiated by competitors concerns mostly basic metals (87%), motor vehicles (86%), chemical products (71%), rubber and plastics (76%), instruments (67%) and computers and electronics (65%). This includes most of the innovative sectors (except aircraft, at 53%), where appropriation considerations are likely to play an important role in the patenting decisions. The result is slightly different with technology negotiation. Here the issue is partly linked to R&D cooperation. The industries that value technology negotiation are ships, aircraft and rail (88%), drugs (75%), fabricated metals (70%), and motor vehicles and basic metals (both 67%). Indeed, we found in a previous study on European patents (DUGUET, [1995]) that motor vehicles, chemicals and equipment goods

---

7. Notice that we do not compute the ratios on the sectoral aggregates but that we take the average of the firm level ratios.

8. The motives for patenting differ according to the country where the survey took place. Compared to European surveys, the Japanese and the American surveys propose an additional motivation to patent: preventing other firms from patenting related inventions (or "blocking"). In the American survey, this motive appeared to be second in importance, after the prevention of copying (COHEN, NELSON and WALSH, [1997]).

account for most European *joint* patents (i.e., patents applied for by several firms at the same time) in French manufacturing. In these sectors, patenting to acquire a strength in technology negotiations and jointly patenting with competitors could represent two alternative strategies for a similar purpose.

The patent deficiencies variables are based on answers to a five-point scale (0 to 4) of the importance of each deficiency. We indicate the mean score for each industry [9]. The strongest limitations are the inability of patents to prevent imitation (2.2) and the disclosure of too much information (1.96). But the costs to get the patent, maintain and defend it are also important, although slightly less than the two other limitations. The industries in which the failure to prevent imitation is of comparatively little importance include instruments (1.67), drugs (1.75) and motor vehicles (1.95), while other innovative sectors such as computers and electronics (2.19) and aircraft (2.35) find this to be a much more important limitation. Notice that the answer seems to be related to the kind of goods produced: more homogenous goods could be easier to imitate than vertically differentiated ones. This could help to explain why patents are less effective in preventing imitation in non metallic mineral products (2.85), fabricated metals (2.35) and basic metals (2.33). The second most important patent deficiency is disclosure. This is a problem when the technology is easy to circumvent from the patent documents. The highest score is for non metallic products (2.77), followed by basic metals (2.47) but high scores are also found in more innovative industries such as chemical products (2.29), drugs (2.07), aircraft (1.94) and computers and electronics (1.89). The industries where this deficiency is the lowest are instruments (1.47) and motor vehicles (1.48). This suggests that, in these two sectors, it would be more difficult to infer a full product from the patent documents, or that other ways to get access to the technology are available to competitors. The assessment of the problem of patent disclosure does not depend on the complexity of the product only (e.g., aircraft), since it also depends on the degree of competition in the final market.

3 The Model

We estimate the following two equations model:

$$\begin{cases} p_i^* = \exp(x_{1i}\pi_1 + v_{1i}) \\ E(n_i|p_i^*, x_{2i}, u_{2i}) = p_i^* \exp(x_{2i}b_2 + u_{2i}) \end{cases} \quad i = 1, \ldots, m$$

9. This type of ordinal data is problematic because of possible differences in the appraisal of the scale by each correspondent. The transformation of the data into dummies using a given threshold allows one to partly solve this problem but at the cost of a loss of information. In the regressions, we compare these two approaches in order to examine the robustness of the results: the first variables used are the original variables of the survey (levels 0 to 4) and the second ones are the corresponding dummies for the highest value (equal to 1 if the answer is 4, 0 otherwise). The statistics that we present in Table 7 use the first convention: the mean of the original variables by industry.

TABLE 1

Propensity to Patent 1990-1992.

Patenting propensity	Number of firms	Percentage
$0 < p_i^* \leq 0.2$	151	50.5
$0.2 < p_i^* \leq 0.4$	51	17.1
$0.4 < p_i^* \leq 0.6$	36	12.0
$0.6 < p_i^* \leq 0.8$	34	11.4
$0.8 < p_i^* \leq 1$	27	9.0
Totals	299	100.0

TABLE 2

Number of European Patent Applications 1990-1992.

Number of patent applications	Number of firms	Percentage
0	118	39.5
1	38	12.7
2	28	9.4
3	21	7.0
4 to 10	26	8.7
11 to 20	24	8.0
21 to 50	26	8.7
51 and more	18	6.0
Totals	299	100.0

TABLE 3

R&D Decile Average.

R&D decile	Average number of patents	Number of patents per million R&D FRF	Average propensity to patent %
1	0.6	0.38	23.3
2	0.9	0.31	29.3
3	1.8	0.39	26.0
4	1.5	0.23	22.0
5	3.1	0.37	35.3
6	3.0	0.19	25.7
7	6.1	0.21	31.3
8	12.1	0.22	30.0
9	23.7	0.17	46.0
10	80.2	0.10	51.4
Sample average	13.1	0.26	32.3

TABLE 4

Industry Contributions.

Industry *% of the sample total*	Number of firms %	Sales %	R&D M RFR
Chemical products	5.7	6.2	4.3
Drugs	9.4	5.5	5.1
Rubber and plastics	5.7	1.7	0.5
Non metallic products	4.3	2.4	0.5
Basic metals	5.0	10.2	1.7
Fabricated metals	7.7	1.0	0.3
Non-electrical machinery	17.7	5.3	1.9
Computers and electronics	21.1	22.0	37.7
Ships, aircraft and rail	5.7	9.8	32.7
Motor vehicles	7.0	32.8	14.2
Instruments	5.0	1.4	0.6
Textile, wood, paper and others	5.7	1.7	0.5
Totals (= 100%)	299 firms	759,423 M	46,224 M

where p_i^* is the share of innovations for which patents have been applied for, n_i the number of European patent applications and m the number of firms. The first relationship explains the propensity to patent by covariates x_1 and the second relationship explains the expected number of European patent applications over 1990-92, which has two components. The first component is p_i^*, the endogenous percentage of innovations that are patented; the second component $\exp(x_{2i}b_2 + u_{2i})$ is the number of innovations times the number of patent applications per patented innovation. This model can be written under the log-linear form:

$$\begin{cases} \ln p_i^* = x_{1i}\pi_1 + v_{1i} \\ \ln E(n_i|p_i^*, x_{2i}, u_{2i}) = \ln p_i^* + x_{2i}b_2 + u_{2i} \end{cases} \quad i = 1,\dots,m$$

We estimate this model in two steps, by asymptotic least square. This method is close to what is known in the econometric literature as Amemiya's method [10] (LEE, [1981]). First, we estimate the reduced form of the model and, secondly, we infer the structural parameters from the reduced form parameters. In the asymptotic least squares terminology the reduced form parameters are the auxiliary parameters and the structural form parameters are the parameters of interest.

The estimation of the reduced form is as follows. The first equation of the model is already under its reduced form, therefore the only estimation problem is that we do not observe p_i^* but the interval it lies in. It implies

---

10. The difference is that we combine maximum likelihood and pseudo maximum likelihood estimators in the first step, so that the estimation of the reduced form is different from the standard one (namely, maximum likelihood).

276

TABLE 5

Industry Averages.

Industry *Averages on firm level data*	Propensity to patent %	Patents per M. R&D FRF	R&D/Sales %	Diversification
Chemical products	28.8	0.14	4.9	2.33
Drugs	33.6	0.09	7.0	1.64
Rubber and plastics	21.8	0.21	1.9	1.98
Non metallic products	22.3	0.16	2.2	1.29
Basic metals	28.7	0.27	1.3	1.55
Fabricated metals	32.6	0.43	3.2	1.54
Non-electrical machinery	31.5	0.34	3.3	1.39
Computers and electronics	38.6	0.19	9.7	1.50
Ships, aircraft and rail	37.0	0.10	11.0	1.57
Motor vehicles	33.8	0.59	3.9	1.30
Instruments	36.7	0.28	3.2	1.65
Textile, wood, paper and others	22.9	0.24	1.8	1.35
Sample	32.3	0.26	5.7	1.55

TABLE 6

Reasons for Patenting
(share of affirmative answers).

Industry *Averages on firm* *level data*	Preventing imitation	Avoiding trials	Technology negotiation	License fees	Rewarding researchers	Entering foreign markets
Chemical products	0.82	0.71	0.47	0.29	0.12	0.24
Drugs	0.89	0.46	0.75	0.43	0.14	0.36
Rubber and plastics	0.88	0.76	0.59	0.24	0.18	0.24
Non metallic products	0.92	0.46	0.54	0.31	0.23	0.23
Basic metals	1.00	0.87	0.67	0.40	0.33	0.27
Fabricated metals	0.96	0.43	0.70	0.26	0.04	0.26
Non-electrical machinery	0.96	0.42	0.45	0.21	0.09	0.23
Computers and electronics	0.92	0.65	0.65	0.25	0.35	0.21
Ships, aircraft and rail	0.94	0.53	0.88	0.29	0.24	0.12
Motor vehicles	0.86	0.86	0.67	0.33	0.05	0.33
Instruments	0.93	0.67	0.60	0.07	0.13	0.13
Textile, wood, paper and others	0.94	0.59	0.53	0.29	0.29	0.35
Manufacturing	0.92	0.62	0.62	0.28	0.18	0.25

TABLE 7

Patent Deficiencies
(mean scores).

Industry *Averages on firm level data*	Costly to get and to maintain	Costly to defend	Does not prevent imitation	Too much disclosure
Chemical products	1.76	1.94	2.29	2.29
Drugs	1.71	1.54	1.75	2.07
Rubber and plastics	2.12	1.76	2.06	1.82
Non metallic products	2.38	1.92	2.85	2.77
Basic metals	1.27	1.73	2.33	2.47
Fabricated metals	2.09	2.22	2.35	1.65
Non-electrical machinery	2.30	2.21	2.30	1.92
Computers and electronics	2.14	1.86	2.19	1.89
Ships, aircraft and rail	1.76	1.47	2.35	1.94
Motor vehicles	1.38	1.81	1.95	1.48
Instruments	2.00	1.67	1.67	1.47
Textile, wood, paper and others	1.53	1.88	2.00	1.71
Manufacturing	1.87	1.83	2.17	1.96

that we cannot use OLS. The "Appropriation" survey provides a *qualitative* variable p_i that is equal to (table 1):

$$p_i = \begin{cases} 1 & \text{if } a_0 < \ln p_i^* \leq a_1 \\ 2 & \text{if } a_1 < \ln p_i^* \leq a_2 \\ 3 & \text{if } a_2 < \ln p_i^* \leq a_3 \qquad i = 1, \ldots, m \\ 4 & \text{if } a_3 < \ln p_i^* \leq a_4 \\ 5 & \text{if } a_4 < \ln p_i^* \leq a_5 \end{cases}$$

where $a_0 = \{-\infty\}$, $a_1 = \ln 0.2$, $a_2 = \ln 0.4$, $a_3 = \ln 0.6$, $a_4 = \ln 0.8$ and $a_5 = \{+\infty\}$. In order to estimate this equation, we use the ordered probit model (see MADDALA, [1992]). This is equivalent to postulate that the distribution of the disturbances v_{1i} are identically and independently distributed as normal variates $N(0, \sigma_1)$. From this assumption, we can estimate the parameters by maximum likelihood [11].

The log-likelihood of the first equation comes directly from the underlying model; it is given by:

$$\ln L_1(p|x_1; \pi_1, \sigma_1) = \sum_{i=1}^{m} \sum_{k=1}^{5} d_{ik} \ln \Pr[p_i = k]$$

---

11. If this assumption does not hold, the estimates may be biased. Then, an extension of this work could look at the robustness of the results with different distributions or turn to non parametric techniques. If, on the contrary, the assumption holds, the maximum likelihood estimator presented below is asymptotically efficient.

with:

$$d_{ik} = \begin{cases} 1 & \text{if } p_i = k \\ 0 & \text{otherwise} \end{cases} \quad i = 1, \dots, m \quad k = 1, \dots, 5$$

and [12]:

$$\Pr[p_i = k] = \Pr[a_{k-1} < \ln p_i^* \leq a_k] = \Pr[a_{k-1} < x_{1i}\pi_1 + v_{1i} \leq a_k]$$
$$= \Pr\left[\frac{a_{k-1} - x_{1i}\pi_1}{\sigma_1} < \frac{v_{1i}}{\sigma_1} \leq \frac{a_k - x_{1i}\pi_1}{\sigma_1}\right]$$
$$= \Phi\left[\frac{a_k - x_{1i}\pi_1}{\sigma_1}\right] - \Phi\left[\frac{a_{k-1} - x_{1i}\pi_1}{\sigma_1}\right] \quad i = 1, \dots, m$$

where Φ is the cdf of the standard normal distribution. We have estimated this first equation with SAS-IML software [13].

The second reduced form equation explains a positive integer dependent variable: the number of patent applications. Following the econometric literature on count data we use a heterogeneous Poisson model (GOURIÉROUX, MONFORT and TROGNON, [1984a]). For this second equation, we do not need to make a specific assumption on the distribution of the residual v_{2i}. We use the specification of the conditional mean of the distribution of the dependent variable only. Therefore, our estimates are robust to the distributional assumptions on the disturbance of the patent numbers equation. We estimate this equation by pseudo maximum likelihood. Based on previous studies on similar data (CRÉPON and DUGUET, [1995a, 1997a]), we use a negative binomial pseudo distribution.

We write the reduced form of the second equation as:

$$\ln E(n_i | p_i, x_i, u_{2i}) = x_i \pi_2 + v_{2i}$$

where x is the full column rank matrix of all exogenous variables in x_1 and x_2.

---

12. Taking the limits, we obtain the specific cases:

$$\Pr[p_i = 1] = \Phi[(a_1 - x_{1i}\pi_1)/\sigma_1] \quad \text{and} \quad \Pr[p_i = 5] = 1 - \Phi[(a_4 - x_{1i}\pi_1)/\sigma_1].$$

13. With known thresholds, the standard error of the disturbance is identified. We make the parameter change $h = 1/\sigma_1$ and $\beta = \pi_1/\sigma_1$ so that the log-likelihood is concave according to h and β. We use a Newton-Raphson algorithm with analytical Hessian. The original parameters (π_1, σ_1) and their covariance are calculated from Slutsky's theorem (so-called "δ-method"). The estimation program we use is %PROBITO, a SAS-IML macro command presented in a previous working paper and available from the authors (CRÉPON and DUGUET, [1995b]).

The pseudo log-likelihood to be maximized is thus [14]:

$$L_2(n|x; \pi_2) = \sum_{i=1}^{m} n_i x_i \pi_2 - (1 + n_i) \ln(1 + \exp(x_i \pi_2))$$

The second step of the estimation is to infer the *structural* parameters of the second equation. We do it by asymptotic least squares also called "minimum distance" (MALINVAUD, [1970]). First, we estimate the correlation matrix of the reduced form estimates. Since we have used different estimation methods and separate regressions, we need a unifying principle. We use M-estimation (see GOURIÉROUX and MONFORT, [1996]). Consider the following function:

$$L(p, n|x; \pi_1, \sigma_1, \pi_2) = L_1(p|x_1; \pi_1, \sigma_1) + L_2(n|x; \pi_2)$$

The first order conditions on this new objective function are exactly the same as the one implied by the separate maximum likelihood and pseudo maximum likelihood estimations of our reduced form [15]. Then, the global asymptotic distribution is the one of the M-estimator defined by the objective above. Let the auxiliary parameter be $\pi = (\pi_1 \, \pi_2 \, \sigma_1)'$, the M-estimator is defined by [16]:

$$\widehat{\pi} = \arg \max_{\pi} L(p, n|x; \pi)$$

Under the usual regularity conditions, given in GOURIÉROUX and MONFORT [1996], the asymptotic distribution of this M-estimator of the auxiliary parameter is [17]:

$$\sqrt{m}(\widehat{\pi} - \pi) \xrightarrow{A} N(0, J^{-1} I J^{-1})$$

with

$$J = \frac{E \; E}{0 \; X} \left[-\frac{\partial^2 L(p^*, n|x; \pi)}{\partial \pi \partial \pi'} \right]$$

---

14. The negative binomial distribution depends on a nuisance parameter θ. Its density is equal to:

$$f_\theta(n) = \frac{\Gamma(n + 1/\theta)}{\Gamma(n + 1)\Gamma(1/\theta)} \, (\theta \mu)^n (1 + \theta \mu)^{-(n+1/\theta)}$$

where μ is the mean of the distribution. In our application we set $\theta = 1$ which does not affect the consistency of our estimates. For more details on count data pseudo maximum likelihood estimation see GOURIÉROUX, MONFORT and TROGNON [1984b]. We also use SAS-IML to estimate this equation, the program is %PMVGNEG and is also available. It uses a Newton-Raphson algorithm with analytical second order derivatives.

15. If there were constraints between the parameters of different equations, this property would not hold. Nevertheless, it would not create a severe problem since it is possible to impose the constraints at the second step of the estimation method. Thus, this method is more general than is seems.

16. This objective is concave.

17. Notice that, since the estimation problem is separable, we have the following simplifications:

$$\frac{\partial^2 L(p^*, n|x; \pi)}{\partial \sigma_1 \partial \pi_{2'}} = 0 \quad \text{and} \quad \frac{\partial^2 L(p^*, n|x; \pi)}{\partial \pi_1 \partial \pi_{2'}} = 0.$$

and

$$E \underset{x}{E} \left[\frac{\partial L(p, n|x; \pi)}{\partial \pi} \frac{\partial L(p, n|x; \pi)}{\partial \pi'} \right]$$

We estimate the J and I matrices by their sample counterparts:

$$\widehat{J} = -\frac{1}{m} \sum_{i=1}^{m} \frac{\partial^2 L(p, n|x; \widehat{\pi})}{\partial \pi \partial \pi'}$$

and

$$\widehat{I} = \frac{1}{m} \sum_{i=1}^{m} \frac{\partial L(p, n|x; \widehat{\pi})}{\partial \pi} \frac{\partial L(p, n|x; \widehat{\pi})}{\partial \pi'}$$

This method can be applied to any mix of well-behaved M-estimators. In the present case, the underlying model is linear so that the relationship between the interest (i.e., structural) parameters and the auxiliary (i.e., reduced form) parameters is obtained as in standard linear models. We have three cases:

(i) Variables present in both equations. If the variable, indexed j, is present in both equations the structural parameter of this variable is simply given by $b_2^j = \pi_1^j - \pi_2^j$.

(ii) Variables present in the first equation only: the parameter is given directly by the reduced form estimate of the first equation.

(iii) Variables present in the second equation only: $b_2^j = \pi_2^j$ and π_1^j must be estimated under this constraint. But it requires a strong exclusion assumption so that we do not use it here. In fact, what we want to do is to test which variable of the "Appropriation" survey is significant in each equation. Then, we use mostly the first case out of the three.

The derivation of the covariance matrix of the structural parameters is straightforward, following Slutsky's theorem.

4 The Results

We study the propensity to patent first, then the innovation function linking the number of patents to research expenditures. We made three groups of regressions, labeled A to C. Each group of regressions includes three tables giving the estimates of, respectively, the propensity to patent equation, the reduced form of the equation for the number of patents and the structural form of the patent numbers equation. The first group of regressions (A) does not control for industry effects. This is used as a benchmark to infer the biases that are likely to arise when the industry effects are omitted.

The first model (A) explains the propensity to patent and the number of patents by R&D expenditures, sales, the average market share, the average Herfindahl concentration index and the diversification index. Two sets of additional firm-level categorical variables, based on the EFAT survey, summarize the reasons to patent and the deficiencies: six dummies for the motivations to patent (see Table 6) and four ordinal variables for the patent deficiencies (see Table 7). We also use a dummy variable that indicates whether the firm has postponed a patent application over 1990-92 in order to achieve a more important innovation. The deficiency variables are five-points categorical variables. In the first regressions (A) they are used directly, without transformation. In the second group of regressions (B), we have added 11 industry dummies in order to control for industry effects. Then, we are able to see which patent deficiencies are really significant at the firm level. In the last group of regressions (C), the deficiency variables are based on dummies that capture the highest response level ("very important" deficiency). In this last group of regressions we compare the model with and without controlling for industry effects.

4.1. The Propensity to Patent

It clearly appears from the regressions that two main factors influence the propensity to patent an innovation: patent disclosure, whose impact is negative, and R&D expenditures, which positively influences this propensity (Tables 8, 11 and 14). A third variable, although with a weaker effect, seems to play a significant negative impact on the propensity to patent: the decision to postpone a patent application. However, it is weakened by the introduction of the industry effects. Another interesting result is the lack of significance of all the reasons to patent. Among the deficiencies, only disclosure is significant.

• Patent Disclosure

The main reason that influences the decision to patent an innovation is disclosure. The effect is present and strong whatever the measure of this deficiency we use (the five-level categorical variable or the dummy). The control for industry effects does not affect this result, although it slightly lowers the coefficient of the disclosure variable. The effect of patent disclosure is always significant at the 5% level in the selected [18] regressions (column 5 in Tables 8, 11 and 14).

The reason why patent disclosure may be such an obstacle to patenting is obvious. Patent disclosure makes the circumvention of innovations by competitors easier since it grants them useful technical knowledge. Although it may demand additional research effort from competitors in order not to infringe the invention, it increases their capacity to reproduce the patented innovation by lowering both the imitation lag and its cost. Yet a patent is supposed to forbid the marketing by competitors of product imitations. However, in numerous cases imitation could be hidden and difficult to detect, moreover the ability to invent around limits the effectiveness of patents. In addition, patent disclosure could be dangerous for the firm when the innovation is a technological breakthrough that can be followed by

---

18. When the strategic postponement dummy is added in the regression, this coefficient falls. However, the latter variable is not significant at the 5% level in the regression, so that we have to retain the column 5 results.

improvements. Although a competitor has no right, theoretically, to market any improvement on the original patent without taking a license on it, the pioneering firm may believe that it will not be able to enforce its rights through litigation. Moreover, it would be unable to block an improvement based upon a non-infringing imitation of its patented invention.

• R&D Expenditures

The level of R&D expenditures has a positive impact on the propensity to patent. However, the effect cannot be assimilated to a pure size effect, since sales are never significant. Moreover, it does not capture sectoral differences since the addition of industry dummies only slightly decreases the R&D coefficient from around 0.19 to 0.15 (see Table 14). It is always significant at the 5% level. Several interpretations can be given to this result. First, we could attribute this effect to the relationship between the research effort of the firm and the magnitude of its innovations or fixed costs in R&D. Second, the highest R&D budgets are found among firms that already have a technical advantage over their competitors, so that they are likely to benefit from better appropriability conditions allowing them to patent a higher share of their innovations. Third, the R&D budget effect could tell us that the larger firms in our sample have internal legal departments responsible for patenting, thus diminishing its cost.

Since R&D, sales and market share logarithms are strongly correlated, we have performed some additional tests presented in appendix 4. The first point to examine is whether R&D captures a size effect or a R&D effect. The second point is simultaneity between the propensity to patent and research investments. From the regressions, it clearly appears that size is significant only when it is the only right-hand variable. Then our results imply that R&D matters, independently from size. For simultaneity, we replace the average R&D expenditures over 1990-1992 by lagged R&D capital in 1989. The results are not affected by this change as well. Overall, what we find is that all the effect of size passes through R&D, not directly.

The elasticity of the patenting propensity to R&D expenditures lies between 0.21 and 0.14, depending on the regression. In regression (3) of Table 11, for instance, where industry dummies and patent deficiency variables are included, the coefficient is around 0.16. Thus a twice bigger R&D budget is associated to a 16% higher patenting share. This effect is relatively low compared to the one of disclosure. Its coefficient in the same regression is around -0.15 and this variable is on a five points scale, from 0 to 4. Thus the difference between firms that suffer the most from disclosure and the ones that do not is $0.15 \times 4 = 60\%$ of the patenting share [19]. This explains stronger differences than the research budget. We can illustrate this point by the following comparison: in order to compensate a simple move from 0 to 1 on the disclosure categorical variable, a firm would need to multiply its R&D budget by a factor $2.5 = \exp(0.15/0.16)$.

---

19. The specification with the corresponding dummy variable gives a close figure of 50% (table 14).

This suggests that under-patenting results mainly from disclosure: the dissemination of knowledge through patents may be strongly undermined by appropriability problems.

• Postponing Patent Applications

The decision of firms to postpone their patent applications in order to achieve more advanced versions of their innovations seems to decrease the proportion of innovations that are patented. The risk that a competitor will patent a similar innovation during the period probably explains the negative sign of the coefficient. The estimated coefficient is –0.30 and significant at the 5% level when it is the only exogenous variable in the model related to the evaluation of patent (column 4 of Table 8). It is –0.24 and significant at the 10% level when industry dummies are added (column 4 of Table 11). This indicates that a part of the effect is sectoral: the low patenting propensity of some sectors could find its origin in postponement tactics.

However the effect is no longer significant when other patent variables are added (column 6 in Tables 8, 11 and 14). The effect is, in fact, captured by the disclosure variable. Simultaneously, the presence of the postponement variable tends to decrease the coefficient of the disclosure variable. Indeed both variables are strongly correlated, and one may infer that patent disclosure is precisely one of the reasons to postpone a patent. One aspect of patent disclosure is that it helps to invent around innovations that are not adequately protected by patents. The quality of the protection strongly depends on the ability of the applicant to associate precise claims with its invention. This ability increases with the maturity of the invention.

• No Effect of the other Patent Motives and Deficiencies

No alleged advantage of patenting seems to make patent applications worthwhile. The unsignificance of the first objective, to prevent imitation, is of particular interest. It is mostly linked to the very high number of firms that do mention this objective, so that it does not explain much variations between firms. Indeed, the coefficient is rather high (around 0.3) but never significant at the 10% level. Therefore, there could be a measurement problem due to the fact that the variables corresponding to the objectives are dummies and contain less information than the other variables used in the regressions. The availability of 5-levels categorical variables for the motives could perhaps alter this result.

Neither patenting costs nor the costs of legal action have a significant effect on the propensity to patent. Firms do not appear to base their decision to patent on the patent costs [20]. Our results suggest looking for other explanatory variables.

---

20. This result may also be linked to the low European patent renewal fees, at least during the first years. For France, it rarely goes over FRF 2000 per year and per patent (about USD 400).

284

Table 8

Propensity to Patent
Model A

Left-hand variable: percentage of innovations patented (logarithm)
With a constant term
Maximum likelihood estimation of the ordered probit model
(Asymptotic t statistic between parentheses).

Variables	(1)	(2)	(3)	(4)	(5)	(6)
R&D Expenditures	0.205	0.189	0.186	0.213	0.172	0.179
(logarithm)	(3.80)	(3.37)	(3.32)	(3.94)	(2.96)	(3.09)
Sales	−0.080	−0.096	−0.079	−0.079	−0.098	−0.101
(logarithm)	(0.89)	(1.05)	(0.84)	(0.88)	(1.03)	(1.27)
Average market share	0.100	0.101	0.095	0.104	0.097	0.101
(logarithm)	(1.35)	(1.34)	(1.20)	(1.38)	(1.23)	(1.28)
Average concentration	−0.032	−0.005	−0.009	−0.039	0.010	0.004
(logarithm)	(0.41)	(0.05)	(0.11)	(0.49)	(0.12)	(0.05)
Diversification	−0.006	−0.029	−0.031	−0.033	−0.049	−0.064
(logarithm)	(0.04)	(0.17)	(0.18)	(0.20)	(0.29)	(0.37)
Reasons for patenting:						
(dummies 0/1)						
1) Preventing imitation		0.402			0.268	0.270
		(1.80)			(1.11)	(1.09)
2) Avoiding trials		0.077			0.099	0.106
		(0.59)			(0.73)	(0.78)
3) Technology negotiation		0.10			−0.013	−0.001
		(0.07)			(0.09)	(0.01)
4) License fees		0.211			0.219	0.210
		(1.51)			(1.52)	(1.45)
5) Rewarding researchers		−0.120			−0.030	−0.038
		(0.73)			(0.17)	(0.21)
6) Entering foreign market		0.095			0.086	0.099
		(0.65)			(0.58)	(0.66)
Patent deficiencies:						
(categorical, 0/4)						
1) Costly to maintain			−0.029		−0.018	−0.019
			(0.43)		(0.26)	(0.27)
2) Costly to defend			0.008		−0.001	−0.001
			(0.12)		(0.01)	(0.01)
3) Does not prevent imitation			−0.056		−0.054	−0.061
			(0.79)		(0.73)	(0.82)
4) Too much disclosure			−0.164		−0.158	−0.134
			(2.69)		(2.51)	(2.09)
Postponing an application				−0.300		−0.207
(dummy 0/1)				(2.33)		(1.49)
$\hat{\sigma}_1$	1.079	1.067	1.045	1.049	1.037	1.033
	(19.3)	(18.4)	(16.6)	(17.2)	(15.6)	(15.6)

TABLE 9

Reduced Form of the Patent Equation
Model A

Left-hand variable: number of patents
With a constant term
Pseudo maximum likelihood estimation of the heterogeneous Poisson model
Negative binomial pseudo distribution
(Asymptotic t statistic between parentheses).

Variables	(1)	(2)	(3)	(4)	(5)	(6)
R&D Expenditures	0.613	0.566	0.601	0.637	0.564	0.577
(logarithm)	(7.96)	(7.45)	(7.91)	(8.61)	(7.52)	(7.80)
Sales	0.288	0.282	0.334	0.288	0.316	0.309
(logarithm)	(2.12)	(2.14)	(2.40)	(2.17)	(2.41)	(2.41)
Average market share	0.024	0.054	0.049	0.021	0.076	0.072
(logarithm)	(0.18)	(0.50)	(0.42)	(0.16)	(0.78)	(2.41)
Average concentration	−0.095	−0.075	−0.107	−0.109	−0.077	−0.085
(logarithm)	(0.86)	(0.79)	(1.04)	(1.00)	(0.86)	(0.94)
Diversification	0.422	0.410	0.425	0.366	0.415	0.376
(logarithm)	(1.83)	(1.90)	(1.96)	(1.61)	(2.03)	(1.87)
Reasons for patenting:						
(dummies 0/1)						
1) Preventing imitation		0.259			0.195	0.161
		(0.80)			(0.60)	(0.48)
2) Avoiding trials		0.487			0.495	0.532
		(2.85)			(2.89)	(3.15)
3) Technology negotiation		0.724			0.687	0.697
		(3.60)			(3.45)	(3.56)
4) License fees		0.040			−0.059	−0.046
		(0.21)			(0.30)	(0.24)
5) Rewarding researchers		−0.097			−0.080	−0.060
		(0.43)			(0.36)	(0.26)
6) Entering foreign markets		−0.041			0.021	0.035
		(0.21)			(0.11)	(0.19)
Patent deficiencies:						
(categorical, 0/4)						
1) Costly to maintain			−0.026		−0.012	−0.005
			(0.32)		(0.14)	(0.06)
2) Costly to defend			0.143		0.118	0.100
			(1.72)		(1.42)	(1.23)
3) Does not prevent imitation			0.042		0.053	0.048
			(0.49)		(0.64)	(0.58)
4) Too much disclosure			−0.262		−0.245	−0.204
			(3.12)		(3.14)	(2.55)
Postponing an application				−0.416		−0.321
(dummy 0/1)				(2.26)		(1.76)

286

TABLE 10

Structural Form of the Patent Equation
Model A

Left-hand variable: number of patents
With a constant term
Asymptotic least squares
(Asymptotic t statistic between parentheses).

Variables	(1)	(2)	(3)	(4)	(5)	(6)
R&D Expenditures	0.409	0.376	0.415	0.424	0.392	0.339
(logarithm)	(4.70)	(4.64)	(4.83)	(5.11)	(4.78)	(4.24)
Sales	0.369	0.378	0.413	0.366	0.392	0.409
(logarithm)	(2.56)	(2.76)	(2.72)	(2.58)	(2.76)	(2.94)
Average market share	-0.077	-0.046	-0.046	-0.083	-0.022	-0.029
(logarithm)	(0.53)	(0.37)	(0.35)	(0.59)	(0.19)	(0.25)
Average concentration	-0.063	-0.069	-0.098	-0.069	-0.087	-0.089
(logarithm)	(0.53)	(0.67)	(0.85)	(0.59)	(0.85)	(0.89)
Diversification	0.429	0.439	0.456	0.399	0.464	0.440
(logarithm)	(1.74)	(1.90)	(1.89)	(1.63)	(2.06)	(1.97)
Reasons for patenting: (dummies 0/1)						
1) Preventing imitation		-0.143			-0.074	-0.109
		(0.47)			(0.23)	(0.33)
2) Avoiding trials		0.410			0.396	0.426
		(2.24)			(2.11)	(2.30)
3) Technology negotiation		0.714			0.700	0.699
		(3.47)			(3.41)	(3.46)
4) License fees		-0.171			-0.277	-0.256
		(0.92)			(1.40)	(1.31)
5) Rewarding researchers		0.023			-0.049	-0.022
		(0.10)			(0.20)	(0.09)
6) Entering foreign markets		-0.136			-0.066	-0.116
		(0.64)			(0.31)	(0.53)
Patent deficiencies: (categorical, 0/4)						
1) Costly to maintain			0.004		0.006	-0.064
			(0.05)		(0.07)	(0.30)
2) Costly to defend			0.135		0.119	0.101
			(1.52)		(1.42)	(1.25)
3) Does not prevent imitation			0.098		0.108	0.109
			(1.08)		(1.19)	(1.20)
4) Too much disclosure			-0.097		-0.086	-0.071
			(1.04)		(0.97)	(0.82)
Postponing an application				-0.116		-0.114
(dummy 0/1)				(0.63)		(0.63)

TABLE 11

Propensity to Patent
Model B

Left-hand variable: percentage of innovations patented (logarithm)
With 12 industry dummies
Maximum likelihood estimation of the ordered probit model
(Asymptotic t statistic between parentheses).

Variables	(1)	(2)	(3)	(4)	(5)	(6)
R&D Expenditures	0.175	0.144	0.163	0.181	0.134	0.139
(logarithm)	(2.73)	(2.18)	(2.47)	(2.83)	(1.97)	(2.04)
Sales	0.005	−0.004	−0.007	0.003	−0.020	−0.023
(logarithm)	(0.05)	(0.04)	(0.06)	(0.03)	(0.19)	(0.21)
Average market share	0.053	0.057	0.047	0.060	0.051	0.056
(logarithm)	(0.61)	(0.64)	(0.51)	(0.69)	(0.55)	(0.60)
Average concentration	0.053	0.076	0.062	0.040	0.083	0.075
(logarithm)	(0.58)	(0.81)	(0.64)	(0.43)	(0.84)	(0.77)
Diversification	−0.008	−0.024	−0.033	−0.019	−0.046	−0.051
(logarithm)	(0.04)	(0.13)	(0.18)	(0.10)	(0.24)	(0.27)
Reasons for patenting:						
(dummies 0/1)						
1) Preventing imitation		0.366			0.223	0.233
		(1.54)			(0.87)	(0.90)
2) Avoiding trials		0.128			0.163	0.170
		(0.92)			(1.15)	(1.19)
3) Technology negotiation		0.010			−0.008	0.002
		(0.07)			(0.05)	(0.01)
4) License fees		0.242			0.242	0.232
		(1.61)			(1.58)	(1.51)
5) Rewarding researchers		−0.118			−0.040	−0.038
		(0.69)			(0.22)	(0.21)
6) Entering foreign markets		0.098			0.094	0.103
		(0.55)			(0.61)	(0.67)
Patent deficiencies:						
(categorical, 0/4)						
1) Costly to maintain			−0.045		−0.037	−0.035
			(0.63)		(0.49)	(0.47)
2) Costly to defend			−0.082		−0.021	−0.001
			(1.17)		(0.29)	(0.01)
3) Does not prevent imitation			−0.062		−0.064	−0.069
			(0.86)		(0.84)	(0.91)
4) Too much disclosure			−0.146		−0.140	−0.122
			(2.28)		(2.12)	(1.82)
Postponing an application				−0.241		−0.165
(dummy 0/1)				(1.72)		(1.10)
$\hat{\sigma}_1$	1.055	1.041	1.025	1.049	1.014	1.012
	(17.3)	(16.5)	(15.3)	(17.2)	(14.7)	(14.7)

4.2. The Number of Patent Applications

The regressions point to several factors that influence the number of patent applications. We distinguish the reduced form of the patent equation (Tables 9, 12 and 15) from its structural form (Tables 10, 13 and 16). The difference is that the latter equation gives the number of patent applications controlled for the propensity to patent: this measure is closer to the number of innovations. However, we cannot disentangle the number of patent applications from the number of patents applications per patented innovation.

Some variables have an effect on both the reduced and structural form of the patent equation. These include R&D expenditures, the use of patents to avoid litigation and the use of patents to strengthen technology negotiations with other firms.

We also find that the significance of firm size, market share and diversification depends on the inclusion of industry dummies. Without industry effects, sales and diversification are significant, while market share is the only significant variable when industry differences are controlled for.

It is important to notice that the postponement variable affects the number of patents through its impact on the patenting propensity only and not directly. In other words, it has a significant coefficient in the reduced form of the model but it is not significant in the structural form. The patent disclosure variable remains significant in the structural form when it is taken as a dummy and not as a five-level variable (Table 16).

The following comments are restricted to the results with industry dummies in the regressions (Tables 12, 13, 15 and 16).

• Size-Linked Effects

An important issue is the R&D elasticity in the patent equation. That is, do we find constant returns in the "innovation production function"? Most cross-section studies exhibit unit elasticities (COHEN and LEVIN, [1989]), contrary to panel data studies. The latter find decreasing returns with coefficients varying from 0.3 to 0.6, depending on the estimation method used (HAUSMAN, HALL and GRILICHES, [1984]; BLUNDELL, GRIFFITH and WINDMEIJER, [1995]; CRÉPON and DUGUET, [1997b]). An explanation for this discrepancy is the propensity to patent: if it remains constant over time while differing between firms, it ends up in a fixed effect and the cross- section estimates that do not account for the differences in patenting propensities are biased. The original features of our data allow to correct for differences in the patenting propensity in a cross-section. The question is then: do we find research elasticities that are closer to the panel data estimates? The answer is positive.

The R&D elasticity (Tables 12-15) is around 0.6-0.7 in the reduced form. Once accounting for the differences in patenting propensities, it lowers to around 0.4-0.5 (Tables 13 and 16). Thus, our regressions suggest that the share of innovations that are patented would indeed intervene in the fixed effect, and would allow for a reduction of the coefficient to around 0.4-0.5. This result is consistent with the panel data estimates mentioned above. The regressions show two types of size effects. One is captured by the R&D

TABLE 12

Reduced Form of the Patent Equation
Model B

Left-hand variable: number of patents
With 12 industry dummies
Pseudo maximum likelihood estimation of heterogeneous Poisson model
Negative binomial pseudo distribution
(Asymptotic t statistic between parentheses).

Variables	(1)	(2)	(3)	(4)	(5)	(6)
R&D Expenditures	0.665	0.581	0.640	0.669	0.570	0.581
(logarithm)	(7.31)	(6.60)	(7.03)	(7.60)	(6.40)	(6.60)
Sales	0.029	0.064	0.078	0.034	0.095	0.085
(logarithm)	(0.20)	(0.48)	(0.52)	(0.23)	(0.69)	(0.63)
Average market share	0.265	0.283	0.281	0.271	0.290	0.296
(logarithm)	(2.23)	(2.60)	(2.36)	(3.11)	(2.64)	(2.69)
Average concentration	−0.062	−0.058	−0.093	−0.091	−0.067	−0.087
(logarithm)	(0.55)	(0.53)	(0.82)	(0.79)	(0.62)	(0.81)
Diversification	−0.001	−0.007	0.032	0.009	0.026	0.026
(logarithm)	(0.01)	(0.03)	(0.15)	(0.04)	(0.12)	(0.12)
Reasons for patenting:						
(dummies 0/1)						
1) Preventing imitation		0.257			0.220	0.219
		(0.83)			(0.75)	(0.74)
2) Avoiding trials		0.333			0.356	0.393
		(0.20)			(2.17)	(2.75)
3) Technology negotiation		0.790			0.764	0.784
		(4.46)			(4.29)	(4.38)
4) License fees		0.177			0.105	0.083
		(0.92)			(0.53)	(0.42)
5) Rewarding researchers		0.016			0.016	0.037
		(0.08)			(0.08)	(0.17)
6) Entering foreign markets		−0.091			−0.025	−0.013
		(0.49)			(0.13)	(0.07)
Patent deficiencies:						
(categorical, 0/4)						
1) Costly to maintain			−0.011		−0.014	−0.008
			(0.13)		(0.16)	(0.09)
2) Costly to defend			0.099		0.072	0.056
			(1.25)		(0.89)	(0.70)
3) Does not prevent imitation			0.019		0.022	0.020
			(0.23)		(0.27)	(0.24)
4) Too much disclosure			−0.183		−0.164	−0.137
			(2.86)		(2.22)	(1.80)
Postponing an application				−0.296		−0.276
(dummy 0/1)				(1.70)		(1.53)

290

TABLE 13

Structural Form of the Patent Equation
Model B

Left-hand variable: number of patents
With 12 industry dummies
Asymptotic least squares
(Asymptotic t statistic between parentheses).

Variables	(1)	(2)	(3)	(4)	(5)	(6)
R&D Expenditures	0.490	0.431	0.477	0.488	0.436	0.442
(logarithm)	(3.95)	(4.31)	(4.42)	(4.69)	(4.27)	(4.38)
Sales	0.024	0.068	0.085	0.032	0.116	0.108
(logarithm)	(0.15)	(0.47)	(0.51)	(0.20)	(0.75)	(0.71)
Average market share	0.211	0.225	0.234	0.211	0.239	0.240
(logarithm)	(1.77)	(2.01)	(1.93)	(2.43)	(2.08)	(2.11)
Average concentration	−0.116	−0.134	−0.154	−0.131	−0.149	−0.162
(logarithm)	(0.98)	(1.17)	(1.24)	(1.09)	(1.25)	(1.37)
Diversification	0.008	0.017	0.066	0.028	0.073	0.077
(logarithm)	(0.03)	(0.07)	(0.27)	(0.11)	(0.30)	(0.31)
Reasons for patenting: (dummies 0/1)						
1) Preventing imitation		−0.109			−0.03	−0.014
		(0.37)			(0.01)	(0.05)
2) Avoiding trials		0.205			0.192	0.223
		(1.13)			(1.04)	(1.23)
3) Technology negotiation		0.780			0.772	0.782
		(4.15)			(4.04)	(4.09)
4) License fees		−0.065			−0.136	−0.149
		(0.33)			(0.66)	(0.72)
5) Rewarding researchers		0.135			0.056	0.075
		(0.58)			(0.23)	(0.30)
6) Entering foreign markets		−0.189			−0.119	−0.116
		(0.89)			(0.055)	(0.53)
Patent deficiencies: (categorical, 0/4)						
1) Costly to maintain			0.034		0.023	0.027
			(0.36)		(0.24)	(0.28)
2) Costly to defend			0.091		0.070	0.089
			(1.01)		(0.80)	(0.96)
3) Does not prevent imitation			0.081		0.087	−0.015
			(0.91)		(0.94)	(0.16)
4) Too much disclosure			−0.037		−0.024	−0.111
			(0.41)		(0.27)	(0.61)
Postponing an application				−0.054		−0.112
(dummy 0/1)				(0.31)		(0.62)

expenditures variable while the other is captured by direct measures of firm size (sales, diversification, market share). Interestingly, when we control for industry effects, the significance of sales and diversification vanishes while the market share remains significant.

Given the impossibility to distinguish the number of innovations from the number of patents per patented innovation, there are two ways to interpret this market share effect: an effect on the number of innovations or an effect on the number of patent applications per innovation. On the one hand, it could be that the number of innovations increases with market power. On the other hand the multiplication of the number of patents may be a way to reinforce the monopoly power provided by the patent system.

• Technology Negotiations and Trials

Some of the reasons to patent have an influence on the corrected (i.e. structural form) patent count: a firm applies for more patents if it uses patents as a tool for negotiations or in order to prevent infringement suits from competitors.

The coefficients apply to dummy variables so that they directly give the differences in percentage between the firms that answered "Yes" and the others. Acquiring a strength in technology negotiations explains an average difference of 75% in the corrected patent number (Table 15, column 6). It is stronger than the effect of R&D (doubling R&D would increase the patent count by 44%). The second effect is also strong: the will to avoid trials by competitors entices firms to patent about 42% more [21].

This result probably means that using patents in negotiations is a motivation to increase the number of applications per innovation. Negotiations may take place with suppliers, customers, and even competitors. The reasons for negotiation may be to fix the license price or other relevant aspects in negotiations with a licensee, to exchange information on technologies under development with a customer or a supplier, to exchange rights with competitors for technologies, or to avoid litigation. Indeed a large portfolio of patents may be an advantage in these kind of negotiations. In the case of a lawsuit, the length and the probable cost of the litigation is correlated with the quantity of technical arguments that each party can provide. Alternatively, when two competing firms develop overlapping technologies, they may be interested in exchanging free licenses rather than entering a conflict.

---

21. The structural form coefficients given in Table 16 are misleading in this case, since when a coefficient is not significant in the patenting propensity equation, its reduced form estimate, given in Table 15, is the right one. This is equivalent to say that the best estimate is obtained by setting the insignificant coefficients to zero in the first (patenting propensity) equation.

292

TABLE 14

Propensity to Patent
Model C

Left-hand variable: percentage of innovations patented (logarithm)
Maximum likelihood estimation of the ordered probit model
(Asymptotic t statistic between parentheses).

Variables	With constant term			With 12 industry dummies		
	(1)	(2)	(3)	(4)	(5)	(6)
R&D Expenditures	0.190	0.176	0.183	0.168	0.141	0.145
(logarithm)	(3.45)	(3.03)	(3.10)	(2.51)	(2.04)	(2.10)
Sales	−0.051	−0.068	−0.067	0.026	0.013	0.011
(logarithm)	(0.57)	(0.73)	(0.71)	(0.25)	(0.12)	(0.10)
Average market share	0.094	0.094	0.098	0.044	0.050	0.056
(logarithm)	(1.21)	(1.21)	(1.26)	(0.48)	(0.54)	(0.61)
Average concentration	−0.015	0.011	0.003	0.063	0.084	0.072
(logarithm)	(0.19)	(0.13)	(0.04)	(0.68)	(0.89)	(0.77)
Diversification	0.006	−0.013	−0.036	0.003	−0.046	−0.017
(logarithm)	(0.04)	(0.08)	(0.20)	(0.02)	(0.24)	(0.09)
Reasons for patenting:						
(dummies 0/1)						
1) Preventing imitation		0.359	0.361		0.326	0.338
		(1.42)	(1.38)		(1.25)	(1.27)
2) Avoiding trials		0.063	0.075		0.117	0.129
		(0.47)	(0.55)		(0.83)	(0.91)
3) Technology negotiation		−0.011	0.008		−0.010	0.008
		(0.08)	(0.06)		(0.07)	(0.05)
4) License fees		0.223	0.210		0.240	0.224
		(1.55)	(1.45)		(1.57)	(1.45)
5) Rewarding researchers		−0.109	−0.108		−0.116	−0.108
		(0.65)	(0.64)		(0.67)	(0.62)
6) Entering foreign markets		0.146	0.155		0.137	0.147
		(0.99)	(1.03)		(0.90)	(0.96)
Patent deficiencies:						
(dummies on the highest level, 0/1)						
1) Costly to maintain	0.075	0.124	0.132	0.038	0.082	0.100
	(0.29)	(0.48)	(0.52)	(0.14)	(0.30)	(0.37)
2) Costly to defend	0.234	0.200	0.175	0.225	0.188	0.170
	(0.97)	(0.82)	(0.72)	(0.87)	(0.72)	(0.65)
3) Does not prevent imitation	0.104	0.192	0.186	0.095	0.169	0.159
	(0.43)	(0.77)	(0.74)	(0.38)	(0.66)	(0.61)
4) Too much disclosure	−0.592	−0.592	−0.457	−0.518	−0.500	−0.471
	(2.61)	(2.52)	(1.90)	(2.13)	(1.98)	(1.83)
Postponing an application			−0.241			−0.221
(dummy 0/1)			(1.80)			(1.50)
$\hat{\sigma}_1$	1.059	1.047	1.039	1.039	1.026	1.021
	(17.6)	(16.9)	(16.5)	(16.2)	(15.5)	(15.5)

TABLE 15

Reduced Form of the Patent Equation
Model C

Left-hand variable: number of patents
Pseudo maximum likelihood estimation of the heterogeneous Poisson model
Negative binomial pseudo distribution
(Asymptotic t statistic between parentheses).

Variables	With constant term			With 12 industry dummies		
	(1)	(2)	(3)	(4)	(5)	(6)
R&D Expenditures	0.593	0.541	0.564	0.643	0.568	0.581
(logarithm)	(7.80)	(7.21)	(7.73)	(7.31)	(6.53)	(6.76)
Sales	0.284	0.287	0.273	0.036	0.064	0.055
(logarithm)	(2.14)	(2.22)	(2.20)	(0.26)	(0.49)	(0.42)
Average market share	0.028	0.048	0.049	0.261	0.269	0.276
(logarithm)	(0.21)	(0.45)	(0.48)	(2.23)	(2.49)	(2.53)
Average concentration	−0.053	−0.040	−0.051	−0.071	−0.058	−0.084
(logarithm)	(0.48)	(0.42)	(0.55)	(0.63)	(0.54)	(0.78)
Diversification	0.405	0.401	0.346	0.021	0.002	0.007
(logarithm)	(1.82)	(1.93)	(1.72)	(0.10)	(0.01)	(0.03)
Reasons for patenting:						
(dummies 0/1)						
1) Preventing imitation		0.164	0.106		0.159	0.143
		(0.54)	(0.31)		(0.54)	(0.49)
2) Avoiding trials		0.501	0.551		0.366	0.416
		(3.04)	(3.36)		(2.27)	(2.60)
3) Technology negotiation		0.663	0.659		0.738	0.749
		(3.44)	(3.45)		(4.27)	(4.28)
4) License fees		0.077	0.073		0.175	0.135
		(0.42)	(0.41)		(0.94)	(0.72)
5) Rewarding researchers		−0.073	−0.054		0.020	0.036
		(0.34)	(0.24)		(0.10)	(0.17)
6) Entering foreign markets		−0.034	−0.001		−0.079	−0.048
		(0.19)	(0.01)		(0.44)	(0.27)
Patent deficiencies:						
(dummies on the highest level, 0/1)						
1) Costly to maintain	−0.320	−0.195	−0.198	−0.078	−0.064	−0.072
	(0.99)	(0.57)	(0.60)	(0.26)	(0.21)	(0.24)
2) Costly to defend	0.208	0.067	0.023	−0.011	−0.114	−0.132
	(0.64)	(0.23)	(0.08)	(0.04)	(0.45)	(0.53)
3) Does not prevent imitation	−0.039	0.097	0.087	−0.037	0.081	0.072
	(0.15)	(0.35)	(0.32)	(0.14)	(0.30)	(0.27)
4) Too much disclosure	−1.288	−1.272	−1.208	−1.154	−1.095	−1.064
	(5.07)	(5.34)	(5.14)	(4.87)	(5.14)	(5.07)
Postponing an application			−0.420			−0.332
(dummy 0/1)			(2.40)			(1.92)

Table 16

Structural Form of the Patent Equation
Model C

Left-hand variable: number of patents
Asymptotic least squares
(Asymptotic t statistic between parentheses).

Variables	With constant term			With 12 industry dummies		
	(1)	(2)	(3)	(4)	(5)	(6)
R&D Expenditures	0.403	0.365	0.380	0.475	0.428	0.436
(logarithm)	(4.63)	(4.45)	(4.75)	(4.52)	(4.32)	(4.45)
Sales	0.335	0.355	0.340	0.011	0.050	0.043
(logarithm)	(2.28)	(2.54)	(2.50)	(0.07)	(0.33)	(0.29)
Average market share	−0.066	−0.046	−0.049	0.217	0.219	0.220
(logarithm)	(0.46)	(0.38)	(0.42)	(1.84)	(1.97)	(1.98)
Average concentration	−0.038	−0.051	−0.054	−0.134	−0.143	−0.156
(logarithm)	(0.32)	(0.48)	(0.52)	(1.13)	(1.23)	(1.34)
Diversification	0.399	0.414	0.382	0.018	0.012	0.023
(logarithm)	(1.62)	(1.78)	(1.68)	(0.07)	(0.05)	(0.09)
Reasons for patenting:						
(dummies 0/1)						
1) Preventing imitation		−0.194	−0.255		−0.167	−0.196
		(0.58)	(0.73)		(0.52)	(0.60)
2) Avoiding trials		0.438	0.476		0.249	0.287
		(2.37)	(2.59)		(1.37)	(1.59)
3) Technology negotiation		0.675	0.651		0.748	0.740
		(3.34)	(3.29)		(4.04)	(3.98)
4) License fees		−0.146	−0.137		−0.065	−0.090
		(0.80)	(0.76)		(0.33)	(0.45)
5) Rewarding researchers		−0.177	0.054		0.136	0.144
		(0.84)	(0.23)		(0.59)	(0.62)
6) Entering foreign markets		−0.189	−0.156		−0.216	−0.195
		(0.90)	(0.75)		(1.02)	(0.91)
Patent deficiencies:						
(dummies on the highest level, 0/1)						
1) Costly to maintain	−0.395	−0.320	−0.330	−0.115	−0.147	−0.171
	(1.38)	(1.09)	(1.13)	(0.41)	(0.53)	(0.61)
2) Costly to defend	−0.027	−0.133	−0.153	−0.236	−0.302	−0.302
	(0.08)	(0.47)	(0.54)	(0.80)	(1.14)	(1.14)
3) Does not prevent imitation	−0.143	−0.05	−0.100	−1.131	−0.088	−0.086
	(0.49)	(0.30)	(0.32)	(3.90)	(0.28)	(0.28)
4) Too much disclosure	−0.695	−0.680	−0.661	−0.636	−0.595	−0.593
	(2.26)	(2.28)	(2.23)	(2.02)	(2.00)	(2.03)
Postponing an application			−0.155			−0.112
(dummy 0/1)			(0.87)			(0.62)

5 Conclusion

The patent numbers embed various components, including the share of innovations that are patented. The "Appropriation" (EFAT) survey allows researchers to correct the patent numbers for this effect and to study the patenting decision at the same time. But the patent numbers are counts and the share of patented innovations are interval data so that one has to use count data and limited dependent variables econometrics.

Using appropriate econometric methods we find that, on the one hand, R&D expenditures and patent disclosure are the main determinants of the share of innovations that are patented. Higher research budgets are associated to higher propensities to patent. On the other hand, the compulsory disclosure implied by the publication of patent documents strongly undermines the incentive to patent. It is not certain however that this implies a welfare loss, since if the disclosure requirement was weakened, less diffusion would occur as well.

Finally, along with research expenditures and market share, two variables newly available in the survey affect the corrected patent numbers: the willingness of firms to avoid trials and to reach a stronger position in technology negotiations with other firms. This clearly confirms that the patent numbers do not rely solely on an innovation function relating innovation inputs to outputs, but also depend on strategic aspects linked to patenting. Securing knowledge benefits seems to be the main problem industrial firms face.

APPENDIX 1

Industry Classification and Representatives of the Sample

The classification is close to OECD's. We give its definition for manufacturing, from the French NAP 100 classification. We also compare the total sales in our sample with that of all manufacturing in 1992 published in the *Tableaux de l'Economie Française* (INSEE, 1994, page 133). The most important selections are the presence in the R&D survey (Frascatti criteria) and to answer to the Appropriation survey.

Classification	NAP 100	Sales (M)		Sample
		Sample	Industry	%
Chemical products	17. Industrie chimique de base 43. Industrie fil et fibres artif. et synthétiques	47112	194788	24.2
Drugs	18. Parachimie 19. Industrie pharmaceutique	41780	273646	15.3
Rubber and plastics	52. Industrie du caoutchouc 53. Transformation des matières plastiques	12862	152024	8.5
Non-metallic products	14. Production de minéraux divers 15. Matériaux de construction, céramique 16. Industrie du verre	18084	158374	11.4
Basic metals	09. Extraction, préparation de minerai de fer 10. Sidérurgie 11. Première transformation de l'acier 12. Extraction et prépar. des minerais non ferreux 13. Métallurgie, 1re transf. des métaux non ferreux	77131	170292	45.3
Fabricated metals	20. Fonderie 21. Travail des métaux	7662	232810	3.3
Non-electrical machinery	22. Fabrication de machines agricoles 23. Fabrication de machines-outils 24. Production d'équipement industriel 25. Fabrication matériel de manutention	40639	270649	15.0
Computers and electronics	27. Fabrication de matériel informatique 28. Fabrication de matériel électrique 29. Matériel électronique ménager et professionnel 30. Fabrication d'équipement ménager	167180	462177	36.2

Classification	NAP 100	Sales (M)		Sample
		Sample	Industry	%
Shipping, aircraft and rail* Motor vehicles*	31B. Autre matériel de transport terrestre 32. Construction navale 33. Construction aéronautique 31A. Construction automobile	323153	652452	49.5
Instruments	34. Fabrication d'instruments de précision	10951	46226	23.7
Miscellaneous	44. Industrie textile 45. Industrie du cuir 46. Industrie de la chaussure 47. Industrie de l'habillement 48. Travail mécanique du bois 49. Industrie de l'ameublement 50. Industrie du papier et du carton 51. Imprimerie, presse, édition 54. Industries diverses	12869	683248	1.9

* No detailed information between industries 31A and 31B is available in the Tableaux de l'Economie Française, so that we have aggregated them in this table.

298

APPENDIX 2

The Patent Numbers Components

The number of patent applications per firm results from three components: the number of innovations, the share of innovations that is patented, and the number of patent applications for each innovation applied for.

In the following, let the subscript i denotes the firm. Let n_i be the number of patent applications of firm i, m_i its total number of innovations, δ_{ik} a dummy variable that equals one when the k-th innovation of firm i is applied for (0 otherwise), and μ_{ik} the number of patent applications for the corresponding innovation ($\delta_{ik} = 1$). Then, we have:

$$n_i = \sum_{k=1}^{m_i} \mu_{ik} = \sum_{k=1}^{m_i} \delta_{ik} \times \mu_{ik} = m_i \times \frac{1}{m_i} \sum_{k=1}^{m_i} \delta_{ik} \times \frac{\sum_{k=1}^{m_i} \delta_{ik} \times \mu_{ik}}{\sum_{k=1}^{m_i} \delta_{ik}} \quad k = 1, \ldots, m_i$$

The first quantity on the right-hand side is the number of innovations of firm i, then comes the share of innovations that are patented $1/m_i \sum_{k=1}^{m_i} \delta_{ik}$ and, finally, the average number of patents per patented innovation.

The share of innovations that are patented is available in the Appropriation survey. Therefore, our econometric model allows to separate the effects of this variable only. The number of patent applications divided by the share of innovations that are patented, will be referred as *the corrected patent number*.

Measurement of Diversification and Domestic Concentration

Accounting for diversification implies to change the market share and concentration measures, since a firm can operate in several industries at the same time. In this study we use weighted averages of the traditional indicators.

The line-of-business *Enquête Annuelle d'Entreprise* (so-called "Fractions EAE") allows us to compute concentration and diversification indicators. Let Q_{ik} be the domestic sales of firm i in industry k, its market shares are equal to:

$$s_{ik} = \frac{Q_{ik}}{\sum_{i=1}^{I} Q_{ik}}, \quad i = 1, \ldots, I \quad k = 1, \ldots, K$$

Notice that in the previous formula, the number of firm is $I > m$, that is we have been computing the market share from the whole data set (size I) and not only from our sample (size m). Here, a diversified firm has a different market share in each industry [22]. To perform our study we need an overall indicator of market power, the average (or weighted) market share, as well as a direct indicator of diversification.

The share of industry k in firm i total sales[23] is:

$$b_{ik} = \frac{S_{ik}}{\sum_{k=1}^{K} S_{ik}}, \quad i = 1, \ldots, I \quad k = 1, \ldots, K$$

This coefficient equals one in the main activity if firm i is not diversified, and 0 in the other activities. Following SCHERER [1983] we compute the equivalent number of activities taken from the Herfindahl index on sales decomposition (one per firm). Our *diversification indicator* d_i thus equals:

$$\frac{1}{d_i} = \sum_{k=1}^{K} b_{ik}^2, \quad i = 1, \ldots, I$$

This equivalent number of activities equals one when the firm is not diversified, and is bounded by the actual number of activities (reached when the activities have equal sales). It is a better measure than the actual number of activities since it eliminates the effect of the industries that contribute weakly to a firm's sales.

We also define the *average market share* as:

$$\bar{s}_i = \sum_{k=1}^{K} b_{ik} \times s_{ik}, \quad i = 1, \ldots, I$$

---

22. We use the NAP 600 French industrial classification that breaks manufacturing in 255 industries. Moreover, we kept industrial activities only to compute the diversification index presented below (services are also available).
23. It includes exports.

From the market share we also compute the average Herfindahl index. First, the Herfindahl index of concentration in market k is defined as usual by:

$$H_k = \sum_{i=1}^{I} s_{ik}^2, \quad k = 1, \ldots, K$$

Since diversified firms operate in different industries at the same time, we use the *average Herfindahl concentration index*:

$$\overline{H}_i = \sum_{k=1}^{K} b_{ik} \times H_k, \quad i = 1, \ldots, I$$

Tests of Robustness on the Propensity to Patent Equation

Correlation Matrix
p-value between parentheses

	R&D Expenditures (logarithm)	Average Market Share (logarithm)	Diversification (logarithm)
Sales (logarithm)	.749 (.001)	.314 (.001)	.723 (.001)
R&D Expenditures (logarithm)		.457 (.001)	.136 (.018)
Average Market Share (logarithm)			.129 (.026)

In all the regressions that follow, we have checked that nor concentration neither diversification is significant at the 5% level. Therefore, we dropped them out of the model in order to reduce possible multicolinearity. More generally, we kept the only variables that are significant at the 5% level in at least one regression.

The selection of firms that have R&D in 1989 reduces the sample size to 242 firms (instead of 299). Therefore, we ran the regression with the R&D expenditures again. No change occurred. For more details on the construction of R&D capital, by the permanent inventory method, see CRÉPON and DUGUET [1997a].

Propensity to Patent
Additional evidence

Left-hand variable: percentage of innovations patented (logarithm)
With 12 industry dummies (242 firms)
Maximum likelihood estimation of the ordered probit model
(Asymptotic t statistic between parentheses)

Variables	(1)	(2)	(3)	(4)	(5)	(6)	(7)	(8)
R&D Expenditures (logarithm)	–	–	.175 (2.53)	.174 (2.50)	.169 (3.04)	–	–	–
R&D Capital in 1989 (logarithm)	–	–	–	–	–	.176 (2.96)	.176 (2.96)	.160 (3.39)
Sales (logarithm)	.203 (3.75)	.140 (1.70)	–.016 (0.16)	.052 (0.66)	–	–.044 (1.01)	.018 (0.23)	–
Average market share (logarithm)	–	.084 (1.00)	.089 (1.08)	–	.081 (1.25)	.083 (1.01)	–	.061 (0.94)

Patent deficiency:								
4) Too much disclosure	-.154	-.148	-.137	-.143	-.137	-.146	-.152	-.146
	(2.35)	(2.25)	(2.11)	(2.21)	(2.12)	(2.27)	(2.37)	(2.28)
$\hat{\sigma}_1$	1.031	1.029	1.011	1.013	1.011	1.003	1.005	1.003
	(12.03)	(12.03)	(12.04)	(12.71)	(12.05)	(12.05)	(12.04)	(12.05)

• References

ARROW, K. (1962). – "Economic Welfare and the Allocation of Resources for Invention". In R. Nelson ed., *The rate and direction of economic activity*, New York: Princeton University Press.

ARUNDEL, A., VAN DE PAAL, SOETE, L. (1995). – *Innovation Strategies of Europe's Largest Industrial Firms*. MERIT, Maastricht, June.

BECK, R. (1986). – "Does Competitive Dissipation Require a Short Patent Life?" *Research in Law and Economics*, vol. 8, pp. 121-129.

BLUNDELL, R., GRIFFITH, R., WINDMEIER, F. (1995). – "Individual Effects and Dynamics in Count Data Models". Institute for Fiscal Studies working paper.

BUSSY, J.-C., KABLA, I., LEHOUCQ, T. (1994). – "La protection technologique dans l'industrie". *Le 4 Pages du SESSI*, n° 34.

COHEN, W., LEVIN, R. (1989). – "Empirical Studies of Innovation and Market Structure". In Schmalensee R. and R. Willig eds, *Handbook of Industrial Organization*, vol. 2, ch. 18, North-Holland.

COHEN, W., NELSON, R., WALSH, J. (1997). – "Appropriability Conditions and why Firm Patent and why they do not in the American Manufacturing Sector". *Mimeo*, June.

CRAMPES, C. (1986). – "Les inconvénients d'un dépôt de brevet pour une entreprise innovatrice". *L'Actualité Economique*, vol. 62, pp. 521-534.

CRÉPON, B., DUGUET, E. (1995a). – "Innovation: Measurement, Returns and Competition". *Insee studies in Economics and Statistics*, 1995, 1, pp. 82-95.

CRÉPON, B., DUGUET, E. (1995b). – "Une bibliothèque de macro commandes pour l'économétrie des données de comptage et des variables qualitatives". *CREST working paper 9525*.

CRÉPON, B., DUGUET, E. (1997a). – "Research and Development, Competition and Innovation: Pseudo Maximum Likelihood and Simulated Maximum Likelihood Methods Applied to Count Data Models with Heterogeneity". *Journal of Econometrics*, 79, pp. 355-378.

CRÉPON, B., DUGUET, E. (1997b). – "Estimating the Innovation Function from the Patent Numbers: GMM on Count Panel Data". *Journal of Applied Econometrics*, vol. 12, pp. 243-263.

CRÉPON, B., DUGUET, E., KABLA, I. (1996). – "A Moderate Support to Schumpeterian Conjecture from Various Innovation Measures". In A. Kleinknecht éd., *Innovation: The Message From New Indicators*. Mac Millan, London.

DE BROCK, L. (1985). – "Market Structure, Innovation and Optimal Patent Life". *Journal of Law and Economics*, vol. XXVIII, April, pp. 223-244.

DUGUET, E. (1995). – "Technical Cooperation through European Joint Patents". *Insee studies in Economics and Statistics*, n° 1, pp. 96-111.

DUGUET, E., IUNG, N. (1997). – "R&D Investment, Patent Life and Patent Value: an Econometric Analysis at the Firm Level". *INSEE Working paper G9705*.

GALLINI, N. (1992). – "Patent Policy and Costly Imitation". *Rand Journal of Economics*, vol. 23, n° 1, Spring, pp. 52-63.

GILBERT, R., SHAPIRO, C. (1990). – "Optimal Patent Length and Breadth". *Rand Journal of Economics*, vol. 21, n° 1, Spring, pp. 106-112.

GOURIÉROUX, C., MONFORT, A. (1996). – *Statistics and Econometric Models*. Cambridge University Press.

GOURIÉROUX, C., MONFORT, A., TROGNON, A. (1984a). – "Pseudo Maximum Likelihood Methods: Application to Poisson Models". *Econometrica* 52 (3), pp. 701-720.

GOURIÉROUX, C., MONFORT, A., TROGNON, A. (1984b). – "Pseudo Maximum Likelihood Methods: Theory". *Econometrica* 52 (3), pp. 681-700.

GRILICHES, Z. (1990). – "Patent Statistics as Economic Indicators: a Survey". *Journal of Economic Litterature*, vol. XXVIII, pp. 1661-1707.

HAUSMAN, J., HALL, B., GRILICHES, Z. (1984). – "Econometric Models for Count Data with an Application to the Patent-R&D Relationship". *Econometrica* 42 (3), pp. 909-938.

HORSTMANN, I., MC DONALD, G., SLIVINSKI, A. (1985). – "Patents as Information Transfer Mechanisms: to Patent or (maybe) not to Patent". *Journal of Political Economy*, 93, pp. 837-858.

KABLA, I. (1997). – "Easiness of Imitation, Patent Disclosure and the Optimal Patent Scope". *Mimeo.*

KAMIEN, M., SCHWARTZ, N. (1982). – *Market structure and innovation*. Cambridge University Press.

KLEMPERER, P. (1990). – "How Broad Should the Scope of Patent Protection be?" *Rand Journal of Economics*, vol. 21, n° 1, Spring, pp. 113-130.

LEE, L.-F. (1981). – "Simultaneous Equations Models with Discrete and Censored Dependent Variables". In C. Manski and Mc Fadden D. eds, *Structural analysis of discrete data with econometric applications*. MIT Press, pp. 346-364.

LEE, T., WILDE, L. (1981). – "Market Structure and Innovation: a Reformulation". *Quaterly Journal of Economics*, 94, pp. 429-436

LEVIN, R., KLEVORICK, A., NELSON, R., WINTER, S. (1987). – "Appropriating the Returns from Industrial Research and Development". *Brookings Papers on Economic Activity*, 3, pp. 783-831.

LOURY, G. (1979). – "Market Structure and Innovation". *Quaterly Journal of Economics*, 93, pp. 395-410.

MADDALA, G. S. (1992). – *Limited Dependent and Qualitative Variables in Econometrics*. Econometric Society Monograph, n° 3, Cambridge University Press.

MALINVAUD, E. (1970). – *Statistical Methods of Econometrics*. North-Holland.

MANSFIELD, E., SCHWARTZ, M., WAGNER, S. (1981). – "Imitation Costs and Patents: an Empirical Study". *Economic Journal*, 91, pp. 907-918.

MANSFIELD, E. (1985). – "How Rapidly does New Industrial Technology Leak Out". *Journal of Industrial Economics*, 34 (2) pp. 217-227.

NORDHAUS, W. (1969). – *Invention, growth and welfare: a theoretical treatment of technological change*. Cambridge, Massachussets: MIT Press.

PAKES, A., SHANKERMAN, M. (1986). – "Estimates of the Value of Patent Rights in European Countries during the post 1950 Period". *The Economic Journal*, December, pp. 1052-1076.

SCHERER, F. (1983). – "The Propensity to Patent". *International Journal of Industrial Organization*, 1, pp. 107-128.

SCOTCHMER, S. (1991). – "Standing on the Shoulders of Giants: Cumulative Research and the Patent Law". *Journal of Economic Perspectives*, 5 (1), pp. 29-41.

SCOTCHMER, S., GREEN, J. (1990). – "Novelty and Disclosure in Patent Law". *Rand Journal of Economics*, 21, n° 1, Spring, pp. 131-146.

304

TANDON, P. (1982). – "Optimal Patents with Compulsory Licensing". *Journal of Political Economy*, 90, n° 3, pp. 470-486.

TAYLOR, SYLBERSTON (1973). – *The Economic Impact of the Patent System*. Cambridge University Press.

VAN DIJK, T. (1994). – *The limits of patent protection*. Maastricht: Universitaire Pers Maastricht.

Patents and R&D
An Econometric
Investigation Using
Applications for German,
European and US Patents
by German Companies

Georg LICHT, Konrad ZOZ *

ABSTRACT. – Based on the data of the first wave of the Mannheim Innovation panel, this paper explores the link between R&D expenditures and patents. Our data allow a detailed analysis of the firm size distribution of R&D and patent applications at different patent offices. It is shown that the share of R&D performing firms is stictly increasing wih firm size. The share of firms applying for patents shows an even steeper increase with firm size. Moreover, large firms are more likely apply for patents in more than one country. The home patent office appears especially important for small firms. Using various count data models, the paper explores the relationship between R&D and patents at the firm level. We carefully test several distributional assumptions for count data models. A negative binomial hurdle model seems to be the most appropriate count data model for our data as the decision to patent inventions and the productivity of R&D are ruled by different mechanisms. Our estimates point towards significant returns to scale of R&D. Furthermore, the empirical results can be interpreted towards minor and insignificant spillover effects. Even after controlling for a variety of firm characteristics, firm size exhibits a large effect on the propensity to patent.

* G. Licht: ZEW, Mannheim; K. Zoz: University of Würzburg. Detailed comments and suggestions by Heinz König, François Laisney and two anonymous referees are gratefully acknowledged. Participants at workshops at Strasbourg University, the OECD in Paris, as well as the Universities of Munich, Constance, Tübingen and Kiel Provided helpful comments and stimulating discussions. Any errors and omissions remain our own.

307

D. Encaoua et al. (eds.), The Economics and Econometrics of Innovation, 307–338.

1 Introduction

Patents and R&D are commonly used indicators in the economic analysis of technical change (see e.g. GRILICHES [1990], PAVITT [1985]). At the aggregate level both measures are used to assess the technological strength of countries and industries. The continual development of these indicators is commonly interpreted towards changes of the innovative capabilities (e.g. NIW [1996], National Science Board [1996]). In firm level analyses, patent numbers and R&D are used as indicators of the technological capacity of firms to study productivity effects of innovation (e.g. LACH [1995]) or to test the famous Schumpeterian hypotheses (see COHEN and LEVIN [1989]).

The use of patent information and R&D figures as economic indicators has been steadily improved and refined in recent years. The quality of both indicators as well as the availability of this kind of data has increased and measurement standards were developed (see e.g. OECD [1993, 1994]). Now, computerisation of patent offices enables detailed analyses of patent information. R&D surveys are performed on a regular basis in all developed economies. Therefore, it seems worthwhile to look more closely at the relationship between both indicators at the firm level.

It has often been recognised that R&D and patents capture different aspects of the innovation process. R&D expenditures or the number of R&D employees can be viewed as a measure of the resources devoted to the innovation process. But R&D represents only a part of the resources necessary to launch new products and processes. In addition, traditional R&D surveys often fail to uncover R&D in small firms (see e.G. KLEINKNECHT AND VAN REIJNEN [1991]). On the other hand patents reflect the results of innovation processes. But as for R&D, only a part of the innovation output is captured by patents. Patents reflect just one aspect: the means by which firms protect an innovation. However, patenting is only one method to protect profits originating from new products or processes from imitation by potential competitors (see LEVIN et al. 1987 for the US, KÖNIG and LICHT [1995] for Germany). Moreover, the computerisation of patent offices has decreased the costs of inferring technological information from patent documents held by competitors in recent years. As a consequence the value of patent protection decreases. As shown by HORSTMANN et al. [1985] it is rational not to patent all inventions if patent applications contain information on technological opportunities.

The relationship between patents and R&D has been studied by various authors in recent years. PAVITT [1985] concludes that small firms tend to patent more per unit R&D than large firms. SCHERER [1983] finds remarkable differences in patenting behaviour within technology groups not being explained by R&D efforts. Using a data set of large German companies, ZIMMERMANN und SCHWALBACH [1991 find only weak correlations between various firm characteristics like risk, diversification, export share and patenting behaviour. In the absence of R&D data, firm size turns out to be an important determinant of the number of patents held by a company. EVENSON [1993] stresses the importance of foreign demand for the propensity to patent. CRÉPON and DUGUET [1996, 1997] study the relation of R&D and patent application at the firm level using a sample of French firms. Using a wide variety of count data models, they find an R&D elasticity of patent numbers of just around 1 and a strong negative effect of R&D rivalry on patent activity.

Our study builds on this literature to explore the relationship between patents and R&D. It extends the literature in at least four aspects. First, previous studies are mainly based on data concerning of US or French enterprises. Our study supplements the literature with the case of the West-German economy which is the world's third largest patentee. Second, we study patent applications at various patent offices for a large sample of manufacturing firms, which enables us to compare patenting behaviour in the home and the export market. Existing empirical evidence only looks at one patent office. Our data set provides us with information on patent applications at various patent offices which allows us to draw some inferences with regard to national and international patenting activities. Third, our data enables us to control for the effect of certain firm characteristics unavailable in most studies. Finally, we distinguish between the decision with respect to the first patent and the decision for additional patents. We carefully test the statistical properties of various count data models and adopt a negative binomial hurdle model to take account of heterogeneity with respect to the propensity to patent as well as the ability of firms to generate inventions.

The paper is organised as follows: Section 2 sets up the problem by describing patenting behaviour and R&D at the firm level. It gives some evidence on differences between patenting and not patenting firms as depicted by indicators of innovation processes. Section 3 shortly outlines a theoretical framework for investigating the relation of R&D and patents at the firm level. In section 4 we describe the necessary steps to apply the theoretical framework to the data set at hand. Section 5 introduces the empirical model. We discuss various count data approaches to the patent-R&D relationship and present some specification tests. In Section 6 we present the regression estimates and take a closer look at the elasticity of patent applications to R&D. Finally, section 7 summarises our results and draws some conclusions for further research.

2 Patents, R&D and Innovation at the Firm Level

Although patents and R&D are regularly used indicators of technical change at the macro and the micro level, only a few studies seek to analyse their relation at a microeconomic level. R&D reflects the input side whereas patents can be viewed as a measure of an intermediate output of innovation processes. Both have their strengths and weaknesses which need not be discussed in detail here. The main problems with patents arise from the fact that not all inventions will be patented. Imitative and incremental innovations are not covered by patent statistics although they represent a large and increasingly important part of innovation activities of firms. The most obvious short-coming of R&D statistics is their undercoverage of innovation activities in small firms (see e.g. KLEINKNECHT and REIJNEN [1991]). [1] As recent research has shown, small firms are less likely to be engaged in R&D; but if they have decided to do so, small firms invest more compared to their size than medium sized firms, but less than large firms. [2]

It is well known from patent application data that a large share of patents is applied for by only a small number of firms and that, therefore, the distribution of patent application numbers is highly skewed. But less is known about the distribution of patenting or not by firm size. Figure 1 shows the size distribution of innovating, R&D performing and patenting firms. As expected, the percentages of innovating, R&D performing and patenting firms increase strongly with firmsize. Slightly more than 50% of all manufacturing companies with more than 4 and less than 50 employees have introduced improved or new products or processes in 1990-1992 or intended to do so in 1993-1995. [3] The share of R&D performing firms amounts to 20% of all firms in this size class. However, just one out of ten innovating firms applies for a patent in 1992 in the smallest size class. In the largest size class the percentage of patenting firms exceeds 65%. When looking at the innovative firms only, the figure demonstrates that the shares of non R&D performing and non patenting companies decline with firm size. Thus the innovation activities of small and medium companies will most certainly be underestimated if only R&D and patents are used as indicators for innovative activities.

The difference between small and large firms is even more pronounced with respect to patent applications at more than one patent office in one year. The overwhelming majority of German patenting firms apply to the German patent office. Just around 10% of the patenting firms use the European procedure only and do not apply to the German office. The share of firms that do not only apply to the German or European Patent office, but also the US Patent and Trademark Office or another patent office, is increasing with firm size for small and medium sized firms. But this share is nearly

---

1. Throughout the paper R&D always refers to the FRASCATI-definition (see OECD [1993]).

2. See e.g. FELDER et al. [1996] who simultaneously model the decision to perform R&D and the R&D intensity. The U-shaped form of the relationship between R&D intensity and firm size strongly depends on the indicators used to measure R&D intensity.

3. These firms are called 'innovating companies'. Our definition of innovation takes a purely firm-specific view. So innovations comprise absolutely new products as well as new products which are pure imitations. We assume that all companies which do not innovate within this six-year-period do not perform R&D in 1992 and do not apply for a patent in 1992.

constant for firms with more than 250 employees. [4] Since the application costs at a foreign patent office are larger than for a patent application at the home office, and exporting is more common in larger enterprises, this result is in line with our expectations. Our data produces two stylised facts already noted by SIRILLI [1987] for the Italian manufacturing sector: the structure of international patenting activities is similar to the structure of international trade; abroad extension of patents is increasing with firm size. So, firm size and export status are expected to be important determinants of patent behaviour in foreign countries.

FIGURE 1

Innovating, R&D-Performing and Patenting Companies in German Manufacturing Industries in 1992-Weighted Data.

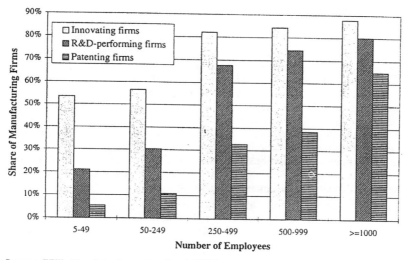

Source : ZEW: Mannheim Innovation Panel (1995).

Patent strategies of firms may strongly depend on firm characteristics. This holds especially for application at different patent offices. But patent statistics regularly lack information on basic firm characteristics. Therefore, not much is known with regard to differences in characteristics between patenting and non patenting firms. We first look at the role various attributes of the innovation process and firm characteristics play for patenting and non patenting firms. Figure 2 documents some differences between non patenting firms, firms which apply for patents in Germany only, as well as

---

4. The European patent procedure is rather expensive (e.g.: patent fees; cost of translating the patent documentation into the languages of the destination countries). As a rule the European patent procedure is cheaper than the direct application via national patent offices if one seeks patent protection in more than three European countries. Therefore, we consider applications at the European Patent Office as applications abroad.

firms which apply for patents at least to one foreign patent office. There are significant differences between patenting and non-patenting firms. However these differences are less significant between firms which only use GPO applications and firms which also apply to foreign patent offices (including EPO).

The first three items in Figure 2 relate to the sources of knowledge used to generate innovations. We distinguish (1) the firm's own R&D department, (2) scientific institutions and (3) other firms, as being an important source of know-how. [5] Own R&D seems to be an important source of know-how especially for patenting firms. A much larger share of patentors regard scientific institutions as an important source of knowledge for innovation processes. This difference is less pronounced with regard to private firms as sources of know-how. To fulfill the novelty requirements patenting firms show a more systematic, R&D based approach to knowledge generation than non patenting firms. These differences on the input side of innovation processes are also confirmed by differences with respect to the results of innovation processes. Figure 2 shows that a larger share of patenting firms introduced products which are not only new to the firm but represent market innovations. When we look at the share of sales of innovative products, [6] we find no difference between patenting and non patenting firms. So, market success with innovative products not only depends on successful technological solutions which are represented by a patent, but also on complementary assets and activities of firms (e.g. superior sales effort). [7] In addition, Figure 2 shows that a lot of firms (40%) introduce products 'new to the market' without applying for patent protection. One of the most prominent explanations maintains that patents are an imperfect tool for protecting innovations. Alternatively, market novelties do not always meet the novelty requirements of patents.

Furthermore, patenting firms spend a larger share of the total R&D budget than non patenting firms on product innovation. Those in turn spend a larger share on process R&D. But this does not imply that patentors devote a higher share of their total innovative activities to new products compared to non patenting companies. Cost saving process innovations and the generation and market introduction of product innovations are viewed as equally important by patenting and non-patenting firms. Figure 2 also shows that patents are an important tool in the strategy of firms. This notion rests on the result that exporting companies and companies with innovative activities devoted to foreign markets are involved in patenting to a larger extent. This is even true when we look at patenting only in Germany. So,

---

5. 'Scientific institutions' and 'other private firms' are aggregated representations of various sources of information (e.g. customers, suppliers, competitors, consultants, universities, government research laboratories). Firms rate the importance of these source for innovation on a five-point scale. The aggregate values are the weighted sum of the scores given to these sources. Weights are obtained by a factor analysis (see FELDER et al. [1996] for details).

6. 'Innovative products' refer to products introduced to the market in the last three years. Innovative products are defined as 'new to the firm'. Therefore, this figure also includes the market success with purely imitative products.

7. Similar results are reported to France by KABLA [1996].

312

FIGURE 2

Innovation Activities and Patent Applications in Germany 1992.

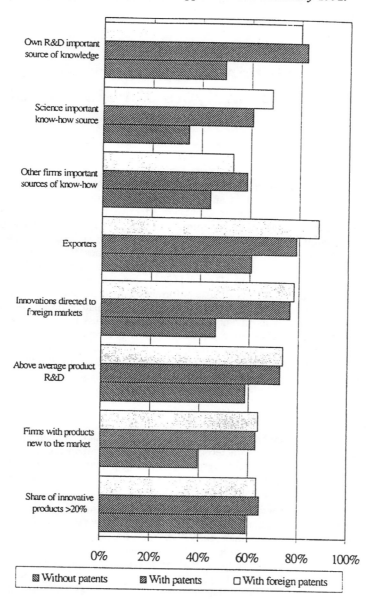

Source : ZEW: Mannheim Innovation Panel (1995).

patenting seems to be especially important in markets which are open to international competition. Protecting the home market by patents is only the first step in gaining intellectual property rights for new products in the world market.

3 A Theoretical Framework for the Econometric Analysis of Patent Applications

A firm will apply for patent protection if the expected marginal return of protection exceeds the cost of an application. The returns from using the patent system depend on whether patents are effective in preventing imitation by competitors. In addition, if competitors profit from the knowledge diffused through publication of patents returns are also adversely affected. Recently, COHEN et al. [1996] provided some evidence that patents are a rather imperfect shelter from imitation. As the theoretical models of HORSTMAN et al. [1985] and HARTER [1993] show, firms will not always apply for a patent if patents diffuse information to competitors. In order to protect its competitive edge, a firm may apply for patent protection for only some fraction of its inventions. Indeed, many firms may not rely on patents at all but on alternative mechanisms like secrecy or complexity of product design. Both arguments lead to the concept of the propensity to patent which states that firms patent only a fraction of their inventions. This is captured by the equation

$$(1) \qquad P_{ij} = g_j(X_i) I_i$$

where P_{ij} is the number of patent applications of firm i at the patent office j. The vector X_i captures characteristics of firms which affect the difference between the marginal expected return from using patents and the costs of applying and holding of a patent. I_i is the number of inventions of firm i which fulfill the novelty test.

The function g represents the propensity to patent and depends on the characteristics of the patent system. The model of HORSTMAN et al. [1985] implies g_j to be smaller than unity. In addition, as the application for patents at a foreign patent office is more expensive than an application at the home office we also suppose that on average foreign patents should be more valuable than patent applications in the home country. So, the expected value of the least valuable patent applied for at a foreign office should exceed the least valuable patent at the home office. Therefore, we should keep in mind that patent applications at foreign offices may be more homogenous w.r.t. to their value than patents applied for at the home patent office.

314

Equation (1) cannot be implemented directly as we do not observe the number of inventions at the firm level. But inventions can be viewed as the outcome of a systematic search process for novelties. The relationship between the outcome of innovative activities and the inputs can be represented by the concept of a production function for inventions. This analytical tool is thought to describe the transformation of R&D into new knowledge which in later stages of the innovation process is used for the development of new knowledge which in later stages of the innovation process is used for the development of new products and processes. We assume R&D to be the most important input into the knowledge generating process. In addition, firms profit from other firms' R&D. The larger this spillover the larger will be the productivity of a firm to generate inventions. To capture this, we assume that R&D capital of the industry enhances the knowledge generating process of firms. Therefore, a simple version of the invention production function is given by

$$(2) \qquad\qquad I_i = f(K_i, K_s, A_i),$$

where I_i represents the number of inventions made by firm i in the period under consideration. K_i denotes the firm's own R&D capital and K_s indicates the R&D capital of all other firms (the industry) from which knowledge spillovers arise. A_i represents other firm-specific factors which influence the R&D productivity of a firm in generating inventions. These factors are referred to as technological opportunities in the literature.

Combining (1) and (2) we derive an equation which relates the number of patents to R&D and various factors which influence the propensity to patent.

$$(3) \qquad\qquad P_{ij} = g_j(X_i) f(K_i, K_s, A_i).$$

To keep the model as simple as possible, we assume that g_j and f are exponential functions of a linear combination of their arguments. Therefore, the log of the number of patents is modelled as a linear function of the arguments of g and f. Given the nature of invention, a random error uncorrelated with the arguments of g and f is added to the loglinear version of equation (3). This random error should also account for unobserved heterogeneity due to the economic value of an invention. As firms probably differ in their ability to assess a priori the economic value of an invention and hence of a patent, their propensity to patent might be affected by this unobserved ability. [8]

Equation (3) relates the number of patent applications to R&D in a rather simple manner but also shows that there probably is a number

---

8. It is well-known from the literature that the economic value of patents varies over a wide range (see LANJOUW, PAKES and PUTNAM [1996] for a survey).

of other variables intervening into the relationship between R&D and patents. Spillovers have an ambiguous effect on the number of patents. On the one hand spillovers will enhance the productivity of R&D and increase the number of inventions. On the other hand spillovers probably reduce the propensity to patent and induce firms to rely on alternative mechanisms to protect their competitive edge. In addition, if patents induce an overinvestment in R&D it can occur that we observe a negative correlation between an industry's R&D and the number of patents.

4 Empirical Implementation

Our data set contains information on the number of patent applications at the German, the European and US Patent Office by German firms in 1992. Unfortunately, we do not observe whether these patent applications refer to the same invention, *i.e.* belong to the same patent family. Moreover, given the rules of inernational patenting, it does not seem reasonable to assume that this is the case. Extensions of patent applications at the home office to foreign patent systems usually do not occur within one year.

We are restricted to a single cross-section of data which implies that the cost of patent applications does not vary much in the sample used. Variation in application costs is mainly present between offices. E.g. it is well-known that patent applications at the European patent office are far more expensive than patent applications at the German office. So, we should expect that firms apply for patent protection for some of the less valuable inventions at the German patent office but hesitate to apply for these inventions at the EPO or foreign patent offices. Therefore, patent applications at foreign patent offices are expected to have a larger mean economic value compared to the patent application at the home patent office. Differences in application costs and the value of patents are only implicitly given as our data set contains patent applications at different patent offices. We should keep this in mind when we interpret the estimation results.

The implementation of various exogenous variables also requires some further comments. [9] Since our data set does not contain any information on past R&D expenditures which would allow the construction of firm specific R&D capital stocks, we use the current R&D expenditures as a proxy for the R&D capital stock. But the data allow us to identify whether or not a firm performs R&D on a continuous basis. This information can be used to account for past R&D, which has a long-lasting effect on the productivity in generating patents.

---

9. The definitions of the variables are summarized in Table 1. Descriptive statistics by firm size are given in Appendix 1.

The construction of the spillover pool is also restricted by data availability. Since no information is available on the technological field (e.g. JAFFE [1988]) or the product groups (e.g. HARHOFF [1994]) in which firms perform R&D, we use the total R&D expenditures of an industry as reported in the official 1992 German R&D statistics (see SV-WISSENSCHAFTSSTATISTIK [1994]). In addition, we account for firm specific differences in the invention production function. Following LEVIN and REISS [1987] we assume that the productivity is higher because of higher technological opportunities, if firms view scientific sources as an important source of information for their innovation activities.

Firm size probably affects the marginal costs of patent application. As many small firms neither have a specialised unit dealing with patents or property rights nor detailed prior information about the patent system, their costs per application are expected to be higher than the marginal application costs of large firms. ZIMMERMANN and SCHWALBACH [1991] show that the number of patents strictly increases with firm size. In addition, it is often argued that small firms hesitate to apply for a patent because of the large patent litigation costs. We test for the effect of firm size on the propensity to patent by including the logarithm of the number of employees.

Several studies argue that the degree of diversification has an impact on the propensity to patent (see e.g. ZIMMERMANN and SCHWALBACH [1991]). The reason for this behaviour is that more diversified firms may use an invention for different products and processes. So the market risk of innovation is lower and the expected marginal returns from patenting are higher.

We consider the impact of the export status of a firm on the propensity to patent. A positive impact of exports on the propensity to patent is expected as the number of competitors gets larger for exporting firms and, therefore, protection of knowledge is more important.

Due to the transformation process in East-Germany, the productivity in generating patents as well as the propensity to patent are likely lower among East-German than among West-German companies. This is most obvious from the fact that within a few years, the number of R&D personnel drops from 88 000 (1989) to around 22 000 (1993). This was accompanied by reorganisations of R&D departments. In addition, new R&D projects have little in common with R&D programmes of the former GDR enterprises which were to a large extent imitations of Western technologies. Therefore, a dummy for East-German firms is included.

Finally, the propensity to patent as well as the patent productivity are affected by other firm characteristics. In some firm groups only the mother company applies for the patent regardless of which subsidiary brought forth the invention. This is especially well known from foreign companies. On the other hand, daughter companies might profit from R&D performed in other parts of the group, which would imply a higher productivity of the observed unit. Therefore, we use dummies for firms which are part of a group and for firms with a foreign mother company.

TABLE 1

Definition of Variables.

Variable name	Short description
PATENT MEASURES	
PATDE	No. of patent applications at the German Patent Office
PATEU	No. of patent applications at the European Patent Office
PATUS	No. of patent applications at the US Patent and Trademark Office
EXPENDITURES FOR R&D	
LR&D:	R&D expenditures in 1992 (in DM 1000; in logs)
LR&DSQ	R&D expenditures in 1992 (in DM 1000; in logs) squared
PERM_R&D	Dummy for firms with permanent R&D activities
SPILLOVER MEASURES	
SPILL	Spillover pool=Total R&D of the industry (in Mill. DM; in logs)
R&D_SPILL	Spillover pool multiplied by the firm's own R&D (in logs)
FIRM SPECIFIC PRODUCTIVITY INDICATORS	
SCIENCE	Importance of scientific institutions as source of knowledge for innovations (factor analysis; see Felder *et al.* [1996]
OTHFIRM	Importance of other firms as source of knowledge for innovations (factor analysis; see Felder *et al.* [1996]
EXPORT STATUS	
EX_SHARE	Export share
EXPORT	Dummy for exporting firm
EX_PLAN	Innovation activities planned for the US, Japanese or other overseas market (Dummy: 1=important or very important)
FIRM SIZE	
LEMP	Number of employees (in logs)
OTHER FIRM CHARACTERISTICS	
EAST	Firm in East-Germany
DIVERS	Degree of diversification calculated as the inverse of the sum of squared sales shares (%) for the 4 major product groups. Therefore a single product firm will have the value 1.
FOREIGN	Foreign subsidiary
GROUP	Part of a group

5 Econometric Modelling

The number of patents is restricted by definition to non-negative integers. Appropriate estimation techniques for this kind of data are given by the family of count data models. Count data models are applied to the patents-R&D relationship by a number of researchers including BOUND *et al.* [1984], HAUSMAN *et al.* [1984] for the US, CRÉPON and DUGUET [1993] for France or ZIMMERMANN and SCHWALBACH [1991] for Germany. Our econometric

318

modelling strategy starts with some basic models for count data which we describe briefly in the first part of the chapter. The second part of this chapter deals with hurdle models for count data. [10]

The economic rationale for applying hurdle models rest on the plausible assumption that the decision to apply for the first patent and the decision to apply for additional patents are ruled by different processes. The decision to apply for a patent has to be made when the yield of holding this patent is not known exactly. Firms often adopt some basic decision about how to protect intellectual property and how to handle patentable inventions. This basic decision is often made in the context of the first invention. The decision to apply for patents for additional inventions is based on this first principle decision. So, we should expect different rules to govern the decisions concerning the first patent and additional patents. The empirical specification of the model should take potentially different decision processes into account. Clearly, all firms included in our sample are assumed to decide whether to patent their innovations or not. Therefore, we restrict the sample to those firms which actually introduced a product or a process innovation in recent years [11].

• Basic Models for Count Data

As a starting point it is often assumed that the data generating process follows a poisson distribution. If the random variable $Y_i \in \{0, 1, 2, ...\}$ is poisson distributed, the probability that exactly y_i counts are observed, is given by

(4)
$$P(Y_i = y_i | \lambda_i) = \frac{\exp(-\lambda_i) \lambda_i^{y_i}}{y_i!},$$
$$y_i = 0, 1, 2, ... \quad \text{with} \quad E[Y_i] = Var[Y_i] = \lambda_i > 0$$

Covariates can be introduced by specifying the individual mean by $\lambda_i = \exp(x_i' \beta)$ to ensure the positiveness of the mean. Here x_i' denotes a $(1 \times k)$ vector of non-stochastic covariates of firm i and β is the corresponding coefficient vector. Assuming a random sample of individual observations (y_i, x_i), the vector β can be estimated by maximum likelihood methods.

In empirical work the equality of conditional mean and conditional variance of the distribution of the dependent variable, implied by the model, often turns out to be too restrictive. In most applications the conditional variance exceeds the conditional mean, which is known as

---

10. Appendix 3 contains an overview of various econometric tests for count data models and reports the results for the data set at hand.

11. If there were firms that would not even think about patenting their innovations, the "zero inflated" count data model of LAMBERT [1992] would be a possible alternative. But this would not correctly model the propensity to patent that we have in mind. Lambert's model would only allow us to distinguish between firms that would never ever patent and others that follow a more conventional pattern comprising the number of patents as well as not to patent at all.

overdispersion. Overdispersion can have at least two distinct statistical sources: positive contagion (occurrences influence future occurences) or unobserved heterogeneity (see WINKELMANN and ZIMMERMANN [1995], McCULLAGH and NELDER [1989]).

A first alternative are models assuming a negative binomial distribution as data generating process. As shown in the literature, the negative binomial model is an extension of the standard poisson model where the poisson parameter for each firm λ_i has an additional random component, accounting for (unobserved) heterogeneity, not yet accounted for by the regressors that determine the individual mean function.

Specifying $\tilde{\lambda}_i = \exp(x_i'\beta + \varepsilon_i) = \exp(x_i'\beta)\,u_i$, where ε_i is an error term uncorrelated with the explanatory variables, captures unobserved heterogeneity and leads to a stochastic mean function with expectation $E[\tilde{\lambda}_i] = \lambda_i$ and variance $Var[\tilde{\lambda}_i] = \lambda_i^2 \sigma_{u_i}^2$. The negative binomial distribution for Y_i results as a compound poisson distribution if the mixing distribution is the gamma distribution. Assuming ε_i to be gamma distributed or equivalently $\tilde{\lambda}_i \sim Gamma(\phi_i, \nu_i)$, one can derive the negative binomial distribution for Y_i with:

$$(5) \qquad P(Y_i = y_i) = \frac{\Gamma(y_i + \nu_i)}{\Gamma(y_i + 1)\Gamma(\nu_i)} \left(\frac{\nu_i}{\phi_i + \nu_i}\right)^{\nu_i} \left(\frac{\phi_i}{\phi_i + \nu_i}\right)^{y_i}$$

with expectation $E[Y_i] = \phi_i$ and variance $Var[Y_i] = \phi_i + \nu_i^{-1}\phi_i^2$.

Specifying the individual mean function as above, $E[Y_i] = \phi_i = \exp(x_i'\beta)$, we get the regression model with an unknown coefficient vector β and an unknown variance parameter ν_i. Choosing different parameterisations for the precision parameter ν_i allows to model different variance to mean ratios of the dependent variable. Setting $\nu_i = \alpha^{-1}$, a constant for all firms, leads to a model with the following form of heteroscedasticity: $Var[Y_i] = E[Y_i](1 + \alpha E[Y_i])$. The variance-mean relationship is linear in the mean. Following CAMERON and TRIVEDI [1986], we call this the type II negative binomial model (negbin II). Similarly, a type I negative binomial model (negbin I) is obtained by setting $\nu_i = \alpha^{-1}\exp(x_i'\beta)$. The variance implied by negbin I can be written as $Var[Y_i] = (1 + \alpha)E[Y_i]$, with a constant variance-to-mean ratio. Negbin I and II are different models and in general lead to different estimates for β.

• Hurdle Models for Count Data

A further alternative modelling strategy in the light of overdispersion is to assume that the decisions of whether or not to patent and to apply for more than one patent are ruled by different processes. This can be done using hurdle models for count data proposed by MULLAHY [1986]. The hurdle takes account of the fact that there may be different distributions which govern the first decision to patent an invention and the decision to apply for patent protection for other inventions. The hurdle specification assumes two different sets of parameter estimates. The underlying idea is that a binomial probability model governs the binary outcome of whether a count variate has a zero or a positive realisation (MULLAHY [1986]). Once the hurdle

320

is crossed and positive counts are observed, the data generating process is governed by a truncated-at-zero count model. The binomial process in the first stage can also be interpreted as a threshold-crossing binary choice model, in which the continuous latent variable is the firm's propensity to enter the second stage of the process, *i.e.* the firm's willingness to patent an invention (see POHLMEIER and ULRICH [1995]).

Assume that f_1 is any probability distribution function for non-negative integers, that governs the decision whether or not to patent, and that f_2 represents the process governing the decision once the hurdle is crossed. Then the probability distribution of the model is given by:

(6)
$$P\left(Y_i = 0\right) = f_1\left(0\right)$$
$$P\left(Y_i = y\right) = \left(1 - f_1\left(0\right)\right)\frac{f_2\left(y\right)}{1 - f_2\left(0\right)}$$

$(1 - f_1\left(0\right))$ gives the probability of crossing the hurdle and $(1 - f_2\left(0\right))$ is the normalisation for $f_2\left(y\right)$ because of the truncation at zero (see WINKELMANN and ZIMMERMANN [1995]).

The likelihood of the model depends on two different parameter vectors: β_1 represents the parameters w.r.t. the decision for the first patent, β_2 the parameter vector which refers to the decision to apply for more than one patent. Let Ω_0 denote the subsample of firms without a patent application and Ω_1 represents the subsample of firms with at least one patent application. Then we can write the likelihood as follows:

(7)
$$L = \prod_{i \in \Omega_0} P\left(Y_i = 0 | x_i' \beta_1, \, \alpha_1\right) \prod_{i \in \Omega_1} \left[1 - P\left(Y_i = 0 | x_i' \beta_1, \, \alpha_1\right)\right]$$
$$\prod_{i \in \Omega_1} \frac{P\left(Y_i = y_i | x_i' \beta_2, \, \alpha_2\right)}{1 - P\left(Y_i = 0 | x_i' \beta_2, \, \alpha_2\right)}$$

The likelihood for the binary process to patent or not to patent is given by the first two expressions in (7), and the last part gives the likelihood of a truncated-at-zero count model.

We choose negbin II as the underlying distribution for both stages for the following reasons: It captures unobserved heterogeneity, allows for overdispersion in its own right and enables us to test the distributional assumptions. In addition, we estimate the poisson hurdle model proposed by MULLAHY [1986], where we assume that the underlying distribution for both stages is poisson. Finally, we also consider a poisson-negbin hurdle model which assumes the poisson distribution for the first stage and the negbin II distribution for the second stage.

The hurdle models comprise the conventional count data models as special cases. If the parameter estimates for both stages are the same the negbin hurdle model as well as the poisson hurdle model collapse to the underlying conventional model (negbin II model in the case of the negbin hurdle model and poisson model in the case of the poisson hurdle model). Furthermore, it can be shown that if the overdispersion parameter converges to zero, $\alpha \to 0$, the negative binomial distribution collapses to the poisson distribution.

FIGURE 3

Comparison of Observed and Predicted Counts for Various Count Data Models

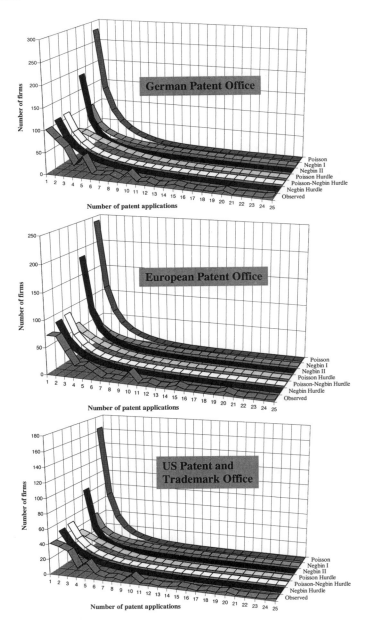

Within the negbin hurdle specification we obtain the poisson-negbin hurdle model if $\alpha_1 = 0$ and poisson hurdle model if $\alpha_1 = \alpha_2 = 0$ (see POHLMEIER and ULRICH [1995]). Hence, it is quite easy to test the various models against each other. More details can be found in Appendix 3 [12.]

As stands out from Appendix 3, our test strategy implies that a negbin hurdle model is preferable. Moreover, this conclusion is confirmed by comparing the observed number of firms with a certain number of patents and the predicted number of firms with a given number of patent applications. These predictions are obtained by first calculating for each observation, the probability to apply for a certain number of patents and then by summing over these individual predicted probabilities for each category (see WINKELMANN and ZIMMERMANN [1995]). The predicted and observed number of firms within each category (number of patents) are compared in Figure 3, details are reported in Appendix 4. We will thus report only the results from the negbin hurdle model, noting that the results for the alternative poisson negbin hurdle model are rather similar.

6 Regression Results

Regression results for the model outlined in equation (7) are reported in Table 2. [13] The model is estimated separately for patent applications at the German, the European and the US patent office. Overall, we find remarkable differences between patent applications at the German Patent Office, the European Patent Office, and the US Patent and Trademark Office. In our opinion this partly reflects peculiarities of the patent procedures of these three offices and can be attributed to the smaller heterogeneity of patents in terms of their value in the case of the EPO and USPTO than at the GPO.

The results demonstrate that the patent strategies of firms are important determinants of patent activities. Therefore, the number of patents produced by an economy in a given year not only reflects technological success but also depends on behavioural patterns of firms. The number of patents of a firm rests not only on its productivity in generating invention but also on the propensity to patent. This can be seen in the differences of estimated parameter vectors for the decision stage and the number of patents part of the hurdle models. Different parameter vectors for both stages are evident from the specification tests reported in Appendix 3.

In addition, the propensity to patent not only affects the decision whether to patent or not, but also affects the number of patents. This is evident from the fact that export share and firm size which were expected to be arguments

---

12. α_1 denotes the overdispersion parameter for the hurdle stage, α_2, for the second stage when the hurdle is crossed.
13. STATA, Version 4.0 was used for estimation.

of the propensity to patent part of the model, are also significant in the second stage. This interpretation is also confirmed by the parameter estimates for the diversification indicator: the higher the degree of diversification the lower will be the number of patents applied for. But the principal decision on whether or not to patent is unaffected by diversification. A possible interpretation of this result could be that diversified firms spend a larger share of their R&D on incremental, non-patentable innovations, so that their 'productivity' in generating patents is lower.

R&D turns out to be a major source in generating new knowledge. The elasticity of the number of patents with respect to R&D is increasing with current R&D expenditures as indicated by the coefficients of log R&D (LR&D) and its square (LR&DSQ) in the patent number part of the model. Our results, therefore, suggest economies of scale with respect to the production of patents. Figure 4 shows the elasticities of the number of patents applied for with respect to R&D. The elasticities are increasing throughout the relevant range of R&D expenditures.

Besides the R&D elasticity of patent numbers, Figure 4 indicates the median value of firms R&D expenditures for those firms which apply to the three patent offices. These calculations show that for the median R&D performer the elasticity is rather close to 0.9. Only for some large R&D spenders, economies to scale are sufficiently large. So, for the majority of firms our results do not deviate too much from recent results for France by CRÉPON and DUGUET [1996] who find an elasticity of patent w.r.t. R&D not deviating significantly from unity.

Moreover, different fixed costs seem to be associated with patent applications at the GPO, the EPO and the USPTO. The parameter estimate

FIGURE 4

Elasticities of the Number of Patent Applications w.r.t. R&D.

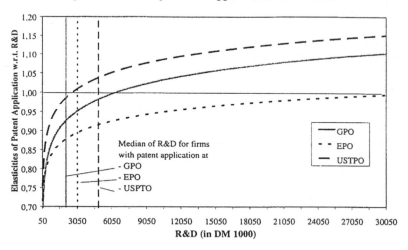

Remark: Calculations are based on regression estimates reported in Table 2. We use the estimates of the "numbers part" only. The value of the spillover-effect is evaluated at he median value for the GPO.

324

for R&D in the hurdle stage is much lower for the GPO than for the EPO and the USPTO. The parameter estimates for the second stage of the hurdle model are far less different between these different kinds of patent applications.

The evidence for positive knowledge spillovers from other firms' R&D investment seems rather weak in our data. No significant impact of the spillover pool (SPILL) on patent activity is observed. Moreover, as the interaction term between own R&D and the spillover pool (R&D_SPILL) is not significant, we conclude that even in high-tech sectors the patent productivity is not affected by spillovers or patent rivalry effects. So, our results do not confirm CRÉPON and DUGUET [1986] who find negative rivalry effects with regard to the number of patents of French companies. They also point out that this effect is especially important for big companies. As many small and medium firms are included in our data set this can be an explanation for this difference in results.

Technological opportunity should reflect interfirm differences in R&D productivity: those firms which regard scientific institutions as primary sources of information for their innovation activities (SCIENCE) apply more often for patents. This reveals that the productivity of R&D is larger in technological areas where the know-how generating process within the firms is enhanced by ongoing research in public scientific infrastructure.

Export activities seem to be one of the major determinants of a firm's propensity to patent. Even in the case of applications at the GPO, the number of patent applications increases with the export share. As one would expect, the effect of exports increases when looking at the EPO and even more when looking at the USPTO. This is even more pronounced if innovation activities are undertaken to protect future competitiveness in foreign markets.

Firm size exhibits a large effect on patenting. The propensity to patent seems to increase with firm size. Even more surprising is the large firm size effect found in the patent number part of our model. This can be interpreted towards a higher productivity in generating inventions in large firms. An alternative explanation could be that rules adopted in larger firms stimulate patent applications even if the economic value of an invention is probably low. [14] Moreover, larger firms are probably more aware of the role played by patents in cross-licensing agreements, R&D cooperations and the strategic dimension of patents. Legal regulations like the German Employee Inventor Law ("Arbeitnehmererfindergesetz") also stimulate to patent applications. Those rules are probably more important considerations for the formalised innovation processes of large companies and, therefore, in line with the larger propensity to patent in large companies.

We should also note that despite of a large correlation of firm size and R&D in a cross-section regression, the coefficients on the R&D variables change only slightly when we drop firm size from the regression.

---

14. GIESE and STOUTZ show that patent applications of large firms are less likely to lead to patent grants.

TABLE 2

Patent Applications at the German Patent Office, European Patent Office and the US Patent and Trademark Office – Results for the Negbin Hurdle Regression Model.

	German Patent Office				European Patent Office				US Patent and Trademark Office			
Summary statistics												
Observations	1685				1689				1694			
Log.Likelihood	−1859.1				−1337.31				−828.18			
χ^2/df/Pseudo R^2	1002.5	56	0.213		913.3	56	0.255		685.4	56	0.293	
	Decision part		Patent numbers		Decision part		Patent numbers		Decision part		Patent number	
Exogenous Variables	Coeff.	t-values	Coeff.	t-values	Coeff.	t-values	Coeff.	t-values	Coeff.	t-values	Coeff.	t-values
LR&D	0.384	1.82	−0.013	−0.09	0.853	2.08	0.107	0.47	1.033	1.72	0.077	0.22
LR&D²	0.019	1.19	0.033	5.87	0.081	2.48	0.022	3.37	0.104	2.24	0.031	3.54
PERM_R&D	0.324	1.21	0.328	1.29	1.014	2.25	−0.302	−0.81	0.105	0.13	0.234	0.33
SPILL	−0.322	−0.62	−0.004	−0.01	−0.784	−0.79	−0.784	−1.44	−0.323	−0.24	−0.669	−1.10
R&D_SPILL	−0.003	−0.13	0.028	1.52	−0.006	−0.17	0.004	0.14	−0.013	−0.24	0.007	0.18
SCIENCE	0.222	2.00	0.199	2.83	0.207	1.20	0.316	3.54	0.544	1.82	0.108	0.95
OTHFIRM	0.135	1.25	0.001	0.01	0.071	0.40	0.068	0.71	−0.362	−1.23	0.101	0.89
EX_SHARE	0.713	1.62	0.550	2.02	2.089	2.54	0.699	2.02	3.969	2.64	1.250	2.73
EXPORTER	0.324	1.11	−0.051	−0.19	0.293	0.55	0.194	0.48	1.306	1.08	−0.578	−0.95
EX_PLAN	0.248	1.33	0.068	0.59	0.500	1.62	0.200	1.36	2.197	3.24	0.081	0.40
LEMP	0.311	3.41	0.351	5.95	0.273	1.82	0.401	5.37	0.356	1.67	0.318	3.34
LEMP*EAST	0.092	0.56	0.008	0.07	0.028	0.08	−0.394	−0.99	−1.154	−1.55	−0.655	−1.18
EAST	−1.458	−1.73	0.398	0.55	−3.025	−1.59	3.599	1.46	1.868	0.53	3.094	0.98
DIVERS	0.027	0.04	−0.923	−2.09	−0.653	−0.59	−0.474	−0.83	0.646	0.36	−1.205	−1.78
FOREIGN	−0.402	−1.13	−0.225	−1.03	−0.451	−0.77	−0.053	−0.21	−0.529	−0.63	0.081	0.26
GROUP	−0.120	−0.61	−0.088	−0.75	0.137	0.42	−0.129	−0.92	0.188	0.38	−0.257	−1.51
Industry dummies	included		included		included		included		included		included	
ln α_1, ln α_2	0.517	1.03	−0.117	−0.88	1.493	3.67	−0.064	−0.39	2.035	4.39	−0.281	−1.40
Constant	−1.001	−0.37	−0.958	−0.48	−0.061	−0.01	2.745	0.98	−4.725	−0.67	2.360	0.71

All models are estimated by maximum likelihood. The likelihood function is given by equation (7). The χ^2-value refers to a test against a model with constants as well as ln α_1 and ln α_2.

Other firm characteristics included in the model show somewhat surprising effects. We do not find a significant negative effect for small or for large East-German firms. Only in the hurdle stage in the regression model for the German Patent Office the East-German dummy variable nearly reaches statistical significance. So, our model does not point to a lower patent productivity nor to a different behaviour owards patents in East-German firms. The small patent numbers of the East-German economy are mainly caused by a low R&D effort and the small number of large firms in East-Germany.

In addition, our expectations with regard to a lower patent activity of group members and subsidiaries of foreign firms are not supported by our results. Given the large differences in the way multinational companies organise their decision processes a more refined modelling seems to be necessary before we can reach more clear-cut conclusions with regard to the patent behaviour of German daughters of multinational companies.

Finally, our specification also includes 12 sector dummies. We omit the discussion of these dummies because it is difficult to interpret whether they reflect interfirm differences in the propensity to patent or in the invention production function.

7 Summary and some Hints on Further Research

Based on the data of the first wave of the Mannheim Innovation Panel, this paper explores the role of patents as appropriability mechanism and the relation between R&D expenditures and patents. This data set generates the possibility to look at the firm size distribution of patent applications at different patent offices.

Before summarizing the main results, some qualifying remarks are in order. First, as shown by various other studies (see e.g. HARHOFF [1994] for German manufacturing) spillovers and appropriability conditions depend crucially on the nature of technology. Further research should more explicitly explore the possibility to estimate our model for high-tech and low-tech sectors separately. Secondly, we neglect technology-specific effects. These effects can be accounted when using the information on technology inherent in the classification of patents by patent offices. Therefore, we should seek to merge available patent application data at the level of patents with our firm level dataset (see e.g. JAFFE [1989]). Finally, R&D expenditures and patent applications may be determined simultaneously (see PAKES [1985]). Future research should try to take this simultaneity into account and test whether the results of this paper suffer from a simultaneous equation bias.

The results of the paper can be summarised in the following way: in the first part of the paper it is shown that the share of R&D performing firms strictly increases with firm size. The share of firms applying for patents exhibits an even steeper increase with firm size. Moreover, the larger a firm, the more likely it is to apply for patents in more than one country. Although large firms apply for a German patent with a higher probability than SMEs, large firms also apply to the European Patent Office whereas SMEs often apply for a patent at the German Patent Office only. The German Patent Office seems to be especially important for small firms.

The second part of the paper explores the relationship between R&D and patents more closely. We find a close relationship between R&D and patents. Our hurdle negbin regression model implies the presence of economies of scale in the patents-R&D relatonship. But the elasticity of patents with respect to R&D significantly exceeds unity only for large R&D spenders. For the majority of firms this elasticity is just around 1. Using the R&D expenditures of the industry, our model is thought to capture spillovers or effects of R&D rivalry on the number of patents. But we failed to find empirical evidence for these effects.

Even after controlling for a variety of firm characteristics, firm size exhibits a large effect on the propensity to patent. Patents also play an important role when looking at export strategies of firms. Exporting firms apply more often for patents at the German patent office and even more at foreign patent offices. Therefore, we should be very careful when using patent numbers as an indicator of the technological capabilities of firms or economies as strategic decisions are important determinants of the number of patent applications. So, a change in the number of patent applications of an economy in a given year can well be the result of a change in the patent strategy of firms and need not to be the result of an increase in the technological capabilities of the economy.

APPENDIX 1

Description of the Data Set

Data were taken from the first wave of the Mannheim Innovation Panel. This innovation survey has been conducted by the 'Zentrum für Europäische Wirtschaftsforschung' (ZEW) and the 'Institut für angewandte Sozialforschung' (infas) since 1993. The sampling frame stems from the records of Germany's largest credit rating company (CREDITREFORM). The sample was stratified by industries and firm size classes as well as West- and East-Germany. The questionnaire follows the guidelines for innovation statistics contained in the OSLO-manual of the OECD (see OECD 1997). Moreover, it is based on the harmonised questionnaire for innovation surveys developed by EUROSTAT. In addition to the harmonised questionnaire, our survey also contains information on patent applications. Firms are asked whether they have applied for patents at German, European and US patent offices, and to estimate the number of patent applications made at each office in 1992. Furthermore, the questionnaire covers a broad range of topics related to the innovation process, such as the objectives behind innovation activities, the obstacles that firms encounter in this connection, characteristics of the know-how generating process, mechanisms for protecting technological knowledge, and firm's expenditure on innovation activities (including R&D).

Approximately 2900 companies participated in the survey and completed the questionnaire. The response rate was about 24%. The survey covers innovative as well as non-innovative firms. An innovative company is defined as a firm which introduced at least one new or improved product or process in 1990-1992 or intended to do so in 1993-1995. To account for a possible bias arising from self-selection of innovative firms into the survey, we conducted a short telephone survey of non-respondents of the initial survey. This telephone survey provided basic information on additional 1000 firms. The non-response survey yielded a response rate of nearly 90% which makes a response bias in this survey rather unlikely. Based on data from the original survey, the sampling frame, and the telephone survey of non-respondents, we use probit models to estimate the participation probability in the original survey. It turned out that innovating and R&D performing firms participate in the survey with a higher probability. Therefore, analyses based only on respondents may be biased as non-R&D performing firms and non-innovators are underrepresented in the sample.

The descriptive statistical analysis contained in section 2 is based on weighted data. To correct for response bias, we calculate the individual weights for the responding firms as follows: let the inclusion probability for the firms of stratum j be denoted by z_j and the participation probability for firm i by r_i, which is estimated by a probit regression model including as regressors firm size, industry affiliation, a credit indicator, as well as dummies for R&D and innovation activities. Weighting factors correcting for the non-response bias are then calculated as $w_i = 1/(z_j r_i)$ i.e. raising factors are given by the inverse of the inclusion probability mutliplied by the inverse of the participation probability. Weighted data are, therefore, less likely subjected to a response bias in favour of innovative and R&D performing firms (for further details see HARHOFF *et al.* [1996]).

About 35% of the firms in our sample belong to the group of non-innovating companies. With the exception of section 2, we restrict our analysis to the group of innovative firms. Furthermore, we delete all service sector firms since their questionnaire contains no information on patents. Overall, data of about 2100 firms are included in this study. [15]

---

15. The largest enterprises in the sample were split into lines of businesses. We refer to these entities in this paper as firms too.

APPENDIX 2

Descriptive Statistics by Firm Size for Data Used in Regression Analysis - Unweighted Data.

Variable	Enterprises with less than 250 employees		Enterprises with 250 employees and more	
	Mean	Std.dev.	Mean	Std.dev.
Share of patenting firms	0.152		0.538	
Firms with patent application at GPO	0.131		0.480	
Number of patent applications at GPO	0.401	1.991	6.248	18.880
Firms with patent application at EPO	0.072		0.364	
Number of patent applications at EPO	0.205	1.020	4.073	16.304
Firms with patent applications at USPTO	0.031		0.230	
Number of patent applications at USPTO	0.085	0.592	2.245	9.511
LR&D	-4.049	2.864	-0.432	3.462
PERM_R&D	0.468		0.801	
SPILL	7.473	1.501	7.701	1.528
R&D_SPILL	-29.219	21.518	-1.400	25.739
SCIENCE	-0.193	0.869	0.288	0.836
OTHFIRM	0.047	0.811	-0.059	0.816
EX_SHARE	0.131	0.194	0.286	0.240
EXPORT	0.609		0.887	
EX-PLAN	0.236	0.425	0.440	0.497
LEMP	3.883	1.029	6.754	1.055
LEMPO	1.691	2.011	1.033	2.394
EAST	0.443		0.160	
DIVERS	1.968	0.942	2.240	1.443
FOREIGN	0.022		0.099	
GROUP	0.166		0.532	
Industries				
Mining. Energy	0.022		0.038	
Food. tobacco	0.092		0.078	
Paper. Pulp. Printing. Wood processing	0.099		0.057	
Chemical industries, refineries	0.071		0.104	
Plastics. rubber	0.075		0.037	
Earth. ceramics	0.042		0.037	
Steal. iron. basic metalls	0.028		0.050	
Metal working	0.109		0.078	
Mechanical engineering	0.207		0.250	
Electrical engineering. computers	0.080		0.083	
Optics. Precision instrumentes	0.085		0.069	
Transport equipment (cars. railroads etc.)	0.053		0.069	
Construction	0.038		0.050	

APPENDIX 3

Model Selection and Tests of Distributional Assumptions for Count Data Models

Count data models assume a dependent variable resulting from an underlying discrete probability function. The econometric toolbox offers a wide range of possible distributional assumptions. This appendix describes our procedure to test these distributional assumptions and to select the most appropriate empirical specification. We restrict ourselves to the poisson distribution and compounds of the poisson distribution. The results are summarised in Figure A1.

As mentioned above several of the models are nested. Testing in this case is done using likelihood ratio tests as well as Hausman tests if applicable. The Hausman test is not applicable to test the negbin models against the poisson model since the poisson and the negbin models (for any fixed value of α) [16] belong to the linear exponential family, which implies consistent pseudo maximum likelihood estimates of the mean function both under the null and the alternative hypothesis. This is not the context in which the Hausman test can be applied. For $H_0 : \alpha = 0$ the true parameter is on the boundary of the parameter space. The asymptotic normality property of the ML estimator does not hold and the conventional LR-, LM- and Wald-tests cannot be applied. However, CHERNOFF [1954] shows that under the null hypothesis the likelihood-ratio statistic for testing $\alpha = 0$ is asymptotically equivalent to a random variable which has a probability mass of 0.5 at zero and a 0,5 χ^2 (1) distribution for positive values (see LAWLESS [1987], WINKELMANN and ZIMMERMANN [1995]). We use this property to test the negbin models (I and II) against the poisson model. This idea is also applied to test the poisson-negbin hurdle model against the poisson hurdle specification and also to test the negbin hurdle specification against the poisson-negbin hurdle specification.

If the models at hand are not nested we apply a likelihood ratio based test for strictly non-nested models proposed by VUONG [1989]. Using the Kullback Leibler Information Criterion to measure the closeness of a model to the truth, Vuong devises a likelihood-ratio based statistic for testing the null hypothesis that the competing models are equally close to the true data generating process against the alternative hypothesis that one model is closer.

We start with testing the basic models discussed in Chapter 5. First, we test the poisson model which implies the equality of conditional mean and conditional variance of the distribution of the dependent variable. In most applications the conditional variance exceeds the conditional mean which is known as overdispersion. We test for overdispersion using the regression-based tests of CAMERON and TRIVEDI [1990]. This is done with the help

---

16. See equation (5) and the adjacent paragraph for the definition of α.

of a standard t-test from an auxiliary regression which is asymptotically equivalent to their optimal test. [17] This test is computed from an OLS regression of $(\sqrt{2}\,\widehat{\lambda}_i)^{-1}\,[(y_i - \widehat{\lambda}_i)^2 - y_i]$ on $(\sqrt{2}\,\widehat{\lambda}_i)^{-1}\,g\,(\widehat{\lambda}_i)$. Two tests are performed concerning the form of heteroscedasticity under the alternative, corresponding to the variance implied by the parametrically richer negative binomial models in the form of the negbin I and negbin-II model. For negbin I we choose $g(\widehat{\lambda}_i) = \widehat{\lambda}_i$ and for negbin II $g\,(\widehat{\lambda}_i) = \widehat{\lambda}_i^2$ (see CAMERON and TRIVEDI [1986]). For patent application at the GPO, we have strong evidence for overdispersion in both versions of the implied variance. The tests indicate weak evidence for overdispersion for patent applications at the EPO only. In the case of patent applications at the USPTO we have strong evidence only in the first version of the implied variance. Additional robust poisson estimations performed for all three dependent variables show large reductions in the estimated t-values of the estimated coefficients, indicating overdispersion too (see WINKELMANN [1994]).

These test results let us search for more general models allowing for overdispersion. A first alternative are models assuming a negative binomial distribution for the data generating process. We estimate both models negbin I and negbin II, which imply different forms of heteroscedasticity. Since it is difficult to tell a priori which of the two models is more appropriate for the data set at hand, we test which one performs better. The two versions of the negbin model are not nested. Therefore, we apply the test proposed by VUONG [1989]. This test is directional: large positive t-values favour negbin I model, large negative values of the t-statistic favour the negbin II model, insignificant t-values in the usual sense mean that one cannot discriminate between the two models. As indicated by insignificant t-statistics in all three cases, we cannot reject the null of no difference between the two models negbin I or negbin II.

We also apply the Vuong-test to decide between poisson hurdle and negbin II model, since these are not nested. Here large positive t-values favour the poisson hurdle model, large negative values of the t-statistic favour the negbin II model. The results show that negbin II is better than poisson hurdle. Since both specifications allow for overdispersion this result justifies the assumption that unobserved heterogenity should be accounted for.

As shown by MULLAHY [1986] and WINKELMANN [1994] the hurdle specification allows for over- and underdispersion at the individual level. This means that every firm in our sample can have its own variance-to mean covariance relationship.

We use the likelihood ratio to test for $H_0 : \theta_1 = \theta_2$, i.e. the equality of the estimated coefficients of the two hurdle stages, to test poisson hurdle against poisson and to test negbin-hurdle against the negbin II model. [18] In addition, we use the Hausman test, which is of special attractiveness to test the negbin hurdle model against the poisson-negbin hurdle model since it

---

17. See CAMERON and TRIVEDI [1990, p. 353] or GOURIÉROUX, MONTFORT and TROGNON [1984].
18. θ is meant to comprise the coefficient vector of the exogenous variables β and the parameter α in case of Negbin hurdle model and to consist of β only in case of Poisson hurdle model.

Testing distributional assumptions for various count data models.

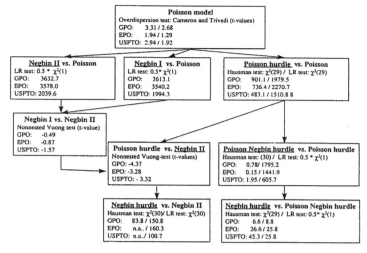

Critical values at the 5% level: : $\chi^2(30)=43.8$; $\chi^2(29)=42.6$; $\chi^2(1)=3.8$;
at the 2.5% level: : $\chi^2(30)=47.0$; $\chi^2(29)=45.2$; $\chi^2(1)=5.0$.

Remark: Cameron/Trivedi-tests reported left to the slash refer to the test against negbin-I, the tests right to the slash refer to the test against negbin-II. Hausman-type tests are performed using estimated parameters and covariance matrices of both stages of the hurdle model. The table reports Hausman-test for the first stage. Using second stage Hausman-tests we never obtain a positive definite matrix of difference of the covariance matrices. The underlined models mean that there is due to our opinion statistical significance in favour of the underlined model.

rests on the parameter vector β, not α, and thus circumvents the boundary problem. In two cases it turned out that the Hausman test could not be applied due to the fact that the difference of the covariance matrices used to compute the statistic failed to be a positive definite matrix.

As obvious from Figure A1 the test strategy implies that a negbin hurdle model is preferable. With respect to the poisson-negbin hurdle model only, the Hausman test and the LR-test do not point in the same direction. Moreover, this conclusion is confirmed by comparing the observed number of firms with a certain number of patents and the predicted number of firms with a given number of patent applications (see Appendix 4). The predictions of count data models are obtained by first calculating for each observation the probability for a certain number of patents and then summing over these individual predicted probabilities for each category (see WINKELMANN and ZIMMERMANN [1995]). The predicted and observed number of firms within each category (number of patents) are compared in Figure 3, details are reported in the appendix 4. Thus we report only the results from the negbin hurdle model, noting that the results for the alternative poisson-negbin hurdle model do not deviate very much.

334

APPENDIX 4

A Comparison of Actual and Predicted Counts

Number	Number Observed	Estimated number of firms having a certain number of patents					
		Negbin Hurdle	Poisson-Negbin Hurdle	Poisson Hurdle	Negbin II	Negbin I	Poisson
German Patent Office							
0	1223	1223.2	1223.8	1223.8	1189.9	1228.4	926.7
1	100	109.6	112	61.1	183.8	98.4	278
2	81	72.3	72.6	60.4	78.1	57.3	134.9
3	63	50.5	60.1	53.1	44.9	40.6	83
4	23	36.8	36.3	44.8	29.8	31.3	56.3
5	48	27.9	27.4	37.1	21.5	25.2	39.8
6	10	21.7	21.2	30.5	16.3	20.9	28.5
7	10	17.2	16.8	24.9	12.9	17.6	20.7
8	13	13.9	13.6	20.3	10.4	15.1	15.2
9	5	11.5	11.2	16.4	8.6	13.1	11.4
10	23	9.6	119.3	13.3	7.3	11.5	8.8
11-15	24	30.3	29.8	37.8	24	40.8	25.2
16-20	16	15.7	15.5	16.1	13.3	24.4	13
21-25	8	9.2	9.21	8.8	8.4	15.7	8.6
European Patent Office							
0	1358	1359	1359.3	1359.3	1189.9	1368.1	1093.6
1	71	85.4	89.6	61.1	183.9	71	240.3
2	71	52.9	43.4	46.6	78.1	40.4	111.3
3	45	35.8	35.3	36.4	44.9	28.3	64.1
4	20	25.6	25	28.6	29.8	21.7	40.9
5	23	19.1	18.5	22.7	21.5	17.4	27.7
6	14	14.7	14.2	18.3	16.3	14.4	19.6
7	4	11.6	11.2	14.9	12.9	12.2	14.3
8	5	9.4	9	12.3	10.4	10.5	10.6
9	3	7.7	7.4	10.2	8.6	9.1	7.9
10	21	6.4	6.2	8.5	7.3	8	6
11-15	24	30.3	29.8	37.8	24	40.8	25.2
16-20	16	15.7	15.5	16.1	13.3	24.4	13
21-25	8	9.2	9.2	8.8	8.4	15.7	8.6
US Patent and Trademark Office							
0	1499	1499.5	1500.4	1500.4	1487.6	1500.2	1325.1
1	40	49.3	51.4	33.4	85.7	44.1	163.5
2	37	32	32.3	29	32	24.5	68.9
3	32	22.1	21.7	23.7	17.5	17	36.7
4	11	15.8	15.3	18.9	11.3	13	22.2
5	20	11.6	11.2	14.7	8	10.4	14.6

6	6	8.8	8.5	11.4	6	8.6	10.2
7	3	6.8	6.5	8.8	4.6	7.3	7.4
8	4	5.4	5.2	6.8	3.7	6.2	5.5
9	1	4.4	4.2	5.3	3.1	5.4	4.2
10	10	3.6	3.4	4.3	2.6	4.8	3.4
11-15	24	30.3	29.8	37.8	24	40.8	25.2
16-20	16	15.7	15.5	16.1	13.3	24.4	13
21-25	8	9.2	9.2	8.8	8.4	15.7	8.6

● References

BOUND, J., CUMMINGS, C., GRILICHES, Z., HALL, B., JAFFE, A. (1984). – "Who Does R&D and Who Patents", in: GRILICHES, Z., (Ed.), *R&D, Patents, and Productivity,* National Bureau of Economic Research, University of Chicago Press, 21-54.

CAMERON, A. C., TRIVEDI, P. K. (1986). – "Econometric Models Based on Count Data: Compariosn and Applications of Some Estimators and Tests", *Journal of Applied Econometrics,* 1, pp. 29-53.

CAMERON, A. C., TRIVEDI, P. K. (1990). – "Regression-Based for Overdispersion in the Poisson Model", *Journal of Econometrics,* 46, pp. 347-364.

CHERNOFF, H. (1954). – "On the Distribution of the Likelihood Ratio", *Annals of Mathematical Statistics,* 25, pp. 573-578.

COHEN, W. M., LEVIN, R. C. (1989). – "Empirical Studies of Innovation and Market Structure", in: R. SCHMALENSEE and R. WILLIG (Eds.), *Handbook of Industrial Organisation,* North-Holland: Amsterdam.

COHEN, W. M., *et al.* (1997). – "Appropriability Conditions and Why Firms Patent and Why They Do Not in the American Manufacturing Sector", *Paper presented at the conference on "Economics and Economics of Innovation",* 3-6 Jun 1996, Strasbourg.

CRÉPON, B., DUGUET, E. (1996). – "Innovation: Measurement, Returns and Competition", *INSEE Studies,* No. 1, pp. 83-96.

CRÉPON, B., DUGUET, E. (1997). – "Research and Development, Competition and Innovation. Pseudo Maximum Likelihood and Stimulated Maximum Likelihood Methods Applied to Count data Models with Heterogeneity", *Journal of Econometrics,* 79, pp. 355-378.

EVENSON, R. E. (1993). – "Patents, R&D, and Invention Potential: International Evidence", *AEA Papers and Proceedings,* 83 No. 2, pp. 463-468.

FELDER, J., LIGHT, G., NERLINGER, E., STAHL, H. (1996). – "Factors Determining R&D and Innovation Expenditure in German Manufacturing Industries", in: KLEINKNECHT, A., (1996), R&D and Innovation. *Evidence from New Indicators,* Macmillan Press: Basingstoke, pp. 125-154.

GIESE, E., STOUTZ, R. V. (1997). – "Indikatorfunktion von Patentanmeldung für regionalanalytische Zwecke in der Bundesrepublik Deutschland", *Studien zur Wirtschaftsgeographie,* Universität Giessen.

GOURIEROUX, C., MONFORT, A., TROGNON, A. (1984). – "Pseudo Maximum Likelihood Methods: Application to Poisson Models", *Econometrica,* 52, pp. 701-720.

GREENE, W. H. (1994). – "Accounting for Excess Zeros and Sample Selection in Poisson and Negative Binomial Regression Models", *New York University Discussion Paper,* EC-94-10.

GRILICHES, Z. (1990). – "Patent Statistics as Economic Indicators: a Survey", *Journal of Economic Literature,* 28, pp. 1661-1707.

336

HARHOFF, D. (1994). – "R&D and Productivity in German Manufacturing Firms", *ZEW-Discussion Paper 94-01*, Mannheim.

HARHOFF, D., LICHT, G., BEISE, M., FELDER, J., NERLINGER, E., STAHL, H. (1996). – *Innovationsaktivitäten kleiner and mittlerer Unternehmen. Ergebnisse des Mannheimer Innovationspanels*, Nomos-Verlag: Baden-Baden.

HARTER, J. F. R. (1993). – "The Propensity to Patent with Differentiated Products", *Southern Economic Journal*, 61, pp. 195-201.

HAUSMAN, J., HALL, B., GRILICHES, Z. (1984). – "Econometric Models for Count Data with an Application to the Patents-R&D Relationship", *Econometrica*, 52, pp. 909-938.

HORSTMANN, I., MACDONALD, G. M., SLIVINSKI, A. (1985). – "Patents as Information Transfer Mechanisms: To Patent or (Maybe) Not to Patent", *Journal of Political Economy*, 93, pp. 837-858.

JAFFE, A. B. (1989). – "Characterizing the 'Technological Position' of Firms, with Application to Quantifying Technological Opportunity and Research Spillovers", *Research Policy*, 18, pp. 87-97.

KABLA, I. (1996). – "The Patent as Indicator of Innovation", *INSEE Studies*, No. 1, pp. 57-72.

KLEINKNECHT, A., REIJNEN, J. O. N. (1991). – "New Evidence on the Undercounting of Small Firm R&D", *Research Policy*, 20, pp. 579-587.

KÖNIG, H., LICHT, G. (1995). – "Patents, R&D and Innovation. Evidence from the Mannheim Innovation Panel", *ifo-Studien*, 41, pp. 521-545.

LACH, S. (1995). – "Patents and Productivity Growth at the Industry Level: A First Look", *Economics Letters*, 49, pp. 101-108.

LAMBERT, D. (1992). – "Zero Inflated Poisson Regression with an Application to Defects in Manufacturing", *Technometrics*, 34, pp. 1-14.

LANJOUW, J. O., PAKES, A., PUTNAM, J. (1996). – "How to Count Patents and Value Intellectual Property: Uses of Patent Renewal and Application Data", *Mimeo*, Yale University, New Haven.

LAWLESS, J. F. (1987). – "Negative Binomial and Mixed Poisson Regression", *The Canadian Journal of Statistics*, Vol. 15, No. 3, pp. 209-225.

LEVIN, R. C., REISS, P. C. (1987). – "Cost-reducing and Demand-creating R&D with Spillovers", *RAND Journal of Economics*, 19, pp. 538-556.

LEVIN, R. C., KLEVORIK, A. K., NELSON, R. R., WINTER, S. G. (1987). – "Appropriating the Returns from Industrial Research and Development", *Brookings Papers on Economic Activity. Special Issue on Microeconomics*, pp. 783-831.

MCCULLAGH, P., NELDER, J. A. (1989). – *Generalized Linear Models*, 2nd ed., Chapman and Hall: London.

MULLAHY, J. (1986). – "Specification and Testing of Some Modified Count Data Models", *Journal of Econometrics*, 33, pp. 341-365.

National Science Board (1996). – *Science & Engineering Indicators 1996*, Washington, DC: U.S. Government Printing Office 1996.

NIW, DIW, ISI, ZEW (1996). – *Germany's Technological Performance*. Updated and expanded report, Hannover/Berlin/Karlsruhe/Mannheim.

OECD (1993). – *Proposed Standard Practice For Surveys of Research and Experimental Development – Frascati Manual*, Paris.

OECD (1994). – *Using Patent Data as Science and Technology Indicators – Patent Manual*, Paris.

OECD (1997). – *OECD Proposed Guidelines For Collecting and Interpreting Technological Innovation Data – OSLO Manual*, Second edition, Paris.

PAKES, A. (1985). – "Patents, R&D, and the Stock Market Rate of Return", *Journal of Political Economy*, 93, pp. 390-409.

PAVITT, K. (1985). – "Patent Statistics as Indicators of Innovative Activities: Possibilities and Problems", *Scientometrics*, 7, pp. 77-99.

POHLMEIER, W., ULRICH, V. (1995). – "An Econometric Model of the Two-Part Decision Process in the Demand for Health", *Journal of Human Resources*, 30, pp. 339-361.

SCHERER, F. M. (1983). – "The Propensity to Patent", *International Journal of Industrial Organisation*, 1, pp. 107-128.

SIRILLI, G. (1987). – "Patents and Inventors: An Empirical Study", *Research Policy*, 16, pp. 157-174.

SV-Wissenschaftsstatistik (1994). – *FuE-Info. Forschung und Entwicklung in der Wirtschaft. Ergebnisse 1992, 1993, Planung 1994*, Essen.

VUONG, Q. H. (1989). – "Likelihood Ratio Tests for Model Selection and Non-Nested Hypotheses", *Econometrica*, Vol. 57, pp. 307-333.

WINKELMANN, R. (194). – "Count Data Models: Econometric Theory and an Application to Labour Mobility", Springer: Heidelberg, Berlin, New York.

WINKELMANN, R., ZIMMERMANN, K. F. (1995). – "Recent Developments in Count Data Modelling: Theory and Application", *Journal of Economic Surveys*, 9, pp. 1-24.

ZIMMERMANN, K. F., SCHWALBACH, J. (1991). – "Determinanten der Patentaktivität", *ifo-Studien*, 37, pp. 201-227.

338

Equilibrium Coalition Structures in Markets for Network Goods

Nicholas ECONOMIDES, Fredrick FLYER *

ABSTRACT. – Firms that produce network goods have strong incentives to adhere to common technical standards. However, adhering to common standards decreases the horizontal differentiation between goods, and that increases market competition. This paper analyzes how these countervailing forces shape firms' decisions to comply to common technical standards under oligopoly. In the model, firms' outputs are identical in non-network characteristics, but firms can adhere to different compatibility standards. Consequently, a good's relative quality level is determined by the total sales of compatible goods. The technical standards coalition structures that form at equilibrium under this framework exhibit interesting characteristics. In particular, coalitions that vary greatly in total sales, profits, and prices often emerge, even though underlying products and cost structures are identical across firms.

* N. ECONOMIDES: Stern School of Business, New York University; F. FLYER: Stern School of Business, New York University. We thank participants of the "The Economics and Econometrics of Innovation" conference, two anonymous referees and the editor for their comments and suggestions.

339

D. Encaoua et al. (eds.), The Economics and Econometrics of Innovation, 339–358.
© 2000 Kluwer Academic Publishers. Printed in the Netherlands.

1 Introduction

A good that derives a portion of its value from the consumption level of related goods is influenced by network externalities. In some cases these externalities determine nearly the entire value of the good. For example, the value of a fax machine largely depends on the number of other compatible fax machines on the network. For other goods, these externalities have more subtle influences. For example, the value of a car can increase with the overall consumption of cars, since this can increase the availability of parts, mechanics, gasoline, roads, maps, and various other related goods and services [1]. The value of nearly every good is influenced by network externalities to some extent [2].

Firms face a unique incentive structure when network externalities are present. On the one hand, a firm can choose to make its output compatible with an established standard, as this increases the value of the product to the consumer. On the other hand, by making its output incompatible with other products, the firm can gain monopoly power, even though its output is less valuable to consumers. The contrasting benefits associated with exploitation of network externalities versus exploitation of monopoly pricing power shapes the equilibrium in these markets.

In this work, a model is developed to solve for these equilibria and is applied to markets where a small number of firms compete. Firms are assumed to produce outputs that are identical in all characteristics except that they may adhere to different compatibility standards. The model is a variation of the GABSZEWICZ and THISSE [1979] or SHAKED and SUTTON [1982] models of vertical differentiation, where firms choose quality in the first stage and prices in the second. Our model differs from the traditional vertical differentiation models in two respects. First, in these vertical differentiation models quality differences reflect inherent differences in the features of products. This differs from our framework, since firms' outputs are identical with respect to inherent characteristics. Second, vertical (quality) differentiation in this model is determined solely by the level of sales of the various coalitions (the group of firms that produce compatible goods), with firms choosing coalition affiliations and output levels simultaneously. Thus, in this model quantity and quality are determined simultaneously.

The central findings of this analysis are: (1) The equilibria are often asymmetric. Despite producing identical goods in terms of inherent characteristics and having identical cost structures, firms' prices, sales and profits can vary dramatically. (2) This asymmetry is more acute for pure network goods than it is in markets where network externalities play a small

---

1. See KATZ and SHAPIRO [1985], ECONOMIDES [1996].
2. While these externalities need not always be positive, as many networks suffer from congestion, this paper examines the effects of positive network externalities under oligopoly.

role. (3) Firms that are in leading coalitions (those with greatest sales) have *less* incentive to make their technical standards available to others when network externalities are large. (4) Full compatiblity is the equilibrium in markets where network externalities play smaller roles. In markets where these externalities are significant, the equilibria tend to support multiple platforms.

We want to underline our result that, in markets with strong network externalities, often the equilibrium exhibits incompatibility and acute differences in production levels and prices of firms that adhere to different technical standards. This leads us to believe that in network industries, acute differences of size are a natural feature of equilibrium rather than a historical aberration. This may explain the historical (pre-divestiture) domination of the telephone industry by AT&T and the current domination of the personal computer software market by Microsoft.

The paper is organized as follows: The model and the corresponding equilibrium concepts are developed in section 2. There are three basic types of coalition structures that can arise at equilibrium [3]. The general characteristics of these structures are described in section 3. In section 4, the equilibrium coalition structures are derived for markets where two or three firms compete. We conclude in section 5.

2 The Model

2.1. Coalition Structures

Given a set of firms $S = \{1, ..., S\}$, and $i = 1, ...$ I technical standards, we identify a subset $C_i \subseteq S$ as a coalition, when the members of C_i adhere to the same technical standard. The partition of S into its subsets defines a coalition structure $C = \{C_1, ..., C_I\}$. Let c_i be the number of firms in coalition C_i. A coalition structure is represented as a vector of the cardinalities of the coalitions, $(c_1, c_2, ..., c_I)$ [4]. In this application, the coalitions are ordered in descending order according to total sales.

Product compatibility by all firms means that a single coalition includes all firms. Total incompatibility, where every firm adheres to its own unique standard, would mean that $s = I$ and every coalition is of cardinality one. Between these two extremes, there is a variety of partial incompatibility

---

3. The three basic types of coalition structures are full compatibility (every firm produces output that is compatible with every other firm's output), total incompatibility (no firm's output is compatible with another firm's output), and partial incompatibility (subgroups of firms, denoted coalitions, produce compatible output).

4. Specific assumptions on the demand and cost structure of our model imply that all firms realize equal profits within the same coalition.

coalition structures. For example, the coalition structure (2, 0) represents full compatibility in two-firm competition. The coalition structure (1, 1, 1) represents total incompatibility in a three-firm industry.

2.2. **The Structure of the Game and the Equilibria**

We analyze two game structures that apply to different regimes of intellectual property rights. In both game structures, firms play a two-stage Cournot-style game. In the first game structure, we assume that all technical standards are non-proprietary, so that firms can coalesce on any standard without restrictions. Thus, the decision of a firm to join a technical standard coalition is only dependent on if it achieves higher profits when it joins. We use the term "non-cooperative equilibrium coalition structure" for the equilibrium of this game. In contrast, in the second game structure, each firm has a technical standard that is proprietary to itself. Thus, if other firms want to join its technical standard coalition, they have to get the consent of the proprietary standard owner. We use the term "consensual equilibrium coalition structure" for the equilibrium of this game, noting, however, that the consent of members of the coalition that a firm leaves is not required.

In the first game structure, each firm chooses sequentially a coalition standard and a quantity of production. We will assume that in making its production decision, each firm considers the technical standard and the output level of all other firms as fixed *a-la-Cournot*. The firms make their choices known simultaneously to each other in the first stage. Each firm j brings to the market its own output in the second stage, and the other firms and the consumers observe these quantities. Firms and consumers also observe which technical standard each firm has chosen, and they calculate total output of each coalition. Given this information, firms and consumers can determine the position of the demand curve for the good of each coalition. In anticipation of consumer demand determined through this process, firms choose technical standards and production levels non-cooperatively. Then output is auctioned *a-la-Cournot*. The second game structure is identical except that entry in a coalition requires the consent of other members. It is instructive to describe the equilibrium through the concept of an "adjacent coalition structure", defined next.

DEFINITION 1 : A coalition structure that results when coalition structure C is changed by the movement of only one firm (across coalitions) is called an *adjacent coalition structure* to C. For example, the coalition structure (3, 0, 0) and (2, 1, 0) are adjacent coalition structures, since the latter coalition structure can be reached from the former by the defection of only one firm to a new compatibility standard.

DEFINITION 2 : A coalition structure C is a *non-cooperative equilibrium* when no firm in C has an incentive to change affiliations by joining a neighboring coalition to form an adjacent coalition structure.

By the last definition, at a non-cooperative equilibrium coalition structure, no firm wants to change its coalition affiliation. Let D_{C_i} be an adjacent coalition structure to C, formed by the movement of firm i to another coalition. Then by definition 2, C is a non-cooperative equilibrium coalition structure if and only if the profit condition $\Pi_i(C) \geq \Pi_i(\boldsymbol{D}_{C_i})$ holds for each firm i and every adjacent coalition structure $\boldsymbol{D}_{C_i}$ formed by a unilateral defection of firm i. By definition, this equilibrium concept considers only moves in and out of coalitions by a single firm. Thus, we do not allow movements of groups of firms.

The concept of the non-cooperative equilibrium implicitly assumes that other firms have no power to stop a firm from joining or leaving a standards coalition. This is an important assumption that applies to many but not all environments. Most importantly, it applies to areas where there are well-known but incompatible technical standards. However, there is a class of cases where an existing coalition has the ability to prevent other firms from joining. For example, if the technical standard is the intellectual property of a coalition, this coalition can prevent others from "joining it" by not authorizing others to use this standard. For such cases, we use the concept of a *consensual equilibrium*.

> DEFINITION 3 : A coalition structure C is a *consensual equilibrium* when either of the following conditions hold: (a) no firm wants to move unilaterally, or (b) no coalition is willing to accept a firm that is willing to join it. We assume that a coalition of null size is willing to accept any firm.

Since condition (a) is necessary and sufficient for a non-cooperative equilibrium, this implies that *any non-cooperative equilibrium is also a consensual equilibrium*. Also note that the consensual equilibrium disregards the interests of firms in the coalition from where a firm may defect; it is assumed that firms in the original coalition are unable to stop a firm from defecting.

2.3. Demand

Let coalition i have total production (market coverage) n_i, normalized so that $0 \leq \sum_{i=1}^{I} n_i \leq 1$. Let the willingness to pay for one unit of a good produced by a firm in coalition i to person of type ω be $u(\omega, n_i) = \omega\, h(n_i)$. Consumer types ω are uniformly distributed over the interval $[0, 1]$ [5]. The *network externalities function*, $h(n_i)$, captures the positive influence on utility associated with network size. The network externalities function is specified to be linear:

$$(1) \qquad h(n_i) = K + An_i.$$

A good's value embodies network and non-network benefits; K represents the non-network benefits that a good provides, since it measures the

---

5. This setup is similar to ECONOMIDES and HIMMELBERG [1995], which focused primarily on perfect competition. Note that the multiplicative specification implies that consumer types vary in the value they attach to the network externality in a network of fixed size.

willingness to pay for a unit of the good when there are no other units sold. A benchmark case of the above function is when $K = 0$. This describes a market for a *pure network good*, since the good has no value in a network of zero size.

2.4. Price Equilibrium for any Coalition Structure

In the model, an industry has S firms, each producing a single good. All firms are assumed to produce goods of equal inherent value (the parameters of the network externality function, K and A, are constant across firms' output), however goods can vary with respect to their compatibility standard. When a collection of firms comply with a common technical standard (a coalition), every firm in the coalition reaps the network externality associated with the coalition's total sales. Since goods are identical in other respects, they are differentiated in quality only by the size of sales of the coalition to which their producer belongs. Let coalition C_i, $i = 1, ..., I$, have c_i firms, total output n_i, with a typical firm in C_i producing output n_{ci} so that $n_i = \sum^{ci} n_{ci}$ [6]. Without loss of generality, we assume that the index i of a coalition is inversely related to the amounts of sales of that coalition; *i.e.*, $n_i > n_{i+1}$, $i = 1, ..., I - 1$ [7]; coalition C_1 has the highest sales. Let ω_i be the marginal consumer who is indifferent between buying good i and good $i + 1$. This indifference implies:

$$\omega_i h(n_{i+1}) - p_{i+1} = \omega_i h(n_i) - p_i$$
(2)
$$\Leftrightarrow \omega_i = (p_i - p_{i+1})/[A(n_i - n_{i+1})],$$
$$i = 1, ..., I,$$

where we define $p_{I+1} \equiv 0$ and $h(n_{I+1}) \equiv 0$. Consumers of types $\omega > \omega_i$ derive greater consumer surplus from good i than from good $i + 1$ (at the going prices). Conversely, consumers of types $\omega < \omega_i$ prefer good $i + 1$ over good i. Thus, consumers of types ω, $\omega_i < \omega < \omega_{i-1}$, buy good i [8]. It follows that higher ω types buy network goods that belong to coalitions with higher sales. Goods from coalitions of higher coverage have higher prices, $p_i > p_{i+1}$ [9]. Sales of each good are:

(3)
$$n_i = \omega_{i-1} - \omega_i, \quad i = 1, ..., I,$$

---

6. For notational simplicity, we suppress an index for firms, although firms within the same coalition may produce different outputs. We will show that at equilibrium, all firms within the same coalition produce the same output.

7. In general we write $n_i \geq n_{i+1}$, but equality is never part of an equilibrium as explained below in footnote 11.

8. These are standard results in models of vertical differentiation.

9. If this were not true, a good from the coalition with lower market coverage would not be purchased.

where $\omega_0 \equiv 1$. Summing these we have

(4) $$\omega_i = 1 - \Sigma^i_{j=1} n_j, \quad i = 1, ..., I,$$

and therefore market coverage is:

(5) $$\Sigma^I_{i=1} n_i = 1 - \omega_I = 1 - p_I/(A\, n_I + K).$$

Inverting the demand system (2), the general form of prices is:

(6) $$p_i = (K + A\, n_i)(1 - \Sigma^i_{j=1} n_j) - \Sigma^{I+1}_{j=i+1}(K + A\, n_j)\, n_j, \quad i = 1, ..., I.$$

Given constant marginal cost m, profits of a firm in C_i are:

(7) $$\Pi_{ci} = n_{ci}(p_i - m).$$

Profits are maximized when [10, 11]

(8) $$\partial\Pi_{ci}/\partial n_{ci} = p_i - m + n_{ci}[A(1 - \Sigma^i_{j=1} n_j) - (K + A\, n_i)] = 0,$$

The solution to the system of equations (6), (7), and (8) defines the equilibrium production levels and prices. It follows directly from equation (8) that all firms in the same coalition produce equal amounts, and therefore $n_i = c_i\, n_{ci}$. Equilibrium profits are

(9) $$\Pi^*_{ci} = n^*_{ci}(p_i - m) = (p_i - m)^2/[(K + A\, n_i) - A(1 - \Sigma^i_{j=1} n_j)].$$

In the following sections, the model is used to analyze alternative market structures; this provides a basis for determining equilibrium coalition structures.

---

10. The second order condition is $\partial^2\, \Pi_{ci}/\partial n^2_{ci} = 2[(1 - \Sigma^i_{j=1} n_j)\, h'(n_i) - h(n_i)] + n_{ci}[(1 - \Sigma^i_{j=1} n_j)\, h''(n_i) - 2h'(n_i)] < 0$. The term in the first brackets is negative because price is greater than marginal cost at the first order condition. The second term in brackets is also negative since $h''(n_i) = 0$.
11. We can now explain why equal production of two coalitions is not possible at equilibrium. If two coalitions C_i and $C_{i'}$ had exactly the same total amount of expected sales, $n^c_i = n^c_{i'}$, then they would define the same marginal consumer $\omega_i = \omega_{i'}$ and would command the same price $p_i = p_{i'}$ givne by (6). (In equation (3) we would have $n_i + n_{i'} = \omega_{i-1} - \omega_i$, and $n_i + n_{i'}$ would similarly appear in the first sum of (6).) Now, given this tie, a firm in coalition C_i has an incentive to expand its output so that the output of the coalition increases from n_i to $n_i + \varepsilon$. If it does so, it reaches a higher quality, and all consumers in $[\omega_i + \delta, \omega_{i-1}]$ switch to it. Since this is better for the firm that expands output, it has a unilateral incentive to deviate from equilibrium. It follows that equal production levels by two or more coalitions are ruled out at equilibrium.

3 Potential Market Structures

3.1. Full Compatibility

Full compatibility refers to the case where all firms in the industry produce compatible output [12]. This coalition structure is denoted $(S, 0)$, since all firms belong to the leading platform. In this case, $I = 1$. The total size of the network is $\Sigma_{s=1}^{S} n_S$, and the willingness to pay by consumer of type ω is $\omega (K + A\Sigma_{s=1}^{S} n_S)$. At equilibrium there is a unique price for all goods, since goods from different firms are identical in every attribute. Given a common price, the marginal consumer ω who purchases the good is defined by

$$(10) \qquad \omega^* = p/(K + A\Sigma_{s=1}^{S} n_s).$$

Since consumers of indices higher than ω^* buy the good, the size of the network (demand) at price p is $\Sigma_{s=1}^{S} n_S = 1 - \omega^*$, or equivalenlty,

$$(11) \qquad \Sigma_{s=1}^{S} n_s = 1 - p/(K + A\Sigma_{s=1}^{S} n_s).$$

The willingness to pay of the last consumer is:

$$(12) \qquad p\left(\Sigma_{s=1}^{S} n_s, \Sigma_{s=1}^{S} n_s\right) = (K + A\Sigma_{s=1}^{S} n_s)(1 - \Sigma_{s=1}^{S} n_s).$$

The j-th oligopolist maximizes the profit function,

$$(13) \qquad \Pi_j = n_j \left[p\left(\Sigma_{s=1}^{S} n_s, n_j + \Sigma_{s\neq j}^{S} n_s\right) - m \right],$$

by solving the following first order condition [13]:

$$(14) \qquad d\Pi_j/n_j = p\left(\Sigma_{s=1}^{S} n_s, n_j + \Sigma_{s\neq j}^{S} n_s\right) + n_j \left(p^1 + p^2\right) - m = 0.$$

At the full compatibility equilibrium, all firms produce equal quantities, since identical first order conditions are solved. Substituting for p, p^1 and p^2 in equation (14) and re-writing it for the typical firm s gives [14]:

$$(15) \qquad (K + Asn_s^*)(1 - sn_s^*) + n_s^* [A(1 - 2sn_s^*) - K] - m = 0.$$

Note that when the externality becomes insignificant, i.e., as $A \to 0$, the market equilibrium converges to the traditional symmetric Cournot equilibrium, since

$$\lim_{A\to 0} n_s^* = [1 - (m/K)]/(S + 1).$$

---

12. This discussion follows ECONOMIDES and HIMMELBERG [1995].
13. We use the notation p^k to signify the partial derivative of the p function with respect to its k-th argument.
14. If the first order condition has two admissible (i.e., non-negative) solutions, we assume that consumers will coordinate to the higher one. It is easy to show that, under full compatibility, there is only one equilibrium with positive sales as long as $m < K$.

For any positive externalities $(A > 0)$ the compatiblity equilibrium production is greater than at the traditional Cournot equilibrium [15].

3.2. Total Incompatibility

In this case, each firm produces a good that is incompatible with output from every other firm. Therefore, all standards coalitions are of size 1, the number of firms in any coalition c_i equals one, and the number of firms S equals the number of coalitions i. Sales, prices, and profits are ordered according to rank in the index of firms, with firm (coalition) 1 having the highest sales, prices and profits.

Notice that in the total incompatibility case, the market equilibrium also converges to the symmetric Cournot equilibrium as the size of the network externality tends to zero. This result is obtained by substituting equation (6) into equation (8), setting $n_{ci} = n_i$, $s = I$, and taking the limit as A tends to zero:

$$\lim_{A \to 0} n_i^* = [1 - (m/K)]/(S + 1),$$

which is the quantity per firm at the S-firm Cournot equilibrium without externalities. Note that as externalities tend to zero, output tends to the same limit under either compatibility or incompatibility; thus, when externalities are very small, whether firms are compatible or not makes little difference.

In the following cases to be analyzed, numerical methods are used to determine equilibrium structures. Without loss of generality, the network externality function is normalized so that $h(n_i) = k + n_i$, where $k = K/A$. The marginal cost is also set equal to zero ($m = 0$). While the simplification regarding marginal costs does not qualitatively affect any of the findings, it does provides a computationaly more convenient structural form. In this specification, the index $1/k$ measures the intensity of the marginal network externality. Thus, a good with small k provides benefits primarily through its associated network externality, while goods with large k have relatively low network externality effects. At the extremes, a pure network good is represented by setting k equal to zero and the standard Cournot case of no externalities is approached when k tends to infinity.

The effects of positive network externalities on market structure are analyzed by solving numerically for the total incompatibility equilibrium for various values of k and s. The first result is that entry has greater effects on incumbent coalitions' (firms') outputs and profits when k is large. The relative effects on profits of entry is seen by comparing figures 1 and 2. These figures depict profits of the leading 3 firms in the market given various number of firms in the industry. In figure 1, k is set equal to 1. In figure 2, k equals 0. Notice that as the number of firms increase, the profits for the leading firms in the industry where k is large (fig. 1) are more dramatically

---

15. Equation (15) is a quadratic in n_s with a well-defined solution n_s^* that is continuous in A. Defining the LHS of equation (15) as $F(A)$, it is easy to show that $F(\lim_{A \to 0} n_s^*) > 0$ and $F'(\lim_{A \to 0} n_s^*) < 0$. It follows that $n_s^*(A) > \lim_{A \to 0} n_s^*$ when $A > 0$.

affected by entrant firms. The intuition is straightforward: the greater non-network benefits associated with high-k industries make goods of different compatibility standards closer substitutes. Therefore, the effect of increased competition on profits is more pronounced for high-k industries.

FIGURE 1

Number of Firms in Marke.

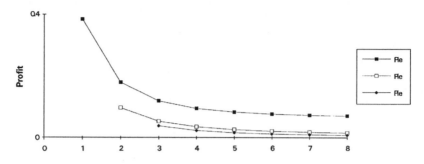

FIGURE 2

Number of Firms in Marke.

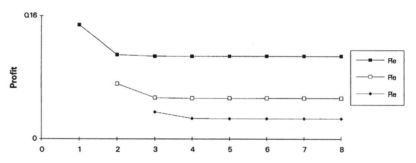

Under total incompatibility, the relative effects that entry has on firms' output is seen in Table 1, which shows the Herfindahl-Hirschman (H) index of market concentration, $H = \Sigma_{i=1}^{S} (n_i / \Sigma_{i=1}^{S} n_i)^2$. Table 1 shows that when k is small there is greater inequality in firms' outputs. The H index decreases in k (increases in $1/k$) for all fixed S [16]. This indicates that the inequality across firms' outputs is larger for markets where network externalities play larger roles. In other words, for the total incompatibility

---

16. Reflecting on the earlier result of convergence to a symmetric Cournot equilibrium as marginal network externalities become negligible, the last column of Table 1 at $k = 5$ gives a concentration index almost equal to that of a symmetric Cournot oligopoly.

case, market concentration, output, and price inequality increase with the extent of the network externality.

The H index is also naturally decreasing in s for fixed k, reflecting more intense competition as more firms compete in the industry. A finding of greater interest is that the H index decreases more significantly in s for markets that exhibit lower network externalities (when k is large). This is because neither the output of firms in leading coalitions or the their prices change very much as more firms enter when k is small. Goods with large network externalities provide large incentives to organize consumers into few platforms. This, however, provides high monopoly power to leading platforms, which are not significantly affected by entry of firms offering incompatible output. However, when network externalities contribute a relatively small portion to a good's value (large k), incompatible output provides a closer substitute to leading platform goods, and consequently have a greater effect on leading firms' output and profits.

3.3. Partial Incompatibility: Two Coalitions

Under partial incompatibility, the number of coalition structures (technical standards) is larger than one and less than the total number of firms ($1 < I < s$). The simplest case is when there are only two coalition structures. For coalition structures of two-layers, we establish that sales of a firm in a coalition of higher market coverage are higher than for any firm in a coalition of lower market coverage [17],

$$(16) \qquad n_{ci} > n_{cj} \Leftrightarrow i < j.$$

TABLE 1

Herfindahl Index for Different Intensities of Marginal Network Externality $1/k$ and Numbers of Firms (Coalitions) S.

		Intensity of Marginal Network Externality $1/k$				
		∞	2	1	0.5	0.2
Number of Firms (Coalitions) S	3	.510	.415	.363	.339	.334
	5	.470	.331	.248	.207	.201
	10	.464	.287	.172	.106	.100

---

17. The numerical proofs of this and subsequent sections were done in *Mathematica* and are available from the authors upon request.

Since prices are always ordered in the same direction as coalition sales, profits of a firm in a coalition of higher market coverage are also higher than for any firm in a coalition of lower market coverage,

$$(17) \qquad \Pi_{ci} > \Pi_{cj} \Leftrightarrow i < j.$$

Equilibrium prices of all goods increase with k. this is expected because an increase in k increases the value of the good to all consumers. Sales of each firm in the upper layer fall in k, while sales of each firm in the lower layer increase in k:

$$(18) \qquad \partial n_{c1}/\partial k < 0, \qquad \partial n_{c2}/\partial k > 0.$$

Fixing the total number of firms in the market to add to a constant, $c_1 + c_2 = s$, we compare prices, sales per firm, sales per coalition, and profits as both c_1 and k vary. The price quoted by firms in the coalition with the largest market share (leading platform), p_1, initially increases in c_1 for low c_1, and later decreases. See figure 3. Sales per firm in the leading platform, n_{c1} decrease in c_1, as seen in figure 4. Market coverage for the leading platform, n_1, increase in c_1, as seen in figure 5.

FIGURE 3

Number of Firms in Leading Platform.

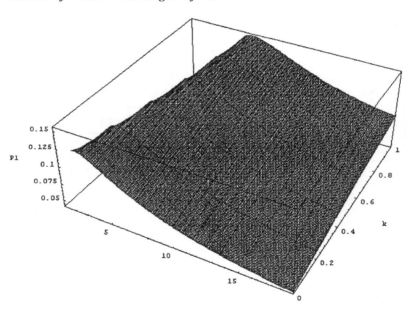

350

FIGURE 4

Number of Firms in Leading Platform.

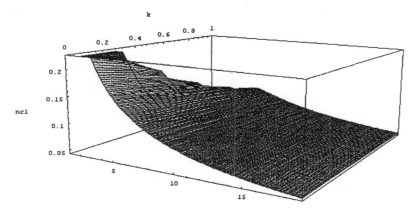

FIGURE 5

Number of Firms in Leading Platform.

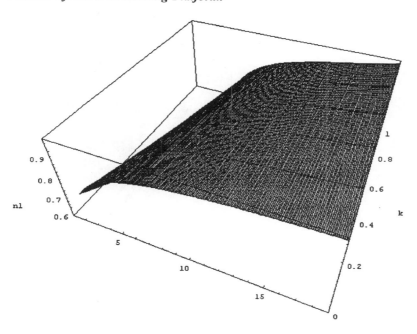

Figure 6 shows how profits in the leading coalition change with c_1 and k. Profits of a firm in the top coalition, Π_1, initially increase in c_1 for low c_1, and later decrease. Therefore, firms in the top coalition benefit from other firms joining them when the top coalition is small. The intuition behind the profit structure depicted in figure 6 is as follows: For low c_1, entry into the leading platform increases market coverage substantially. The network externalities for the leading platform subsequently increase sharply, while the externality benefits for the lower platform decline. This change in the network externalities more than offsets the effects of greater competition in the top coalition, and the price of the top coalition's output rises. Initially, higher prices dominate the drop in per firm output, and consequently firms' profits rise. However, as additional firms enter the leading platform, the marginal increases in total output diminish, and the effects of greater competition in the top platform dominates increases in the network externality benefits, and both prices and profits fall.

Figure 6

Number of Firms in Leading Platform.

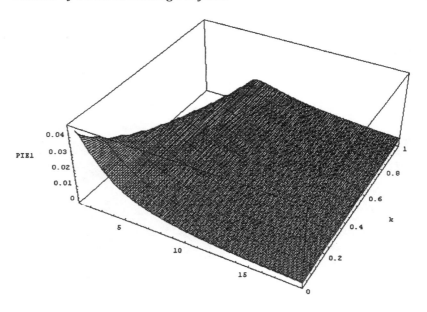

The equilibrium profit structure, and, in particular the profit incentives of firms in the leading coalition to encourage entry into their coalition when c_1 is small, counters the usual oligopoly result that prices and profits decrease with additional entry. This is an important feature of network good markets, and is probably understated in figure 6 because marginal costs are assumed to be zero. If firms in the top coalition have rising marginal costs, then the economic forces behind additional entry into the top coalition will be even stronger, since this would imply efficiency gains in production.

352

4 Application of Equilibrium Concepts

4.1. Special Case: Two Firms

In an industry with two firms, there are two possible coalition structures: (i) compatibility–denoted (2, 0); and (ii) incompatibility–denoted (1, 1). To analyze the non-cooperative equilibrium structures that arise, we calculate profits conditional on coalition affiliation. Figure 7 shows equilibrium profits under both coalition structures for each firm as k varies [18]. This plot illustrates that, for large k, $k > 1.1$, both firms earn more under compatibility than the leading firm earns under incompatibility. Therefore for large k, compatibility is the coalition structure equilibrium. Since it is a non-cooperative equilibrium, compatibility is also a consensual equilibrium.

For small k, when there are strong network externalities, compatibility profits lie between the incompatibility profits of the first and the second firm. In this case, firm 2 wants compatibility and firm 1 wants incompatibility. Therefore, for small k, there is no non-cooperative equilibrium. Incompatibility is a consensual equilibrium, which arises when the leading firm has the power to restrict the second firm from entering its coalition.

FIGURE 7

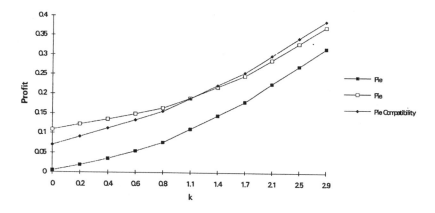

These results may seem paradoxical, since the incentive to break from compatibility is higher in goods with strong network externalities, when one expects the highest benefits from compatibility. The intuition behind this

---

18. We can show uniqueness of all production equilibria (given coalition structure) in the two- and three-firm cases.

finding is as follows: The differences across firms in the equilibrium outputs and prices under incompatibility increase as network externalities play a larger role in the goods value (when k is small). With large externalities, goods where k is close to zero, the top firm sells to the vast majority of consumers and receives a very high price. Thus, the incentive to deviate from the equal quantities, prices, and profits compatibility equilibrium and become the top firm under incompatibility is greater when network externalities are large. Table 2 summarizes the equilibrium coalition structures for the two-firm industry as k varies.

4.2. Special Case: Three Firms

4.2.1. Non-Cooperative Coalition Structure Equilibria

In an industry with three firms, the potential coalition structures are as follows: full compatibility, (3, 0, 0); total incompatibility, (1, 1, 1); and partial incompatibility, (2, 1, 0) or (1, 2, 0). Equilibrium profits associated with the different coalition structures are presented in figure 8. This graph can be used to determine which coalition structures qualify as non-cooperative equilibria. We first eliminate those coalition structures that do not qualify. Three coalition structures can be immediately eliminated as candidates for non-cooperative equilibrium. In each of these cases, a firm has an incentive to deviate and join another coalition, thus creating an adjacent coalition structure.

FIGURE 8

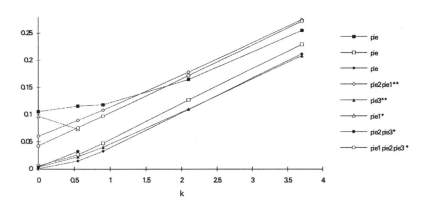

• (1, 1, 1) is *not* a non-cooperative equilibrium because profits at (2, 1, 0) are higher for a firm in the top layer than for the middle firm in (1, 1, 1); thus, there is an incentive for the middle firm to join the top layer.

• (2, 1, 0) is *not* a non-cooperative equilibrium because profits at (2, 1, 0) are lower for a firm in the middle layer than at full compatibility at (3, 0, 0), and therefore the middle firm has an incentive to join the top coalition.

354

TABLE 2

Coalition Structure Equilibria in a Two-Firm Industry

Range of k	Intensity of Marginal Network Externality $1/k$	Non-Cooperative Equilibria	Consensual Equilibria
[0, 1.1]	[0.909, ∞]	None	(1, 1)
[1.1, ∞]	[0, 0.909]	(2, 0)	(2, 0)

• (1, 2, 0) is *not* a non-cooperative equilibrium because profits for a firm at the top layer at (2, 1, 0) are higher than for a firm in the lower layer of (1, 2, 0).

We now establish under what conditions the remaining coalition structure, (3, 0, 0) (*i.e.,* full compatibility), *is* a non-cooperative equilibrium. For $k > 0.5$, the firm in the top layer in coalition structure (1, 2, 0) is worse off than at (3, 0, 0). Thus, for $k > 0.5$, a defection from (3, 0, 0) to (1, 2, 0) or to (2, 1, 0) is not desirable for the defecting firm. Therefore, *for $k > 0.5$, full compatibility is a non-cooperative equilibrium.* For $k < 0.5$, the firm in the top layer at (1, 2, 0) is better off than at (3, 0, 0), and therefore (3, 0, 0) is *not* a noncooperative equilibrium. Since all other coalition structures have been shown not to be non-cooperative equilibria, *for $k < 0.5$, there is no non-cooperative equilibrium in pure strategies.*

In summary, we find that the only non-cooperative equilibrium is at full compatibility, and that it is achieved only for goods that have some value on their own irrespective of sales to other customers. For pure two-way network goods where $k = 0$, there is no non-cooperative equilibrium coalition structure. This is because in any coalition structure, there is some firm that has an incentive to deviate from the coalition that it belongs to and join another coalition.

4.2.2. Consensual Coalition Structure Equilibria

Figure 8 is now used to determine which coalition structures are *consensual* equilibria. Since the consensual equilibrium is defined by less restrictive conditions, there are more consensual equilibria than non-cooperative equilibria. First note that *for $k > 0.5$, (3, 0, 0) is a consensual equilibrium* because it is a non-cooperative equilibrium. For $k < 0.5$, a firm in (3, 0, 0) wants to defect and be by itself in the top layer in (1, 2, 0). Therefore for $k < 0.5$, (3, 0, 0) is *not* a consensual equilibrium.

We now establish the conditions under which (2, 1, 0) is a consensual equilibrium. Profits at (2, 1, 0) are higher for a firm in the top layer than at full compatibility (3, 0, 0). A firm in the top layer of (2, 1, 0) has an incentive *not* to accept the firm from the lower layer. As noted earlier, a firm in the top layer of (2, 1, 0) does not want to move to the middle layer of (1, 2, 0). Furthermore for large k, $k > 1.5$, the firm in the top layer of (1, 1, 1) prefers to be together with the firm in the second layer rather than apart. Therefore, *for $k > 1.5$, partial compatibility (2, 1, 0) is a consensual* *equilibrium.* For small k, $k < 1.5$, the firm in the top layer of $(1, 1, 1)$ prefers to be apart from the firm in the second layer. Therefore, for $k < 1.5$, $(2, 1, 0)$ is *not* a consensual equilibrium.

We now establish the conditions under which $(1, 2, 0)$ is a consensual equilibrium. For very small k, $k < 0.5$, a firm in the top layer of $(1, 2, 0)$ does not want anyone to join it (and form $(2, 1, 0)$), even though a firm in the second layer wants to join. For $0.1 < k < 0.5$, a firm in the second layer does not want to defect and be by itself (thus forming $(1, 1, 1)$). A firm in the top layer of $(1, 2, 0)$ does not want to join the second layer, thus forming $(3, 0, 0)$. Therefore, *for 0.1 < k < 0.5, partial compatibility (1, 2, 0) is a consensual equilibrium.* For $k > 0.5$, the firm in the top layer of $(1, 2, 0)$ wants to join the middle layer, and the middle layer wants to accept it, thus forming $(3, 0, 0)$. Therefore for $k > 0.5$, $(1, 2, 0)$ is *not* a consensual equilibrium.

We now establish the conditions under which $(1, 1, 1)$ is a consensual equilibrium. For extremely small k (very high externalities), $k < 0.1$, the middle firm does not want the bottom firm to join it, and the top firm does not want the middle firm to join it, even though any lower firm wants to join a higher layer. This establishes that for *k < 0.1, (1, 1, 1) is a consensual equilibrium.* For $k > 0.1$, the middle firm will accept the lowest layer firm, and therefore $(1, 1, 1)$ is *not* a consensual equilibrium.

In summary, we found that each coalition structure can be a consensual equilibrium for some range of k. In particular, coalition structures of partial compatibility are consensual equilibrium coalition structures for different values of k: for $k < 0.5$ the consensual equilibrium is $(1, 2, 0)$, and for $k > 1.5$, the consensual equilibrium is $(2, 1, 0)$. Full compatibility $(3, 0, 0)$ is a consensual equilibrium whenever it is a non-cooperative equilibrium, *i.e.*, for $k > 0.5$. Finally, total incompatibility $(1, 1, 1)$ is an equilibrium for $k < 0.1$. These results are summarized in Table 3.

TABLE 3

Coalition Structure Equilibria in a Three-Firm Industry.

Range of k	Intensity of Marginal Net work Externality $1/k$	Non-Cooperative Equilibria	Consensual Equilibria
[0, 0.1]	[10, ∞]	None	(1, 1, 1)
[0.1, 0.5]	[2, 10]	None	(1, 2, 0)
[0.5, 1.5]	[0.666, 2]	(3, 0, 0)	(3, 0, 0)
[1.5, ∞]	[0, 0.666]	(3, 0, 0)	(3, 0, 0), (2, 1, 0)

Note that, for some regions of the parameters, there is multiplicity of consensual equilibria. Given the nature of consensual equilibrium, this should not be surprising and does not create a contradiction even though the equilibria are adjacent coalition structures. For example, for high externalities, both total incompatibility $(1, 1, 1)$ and partial compatibility

356

(1, 2, 0) are consensual equilibria. Although under total incompatibility (i) no one from a higher platform wants to join a lower platform, and (ii) every firm in a lower platform wants to join a higher one, (1, 1, 1) is a consensual equilibrium because (iii) no firm in a higher platform wants to admit one form a lower platform. At the same time, (1, 2, 0) is a consensual equilibrium as well, because (among other reasons) no middle platform firm wants to go lower by itself thus forming (1, 1, 1).

5 Conclusion

Firms that compete in markets where network externalities are present face unique tradeoffs regarding the choice of a technical standard. Adhering to a leading compatibility standard allows a firm's product to capture the value added by a large network, however, simultaneously the firm loses direct control over the market supply of the good. Alternatively, adhering to a unique standard allows the firm to control the market supply of the product, but it sacrifices the added value associated with a large network. The tension between these economic forces shapes the coalition formation equilibrium in these markets.

In this work, we developed a model that can be used to solve for the potential coalition formation equilibria in markets for network goods. The model is then implemented on several different market structures and provides some insight regarding the characteristics of the equilibria that emerge. The principal findings of this analysis are: (1) Industry output is larger under the full compatibility equilibrium than it is under the standard Cournot equilibrium when network externalities are present. (2) The coalition formation equilibria that emerge are often very asymmetric in firms' profits and output, despite firms producing identical goods in terms of inherent qualities and using the same production technology. The acuteness of these asymmetries increases as the portion of a goods value that derives from the network increases. (3) The conflicting benefits associated with joining a leading coalition versus adhering to a unique standard also influences a firm's decision on whether to make their technical standards available to competitors. In many instances, firms in leading coalitions earn higher profits by allowing additional firms enter that platform, despite the increase in direct competition and the fact that no side payments are allowed. (4) Full compatibility can be a consensual equilibrium for pure network goods in markets with two or three firms. However, full compatibility is not a non-cooperative equilibrium in these markets. This follows because the potential monopoly rents associated with the leading platform in a pure network good market are very large, and this creates an enormous incentive for firms to be the sole producer in the leading platform. (5) When a coalition is able to exclude entrants (because it holds proprietary standards), in markets with very strong externalities, the equilibrium is characterized by either total or partial incompatibility. This result indicates that market dominance by one or few firms may be an inherent characteristic of market equilibrium in network industries.

• References

D'ASPREMONT, C., JACQUEMIN, A., JASKOLD-GABSZEWICZ, J., WEYMARK, J. (1983). – "On the Stability of Collusive Price Leadership", *Canadian Journal of Economics,* vol. 16, pp. 17-25.

DENECKERE, R., CARL, D. (1985). – "Incentives to Form Coalitions with Bertrand Competition", *Rand Journal of Economics,* vol. 16, no. 4, pp. 473-486.

DONSIMONI, M.-P., ECONOMIDES, N., POLEMARCHAKIS, H. (1986). – "Stable Cartels", *International Economic Review,* vol. 22, no. 2, pp. 317-327.

ECONOMIDES, N. (1984). – "Equilibrium Coalition Structures", *Discussion Paper No. 273,* Columbia University, Department of Economics.

ECONOMIDES, N. (1996). – "The Economics of Networks", *International Journal of Industrial Organization,* vol. 16, no. 4, pp. 675-699.

ECONOMIDES, N., HIMMELBERG, C. (1995). – "Critical Mass and Network Size with Application to the US Fax Market", *Discussion Paper no. EC-95-10,* Stern School of Business, N.Y.U.

ECONOMIDES, N., WHITE, L. J. (1994). – "Networks and Compatibility: Implications for Antitrust", *European Economic Review,* vol. 38, pp. 651-662.

JASKOLD-GABSZEWICZ, J., THISSE, J.-F. (1979). – "Price Competition, Quality, and Income Disparities", *Journal of Economic Theory,* vol. 20, pp. 340-359.

MUSSA, M., SHERWIN, R. (1978). – "Monopoly and Product Quality", *Journal of Economic Theory,* vol. 18, pp. 301-317.

SHAKED, A., SUTTON, J. (1982). – "Relaxing Price Competition Through Product Differentiation", *Review of Economic Studies,* vol. 49, pp. 3-14.

YI, S.-S., HYUKSEUNG, S. (1992). – "Endogenous Formation of Coalitions Part I: Theory", *mimeo.*

Does Standardization Really Increase Production?

Katz and Shapiro's result revisited

Hubert STAHN *

ABSTRACT. – In market structures with network externalities, it is often asserted that there is a natural tendency toward standardization. In this paper it is argued that incompatible products may survive in static models. Like KATZ and SHAPIRO [1985], I develop a simple multi-product oligopoly in which the demand for one of these commodities increases with the number of agents consuming this good. Instead I introduce a variety of cost functions and discuss the limitations of their results of Katz and Shapiro and exhibit an example that reverses their conclusions.

* H. STAHN: BETA University Louis Pasteur, Strasbourg 1. Comments by a number of colleagues and two anonymous referees have been extremely helpful. Research support from France Telecom is also gratefully acknowledged.

D. Encaoua et al. (eds.), The Economics and Econometrics of Innovation, 359–366.
© 2000 Kluwer Academic Publishers. Printed in the Netherlands.

1 Introduction

For many products, the utility that a consumer derives from consumption is affected by the number of the other consumers buying the same commodity. These markets are said to exhibit *"network externalities"* [1]. These externalities are generated through a direct or an indirect effect of the number of consumers on the quality of the product or of products which complement this one [2]. The behavior and the performance of the network good markets are therefore profoundly affected by the presence of these adoption effects. If several network incidently complete, the standardization problem becomes an interesting issue. If one restricts oneself to static models in which the demand for a network good is a function of both its price and the expected size of the network, it is often asserted that there is a natural tendency toward de facto standardization. Multiple incompatible products only last if there exists a trade off between profits today and losses in the future related for instance to a reduction of variety or to an increase in the degree of competition.

In this note, I want to point out that there is no natural tendency toward standardization. As KATZ and SHAPIRO [1985], I develop a multi-product Cournot model in which the utility that an agent derives from consumption increases with the number of consumers. In this framework, these two authors show that the level of total output is greater under industrywide compatibility than in any equilibrium with less than complete compatibility. Moreover they also prove that if two groups of firms make their products mutually compatible then (a) the average output of the firms in the merging coalition will rise (b) the output of any firm not in the merging coalition will fall and (c) industry output will rise. Combined with a surplus analysis, these facts engender a natural tendency toward standardization. But, to obtain these results, they assume that the firms do not supports production costs. The purpose of this note is to show that their results break down if cost functions are introduced.

In order to verify this statement, this paper will be organized as follows. In section 2, I briefly introduce a model which is very closed to the one used by these authors. In section 3, I present the limits of their argument if cost function are introduced. Section 4 is devoted to a counter-example. Section 4 concludes this note.

---

1. For an overview of this litterature see BESSEN-FARREL [1994], KATZ-SHAPIRO [1994] or PERROT [1993].
2. To illustrate direct effects, the reader is referred to ROHLFS [1974] or KATZ-SHAPIRO [1985]. Examples of indirect effects can be based on the *"Hardware/Software"* paradigm (see CHOU-SHY [1990] or CHURCH-GANDAL [1991]) or on lock-in effects (see FARREL-SHAPIRO [1989]).

2 The Model

In order to make their point, Katz and Shapiro develop a partial equilibrium oligopoly model in which each commodity delivered to the market is characterized by one of the m available standards or brands (indexed by i). These goods are produced by n firms (indexed by j). Producer j). Product j only delivers one brand in quantity q_j. Let me denote by N_i the set of firms selling goods of standard i.

With regards to the demand side, each consumer purchases one unit of this good and his willingness to pay for one commodity of standard i is given by $r + v_i$. These agents are heterogeneous in r but homogeneous in their valuations of the anticipated network externality v_i. In order to handle with externalities, I also assume that v_i is related to the anticipated market size y_i^e of brand i by a function $v(y_i^e)$ satisfying $v(0) = 0$, $v'(x) > 0$, $v''(x) < 0$ and $\lim_{x \to +\infty} v'(x) = 0$. As Katz and Shapiro, I do not explicitly model the process through which consumer's expectations are formed. I however require that these expectations are fulfilled at equilibrium. Finally, if r which varies across consumers is assumed to be uniformly distributed between $-\infty$ and $A > 0$, the inverse demand for each brand i is given by $P_i\left(\sum_{j=1}^n q_j, v_i\right) = \max\left\{A + v_i - \sum_{j=1}^n q_j, 0\right\}$.

Concerning the supply side, each producer chooses his production level q_j by taking for given (a) the expectations about the sizes of the networks (or equivalently the $(v_i)_{i=1}^m$), and (b) the output level of the other firms. In order to produce q_j, he however supports a production cost. This one is assumed to be the same across firms and is given by a function $c(q)$ which satisfies $c'(q) > 0$, $c''(q) \geq 0$.

At equilibrium, no firm has an incentive to change his production level and the expectation are fulfilled. Hence

> DEFINITION: A rational expectation Cournot equilibrium is a vector $(\hat{q}_j)_{j=1}^n \in \mathbb{R}_+^n$ which satisfies:
> (i) $\forall i = 1, ..., m, \forall j \in N_i \; \hat{q}_j \in \arg\max_{q_j \in \mathbb{R}_+} P_i\left(\sum_{j=1}^n q_j, v_i\right) \cdot q_j - c(q_j)$
> (ii) $\forall i = 1, ..., m, \; v_i = v\left(\sum_{j \in N_i} \hat{q}_j\right)$

Having in mind this definition, one immediately notices that some firms may not produce at equilibrium because their inverse demand function which is defined by $\max\left\{A + v_i - \sum_{j=1}^n q_j, 0\right\}$ can be zero. To simplify the presentation, let me only concentrate, as Katz and Shapiro, on equilibria in which all firms are active [3]. In this case, the behavior of each producer can be summarized by the first order condition of this maximization

---

3. Because the cost functions are the same across firms, if one firm is inactive, the same must be true for all the other firms producing the same standard. The inactivity simply induces a reduction of the number of available standards.

program [4]. If one also takes into account that the expectations are fulfilled, an equilibrium simply satisfies:

$$(1) \quad \forall i = 1, ..., m, \ \forall j \in N_i, \quad q_j + c'(q_j) = A + v\left(\sum_{j \in N_i} q_j\right) - \sum_{j=1}^{n} q_j$$

Moreover, because prices $p_i = A + v(\sum_{j \in N_i} q_j) - \sum_{j=1}^{n} q_j$ are unique for one standard and because $q_j + c'(q_j)$ is increasing, every firm belonging to N_i produces in equilibrium the same amount of output. If one denotes by Q_i the total production of goods of standard i, an equilibrium reduces to this new set of equations;

$$(2) \quad \forall i = 1, ..., m, \ \frac{Q_i}{n_i} + c'\left(\frac{Q_i}{n_i}\right) = A + v(Q_i) - \sum_{i=1}^{m} Q_i$$

3 The Limits of Katz and Shapiro's Argument

In order to make their point, Katz and Shapiro sum up the preceding set of equation. Doing the same and rearranging the terms, one obtains:

$$(3) \quad \sum_{j=1}^{m} Q_i = \frac{n}{n+1}\left(A + \sum_{i=1}^{m} \frac{n_i}{n} \cdot \left(v(Q_i) - c'\left(\frac{Q_i}{n_i}\right)\right)\right)$$

if m standards coexist and

$$(4) \quad Q = \frac{n}{n+1}\left(A + v(Q) - c'\left(\frac{Q}{n}\right)\right)$$

under industrywide compatibility. Without cost functions, their argument is immediate. Because v is concave and increasing, one can state that:

$$(5) \quad \frac{n}{n+1}\left(A + \sum_{i=1}^{m} \frac{n_i}{n} \cdot v(Q_i)\right) \leq \frac{n}{n+1}\left(A + v\left(\sum_{i=1}^{m} Q\right)\right)$$

The curve $\frac{n}{n+1}(A + v(Q))$ therefore lies above $\frac{n}{n+1}(A + \sum_{i=1}^{m} \frac{n_i}{n} \cdot v(Q_i))$ where $Q = \sum_{i=1}^{m} Q_i$. As long as $\frac{n}{n+1}(A + v(0)) = \frac{n}{n+1} \cdot A > 0$. The

---

4. Because each producer takes as given the expected size of his network, the second order condition $\frac{d\pi}{dq_j} = -2 - c''(q_j) < 0$ is always satisfied.

total production equilibrium level which corresponds to the intersection of these curves with the 45 degree line must be greater under industry-wide compatibility than under incomplete compatibility.

Now if one tries to extend Katz and Shapiro's proof to situations in which cost functions matter, one has to verify that (i) $v(Q) - c'\left(\frac{Q}{n}\right)$ is concave and (ii) $A > c'(0)$. But neither of these two requirements are convincing. Concerning point (i), one immediately notices that $v(Q) - c'\left(\frac{Q}{n}\right)$ is concave if one assumes that the marginal cost function is not too concave. But this condition induces a non standard restriction on the cost function (*i.e.* on its third derivative). Let me now turn to restriction (ii). In network economies, the size of each network crucially affects each consumer's willingness to pay. It seems therefore difficult to exclude situations in which markets for network goods are not viable (*i.e.* $A + v(0) \leq c'(0)$) for small production levels. For many network goods, the highest reservation price which do not make into account the externalities if often close to zero [5]. It is for instance not very interesting to be the only one to have a phone.

4 A Simple Counter-Example

Let me consider a market structure composed by three firms characterized by the following cost function $c(q) = 1/2 \cdot a \cdot q^2 + b \cdot q$. The network externality are described by $v(x) = c \cdot x - d \cdot x^2$ for $x \leq \frac{c}{2d}$ and $v(x) = \frac{c^2}{4d}$ for $x \geq \frac{c}{2d}$. In this simple example, three levels of standardization are available. The products of these firms are neither compatible, partially compatible or totally incompatible. As long as $q_i \in [0, \frac{c}{2d}]$, one easily verifies, by computation, that an equilibrium in each of these three situations is respectively given by:

- $(q_1, q_2, q_3) = (q/3, q/3, q/3)$ and q satisfies

(6)
$$d \cdot q^2 + \left(\frac{4+a}{3} - c\right) \cdot q + b - A = 0$$

- $(q_1, q_2, q_3) = (q_C/2, q_C/2, q_I)$ and (q_C, q_I) satisfies

(7)
$$\begin{cases} d \cdot q_C^2 + \left(\frac{3+a}{2} - c\right) \cdot q_C + q_I + b - A = 0 \\ d \cdot q_I^2 + (2 + a - c) \cdot q_I + q_C + b - A = 0 \end{cases}$$

---

5. It is even possible to assume that A is negative if one wants to capture the idea that a network good is only viable if a minimal number of people are interested.

• $(q_1, q_2, q_3) = (q, q, q)$ and q satisfies

(8) $$d \cdot q^2 + (4 + a - c) \cdot q + b - A = 0$$

If one chooses [6] $a = 1$, $b = 13$, $c = 8$, $d = .05$, $A = 10$, the equilibrium production levels [7] are, in these three cases, respectively given by (.158, .158, .158), (.313, .313, .730), (1.017, 1.017, 1.017) and the profits are respectively (.036, .036, .036), (.149, .149, .797), (1.551, 1.551, 1.551). This simple example induces the following remarks:

• The aggregated production level is smaller under industrywide compatibility then in an equilibrium with less than complete compatibility. This total production level is even increasing with the number of incompatible standards.

• Let me now suppose that two firms decide to make their products mutually compatible (i.e. compare cases (ii) and (iii)). In the postmerger equilibrium, (a) the average output of the firms in the merging coalition will fall from 1.017 to .313, (b) the market size of the firm not in the merging coalition will rise from 33% to 54% and of course (c) the total output will fall.

• If one takes the sum of the producers' and consumers' surplus as a social welfare measure, one obtains in this three cases .220, 2.014, 9.307. This quantity increases with the number of incompatible standards. There is therefore a strong social incentive for network incompatibility.

• Keeping in mind that the compatibility or incompatibility of the products is the result of explicit decisions by the firms, one also notices that the equilibrium profits are increasing for each firm with the number of incompatible standards. If the switching costs are not too high, there are also private incentives for network incompatibility.

One can also notices that if one chooses $a = 0$, $b = 13$, $c = 8$, $d = .05$, $A = 10$, the model produces the following equilibrium values. With full compatibility the production levels are (.151, .151, .151), the profits are given by (.024, .024, .024) and the total surplus is 0.175. With partial compatibility one respectively observes (.278, .278, .595), (.078, .078, .352),

---

6. By computation one can also verify that these results are robust. They remain true for instance by choosing $a \in [0, 3]$, $b \in [11, 15]$ and $c \in [6, 10]$.

7. The reader surely notices that their is another root to these equations which lead to higher production levels. This multiplicity is not really surprising if one keeps in mind that the equilibrium production plan must be consistent with the expectations. Moreover because the objective of this note is to build a counter-example, one can of course select the bad-behaved equilibria.

and 1.172. Finally with incompatibility one obtains (.757, .757, .757), (.573, .573, .573), and 4.298. The reader immediately notices that the preceding remarks remain true and that the cost function reduces, in this example, to a function characterized by a constant marginal cost equal to 13. Katz and Shapiro's result can therefore not even be extended to the class of constant marginal cost functions [8].

5 Conclusion

In market structures in which network externalities occur, it is often asserted that there is a natural tendency toward de facto standardization. Consequently, several incompatible systems only survive, if the decision of producing these goods is a part of a more complex intertemporal strategy. In this paper it was argued that incompatible products may survive in static models.

To illustrate this case I have developed a simple multi-product Cournot model with network externalities. The model presented in this paper was very close to the one introduced by KATZ and SHAPIRO [1985]. The only difference consists in the addition of cost functions. In this setting, I have exhibited an example which invalidate their conclusions.

• References

BESSEN, S., FARRELL, J. (1994). – "Choosing How to Compete: Strategies and Tactics in Standardization", *Journal of Economic Perspective,* 8, 2, pp. 117-131.

CHOU, C., SHY, O. (1990). – "Network effects without Network Externalities", *International Journal of Industrial Organization,* 8, pp. 259-270.

CHURCH, J., GANDAL, N. (1991). – "Network effects, Software Provision and Standardization", *Journal of Industrial Economics,* 40, pp. 85-103.

FARREL, J., SHAPIRO, C. (1989). – "Optimal contracts with lock-in American", *Economic Review,* 79, pp. 51-68.

KATZ, M., SHAPIRO, C. (1985). – "Network Externalities, Competition and Compatibility", *American Economic Review,* 75, pp. 424-440.

KATZ, M., SHAPIRO, C. (1994). – "System Competition and Network Effects", *Journal of Economic Perspective,* 8, 2, pp. 93-115.

---

8. To be more precise, these two authors introduced a linear cost function $c(q) = a + c \cdot q$. They assumed that the fixed cost can be set to zero as long as this one is smaller than the firm's equilibrium revenues minus variable costs. But they also claim that the variable costs can be set to zero without loss of generality. In fact, they argued that it is equivalent to rescale r the willingness to pay. But in this case one also needs to redefine its upper bound and this one can become negative.

PERROT, A. (1993). – "Compatibility, Network and Competition: a Review of Recent Advances", *Transportation Science,* 27, pp. 62-72.

ROHLFS, J. (1974). – "A theory of Interdependent Demand for a Communication Service", *Bell Journal of Economics,* 10, pp. 16-37.

Accumulation of R&D Capital and Dynamic Firm Performance: a Not-so-Fixed Effect Model

Tor Jakob KLETTE, Frode JOHANSEN*

ABSTRACT. – Considering the observed patterns of R&D investment, we argue that a model which allows for a positive feedback from already acquired knowledge to the productiveness of current research, fits the empirical evidence better than the standard model that treats knowledge accumulation symmetrically with the accumulation of physical capital. We present an econometric framework consistent with a positive feedback in the accumulation of R&D capital. The empirical model is econometrically simple and less data-demanding than the standard framework. Our estimates show a significant positive effect of R&D on performance and a positive feedback effect from the stock of knowledge capital. We calculate the depreciation rate and the rate of return to knowledge capital for our alternative framework, and compare our estimated rates of return to results obtained within the standard framework.

* T. J. KLETTE : University of Oslo and Statistics Norway, Norwegian School of Economics; F. JOHANSEN : Statistics Norway. We have benefited from comments from B.H. Hall, S. Machin, J. Mairesse, J. Møen, Ø.A. Nilssen and two anonymous referees, and from participants at the "Economics and econometrics of innovation" conference in Strasbourg, June 3-5, 1996, the "CAED'96" conference in Helsinki, June 17-19, 1996, and the "First Bergamo workshop on applied economics" in Bergamo, October 11-12, 1996. The project has received financial support from the Norwegian Research Council (Nærings-LOS).

D. Encaoua et al. (eds.), The Economics and Econometrics of Innovation, 367–397.
© 2000 *Kluwer Academic Publishers. Printed in the Netherlands.*

1 Introduction

Over the last 10-15 years, we have seen an outburst of econometric research on R&D investment and productivity; see GRILICHES [1995] for a recent survey of the many insights that have emerged from this line of research. Much of this research follows the framework outlined in GRILICHES [1979]. In this paper we argue that this econometric framework should be modified and extended in various ways. In particular, considering the empirical evidence on the patterns of R&D investment, we argue that a model which allows for a positive feedback from already acquired knowledge to the productiveness of current research fits the empirical evidence better than the standard model that treats knowledge accumulation symmetrically to the accumulation of physical capital. Positive feedbacks in knowledge accumulation have recently been considered in the literature on macroeconomic growth by ROMER [1990], MILGROM, QIAN and ROBERTS [1991], and JONES [1995]. Their argument is that this feedback mechanism can explain the persistent differences in productivity between countries or industries, and why some industries or countries suddenly gain momentum and go through phases of high growth.

Our analysis is concerned with a related phenomenon at the micro level; how can we rationalize that some firms are persistently, often for a long period, more productive than other firms, as shown e.g. by BAILEY, HULTEN and CAMPBELL [1992]. Similarly, why do some firms persistently carry out considerable R&D, while other firms in the same industry never report any R&D investments? Empirically, it is widely observed that there are large differences in R&D effort across firms within narrowly defined industries, and that these differences in R&D effort are persistent over time. NELSON [1988] has pointed out that this co-existence of innovators and imitators - as he calls them - is a puzzle for the standard framework for productivity analysis at the micro level.

We argue that positive feedbacks in knowledge accumulation can be one explanation for the persistency of performance differences at the micro level, parallel to the cited arguments presented in the macro growth literature. The co-existence of innovators and imitators can within our framework be considered a consequence of the stochastic nature of knowledge production in combination with a positive feedback from past R&D success to the productiveness of current R&D. That is, a lucky draw in the R&D activity in one year tends to make R&D investments in the following years more productive and profitable. This positive feedback from past R&D success to the productivity of current R&D can explain how an innovation in a firm can stimulate the firm's R&D activity and start a cumulative process of several subsequent innovations and high productivity growth. Our alternative model of R&D accumulation tries to capture this cumulative nature of research.

The model presented below is attractive as it leads to an estimating equation which is empirically more tractable than the standard framework. In particular, one does not need to construct the knowledge stock variable which is often quite problematic since the calculation requires a long history of R&D investments for each firm. Our empirical model also alters and augments the standard framework as presented in GRILICHES (1979, 1995) by explicitly incorporating the demand side and both process and product innovations.

We have estimated our model on a new data set that links R&D investment at the line-of-business level (within each firm) to plant level data on productivity. The results show that R&D investment is a significant determinant of dynamic performance and that the appropriable part of R&D capital depreciates quite rapidly.

The analysis presented here is in several ways an extension of the analysis presented in KLETTE [1996]: First, the present paper presents a formal analysis of optimal R&D investment when the accumulation process allows for the feedback mechanism in our alternative specification. Second, we present an empirical analysis of R&D investment to illustrate the empirical importance of our respecification. Third, the formal analysis of optimal R&D investment leads us to a formula for calculating the private rate of return to R&D investment. Finally, the empirical analysis in section 4 is carried out on a new data set that links R&D data at the line of business level to plant level data for the period 1980-92 (while KLETTE [1996], used only a single cross section of R&D data for 1989). This new, larger data set allows us to explore a number of specification issues and formal econometric tests that were not possible with the limited data set used in KLETTE [1996].

The rest of our paper is organized as follows: In section 2, we examine patterns of R&D investments. After discussing R&D investment in the standard model of knowledge accumulation, we present a dynamic programming analysis of optimal R&D investment for our alternative specification of the accumulation process. This theoretical analysis is confronted with empirical patterns of R&D investment in the second half of section 2. We proceed to the empirical analysis of R&D, productivity and performance in sections 3 and 4. For comparison, we start in section 3 with a standard analysis of R&D and productivity, following GRILICHES (1979, 1995) and HALL and MAIRESSE [1995]. Section 4 contains the main part of our analysis of R&D and performance, where we spell out the empirical framework and present the econometric results. We add some final comments in section 5.

2 Investment in R&D Capital and Performance

2.1. Persistent cross sectional differences in R&D investment: Theory

The standard framework treats the accumulation of knowledge capital in the same way as that of physical capital, using the "perpetual inventory" specification as a common framework. Formally,

$$(1) \qquad K_{it+1} = K_{it}(1 - \delta) + R_{it} \ ,$$

where K_{it} and R_{it} represent knowledge capital and R&D investment for firm i in year t [1].

We will argue that the standard framework contradicts the widely observed pattern that the same firms tend to persistently carry out above (or below) average amounts of R&D, say, relative to their sales. This persistence in the differences in R&D intensities between firms within the same industry is hard to rationalize on the basis of a knowledge accumulation process as specified in equation (1). To clarify our point, assume a Cobb-Douglas production function,

$$(2) \qquad Q_{it} = \Phi_{it} X_{it}^{\alpha^X} K_{it}^{\alpha^K},$$

where Q_{it} is output, Φ_{it} a productivity term, and X_{it} inputs. A firm's rate of return to knowledge capital can then be calculated as $\alpha^K Q_{it}/K_{it}$. This expression implies that if we consider two firms which differ only in their output-knowledge ratios at the beginning of a period, the firm with the lowest output-knowledge ratio should have the highest marginal return on its knowledge capital. Hence, one should expect the highest R&D-intensity for the firm with the lowest knowledge-output ratio at the beginning of the period [2]. Our point is that the standard model, based on (1) and (2), is difficult to reconcile with widely observed patterns of *persistent cross-sectional differences in R&D-intensities* within the same industry. That is to say, it is difficult to rationalize the co-existence of high R&D-intensity firms with low R&D-intensity firms year after year within this model. See NELSON [1988] for an elaborate discussion of this question.

One possible resolution is to add convex adjustment costs for R&D capital to the model above. Firms starting with different initial conditions would then *slowly* converge towards the same ratio Q_{it}/K_{it}, with persistent differences in their R&D-intensities on their transition paths. However, given the relatively poor empirical performance of Euler equations for R&D investments we find it attractive to examine alternative models.

The treatment of heterogeneity is a more general problem with models such as (1) and (2). Heterogeneity is often captured by so-called fixed effects in empirical research on firm level data. While the presence of fixed effects can make the model consistent with the observed cross sectional differences in R&D activity, they are not very satisfactory. First, econometric studies of R&D and productivity based on models with fixed effects often give weak, if significant results, and the estimates are often not robust; see the survey by MAIRESSE and SASSENOU [1991]. Second, while our model suggests a mechanism generating persistent differences in R&D investment, models

---

1. It follows from (1) that this knowledge capital is a beginning-of-period capital.
2. Note that this result is valid even if firms differ in terms of productivity, Φ_{it}.

with fixed effects only account for such differences without offering any explanation how such differences have been generated.

2.1.1. An Alternative Specification of Knowledge Accumulation

A possible explanation for the observation that a high return on knowledge capital does not lead to R&D investments is that the relationship between R&D investment and knowledge capital is more complex than in equation (1). There is an alternative to the perpetual inventory model of capital accumulation that suggests that old capital and new investment are *complementary* inputs in the production of new capital. This view seems particularly relevant for the accumulation of knowledge capital, as noticed by GRILICHES [1979], HALL and HAYASHI [1989], ROMER [1990], JONES [1995] and KLETTE [1996]. The basic idea is that greater initial knowledge will tend to increase the amount of knowledge obtained from a given amount of R&D. The specific model of capital accumulation we will consider here was originally presented by UZAWA [1969], who attributed the idea to PENROSE [1959] [3].

Formally, we will assume that knowledge capital can be accumulated according to the equation [4]

$$(3) \qquad K_{t+1} = K_t^{(\rho-\nu)} R_t^{\nu}.$$

ν is a parameter capturing the productiveness of R&D in generating new knowledge, while ρ reflects scale economies in the production of knowledge. The interpretation of these parameters will be discussed further in section 4.1.3. We recognize that (3) has the rather extreme and unrealistic implication that a firm which stops its R&D in a single year will loose all its knowledge capital. A better specification is perhaps $K_{t+1} = K_t^{(\rho-\nu)} (R_t + c)^{\nu}$, where c is some positive parameter, but this respecification creates a non-linear estimation problem that we have not addressed in this paper. We will however add some further comments on this specification in section 4.

The firm maximizes its net present value; $V(K_0)$, given its initial knowledge capital stock (K_0):

$$(4) \qquad V(K_0) = \max_{\{R_t\}} \sum_{t=0}^{\infty} \beta^t (\pi_t(K_t) - w_t R_t),$$

subject to the accumulation equation (3). β is the discount factor, $\pi_t(K_t)$ is the profit function conditional on the knowledge capital stock, excluding

---

3. Penrose and Uzawa put the model forward as a model of physical capital accumulation. Their argument was that physical capital investment requires organizational skills or capital as a complementary input, and organizational capital involves an accumulation process where past knowledge gives a positive feedbacks to the acquisition of new knowledge.
4. It can be shown that the log-linear specification is not essential for the argument below.

R&D investment cost, while w_t is the unit cost of R&D investment. For convenience, we have not included other kinds of capital or uncertainty in the model. This can be done without changing the argument; it only involves more notation.

As shown for instance by STOKEY and LUCAS (1989, ch. 4), under mild regularity conditions the value function satisfies the Bellman-equation:

(5) $$V(K_t) = \max_{R_t}[\,\pi_t(K_t) - w_t R_t + \beta V(K_{t+1})\,],$$

where K_{t+1} is a function of K_t and R_t as specified in (3). Assuming strict concavity of the short run profit function (in K_t), the optimal R&D investment must satisfy the first-order condition:

(6) $$-w_{t-1} + \beta V'(K_t)\frac{\partial K_t}{\partial R_{t-1}} = 0$$

Furthermore, as the Bellman equation (5) is supposed to hold for all initial knowledge capital stocks, we have that

(7) $$V'(K_t) = \pi_t'(K_t) + \beta V'(K_{t+1})\frac{\partial K_{t+1}}{\partial K_t}.$$

Eliminating the V's from this equation by equation (6), we find that

(8) $$\frac{1}{\beta}w_{t-1}\left(\frac{\partial K_t}{\partial R_{t-1}}\right)^{-1} = \pi'(K_t) + w_t\left(\frac{\partial K_{t+1}}{\partial R_t}\right)^{-1}\frac{\partial K_{t+1}}{\partial K_t}$$

Or, using (3), and rearranging some terms:

(9) $$w_{t-1}R_{t-1} = \beta[\nu\,\pi'(K_t)K_t + (\rho - \nu)w_t R_t]$$

A common specification of the profit function implies that $\pi'(K_t) = \gamma S_t/K_t$, where S_t is sales (see KLETTE [1996]). In this case

(10) $$\frac{w_{t-1}R_{t-1}}{S_t} = \beta\left[\nu\gamma + (\rho - \nu)\frac{w_t R_t}{S_t}\right].$$

Cross-sectional differences in sales are highly autocorrelated i.e. $S_{t-1} \simeq S_t$. Hence, equation (10) predicts that differences in the R&D intensity between different firms should be highly correlated over time. In section 2.2, we will provide empirical support for this prediction.

To summarize, the multiplicative model of knowledge accumulation considered in this section rationalizes why the same firms persistently invest above (or below) average in R&D. The main reason identified here is the intertemporal complementarity in the R&D activity; past experience makes current R&D effort more productive. We have formally shown that this mechanism leads to a pattern of persistent differences in R&D intensities between firms, a well known empirical pattern which is hard to rationalize in the standard framework.

2.2. Persistent Cross Sectional Differences in R&D Investment: Empirical Evidence

This section provides empirical evidence on two features of R&D investment behavior which motivate the alternative model of knowledge accumulation: The heterogeneity and persistence in R&D intensities.

The empirical analysis is based on two primary data sources; the annual manufacturing census carried out by Statistics Norway and the R&D survey carried out by the Norwegian Research Council for Science and Technology (NTNF) until 1989 and by Statistics Norway from 1991. Our analysis covers the period 1980-92 and the following industries: "Chemicals", "Mineral products", "Basic metals" and "Metal products". These industries account for almost all R&D in Norwegian manufacturing. Further details on our data sources and samples are given in the appendix.

One of the advantages with the Norwegian R&D data is that R&D is reported at the *line of business level within each firm.* The production data are reported at the plant level, and they have been aggregated to the line-of-business level for the analysis in this section where we will examine cross sectional and longitudinal patterns in R&D intensities.

Figure 1 shows the distribution of R&D intensities with the line-of-business within each firms as the unit of observation. The figure presents the

FIGURE 1

Distribution of R&D Intensities by Industry.

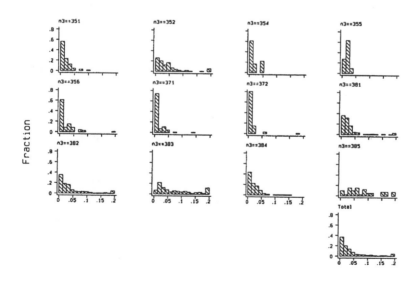

Notes: *Observations at line of business level. Observations with no R&D not shown.*

distribution of R&D intensities for each 3-digit industry and for the complete sample. We see from figure 1 that even within relatively narrowly defined industries there is a large amount of heterogeneity in R&D intensities. As COHEN and KLEPPER [1992] found, the distribution of R&D intensities is highly skewed in most industries, with a large fraction of the line-of-businesses reporting little or no R&D [5]. There is a censoring problem for line-of-businesses that are not reporting R&D. Most of these firms are probably accumulating new knowledge, but often by other means than formal R&D. The firms without R&D create well-known problems for empirical analysis that we will return to in section 4.

Cohen and Klepper examined only a single cross section of firms. With a set of panel data, we can push the issue a step further. Table 1 shows that not only is the distribution of R&D intensities highly skewed; it is also the same firms that invest heavily in R&D year after year. Table 1 shows transition probabilities for categories of R&D intensities. The table shows that 90% of the plants which have no R&D in a given year, have no R&D two years later. More than 60% of the plants in the highest quartile of R&D plants are in this quartile two years later. This persistence in R&D intensities indicates that there are persistent differences in R&D investment opportunities across firms.

TABLE 1

Matrix of Transition Probabilities for Categories of R&D-Intensity.

t	$t+2$ No R&D	1	2	3	4	Total
No R&D	2170	65	46	68	47	2396
	90.57	2.71	1.92	2.84	1.96	100.00
1	42	98	17	4	1	162
	25.93	60.49	10.49	2.47	0.62	100.00
2	38	24	42	16	3	123
	30.89	19.51	34.15	13.01	2.44	100.00
3	29	3	20	73	28	153
	18.95	1.96	13.07	47.71	18.30	100.00
4	21	1	4	26	91	143
	14.69	0.70	2.80	18.18	63.64	100.00
Total	2300	191	129	187	170	2977
	77.26	6.42	4.33	6.28	5.71	100.00

Another way to illustrate the same point is presented in figure 2; the figure shows ranks of R&D intensities in year t vs. year $t + 2, \ldots , t + 8$.

---

5. See also BOUND et al. (1984), KLETTE (1994b), and PAKES and SCHANKERMAN (1984).

The figure shows a positive autocorrelation pattern. For comparison, the analysis is repeated for physical capital investment intensities in figure 3. The autocorrelation pattern for fixed investment (intensities) is weak. A comparison of figures 2 and 3 shows that R&D investments are much more persistent than for physical capital investments. High persistence in the short run could also be explained by adjustment costs, as mentioned above. However, the fact that the degree of persistence is quite high over a large number of years for R&D suggests that standard convex adjustment costs are an inadequate explanation. The positive feedback effect incorporated in the model presented in section 2.1 is consistent with persistent differences in investment opportunities in R&D, cf. equation (10).

FIGURE 2

Ranks of R&D Intensities. Time t vs. $t + 2$, $t + 4$, $t + 6$, $t + 8$.

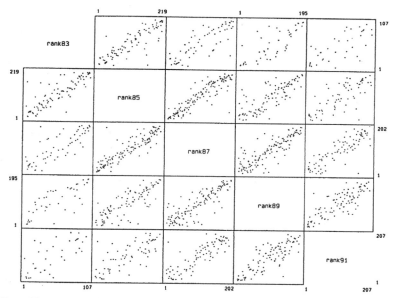

Notes: Observations at line of business level. Observations with no R&D not shown.

We noticed above that the positive feedback effect incorporated in the multiplicative model for capital accumulation was originally put forward as a model for physical capital investments by PENROSE [1959], UZAWA [1969]; see also SHEN [1970] who examined the empirical performance of the model. Our comparison of the patterns in figures 2 and 3 suggests that the positive feedback effect is much weaker in the accumulation of physical capital as compared to the case with R&D capital.

FIGURE 3

Ranks of Investment Intensities. Time t vs. $t + 2$, $t + 4$, $t + 6$, $t + 8$.

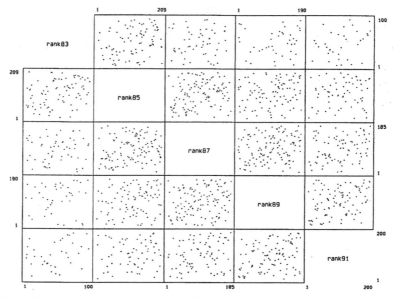

Notes: *Observations at line of business level. Observations with no R&D not shown.*

3 R&D and Productivity: a Standard Analysis

Before we present our main analysis, it is useful to present an econometric analysis of productivity and R&D based on the standard framework. By estimating some of the traditional models in the literature we want to illustrate two points: In the cross section, there is a positive relationship between R&D and productivity, while this relationship is quite weak in the longitudinal dimension.

In columns 1-8 of table 2 we estimate the output elasticity of the R&D capital stock, following the standard approach in the literature [6]. The R&D capital stock is constructed by accumulating R&D investments according to equation (1) from an initial year. We assume a 15% depreciation rate for R&D and an R&D expenditure growth rate of 10% prior to the first

---

6. See GRILICHES (1979, 1995) and HALL and MAIRESSE (1995).

observation for each line of business (firm) [7]. The first six columns of the table give results for a log-linear (i.e. Cobb-Douglas) technology for two different measures of output, i.e. from estimating

$$y_{it} = \alpha + X_{it}\beta + \gamma k_{it} + e_{it},$$

where y_{it} is log output (either gross output or value added), X_{it} is a vector representing (log) capital and labor, as well as materials if output is measured by gross output. k_{it} is log of the R&D capital stock and γ is the parameter of primary interest.

Column (1) shows that R&D has a significant effect on value added. Including time and industry dummies as in column (2) gives almost identical results. A positive cross sectional relationship between productivity and the stock of knowledge capital has been found in a number other studies; see the surveys by MAIRESSE and SASSENOU [1991] and GRILICHES [1988, 1995]. In column (3), we see that when fixed effects are included, the relationship between R&D and productivity becomes weaker. This result is not surprising given the high persistence in R&D investments discussed above, and is well recognized in the literature (cf. the survey by SASSENOU and MAIRESSE [1991]. In columns (4) through (6) we repeat these regressions for a gross output specification of output. The (gross) output elasticities are similar to the estimates based on value added, but somewhat lower as expected.

The next two columns, (7) and (8) show similar results for a more general specification of the technology than the log-linear specification used in columns (1)-(6). Here we regress a productivity index on the stock of knowledge capital. This index of total factor productivity will be defined in section 4.1.2 below (cf. equation (18)). Again we find a significant relationship between R&D and productivity in the cross section, but R&D capital is insignificant when firm effects are included.

Finally in column (9) we regress productivity growth on R&D intensity. In this model the coefficient on R&D intensity can be interpreted as the private rate of return to R&D, see GRILICHES [1979]. We find essentially a zero rate of return. The implied rates of return for the estimates in columns (1)-(8) are presented in table 3. We will comment on these rates of return in section 4.5 below.

To summarize, our analysis based on the standard framework shows results similar to what comparable studies have found for other countries. R&D is positively correlated with productivity levels, while the longitudinal correlation between R&D and productivity growth is much weaker, in some cases even statistically insignificant. The basic message is that R&D firms are ahead and tend to stay ahead in terms of both R&D and productivity. The dynamic, econometric model we present in the next section fits very well with such a pattern.

---

7. See HALL and MAIRESSE (1995) for an extensive analysis of the sensitivity of the parameter estimates to changes in assumptions about this growth rate, the depreciation rate and other specification issues.

Results for Log-linear Models with Standard R&D Capital Accumulation.

	ln(Value added)			ln(Gross output)			$\hat{a}_t$		$\Delta\hat{a}_t$
	(1)	(2)	(3)	(4)	(5)	(6)	(7)	(8)	(9)
ln(Materials)				.556	.528	.485			
				(.007)	(.007)	(.011)			
ln(Capital)	.201	.125	.127	.073	.040	.051			
	(.007)	(.009)	(.017)	(.005)	(.005)	(.006)			
ln(Labor)	.819	.903	.781	.349	.423	.397			
	(.008)	(.010)	(.023)	(.006)	(.008)	(.014)			
ln(R&D Capital)	.066	.053	.018	.036	.030	.004	.018	−.002	
	(.005)	(.005)	(.007)	(.002)	(.002)	(.003)	(.002)	(.002)	
R&D Intensity									.004
									(.020)
D(R&D Capital = 0)	.422	.335	.105	.243	.198	.020	.115	−.005	
	(.039)	(.038)	(.054)	(.019)	(.019)	(.020)	(.015)	(.017)	
D(R&D Int. = 0)									.000
									(.003)
Time dummies	No	Yes	Yes	No	Yes	Yes	No	No	No
Industry dummies	No	Yes	No	No	Yes	No	No	No	No
Fixed effect	No	No	Yes	No	No	Yes	No	Yes	No
Adjusted R^2	.90	.91	.94	.97	.98	.99	.02	.52	.00
Observations	11289	11289	11289	11343	11343	11343	11343	11343	9970

Notes: R&D Intensity is defined as R&D investment divided by the average of output in period t and $t + 1$.

T<small>ABLE</small> 3

Implied rates of return to R&D investments from models in table 2.

	ln(Value added)			ln(Gross output)			$\hat{a}_t$	
	(1)	(2)	(3)	(4)	(5)	(6)	(7)	(8)
For mean value of Output/R&D Capital	24%	22%	2%	51%	45%	6%	28%	−17%
For median value of Output/R&D Capital	6%	5%	1%	11%	10%	1%	6%	−4%

4 R&D, Productivity and Performance: the Not-So-Fixed Effect Model

4.1. R&D, Productivity and Dynamic Performance

This section will present a modification of the standard econometric model used to estimate the relationship between R&D and productivity.

The modification involves the R&D accumulation process discussed in section 2 as a replacement for the R&D stocks based on the perpetual inventory model. Our framework is attractive as the estimating equation is simple to implement, and the parameters have a structural interpretation. The presentation bellow follows KLETTE [1996] closely. Our framework is made up of three components: (i) a model of production; (ii) a simple specification of product demand; and (iii) the specification of knowledge accumulation, already discussed in section 2.

4.1.1. Production, R&D Capital and Process Innovations

The first component of the modified framework is a model of short-run producer behavior, a specification that is based on the assumption of short-run, profit-maximizing behavior, allowing for scale economies and imperfect competition in the output market. In this section, we will use the term firm without making any distinction between plants and the line of business within a firm. The distinction between the plant and the line of business (within the firm) will be introduced when we present the estimating equation in section 4.1.4.

Consider a firm that produces an output (Q_t) by means of the three inputs, labor, materials and capital, according to the production function $\Phi_t F(X_t)$, where X_t is a vector representing the three inputs $(X_t^l, l = L, M, C)$. Let a hat above a variable denote logarithmic deviations from a reference input-output vector, (Q_{0t}, X_{0t}); i.e. $\hat{q}_t = \ln(Q_t/Q_{0t})$. We will refer to this reference point as the *reference firm*. We have dropped the index referring to the firm (the subscript "i"). It can be shown that the following relationship holds under quite general conditions [8]:

$$(11) \qquad \hat{q}_t = \sum_{l=L,M,C} \alpha_t^l \hat{x}_t^l + \widehat{\phi}_t$$

where $\alpha_t^l \equiv [\partial \ln(F_t)/\partial \ln(X_t^l) + \partial \ln(F_{0t})/\partial \ln(X_{0t}^l)]/2$. $\widehat{\phi}_t$ is the (logarithmic) productivity difference between the firm we consider and the reference firm.

With profit maximization, the output elasticity for a fully adjustable factor of production is equal to the markup (on marginal costs) times the factor's cost share, assuming price taking firms in the *factor* markets (see KLETTE, 1994a, for details). It follows that

$$(12) \qquad \alpha_t^l = \mu(\theta_t^l + \theta_{0t}^l)/2 \equiv \mu\, \bar{\theta}_t^l,$$

where θ_t^l is the cost for factor l as a share of revenue, for the firm we consider; θ_{0t}^l is the corresponding share for the reference firm. μ is the markup, i.e. the ratio of price and marginal costs. It is not reasonable

---

8. See KLETTE (1994a).

to assume capital to be fully adjusted in every period, so we should treat capital differently from the fully adjustable factors. If ϵ is the elasticity of scale, we have that the output elasticity of capital (α_t^C) can be expressed: $\alpha_t^C = \epsilon - \sum_{l \neq C} \alpha_t^l = \epsilon - \sum_{l \neq C} \mu \bar{\theta}_t^l$, where the last equality follows from (12). Inserting this expression and (12) into equation (11):

$$(13) \qquad \hat{q}_t = \mu \sum_{l=L,M} \bar{\theta}_t^l (\hat{x}_t^l - \hat{x}_t^C) + \epsilon \hat{x}_t^C + \widehat{\phi}_t$$

We will decompose the productivity term $(\widehat{\phi}_t)$ into two parts: One term reflects productivity differences due to differences in knowledge capital $(\alpha^K \hat{k}_t)$, whereas the second term $(\hat{u}_t)$ captures the remaining differences in productivity:

$$(14) \qquad \hat{q}_t = \mu \sum_{l=M,L} \bar{\theta}_t^l (\hat{x}_t^l - \hat{x}_t^C) + \epsilon \hat{x}_t^C + \alpha^K \hat{k}_t + \hat{u}_t.$$

α^K is the output elasticity of knowledge capital. This parameter reflects the opportunities for *process innovation*.

4.1.2. Demand, R&D Capital and Product Innovations

As usual with firm level data, we do not have information about real output, only nominal sales [9]. We will now show how to reformulate equation (14) in terms of nominal sales instead of real output. Let us start with a demand function with price, knowledge capital and other demand shifters as its arguments. A firm's knowledge capital is assumed to affect demand through differences in product quality. Consider a (first order) log-linear expansion of the demand function around the reference firm [10]:

$$(15) \qquad \hat{q}_t = \eta \hat{p}_t + \xi \hat{k}_t + \hat{d}_t,$$

where $\hat{p}_t$ and $\hat{k}_t$ are the firm's price and knowledge capital relative to the reference firm. η is the price elasticity of demand, while ξ is the elasticity of demand with respect to a change in the firm's relative "product quality". The parameter ξ also captures the relationship between knowledge and product quality. $\hat{d}_t$ is a demand shifter. From the relationship $S_t = P_t Q_t$, it follows that $\hat{s}_t = \hat{p}_t + \hat{q}_t$. Using this relationship, we can eliminate the unobservable $\hat{p}_t$ in equation (15):

$$(16) \qquad \hat{q}_t = \frac{1}{\eta+1} \hat{d}_t + \frac{\eta}{\eta+1} \hat{s}_t + \frac{\xi}{\eta+1} \hat{k}_t.$$

---

9. Deflated sales will not alter the argument as long as the deflation is based on industry wide deflators. See KLETTE and GRILICHES (1996) for a discussion in a slightly different context.
10. One might argue that knowledge capital affects the price elasticity of demand and not only the level of demand. This could be incorporated by allowing for interaction terms between $\hat{p}_t$ and $\hat{k}_t$ in (15). However, this extension of the model will substantially complicate the subsequent analysis and must be left as a topic for future research.

380

Optimal price setting implies a markup: $\mu = \eta/(1+\eta)$. Using this expression and combining (14) and (16) to eliminate the unobservable $\widehat{q}_t$, we have that

$$(17) \qquad \hat{s}_t = \sum_{l=M,L} \overline{\theta}_t^l (\hat{x}_t^l - \hat{x}_t^C) + \frac{\epsilon}{\mu}\hat{x}_t^C + \gamma\hat{k}_t - \frac{1}{\eta}\,\hat{d}_t + \frac{1}{\mu}\hat{u}_t,$$

where $\gamma = \alpha^K/\mu - \xi/\eta$ (notice that η, the price elasticity, is negative by definition). The two terms that make up the γ-parameter capture the effect of both process and product innovations.

Define the performance index:

$$(18) \qquad \hat{a}_t \equiv \hat{s}_t - \sum_{l=M,L} \overline{\theta}_t^l (\hat{x}_t^l - \hat{x}_t^C) - \hat{x}_t^C.$$

Notice that this performance index can be calculated directly from observations on output, factor inputs and factor costs (cf. the right hand side of 17), as we have done in the empirical analysis we present below [11]. We can rewrite equation (17) in terms of the performance index (18):

$$(19) \qquad \hat{a}_t = \left(\frac{\epsilon}{\mu} - 1\right)\hat{x}_t^C + \gamma\hat{k}_t + \widehat{\varepsilon}_t,$$

where $\widehat{\varepsilon}_t = \hat{u}_t/\mu - \hat{d}_t/\eta$. Having calculated the performance index according to (18), we will now show how it can be embedded in an estimating equation to identify $(\rho - \nu), \nu, \gamma$ and other parameters of primary interest [12].

4.1.3. R&D Investment and the Production of Knowledge Capital

Knowledge accumulation is assumed to take place according to (3). Since the log-linear relationship is assumed to hold for all firms we have that:

$$(20) \qquad \hat{k}_{t+1} = (\rho - \nu)\hat{k}_t + \nu\hat{r}_t + \hat{v}_t,$$

where $\hat{v}_t$ captures stochastic elements in the innovation process. As above, a hat above a variable represents logarithmic deviations from the reference firm. Hence, the specification suggests that a firm's knowledge capital stock next year, measured *relative to the reference firm*, depends on its *relative* capital stock from the past, as well as the firm's *relative* R&D effort.

---

11. To calculate the right hand side of (18), we need to identify the reference firm. How this is done will be explained in section 4.2.1. The performance index (18) is essentially a Tornquist index for the Solow residual, except that sales ($\hat{s}_t$) has replaced real output ($\hat{q}_t$) in the Solow residual; see KLETTE (1996) for a discussion.

12. As we show below, it is only possible to identify ν and γ if we assume $\rho = 1$.

Note that though the accumulation equation for R&D capital collapses for zero R&D investment, our empirical analysis includes firms which do not report any R&D. We circumvent this problem by including a dummy variable for these firms. The interpretation is that these firms also accumulate knowledge, but not by means reported as formal R&D [13].

The term $(\rho - \nu)$ reflects the depreciation rate for the private (i.e. the appropriable) part of a firm's knowledge capital. Below, we will refer to $1 - (\rho - \nu)$ as the depreciation rate. $(\rho - \nu)$ determines *cet.par.* the speed of decay of a firm's knowledge advantage (or disadvantage) [14]. As pointed out in section 2.1.1, the ρ parameter reflects scale economies in knowledge production, while the ν-parameter reflects the innovative opportunities of R&D effort. Hence, the two parameters ρ and ν reflect three different aspects of the process for generating R&D capital; scale economies in R&D, depreciation, and the potency of R&D in generating new knowledge. This suggests that a more general specification of the production function for R&D capital might be desirable. We must leave this as a topic for future research.

PAKES and ERICSON [1989], among others, have argued that firm specific stochastic elements in knowledge accumulation (in a broad sense) represent an important aspect of firm dynamics. The possibility of incorporating stochastic shocks in the knowledge accumulation process (cf. the last term in 20), in a clean and consistent way, is a benefit of the alternative framework here as compared to the standard ("perpetual inventory") framework.

It might be undesirable to impose the assumption that there is a one-year lag between R&D and new profit making knowledge, as in (20). It is not difficult to generalize the specification in (5) (and (20)) with a more flexible lag-structure, i.e. $K_{it+1} = K_{it}^{(\rho - \nu_1)} R_{it}^{\nu_1} R_{it-1}^{\nu_2} R_{it-2}^{\nu_3} \cdots$ We will present some estimates with this more general specification below. However, as others have experienced before us, empirically it turns out to be hard to determine the appropriate lag structure, since R&D investments tend to be highly autocorrelated, as we showed in section 2.

4.1.4. The Estimating Equation: A Not-So-Fixed Effect Model

We can eliminate the unobservable knowledge capital stocks in equation (19) by using equation (20):

$$(21) \qquad \hat{a}_{it} = (\rho - \nu)\hat{a}_{it-1} + \gamma \nu \hat{r}_{It-1}$$
$$+ (\epsilon/\mu - 1)\hat{x}_{it}^C + (\rho - \nu)(\epsilon/\mu - 1)\hat{x}_{it-1}^C + \hat{e}_{it}.$$

---

13. As noticed above, an alternative way to handle firms that do not carry out R&D is to consider a knowledge accumulation process as discussed in section 2.1.1, where $K_{t+1} = K_t^{(\rho - \nu)}(R_t + c)^\nu$ (which creates a non-linear estimation problem).

14. See PAKES and SCHANKERMAN (1984) for a discussion of knowledge depreciation. More precisely, $(\rho - \nu)$ is the speed of decay for the *logarithm* of the knowledge capital stock relative to the reference firm.

The two last terms in (21) can be manipulated to reduce the multicolinearity problem between the variables representing the capital stock in two subsequent years [15]:

$$(22) \qquad \hat{a}_{it} = (\rho - \nu)\hat{a}_{it-1} + \gamma\nu\,\hat{r}_{It-1} + \lambda_1\widehat{i}_{it-1} + \lambda_2\hat{x}^C_{it-1} + \hat{e}_{it}.$$

The two first terms on the right hand side of (22) capture the essence of our model, while the next two terms are included to control for market power and scale economies.

Equation (22) is our estimating equation incorporating the performance index which must be calculated according to (18). We have in this equation introduced a notation that distinguishes between plants and the line-of-business (within a firm) to which the plant belongs. The subscript i refers to a plant, while the upper case subscript I refers to the line-of-business within the firm to which the plant belongs. If a firm operates several plants within a line-of-business, we assume that they all have access to the same knowledge capital stock; see KLETTE [1996] for a related analysis of scope economies in R&D [16].

The difference equation (22) corresponds to a dynamic process where there are persistent differences in performance between plants, but not quite as persistent as in the fixed-effect case. The equation portrays a process where there is a tendency for differences in productivity to disappear with time, if there are no differences in R&D effort. Externalities, i.e. diffusion of knowledge is the cause for this tendency to converge, in our interpretation. Hence, the property that an above average firm tend to decline to average performance reflect only a relative decline rather than an absolute decline - in other words, the average level of performance is persistently improving. We should emphasize that this tendency to convergence only holds when there are no differences in R&D effort. We argued, however, in section 2 that there is a feedback mechanism built into this model that will give incentives to preserve (cross sectional) differences in R&D effort over time. This suggest that the model can rationalize persistent differences in performance between firms. A complete dynamic analysis of the model presented here requires an analysis of the two coupled difference equations (10) and (22), a task beyond the scope of this paper.

We notice that equation (22) is similar to equations widely studied and estimated within the standard framework. As noticed in KLETTE [1996], equation (22) picks up two correlation patterns which are not new or surprising; i.e. that productivity growth is positively related to lagged R&D, and negatively related to initial productivity. The contribution of the present framework is to show how these two patterns can been related within a fully specified *structural* model.

---

15. Use the approximation $x^C_{it} = \ln X^C_{it} = \ln(X^C_{it-1} + I_{it-1}) \simeq \ln X^C_{it-1} + (I_{it-1}/X^C_{it-1})$, where we have introduced the variable $i_{it-1} = I_{it-1}/X^C_{it-1}$. The parameters should then be interpreted as follows: $\lambda_1 = (\epsilon/\mu - 1)$ and $\lambda_2 = [1 - (\rho - \nu)](\epsilon/\mu - 1)$.

16. See also ADAMS and JAFFE (1996). Notice that ADAMS and JAFFE (1996) do not have access to R&D broken down at the line-of-business level as we do.

4.2. Econometric Issues

4.2.1. Data and Variable Construction

Our data sources were briefly presented in section 2.2; more details are available in the appendix. In our empirical analysis we present estimates based on equation (22), with the plant as the unit of observation. One major reason why we have chosen the plant rather than the line-of-business within each firm, is that there is a significant amount of corporate restructuring going on among R&D intensive firms [17]. This makes it hard to keep track of the firms over time, while the problem is less severe for the plants which keep their identification number irrespective of the changes in ownership and the corporate structure.

To calculate the performance index (18), we have used the time-industry median values for output and each of the inputs in defining the reference plant (firm), cf. e.g. $\hat{q}_t$ and $\hat{x}_t^l$ in equation (11). That is to say, output and inputs are constructed as logarithmic deviations from the corresponding time-industry median values, and the factor shares θ_{0t}^l in (12) are also calculated as the time-industry median values.

4.2.2. Instrumental Variables, Fixed Effects and GMM

Equation (22) can not be estimated directly by OLS since the equation contains a lagged dependent variable and the error term is autoregressive [18], i.e. $\hat{e}_{it} \equiv \hat{\varepsilon}_{it} - (\rho - \nu)\hat{\varepsilon}_{it-1} + \hat{v}_{it}$. The estimation is instead carried out by instrumental variables, or more precisely by GMM.

The model is estimated in levels. As instruments for the lagged endogenous variable we use lagged values of output and employment in levels or growth rates (first differences). The preferred specification is based on growth in output and employment rather than their levels since the specification tests which we will present below indicate that the variables in levels are correlated with the error term. BLUNDELL and BOND [1995] have recently argued that growth rates can be quite powerful and attractive instruments in GMM-estimation with panel data. No instrument is used for the R&D variable, as it is assumed to be determined before the knowledge shock (and the performance shock) is revealed. As mentioned, both formal overidentification tests and estimates based on alternative instrument sets will be presented below.

---

17. GRILICHES and MAIRESSE (1984) discussed this problem with firm level data, and argued that the problem might significantly affect the estimated rate of return to R&D capital. One tends to loose many of the most successful R&D performers when constructing R&D capital stocks from past R&D expenditures, as many of the most successful R&D performers tend to restructure more often than other firms. A major benefit of the not-so-fixed effect model presented in this paper is that it only requires short panels of R&D investment. This is a useful property when we want to trace the performance of restructuring firms. KLETTE (1996) exploits and discusses this aspect of the not-so-fixed effect model.

18. See GRILICHES (1961).

As can be seen from the estimating equation (22), we are able to identify $(\rho - \nu)$ and $\gamma\nu$ which are the parameters required e.g. to calculate the rate of return to R&D investment, as we show below. If we assume constant returns to scale in knowledge production [19], i.e. $\rho = 1$, we can clearly identify γ and ν. There are some cross-coefficient restrictions that appear to provide a means for specification testing, and more efficient estimation of the parameters. However, one should notice that if the ratio between the scale elasticity and the markup (cf. ϵ/μ) changes between periods, this cross-coefficient restriction disappears.

4.3. The Potency of R&D and Persistent Performance Differences

4.3.1. Estimates from First Differences

The first results from our estimation of equation (22) can be found in table 4 [20]. For completeness, column (1) shows OLS results which for reasons explained above are biased. The instrument sets based on variables in levels, used in columns (2)-(4), are rejected in favor of instruments

TABLE 4

Dynamic performance and R&D. Eq. (22). One Year Differences, GMM-Results.

Dependent variable: $\hat{a}_{t+1}$

	(1)	(2)	(3)	(4)	(5)	(6)	(7)
$\hat{a}_t$	.6604	.8828	.9342	.9310	.8248	.8497	.8461
	(.0171)	(.0144)	(.0161)	(.0186)	(.0265)	(.0307)	(.0355)
$\hat{r}_t$	.0115	.0061	.0046	.0048	.0065	.0066	.0069
	(.0021)	(.0013)	(.0013)	(.0013)	(.0017)	(.0015)	(.0017)
$\hat{\imath}_t$	.0311	−.0043	−.0109	−.0093	−.0028	−.0075	−.0062
	(.0121)	(.0095)	(.0105)	(.0111)	(.0108)	(.0117)	(.0126)
$\hat{x}_t^C$	−.0025	−.0020	−.0015	−.0013	−.0022	−.0026	−.0028
	(.0018)	(.0009)	(.0009)	(.0010)	(.0012)	(.0012)	(.0012)
$D(R_t = 0)$	.0641	.0358	.0264	.0281	.0364	.0361	.0381
	(.0144)	(.0090)	(.0087)	(.0089)	(.0111)	(.0109)	(.0113)
Obs	9991	9991	9991	9991	9991	9991	9991
Sargan/Hansen		p=.002	p=.016	p=.059	p=.000	p=.000	p=.000
IV	OLS	$n_{t-1,2,..}$	$n_{t-2,3,..}$	$n_{t-3,4,..}$	$\Delta n_{t-1,2,..}$	$\Delta n_{t-2,3,..}$	$\Delta n_{t-3,4,..}$
		$q_{t-1,2,..}$	$q_{t-2,3,..}$	$q_{t-3,4,..}$	$\Delta q_{t-1,2,..}$	$\Delta q_{t-2,3,..}$	$\Delta q_{t-3,4,..}$

Notes: Robust standard errors in parentheses. Time, industry, age, foreign ownership and plant type dummies not reported.

---

19. Notice that this is a maintained hypothesis in the standard framework based on the perpetual inventory formula (1).
20. The estimates have been obtained by means of the GAUSS-program DPD, developed by Manuell Arellano and Steve Bond; see ARELLANO and BOND (1988).

in differences used in columns (5)-(7). The results in columns (5), (6) and (7) are quite similar and imply a depreciation rate of 15-18 percent, and a statistically highly significant, positive effect of R&D on next periods productivity [21].

In table 5 we try to explore the timing pattern of R&D by including several lags of R&D. From columns (5)-(7) it is clear that the lag structure is difficult to identify. It is not surprising that we encounter this well known problem given the persistence in R&D intensities found in section 2.2.

TABLE 5

Dynamic performance and R&D. Eq. (22).   One Year Differences, GMM-Results, Extended R&D-lags.

Dependent variable: $\hat{a}_{t+1}$

$\hat{a}_t$	.8310
	(.0267)
$\hat{r}_t$	.0023
	(.0039)
$\hat{r}_{t-1}$	.0026
	(.0059)
$\hat{r}_{t-2}$	−.0013
	(.0034)
$\hat{\imath}_t$	−.0088
	(.0123)
$\hat{X}_t^C$	.0023
	(.0012)
$D(R_t = 0)$	.0101
	(.0239)
$D(R_{t-1} = 0)$	.0140
	(.0366)
$D(R_{t-2} = 0)$	−.0012
	(.0228)
Wald test: $\hat{r}_t = \hat{r}_{t-i} = 0$	p=.156
Obs	8552
Sargan/Hansen	p=.011
IV	$\Delta n_{t-1,2,..}$
	$\Delta q_{t-1,2,..}$

Notes: Robust standard errors in parentheses. Time, industry, age, foreign ownership and plant type dummies not reported.

4.3.2. Estimates from Longer Differences: Reducing Problems with Lag Specification

To reduce the problems with the lag specification, we have estimated the model for three year productivity differences. We recognize that even though

---

21. The No-R&D dummy is positive indicating that plants with high R&D drive this result.

386

the timing issue favor longer differences, problems with sample selection pulls in the opposite direction. The survival rate is lower for the no-R&D plants as we have documented in the working paper version of this paper; going to longer differences will consequently select a less representative group of no-R&D plants compared to the group of R&D plants.

The results based on the model for three year productivity differences can be found in table 6. The OLS results can again be rejected. There are large differences in the parameter estimate for the lagged dependent variable, when we compare the estimates based on instruments in levels (cf. columns. 2 and 3) with the estimates based on instrument in growth rates (cf. columns. 4 and 5). As the differences in these parameter estimates are large relative to their standard errors, it is clear that a formal Hausman test will reject the models based on instruments in levels. Our preferred specification is thus column (4) which implies an annual depreciation rate similar to what we found using one year differences, 18 percent [22], and a highly significant, positive effect of R&D on productivity.

TABLE 6

Dynamic performance and R&D. Eq. (22). Three Year Differences, GMM-Results.

Dependent variable: $\hat{a}_{t+3}$

	(1)	(2)	(3)	(4)	(5)
$\hat{a}_t$	.4476	.7176	.7989	.5576	.6206
	(.0222)	(.0301)	(.0408)	(.0571)	(.0698)
$\ln(\sum R_t)$	.0160	.0102	.0086	.0136	.0127
	(.0031)	(.0025)	(.0025)	(.0027)	(.0027)
$\sum \hat{i}_t$	.0263	.0040	−.0044	.0112	.0070
	(.0108)	(.0099)	(.0110)	(.0111)	(.0124)
$\hat{x}_t^C$	−.0034	−.0030	−.0021	−.0046	−.0041
	(.0026)	(.0020)	(.0020)	(.0021)	(.0021)
$D(\sum R_t = 0)$	.1017	.0655	.0555	.0883	.0819
	(.0238)	(.0190)	(.0190)	(.0206)	(.0205)
Obs	7287	7287	7287	7287	7287
Sargan/Hansen		p=.018	p=.068	p=.001	p=.001
IV	OLS	$n_{t-1,2,..}$	$n_{t-2,3,..}$	$\Delta n_{t-1,2,..}$	$\Delta n_{t-2,3,..}$
		$q_{t-1,2,..}$	$q_{t-2,3,..}$	$\Delta q_{t-1,2,..}$	$\Delta q_{t-2,3,..}$

Notes: Robust standard errors in parentheses. Time, industry, age, foreign ownership and plant type dummies not reported.

22. I.e., $0.18 = 1 - (.558)^{1/3} = 1 - .82$.

4.4. Parameter Stability Over Time and Across Industries

4.4.1. Differences over Time

It has been argued that the innovative opportunities and the potency of R&D has been declining over the last 10 to 20 years; see GRILICHES [1994] for a survey of this discussion based on evidence for the US. In Norway, it is well known that a number of the large firms in the R&D intensive electronics industry in Norway faced severe problems at the end of the 1980s, after some successful years in the early 1980s. KLETTE and FØRRE [1995] found that R&D intensive firms eliminated more jobs than other firms in the late 1980s, while the opposite was true in the first half of the 1980s. It is therefore interesting to know whether the potency of R&D investments has changed over the period we consider. The results in table 7 suggests, that if anything, R&D became more potent from 1987 onwards. The negative relationship between R&D and performance in terms of job creation documented in Klette and Førre, does not carry over when we consider performance in terms of productivity. Indeed, some of the improvements in performance and productivity for R&D firms might take the form of labor saving.

TABLE 7

Dynamic performance and R&D. Eq. (22). Three Year Differences, GMM-Results, R&D effects by time period.

Dependent variable: $\hat{a}_{t+3}$

$\hat{a}_t$	.5530
	(.0571)
$\ln(\sum R_t)D(81-86)$	.0132
	(.0026)
$\ln(\sum R_t)D(87-91)$	.0157
	(.0030)
$\sum \hat{\imath}_t$	.0117
	(.0111)
$\hat{x}_t^C$	−.0047
	(.0021)
$D(\sum R_t = 0)$	.0916
	(.0206)
Obs	7287
Sargan/Hansen	p=.002
IV	$\Delta n_{t-1,2,..}$
	$\Delta q_{t-1,2,..}$

Notes: Robust standard errors in parentheses. Time, industry, age, foreign ownership and plant type dummies not reported.

4.4.2. Differences Across Industries

We have examined differences in the effect of R&D across industries. Tables 8 and 9 present our results from estimating the model industry by industry. Table 8 is based on instruments in levels, while table 9 is based on instruments in difference form. The estimated R&D coefficients are quite similar in the two sets of estimates, while the estimated coefficients on the lagged dependent variable tend to be lower when we apply instruments based on differences. For most industries, a formal Hausman test based on this coefficient will tend to reject the specification in table 8.

TABLE 8

Dynamic performance and R&D. Eq. (22). Instruments in levels. Three Year Differences, GMM-Results by Industry.

Dependent variable: $\hat{a}_{t+3}$

Industry	(1) 351-352	(2) 354-356	(3) 37	(4) 381	(5) 382	(6) 383	(7) 384-385
$\hat{a}_t$	.6391	.5726	.7396	.5000	.7958	.6532	.6981
	(.0149)	(.0355)	(.0208)	(.0493)	(.0392)	(.0271)	(.0374)
$\ln(\sum R_t)$	.0185	.0185	.0084	.0028	.0063	.0070	.0021
	(.0012)	(.0040)	(.0021)	(.0060)	(.0037)	(.0026)	(.0042)
$\sum \hat{i}_t$	.0833	−.0009	.0695	.0168	.0001	−.0052	.0423
	(.0104)	(.0055)	(.0104)	(.0106)	(.0132)	(.0106)	(.0175)
$\hat{x}_t^C$	−.0379	.0030	.0141	−.0122	.0040	−.0039	−.0025
	(.0021)	(.0028)	(.0022)	(.0037)	(.0029)	(.0035)	(.0033)
$D(\sum R_t = 0)$	.1275	.1355	.0480	.0282	.0374	.0182	.0109
	(.0123)	(.0307)	(.0159)	(.0462)	(.0303)	(.0215)	(.0312)
Obs	578	866	496	1451	1481	723	1488
Sargan/H.	p=.420	p=.390	p=.802	p=.253	p=.341	p=.296	p=.086
IV	$n_{t-1,2,..}$	$n_{t-1,2,..}$	$n_{t-1,2,..}$	$n_{t-1,2,..}$	$n_{t-1,2,..}$	$n_{t-1,2,..}$	$n_{t-1,2,..}$
	$q_{t-1,2,..}$	$q_{t-1,2,..}$	$q_{t-1,2,..}$	$q_{t-1,2,..}$	$q_{t-1,2,..}$	$q_{t-1,2,..}$	$q_{t-1,2,..}$

Notes: Robust standard errors in parentheses. Time, industry, age, foreign ownership and plant type dummies not reported.

The R&D coefficients presented in table 9 show that R&D investment is most important for performance in "Industrial chemicals and Pharmaceuticals" (ISIC 351-2) and "Plastic and petroleum products" (ISIC 354-6), while somewhat lower in the other industries. There are also significant differences in the depreciation rate of knowledge capital; cf. the coefficient on the lagged dependent variable. We find the lowest depreciation rate in "Metals" (ISIC 37) and the highest depreciation rate in "Plastic and petroleum products" (ISIC 354-6).

TABLE 9

Dynamic performance and R&D. Eq. (22). Instruments in differences. Three Year Differences, GMM-Results by Industry.

Dependent variable: $\hat{a}_{t+3}$

Industry	(1) 351-352	(2) 354-356	(3) 37	(4) 381	(5) 382	(6) 383	(7) 384-385
$\hat{a}_t$	.4700	.2996	.8450	.4427	.7607	.7122	.4443
	(.0129)	(.0296)	(.0313)	(.0511)	(.0489)	(.0323)	(.0509)
$\ln(\sum R_t)$	.0178	.0148	.0075	.0062	.0067	.0039	.0080
	(.0013)	(.0034)	(.0021)	(.0061)	(.0046)	(.0025)	(.0046)
$\sum \hat{i}_t$	.1186	.0096	.0711	.0189	−.0045	.0070	.0521
	(.0107)	(.0073)	(.0056)	(.0106)	(.0143)	(.0112)	(.0196)
$\hat{x}_t^C$	−.0382	−.0047	.0138	−.0128	.0031	−.0008	−.0064
	(.0016)	(.0027)	(.0029)	(.0039)	(.0037)	(.0041)	(.0040)
$D(\sum R_t = 0)$	.1317	.0984	.0510	.0526	.0308	.0007	.0510
	(.0128)	(.0262)	(.0131)	(.0463)	(.0371)	(.0219)	(.0332)
Obs	578	866	496	1451	1481	723	1488
Sargan/H.	p=.224	p=.161	p=.720	p=.599	p=.510	p=.347	p=.896
IV	$\Delta n_{t-1,2,..}$ $\Delta q_{t-1,2,..}$	$\Delta n_{t-1,2,..}$ $\Delta q_{t-1,2,..}$	$\Delta n_{t-1,2,..}$ $\Delta q_{t-1,2,..}$	$\Delta n_{t-1,2,..}$ $\Delta q_{t-1,2,..}$	$\Delta n_{t-1,2,..}$ $\Delta q_{t-1,2,..}$	$\Delta n_{t-1,2,..}$ $\Delta q_{t-1,2,..}$	$\Delta n_{t-1,2,..}$ $\Delta q_{t-1,2,..}$

Notes: Robust standard errors in parentheses. Time, industry, age, foreign ownership and plant type dummies not reported.

4.5. Rates of Return to R&D Investments

In this section, we will illustrate how equation (10) and the estimated coefficients can be used to estimate the rate of return to R&D investments. Rearranging terms in (10), we find that

$$\beta = \frac{w_{t-1}R_{t-1}}{\nu\gamma S_t + (\rho - \nu)w_t R_t}$$

or since $\beta = 1/(1+r)$:

$$(23) \qquad r = \frac{\nu\gamma S_t + (\rho - \nu)w_t R_t}{w_{t-1}R_{t-1}} - 1$$

Using the parameter estimates presented above and the summary statistics in table 10, we can calculate the right hand side of this expression and thereby estimate the rates of return to R&D investments. The discount factor β in equation (10) reflects the required rate of return to R&D investments, and corresponds therefore to an *ex-ante* rate of return. However, the variables dated t in equations (10) and (23) refer to the expected values at time $t-1$ (or more generally, at the time when the R&D investment decision for period $t-1$ is made). Since we use realized rather than expected values in our estimates of the rate of return, it is more correct to consider this rate of return as an *ex-post* rate.

TABLE 10

Summary Statistics.

Variable	Sample	Obs.	Mean	Median	S.Dev.
$\hat{a}_t$	All	11343	−0.050	−0.055	0.183
	R&D plants	4316	−0.026	−0.038	0.178
	No R&D plants	7027	−0.066	−0.066	0.185
i_t	All	11343	0.059	0.019	0.140
	R&D plants	4316	0.055	0.026	0.120
	No R&D plants	7027	0.061	0.014	0.150
$\hat{x}_t^C$	All	11326	9.557	9.502	1.793
	R&D plants	4316	10.586	10.530	1.706
	No R&D plants	7010	8.924	9.061	1.533
Employment	All	11343	108	48	189
	R&D plants	4316	185	93	269
	No R&D plants	7027	61	36	86
$\hat{r}_t$	R&D plants	4316	4.261	5.606	4.001
$w_t R_t / S_t$	R&D plants *	1609	0.126	0.038	0.982
$w_t R_t / w_{t-1} R_{t-1}$	R&D plants *	1187	1.248	1.094	1.310

Notes: * Observations at line of business level.

As we noticed in figure 1, the distribution of R&D intensities across plants is highly skewed. We therefore calculate rates of return for mean and median values of the R&D intensities as presented in the summary statistics in table 10. The resulting rates of return are given in table 11.

TABLE 11

Rates of Return to R&D investments.

	All Industries		Returns by Industry						
	(1)	(2)	(3) 351-352	(4) 354-356	(5) 37	(6) 381	(7) 382	(8) 383	(9) 384-385
Mean value	9%	11%	8%	4%	23%	0%	19%	15%	2%
Median value	9%	6%	7%	−3%	11%	−8%	7%	2%	−5%

In the first column we use the estimate of the structural parameters in table 4, column (6). For a plant with the mean R&D intensity and mean R&D growth our results imply a rate of return of 9 percent. For median values of R&D intensity and R&D growth the return is also 9 percent.

In the next column we use the estimate of the structural parameters in table 6, column (4). For a plant with the mean R&D intensity and mean R&D growth our results imply an annual rate of return of 11 percent. For median values of R&D intensity and R&D growth the return is 6 percent. We also give results for each industry using the structural parameters from table 9.

Considering the estimated private rates of return in table 11, they are quite low compared to estimates based on the standard model; see GRILICHES [1994, 1995]. The rates of return in table 11 are much closer to normal rates of return e.g. on physical investment [23] than the estimates that Griliches refers to. Taking the estimates in table 11 at face value, they e.g. suggest significantly smaller imperfection in the capital market than previous estimates.

In table 3, we have presented estimates for the rate of return to R&D investments based on the standard model. We can use these estimates to make a more clear cut comparison of the rate of return derived from the standard framework to the estimates based on our alternative specification. The results in columns 4-6 in table 3 are *a priori* most comparable to those we have presented in table 11 [24]. We must recognize that the rates of return in table 3 are *gross* rates and should be adjusted for depreciation to be comparable to the results in table 11. Considering the rates of return for the mean output-R&D capital ratio in columns 4 and 5 in table 3, the estimates are much higher than the estimates in table 11. This is true even if we subtract a 15 percent depreciation rate from the estimates in table 3 (i.e. the depreciation rate used to construct the R&D capital stocks). It is, however, evident that the rates of return to R&D investment presented in table 3 are not very robust and that allowing for fixed effects in the estimation (as in columns 3, 6, 7 and 8) has a very dramatic effect on the rates of return. This is to a large extent also true for the estimates in table 11 based on our alternative specification. The lack of robust estimates of rates of return to R&D has been observed in a number of similar studies; see the survey by MAIRESSE and SASSENOU [1991].

A striking pattern in table 11 is the large differences in the rates of return between industries. Since these are *ex-post* rates of return, this variation might reflect a substantial amount of randomness in the innovation process, that we also emphasized above. Similarly, the mean rate of return to R&D investment is much higher than the estimates for the median line of business. This suggests a distribution of rates of return skewed to the right. That is to say, a low fraction of firms experience rates of return to R&D that are sufficiently high to pull the average rate of return substantially above the median. This result is related to SCHANKERMAN and PAKES [1986] who also found that the value of innovations, measured by the value of patents, is highly skewed with a few very profitable innovations and a large fraction that are close to worthless. Clearly, the variations in our estimated rates of return to R&D investment could also reflect a problem with our framework.

Before we pull the interpretation of our estimates too far we should point out a caveat that our model shares with the standard framework. It is clear from equation (23) that a firm with sufficiently low R&D investment (cf. the denominator) relative to its sales, will have a high rate of return to its R&D (even if its planned R&D investment in the next period is zero). A

---

23. The rate of return on physical capital investment has been estimated to around 7 percent for the Norwegian economy.
24. Since both are based on gross output rather than value added.

similar problem is present in the standard model where the rate of return to R&D capital is estimated as proportional to the ratio of sales to R&D capital; a firm with little R&D capital, i.e. little past R&D investment will therefore have a high rate of return and vice versa. We find this implication of the model puzzling and it might reveal a problem with the log-linear specification where the marginal product of knowledge capital is proportional to the average product of knowledge capital. Alternatively, a respecification of the knowledge production function as suggested in section 2.1.1 (and footnote 13) might reduce the problem. This issue deserves further analysis before too much is made out of estimated rates of return to R&D investment.

5 Conclusions

The point of departure for our analysis are some well known observations on the empirical patterns of R&D investment and productivity: First, there are substantial cross sectional differences in R&D activity within narrow industries, and these cross sectional differences tend to be quite persistent over time. Second, there are quite strong cross sectional correlations between R&D and productivity, while the longitudinal correlations are much weaker. We have argued that the first observation questions the validity of the standard framework for R&D productivity studies that treat the accumulation of knowledge capital as identical to the accumulation of physical capital (based on the perpetual inventory model). We also argued that the empirical pattern of R&D investment can be better accommodated by a simple, alternative accumulation process for R&D capital that allows for a positive complementarity between already acquired knowledge and current R&D in the generation of new knowledge [25].

The second step in our analysis shows how this alternative specification of knowledge accumulation leads to a simple, structural and dynamic econometric model, where next year's performance (roughly speaking, productivity) depends on current performance and current R&D activity. We have estimated this model on a new data set, where plant level production data have been linked with R&D data broken down by product line within each firm. Our empirical framework merges the cross sectional and the longitudinal patterns identified in the second observation mentioned above, and permits a structural interpretation of the estimated coefficients. We find that the appropriable part of R&D capital depreciates quite rapidly, with an

---

25. We have shown that intertemporal complementarity in R&D can rationalize the observed persistency in R&D. However, persistency in R&D does not necessarily imply persistency in innovations. Indeed, Geroski, Van Reenen and Walters (1996) have shown, on the basis of innovation data for UK, that there is little persistence in *large* innovations. There might be a high degree of persistence in smaller innovations, while the persistence in major breakthroughs and innovations is low.

estimated annual depreciation rate around 18 percent on average. We should point out that this high rate of depreciation of the appropriable part of R&D capital suggests significant spillover effects according to our model. Our estimates also show that R&D investment has a significant effect on firm (or plant) performance, but the estimated private rates of return to R&D investment is substantially lower than the rates of return found in many of the studies surveyed by GRILICHES [1995]. However, we point out a puzzle or problem with our estimates of the rate of return to R&D investment that we have not managed to resolve. That is, the rate of return to R&D investment is estimated to be very high for firms that invest very little in R&D relative to their sales. This implication of the model is due to the assumption of diminishing returns to knowledge capital for all values of this capital, an assumption or property that our alternative specification shares with the standard framework.

The estimated model did not incorporate the R&D investment equation. An obvious extension of the empirical analysis presented in this paper will be to estimate the R&D investment equation (equation 9 or 10) jointly with the not-so-fixed effect model (equation 22).

APPENDIX

• Data sources

Our empirical analysis uses merged data from the Manufacturing Statistics and R&D surveys. The Manufacturing Statistics of Statistics Norway is an annual census of all plants in the Norwegian manufacturing industry. See HALVORSEN et al. [1991] for documentation. From this source we use information on outputs and other inputs than R&D. The unit of observation in the analysis is the plant, so to each plant we merge the R&D expenditures at the line of business level within each firm.

Information about R&D expenses at the line of business level of each firm is obtained from R&D surveys for the years 1982, -83, -84, -85, -87, -89 and -91. This survey was carried out by the Norwegian Research Council for Science and Technology (NTNF) until 1989 and by Statistics Norway in 1991. See SKORGE et al. [1996] for definitions and industry level figures.

• Sample construction

Our analysis covers the period 1980-92 and the following industries: "Chemicals" (ISIC 35) [26], "Basic metals" (ISIC 37) and "Metal products" (ISIC 38). These industries account for almost all R&D in Norwegian manufacturing [27].

Since the coverage of the R&D survey is quite low for firms with less than 20 employees, our analysis covers only plants that belong to firms with at least 20 employees in at least one year in the sample period. Note that the analysis also includes plants which report no R&D. Since we use lagged variables as instruments when estimating the model, we limit the analysis to plants where we have at least four consecutive years of observations.

• Variable construction

Output is measured as the value of gross production corrected for taxes and subsidies. Inputs are labor (man hours), materials including energy, rentals and fire insurance value of capital. Constructing our performance index, all nominal variables are deflated using industry level deflators from Norwegian national accounts.

In addition to investments, each plant reports the fire insurance values and rental costs for machinery and buildings. We have constructed a simple filter to eliminate some of the noise that is known to exist in the fire insurance values. The capital values have been transformed to rental costs by a

---

26. We have not included "Petroleum refining" (ISIC 353) in our analysis, as it is a sector with a very low R&D intensity (in Norway).

27. In 1991, these industries accounted for 91 per cent of total R&D expenditures in manufacturing.

standard user cost formula, to account for the differences in depreciation between buildings and machinery and to make it possible to sum these costs together with the reported rental costs of capital. The final measure of capital for year t is the mean of capital values at the end of years $t-2$, $t-1$, and t

The R&D variable includes all intramural and extramural R&D expenditures. The R&D expenditures are deflated with a wage deflator. To avoid double counting of the R&D inputs, we have pulled out R&D labor from the man hours before constructing the performance measure. Finally for the three years without a R&D survey, we interpolate R&D expenses plant by plant.

● References

ADAMS, J., JAFFE, A. (1996). – "Bounding the Effects of R&D: An Investigation Using Matched Establishment-Firm Data", *RAND Journal of Economics*, 27, pp. 700-721.

ARELLANO, M., BOND, S. (1988). – "Dynamic Panel Data Estimation Using DPD - A Guide for Users", Institute for Fiscal Studies, *Working Paper 88/15*, London.

BAILEY, M., HULTEN, C., CAMPBELL, D. (1992). – "Productivity Dynamics in Manufacturing Plants", *Brookings Paper on Economic Activity, Microeconomics*, pp. 187-268.

BLUNDELL, R., BOND, S. (1995). – "Initial Conditions and Moment Restrictions in Dynamic Panel Data Models", *Working Paper no. 95/17*, Institute of Fiscal Studies.

BOUND, J., CUMMINS, C., GRILICHES, Z., Hall, B. H., Jaffe, A. (1984). – "Who does R&D and Who Patents?", In Z. Griliches (ed.), *R&D, Patents and Productivity*, Chicago: Chicago University Press.

COHEN, W. M., KLEPPER, S. (1992). – "The Anatomy of Industry R&D Intensity Distributions", *American Economic Review*, 82, pp. 773-99.

GEROSKI, P., VAN REENEN, J., WALTERS, C. F. (1996). – "How Persistently do Firms Innovate?", *CEPR Discussion Paper no. 1433*.

GRILICHES, Z. (1961). – "A Note on Serial Correlation Bias in Estimates of Distributed Lags", *Econometrica*, 29, pp. 65-73.

GRILICHES, Z. (1979). – "Issues in Assessing the Contribution of Research and Development to Productivity Growth", *Bell Journal of Economics*, 10, pp. 92-116.

GRILICHES, Z. (1988). – "Productivity Puzzles and R&D: Another Nonexplanation", *Journal of Economic Perspectives*, 2, pp. 9-21.

GRILICHES, Z. (1994). – "Productivity, R&D, and the Data Constraint", *American Economic Review*, 84, pp. 1-23.

GRILICHES, Z. (1995). – "R&D and Productivity: Econometric Results and Measurement Issues", In P. Stoneman (ed.), *Handbook of the Economics of Innovation and Technical Change*, Oxford: Blackwell.

GRILICHES, Z., MAIRESSE, J. (1984). – "Productivity and R&D at the Firm Level", In Z. Griliches (ed.), *R&D, Patents and Productivity*, Chicago: Chicago University Press.

HALL, B. H., HAYASHI, F. (1989). – "Research and Development as an Investment", *NBER Working paper no. 2973*.

HALL, B. H., MAIRESSE, J. (1995). – "Exploring the Relationship Between R&D and Productivity in French Manufacturing Firms", *Journal of Econometrics*, 65, pp. 263-94.

396

Jones, R. (1995). – "Models of R&D and Endogenous Growth", *Journal of Political Economy*, 103, pp. 759-784.

Klette, T. J. (1994a). – "Simultaneous Estimation of Price-Cost Margins and Scale Economies from a Panel of Microdata", *Discussion Papers no. 130*, Statistics Norway.

Klette, T. J. (1994b). – "R&D, Spillovers and Performance among Heterogeneous Firms. An Empirical Study Using Microdata", *Discussion Papers no. 133*, Statistics Norway.

Klette, T. J. (1996). – "R&D, Scope Economies and Plant Performance", *RAND Journal of Economics*, 27, pp. 502-522.

Klette, T. J., Førre, S. E. (1995). – "Innovation and Job Creation in a Small Open Economy: Evidence from Norwegian Manufacturing Plants 1982-92", *Discussion Papers 159*, Statistics Norway. (Forthcoming in The Economics of Innovation and New Technology).

Klette, T. J., Griliches, Z. (1996). – "The Inconsistency of Common Scale Estimators when Output Prices are Unobserved and Endogenous", *Journal of Applied Econometrics*, 11, pp. 343-361.

Mairesse, J., Sassenou, M. (1991). – "R&D and Productivity: A Survey of Econometric Studies at the Firm Level", *STI Review no. 8*, Paris: OECD.

Milgrom, Qian, P. Y., Roberts, J. (1991). – "Complementarities, Momentum, and the Evolution of Modern Manufacturing", *American Economic Review, Papers and Proceddings*, 81, pp. 84-88.

Nelson, R. R. (1988). – "Modelling the Connections in the Cross Section between Technical Progress and R&D Intensity", *RAND Journal of Economics*, 19, pp. 478-85.

Pakes, A., Ericson, N. (1989). – "Empirical Implications of Alternative Models of Firm Dynamics", *NBER Working paper no. 2893*.

Pakes, A., Schankerman, M. (1984). – "An Exploration into the Determinants of Research Intensity", In Z. Griliches (ed.), *R&D, Patents and Productivity*, Chicago University Press (Chicago).

Penrose, E. T. (1959). – *The Theory of the Growth of the Firm*, Basil Blackwell (Oxford).

Romer, P. M. (1990). – "Endogenous Technological Change", *Journal of Political Economy*, 98, pp. 71-102.

Schankerman, M., Pakes, A. (1986). – "Estimates of the Value of Patent Rights in European Countries During the Post-1950 Period", *Economic Journal*, 96, pp. 1052-76.

Shen, T. Y. (1970). – "Economies of Scale, Penrose Effect, Growth of Plants and their Size Distribution", *Journal of Political Economy*, 78, pp. 702-16.

Skorge, O., Foyn, F., Frengen, G. (1996). – *Reasearch and Development in Norwegian Manufacturing Industry 1993*. Reports 96/14. (In Norwegian). Statistics Norway (Oslo).

Stokey, N. L., Lucas, R. E., with Prescott, E. (1989). – "Recursive Methods in Economic Dynamics", *Harvard University Press*, (Cambridge, U.S.).

Uzawa, H. (1969). – "Time Preference and the Penrose Effect in a Two-Class Model of Economic Growth", *Journal of Political Economy*, 77, pp. 628-52.

Are There Financing Constraints for R&D and Investment in German Manufacturing Firms?

Dietmar HARHOFF *

ABSTRACT. – Using a newly constructed panel dataset of German enterprises, I estimate R&D and capital investment equations for the time period from 1990 to 1994. Simple accelerator specifications indicate considerable sensitivity of R&D and investment to cash flow for relatively small firms. Much of this effect vanishes once error-correcting behavior is taken into account, but a significant positive relationship between cash flow and investment remains for relatively small firms. In the case of R&D, weak but significant cash flow effects persist both for small and large firms. The evidence from Euler equation estimates is not conclusive. The investment Euler equation for large firms appears to perform relatively well and yields results close to those expected under the null hypothesis of no financing constraints. The estimates from the Euler equation for R&D are not informative. Additional evidence from survey data suggests that the cash flow sensitivity of investment in small firms is likely to reflect financing constraints.

---

* D. HARHOFF: ZEW, University of Mannheim, CEPR. This research has been supported by grants from the German Research Council (DFG) and the ZEW. I would like to thank conference and seminar audiences in Bonn, Strasbourg, Konstanz, Mannheim, at the NBER Summer Institute, the Wissenschaftszentrum Berlin, the EEA meeting in Istanbul, and a DFG workshop in Heidelberg for helpful comments. I am grateful to Wesley Cohen, Christian Dustmann, Zvi Griliches, Martin Hellwig, Bronwyn Hall, Olaf Hübler, Tor Jacob Klette, Jan Pieter Krahnen, Dennis Mueller, Ishaq Nadiri, Manfred Neumann, and Lars-Hendrik Röller for their helpful suggestions. Steve Bond and John Van Reenen were particularly supportive in discussing this work. I also acknowledge insightful and detailed comments made by two anonymous referees and the editor, Francois Laisney. The construction of the database has been competently performed and supported by Christiane Bühler, Marc Dehoust, Andreas Fier, Urs Finger, Lydia Irrgang, Oliver Schmale, and Julia Wienbeck. All remaining errors are my responsibility.

D. Encaoua et al. (eds.), The Economics and Econometrics of Innovation, 399–434.
© 2000 *Kluwer Academic Publishers. Printed in the Netherlands.*

1 Introduction

This paper is concerned with an aspect of firm behavior that has only recently reemerged as a central problem in corporate finance and industrial organization - the potential existence of financing constraints and their implications for investment and innovation at the firm and the aggregate level. As early as in the Sixties, a number of researchers (e.g., MEYER and KUH [1957], DUESENBERRY [1958], MEYER and GLAUBER [1964]) had proposed informal theories of liquidity and investment and had tried to test these models empirically. But the notion of financing constraints did not receive major support among economists until highly influential papers by JAFFEE and RUSSELL [1976], KEETON [1979], and STIGLITZ and WEISS [1981] pointed to possible equilibrium credit rationing by lenders. The key assumption driving the results of these papers concerns asymmetric information between borrower and lender. Papers by MYERS and MAJLUFF [1984] and MYERS [1977, 1984] also suggested a causal relationship between asymmetric information and the firm's preference for internal finance.

The paper by FAZZARI, HUBBARD, and PETERSEN [1988] has been the first empirical study explicitly building on these theoretical contributions. Since then, there has been a large number of empirical investigations in this field, mostly focusing on financing constraints for capital investment. The overall picture is still clouded by difficult econometric and conceptual problems. In a recent debate, some doubts have been expressed that the cash flow effects detected by these studies can be interpreted as evidence of financing constraints (KAPLAN and ZINGALES 1997). In any case, it has been difficult to quantify the extent of these constraints precisely, or to assess their interaction with the institutional framework, e.g. the role of intermediaries in general and of banks in particular. Therefore it is still difficult to gauge the overall economic implications of financing constraints in a reliable manner.

Investment in capital goods may not be the only firm activity where financing constraints can be of importance. Actually, since investments in intangible assets (like know-how or consumer goodwill) are presumably more risky and provide less collateral to lenders than capital goods do, liquidity effects might be even more pronounced for these activities. GRABOWSKI [1968] provided some early cross-sectional support for this view, while MUELLER [1967] and HAMBURG [1966] did not find such an effect. In more recent work, BERNSTEIN and NADIRI [1986], HALL [1992], HAO and JAFFE [1993], HIMMELBERG and PETERSEN [1994], and KATHURIA and MUELLER [1995] have produced evidence that liquidity effects may also be at work in determining R&D activities. But the evidence on this point is still very tentative and warrants further attention, given that R&D is already subject to a number of externalities which may lead to under-investment in a market economy.

Due to data constraints, the empirical evidence for Germany has been particularly scarce. A few studies have analyzed the financing aspects of capital investment in Germany (ELSTON [1995], ELSTON and ALBACH [1994],

400

AUDRETSCH and ELSTON [1994]). These investigations have been based on the *Bonn Database* which contains comprehensive data on publicly traded German enterprises. These studies have pointed to the existence of cash flow effects for the investment activities of even the largest enterprises, but have so far excluded the firm's innovation activities. Moreover, only the investment behavior of publicly traded firms has been analyzed so far. This may not be a serious problem in the United States where a relatively large number of small and medium-sized firms have access to equities markets. It is definitely a concern in Germany where access to the stock market is tight and market capitalization is relatively low. The prominent role that small and medium-sized firms have in the German economy makes a study of their investment and R&D behavior an appealing exercise.

The purpose of this paper is to provide an analysis of the relationship between finance and investment behavior using a new dataset describing the R&D and investment decisions of German firms, including independent medium-sized enterprises whose shares are not traded in the stock market. In the first part of the empirical exercise, I estimate accelerator and error-correction models for investment and R&D. The cash flow effects obtained from these regressions cannot be interpreted without ambiguity. In particular, cash flow may also be correlated with investment opportunities [1]. It is nonetheless instructive to study the variation of these coefficients across firms of different size. Below I present results which suggest that the investment policies of smaller firms are indeed more sensitive to cash flow variations than those of relatively large firms. In order to test whether these results from accelerator and error-correction models point to the existence of financial constraints, I also derive and implement structural Euler equation models for investment and R&D, but the estimation results are unfortunately not satisfactory. However, additional evidence from other data sources suggests that the size-contingent cash-flow effects actually mirror financing constraints at the firm level.

The paper proceeds as follows. Theoretical aspects and some previous empirical results will be summarized briefly in section 2. In section 3, I describe the data used in this study and central descriptive statistics. Three econometric specifications are discussed briefly in section 4, and estimation results are presented in section 5. The central results are based on accelerator and error-correction specifications, but I also derive and estimate Euler equations for R&D and investment. The final section summarizes the results and concludes with a number of suggestions for further work.

---

1. The interpretation of cash flow as an indicator of investment opportunities is not the only source of ambiguity. As JENSEN [1985] has argued, managers may have incentives to let firms grow beyond optimal size. Cash flow in excess of what is needed to fund the optimal level of investment will then not be turned over to share-holders, but managers will invest at below the cost of capital. In such a case, externally imposed financing constraints may actually have positive implications in that they prevent management from making such investments. The Jensen hypothesis is clearly a serious contender in interpreting what the implications of financing constraints will be. But the paper presented here will - for now - merely attempt to explore whether there is reason to believe that such constraints exist.

2 Theoretical Aspects and Previous Studies

2.1. Asymmetric Information, Credit Rationing and Financing Hierarchies

Credit markets are different from standard commodity markets in that the lender delivers a loan on the borrower's promise to pay back the loan and interest. The lender's evaluation of the borrower's capability to pay back is crucial for the lending decision [2]. Equilibrium quantity rationing thus emerges endogenously due to asymmetric information (the lender knows less about the borrower than the borrower herself) and incompleteness of contracts (contractual agreements to control all aspects of borrower behavior are infeasible). In the case of rationing, the lender will decide not to grant a loan to the borrower, even if the borrower offers a higher interest rate than is observed in the market for loans. Thus, the supply of loans does not equate the demand at the market interest rate.

The underlying logic for all credit rationing phenomena are the self-selection and incentive effects imposed by interest rates. Adverse selection occurs, since the average quality of borrowers will be a decreasing function of the interest rate charged by the lender. Moreover, as the interest rate increases the borrower will be tempted to undertake riskier projects unless the loan is fully collateralized. In this context, there may exist an interest rate that maximizes the lender's profit although supply does not equal demand. Either some lenders are not able to obtain any loan, or the loan size will be below the one demanded by the borrower (BESTER and HELLWIG [1987]).

Asymmetric information may also lead managers not to issue new equity. In an influential paper, MYERS and MAJLUF [1984] analyze the effect of asymmetric information if managers have privileged knowledge about the true value of investment projects and the firm's other assets while investors (or lenders) only know the joint distribution of these values until the ex ante random characteristics of the projects are revealed. Managers are assumed to act on behalf of existing shareholders. Managers will issue new shares only if this is not to the disadvantage of existing stockholders, *i.e.* if the market's evaluation of the new stock is above the respective value for the existing stockholders. Thus, managers will only issue shares for investments with less than expected value. Consequently, issuing shares will be seen by the new investors as a bad signal. Hence, the firm will not issue new shares even if the projects have positive net present value. Thus, financing constraints have negative welfare effects in this model [3].

---

2. For surveys, see CLEMENZ [1986], BALTENSPERGER and DEVINNEY [1985], and BESTER and HELLWIG [1987].
3. Variations of the fundamental theme of the Myers/Majluf paper have been developed in large numbers, but the basic idea is the same in these extensions. For example, KRASKER [1986], BESANKO and THAKOR [1987], THAKOR [1993].

The conclusions that can be derived from the Myers/Majluf and other models are quite strong. Given that management acts in the interest of existing shareholders, firms will prefer internal finance over debt financing, and debt financing over the issuance of new shares. Furthermore, issuing new shares will typically lead to a decline in the stock price. Both predictions have found some empirical support[4]. As a result of some of these arguments, MYERS and MAJLUF [1984], *inter alia*, have postulated a financial "pecking order" model which deviates considerably from either the static equity-debt tradeoff model or the ranking of capital costs suggested by AUERBACH [1983]. Once slack resources are exhausted, the firm will have to borrow to satisfy its capital needs. The most expensive type of capital will be new equity. In some cases, the firm will rather forego an investment opportunity than to issue debt. Positive shocks to cash flow will lead to more investment in such a situation. Note that in the pecking order model, there is no well-defined optimal capital structure as it exists in the static Modigliani-Miller model with taxation. The model developed by Myers and Majluf does not directly relate long-term capital structure, but the availability of slack resources to investment spending. Indirectly, though, the model suggests a motive for precautionary corporate saving ("cash stock-piling").

In another paper, MYERS [1977] also comments on the relationship between capital structure and the nature of the firm's projects. Suppose that the true value of the firm is given by the value of its assets in place and the value of future investment opportunities. The extent to which the latter can be exploited depends on discretionary spending by the firm's management. In essence these opportunities represent call options. Suppose that the firm issues risky debt to finance such an investment opportunity. The existence of risky debt introduces a wedge between the firm's marginal value and the marginal value of equity. On average, this will lead to underinvestment. The stock market's evaluation of the prospective behavior of the shareholders will lead to an ex ante reduction of the value of the firm. Moreover, lending may be rationed in this context. To rational lenders and equity owners the value of a firm with relatively important growth opportunities will decline with leverage. Myers concludes that the more the firm's value is determined by future investment opportunities relative to assets in place, the more it will favor equity financing in order to avoid the underinvestment effect. In empirical terms, this theory suggests that innovative firms with few assets already in place (say small companies with a promising new product, but no established products) should be mostly equity-financed. It is beyond the scope of this paper to test this theory thoroughly, but it is an interesting question to be pursued in future work.

2.2. Different Types of Investment: Capital Goods versus Know-How

It is by now generally acknowledged that externalities in the form of

---

4. See the review of empirical evidence in THAKOR [1993, p. 461].

information or knowledge "spillovers" play a potentially important role in shaping the incentives for research and development activities (R&D) of private firms. Much less is known about the potential effects of financing constraints on innovation. Can liquidity constraints - if they exist–be particularly important for investments in research and development (R&D) or innovation projects? The literature lists a number of reasons why investment in physical capital and investment in knowledge capital should be affected differently by financing constraints, and why obtaining external finance for innovation and R&D projects may be more costly than obtaining such funding for capital investment. At the same time, fundamental technological differences with respect to the adjustment costs of investment and R&D may work against pronounced sensitivity of R&D spending to *transitory* shocks in cash flow.

As HALL [1992] points out, contrary to most capital investment goods (plant, property, and equipment), R&D results such as a new prototype or a design cannot be used easily as collateral. The investment share of R&D expenditures is on the order of ten per cent of total R&D expenditures, and most inputs to the innovation process are likely to be firm-specific or specific to the new product or process to be developed. Thus, an external financier cannot expect to recover a significant share of her funds if it is used to finance an unsuccessfull innovation project.

Second, for obvious reasons firms are unlikely to reveal content and objectives of their R&D efforts, since this knowledge may leak out to competitors [5]. Strategic considerations of this kind will tend to maintain and reinforce informational asymmetries. But even without secrecy undermining the incentives to share information about R&D projects, the evaluation of long-term risky projects by external financiers may be more costly than the assessment of more short-term oriented ones. Thus, if providers of finance face greater uncertainty with respect to R&D than to investment projects, they will require a higher lemon's premium for the former type of investment. Hence, even without rationing behavior on behalf of banks and other financial institutions, there will be a premium to be paid for obtaining external funding. This is of course the classical argument that leads MYERS and MAJLUFF [1984] to postulating a financial hierarchy in which internal funds are the cheapest source of capital.

While the above arguments may suggest that R&D will be more susceptible to cash flow variations, there are other considerations that work in the opposite direction. It is likely that the R&D process cannot be delayed or accelerated to the extent to which this may be possible for capital investment. Scientists cannot be fired and rehired without substantial loss of human capital to the firm (and potential gains to competitors), and due to their high degree of specialization, resources employed in R&D cannot simply be used in production (or vice versa). Thus, adjustment costs are likely to be higher for R&D than for investment. We would expect to

---

5. See MANSFIELD [1985] for some evidence on the speed of information dissemination. Theoretical models of knowledge dissemination are presented by BHATTACHARYA and RITTER [1985] and BHATTACHARYA and CHIESA [1994].

see relatively high persistence in R&D data – an expectation that is indeed born out by the empirical evidence (e.g., LACH and SCHANKERMAN [1989]). Moreover, this effect will actually dampen the long-term response of R&D to cash flow variation.

However, the extent of adjustment costs may well be a function of the type of projects undertaken – and thus a choice variable for firm managers. If a firm anticipates that its cash flow may be highly fluctuating and that external finance will not be available to fund R&D projects, then the respective R&D budget may favor projects that have a relatively short duration or are relatively flexible in terms of adjustment opportunities. One branch of the theoretical literature has considered the effect of different project duration for investor response and managerial choices. SHLEIFER and VISHNY [1990] show that if long-term projects stay mis-priced for a longer period than projects with short duration, then managers may select short-term projects. THAKOR [1993] distinguishes between "late bloomer" projects (high payoff in the more distant future) and "early winners" (projects with lower returns in the near future). If managers care about existing stockholders, then the stock price reaction to an equity issue for a "late bloomer" project will be negative while it might be positive for the other type of project. R&D projects are – when compared to investment projects – such late bloomers (THAKOR [1993]). But R&D itself may be heterogeneous, and managers may be able to choose short-term R&D projects over ultimately more profitable long-term ones if financing constraints are anticipated. A sequence of short-term projects can be adjusted far more easier than long-term projects which cannot be accelerated or slowed down without some penalty.

As mentioned before, there are only few studies to date that have analyzed the potential impact of financing constraints on the firm's innovation policy. HALL [1992] finds that the elasticity of investment and R&D with respect to cash flow is positive and significant in a large sample of U.S. manufacturing firms. Interestingly, the results suggest that the effect on investment is stronger than the effect on R&D. She computes long-term cash flow elasticity values of 0.46 for investment and 0.28 for R&D spending. HIMMELBERG and PETERSEN [1994] present an investigation of the effect of financing constraints on relatively small U.S. firms in high-technology industries. The elasticities (at the sample mean) implied by their estimates are noteworthy: in the case of investment, HIMMELBERG and PETERSEN calculate a cash flow elasticity of 0.83. For R&D, the elasticity is on the order of 0.36. Investment in these companies appears to react to transitory movements in cash flow, while R&D expenditures are being smoothed according to the permanent component of cash flow. Himmelberg and Petersen argue that firms face relatively large adjustment costs in their R&D activities and cannot adjust the intensity of these efforts to short-term liquidity shocks. As argued before, these results are subject to the critique that cash flow effects cannot be interpreted unambiguously as indicators of financial constraints.

2.3. Firm Size and Financing Opportunities

Firm size plays a central role in this study. I argue in this paper that small firms are more likely to be characterized by excess sensitivity to the availability of internal finance [6]. First, smaller firms will be characterized by idiosyncratic risk which would raise the cost of external capital. In addition, a randomly chosen group of small firms will include a relatively large number of young firms, hence outside investors may not yet have sufficient information to distinguish good from bad performers. Second, these firms may also have more limited access to external financial markets, in particular in Germany where entry into the stock market by young or small firms has been a rare event. Third, these firms have less collateral (in terms of existing assets) which could be used for obtaining external loans. Moreover, smaller firms may employ more flexibly adjustable R&D and investment processes than large firms do. Thus, the response to liquidity effects should be faster, i.e. the respective processes should display less persistence, even after accounting for presumably larger fluctuations in sales or other determinants of investment.

While there is a considerable number of studies looking at the relationship between investment, finance and firm size [7] only very little evidence is available on the impact of firm size on the finance-R&D relationship. HAO and JAFFE [1993] find evidence that small firms' R&D expenditures react more strongly to measures of cash flow or working capital than R&D performed by larger enterprises. However, they do not compare R&D and investment behavior, and their empirical test does not take adjustment processes into account. WINKER [1996] uses managerial survey responses as indicators of financial constraints. He finds that managers are more likely to indicate that their firms are financially constrained if the respective firm is small, and if demand expectations are *positive*. In regressions using investment and innovation expenditures as the dependent variables, the financial constraints variables yield a significant negative effect.

3 Data Source and Descriptive Statistics

3.1. Data Sources and Data Collection

Data on R&D expenditures at the firm level are difficult to obtain in Germany. In previous work, I used the most comprehensive database – provided by the Stifterverband für die Deutsche Wissenschaft – to study productivity and spillover effects (HARHOFF 1996, 1998). Containing detailed information on the firm's R&D expenditures and their breakdown,

---

6. These arguments are not new. See, for example, SCHIANTARELLI (1995, pp. 31-33) and the references cited therein.
7. See SCHIANTARELLI [1995] for a summary of results.

those data do unfortunately not offer information on the financial performance of firms. For the purpose of this study, an entirely new panel dataset was constructed from publicly available sources and complemented – if necessary – with confidential data from other sources (see the appendix). The most important public source for R&D information were financial statements, published in the *Bundesanzeiger*. In some cases additional data were obtained from yearly business reports. The final dataset is an unbalanced panel of 236 German firms and covers the period from 1987 to 1994. Due to the recession of the German economy following the reunification boom, the data span a period that is characterized by rather divergent business conditions and considerable changes in firms' liquidity.

Details regarding sample composition, variable definitions and other important aspects of "data cleaning" are relegated in the data appendix. Due to a number of exclusion restrictions, the initial sample of about 2300 observations of R&D expenditure data shrinks to a sample of 1755 observations and 299 firms. Applying the constraint that at least three consecutive observations have to exist on all relevant variables and using "cleaning" procedures described in the appendix, we have finally a sample of 1365 observations for 236 firms. There are seven or eight observations for 90 firms; another 86 firms have either 5 or 6 observations; and 60 firms have either 3 or 4 observations. The sectoral composition of the panel is described in Table 1. It reflects the particular specialization of German industry in the production of chemicals and pharmaceuticals, machinery, and electrical products quite well – 161 of the total of 236 firms are operating in these sectors.

TABLE 1

Sectoral Composition of the Sample.

SYPRO	Sector	Number of Firms
24, 40	Chemicals, Pharmaceuticals	46
58, 59	Plastic and Rubber Products	12
25, 51, 52	Mining, Quarrying, Ceramic Products	12
21, 22	Petroleum Refineries	7
27, 28, 29	Metal and Metal Products	11
30, 31	Structural Steel Products	7
32, 50	Machinery	66
33, 34, 35	Road Vehicles	15
36, 37	Electrical Products, Precision and Optical Goods	49
38, 39	Ironware, Sheet Metal	5
53-57, 61-64	Wood Products, Pulp, Paper and Paperboard, Printing and Duplication, Leather, Leatherware, Footware, Textiles and Apparel	3
68, 69	Food, Beverages and Tobacco	3
Total		236

3.2. Descriptive Statistics

This paragraph briefly describes the sample in terms of its properties and descriptive statistics. A number of points need to be stated at the outset. First, the sample is not representative. Quite to the contrary, it has emerged from a complex selection process. Moreover, German corporate law gives firms some leeway in choosing how to comment on their R&D activities. The reporting may range from precise data on expenditures, R&D personnel and patenting activity to simple comments like "R&D was performed". Only firms with information that would allow the computation of R&D expenditures are included in the sample. Nonetheless, due to the inclusion of large enterprises, the sample captures in each of the years from 1987 to 1994 slightly more than 50 percent of private R&D spending in the Federal Republic. This is not surprising, given the concentration of R&D spending in large firms.

Table 2 presents means, medians and the interquartile ranges of the most important variables. Most distributions are highly skewed due to the presence of very large enterprises. At the median of the 1990 sample, firms have sales of about DM 445 million (in 1985 prices). The size distribution thus seriously restricts the possibility of analyzing financing problems of small firms. The empirical strategy to do so with this sample relies on splitting the sample at the median of the initial year sales distribution. The lower quartile of the 1990 sales distribution for smaller firms is at DM 95 million, the upper quartile at DM 260 million.

The overall sample is also fairly research-intensive. The mean of R&D intensity (real R&D expenditures divided by real sales) is 5.1 percent. This is considerably above the average R&D intensity among German R&D-performing firms which is on the order of 2.2 percent. Figure 1 plots the R&D intensity distribution of all firms with data for 1990. The shape of the distribution conforms to the plots presented by COHEN and KLEPPER [1992] for the United States: it is roughly unimodal and highly skewed.

The firm's willingness to reveal its R&D expenditures in a consistent way may be correlated with the firm's size and the extent of innovation in the industry. For small, specialized firms any revelation of the extent of innovation may generate information for competitors that may be deemed harmful by the firm's management, thus leading to a preference for secrecy. As to the above-average R&D intensity, it is well-known that pharmaceutical and chemical companies have published R&D- related data for some decades. In some industries, the signalling value of revealing the firm's R&D expenditures may be significant. As Table 1 shows, the dominant industries in the sample used here are indeed chemicals and pharmaceuticals, electrical products, and machinery. Simple productivity regressions also show that the elasticity of revenues with respect to the R&D capital stock is on the order of 10 percent in fixed-effects estimates. This result is consistent with elasticities computed for a panel of firms in high-technology industries in the Stifterverband data (HARHOFF [1998], Table 4). Table 2 suggests that the sample firms spend on average slightly less on R&D than on investment. In conclusion, R&D is an important activity for the firms in this sample.

The key feature of the dataset is the combination of financial performance data with R&D and investment expenditure information. Partial correlation

TABLE 2

Descriptive Statistics (215 Firms – 1990).

Variable	Mean	S.E.	Lower Quartile	Median	Upper Quartile
I/C	0.139	0.105	0.075	0.108	0.174
CF/C	0.302	0.256	0.160	0.232	0.341
Y/C	2.637	2.083	1.400	1.949	2.965
R/C	0.136	0.139	0.050	0.093	0.179
R/K	0.199	0.093	0.173	0.201	0.221
I/R	1.824	2.439	0.618	1.156	2.024
Y	3660.4	10620.0	157.8	445.7	1695.2
I	229.1	698.6	7.8	28.0	91.5
R	163.6	577.0	7.2	18.8	72.5
C	2246.1	7110.4	74.5	196.9	870.1
K	831.8	3013.2	36.8	94.2	327.4
Employees	15006	43862	791	2291	6909
Net Book Value (PPE)	1000.9	3222.5	32.6	94.9	477.1

Note : Absolute values for Y, I, R, C, K and net book value (PPE) in 1985 million DM. All capital ratios for physical capital were computed using the capital stock measure computed from historical cost data.

FIGURE 1

R&D Intensity Distribution (1990).

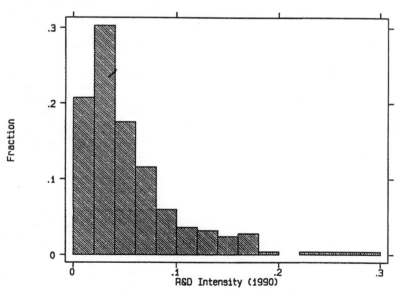

coefficients can be used to establish a number of stylized facts. In simple OLS regressions using R&D scaled over capital as the dependent variable and including time dummies, firm size, and revenue growth among the right-hand side variables, the coefficient (standard error) of cash flow is 0.45 (0.012). Using investment over capital as the dependent variable, the respective cash flow coefficient (standard error) is given by 0.12 (0.011). Including detailed industry dummy variables at the two-digit SYPRO level does not change these results by much. Thus, after controlling for observable firm characteristics, the cross-sectional relationship between cash flow and R&D is much stronger than between cash flow and investment in tangible capital.

A causal interpretation of this correlation is obviously subject to a number of problems. First, the OLS estimates completely neglect the possibility that firm-specific effects can render the estimated coefficients inconsistent. For example, the relationship between cash flow and R&D may be spurious, since profitability (and thus cash flow) may simply be correlated with the extent of firm-specific technological opportunities, and therefore with the firm's propensity to invest in R&D. Second, since the symmetric treatment of R&D and investment requires a correction of the cash flow variable (R&D has been expensed and must be added back to cash flow), measurement error in the R&D variable will lead to a positive, but meaningless correlation. These complications will be addressed below in more refined dynamic specifications.

As pointed out in the previous section, it would be interesting to compare the capital structure of firms with respect to the kind of investments undertaken by these enterprises. Most of the theoretical arguments presented in section 2 imply that debt finance is not conducive to R&D spending. To explore the relationship between capital structure and the firm's investment policy, the correlation between debt and R&D spending (or R&D capital stock) can be analyzed. This has not been undertaken in a systematic way in this project, but preliminary results indicate that the correlation between R&D activity (measured as the ratio of R&D capital over the sum of R&D capital and physical capital) and the firm's longterm debt (measured as longterm debt divided by the sum of R&D capital and physical capital) is consistently negative in all years. The respective correlation coefficients range between -0.05 and -0.15 and are thus weaker than the correlations found in US data by HALL [1992] which were on the order of -0.2 to -0.3 [8]. A more detailed analysis of the link between capital structure and innovation in this sample is left to a separate study.

---

8. The results are preliminary, since the balance sheet data used so far are too coarse to adjust the debt variable for reserve holdings for pensions. Such a correction is currently under way.

4 Econometric Specifications for Investment and R&D Spending

This section briefly describes the econometric framework used in the analysis. While cash flow-investment elasticities are potentially ambiguous, non-structural models like accelerator (section 4.1) or error-correction specifications (section 4.2) are nonetheless informative starting points. Clearer evidence should in principle come from a structural Euler equation model introduced in section 4.3.

4.1. Accelerator Models

Investment accelerator specifications have been used, *inter alia*, by BOND *et al.* [1994]. The derivation of such a model follows the usual logic which postulates a relationship between the logarithm of output $j_{i,t}$, the logarithm of the desired stock of capital $c_{i,t}$, and the user cost of capital $j_{i,t}$

$$(1) \qquad c_{i,t} = a + y_{i,t} - \sigma\, j_{i,t}.$$

This model can be derived from a profit maximization problem, given a CES production function with elasticity of substitution σ. By taking first differences and applying the usual approximation $\Delta c_{i,t} \approx I_{i,t}/K_{i,t-1} - \delta$ one arrives at

$$(2) \qquad \frac{I_{i,t}}{C_{i,t-1}} = \delta + \Delta y_{i,t} - \sigma\, j_{i,t}$$

where $I_{i,t}$ is investment, $C_{i,t-1}$ is the firm's capital stock and δ is the rate of depreciation. In the empirical specifications, the user cost of capital are modelled as a function of time dummy variables and firm-specific effects. Following BOND *et al.* [1994], I use a generalized dynamic version which nests equation (2) in the empirical equation

$$(3) \qquad \frac{I_{i,t}}{C_{i,t-1}} = \delta^I \frac{I_{i,t-1}}{C_{i,t-2}} + \beta_1^I \Delta y_{i,t} + \beta_2^I \Delta y_{i,t-1} + d_t^I + \eta_i^I + \varepsilon_{i,t}^I$$

where $\varepsilon_{i,t}^I$ is an error term, d_t^I represents time dummies, and η_i^I captures unobserved heterogeneity at the firm level. The inclusion of cash flow effects then renders the basic empirical specification

$$(4a) \qquad \frac{I_{i,t}}{C_{i,t-1}} = \rho^I \frac{I_{i,t-1}}{C_{i,t-2}} + \beta_1^I \Delta y_{i,t} + \beta_2^I \Delta y_{i,t-1}$$
$$+ \beta_3^I \frac{CF_{i,t}}{C_{i,t-1}} + \beta_4^I \frac{CF_{i,t-1}}{C_{i,t-2}} + d_t^I + \eta_i^I + \varepsilon_{i,t}^I.$$

The corresponding R&D equation can be derived in the same way by treating R&D and investment completely symetrically. Thus,

$$
\text{(4b)} \quad \frac{R_{i,t}}{K_{i,t-1}} = \rho^R \frac{R_{i,t-1}}{K_{i,t-2}} + \beta_1^R \Delta y_{i,t} + \beta_2^R \Delta y_{i,t-1}
$$
$$
+ \beta_3^R \frac{CF_{i,t}}{K_{i,t-1}} + \beta_4^R \frac{CF_{i,t-1}}{K_{i,t-2}} + d_t^R + \eta_i^R + \varepsilon_{i,t}^R.
$$

Here, $R_{i,t}$ denotes the firm's R&D expenditures and $K_{i,t}$ is the respective knowledge capital stock. The computation of this variable and potential complications are described in the data appendix.

These equations can be estimated in first differences in order to eliminate the firm-specific effects. ARELLANO and BOND [1991] describe a family of GMM estimators which can be employed for this purpose and have a number of desirable properties. Since we want to allow for endogenous relationships between the right-hand side variables and the error terms, suitable instruments have to be devised to estimate the equation. Arellano and Bond suggest using lagged values of the right-hand side variables and of the autoregressive term. If the original error term $\varepsilon_{i,t}$ follows a white noise process, then values (in levels) of these variables lagged two or more periods will be admissible instruments. If the error term has a moving average structure, longer lags will have to be considered. Arellano and Bond also propose a number of test statistics that can be used to test for violations of various assumptions, in particular for serial correlation and validity of the instruments [9].

4.2. Error-Correction Models

BOND et al. [1994] follow BEAN [1981] and nest equation (1) directly in an error-correction framework of the type

$$
\text{(5a)} \quad \frac{I_{i,t}}{C_{i,t-1}} = \rho^I \frac{I_{i,t-1}}{C_{i,t-2}} + \beta_1^I \Delta y_{i,t} + \beta_2^I \Delta y_{i,t-1} + \phi^I (c_{i,t-2} - y_{i,t-2})
$$
$$
+ \beta_3^I \frac{CF_{i,t}}{C_{i,t-1}} + \beta_4^I \frac{CF_{i,t-1}}{C_{i,t-2}} + d_t^I + \eta_i^I + \varepsilon_{i,t}^I
$$

$$
\text{(5b)} \quad \frac{R_{i,t}}{K_{i,t-1}} = \rho^R \frac{R_{i,t-1}}{K_{i,t-2}} + \beta_1^R \Delta y_{i,t} + \beta_2^R \Delta y_{i,t-1} + \phi^R (k_{i,t-2} - y_{i,t-2})
$$
$$
+ \beta_3^R \frac{CF_{i,t}}{K_{i,t-1}} + \beta_4^R \frac{CF_{i,t-1}}{K_{i,t-2}} + d_t^R + \eta_i^R + \varepsilon_{i,t}^R
$$

which has equation (1) as its long-run solution. Negative estimates for the coefficients ϕ^R and ϕ^I would indicate error-correcting behavior for the respective type of investment. Since (5a) and (5b) also nest the respective

---

9. For details on the estimation technique, see ARELLANO and BOND (1991).

accelerator models, this specifation is particularly convenient. Deviations from constant returns can be tested by including the logarithm of output as an additional regressor in (5a) and (5b). Deviations of the respective coefficient from zero would indicate a violation of the constant-returns assumption (see BEAN [1981]).

4.3. Euler Equations

Due to the aforementioned ambiguities regarding the interpretation of the cash flow effects in reduced-form equations, possibly significant cash flow coefficients in the accelerator and error-correction specifications are not fully convincing. In particular, they cannot unambiguously be interpreted as evidence for financing constraints, since cash flow may be correlated, with investment demand.

It is therefore desirable to employ a structural framework in order to confirm or reject findings from the accelerator and error correction equation models. Such models have been used successfully by BOND and MEGHIR [1994] and WHITED [1992], among others. Including R&D activity in a *structural* estimation approach requires that the theoretical framework encompass at least [10] two distinct types of capital (knowledge capital and tangible capital). Studies of this type are still rare in the literature [11], but such a model – based on the work of BOND and MEGHIR [1994] – is derived and described in the appendix where I show that – under suitable assumptions – the empirical Euler equation for investment in tangible capital can be written as

$$(6a) \quad \left(\frac{I}{C}\right)_{t+1} = \beta_1^I \left(\frac{I}{C}\right)_t + \beta_2^I \left(\frac{I}{C}\right)_t^2 + \beta_3^I \left(\frac{X}{C}\right)_t$$
$$+ \beta_4^I \left(\frac{Y}{C}\right)_t + \beta_5^I \left(\frac{R}{C}\right)_t + \beta_6^I \left(\frac{R}{C}\right)_t^2 + \alpha_t^I + \alpha_i^I + \psi_t^I.$$

Analogously, one can derive the empirical equation for the firm's R&D spending

$$(6b) \quad \left(\frac{R}{K}\right)_{t+1} = \beta_1^R \left(\frac{R}{K}\right)_t + \beta_2^R \left(\frac{R}{K}\right)_t^2 + \beta_3^R \left(\frac{X}{K}\right)_t + \beta_4^R \left(\frac{Y}{K}\right)_t$$
$$+ \beta_5^R \left(\frac{I}{K}\right)_t + \beta_6^R \left(\frac{I}{K}\right)_t^2 + \alpha_t^R + \alpha_i^R + \psi_t^R.$$

---

10. It is not clear that labor can be treated as adjustable without causing adjustment costs to the firm. This problem applies obviously to industries with high human capital, but it could be particularly pronounced in the Federal Republic where legislation heavily restricts employer's ability to layoff workers. The Euler equation model in the appendix is in principle amenable to an extension which would allow for costs in adjusting the labor force, but such an extension is beyond the scope of this paper.
11. See the survey by CHIRINKO [1993a]. CHIRINKO [1993b] estimates a model with multiple capital stocks on the basis of the *q* approach.

In these equations, K is the knowledge capital stock, and C is the stock of physical capital, I is investment in physical capital and R the firm's R&D expenditures. Y denotes the firm's output (measured as sales) and X is the firm's gross profit [12]. For both equations, the theoretical model yields the parameter restrictions $\beta_1 > 1$, $\beta_2 < -1$, $\beta_3 < 0$, $\beta_4 > 0$, $\beta_5 > 0$, and $\beta_6 < 0$. Details are provided in the appendix. These coefficients are themselves functions of underlying structural parameters. However, as in most other papers using Euler equations of this type, the resulting restrictions across coefficients will not be tested or enforced in this paper.

The Euler equations derived in the appendix specify investment and R&D equations under the null hypothesis of no financing constraints. There is no explicit structural model of the firm's investment behavior under the alternative. The logic of testing the model is the following. Presumably, if financing constraints exist for at least a subsample of firms, then the parameter restrictions just described will not be satisfied. Moreover, in that case other specification tests, e.g. the Sargan test and tests for serial correlation may also yield significant test statistics [13]. If the subsample of firms affected by financing constraints can be identified, then separate estimates for the respective groups of firms should lead to a rejection in one case, and acceptance of the Euler equations in the other. In practice, it may be difficult to achieve a full acceptance of the model, since any deviation from the assumptions underlying the structural model may lead to deviations from the expected coefficient patterns. Thus, obtaining the right signs on the parameters and moving closer to the expected coefficient size after the sample-split has been implemented can be seen as an imperfect, but still positive result.

5 Estimation Results

5.1. Accelerator and Error-Correction Models

In Table 3, I report estimates based on the accelerator specifications in equations (4a) and (4b). In the overall sample, there are significant cash flow effects in investment, but not in R&D spending. Splitting the sample according to size reveals a more complex pattern. Apparently, the significant effects in the investment equation are driven by the subsample of smaller firms where cash flow effects remain highly significant while there is no statistically significant effect for the subsample of larger firms. A similar result is obtained for the R&D equations, but the associated cash flow coefficients are considerably smaller. The test statistics for these results do

---

12. See the data appendix and the derivation of the Euler equations for details on the variable definition.
13. For details on the logic of testing these models see ZELDES [1989] and BOND and MEGHIR [1994].

414

not suggest any problems with the choice of instruments and/or their time structure. The Sargan test statistic is never significant at the 5 percent level, nor are the tests for second order serial correlation. However, one should note that the output accelerator effects are not particularly convincing if the underlying model is taken at face value. These coefficients are either quite small and typically insignificant, or they carry the wrong sign. This may indicate a problem with the choice of the output variables (sales) which does not account for changes in inventories or with the industry-specific sales deflators used in this study [14].

The implications of allowing for error-correcting behavior are analyzed in Table 4. Note that this equation nests the previous specification. The error

TABLE 3

Accelerator Models.

Dependent Variable	I_t/C_{t-1}			Dependent Variable	R_t/K_{t-1}		
	Full Sample	Smaller Firms	Larger Firms		Full Sample	Smaller Firms	Larger Firms
I_{t-1}/C_{t-2}	−0.051	−0.087	0.429	R_{t-1}/K_{t-2}	0.152	0.054	0.258
	(0.055)	(0.051)	(0.178)		(0.114)	(0.132)	(0.137)
CF_t/C_{t-1}	0.178	0.126	0.072	CF_t/K_{t-1}	0.022	0.065	0.025
	(0.192)	(0.199)	(0.104)		(0.021)	(0.024)	(0.015)
CF_{t-1}/C_{t-2}	0.314	0.322	0.080	CF_{t-1}/K_{t-2}	0.027	0.032	0.014
	(0.063)	(0.065)	(0.138)		(0.020)	(0.036)	(0.010)
Δy_t	−0.016	−0.021	−0.012	Δy_t	0.020	−0.007	0.029
	(0.082)	(0.096)	(0.056)		(0.035)	(0.033)	(0.030)
Δy_{t-1}	−0.002	−0.006	0.012	Δy_{t-1}	0.007	0.008	−0.008
	(0.073)	(0.093)	(0.012)		(0.016)	(0.019)	(0.017)
Test Statistics				Test Statistics			
Sargan Test	39.0 (37)	41.3 (37)	43.2 (37)	Sargan Test	44.9 (37)	39.5 (37)	35.5 (37)
	$p = 0.381$	$p = 0.287$	$p = 0.224$		$p = 0.176$	$p = 0.361$	$p = 0.540$
1st Order Serial Corr.	−2.219	−2.363	−1.832	1st Order Serial Corr.	−2.053	−1.458	−2.809
2nd Order Serial Corr.	−1.753	−1.616	0.410	2nd Order Serial Corr.	1.246	0.649	0.875
Wald Test on Cash Flow Terms	$p < 0.001$	$p < 0.001$	$p = 0.785$	Wald Test on Cash Flow Terms	$p = 0.161$	$p = 0.017$	$p = 0.057$
Observations	673	306	367	Observations	673	306	367
Firms	(213)	(106)	(107)	Firms	(213)	(106)	(107)
Instruments	t–2,...t–5	t–2,...t–5	t–2,...t–5	Instruments	t–2,...t–5	t–2,...t–5	t–2,...t–5

Note : Estimation in first differences using the DPD software (Arellano and Bond 1988). All regressions include time dummy variables for the respective years of observation. The sample was split at the median of initial year sales.

---

14. For firms that sell products from accumulated stocks, output is biased upwards, and vice versa for firms accumulating stocks of finished and semi-finished products.

correction terms have the expected negative signs, and they are significant in all equations, except for the investment equations for the overall sample and the group of smaller firms. The test statistics do not point to any misspecification, once the equations are estimated separately for the two subsamples. However, it is disturbing that the coefficient of $\log(Y_{t-2})$ is also significantly negative in most of the columns of Table 4. This would suggest strong decreasing returns to scale which appears implausible. Again, this effect might be triggered by problems with the output variable used in this study or by the fact that the time series is too short. One can enforce the constant returns to scale assumption in these data by simply omitting the variable $\log(Y_{t-2})$, but this does not change the coefficients of the remaining variables strongly, although cash flow effects become slightly stronger in the restricted specification. For larger firms, the accelerator terms assume reasonable values in Table 4.

For the ECM specification, there is little evidence of any cash flow effects for investment or R&D in the overall sample. The test statistic for the joint test of the cash flow terms in the investment and R&D equations is insignificant. The admission of error-correcting behavior appears to lead to lower cash flow effects in all of the specifications. For smaller and larger firms, cash flow does not appear to have a significant effect on investment. However, in the R&D equation, there are significant cash flow effects for both subsamples. The cash flow coefficients are considerably larger for the smaller companies, but their overall size $0.079\,(=0.050+0.029)$ is still quite small.

Experimenting with different sample splits provided evidence of a size-contingent cash flow effect in the subsample of smaller firms. In Table 4, the significance level of the test statistic for the joint effect of cash flow variables in the investment equation for smaller firms is $p=0.077$. Reestimating the error-correction model for investment with a sample split into three groups (see Table 5) yields significant cash flow effects at the confidence level of $p=0.005$ for the group consisting of the 71 smallest firms in the sample while no significant effects emerge for the two other groups. Moreover, it is interesting that error-correcting behavior appears to be relevant for the investment decisions of larger firms, but not for the very smallest firms in this sample. This result would support the presumption that smaller firms employ rather flexible investment processes. As to the R&D equations, splitting the sample into three groups did not provide qualitatively new results. Small but significant cash flow effects persist, and they tend to be slightly larger for the smaller firms.

These results suggest that the data may not be ideal to test for financing constraints: if they are present and indeed apparent in the form of cash flow effects, they are likely to affect only the very smallest firms in this sample. This does not mean that these firms are of little relevance: small and medium-sized firms with fewer than 500 employees constitute the lion's share of Germany's firm population and account for about 70 percent of employment, and a reliable assessment of their financing situation would be quite important. But these firms tend to be systematically underrepresented in financial accounts data of the form used here.

416

TABLE 4

Error Correction Models.

Dependent Variable I_t/C_{t-1}	Full Sample	Smaller Firms	Larger Firms
I_{t-1}/C_{t-2}	-0.204 (0.114)	-0.223 (0.124)	-0.129 (0.153)
CF_t/C_{t-1}	0.010 (0.263)	-0.001 (0.263)	-0.088 (0.134)
CF_{t-1}/C_{t-2}	0.141 (0.113)	0.214 (0.136)	-0.117 (0.129)
Δy_t	-0.069 (0.114)	-0.038 (0.090)	0.113 (0.054)
Δy_{t-1}	-0.003 (0.132)	-0.024 (0.124)	0.231 (0.097)
$c_{t-2} - y_{t-2}$	-0.252 (0.158)	-0.240 (0.207)	-0.417 (0.090)
y_{t-2}	-0.224 (0.196)	-0.257 (0.182)	-0.147 (0.062)
Test Statistics			
Sargan Test	37.2 (37) $p=0.462$	39.4 (37) $p=0.364$	40.0 (37) $p=0.340$
1st Order Serial Corr.	-1.935	-2.181	-1.717
2nd Order Serial Corr.	-1.756	-1.385	0.061
Wald Test on Cash Flow Terms	$p=0.228$	$p=0.077$	$p=0.640$
Observations	673	306	367
Firms	(213)	(106)	(107)
Instruments	t-2,...t-5	t-2,...t-5	t-2,...t-5

Dependent Variable R_t/K_{t-1}	Full Sample	Smaller Firms	Larger Firms
R_{t-1}/K_{t-2}	-0.234 (0.104)	-0.244 (0.154)	-0.191 (0.157)
CF_t/K_{t-1}	0.003 (0.027)	0.050 (0.019)	0.023 (0.015)
CF_{t-1}/K_{t-2}	0.025 (0.018)	0.029 (0.024)	0.018 (0.010)
Δy_t	0.078 (0.057)	0.026 (0.054)	0.080 (0.034)
Δy_{t-1}	0.136 (0.080)	0.044 (0.079)	0.124 (0.060)
$k_{t-2} - y_{t-2}$	-0.248 (0.070)	-0.229 (0.067)	-0.236 (0.042)
y_{t-2}	-0.096 (0.055)	-0.175 (0.087)	-0.076 (0.025)
Test Statistics			
Sargan Test	30.7 (37) $p=0.756$	38.2 (37) $p=0.414$	30.9 (37) $p=0.751$
1st Order Serial Corr.	-0.298	-0.237	-0.763
2nd Order Serial Corr.	0.928	0.933	0.343
Wald Test on Cash Flow Terms	$p=0.341$	$p=0.031$	$p=0.041$
Observations	673	306	367
Firms	(213)	(106)	(107)
Instruments	t-2,...t-5	t-2,...t-5	t-2,...t-5

Note: Estimation in first differences using the DPD software (Arellano and Bond 1988). All regressions include time dummy variables for the respective years of observation. The sample was split at the median of initial year sales.

Summarizing the results from the accelerator and error correction specifications used here, there is some evidence pointing to size-contingent cash flow effects, both for R&D and investment. These effects persist even after accounting for relatively complex dynamics, although the effects are clearly reduced in size once such adjustment mechanisms are allowed for. This result has been described before by BOND *et al.* [1997]. Even without attempting to interpret the cash flow effects in one way or another, one lesson from these results is certainly that simple linear specifications (such as the accelerator model) will tend to deliver inflated cash flow effects, and that the results from studies not introducing more complex (and presumably realistic) adjustment processes ought to be viewed with caution.

TABLE 5

Alternative Sample Split for Investment Error Correction Model.

	Dependent Variable	I_t/C_{t-1}	
	Initial Year Sales <208 Mill. DM	208 Mill. DM<= Initial Year Sales< 950 Mill. DM	initial Year Sales >=950 Mill. DM
I_{t-1}/C_{t-2}	−0.078	−0.412	−0.106
	(0.160)	(0.122)	(0.160)
CF_t/C_{t-1}	0.221	0.048	−0.031
	(0.377)	(0.091)	(0.067)
CF_{t-1}/C_{t-2}	0.252	0.157	−0.069
	(0.087)	(0.080)	(0.101)
Δy_t	0.014	0.110	0.135
	(0.186)	(0.061)	(0.056)
Δy_{t-1}	−0.149	0.147	0.182
	(0.201)	(0.087)	(0.073)
$c_{t-2} - y_{t-2}$	−0.073	−0.351	−0.339
	(0.226)	(0.102)	(0.069)
y_{t-2}	−0.245	−0.211	−0.125
	(0.249)	(0.115)	(0.059)
Test Statistics			
Sargan Test	36.8 (37)	33.0 (37)	37.0 (37)
	$p = 0.481$	$p = 0.656$	$p = 0.117$
1st Order Serial Corr.	−1.966	−1.214	−2.035
2nd Order Corr.	−1.354	−2.195	−1.088
Wald Test on all Cash Flow Terms	$p = 0.005$	$p = 0.142$	$p = 0.780$
Observations	206	205	262
Firms	(71)	(71)	(71)
Instruments	t–2,...t–5	t–2,...t–5	t–2,...t–5

Note : Estimation in first differences using the DPD software (Arellano and Bond 1988). All regressions include time dummy variables for the respective years of observation.

5.2. Euler Equation Results

Results from Euler equation estimates for investment in tangible capital are presented in the left-hand panel of Table 6. The GMM technique used in the previous sections is again chosen to estimate the equations. In each case I start with the assumption that values of the right-hand side variables lagged two or more years are admissible instruments. Both the admissibility of instruments and the serial correlation structure are tested. If serial correlation of second order is detected, the error term in (6a) or (6b) may be MA(1), and valid instruments have to be lagged at least three periods. The choice of instruments is indicated in the last line of each column in Table 6.

For the overall sample, the coefficient estimates are nowhere close to their expected size, and in many cases the signs do not correspond to the

418

TABLE 6
Euler Equation Results.

Investment Equation

	Full Sample	Smaller Firms	Smaller Firms	Larger Firms
$(I/C)_t$	0.364	0.191	0.081	0.674
	(0.148)	(0.170)	(0.325)	(0.153)
$(I/C)_t^2$	-0.280	-0.074	-0.256	-0.791
	(0.275)	(0.307)	(0.744)	(0.327)
$(Y/C)_t$	0.022	0.021	0.013	0.022
	(0.009)	(0.013)	(0.015)	(0.007)
$(X/C)_t$	-0.010	-0.009	0.0001	-0.001
	(0.006)	(0.007)	(0.0069)	(0.014)
$(R/C)_t$	0.340	0.853	0.576	-0.349
	(0.300)	(0.453)	(0.454)	(0.393)
$(R/C)_t^2$	-0.093	-0.538	-0.259	0.876
	(0.265)	(0.407)	(0.290)	(0.678)
Test Statistics				
Sargan Test	114.0 (102)	103.7 (102)	72.4 (66)	98.2 (102)
	p = 0.196	p = 0.435	p = 0.275	p = 0.589
1st Order Serial Corr.	-5.410	-4.644	-1.796	-4.532
2nd Order Serial Corr.	-2.256	-2.329	-3.018	-0.828
Observations	893	420	298	473
Firms	(236)	(122)	(103)	(114)
Instruments	t-2,...t-5	t-2,...t-5	t-3,...t-5	t-2,...t-5

R&D Equation

	Full Sample	Smaller Firms	Smaller Firms	Larger Firms
$(R/K)_t$	-0.058	0.171	0.292	-0.064
	(0.304)	(0.301)	(0.348)	(0.259)
$(R/K)_t^2$	0.381	-0.113	-0.215	0.612
	(0.706)	(0.726)	(0.805)	(0.689)
$(Y/K)_t$	-0.001	0.001	0.001	-0.002
	(0.001)	(0.001)	(0.002)	(0.001)
$(X/K)_t$	0.0002	0.0002	0.0007	0.0003
	(0.0001)	(0.0001)	(0.0021)	(0.0008)
$(I/K)_t$	0.0005	-0.0081	-0.0086	0.0385
	(0.0088)	(0.0101)	(0.0116)	(0.0163)
$(I/K)_t^2$	0.0004	0.0015	0.0013	-0.0071
	(0.0012)	(0.0011)	(0.0014)	(0.0033)
Test Statistics				
Sargan Test	128.6 (102)	110.7 (102)	79.4 (66)	98.9 (102)
	p = 0.278	p = 0.717	p = 0.434	p = 0.920
1st Order Serial Corr.	-3.361	-2.858	-2.630	-5.822
2nd Order Serial Corr.	-1.966	-1.902	-0.386	-0.463
Observations	893	420	298	473
Firms	(236)	(122)	(103)	(114)
Instruments	t-2,...t-5	t-2,...t-5	t-3,...t-5	t-2,...t-5

Note : Estimation in first differences using the DPD software (Arellano and Bond 1988). All regressions include time dummy variables for the respective years of observation. The sample was split at the median of initial year sales for the sample used in Table 3 (see text).

theoretical predictions. This should be expected if financing constraints are present. But it is more likely that it indicates general data problems, or simply some mismatch between the assumptions of the theoretical model and real-world investment behavior. Introducing the distinction between small and large firms goes some way to produce clearer patterns and to support the notion that the Euler equation is more likely to fail for smaller firms. For larger firms, the coefficient sizes of the first two terms are still far from the unit value [15]. The cash flow term assumes the predicted negative sign for the larger firms while it is positive in the other subsample, but the coefficients are insignificant in both cases. While the estimates are quite imprecise overall, it is nonetheless clear that the subsample of larger firms corresponds much better to the expected patterns. In terms of sign restrictions derived from theory, only the last two R&D terms carry the wrong sign, but they are jointly insignificant ($p = 0.302$). Nesting both estimates by using a full set of size interaction terms and testing the significance of the interacted terms indicates that the coefficient vectors for the two subsamples differ in statistical terms ($p = 0.030$). Since the test statistics indicate second-order serial correlation in the subsample of smaller firms, I also estimated the Euler equation with instruments lagged at least 3 periods. However, there was no improvement in the test statistic, suggesting that other sources of misspecification may be present as well. Recall that the larger firms did not show any sign of financing constraints for investment in Table 4 and 5, while the smaller firms appeared to be affected by such effects. Thus, while the investment estimates in Table 6 are still far from being satisfactory, they are not grossly inconsistent with the previous results.

The results from the R&D Euler equations are not informative. Again, the specification for the overall sample does not perform well, and in this case there is no sign of major improvement once the equation is estimated for the subsamples. Changing the instrument set (e.g. in the third column of the right-hand side panel in Table 6) in order to avoid problems from second-order correlation of the error terms also did not lead to any improvement.

Taken together, the results of the Euler tests are disappointing. Clearly, the sample is still relatively small, and the estimation approach required consumes a large number of degrees of freedom. Differencing and the use of lagged values as instruments subtracts at least two observations from each time series. On the positive side, the sample split according to firm size appears to move the coefficient estimates for capital investment by larger firms in the right direction. But they are still far from the expected value under the null hypothesis of no financing constraints. Note that this result is consistent with the previous estimates – the weakest evidence of cash flow effects on investment was found for large firms.

---

15. In preliminary experiments using the GMM estimator proposed by ARELLANO and BOVER [1995], the estimated coefficients were closer to the theoretical expectations. But even in this case, the coefficients for the subsample of smaller firms are significantly below the values suggested by the theory. See BLUNDELL and BOND [1995] for a discussion of the different estimators and of the potential advantage of the ARELLANO-BOVER estimator.

Assuming that the rejection of the Euler equations for smaller firms is driven by financing constraints, there are a number of explanations why they also fail for larger firms. That subsample may still contain some firms which experience genuine financing constraints. Detection and identification of these firms may require the use of additional variables on capital structure and other firm characteristics. Note also that the failure of the Euler equations is particularly clear for the R&D equation. This may point to problems in either the theoretical formulation of the R&D law of motion (see the appendix) or in the measurement of the capital stock. Longer time series would definitely be helpful towards mitigating existing data problems and exploring alternative specifications.

5.3. **Additional Evidence from Survey Data**

Given that the cash flow effects emerging from Table 4 and 5 are not unambiguous and that the Euler equation framework does not deliver completely reliable results either, it may be helpful to look for additional evidence on the role of firm size for the relationship between finance and investment. Such indirect evidence is available from an innovation survey conducted in 1995 in Germany. For details on this data source, see HARHOFF and LICHT [1994]. In this postal survey, respondents (mostly R&D managers) were asked whether a lack of equity or of debt finance was a serious impediment to their innovation projects. The answers ranged from "not at all" to "very much" with five ordinal response categories. For 51 firms in the sample used in this study, data from the 1995 survey could be matched. 29 percent of the small firms (according to the definition used in Table 5) in this sample responded that there were debt constraints (*i.e.* marked either of the two highest response categories), but only 5 percent of the larger firms did so. The difference is significant at the level of $p = 0.022$. Similarly, 36 percent of the smallest firms indicated that lack of equity capital was an impediment for innovation activities, while again only 5 percent of the larger firms did so ($p = 0.005$). I also employed ordered logit models with a dummy variable for the group of the smallest firms (as in Table 5) as the independent variable. It turns out that the coefficient for this dummy variable is significant at the level of $p = 0.011$ for the equity question and at the level of $p = 0.023$ for the debt question. Thus, these subjective responses appear to support the result that small firms have a higher propensity of being financially constrained.

Much can be said against the cash flow effects presented above in Table 4 and Table 5, and serious objections may be raised against using subjective survey responses [16]. Nonetheless, the evidence from both sources is consistent and provides tentative support that the cash flow effects detected

---

16. The evidence concerning the subjective responses is ambiguous because even in the absence of any informational asymmetries, one would expect that the group of small firms includes a relatively large number of "lemons". Whether the identity of these is known to external financiers or not, enterprises in this group of small firms will – on average – face greater financing problems than larger firms would.

in the panel data are indeed an outcome of financing constraints at the firm level.

6 Conclusions and Extensions

The present analysis has been limited in many ways, mostly due to data constraints that will hopefully be relaxed over time. The sample used here is not representative, and thus the results need to be taken with a grain of salt. While all of these caveats call for a cautious interpretation of the results, the existing evidence suggests that firm size has a potentially strong impact on the relationship between cash flow and investment in physical and knowledge capital. For the group of smaller firms, there appears to be some sensitivity of R&D and of investment to the firm's cash flow. While this result can be rationalized by pointing to the basic ambiguity in interpreting cash flow effects, it is much harder to explain the differences between results for smaller and larger firms on this basis. Explaining this result away would amount to assuming that cash flow has no (or a negligible) investment demand component for larger firms, but indeed some informational content about investment opportunities for the group of smaller firms. This notion appears somewhat odd. Moreover, the survey evidence summarized in section 5.3 provides suggestive evidence that smaller firms may indeed be facing financing constraints in Germany. For larger firms, the evidence is broadly consistent with the results reported by BOND et al. [1997] for a sample of German stock market firms. One should also note that the Jensen hypothesis of free cash flow would not lend itself easily to an explanation of these results, either, unless one assumes that free cash flow is a particularly astute problem for relatively small firms. Since these firms are presumably less likely to suffer from intransparencies of managerial behavior than larger ones, this explanation does not seem particularly plausible.

However, to distinguish between the competing hypotheses more clearly, it is necessary to implement structural models of investment and R&D behavior. This paper attempted to do so by deriving specifications for investment and R&D Euler equations. With the exception of the subsample of large firms in the case of capital investment, the parameter restrictions implied by this model do not appear to be consistent with the data. While such a rejection could be caused by financing constraints, it is probably more realistic to argue that the sample is too small for a precise estimation of the Euler equation coefficients, or that the model itself is too restrictive to describe the complexity of investment processes in a satisfactory way. Since it is desirable to include German firms not traded in the stock market, it would be fruitful to explore as an alternative the applicability of the structural approach pioneered by ABEL and BLANCHARD [1986]. In this approach a separate equation for estimating the shadow value of capital needs to be implemented, and the predicted values are then used as a substitute of Tobin's q.

422

Finally, international comparisons as in BOND *et al.* [1997] may constitute a productive approach to the question posed in this paper. It should be particularly instructive to study differences between firms in countries with market-based financing systems (e.g. the U.S. and the United Kingdom) and systems which rely strongly on links between banks and firms (e.g. in continental Europe). In such a comparison, the investment demand component of the cash flow variable can presumably be controlled for by choosing appropriate groups of firms for between-country comparisons.

If these avenues are pursued further, a stronger case *for or against* the existence of financing constraints in German firms can presumably be made. At this point, there is some evidence that such constraints exist, in particular for capital goods investment in relatively small firms, but the empirical results are still less than satisfactory.

APPENDIX A

The Data

In 1985, several changes were introduced into German corporate law (§289 *Handelsgesetzbuch*), most of them triggered by the European Community's Fourth Company Law directive on harmonization of national requirements pertaining to financial statements. Thus starting in the fiscal year of 1987, all limited liability corporations (*Gesellschaften mit beschränkter Haftung-GmbHs*) and stock-based corporations (*Aktiengesellschaften-AGs*) had to submit their annual financial statements to the Commercial Register. Only the larger firms have to have their statements audited, smaller ones need not submit a statement of profits and losses, and the balance sheet can be abbreviated significantly. Medium-sized and large *GmbHs* are required to publish their statements in the *Bundesanzeiger*. The size requirements are satisfied if two or more of the following conditions are met: revenues in excess of DM 32 million, more than 250 employees, or balance-sheet total in excess of DM 15 million.

A discussion of the situation of the business (*Lagebericht*) is part of the published statement. Besides establishing new publication requirements, the 1985 law also requires firms to comment on their R&D acitivities (§289 *Handelsgesetzbuch*, para 2). However, there is no legal specification as to the format of R&D reporting.

The data used in this paper originate with financial statements and respective appendices published in the *Bundesanzeiger*. To obtain the respective data, the 1993 volume of the *Bundesanzeiger* was searched for any published statements that indicated R&D activities. These roughly 900 records provided the "master list" of companies for the data collection. The statements of these companies were then tracked backwards to 1987 and forward to 1994. Whenever companies provided quantitative items on their R&D activities, the record was entered into the database. A list of companies which had published similar information in 1987 was provided by B. SCHWITALLA and H. GRUPP and used to check the completeness of our own data search. See SCHWITALLA [1993] for a description of the 1987 cross-section.

Quantitative data on R&D activity were recorded from the *Bundesanzeiger* if one or several of the following items were available: i) R&D expenditures, ii) R&D employees, iii) R&D intensity with respect to sales, iv) R&D intensity with respect to total number of employees, v) growth rates of any of these indicators. For about 200 firms, comparable data from the Mannheim Innovation Panel (MIP) were available for two or more years. See HARHOFF and LICHT [1994] for a discussion of these data. A comparison of the R&D figures from the two sources yielded the result that the Bundesanzeiger figures were less frequently rounded off than the survey data. Moreover, whenever the business responding to the survey could be matched in terms of employees and revenues (about 150 cases), the R&D figures were nearly identical, leaving aside rounding errors in the survey responses. Since the

424

MIP survey explicitly asks for R&D according to the Frascati definitions, the correspondence between the two sources is reassuring.

Since the operationalization of the theoretical model requires data on R&D expenditures, the respective information had to be imputed for a small number of cases (105 out of 2300) for which it was not available directly. In the case of items ii) and iv), industry-specific regression coefficients from a previous analysis of the 1987 and 1989 Stifterverband surveys were used to impute R&D expenditures from R&D personnel data. These regression results are available upon request. As one should expect, the number of R&D employees and R&D expenditures are highly correlated ($\rho = 0.98$), and inclusion of time and industry dummies in these regressions generates a good fit.

The data obtained from the *Bundesanzeiger* were matched to commercially available balance sheet data published by Creditreform, a large credit rating agency. While the *Bundesanzeiger* entries contain in principle all of the necessary data, it was not feasible to enter the full balance sheet information for these companies. Thus the availability of the matching information in the Creditreform database is currently still a constraint for about 300 observations.

Investment (I). The data on additions to plant, property and equipment came from the detailed *Anlagenspiegel* tabulation of assets in each of the *Bundesanzeiger* entries. The tabulation also includes their value at historical cost.

Output (Y). Computing time series for output (sales) followed the suggestions in the data appendix of BOND *et al.* [1994]. The deflators used for computing real output were at the two-digit SYPRO level.

Cash Flow (CF). For the purpose of the regressions in sections 4.1 and 4.2, cash flow is computed as funds available for investment and R&D spending, *i.e.* as net income plus depreciation plus R&D expenditures. The latter correction is necessary, since R&D is expensed in Germany (as in the U.S., see HIMMELBERG and PETERSEN [1994], HALL [1992]). Obviously, this does not hold for the investment portion (buildings, plant and equipment) of R&D laboratories, but the respective share of these expenditures is below 10 percent. Note that a correction of the cash flow variable would also necessitate reducing the physical investment figures by the corresponding amount. I experimented with such a correction of the investment and cash flow variables for the investment share of the R&D budget, but the results presented in this paper do not change in any major way. For that reason, the simpler procedure is followed here.

Gross Profit (X). For the estimation of the Euler equations described in section 4.3, the theoretical derivation of the model implies that the most appropriate measure is given as gross operating profits. For the data used here, the measure was computed as cash flow (see above) plus interest plus tax payments.

The capital stock (C) measure was computed by adjusting the historic cost values taken from the Anlagenspiegel for inflation, and by applying a perpetual inventory procedure with a depreciation of 8 percent per annum for all years following the first year for which historic cost data were available. The choice of this depreciation rate reflects average economic depreciation across German industries.

The knowledge capital stocks (K) in 1987, the initial year of most of the time series observations, were again computed from a permanent growth approximation as in HARHOFF [1998], assuming a pre-sample growth rate of 6 percent for all firms. Stock data for the following years were computed on the basis of perpetual inventory calculations, using a depreciation rate of 15 percent. Note that the data do not allow for a correction of the double-counting problem – a small portion of R&D expenditures (on average about 10 percent in Germany) is capital investment and thus included in the stock of phyisical capital. See SCHANKERMAN [1981] for a discussion of potential distortions arising from this problem.

Exclusion procedures. From the data thus constructed, any overlapping entries were deleted. Priority was given to consolidated financial statements whenever possible, though the database still contains a large number of nonconsolidated statements, in particular when comparability over time requires their use. Non-profit firms and subsidiaries of foreign firms were deleted as well. For the purpose of this study, only manufacturing firms were included.

Cleaning procedures and sample trimming. Observations were excluded if the following variables were below the lower centile or beyond the upper centile of the respective distribution: I/C, CF/C and the output growth rate.

Final Analysis at the Firm Level. The fact that some subsidiaries report their R&D expenditures in the Bundesanzeiger can be troublesome for any kind of analyis of R&D or financial performance. In this particular case, the relationship between cash flow and R&D might be affected by strategic issues or attempts to minimize overall taxes by strategic choice of transaction prices, etc. Moreover, the delination of R&D-performing units may be affected. In order to exclude cases in which problems were likely to occur, all firms that had passed the above selection and cleaning procedures were analyzed individually. Data on ownership structure from Creditreform was used to detect subsidiaries. Data from the Mannheim Innovation Panel was consulted to rule out cases in which R&D for a subsidiary was conducted by other business units or centralized R&D facilities. Cases that were deemed to problematic to deal with or sufficiently suspect were discarded. By applying this final cleaning procedure, the sample shrank again from about 1640 observations to 1365 observations.

426

APPENDIX B

Derivation of the Euler Equations

This section derives a structural model of investment and R&D spending in the presence of financing constraints. To avoid cluttered notation, I will only write subscripts for years and not use firm subscripts unless clarity requires it. The firm under consideration in this section has four choice variables. It can determine its level of R&D, investment, labor, and borrowing. R&D and investment contribute to the build-up of the respective capital stocks. For simplicity, I will refer to the capital stock (stock of physical capital) and the knowledge stock (stock of R&D capital). The firm faces two constraints. First, dividend payments are non-negative. The respective shadow value of dividends is then equivalent to the shadow value of internal funds. Second, the firm possibly faces an exogenously given borrowing constraint which limits investment spending if internal funds are exhausted. By definition, the firm cannot issue new equity. This restriction simply acknowledges that issuing of new equity is a rare event in German corporations and therefore not too interesting for the model at hand.

The per period profit of the firm is given by

(A.1)
$$\Pi_t = p_t F\left(C_t, K_t, L_t\right) - p_t G\left(I_t, R_t, C_t, K_t\right) - w_t L_t - p_t^I I_t - p_t^R R_t$$

where p_t is the price of one unit of output, C_t is the stock of physical capital, K_t is the knowledge capital stock, and L_t is labor with unit cost w_t. The firm utilizes a production function $F\left(C_t, K_t, L_t\right)$ with constant returns to scale and faces adjustment costs captured by the cost function $G\left(I_t, R_t, C_t, K_t\right)$ where I_t is investment in physical capital and R_t is the firm's R&D expenditures. The effective prices of investment and R&D are given by p_t^I and p_t^R, respectively.

The balance of sources and uses of funds is specified in

(A.2)
$$D_t = \Pi_t + B_t - \left(1 + \left(1 - \tau_t\right) i_{t-1}\right) B_{t-1}$$

where D_t are the firm's dividend payments, B_t is the amount borrowed in period t, τ_t is the corporate tax rate, and i_t is the interest on borrowed funds. Capital market arbitrage (neglecting capital gains and new equity issues) requires the cumulated dividend value of the firm V_t to satisfy

(A.3)
$$\left(1 + \left(1 - m_{t+1}\right) i_t\right)\left(V_t - \left(1 - m_t\right) D_t\right) = E_t V_{t+1}$$

where m_t is the personal tax rate on interest and dividend income and i_t is the interest rate. Solving the arbitrage condition backwards, we can write the value of the firm as

$$(A4) \qquad V_t = E_t \left\{ \sum_{j=0}^{\infty} \beta_{t+j}^t \left(\gamma_{t+j} D_{t+j} \right) \right\}$$

where $\gamma_t = (1 - m_t)$ is the tax preference parameter in the absence of capital gains taxation and $\beta_{t+j}^t = \prod_{i=1}^{j} (1 + r_{t+i-1})^{-1}$ is the j-period discount factor with $j \geq 1$, $\beta_t^t = 1$ and $r_t = (1 - m_{t+1}) i_t$. Note that these expressions are simplified versions of the tax parameters and discount factor in BOND and MEGHIR [1994].

The transformation laws for physical and knowledge capital follow the perpetual inventory rules

$$(A.5) \qquad C_t = (1 - \delta^I) C_{t-1} + I_t$$

$$(A.6) \qquad K_t = (1 - \delta^R) K_{t-1} + R_t$$

where δ^R and δ^I are the respective rates of depreciation. Note that knowledge capital and physical capital are treated analogously here, as has been done in most of the R&D literature [17]. In order to prevent the firm from borrowing and paying the borrowed funds out as dividends, we also require that the following transversality condition

$$(A.7) \qquad \lim_{T \to \infty} \left(\prod_{j=0}^{T-1} \beta_{t+j}^t \right) B_T = 0, \, \forall t$$

holds. Given initial conditions at the beginning of period t, the Bellmann equation characterizes the net present value of the firm as

$$(A.8) \qquad V_t (C_{t-1}, K_{t-1}) = \max_{I_t, K_t, L_t, B_t} \left\{ D_t + \beta_t^{t+1} E_t V_{t+1} (C_t, K_t) \right\}$$

subject to the laws of transformation (A.5) and (A.6), and the borrowing and dividend constraints

$$(A.9) \qquad B_t \leq B_t^*$$

$$(A.10) \qquad D_t \geq 0.$$

---

17. This specification for the R&D capital stock is not the only feasible way to portray the transformation law for knowledge capital. For example, HALL and HAYASHI [1989] and KLETTE [1996] have suggested to specify the law of motion as $K_t = K_{t-1}^{1-\alpha} R_t^{\beta}$, α, $\beta \in (0, 1)$ where α is the rate of depreciation of the log capital stock. This functional form assumption has been proposed to capture the non- exclusive character of the existing knowledge stock which presumably does not only enter in production of output but also in the production of new knowledge.

As STOKEY and LUCAS (1989, ch. 9) show, solving the maximization program in (A.8) is a necessary condition for maximizing the value of the firm given in (A.4). They also state the corresponding regularity conditions on functional forms and stochastic shocks.

Assuming that managers maximize the value of the firm, we obtain the first-order condition for optimal borrowing

$$(A.11) \quad (\gamma_t + \lambda_t^D) - \beta_{t+1}^t E_t \left\{ (1 + (1 - \tau_{t+1}) i_t) (\gamma_{t+1} + \lambda_{t+1}^D) \right\} - \lambda_t^B = 0.$$

Note that the last left-hand side term stems from the assumed borrowing constraint. While the equations will not be estimated under the alternative hypothesis of binding financing constraints, it is nonetheless instructive to study (A.11) in detail. Consider the case in which borrowing constraints are not binding, i.e. $\lambda_t^B = 0$. With perfect capital markets and risk neutrality, the after tax return on equity and the after-tax return on debt will be equal and (A.11) simplifies to $(\gamma_t + \lambda_t^D) - E_t \left\{ (\gamma_{t+1} + \lambda_{t+1}^D) \right\} = 0$, i.e. the marginal value of dividend payments will be equalized over time. Once borrowing constraints are present, the respective shadow values will no longer be equal. Again assuming perfect capital markets and risk neutrality, we have $(\gamma_t + \lambda_t^D) - E_t \left\{ (\gamma_{t+1} + \lambda_t^B + \lambda_{t+1}^D) \right\} = 0$ in this case. The multiplier λ_t^B simply reflects the change in the value of the firm if the debt constraint were relaxed by one unit.

The two Euler equations for investment and R&D can be written as

$$(A.12) \quad \frac{\partial V_t}{\partial C_{t-1}} = (1 - \delta^I)(\gamma_t + \lambda_t^D) \frac{\partial \Pi_t}{\partial C_t} + (1 - \delta^I) \beta_{t+1}^t E_t \left[\frac{\partial V_{t+1}}{\partial C_t} \right]$$

$$(A.13) \quad \frac{\partial V_t}{\partial K_{t-1}} = (1 - \delta^R)(\gamma_t + \lambda_t^D) \frac{\partial \Pi_t}{\partial K_t} + (1 - \delta^R) \beta_{t+1}^t E_t \left[\frac{\partial V_{t+1}}{\partial K_t} \right].$$

Combining these with the first-order conditions for investment and R&D yields

$$(A.14) \quad -(1 - \delta^I) \beta_{t+1}^t E_t \left\{ (\gamma_{t+1} + \lambda_{t+1}^D) \frac{\partial \Pi_{t+1}}{\partial I_{t+1}} \right\}$$
$$= -(\gamma_t + \lambda_t^D) \frac{\partial \Pi_t}{\partial I_t} - (\gamma_t + \lambda_t^D) \frac{\partial \Pi_t}{\partial C_t}$$

$$(A.15) \quad -(1 - \delta^R) \beta_{t+1}^t E_t \left\{ (\gamma_{t+1} + \lambda_{t+1}^D) \frac{\partial \Pi_{t+1}}{\partial R_{t+1}} \right\}$$
$$= -(\gamma_t + \lambda_t^D) \frac{\partial \Pi_t}{\partial R_t} - (\gamma_t + \lambda_t^D) \frac{\partial \Pi_t}{\partial K_t}.$$

Towards an empirical implementation, the expectations term will be replaced by observables and a rational expectations error. Expectations E_t

are formed over future prices, technologies, and interest rates on the basis of information available at the beginning of period t.

To obtain an empirically useful specification, several other functional form assumptions are necessary. The adjustment cost function is specified as

$$(A.16) \quad G\left(I_t, R_t, C_t, K_t\right) = \frac{b^C}{2}\left[\frac{I_t}{C_t} - \nu^C\right]^2 C_t + \frac{b^K}{2}\left[\frac{R_t}{K_t} - \nu^K\right]^2 K_t$$

which is linearly homogeneous in its arguments. Additive separability is a matter of convenience here, since one may very well construct cases in which interaction between physical capital and R&D capital could matter. The output price p_t depends on the volume of output in order to allow for imperfect competition, *i.e.* $p_t = Y_t^{-1/\varepsilon}$ where ε is the price elasticity of demand and $Y = F - G$ is net output. Then the profit derivatives of the firm's profit with respect to investment and capital stock are given by

$$(A.17) \qquad \frac{\partial \Pi_t}{\partial I_t} = -b^C \mu\, p_t \frac{I_t}{C_t} + b^C \nu^C \mu\, p_t - p_t^I$$

$$(A.18) \qquad \frac{\partial \Pi_t}{\partial C_t} = \mu\, p_t \left(\frac{\partial F}{\partial C_t} - \frac{\partial G}{\partial C_t}\right)$$

where $\mu = (1 - 1/\varepsilon)$. The expressions for R&D are analogous. We still have to find an operationalization for the marginal terms in equation (A.18). Note that both gross output F and adjustment costs G are homogeneous of degree one. Let $\varphi^C = (\partial Y/\partial C_t)\,(C_t/Y_t)$ denote the elasticity of net output with respect to physical capital. Taking account of the functional form specification for adjustment costs and of the first-order condition for the optimal allocation of variable factors L we can show that

$$(A.19) \quad \frac{\partial \Pi_t}{\partial C_t} = \mu\, p_t \left((1 - \varphi^K)\frac{Y}{C_t} - \frac{1}{\mu\, p_t}\frac{w\, L_t}{C_t} + b^K \left(\frac{R_t}{C_t}\right)^2\right.$$
$$\left. - b^K \nu^K \frac{R_t}{C_t} + b^C \left(\frac{I_t}{C_t}\right)^2 - b^C \nu^C \frac{I_t}{C_t}\right)$$

Again, the R&D equation is analogous. Under the *null hypothesis* of no financing constraints and time-invariant tax regimes, the derived expressions can be used to obtain the following equation:

$$(A.20) \quad -\left(1 - \delta^I\right)\beta_{t+1}^t\, E_t \left\{-b^C \mu\, p_{t+1} \frac{I_{t+1}}{C_{t+1}} + b^C \nu^C \mu\, p_{t+1} - p_{t+1}^I\right\}$$
$$= -\left(-b^C \mu\, p_t \frac{I_t}{C_t} + b^C \nu^C \mu\, p_t - p_t^I\right)$$
$$- \mu\, p_t \left((1 - \varphi^K)\frac{Y}{C_t} - \frac{1}{\mu\, p_t}\frac{w\, L_t}{C_t} + b^K \left(\frac{R_t}{C_t}\right)^2\right.$$
$$\left. - b^K \nu^K \frac{R_t}{C_t} + b^C \left(\frac{I_t}{C_t}\right)^2 - b^C \nu^C \frac{I_t}{C_t}\right)$$

430

Replacing the expectations operator by a rational expectations error term and collecting terms we have:

$$(A21) \quad \frac{I_{t+1}}{C_{t+1}} = \nu^C \left(1 - \phi_{t+1}^C\right) + \left(1 + \nu^C\right) \phi_{t+1}^C \left(\frac{I_t}{C_t}\right)$$

$$- \phi_{t+1}^C \left(\frac{I_t}{C_t}\right)^2 - \frac{\phi_{t+1}^C}{\mu \, b^C} \left(\frac{X_t}{C_t}\right)$$

$$+ \frac{\phi_{t+1}^C \left(1 + \varphi^K \left(\varepsilon - 1\right)\right)}{b^C \left(\varepsilon - 1\right)} \left(\frac{Y_t}{C_t}\right) + \frac{b^K \, \nu^K}{b^C \, \nu^C} \phi_{t+1}^C \left(\frac{R_t}{C_t}\right)$$

$$- \frac{b^K}{b^C} \phi_{t+1}^C \left(\frac{R_t}{C_t}\right)^2 + \frac{\phi_{t+1}^C}{\mu \, b^C} J_t^C + \psi_{it}^I$$

where

$$(A.22) \qquad \phi_{t+1}^C = \frac{p_t \left(1 + r_{t+1}\right)}{p_{t+1} \left(1 - \delta^C\right)}$$

which will be greater than one for realistic values of the variables. The ratio of gross profit to capital, evaluated in real terms, is given by $(X_t/C_t) = (p_t \, Y_t - w_t \, L_t)/p_t \, K_t$. The user costs of physical capital are captured in

$$(A.23) \qquad J_t^C = \left(1 - \frac{p_{t+I}^I \left(1 - \delta^I\right)}{\left(1 + r_t\right) p_t^I}\right) \frac{p_t^I}{p_t}.$$

This term will not be included explicitly, since price and depreciation data are not available at the firm level. The user cost term is simply captured by firm-specific effects and time dummies. The empirical specification for the investment equation under the null hypothesis of no financing constraints is thus given by

$$(A.24) \quad \left(\frac{I}{C}\right)_{t+1} = \beta_1^I \left(\frac{I}{C}\right)_t + \beta_2^I \left(\frac{I}{C}\right)_t^2 + \beta_3^I \left(\frac{X}{C}\right)_t$$

$$+ \beta_4^I \left(\frac{Y}{C}\right)_t + \beta_5^I \left(\frac{R}{C}\right)_t + \beta_6^I \left(\frac{R}{C}\right)_t^2 + \alpha_t^I + \alpha_i^I + \psi_{it}^I.$$

Analogously, one can derive the empirical equation for the firm's R&D spending

$$(A.25) \quad \left(\frac{R}{K}\right)_{t+1} = \beta_1^R \left(\frac{R}{K}\right)_t + \beta_2^R \left(\frac{R}{K}\right)_t^2 + \beta_3^R \left(\frac{X}{K}\right)_t$$

$$+ \beta_4^R \left(\frac{Y}{K}\right)_t + \beta_5^R \left(\frac{I}{K}\right)_t + \beta_6^R \left(\frac{I}{K}\right)_t^2 + \alpha_t^R + \alpha_i^R + \psi_{it}^R$$

The coefficients should – under the null hypothesis – satisfy the restrictions $\beta_1 > 1$, $\beta_2 < -1$, $\beta_3 < 0$, $\beta_4 > 0$, $\beta_5 > 0$, and $\beta_6 < 0$ where superscripts have been neglected, since these restrictions apply to both equations symmetrically.

• References

ABEL, A., BLANCHARD, O. (1986). – "The present value of profits and cyclical movements in investment," *Econometrica*, Vol. 54, pp. 302- 337.

ARELLANO, M., BOND, S. R. (1991). – "Some Tests of Specification for Panel Data: Monte Carlo Evidence and an Application to Employment Equations", *Review of Economics and Statistics*, Vol. 58, pp. 277-297.

ARELLANO, M., BOND, S. R. (1988). – "Dynamic panel data estimation using DPD: a Guide for Users", *IFS Working Paper No. 88/15*, Institute for Fiscal Studies, London.

ARELLANO, M., BOVER, O. (1995). – "Another Look at the Instrumental Variable Estimation of Error-Components Models", *Journal of Econometrics*, Vol. 68, pp. 29- 51.

AUDRETSCH, D. B., ELSTON, J. A. (1994). – "Does Firm Size Matter? Evidence on the Impact of Liquidity Constraints on Firm Investment Behaviour in Germany", *CEPR Discussion Paper No. 1072*. Centre for Economic Performance Research, London.

AUERBACH, A. J. (1983). – "Taxation, Corporate Financial Policy and the Cost of Capital", *Journal of Economic Literature*, Vol. 21, pp. 905-940.

BALTENSPERGER, E., DEVINNEY, T. (1985). – "Credit Rationing Theory. A Survey and Synthesis", *Zeitschrift für die gesamte Staatswissenschaft*, Vol. 141, pp. 475-502.

BEAN, C. R. (1981). – "An Econometric Model of Manufacturing Investment in the UK", *Economic Journal*, Vol. 91, pp. 106-121

BERNSTEIN, J. I., NADIRI, M. I. (1986). – "Financing and Investment in Plant and Equipment and Research and Development", in: M. H. Feston and R. E. Quandt (eds.): *Prices, Competition and Equilibrium*, pp. 233-248. Philip Allan Publishers.

BESANKO, D., THAKOR, A. V. (1987). – "Competitive Equilibrium in the Credit Market under Asymmetric Information", *Journal of Economic Theory*, Vol. 42 (1), pp. 167-182.

BESTER, H., HELLWIG, M. (1987). – "Moral Hazard and Equilibrium Rationing: An Overview of the Issues", in: G. Bamberg and K. Spreman (eds.): *Agency Theory, Information and Incentives*. Berlin: Springer, pp. 136-166.

BHATTACHARYA, S., CHIESA, G. (1994). – "Proprietary Information, Financial Intermediation and Research Incentives", *LSE Financial Markets Group Discussion Paper No. 186*, London School of Economics.

BHATTACHARYA, S., RITTER, J. R. (1985). – "Innovation and Communication: Signalling with Partial Disclosure", *Review of Economic Studies*, Vol. 50, pp. 331-346.

BLUNDELL, R., BOND, S. (1995). – "Initial Conditions and Moment Restrictions in Dynamic Panel Data Models", *IFS Working Paper No. W95/17*, Institute for Fiscal Studies, London.

BOND, S., MEGHIR, C. (1994). – "Dynamic Investment Models and the Firm's Financial Policy", *Review of Economic Studies*, Vol. 61, (2), S. 197-222.

BOND, S., ELSTON, J. A., MAIRESSE, J., MULKAY, B. (1997). – "A Comparison of Empirical Investment Equations using Company Panel Data for France, Germany, Belgium and the UK", *NBER Working Paper* National Bureau of Economic Research, Cambridge, Mass.

432

Chirinko, R. (1993a). – "Fixed Business Investment Spending: Modeling Strategies, Empirical Results, and Policy Implications", *Journal of Economic Literature*, Vol. 31, pp. 1875-1911.

Chirinko, R. (1993b). – "Multiple Capital Inputs, *Q*, and Investment Spending", *Journal of Economic Dynamics and Control*, Vol. 17, pp. 907-928.

Clemenz, G. (1986). – *Credit Markets with Asymmetric Information*. Berlin: Springer.

Cohen, W. C., Klepper, S. (1992). – "The Anatomy of Industry R&D Distributions", *American Economic Review*, Vol. 82, pp. 773-799.

Duesenberry, J. S. (1958). – *Business Cycles and Economic Growth*. McGraw Hill.

Elston, J. A. (1995). – "Investment, Liquidity Constraints and Bank Relationships: Evidence from German Manufacturing Firms", *unpublished manuscript*, Wissenschaftszentrum Berlin.

Elston, J. A., Albach, H. (1994). – "Bank Affiliations and Firm Capital Investment in Germany", *WZB Discussion Paper No. FS IV 94-10*, Wissenschaftszentrum Berlin.

Fazzari, S. M., Petersen, B. C. (1993). – "Working Capital and Fixed Investment: New Evidence on Financing Constraints", *RAND Journal of Economics*, Vol 24, No. 3, pp. 328-342.

Fazzari, S. M., Hubbard, G. R., Petersen, B. C. (1988). – "Financing Constraints and Corporate Investment", *Brookings Papers on Economic Activity*, 1994 (1), pp. 141-195.

Grabowski, H. (1968). – "The Determinants of Industrial Research and Development: A Study of the Chemical, Drug and Petroleum Industries", *Journal of Political Economy*, Vol. 76, pp. 292-306.

Hall, B. H. (1992). – "Investment and Research and Development at the Firm Level: Does the Source of Financing Matter", *NBER Discussion Paper No. 4096*, National Bureau of Economic Research, Cambridge, Mass.

Hall, B. H., Hayashi, F. (1989). – "Research and Development as an Investment", *Working Paper No. 89-108*, University of California, Berkeley.

Hamburg, D. (1966). – *Essays on the Economics of Research and Development*. New York: Random House.

Hao, K. Y., Jaffe, A. B. (1993). – "Effect of Liquidity on Firms' R&D Spending", *Economics of Innovation and New Technology*, Vol. 2, pp. 275-282.

Harhoff, D. (1996). – "R&D Spillovers, Technological Proximity and Productivity Growth - Evidence from German Panel Data", *mimeo*, Zentrum für Europäische Wirtschaftsforschung, Mannheim.

Harhoff, D. (1998). – "R&D and Productivity in German Manufacturing Firms", *Economics of Innovation and New Technology*, forthcoming.

Harhoff, D., Licht, G. (1994). – "Das Mannheimer Unternehmenspanel", in: U. Hochmuth and J. Wagner (eds.): *Firmenpanelstudien in Deutschland-Konzeptionelle Überlegungen und empirische Analysen*. Tübingen: Francke, pp. 255-284.

Himmelberg, C. P., Petersen, B. C. (1994). – "R&D and Internal Finance: A Panel Study of Small Firms in High-Tech Industries", *Review of Economics and Statistics*, Vol. 76 (1), pp. 38-51.

Jaffee, D., Russell, T. (1976). – "Imperfect Information, Uncertainty, and Credit Rationing", *Quarterly Journal of Economics*, Vol. 90, pp. 651-666.

Jensen, M. C. (1985). – "Agency Costs of Free Cash Flow, Corporate Finance and Takeovers", *American Economic Review*, Vol. 76, pp. 323-329.

Kaplan, S. N., Zingales, L. (1997). – "Do Investment-Cash Flow Sensitivities Provide Useful Measures of Financing Constraints?", *Quarterly Journal of Economics*, Vol. CXII, No. 1, pp. 169-216.

Kathuria, R., Mueller, D. C. (1995). – "Investment and Cash Flow: Asymmetric Information or Managerial Discretion", *Empirica*, Vol. 22, p. 211-234.

KEETON, W. R. (1979). – *Equilibrium Credit Rationing.* New York: Garland.

KLETTE, T. J. (1996). – "R&D, Scope Economies, and Plant Performance", *RAND Journal of Economics,* Vol. 27, No. 3, pp. 502-522.

KRASKER, W. S. (1986). – "Stock Price Movements in Response to Stock Issues under Asymmetric Information", *Journal of Finance,* Vol. 41, pp. 93-105.

LACH, S., SCHANKERMAN, M. (1989). – "Dynamics of R&D and Investment in the Scientific Sector", *Journal of Political Economy,* Vol. 97, (4), pp. 880-904.

LELAND, H. E., PYLE, D. H. (1977). – "Informational Asymmetries, Financial Structure, and Financial Intermediation", *Journal of Finance,* Vol. 32, pp. 371-387.

MANSFIELD, E. (1985). – "How Rapidly Does New Industrial Technology Leak Out?", *Journal of Industrial Economics.* Vol. 34, pp. 217-223.

MEYER, J. R., KUH, E. (1957). – *The Investment Decision: An Empirical Study.* Cambridge, Mass.: Harvard University Press.

MEYER, J. R., GLAUBER, R. R. (1964). – *Investment Decisions, Economic Forecasting, and Public Policy.* Cambridge, Mass.: Graduate School of Business Administration, Harvard University.

MUELLER, D. C. (1967). – "The Firm Decision Process: An Econometric Investigation", *Quarterly Journal of Economics,* Vol.. 81, pp. 58-87.

MYERS, S. C. (1977). – "Determinants of Corporate Borrowing", *Journal of Financial Economics,* Vol. 5, pp. 147-175.

MYERS, S. C. (1984). – "The Capital Structure Puzzle", *Journal of Finance,* Vol. 39, pp. 575-597.

MYERS, S. C., MAJLUFF, N. S. (1984). – "Corporate financing and investment decisions when firms have information that investors do not have", *Journal of Financial Economics,* Vol. 13, pp. 187-221.

SCHANKERMAN, M. (1981). – "The effects of double-counting and expensing on the measured returns to R&D", *Review of Economics and Statistics,* Vol. 63, No. 3, pp. 454-458.

SCHIANTARELLI, F. (1995). – "Financial Constraints and Investment: A Critical Review of Methodological Issues and International Evidence", Boston College, Department of Economics, *Working Paper No. 293.*

SCHWITALLA, B. (1993). – *Messung und Erklärung industrieller Innovationsaktivitäten.* Heidelberg: Physica.

SHLEIFER, A., VISHNY, R. (1990). – "Equilibrium Short Horizons of Investors and Firms", *American Economic Review,* Vol. 80, pp. 148-153.

STIGLITZ, J. E., WEISS, A. (1981). – "Credit Rationing in Markets with Imperfect Information", *American Economic Review,* Vol. 71, pp. 393-410.

STOKEY, N. L., LUCAS, R. E. (1989). – *Recursive Methods in Economic Dynamics.* Cambridge, Mass.: Harvard University Press.

THAKOR, A. V. (1990). – "Investment 'Myopia' and the Internal Organization of Capital Allocation Decisions", *Journal of Law, Economics and Organization,* Vol. 6, pp. 29-53.

THAKOR, A. V. (1993). – "Information, Investment Horizon, and Price Reactions", *Journal of Financial and Quantitative Analysis,* Vol. 28 (4), pp. 459-482.

WHITED, T. M. (1992). – "Debt, Liquidity Constraints, and Corporate Investment: Evidence from Panel Data", *Journal of Finance,* Vol. XLVII (4), pp. 1425-1460.

WINKER, P. (1996). – *Rationierung auf dem Markt für Unternehmenskredite in der BRD.* Tübingen: Mohr.

ZELDES, S. P. (1989). – "Consumption and Liquidity Constraints: an Empirical Investigation", *Journal of Political Economy,* Vol. 97, pp. 305-346.

The Commercial Success of Innovations: an Econometric Analysis at the Firm Level in French Manufacturing

Corinne BARLET, Emmanuel DUGUET,
David ENCAOUA, Jacqueline PRADEL*

ABSTRACT. – This paper offers some empirical evidence on how do product and process innovations affect manufacturing sales and exports. Accounting for differences in technological opportunities between industries, and the "market pull" or "technology push" nature of firms' innovations, we explain the share of new products in total sales and exports by the innovation types firms have implemented. The data come from the French Ministry of Industry's Innovation survey 1986-1990. The left-hand variables are the sales revenues and the export revenues of the firms that are attributable to products introduced within the last 5 years. Given that the survey reports only interval data, our estimates were obtained by maximum likelihood on the ordered probit model. The following results are obtained: (i) The contribution of products less than 5 years old is lower to overall exports than to total sales but the innovative content is stronger in exports than in domestic sales; (ii) The greater the underlying technological opportunities, the less successful are product imitations; (iii) Both domestic sales and exports are mostly made of product improvements; (iv) Firm size has a positive effect on innovation output only when the technological opportunity is strong.

---

* C. BARLET : CEME-Université de Paris 1, CRESE-Université de Besançon ; E. DUGUET : CEME-Université de Paris 1, INSEE-DMSE. D. ENCAOUA et J. PRADEL : CEME-Université de Paris 1.
We thank W. J. ADAMS, B. H. HALL, N. IUNG, F. LAISNEY, F. MELESE and two anonymous referees for helpful suggestions and comments as well as the participants at the *Xth ADRES Conference on the Economics and Econometrics of Innovation* (Strasbourg, June 1996) and at the *XIVth Journées de Microéconomie Appliquée* (Marrakech, May 1997). The usual disclaimer applies.

D. Encaoua et al. (eds.), The Economics and Econometrics of Innovation, 435–456.
© 2000 *Kluwer Academic Publishers. Printed in the Netherlands.*

1 Introduction

Economic effects of innovation are often appraised in the context of labor or total factor productivity (GRILICHES, [1986]; HALL and MAIRESSE, [1995]). This permits the evaluation of the impact of innovation on productive efficiency, but it ignores the degree to which an innovation is received favorably in the marketplace. Yet, commercial success is a crucial aspect of product innovations. Potential innovators often face considerable product market risk as they make their R&D decisions. In fact, it is precisely the existence of product market risk that distinguishes product innovation from product invention. Such risk explains why product innovators seek linkages with potential customers well before their innovations are ready for market. The success of an innovator's R&D project depends heavily on acceptance in the marketplace. In the case of a firm that produces a large number of products, introduced at various points in time, the commercial success of these innovations can be measured in terms of the sales revenue of the firm that is attributable to products introduced relatively recently – say, within the last five years. We shall refer to this measure, defined as a fraction of total revenue, as the new product ratio (NPR) of the firm. Although business enterprises attach a great deal of importance to NPR, it has received little attention in the applied econometric literature given the relative scarcity of data.

The purpose of this paper is to study the determinants of commercial success of various product innovation strategies using NPR as the measure of commercial success. It is important to know why firms differ in the commercial success they derive from their innovations. On the one hand, such an understanding reveals the compatibility of research incentives and market performance. It reveals how the ex ante market risk of product innovation gets resolved after innovation occurs. On the other hand, NPR is a unique feature of business enterprises. At any given moment, each firm offers a variety of products for sale, each one conceived and introduced in a different period. NPR can be interpreted as a measure of the firm's ability to replenish its stock of products. The larger NPR, the greater the degree to which the firm has replenished its stock of products, and the lower the average age of its products.

The first question of interest is whether different types of innovation enjoy different degrees of commercial success. Innovations can be distinguished on the basis of their degree of novelty. Novelty is a concept difficult to define precisely, but the intuition behind it is quickly understood by exploring some of its properties. To begin with, the degree of novelty is an ordinal concept, implying a value judgment on the degree of novelty of the innovation. Second, this judgment might differ depending on whether one's point of view is that of the innovator or that of the marketplace. Let us examine three types of product innovations, ranked in order of increasing novelty from the consumer's point of view.

First, a firm can launch a product that is new for the firm but not for the market. In other words the firm can launch a product that has close

436

substitutes already offered by other firms. For example, a pharmaceutical firm might introduce a new antihistamine. The firm is seeking to broaden its product line to include antihistamines, but very similar antihistamines are already offered by other pharmaceutical companies.

Second, a firm can launch a product that represents considerably higher quality than other versions of the product that already exist in the marketplace. The other versions of the product might be those of the firm itself. Returning to the example presented in the previous paragraph, a pharmaceutical company might introduce a new antihistamine that represents considerable therapeutic improvement over the other antihistamines already offered by the firm. From the firm's perspective, such an innovation might be considered a product improvement; from the market's perspective, it might be considered a real novelty.

Third, a firm can launch a product that is new both for the firm and for the market. This is the most novel of all new products.

This categorization of new products can also be used in the context of new methods of production. Some new methods represent improvements on existing methods. Others embody greater novelty such as a technological breakthrough in production methods.

With these categories in mind, the first goal of the paper is to explore the effects of product novelty on the degree of commercial success. A priori, one can imagine two distinct and opposite effects. The first, which one might call the *inertia* effect, suggests that the greater the novelty the greater the risk. The market's acceptance of novel products will occur only very gradually over time. The second effect, which one might call the *efficiency* effect, suggests that novelty is valued, at least to the extent to which it responds to market demand. Knowledge of how these two effects balance out in practice will improve our understanding of innovative strategy.

One can also evaluate the effects of innovations on commercial success using other schemes of categorization. These include whether the innovation is product or process in nature, and whether the innovation is market- or knowledge- driven (demand- pull or technology push in nature, SCHMOOKLER [1966]).

The effect of different types of innovation on commercial performance likely depends on the specific economic environment facing the firm. For example, underlying technological opportunities differ among industries. Technological opportunity is another concept that is difficult to define precisely but easy to describe intuitively. Technological opportunity of an industry relates to its innovative potential. The innovative potential of an industry depends on the stock of, and rate of change of the corresponding scientific base. It also depends on the level and rate of change of the demand for differentiated products embodied in the demand function.

Here we study the effect of novelty on commercial performance while controlling for technological opportunity. If the inertia effect prevails when there are little technological opportunities, while the efficiency effect prevails when there are abundant technological opportunities, then novelty is likely to reduce commercial performance in the former case and increase it in the latter.

Until now, commercial success has been defined in terms of NPR – the value of new products as a fraction of total sales. But total sales include both domestic and foreign sales. It may well be that the determinants of commercial success differ between the two markets. Foreign markets can either be more or less receptive to novelty than their domestic counterpart. If the domestic market is the more receptive to novelty, one would expect the firm to concentrate sales of its newest products at home. If this is the case, then the existence of a domestic market ready to absorb new products could be a crucial prerequisite to high levels of export performance.

To study these questions we use the Innovation Survey in French manufacturing firms that covers the period 1986-1990. Most of the data in the survey are available only in ordinal form. For example, NPR is not measured continuously in the interval [0,1]; rather, the interval is divided arbitrarily into several sub- intervals, and each firm is then assigned to answer in one of those sub- intervals. As a result, it is necessary to use ordered probit methods, applied to transforms of the primitive ordinal variables.

The article is organized as follows: section 2 describes the dataset and the economic specification of the model. Section 3 describes the estimation procedure. Section 4 presents the empirical results regarding the determinants of NPR. Section 5 presents the empirical results regarding the determinants of export NPR. Conclusions appear in section 6.

2 Types of Innovation, Technological Opportunities and the New Product Ratio

2.1. Sources, Data and Variables Definitions

The main variables used in this paper come from the Innovation Survey, gathered by the French Ministry of Industry in 1991. The survey consists of a qualitative questionnaire on the different types of innovation implemented by manufacturing firms in France over the period 1986- 90. Unfortunately, no yearly information was collected for the period.

The first question focused on the different types of product and process innovations introduced by firms over the five-year period from January 1986 to December 1990. Product and process innovations are distinguished according to their degree of novelty. Each firm was asked to answer the following three questions with a "yes" or a "no":

During the last five years, has the firm:
– substantially improved, from a technological viewpoint, on existing products?
("yes" or "no")

438

– launched new products embodying technological innovations (excluding packaging) that were :
   – new for the firm but not for the market? ("yes" or "no")
   – new for the firm and for the market? ("yes" or "no")

Two additional questions are related to the process innovation types which occurred during the same five-year period:
– has the firm implemented a technological breakthrough? ("yes" or "no")
– has the firm substantially improved, from a technological viewpoint, on existing production methods? ("yes" or "no")

Thus, five innovation types are introduced in the analysis. From the market point of view, the degree of novelty allows a ranking of product innovations from products new for the firm and for the market, followed by products substantially improved and products which are new for the firm but not for the market.

The other questions are related to "market pull", "technology push" and the innovative potential of the firm's activity. At the firm level, market pull and technology push variables are provided through the answers to the following questions:

Does your firm estimate that innovation is determined by:
– market impetus (relationships with customers, competitors) ("no", "weakly", "moderately" or "strongly")
– the own dynamics of technology ("no", "weakly", "moderately" or "strongly")

The question regarding the innovative potential of the firm's activity, which Dasgupta (1986) calls "technological opportunity" of the industry is:

Do you consider that your activity is technologically:
– not innovative
– weakly innovative
– moderately innovative
– strongly innovative

The technological opportunities for undertaking innovations are clearly linked to advances in basic scientific knowledge. ROSENBERG [1974] has emphasized the importance of progress in the underlying scientific base for facilitating innovative possibilities. We have grouped the first two levels of responses (" no " and " weakly ") so that we classify firms into three categories [1].

Our dependent variable is the New Product Ratio (NPR). In the Innovation survey, it is a categorical variable, given into four classes: 0-10%, 10-30%, 30-70% and 70-100%. NPR is defined as the share of sales revenues attributable to product innovations introduced within the last five years.

---

1. This question is an assessment of the technological opportunities of the *activity* of the firm, not of the firm itself. Indeed, the questionnaire includes two questions about technological opportunities: one on the activity of the firm and one on the firm itself. Since our innovation variables already assess the innovation level of the firm, we have kept the environment variable only.

2.2. Description of the Sample and Preliminary Evidence

In order to assess the importance of NPR we have selected the responses of firms which were product innovators. Moreover, as the whole questionnaire is related to the 5-year period 1986-1990, we have kept the firms that were present in the same period. After these two selections, our sample includes 5402 manufacturing firms.

The median firm in the sample is relatively small with sales of FRF 43 millions [2] in 1989 (table 1). However, since the mean is much higher than the median (293 millions of FRF), the distribution of firm size in the sample is skewed. Moreover, the median and average firm sizes vary according to innovation types. The largest firms have implemented the most innovative products and processes. For instance, firms that claim to have implemented a technological breakthrough have median sales of 60 FRF millions and average sales of 600 FRF millions. A difference of the same order of magnitude exists between firms that launched new products in the market and those that didn't. As a result, we have to control for differences in firm size when we estimate the model. Since similar data exists for industries, along with our measure of firm size, we include 18 industry dummies in each of our regressions.

The first table shows the distribution of the New Product Ratio for total sales. Firms that have implemented process breakthroughs or launched new products appear to have a higher NPR. But since they also have a different size and operate in different industries, only a regression that controls for these two effects can tell us if these innovation types explain the success of innovation in the marketplace.

The second part of table 1 shows the marginal and conditional frequencies for each innovation type. These frequencies are similar to the correlation analysis for qualitative data (although the frequencies are not symmetric). More common innovations tend to be less innovative, which is not surprising. More interesting is the finding that the introduction of the most novel innovations – either product or process – are strongly correlated. But the relation is not symmetric: while 43% of the firms that launched a new product on the market also implemented a process breakthrough, 75% of process breakthrough firms also launched a new product on the market.

These results suggest that it is harder to change a process without changing the product than to change the product while improving on the production process. Globally, the data exhibit imperfect correlations between product and process innovations. This explains why we introduce both product and process innovations in our model when explaining the commercial success of product innovations. A more innovative process may contribute to the success of a new product by, say, lowering its price or allowing for stronger scale economies. It may also be the only way to produce the new good.

---

2. About 8.6 USD millions (1 USD ≈ 5 FRF).

440

TABLE 1

Sample Statistics (all firms)

Conditioning	All Firms	Product Innovators			Process Innovators	
Sample: 5402 firms		Impro-vements	New for the firm but not for the market	New for the market	Impro-vement	Break-through
Sales (Millions 1989 FRF):						
– Median	43	45	45	55	48	60
– Average	293	308	269	427	380	600
Less than 5 years old products in total sales:						
– less than 10%	45.1	41.0	43.4	36.1	42.0	33.6
– between 10 and 30%	35.4	37.2	36.7	38.1	37.0	37.5
– between 30 and 70%	16.1	18.1	16.6	21.5	17.5	23.6
– more than 70%	3.3	3.7	3.2	4.3	3.4	5.2
Conditional frequencies (%)						
Product innovations:						
– Improvements	80.3	100.0	77.8	83.5	86.9	87.1
– New for the firm, not for the market	67.0	64.9	100.0	63.4	68.0	64.3
– New for the market	51.8	53.9	49.0	100.0	51.8	74.7
Process innovations:						
– Improvements	67.1	72.6	68.2	67.2	100.0	75.8
– Breakthrough	30.1	32.6	28.9	43.4	34.0	100.0

We also examine the innovation content of exports (table 2). This is defined as the share of exports revenues attributable to products introduced within the last five years (exports NPR). Among the 3893 exporters, the median export rate is 14% while the average is 22%. Firms that have implemented more inventive innovations also tend to have a higher export NPR. But do exported products include more innovations than other products? An examination at the export New Product Ratio provides a first answer: the innovation content is lower in exports than in total sales, which implies that the domestic NPR is higher than the export NPR. A comparison between total sales NPR and export NPR shows that the distribution of the last variable includes more firms in the two end classes. For the export NPR, 61% of the firms are in the lowest class (0-10%) and 5% in the highest category (more than 70%). For total sales NPR the corresponding figures are respectively 45% and 3%.

All these issues can be examined more precisely using appropriate econometric methods, that allows to control for the effects of more variables, and to separate out the effect of each innovation type on the new product

TABLE 2

Sample Statistics (exporters)

Conditioning	Exporter	Product Innovators			Process Innovators	
Sample: 3893 exporters		Impro-vements	New for the firm but not for the market	New for the market	Impro-vement	Break-through
Exports (Millions 1989 FRF)						
– Median	9	9	9	12	10	14
– Average	137	143	120	197	179	213
Export rate (%):						
– Median	14.4	15.2	14.3	16.1	15.1	17.7
– Average	22.0	20.9	20.5	23.5	22.6	25.3
Less than 5 years old products in exports:						
– less than 10%	60.9	57.6	59.6	53.9	58.9	49.2
– between 10 and 30%	21.4	22.8	22.7	23.5	22.8	25.5
– between 30 and 70%	12.9	14.2	13.1	16.3	13.4	17.5
– more than 70%	4.8	5.4	4.6	6.3	4.9	7.8
Conditional frequencies (%)						
Product innovations:						
– Improvements	81.6	100.0	79.9	84.3	87.9	87.1
– New for the firm, not for the market	67.8	66.4	100.0	64.5	64.6	69.2
– New for the market	55.9	57.8	53.3	100.0	76.5	55.5
Process innovations:						
– Improvements	68.4	73.0	69.8	67.9	100.0	36.1
– Breakthrough	32.2	34.7	30.7	44.0	76.7	100.0

ratio (NPR). The next section presents the estimation method applied. The following sections present the results.

3 An Econometric Model of Commercial Success of Innovations

In this section we construct an empirical model of NPR which attempts to unravel the relative importance of the different variables presented above and their specific effect on the commercial success of innovations.

3.1. The Model

The left hand variable is the NPR in 1990 (φ_i^*). In order to insure that this proportion lies between 0 and 1, we set:

$$\varphi_i^* = \frac{\exp(x_i b + u_i)}{1 + \exp(x_i b + u_i)}, \qquad i = 1, \cdots, n$$

where x_i is the vector of explanatory variables for firm i, b is the corresponding vector of coefficients, u_i a disturbance that summarizes unobserved firm-level heterogeneity and n the number of firms. The logistic form of the NPR is not a distributional assumption but a mere functional form assumption. The logistic function assumed is strictly increasing, so that a positive coefficient for b implies a positive effect of the corresponding variable on the ratio. The explanatory variables x_i are:

1) size, measured by the logarithm of total sales in 1989 in the total sales NPR model, or by the logarithm of exports in 1989 in the export NPR model.

2) firm level dummies indicating the implementation of the 5 innovation types over 1986-1990.

3) firm level dummies indicating the importance of the "demand pull" and "technology push" (3 levels for each variable).

4) 18 industry dummies.

In order to avoid perfect multicolinearity, we drop the lowest level of the "demand pull" and "technology push" dummies. Since the dependent variable φ_i^* is only reported with intervals, a discussion of the econometric method applied is provided.

3.2. Estimation

Our model can also be written in the form:

$$p_i^* = \ln \frac{\varphi_i^*}{1 - \varphi_i^*} = x_i b + u_i, \qquad i = 1, \cdots, n$$

This transformed model is linear, hence the estimation problem comes from the fact that we do not observe φ_i^* but only the interval it lies in, namely]0,0.1],]0.1,0.3],]0.3,0.7] or]0.7,1]. Therefore, some knowledge of the distribution of the disturbances is needed. We assume that the disturbances are independently and identically normally distributed:

$$u_i \quad \text{i.i.d.} \quad N(0, \sigma_u^2), \qquad i = 1, \cdots, n$$

We do not observe p_i^* but the qualitative variable p_i:

$$p_i = \begin{cases} 1 & \text{if} \quad a_0 < p_i^* \leq a_1 \\ 2 & \text{if} \quad a_1 < p_i^* \leq a_2 \\ 3 & \text{if} \quad a_2 < p_i^* \leq a_3 \\ 4 & \text{if} \quad a_3 < p_i^* \leq a_4 \end{cases}$$

with $a_0 = \{-\infty\}$, $a_1 = \ln 0.1/0.9$, $a_2 = \ln 0.3/0.7$, $a_3 = \ln 0.7/0.3$ and $a_4 = \{+\infty\}$. The log-likelihood of the sample comes directly from the underlying model and is given by:

$$\ln L\left(p|x;\ b,\ \sigma_u^2\right) = \sum_{i=1}^{n} \sum_{k=1}^{4} d_{ik} \ln \Pr\left[p_i = k\right]$$

with

$$d_{ik} = \begin{cases} 1 & \text{if} \quad p_i = k \\ 0 & \text{otherwise} \end{cases} \qquad i = 1, \cdots, n, \qquad k = 1, 2, 3, 4$$

$$\Pr\left[p_i = k\right] = \Pr\left[a_{k-1} < p_i^* \le a_k\right] = \Pr\left[a_{k-1} < x_i b + u_i \le a_k\right]$$

$$= \Pr\left[\frac{a_{k-1} - x_i b}{\sigma_u} < \frac{u_i}{\sigma_u} \le \frac{a_k - x_i b}{\sigma_u}\right]$$

$$= \Phi\left[\frac{a_k - x_i b}{\sigma_u}\right] - \Phi\left[\frac{a_{k-1} - x_i b}{\sigma_u}\right]$$

where Φ is the cdf of the standard normal [3] distribution. Notice that, when the thresholds are known, the standard error of the disturbances σ_u is identified. We estimate this model by maximum likelihood under SAS-IML [4]. Two goodness-of-fit measures are provided: the Mc Fadden R^2 and the R^2 of the underlying linear model (denoted R_*^2), defined here as:

$$R_*^2 = \frac{V_e(\widehat{p_i^*})}{V_e(\widehat{p_i^*}) + \widehat{\sigma}_u^2}$$

where $\widehat{\sigma}_u^2$ is the maximum likelihood estimate of σ_u^2, and V_e denotes the empirical variance [5].

3.3. Direct Impact of Each Innovation Type

The relationship between the innovation ratio φ_i^* and the explanatory variables x_i is not linear (because of the logistic transformation) so that we need to evaluate the impact of each innovation type, firm by firm. We proceed as follows: let I_{si} be a dummy equal to 1 if firm i implemented

---

3. Taking the limits, we obtain the specific cases:

$$\Pr\left[p_i = 1\right] = \Phi\left[(a_1 - x_i b)/\sigma_u\right] \qquad \text{and} \qquad \Pr\left[p_i = 4\right] = 1 - \Phi\left[(a_3 - x_i b)/\sigma_u\right]$$

4. We make the parameter change $h = 1/\sigma_u$ and $\beta = b/\sigma_u$ so that the log-likelihood is concave in h and β (MADDALA, 1992). We use a Newton-Raphson algorithm with the analytical Hessian, which is used to estimate the covariance matrix of the parameters. The original parameters and their covariance are calculated from Slutsky's theorem once the maximum is reached. The estimation program we use is a slight extension of %PROBITO, a SAS-IML macro command presented in a previous working paper (CRÉPON and DUGUET, 1995).

5. For a discussion of these measures and other goodness-of-fit measures, see the survey by WINDMEIJER [1995].

a type s innovation ($s = 1, \cdots, 5$). The firm's transformed NPR can be written:

$$p_i^* = \ln \frac{\varphi_i^*}{1 - \varphi_i^*} = z_i c + d_s I_{si} + u_i, \qquad i = 1, \cdots, n$$

where z_i includes all the explanatory variables except I_{si}. The predicted innovation ratio of firm i when it implements a type s innovation is thus ($I_{si} = 1$):

$$\widehat{\varphi}_{is}^* = \frac{\exp(z_i \widehat{c} + \widehat{d_s})}{1 + \exp(z_i \widehat{c} + \widehat{d_s})}$$

If the same firm had not implemented a type s innovation ($I_{si} = 0$), its innovation ratio would be equal to:

$$\widehat{\varphi}_{0is}^* = \frac{\exp(z_i \widehat{c})}{1 + \exp(z_i \widehat{c})}$$

Hence the direct impact of a type s innovation on the innovation ratio of firm i (everything else equal) is given by:

$$\Delta \widehat{\varphi}_{is}^* = \widehat{\varphi}_{is}^* - \widehat{\varphi}_{0is}^*$$

We compute these quantities for all the firms which have implemented the type s innovation and report the distribution of the direct impacts $\Delta \widehat{\varphi}_{is}^*$. Notice that if the innovation coefficient $\widehat{d_s}$ is positive, the direct impact is also positive since $\widehat{\varphi}_{is}^*$ is strictly increasing with $\widehat{d_s}$.

4 The Results

4.1. Total Sales Innovation Ratio

The estimations are presented in table 3. The first column presents the model estimated from all the observations. The first finding, consistent with the previous empirical literature on innovation (COHEN and LEVIN, [1989]) is that industry effects are always significant. Once these effects are controlled for, we find a size effect that suggests larger firms may have a commercial advantage in getting their innovations to the market.

Once sector and size differences are controlled for, we find that all the innovation types contribute to the NPR, except process improvements. The strongest innovation coefficient is for product improvements, but the other innovation types still have a significant effect. We uncover some other interesting results. One of the reasons why the industry dummies have been introduced in the regression is that firms may face different demand conditions and are confronted with different technological bases. The Innovation survey provides proxies for these variables at the firm level, so that we can test whether the industry dummies fully control for these effects or not.

More precisely we use three new indicators. The first one, "market pull", indicates whether the innovation arose from a demand impetus and/or from rivalry. The second indicator, "technology push", is related to the importance of the dynamics of technology as a determinant of innovation. The last indicator, "technological opportunities", reveals whether the firm considers itself to belong to a weakly, a moderately or a strongly innovative activity. The first two indicators are often used at the industry level in previous empirical studies (COHEN and LEVIN, [1989]). However, until now no such measures were available at the firm level. The third indicator is different. Although the market pull and technology push indicators refer to the nature of the determinants of a firm's innovations, the technological opportunities variable is not a characteristic of the firm but rather of its level of activity. This activity is not identical to the industry. Since the firm answers directly to the question, the activity is closer to the relevant market definition than the industry to which the firm belongs. Then, we can examine whether the decomposition in 18 industries [6] is enough to summarize the sectoral variations in innovation commercial successes or not. We find that they are not: there remains a significant heterogeneity among firms inside the same industry.

TABLE 3

Sales from Innovations.

Left-hand variable: percentage of less than 5 years old products in total sales 1990
Transformation: $\ln[\varphi/(1-\varphi)]$
18 industry dummies are included in all the regressions
Maximum likelihood estimates on the ordered probit model
(asymptotic t statistic between parentheses)

Firm level innovation Opportunities: Estimates:	All (1)	All (2)	Weak (3)	Moderate (4)	Strong (5)
Sales logarithm 1989	0.056*	0.066*	0.004	0.046*	0.123*
	(12.1)	(4.0)	(0.11)	(2.15)	(3.57)
Product innovation (dummies):					
– Improvement of an existing	0.379*	0.500*	0.518*	0.388*	0.003
product	(6.67)	(9.03)	(5.38)	(4.94)	(0.02)
– New for the firm but not	0.133*	0.148*	0.200	0.193*	– 0.119
for the market	(3.00)	(3.27)	(2.21)	(3.36)	(1.11)
– New for the market	0.283*	0.410*	0.259*	0.311*	0.263*
	(6.33)	(9.03)	(2.92)	(5.47)	(2.18)
Process innovation (dummies):					
– Improvement of an existing	0.038	0.077	– 0.041	0.120*	0.013
process	(0.82)	(1.62)	(0.47)	(1.96)	(0.11)
– Technological breakthrough	0.178*	0.303*	0.212	0.120*	0.256*
	(3.71)	(6.25)	(1.93)	(1.97)	(2.47)

---

6. This industry classification is the French NAP 40.

446

TABLE 3 (continued)

Firm level innovation Opportunities: Estimates	All (1)	All (2)	Weak (3)	Moderate (4)	Strong (5)
Firm-level market pull (dummies):					
– Moderate	0.217*	0.241*	0.284*	0.225*	0.038
	(3.04)	(3.29)	(2.19)	(2.32)	(0.20)
– Strong	0.349*	0.452*	0.501*	0.381*	– 0.004
	(5.43)	(6.88)	(4.26)	(4.37)	(0.03)
Firm-level Technology push (dummies):					
– Moderate	0.169*	0.268*	0.139	0.163*	0.273
	(3.45)	(5.23)	(1.48)	(2.63)	(1.85)
– Strong	0.212*	0.469*	0.084	0.235*	0.207
	(3.78)	(8.43)	(0.66)	(3.24)	(1.49)
Firm-level innovation opportunities (dummies):					
– Moderate	0.559*	–	–	–	–
	(10.88)				
– Strong	1.146*	–	–	–	–
	(16.52)				
σ_u	1.314*	1.358*	1.372*	1.231*	1.393*
	(62.93)	(63.06)	(27.05)	(47.01)	(31.60)
Number of firms	5 402	5 402	1 720	2 715	967
Log-likelihood	– 5 628.98	– 5 767.74	– 1 436.13	– 2 940.08	– 1 201.79
Test: sectoral dummies [a]	649.2	669.0	130.6	280.0	123.5
Mc Fadden R^2	0.084	0.062	0.036	0.038	0.047
Latent model R^2	0.212	0.161	0.092	0.101	0.133
Estimated φ (%):					
– 1st quartile	7.3	7.9	4.4	10.1	18.2
– Median	11.5	11.5	5.9	13.2	24.0
– 3rd quartile	17.2	16.6	7.8	16.6	31.6

* Significant at the 5% level.
a. The null hypothesis is that the sectoral dummies can be replaced by a constant term. Under the null the statistic is chi-square distributed with 17 degrees of freedom. The critical value at the 5% level is 27.6.

The first column clearly shows that there are significant differences between firms in the same industry: in terms of market pull, technology push, but mostly in terms of technological opportunities. The coefficients of the latter indicator are 5 to 6 times higher than the ones of market pull and technology push. This suggests that it is appropriate to run separate regressions on each of the classes defined by the levels of technological opportunity. In fact, the entire relationship depends on firms' technological opportunities [7]. This implies that the different innovation types have returns that depend on the technological environment facing the firms.

---

7. An interesting comparison could be made between this "technological opportunities" variable and more disaggregated industry classifications, using data analysis.

Columns 3 to 5 present the separate regressions [8]. Since, the size effect [9] increases with technological opportunities (with no significant effect in the lowest class), the largest firms enjoy an advantage when innovations are commercialized in activities characterized by a high level of technological opportunity. We also find remaining (positive) differences stemming from more favorable demand and technology conditions, except in the highest technological opportunity class. The meaning of this last result may be simply that in this class, both market pull and technology push achieve strong levels for a majority of firms. The performance differences are therefore to be found elsewhere, namely in the type of innovations that the firms have implemented.

The effect of innovation types on the NPR vary according to the level of technological opportunities. First, innovation profiles differ between regressions. When we restrict our attention to comparisons between significant coefficients [10], the remaining coefficients are significantly different at the 5% level [11].

Second, our results clearly illustrate the effect of what has been classified as "weak", "moderate" and "strong" technological opportunities. We find significant differences in median predicted [12] NPR between these three classes: 6%, 13% and 24%. The median nearly doubles each time one gets in the upper class.

Under weak technological opportunities, the product innovations sold by the firms are mostly improvements on an existing product, followed by the more innovative products. Process innovations are not significant at the 5% level. As technological opportunities increase, improvements and new products for the market have an equal contribution to innovative sales, followed by product imitation (that are new for the firm but not

---

8. We have kept the sectoral dummies in the model since their coefficients always significantly differ at the 5% level.

9. Size is measured by total sales, since it is the denominator of the innovation ratio.

10. The specification tests are presented in tables 5 (total sales) and 8 (for exports). We first test the equality of coefficients among different technological opportunity classes. We always reject the equality of all coefficients at the 5% level. Sometimes, we find that some innovation coefficients are equal among regressions, but it is often because one of the coefficients is not significant (with a large standard error). Following a suggestion by a referee, we have also performed a second test. We examine if our "known threshold" model is compatible with the standard ordered probit model (with unknown threshold). We find that the separate regressions nearly always accept this model: the only exception is for the regression of total sales NPR under moderate technological opportunities. In this last case, however, the innovation coefficients are not very different from the ones presented here.

11. When a coefficient is not significant, it has a relatively large standard error, so that the equality test between this coefficient and the other coefficients are often accepted. It is a misleading result since one of the coefficient is significant while the other is not. This is why we comment on the statistics dealing with significant coefficients only.

12. The ratios cannot be observed, but a prediction can be computed for each firm. This comes from the fact that the variance parameter σ_u is identified when the truncation thresholds are known.

448

for the market). Moreover, process innovations have a modest although significant contribution to innovation sales. Finally, when technological opportunities are strong, only new products for the market and technological breakthrough contribute significantly to the NPR. Moreover, these two innovation types have equal effects. To sum up, an innovation of a given type will not necessarily achieve the same commercial success in different activities. The impact of an innovation type will differ according to the level of technological opportunity. In strongly innovative activities product imitations or improvements have no significant effect on the NPR. Conversely, in the same activities, real product innovation and process breakthrough have a significant impact on NPR.

Since these regressions do not allow for a direct measurement of the return on each innovation type, we have performed additional computations to assess the gains from innovation. They are computed for innovation performers only (defined by type) and presented in table 4.

Table 4 reveals the NPR variations that can be attributed to each innovation type [13]; controlling for size, sector, market pull, technology push, and the implementation of all the other innovations types. Since these computations must be done for each firm, we report the quartiles of the gains distributions. The main question to be examined in this table is: when does an innovation reach its maximum return (i.e., its maximum direct impact)?

Product improvements achieve a strong commercial return under moderate technological opportunities only, with a median gain of 4%. Products that are new for the firm but not for the market never achieve a strong gain. This suggests that, overall, "imitation" is a small contributor to NPR. Its maximum value lies in moderate technological opportunities, but it is only 2%.

The strongest contribution to the NPR comes from products that are new for the market: 1.6% under low technological opportunities, 3.7% under moderate technological opportunities and 4.7% when they are strong. This demonstrates that commercial returns on real innovations increase with the technological opportunity basis of a firm's activity.

A comparable result holds for process innovations: improvements make a small contribution to NPR, and only in activities with moderate technological opportunities. Conversely, process breakthrough have greater returns: from 1.5% under moderate technological opportunities activities to 4.7% in strong ones.

These results demonstrate that not all innovation types are efficient for a given market environment. In particular, product imitations and process improvements never contribute much to the commercial success of innovations. Moreover, the commercial impact of real innovations increases with the level of technological opportunities.

Since innovation is often considered as favoring exports, we undertake a similar analysis for the export NPR, the share of exports attributable to products introduced within the last five years.

---

13. The variation is expressed in percentage points, so that it can be added directly to the median NPR *without* the corresponding innovation type (also given in the table).

TABLE 4

Direct Effect of Each Innovation Type on the % of less than 5 years old products in total sales 1990 (φ)

(firms with innovations, computed from the estimates in table 3 *ceteris paribus*)

All figures are %	Product Innovations			Process Innovations	
	Impro-vements	New for the firm but not for the market	New for the market	Impro-vement	Break-through
Low Innovation Opportunities:					
Innovators (1 720 firms)	68.0	66.6	35.2	57.5	17.3
Median φ without the direct effect	4.4	5.1	5.7	6.5	6.4
$\Delta\varphi$ direct effect:					
– 1st quartile	0.2	0.8	1.2	– 0.3	1.0
– Median	0.3	1.1	1.6	– 0.2	1.4
– 3rd quartile	0.3	1.4	2.0	– 0.2	1.8
Moderate Innovation Opportunities:					
Innovators (2 715 firms)	84.6	67.0	54.5	70.3	29.3
Median φ without the direct effect	10.0	11.8	11.9	12.4	14.0
$\Delta\varphi$ direct effect:					
– 1st quartile	3.3	1.7	3.3	1.1	1.3
– Median	4.1	2.2	3.7	1.4	1.5
– 3rd quartile	4.9	2.6	4.3	1.6	1.8
Strong Innovation Opportunities:					
Innovators (967 firms)	90.2	67.7	73.4	79.0	55.1
Median φ without the direct effect	24.3	23.2	21.4	23.8	22.2
$\Delta\varphi$ direct effect:					
– 1st quartile	0.4	– 2.6	4.0	0.2	4.1
– Median	0.5	– 2.1	4.7	0.2	4.7
– 3rd quartile	0.6	– 1.8	5.6	0.3	5.6

4.2. **Export Innovation Ratio**

Examining the innovation intensity of exports, we retain only firms that export [14]. Exporters represent 72% of firms in the sample. Similar regressions are run. Once again we find significant differences in the regressions, although the first two innovation opportunity classes exhibited similar patterns [15] (tables 6 and 8).The median export NPR is lower than the one obtained on total sales. Ranked from weak to strong technological opportunities we get increases in export NPR of 2%, 7% and 14% respectively. A comparison with figures in table 3 shows that every quartile

---

14. We keep the firms with an export rate of at least 1%.
15. The rejection of the test comes mostly from the coefficients of the industry dummies.

TABLE 5

Specification Tests

Model (table 3): Statistics:	(1)	(2)	(3)	(4)	(5)
LRT: Equality of product innovation coefficients (df = 2, critical value 5% = 5.99)	14.28*	31.54*	7.72*	4.88	6.44*
LRT : Equality of process innovation coefficients (df = 1, critical value 5% = 3.84)	4.06*	10.16*	3.04	0.02	2.10
LRT: Equality with the unknown thresholds model (df = 3, critical value 5% = 7.81; 2.5% = 11.14)	37.75*	38.74*	2.70	22.22*	9.41*
Equality of all the coefficients:		(3)=(4)=(5)	(3)=(4)	(3)=(5)	(4)=(5)
LRT Statistic		379.48*	157.88*a	261.68a	157.88*
(df, critical value 5%)		(56, 78.1)	(28, 41.3)	(28, 41.3)	(28, 41.3)
Equality of all the coefficients except innovation opportunities					
LRT Statistic		101.96*	–	–	–
(df, critical value 5%)		(52, 73.3)			
Equality of the innovation coefficients only:					
Wald Statistic [b]		18.98*	3.39	11.95*	14.49*
(df, critical value 5%)		(10, 18.31)	(5, 11.07)	(5, 11.07)	(5, 11.07)

a. This is not an error, both statistics are found to be equal.
b. The estimations are made on separate cross-sections, so that the estimators are independent and the test is straightforward.
* We reject the null at the 5% level.

of the export NPR is lower that the one of total sales NPR. This suggests that commercial success in the domestic market precedes the introduction of a corresponding innovation in foreign markets. This result is interesting in the current debate about the relative commercial success of innovations in domestic and foreign markets.

Since the effect of firm size on NPR is greater for export NPRs, this suggests that large exporters are better at commercializing their innovations. Let us now turn to the innovation types that have a significant effect on the export NPR. Two patterns emerge: first, with weak and moderate technological opportunities, only product improvements and product imitations are significant. Moreover, no process innovation is significant. Thus, most of the innovative products exported by firms in the activities that have low technological opportunities are either improvements or imitations. This profile is representative of 81% of exporters. The previous finding that the domestic market is used as a basis for exports is thus confirmed.

TABLE 6

Exports from Innovations.

Left-hand variable: percentage of less than 5 years old products in total exports 1990
Transformation: $\ln [\varphi/(1 - \varphi)]$
18 industry dummies are included in all the regressions
Maximum likelihood estimates on the ordered probit model
(asymptotic t statistic between parentheses)

Firm level innovation Opportunities: Estimates	All (1)	All (2)	Weak (3)	Moderate (4)	Strong (5)
Exports logarithm 1989	0.272*	0.288*	0.215*	0.257*	0.358*
	(13.4)	(14.0)	(4.75)	(9.91)	(8.06)
Product innovation (dummies):					
– Improvement of an existing	0.429*	0.591*	0.517*	0.420*	0.297
product	(3.98)	(5.46)	(2.82)	(2.85)	(0.92)
– New for the firm but not	0.127	0.128	0.463*	0.258*	– 0.112
for the market	(1.58)	(1.57)	(2.60)	(2.54)	(0.60)
– New for the market	0.284*	0.428*	0.147	0.096	0.563*
	(3.48)	(5.22)	(0.88)	(0.93)	(2.55)
Process innovation (dummies):					
– Improvement of an existing	– 0.096	– 0.082	– 0.100	– 0.017	– 0.222
process	(1.14)	(0.96)	(0.58)	(0.15)	(1.08)
– Technological breakthrough	0.276*	0.411*	0.306	0.183	0.404*
	(3.30)	(4.90)	(1.49)	(1.75)	(2.24)
Firm-level market pull (dummies):					
– Moderate	0.136	0.179	0.035	0.237	– 0.004
	(0.99)	(1.29)	(0.14)	(1.28)	(0.01)
– Strong	0.358*	0.483*	0.403	0.485*	– 0.029
	(2.89)	(3.84)	(1.76)	(2.88)	(0.10)
Firm-level Technology push (dummies):					
– Moderate	0.345*	0.455*	0.242	0.398*	0.256
	(3.87)	(5.07)	(1.34)	(3.61)	(1.01)
– Strong	0.339*	0.614*	0.292	0.488*	– 0.007
	(3.33)	(6.14)	(1.21)	(3.75)	(0.03)
Firm-level innovation opportunities (dummies):					
– Moderate	0.638*	–	–	–	–
	(6.60)				
– Strong	1.243*	–	–	–	–
	(9.95)				
σ_u	1.880*	1.920*	1.967*	1.747*	1.991*
	(43.0)	(43.0)	(17.8)	(32.4)	(21.9)
Number of firms	3 893	3 893	1 166	1 991	736
Log-likelihood	– 3 681.82	– 3 732.40	– 807.43	– 1 959.98	– 874.29
Test: sectoral dummies [a]	1 040.4	1 051.0	224.7	483.6	178.4
Mc Fadden R^2	0.093	0.080	0.044	0.064	0.088
Latent model R^2	0.236	0.210	0.156	0.172	0.246

452

TABLE 6 (continued)

Firm level innovation Opportunities: Estimates	All (1)	All (2)	Weak (3)	Moderate (4)	Strong (5)
Estimated φ (%):					
– 1st quartile	2.8	2.9	1.5	4.0	7.5
– Median	5.6	5.6	2.3	6.9	14.4
– 3rd quartile	10.9	10.5	3.7	11.1	25.6

* Significant at the 5% level.
a. The null hypothesis is that the sectoral dummies can be replaced by a constant term. Under the null the statistic is chi-square distributed with 17 degrees of freedom. The critical value at the 5% level is 27.6.

The remaining 19% of exporters, from activities with strong technological opportunities, exhibit entirely different results. For these firms, products that are new to the market are the only significant contributors to the export NPR. Process breakthroughs are also significant with a comparable coefficient. In those activities, firms do tend to export 'high-tech' goods, thus contributing to the diffusion of up-to-date products in the other countries.

The commercial gains associated to innovation are low for improvements and imitations (table 7): from 1% to 2%. In contrast, firms that bring strong innovations to the market make strong gains under strong technological opportunities: the median is 6.6% for new products and 5.4% for process breakthroughs. Clearly, nearly all gains accrue to the strongest innovators located in activities with strong technological opportunities.

These results undermine the usual view that imitations of innovations are always successful. ROSENBERG and STEINMUELLER [1986] also argue against this view. In fact, our results clearly demonstrate that there are two types of activities in an economy: ones with strong underlying technological opportunities, and ones with weak or moderate underlying technological opportunities. In the first category, only product innovations that appear as new products to the market are successful. In the second category, only imitations and improvements have a significant effect on the NPR. The dynamics of manufacturing in France thus results from a combination of these two types of activities. The figures obtained for the French industry show that 19% of the exporters fall in the first category while 81% belong to the second category. Further research efforts that would provide a comparison with other countries would be very valuable.

Finally, if one assumes that firms in the different technological opportunities classes do not export their production to the same countries, the results of this paper support the view that exporters of product improvements contribute to the diffusion of innovations by exporting to countries with a lower innovation level. By contrast, firms with strong technological opportunities would tend to be more involved in intra-industry trade between developed countries where the diffusion of innovations involves more innovative products.

TABLE 7

Direct Effect of Each Innovation Type on the % of less than 5 years old products in total exports 1990 (φ)

(firms with innovations, computed from the estimates in table 6 *ceteris paribus*)

All figures are %	Product Innovators			Process Innovators	
	Impro-vements	New for the firm but not for the market	New for the market	Impro-vement	Break-through
Low Innovation Opportunities:					
Innovators (1 166 firms)	68.0	67.8	37.9	61.0	18.4
Median φ without the direct effect	1.7	1.7	2.4	2.7	2.6
$\Delta\varphi$ direct effect:					
– 1st quartile	0.7	0.6	0.2	– 0.4	0.5
– Median	1.1	1.0	0.4	– 0.3	0.9
– 3rd quartile	1.7	1.4	0.6	– 0.2	1.3
Moderate Innovation Opportunities:					
Innovators (1 991 firms)	86.0	67.6	58.3	70.6	31.0
Median φ without the direct effect	5.0	6.6	6.4	7.3	7.8
$\Delta\varphi$ direct effect:					
– 1st quartile	1.5	0.4	1.1	– 0.1	0.9
– Median	2.4	0.6	1.7	– 0.1	1.4
– 3rd quartile	3.7	0.9	2.7	– 0.1	2.1
Strong Innovation Opportunities:					
Innovators (736 firms)	91.0	68.2	78.1	73.9	57.1
Median φ without the direct effect	12.1	15.1	10.7	17.0	13.8
$\Delta\varphi$ direct effect:					
– 1st quartile	1.9	– 0.2	3.9	– 4.3	3.1
– Median	3.5	– 0.1	6.6	– 2.9	5.4
– 3rd quartile	5.2	– 0.1	9.8	– 1.6	7.7

5 Conclusion

The French Ministry of Industry's innovation survey provides much of new information on the outputs of innovation. Besides the usual measures of innovation, such as patents and R&D expenditures, this survey offers the possibility of examining the commercial success of different types of innovations. Although the Innovation survey provides only qualitative variables, based on subjective answers to objective questions, the careful use of these variables yields sensible results.

TABLE 8

Specifications Tests (Exports)

Model (table 6): Statistics:	(1)	(2)	(3)	(4)	(5)
LRT: Equality of product innovation coefficients (df = 2, critical value 5% = 5.99)	5.61 +	14.46*	2.64	3.60	6.43*
LRT : Equality of process innovation coefficients (df = 1, critical value 5% = 3.84)	9.00*	15.51*	2.12	1.64	4.70*
LRT: Equality with the unknown thresholds model (df = 3, critical value 5% = 7.81; 2.5% = 11.14)	3.93	4.40	0.69	2.67	2.77

Equality of all the coefficients:	(3)=(4)=(5)		(3)=(4)	(3)=(5)	(4)=(5)
LRT Statistic	181.40*		74.56*	112.60*	84.89
(df, critical value 5%)	(56, 78.1)		(28, 41.8)	(28, 41.3)	(28, 41.3)
Equality of all the coefficients except innovation opportunities					
LRT Statistic	80.24*				
(df, critical value 5%)	(52, 73.3)		–	–	–
Equality of the innovation coefficients only:					
Wald Statistic [a]	11.89		3.91	9.58 +	6.16
(df, critical value 5%)	(10, 18.31)		(5, 11.07)	(5, 11.07)	(5, 11.07)

a. The estimations are made on separate cross-sections, so that the estimators are independent and the etest is straightforward.
* We reject the null at the 5% level.
+ We reject the null at the 10% level.

This study suggests that the commercial success of an innovation depends on the following factors. First, large firms have an advantage in selling their new products, and this size effect increases with the scope of underlying technological opportunities. Second, the contents of innovative sales and exports are different and both depend on the level of technological opportunities. A new product is not always the best way to penetrate a market, our results suggest that this strategy only works under strong technological opportunities. But in activities with low technological opportunities, product improvements and imitations contribute significantly to increase both total sales and export NPRs. Thus the efficiency effect is dominant in the former activities while the inertia effect dominates the latter. This does not mean that new product innovation don't prevail in low technological opportunities activities. It only means that this type of innovation does not constitute a commercial success in these activities, possibly because the demand for variety is low or because the technology does not allow for important changes. Indeed these last two elements characterize the level of technological opportunities.

Finally, our results tend to support the view that commercial success in the domestic market precedes the introduction of a corresponding innovation in foreign markets. However, this interpretation points the need for additional theoretical and empirical research.

• References

COHEN, W., LEVIN, R. (1989). – "Innovation and Market Structure". In R. Schmalensee and R. Willing eds., *Handbook of Industrial Organization*, vol. 2, ch. 18, pp. 1060-1107.

CRÉPON, B., DUGUET, E. (1995). – "Une bibliothèque de macro commandes pour l'économétrie des données de comptage et des variables qualitatives". *CREST working paper 9525*.

DASGUPTA, P. (1986). – "The Theory of Technological Competition". In J. Stiglitz and F. Mathewson eds., *New Developments in the Analysis of Market Structure*. The MIT Press

FRANÇOIS, J.-P. (1991). – "Une enquête sur l'innovation". *Courrier des Statistiques*, n° 57.

GRILICHES, Z. (1986). – "Productivity, R&D and Basic Research at the Firm Level in the 1970's", *American Economic Review*, vol. 76, n° 1, pp. 141-154.

HALL, B. H., MAIRESSE, J. (1995). – "Exploring the Relationship between R&D and Productivity in French Manufacturing Firms". *Journal of Econometrics*, vol. 65, pp. 263-293.

MADDALA, G. (1992). – *Limited Dependent and Qualitative Variables in Econometrics*, Econometric Society Monograph, n° 3, Cambridge University Press.

ROSENBERG, N. (1974). – "Science, Innovation and Economic Growth". *Economic Journal*, 84, pp. 90-108.

ROSENBERG, N., STEINMUELLER E. (1988). – "Why are Americans such poor imitators?", *American Economic Review*, Papers and Proceedings, vol. 78, pp. 229-234.

SCHMOOKLER, J. (1966). – "Invention and Economic Growth". Harvard University Press.

WINDMEIJER, F. (1995). – "Goodness-of-Fit Measures in Binary Choice Models". *Econometric Reviews*, Vol. 14, n° 1, pp. 101-116.

Incentives for Cost Reducing Innovations Under Quantitative Import Restraints

Célia COSTA CABRAL,
Praveen KUJAL, Emmanuel PETRAKIS*

ABSTRACT. – The effect of trade quotas on firms' incentive to invest in cost-reducing R&D is studied in a two-stage price-setting duopoly game. A domestic and a foreign firm first choose R&D levels and then set the prices of their differentiated products in the domestic market. With a quota imposed at, or close to, the free-trade level of imports, the domestic firm faces less competition than under free-trade and invests less in R&D. Contrarily, the constrained foreign firm invests more in R&D as the negative strategic effect of a reduction in its cost is now absent. These results differ partially from the Cournot duopoly case in which R&D expenditures are lower for both the firms. As the quota becomes more restrictive, the domestic firm increases and the foreign firm decreases its expenditures on R&D. Domestic welfare is always higher under free-trade than under any quota regardless of the degree of product substitutability.

* C. COSTA CABRAL: Universidade Nova de Lisboa; P. KUJAL: Universidad Carlos III de Madrid; E. PETRAKIS: Universidad Carlos III de Madrid. The authors acknowledge the comments received from Peter Neary and other participants at the CEPR ERWIT meeting in Thessaloniki, 1995, the Jornadas de Economía Industrial in Madrid, 1995, the ADRES conference at Strasbourg, June 1996, FEDEA and two anonymous referees. Kujal and Petrakis acknowledge support from the DGICYT grant PB95-287 and financial support from the grant Acción Integrada Hispano-Portuguesa 1996, 29 B. Cabral acknowledges financial support from the grant Açòes Integradas Luso-Espanholas E-63/96.

D. Encaoua et al. (eds.), The Economics and Econometrics of Innovation, 457–471.

1 Introduction

The use of trade policies aimed at protecting domestic industries is sometimes justified using the "infant industry" argument. Those in favor of this type of policy argue that trade protection is industry-promoting in the sense that domestic producers, sheltered from foreign competition, can choose long-run strategic variables [1], that ensure long-run gains in profitability [2]. Investment in cost-reducing innovation is one of such strategic variables. Protectionist measures have been shown to affect this variable choice in the "wrong" direction, as shown by REITZES [1991].

REITZES [1991] looks at the impact of quotas (and tariffs) on strategic R&D behavior. Using a two-stage Cournot duopoly game, where firms initially choose R&D levels and subsequently compete in quantities, Reitzes shows that both the domestic and the foreign firm choose lower levels of cost-reducing R&D when a quota is set at the free trade level of production than under free trade. The reason for the decline in R&D is that, in the presence of a quota, the strategic value of R&D vanishes. With a quota, the domestic firm becomes a monopolist on the residual demand, and thus chooses its cost-minimizing level of R&D expenditures. The foreign firm, constrained by the quantity it may sell, will also have less incentives to invest in cost reduction. Note that, although domestic productive efficiency deteriorates as a consequence of the quota, its relative (to the foreign country) efficiency does not necessarily become worse. With the exception of REITZES [1991], very little has been written on the effects of this type of protection on firms' investment in cost-reducing assets.

In this paper, the objective is to study whether REITZES' [1991] results still hold under price competition, since it is known that price competition produces effects on incentives to innovate which are usually the reverse from Cournot competition. For instance, with respect to the well known BRANDER and SPENCER [1985] result where they show that in a Cournot model the domestic government should subsidize exports EATON and GROSSMAN [1986] show that changing the assumption to price competition results in the domestic government taxing exports. Further, BESTER and PETRAKIS [1993] show that if the domestic and the foreign goods are relatively close substitutes, Cournot competition provides weaker incentives to invest in cost-reducing R&D than Bertrand competition, and vice versa for high substitutability among goods. Note, that in all these papers changing the choice variable results in a complete reversal of the outcomes.

---

1. Examples of strategic variables are quality, R&D investment, expenditure on innovation etc.
2. This is the political economy argument towards infant industry protection. The economic argument for industry protection refers to spillovers. Either of these two arguments may be behind protectionist practices. In this paper, we are concerned with the former argument. The case of India, where industrialists wholeheartedly supported the erection of import barriers, leading to the erection of substantial regulatory barriers, is an example of the desire to ensure the 'growth' of domestic industry through protection (KUJAL, 1996).

458

We show that in a price setting game, when a quota is set at the free trade level, the domestic firm *lowers* and the foreign firm *increases* its expenditures on R&D. This result (unlike the complete reversal obtained in other papers) is a partial reversal from REITZES' [1991], where *both* firms invest less in R&D. Under price competition, foreign investment in R&D has a negative indirect (strategic) effect on foreign firm's profits: higher foreign firm's investment in R&D makes the domestic firm lower its price, which in turn results in lower price and profits for the foreign firm. This makes the foreign firm "underinvest" in R&D. With the introduction of a quota, the negative effect disappears for the foreign firm and investment in R&D increases necessarily for the constrained case. Under Cournot competition, the strategic effect has just the opposite sign, which explains the reversal of the results for the foreign firm. Contrarily (as in REITZES [1991]), as the domestic firm faces less competition from the foreign firm after the imposition of the quota it underinvests in R&D. As a consequence, under price competition the domestic industry's absolute and relative productive efficiency necessarily decreases in the presence of a quota. Then the infant industry argument cannot be even partially justified as in Reitzes ' case.

We further show that these qualitative results depend also on how restrictive the quota is. As the quota becomes more restrictive the domestic firm increases and the foreign firm decreases its expenditures on R&D. For a restrictive enough quota, the domestic firm's level of R&D expenditure may exceed the free trade level, and the foreign firm's may decrease relatively to the free trade case. These results are important since, unlike suggested by the infant industry protection argument, strategic variable choices may change in the "wrong" direction: if less R&D takes place domestically while the foreign firm increases its own effort to reduce costs, the relative domestic production cost increases. This also renders less likely that protection will be just temporary, if the domestic firm is to survive future competition. Domestic R&D efforts may increase, but this can only be achieved if the quota is restrictive enough.

Finally, we show that domestic welfare is *always* higher under free trade independently of the degree of product differentiation. This result constitutes a strong argument against this type of protectionist policies. However, if the quota is to be imposed, the right level of quota will depend on the degree of product differentiation. If the goods are close enough substitutes the domestic government may want to completely shut the foreign firm out of the domestic market. If the goods are significantly differentiated, then the right level of the quota will be at the free-trade level of production. This may explain why in many developing countries, close substitutes to domestic production were completely shut out of the market.

The paper is organized as follows. In Section 2 the model is presented and equilibrium under free trade determined. In Section 3, equilibrium after the imposition of an import quota is determined for a sequential move price setting game. Section 4 presents the welfare analysis and Section 5 concludes.

2 The Model under Free Trade

There are two firms, one domestic and one foreign. Firms produce goods which are imperfect substitutes and sell their production in the domestic market only [3]. Firms face the following (symmetric) demand functions [4]:

$$(1) \qquad x_i = \frac{1}{1 - \gamma^2}[a(1 - \gamma) - p_i + \gamma p_j], \quad i, j = 1, 2.$$

γ measures the degree of product differentiation. As γ goes to zero, each firm becomes a local monopolist. When γ goes to one, firms' goods are almost perfect substitutes. To avoid corner solutions, we shall assume that $\gamma \leq 0.827891$. The domestic firm is denoted by $i = 1$, and the foreign firm by $i = 2$. Both firms have initially the same unit production costs, c. Firms can invest in R&D in order to reduce their unit cost. In particular, by investing $\frac{\Delta_i^2}{2}$ firm i will reduce its cost by Δ_i.

Firms play a two-stage game. In stage one, firms simultaneously decide on how much to invest in cost-reducing R&D. In stage two, given the (reduced) unit cost, firms decide simultaneously on which price to set. It should be noted that R&D has a commitment value in this context. Firms can use R&D strategically to improve their position in the subsequent market competition game. The problem is solved recursively for the equilibrium outcomes, i.e., we restrict our attention to the subgame perfect equilibria.

(i) the market competition stage

Firm i chooses p_i to maximize profits:

$$\max[p_i - (c - \Delta_i)]x_i(p_i, p_j).$$

p_j and Δ_i are taken as given. This defines each firm's reaction function:

$$(2) \qquad p_i = b_i(p_j; \Delta_i) \equiv \frac{a(1 - \gamma) + c - \Delta_i + \gamma p_j}{2}.$$

In figure 1, firms' reaction functions under free trade are depicted. The dashed line $b_i(p_j)$ represents the price firm i will choose to set given firm j's price p_j.

---

3. This approach to modelling the effects of trade policies is standard to the literature. Of course, the issue of retaliation is important in trade policy (we would like to thank one of the referees for pointing this out). However, conditions under which quantity restrictions are only imposed by the home country has many parallels in real world situations. For example, VERs by definition are not retaliatory in nature and have been the accepted mode of quantity controls both in the U.S. and the E.U in their trade with Japan and South Korea. Given that in the presence of quantity restrictions trade between countries co-exists provides us with ample evidence that justifies the use of only one active government.
4. These are the demand functions of a representative consumer with utility $u(x_i, x_j) = a(x_i + x_j) - (x_i^2 + x_j^2 + 2\gamma x_i x_j)/2 + m$ with m representing money, following DIXIT (1979). Resulting inverse demand is $p_i = a - x_i - \gamma x_j$.

Then equilibrium prices and profits are:

(3) $$p_i = \frac{1}{4-\gamma^2}\{[a(1-\gamma)+c](2+\gamma) - 2\Delta_i - \gamma\Delta_j\},$$

and

(4) $$\pi_i = \frac{(p_i - c + \Delta_i)^2}{1-\gamma^2} - \frac{\Delta_i^2}{2}.$$

FIGURE 1

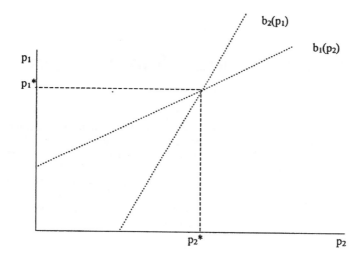

(ii) the R&D stage

Firm i, given Δ_j, chooses Δ_i to maximize its profits (defined in (4)). From the first-order conditions and symmetry we obtain optimal R&D spending, output and price for each firm:

(5) $$\Delta^* = \frac{2(2-\gamma^2)}{D(\gamma)}(a-c),$$

(6) $$x^* = \frac{(4-\gamma^2)}{2(2-\gamma^2)}\Delta^*,$$

(7) $$p^* = \frac{1}{2-\gamma}[a(1-\gamma) + c - \Delta^*].$$

Firms' profits are then given by

$$(8) \qquad \pi^* = \frac{8 - 16\gamma^2 + 7\gamma^4 - \gamma^6}{D(\gamma)^2}(a - c)^2.$$

where $D(\gamma) = (1 + \gamma)(2 - \gamma)(4 - \gamma^2) - 2(2 - \gamma^2)$.

Note, that under price competition a firm has less incentives to invest in cost-reducing R&D than under a pure cost-minimizing strategy. There is a negative strategic effect when firms compete in prices. As a response to firm i's reduction of unit cost, its rival decreases its price (see (3)), thus shifting-in i's demand function. Firm i has now to reduce its price in order to sell the same output. By lowering its R&D expenditures beyond the cost-minimizing level, a firm can commit to softer competition in the subsequent market game.

3 Equilibrium under Import Quotas

In this section we assume that the domestic government precommits to a given quota level $\bar{x}$ (or, the foreign government precommits to a level of VER) before the firms decide how much to invest in R&D. For illustrative purposes we shall concentrate on the analysis of the case where a quota is set at the free-trade level of imports. A similar reasoning applies to the case of more restrictive quotas. Henceforth, firm 2 (the foreign firm) is assumed to be restricted to sell no more than $\bar{x}$ units, with $\bar{x}$ being set at the free-trade level of imports as defined by (6).

3.1. The Best Response Functions

As shown by KRISHNA [1989], the imposition of quantity restrictions alters firms' best response functions in the market competition stage [5]. Let us define $f(p_1, \bar{x})$ as the foreign firm's price level that yields a demand for its good just equal to $\bar{x}$. Clearly, this is a function of the price selected by the domestic firm p_1. In figure 2, $f(p_1, \bar{x})$ is represented by the dashed line between $b_2(p_1)$ and $b_1(p_2)$. Since the quota is set at the free-trade equilibrium level of production, this line has to go through the free-trade equilibrium point (the point where the original reaction functions $b_i(p_j)$ intersect). Above $f(p_1, \bar{x})$, the foreign firm is bound by the restriction while below it the restriction is not binding. Firm 2's best response is not altered from the free-trade case if $p_1 < p^*$ since optimal pricing decisions do not involve firm 2's production exceeding $\bar{x}$: the domestic firm's price is low

---

5. The derivation of the best response functions that follows draws on KRISHNA (1989).

enough for firm 2's production to be below its free trade level, now the quota level. However, if the domestic firm's price exceeds the free-trade equilibrium price, i.e., if $p_1 > p^*$, then, in the absence of a quota, the foreign firm would like to produce more than $\bar{x}$. But, that is no longer possible. The foreign firm's best response is then to select a price high enough so that its demand is just equal to the quota level $\bar{x}$. In this case, the best response function coincides with the $f(p_1, \bar{x})$ line. Firm 2's best response function is depicted in figure 2, given by the kinked full line and is defined by:

$$\hat{b}_2(p_1, \bar{x}) = \begin{cases} b_2(p_1) & \text{if } p_1 \leq p^*, \\ f(p_1, \bar{x}) & \text{if } p_1 > p^*. \end{cases}$$

Using (1) this can be written as:

$$\hat{b}_2(p_1, \bar{x}) = \max\left\{ \frac{a(1-\gamma) + c - \Delta_2 + \gamma p_1}{2}, a(1-\gamma) - (1-\gamma^2)\bar{x} + \gamma p_1 \right\}.$$

FIGURE 2

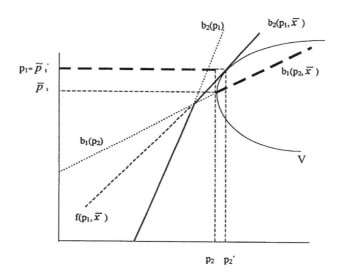

Let us now turn to the determination of the domestic firm's best response function. Let us define $F(p_2, \bar{x})$ as the function that determines the domestic price level which, given p_2, yields a demand level for the foreign product exactly equal to $\bar{x}$. Graphically, $F(p_2, \bar{x})$ coincides with $f(p_1, \bar{x})$, since, by definition one function is the inverse of the other. When firm 2 is bound by the quota level, then domestic firm's demand depends only on its own price: $p_1 = a - x_1 - \gamma\bar{x}$. Hence, above $F(p_2, \bar{x})$, the domestic firm's isoprofit curves are horizontal and there is a unique price, $\bar{p}_1$, which maximizes its profits. In this case, some consumers are rationed by the (low-priced) foreign firm. Assume the following rationing rule: consumers lucky enough to buy the foreign firm's good, are able to resell it costlessly in the market. This situation is equivalent to the foreign firm selecting a best reply to $\bar{p}_1$. This, in turn, guarantees a profit level of V to the domestic firm, the same as the profits that a Stackelberg leader, who makes the quota bind on the foreign firm, can achieve.

Below $F(p_2, \bar{x})$, the domestic firm's isoprofit curves remain the same as under free-trade. As a result, isoprofit curves are kinked along $F(p_2, \bar{x})$, and moreover they are not convex anymore. If the foreign firm's price is higher than p_2', then the domestic firm can reach a profit level higher than V by choosing not to make the foreign firm bound by the quota. If, however, the foreign firm's price is lower than p_2', the domestic firm can always guarantee profits of V by choosing $\bar{p}_1$. Firm 1's best response function is given by the two dark dashed lines in figure 2 and is defined by $\hat{b}_1(p_2, \bar{x})$:

$$
p_1 = \hat{b}_1(p_2, \bar{x}) = \begin{cases} \bar{p}_1 & \text{if } p_2 \leq p_2' \\ b_1(p_2) & \text{if } p_2 \geq p_2' \end{cases}
$$

It should be noted that firm 1's best response function is not continuous and that it assumes two values when $p_2 = p_2'$ (the same profit level V can be reached charging either $\bar{p}_1$ or $\tilde{p}_1$).

3.2. Equilibrium with Sequential Moves

When firms choose prices simultaneously, there is a unique equilibrium in mixed strategies in the market competition game where the foreign firm chooses p_2' and the domestic firm randomizes over $(\bar{p}_1, \tilde{p}_1)$, (see KRISHNA [1989]). In this equilibrium the domestic firm always obtains profits of V: the profit level that a domestic firm could attain as a Stackelberg leader that makes the quota bind on the foreign firm. The domestic firm is, thus, indifferent between being a price leader or choosing its price simultaneously with its rival. The foreign firm, playing simultaneously, obtains strictly lower profits than the Stackelberg follower's profits [6].

Thus, we can imagine that there exist two stages, 1 and 2, before the good is sold in the market. Since by acting as a Stackelberg follower in the price competition game it is guaranteed higher profits the foreign firm will let the domestic firm set its price before it chooses its own. Our justification for this sequence of moves is along the lines of the existing literature on

---

6. This is true since a Stackelberg follower (foreign) firm sets a higher price than in the simultaneous move game ($\hat{p}_2 > p_2'$) and, moreover, it always sells at the quota level $\bar{x}$. As we saw, under simultaneous choice of prices, the foreign firm sells at the quota level only when the domestic firm sets its price at $\bar{p}_1$, while it sells less than $\bar{x}$ when the domestic price is $\tilde{p}_1$, in the mixed strategy equilibrium. Thus, the foreign firm attains higher profits whenever it acts as a Stackelberg follower.

the endogeniety of moves. In fact, FURTH and KOVENOCK [1993] [7] use similar arguments to ours to show endogeniety of moves in a much more general setting. They also show that precisely in the structure of the Krishna paper mentioned above the endogenous outcome of player moves is in-fact along the lines of our argument. That is, the domestic firm emerges as the Stackelberg leader and the foreign firm the Stackelberg follower.

The imposition of the quota thus changes the timing of player moves. We, therefore, assume that the firms choose their prices sequentially with the domestic firm being the Stackelberg leader and the foreign firm the Stackelberg follower in the price setting game (as in HARRIS [1985]) [8].

So far we have only treated the case of a quota imposed at the free-trade level of imports. A similar analysis applies to more restrictive quotas. In what follows, we take as given that the imposition of any quota alters the sequence of price choices in the market game.

The game becomes a 3-stage game. In the first stage, both firms select R&D levels. In the second stage, the domestic firm sets its price, and in the third stage, the foreign firm selects its price.

(i) stage-3

Given Δ_1, Δ_2 and p_1, the foreign firm sells $\bar{x}$, and charges the market clearing price:

$$(9) \qquad p_2 = f(p_1, \bar{x}) = a(1 - \gamma) - (1 - \gamma^2)\bar{x} + \gamma p_1$$

(ii) stage-2

The domestic firm is now a constrained monopolist facing a residual demand $x_1 = D_R(p_1) = a - \gamma\bar{x} - p_1$. Then its profit maximizing price and output levels are:

$$(10) \qquad p_1 = \frac{a + c - \gamma\bar{x} - \Delta_1}{2},$$

$$(11) \qquad x_1 = \frac{a - c - \gamma\bar{x} + \Delta_1}{2}.$$

Resulting profits are

$$(12) \qquad \pi_1 = \frac{(a - c - \gamma\bar{x} + \Delta_1)^2}{4} - \frac{\Delta_1^2}{2}.$$

It should be noted that the domestic price and profits do not depend on Δ_2. Note, also that, when the quota is binding on the foreign firm, R&D

---

7. Also see CORNEO (1995), DENECKERE and KOVENOCK (1992) and SYROPOULOS (1996).
8. Note, that qualitatively similar results hold even when firms set their prices simultaneously. For the reasons mentioned above and given that mixed strategies in the simultaneous move game significantly complicate the analysis, we have opted for exposing the sequential move game only. The analytical treatment of the Bertrand game is available upon request.

has no strategic value for the domestic firm. Hence, it will simply choose the cost-minimizing level of R&D, acting as a constrained monopolist.

Substituting (10) into (9), we obtain the foreign firm's price and profits:

$$(13) \qquad p_2 = \frac{a(2 - \gamma) - (2 - \gamma^2)\bar{x} + (c - \Delta_1)\gamma}{2}$$

$$(14) \quad \pi_2 = \left\{ \left[\frac{a(2 - \gamma) - (2 - \gamma^2)\bar{x} + (c - \Delta_1)\gamma}{2} \right] - c + \Delta_2 \right\} \bar{x} - \frac{\Delta_2^2}{2}$$

Note that, whatever the reduction of its unit cost, the foreign firm always sells at the quota level. As a result, its marginal revenue from a reduction in its unit cost is simply equal to the quota level itself. Hence, the imposition of the quota removes the negative strategic effect which was present under free-trade price-competition.

(iii) stage-1

Maximizing profits as defined by (12) and (14), and solving the first-order conditions, we get the optimal R&D levels for the domestic and the foreign firms:

$$(15) \qquad\qquad \tilde{\Delta}_1 = a - c - \gamma\bar{x}$$

$$(16) \qquad\qquad \tilde{\Delta}_2 = \bar{x}$$

Domestic R&D decreases with the quota level. As the quota becomes more restrictive on the foreign firm, the domestic firm's residual demand increases and thus also the profitability of a reduction in its unit cost. Contrarily, foreign R&D levels increase with the quota level and in a one-to-one relation. This is because, as we saw, the foreign firm's marginal revenue of a reduction in unit cost is equal to the quota, while the marginal cost is Δ_2.

Figure 3 depicts $\tilde{\Delta}_i$ as a function of the level of the quota $\bar{x}$ imposed on the foreign firm.

FIGURE 3

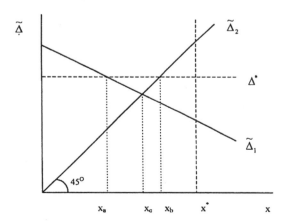

Finally, prices, quantities and profits can now be determined:

$$(17) \qquad \hat{p}_1 = c$$

$$(18) \qquad \hat{p}_2 = a(1 - \gamma) - \bar{x}(1 - \gamma^2) + c\gamma$$

$$(19) \qquad \hat{x}_1 = a - c - \gamma\bar{x}$$

$$(20) \qquad \hat{x}_2 = \bar{x}$$

$$(21) \qquad \hat{\pi}_1 = \frac{(a - c - \gamma\bar{x})^2}{2}$$

$$(22) \qquad \hat{\pi}_2 = \frac{\bar{x}}{2}[2(a - c)(1 - \gamma) + \bar{x}(2\gamma^2 - 1)]$$

Domestic profits increase as the quota becomes more restrictive, since more residual demand allows the domestic firm to attain higher profit levels, while foreign profits decrease [9].

> PROPOSITION 1 : The domestic firm invests less in cost reduction ($\tilde{\Delta}_1 < \Delta^*$) for a quota set at, or close to, the free-trade level ($\bar{x} = x^*$) than under free trade. As the quota ($\bar{x}$) becomes more restrictive, $\tilde{\Delta}_1$ increases.

Proof: With a quota set at the free-trade level, i.e., with $\bar{x} = x^*$, the resulting investment in cost-reducing tecnology ($\hat{\Delta}_1$) will be below the free trade value (Δ^*):

$$\hat{\Delta}_1(\bar{x} = x^*) = \frac{(2 - \gamma^2)^2(a - c)}{D(\gamma)} < \frac{2(2 - \gamma^2)(a - c)}{D(\gamma)} = \Delta^*.$$

$\hat{\Delta}_1$ is decreasing in $\bar{x}$ since $\hat{\Delta}_1 = a - c - \gamma\bar{x}$. $\quad\square$

> PROPOSITION 2 : The foreign firm invests more in cost reduction ($\tilde{\Delta}_2 > \Delta^*$) than under free-trade when a quota is set at, or close to, the free-trade level. Investment in R&D decreases with the restrictiveness of the quota. If the quota is sufficiently restrictive (in particular for $\bar{x} < \Delta^*$), the foreign firm invests less than under free trade.

Proof: With a quota set at the free-trade level, i.e., with $\bar{x} = x^*$, the resulting investment in cost-reducing technology ($\hat{\Delta}_2$) will be above the free-trade level (Δ^*): $\hat{\Delta}_2(\bar{x} = x^*) = x^* > \Delta^*$ (from (6)). Since $\hat{\Delta}_2 = \bar{x}$,

---

9. this is easily shown.

this implies that, for levels of restriction less than free trade level of innovation $\bar{x} < \Delta^*$, the foreign firm will invest less than it does under free trade. $\square$

When a restraint is set at the free-trade level of imports the foreign firm chooses to innovate more and the domestic firm less [10]. The results under price competition differ from those obtained under Cournot competition, where both the domestic and the foreign firm lower their R&D expenditures after the imposition of the quota (REITZES [1991]). The reason is that, under Cournot competition, foreign R&D spending has a positive indirect (strategic) effect on foreign firm's profits, while under Bertrand competition this effect is a negative one. Under price competition, a foreign firm's increase in R&D spending leads the domestic firm to lower its price, which in turn results in lower price and profits for the foreign firm. The foreign firm thus "underinvests" in R&D when there is free trade. Once a quota is imposed this strategic effect vanishes, since the domestic price no longer depends on foreign firm's choice of R&D spending. Consequently, more investment in cost-reducing R&D takes place in the constrained case than in the unconstrained case. The effect on the unconstrained domestic firm is just the opposite. It spends less on R&D after the imposition of the quota because it faces less competition (since the foreign firm is now constrained).

4 Welfare

In this section we analyze the effect of imposing a quota on domestic welfare versus free trade. It is shown that total welfare is always the highest under free trade than under any level of quota for any degree of product differentiation.

To compute the consumer surplus, recall that preferences are quasi-linear [11]. Hence,

$$CS = a(\hat{x}_1 + \hat{x}_2) - \frac{\hat{x}_1^2 + \hat{x}_2^2 + 2\gamma\hat{x}_1\hat{x}_2}{2} - \hat{p}_1\hat{x}_1 - \hat{p}_2\hat{x}_2,$$

Using (17)-(20) and simplifying, we get:

(23) $$CS = \frac{1}{2}[(a - c)^2 + (1 - \gamma^2)\bar{x}^2].$$

Total domestic welfare (TW) is defined as the sum of the consumer surplus and the domestic firm's profits:

$$TW = CS + \hat{\pi}_1.$$

---

10. It should at this point be stressed that both propositions 1 and 2 also hold under the simultaneous move game.
11. See footnote 2.

468

Then, using (21) we get

$$(24) \qquad TW = (a - c)^2 - \gamma\bar{x}(a - c) + \frac{\bar{x}^2}{2}.$$

It can easily be seen that total domestic welfare under the quota initially decreases with $\bar{x}$, it reaches a minimum at $\bar{x} = \gamma(a - c)$ and then increases with $\bar{x}$. Hence, it reaches its maximum either at $\bar{x} = 0$ or at $\bar{x} = x^*$ depending on the degree of product substitutability.

Figure 4 represents total welfare as a function of the product differentiation parameter, γ [12]. TW_F represents total welfare under free trade. $TW(\bar{x} = 0)$ represents total welfare when the foreign firm is shut out of the market, which is given by $(a - c)^2$ and is independent of the degree of product differentiation. $TW(\bar{x} = x^*)$ represents welfare when the quota is set at the free-trade level of production.

FIGURE 4

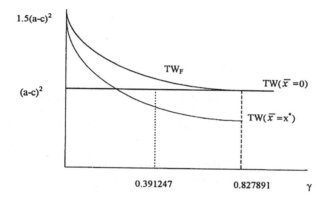

Total welfare under free trade is $TW_F = CS_F + \pi^*$, where (see footnote 2)

$$CS_F = 2ax^* - x^{*2} - \gamma x^{*2} - 2p^* x^*$$

Using (6)-(8) and simplifying, we get:

$$(25) \qquad TW_F = \frac{24 + 16\gamma - 24\gamma^2 - 8\gamma^3 + 8\gamma^4 + \gamma^5 - \gamma^6}{(4 + 4\gamma - 4\gamma^2 - \gamma^3 + \gamma^4)^2}(a - c)^2$$

In figure 4, total domestic welfare under free trade, TW_F, is represented by the upper line. Free trade leads to a higher domestic welfare than the optimal restriction for *any* value of the product substitutability parameter.

---

12. We will restrict our attention to $\gamma < 0.827891$ since this condition is necessary to guarantee $\pi_i^* \geq 0$.

Welfare is higher under free trade. This result is true for any degree of product differentiation. The reason is that quotas act as collusion facilitating practices. As a result, consumers pay much higher prices after the imposition of the quota, and thus consumer surplus is reduced substantially. The increase in domestic firm's profits, on the other hand, is not enough to compensate for the loss in the consumer surplus. This constitutes a very strong result against the imposition of quotas. However, if a quota has to be imposed, then the size of the restriction depends on the degree of substitutability between the two goods. For sufficiently differentiated goods, $\gamma < 0.391247$, the quota should be set at the free trade level of output of $\bar{x} = x^*$. However, when the goods are close substitutes, $\gamma > 0.391247$, it should be set at $\bar{x} = 0$. This is along the line of the import substitution argument: closer substitutes to domestic goods are subject to tighter import restrictions. Note, the imposition of a quantity restriction (KRISHNA [1989]) facilitates collusion between the foreign and the domestic firm. Thus, it is reasonable to assume that a foreign country has the incentives not to in-fact retaliate to the quantity restriction as it makes a higher level of profits.

5 Conclusions

This paper shows that, under price competition, when a quantity constraint is imposed at the free trade level of production, or close to it, the foreign firm increases its expenditures on R&D. The domestic firm, however, chooses to spend less than in the absence of that quantity restriction. These results partially differ from the Cournot competition case analyzed by REITZES [1991] where both the foreign and domestic firm lower their R&D expenditures. Under price competition, foreign investment in R&D has a negative strategic effect on foreign firm's profits: more investment in R&D by the foreign firm makes the domestic firm lower its own price, which in turn results in lower price and profit levels for the foreign firm. With the introduction of a quota this negative effect disappears and foreign firm's investment in R&D necessarily increases. Under Cournot competition, the strategic effect has the opposite sign, which explains this reversal in results for the foreign firm.

We further show that, as the quota becomes more restrictive, the domestic firm increases its spending on R&D while the foreign firm decreases it. In this sense, results in line with the "infant-industry" argument in favor of protection can be achieved with a quota but only if it is sufficiently restrictive. As in the "infant industry" argument, industries producing close substitutes to potential imports desire protection. Finally, it is shown that domestic welfare is always lower in the presence of a quantity restriction than under free trade. This result is independent of the degree of product differentiation and the level of the quantity restriction. This constitutes a strong argument against the imposition of quantity restrictions, such as quotas and VERs. The empirical evidence from countries that used this type of regulatory policy clearly does not lend support to the infant industry protection argument either.

● References

BESTER, H., PETRAKIS, E. (1993). – "The Incentive for Cost Reduction in a Differentiated Industry", *International Journal of Industrial Organization*, 11, pp. 519-34.

BRANDER, J., SPENCER, B. (1985). – "Export Subsidies and International Market Share Rivalry", *Journal of International Economics*, 16, pp. 227-42.

CORNEO, G. (1995). – "National Wage Bargaining in an Internationally Integrated Product Market", *European Journal of Political Economy*, 11, 3.

DENECKERE, R., KOVENOCK, D. (1992). – "Price Leadership", *Review of Economic Studies*, 59, pp. 143-62.

DIXIT, A. (1979). – "A Model of Oligopoly Suggesting a Theory of Entry Barriers", *Bell Journal of Economics*, 10.

EATON, J., GROSSMAN, G. (1986). – "Optimal Trade and Industrial Policy under Oligopoly", *Quarterly Journal of Economics*, 101, pp. 383-406.

FURTH, D., KOVENOCK, D. (1993). – "Price Leadership in a Duopoly with Capacity Constraints and Product Differentiation", *Journal of Economics*, 57, 1, pp. 1-35.

HARRIS, R. (1985). – "Why Voluntary Export Restraints Are Voluntary?", *Canadian Journal of Economics*, 18, pp. 799-809.

KUJAL, P. (1996). – "The Impact of Regulatory Control on Industry Structure: A Study of the Car and Scooter Industry in India", *Working Paper 96-15*, Universidad. Carlos III de Madrid.

KRISHNA, K. (1989). – "Trade Restrictions and Facilitating Practices", *Journal of International Economics*, 26, pp. 251-70.

REITZES, J. D. (1991). – "The Impact of Quotas and Tariffs on Strategic R&D Behavior", *International Economic Review*, 32(4).

SYROPOULOS, C. (1996). – "Nontarriff Trade Controls and Leader Follower Relations in International Competition", *Economica*, 63, pp. 633-48.

The Size Distribution of Profits from Innovation

Frederic M. SCHERER*

ABSTRACT. – This paper reports on research seeking to determine how skew the distribution of profits from technological innovation is – *i.e.*, whether it conforms most closely to the Paretian, log normal, or some other distribution. The question is important, because high skewness makes it difficult to pursue risk-hedging portfolio strategies, and it may have real business cycle consequences. Data from several sources are examined: the royalties from U.S. university patent portfolios, the quasi-rents from marketed pharmaceutical entities, the stock market returns from three large samples of high-technology venture startups, and preliminary results from a survey of German patents on which renewal fees were paid until full-term expiration in 1995. The evidence reveals a mixture of distributions, some close to log normality and some Paretian. Preliminary hypotheses about the underlying behavioral processes are advanced.

* F. M. SCHERER: Harvard University. The support from a Sloan Foundation grant is gratefully acknowledged, as are comments from three anonymous referees.

D. Encaoua et al. (eds.), The Economics and Econometrics of Innovation, 473–494.
© 2000 *Kluwer Academic Publishers. Printed in the Netherlands.*

1 Introduction

It is now widely recognized that the size distribution of profit returns from technological innovation is skewed to the right. The most profitable cases contribute a disproportionate fraction of the total profits from innovation. The exact form the distribution function takes remains a mystery. In an early analysis (SCHERER [1965]), I reported that the profits measured through a small survey of U.S. patents conformed tolerably well to the Pareto-Levy distribution:

$$(1) \qquad\qquad N = kV^{-\alpha},$$

where V is the value of profits from an innovation, N is the number of cases with value V or greater, and k and α are positive parameters. The equation is linear in the logarithms. For the sample analyzed, the linear slope coefficient α appeared to be less than 0.5. Since then economists have sought to discern the size distribution's form by analyzing the rate at which patents have been allowed to expire before full term due to non-payment of the periodic maintenance fees imposed by many national patent offices. Early evidence analyzed by PAKES and SCHANKERMAN (1984, p. 78) favored the Pareto-Levy distribution, but later work by SCHANKERMAN and PAKES [1986] found mixed but stronger support for the log normal distribution [1].

The difference between distributions is important. When the distribution is Pareto-Levy and α is less than 2.0, the variance is not asymptotically finite, and for $\alpha < 1$, the mean is also not asymptotically finite. What this implies is that as one draws ever larger samples, there is an increasing chance that some unprecedentedly large value (e.g., an extraordinarily large profit) will be included, overwhelming the observations drawn previously and forcing the mean and variance upward, contrary to conventional expectations under the law of large numbers. With finite variances and means, log normal and similar skew distributions are better behaved statistically. Still the more rightward-skewed the distribution is, whether Pareto-Levy, log normal, or some related form, the more difficult it is to hedge against risk by supporting sizable portfolios of innovation projects. The potential variability of economic outcomes with Pareto-Levy distributions is so great that large portfolio draws from year to year can have consequences for the macroeconomy. In a simulation experiment, NORDHAUS (1989, p. 324) discovered that aggregated Pareto-distributed productivity effects from samples approximating in size the number of patents issued annually in the United States mimicked the long-term productivity fluctuations actually experienced by the U.S. economy between 1900 and 1985 [2].

Crucial to the portfolio properties of large invention samples is the value distribution of observations in the right-hand (most valuable) tail.

---

1. See also PAKES (1986, p. 777), SCHANKERMAN [1991] and LANJOUW [1992], all of whom find distributions less skew than the Pareto-Levy.
2. On the aggregation properties of Pareto-Levy distributions, see MANDELBROT (1963).

On this, studies of patent renewals provide only limited insight. Even in nations with relatively high maintenance fees that rise over the patent's life span, only 10 to 20 percent of the issued patents survive to full term (*i.e.*, 18 to 20 years) after paying all fees. Such patents are clearly of relatively high value. However, the distribution of values within the full-term cohort is ascertained in renewal studies only by extrapolation, not by direct measurement. Because, as we shall see, it is difficult under even the best of circumstances to discriminate among size distributions on the basis of right-hand tail characteristics, extrapolation is hazardous. Also, the mapping from patents to innovations is far from simple. Many innovations are covered by numerous patents, some with a crucial imitation-blocking role, some not. Although patents cannot add significant value to a worthless technology, they enhance the rewards appropriated from certain valuable innovations, but in other cases are unimportant because there are alternative barriers to competitive imitation. See SCHERER [1977] and LEVIN *et al.* [1987].

This paper reports the first results from an ongoing attempt to surmount the limitations of prior research. It probes the right-hand tail, analyzing detailed innovation data across the full spectrum of positive payoff outcomes (while discarding negative outcomes). It examines not only individual patents, but technological innovations construed more broadly. Specifically, evidence will be presented from three patent samples, in two or which complementary patents are bundled together; two nearly exhaustive samples of new pharmaceutical entities introduced into the U.S. market; and two large samples of high-technology venture capital investments.

The approach pursued here is inductive, seeking not to impose an a priori theory upon the data, but merely to see what general patterns the data reveal as a first step toward sorting out plausible from implausible theories [3]. Parallel research is exploring alternative models (such as Gibrat and Einstein-Bose processes) in an attempt to identify stochastic regimes most consistent with the observed distribution of profit outcomes [4].

Preliminary insight is maximized by plotting the data graphically, although statistical tests will also be reported. The Pareto-Levy distribution will be emphasized in part because of its simplicity, plotting linearly on doubly logarithmic coordinates, and partly because it has the most radical implications for risk-pooling under a large-numbers strategy. When the data permit, the log normal distribution (which emerges from Gibrat stochastic processes) and the exponential and Weibull distributions will be considered as alternative hypotheses. The focus, again, will be on the high-value tails of the observed distributions.

---

3. This methodology is more typical of the natural sciences than economics. See IJIRI and SIMON (1977, pp. 4-5 and 109-111); SCHERER [1986] (on Kepler, Einstein, Watson, and Crick), and more generally HANSON [1961].

4. See e.g. GIBRAT [1931], De VANY and WALLS [1996], and IJIRI and SIMON [1977].

2 Patent Data

Figure 1 plots on log-log coordinates the profitability data analyzed in my 1965 article [5]. The profit estimates were drawn from a survey of 600 U.S. patents by SANDERS *et al.* (1958, p. 355; 1964, p. 53), among which 74 useable responses with positive profits were received. (For 149 additional patents, net losses, typically small, were quantified.) The data were reported as patent counts over seven profit intervals. Consistent with the Pareto distribution assumptions of equation (1), the dotted line plots the data points at lower interval bounds. Since the lowest (under $5,000) interval was bounded at zero, for which no logarithm exists, an arbitrary lower bound of $1,000 is assumed. The distribution function's implied left-hand shape is sensitive to that assumption. The highest profit value interval, "over $1 million", included five patents, but a later (1964) article revealed the maximum value to be $15 million. Since that largest observation is a point rather than a lower bound, the solid line plots for consistency the data points at the geometric means of class intervals, assuming a value of $3,000 for the lowest-profit interval.

FIGURE 1

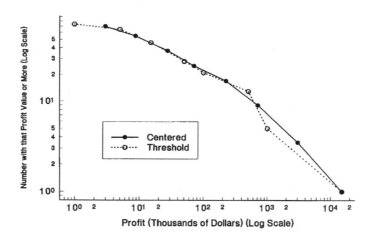

For the dotted lower-interval-bound plot, a straight line fitted by least squares yields an α value of 0.454, with standard error of 0.050 and r^2 of 0.931. For the solid geometric mean plot, $\alpha = 0.497$, with standard error of

---

5. For ease of plotting, all logarithms used in this article are taken to the base ten.

0.040 and $r^2 = 0.963$ [6]. If the distribution is in fact Paretian, both α values lie within the range where neither means nor variances are asymptotically finite. However, both plots reveal a modest degree of concavity inconsistent with the Pareto-Levy hypothesis. Adding a quadratic term to the centered value regression raises R^2 by 0.0343, which, despite retaining only five residual degrees of freedom, is highly significant in an F-ratio test.

For a first extension of the patent value analysis, a novel data source was tapped. The Bayh-Dole Act of 1980 changed U.S. law, permitting researchers in universities and other non-profit institutions supported by federal government grants to receive and assign exclusive rights to inventions resulting from their government-funded research. Many universities established technology licensing offices to apply for patents on such inventions and to negotiate licenses with private sector enterprises for their commercial exploitation. By 1993, the royalty revenues received by 117 U.S. universities from their outstanding technology licenses had reached an annual rate of $242 million [7]. Among those 117, the top ten institutions had royalty revenues of $171 million, or 70.6 percent of the total.

One of the top ten on this list was Harvard University, my emplyer. The Harvard Office of Technology Licensing kindly provided to me a detailed confidential tabulation of the total royalties received between 1977 and May 1995 on 118 technology "bundles" with non-zero royalties whose patents had been applied for by the end of 1990. Among the 118 bundles, 27 included more than one patent, and six included five or more patents. The twelve bundles with the largest cumulative royalties originated nearly 84 percent of total portfolios royalties – characteristic evidence of high royalty distribution skewness.

Figure 2 plots the royalty income (multiplied by a constant disguise parameter) from individual invention bundles. The plot is clearly not linear, as would be expected with a Pareto-Levy distribution, but shows considerable downward concavity. If a straight line (in the logarithms) is forced by least squares to the data, the indicated slope is 0.41, with standard error of 0.015 and r^2 of 0.865 [8]. Adding a quadratic term to the regression raises R^2 to 0.983; the increment is significant at the 0.01 level. The slope is plainly steeper in the higher-value tail of the distribution. A linear regression on the 39 most valuable invention bundles (*i.e.,* the top third of the distribution) yields a slope of 0.71, with the standard error of the coefficient being 0.016 and $r^2 = 0.981$. A further analysis of all 118 Harvard technology bundles revealed the fitted Pareto-Levy line to be insignificantly influenced by the number of patents in the bundles and (surprisingly) by the age of the patent bundles.

---

6. Since each group has different numbers of observations, one might prefer to use weighted least squares, where the weights are the square roots of the number of observations. This places relatively more weight on the lower-value observations, which are more numerous. The estimated α values (and standard errors) are 0.377 (0.048) and 0.433 (0.036) for the bounded and centered observations respectively.

7. Aggregated university data were provided by the Association of University Technology Managers.

8. Despite the poor fit, double-log slopes are reported here becaused they will be used in a later paper as part of a benchmark for evaluating alternative stochastic processes.

FIGURE 2

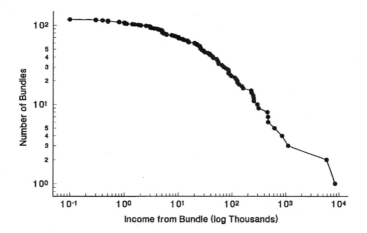

Figure 3 plots the Harvard royalty data on log normal probability coordinates, with the cumulative probability given on the horizontal axis and the cumulative number of invention bundles required to reach that

FIGURE 3

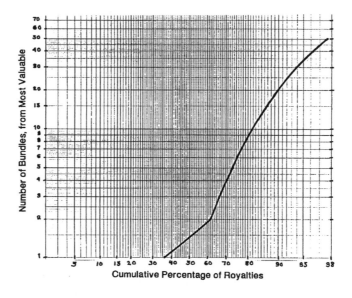

478

probability, starting from the most valuable bundle (*i.e.*, from the right-hand tail), on the vertical axis. The linear fit one would expect if the distribution were exactly log normal is absent. Letting μ_i be the i-th moment of a distribution, we define the coefficient of skewness to be $\sqrt{\beta_1} = \mu_3/\mu_2^{3/2}$. Taking logarithms of the royalty distribution, we find $\sqrt{\beta_1} = +0.17$, which rejects the hypothesis of log normality only at a confidence level short of 80 percent. See D'AGOSTINO and STEPHENS [1986], p. 380. The coefficient of kurtosisis is defined as $\beta_2 = \mu_4/\mu_2^2$. Its value for the log royalty distribution is 2.99, which is not significantly different from the 3.00 value associated with log normality.

Figure 4 subjects the Harvard data to a further graphic test attributable to M. C. BRYSON [1974] [9]. The horizontal axis measures royalties logarithmically. The vertical axis is scaled as one minus the cumulative probability integral, beginning with the lowest-royalty observation, but truncating at the midpoint of the distribution so that only the highest-value observations are plotted. If the underlying distribution were negative exponential, the plot would be linear; if the distribution were two-parameter Weibull, the plot would be concave downward. Both hypotheses are clearly rejected. The downward convexity exhibited in Figure 4 is consistent with log normal, Paretian, or other highly skew distributions. The analysis of the preceding paragraph favors an inference of log normality.

FIGURE 4

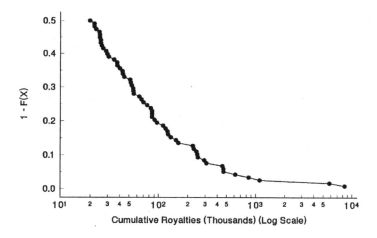

Cumulative Royalties (Thousands) (Log Scale)

Eleven university technology licensing offices, including the top ten royalty recipients of 1993, were asked to provide information on the distribution of their technology license royalties, divided into nine value ranges, and on total royalty income, for each of their fiscal years 1991

9. See also D'AGOSTINO and STEPHENS [1986], pp. 18-23.

through 1994 [10]. Six of the eleven, with total royalties of nearly $83 million in 1993 on 466 positive-royalty cases, responded favorably. All six accounted for their licensed technologies as bundles of patents and disclosures rather than single patents, although, as in the Harvard case, most of the bundles contained only one patent. The largest royalty interval, "more than $5 million", was open-ended. Because data on total royalty receipts per year were obtained, however, it was possible to approximate the values of individual bundles in that tail of the distribution. The approximation was carried out by assigning to closed intervals the mean value of Harvard patents in that interval (which in every case was close to the geometric mean of the interval extremes). Interval totals were found by multiplying the number of patents in an interval by the mean values, and the sum of such totals for all closed intervals was subtracted from total royalties to estimate royalties in the right-hand tail (with at most one observation per university per year).

The fractions of total sample royalties contributed by the top six technology bundles in each year were as follows:

	1991	1992	1993	1994
Percent of royalties	66.2%	70.9%	75.6%	74.4%
Total number of royalty-paying bundles	350	408	466	486

The most lucrative bundle licensed by any university contained the process and product patents on gene splicing methods granted in 1980, 1984, and 1988 to Stanley Cohen of Stanford University and Herbert Boyer of the University of California (and administered by the Stanford Technology Licensing Office). At the end of fiscal year 1994, 290 non-exclusive licenses to that bundle had been issued. Over the four years covered by our sample, the bundle yielded royalty payments of roughly $75 million [11]. Since licenses to the Cohen-Boyer patents, which had a revolutionary impact on the biotechnology industry's development, carried only modest royalty payments [12], the social surplus contributed by the inventions was vastly in excess of royalties appropriated by the patent-holding institutions.

Figure 5 arrays the six universities' royalty distributions on double logarithmic coordinates. Over the four years sampled, the distributions are reasonably stable. They are clearly not linear as predicted under the Pareto-Levy law; considerable concavity is evident. However, it would be premature to reject the linearity hypothesis for the most valuable tail. Fitting log-linear regressions to bundles with annual royalties of $50,000 or more, the results are as follows:

---

10. In interpreting data published by the Association of University Technology Managers, one must be careful to eliminate royalties from trademark licensing, e.g., from firms printing university seals on their garments.
11. See WINSTON-SMITH [1996] and ALDRIDGE [1996], pp. 104-108. Aldridge's account confuses annual with total royalties.
12. The original terms called for a $10,000 advance payment plus royalty rates ranging from 0.5 percent (on the sale of end products such as injectable insulin) to 1-3 percent on bulk products and 10 percent on basic genetic vectors and enzymes.

	1991	1992	1993	1994
Estimated α	0.665	0.660	0.583	0.649
Standard error	(.038)	(.036)	(.039)	(.029)
r^2	0.963	0.971	0.949	0.974
Observations	14	12	14	15
Bundles included	64	75	65	76

FIGURE 5

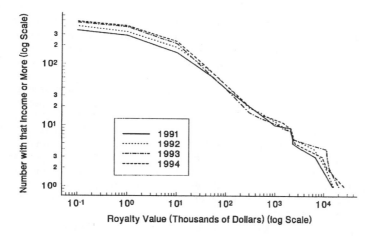

Again, the slope values lie in the range within which, asymptotically, Pareto-Levy distributions have neither finite means nor variances. Adding quadratic royalty value terms to the regressions effected variance reductions statistically significant (at the 0.05 level) only for 1991, with $F(1, 11) = 7.58$. Incremental F-ratios for the other years were 2.69, 0.3, and 3.64.

3 The Profitability of Approved New Pharmaceutical Entities

New chemical entities for use as pharmaceuticals in the United States must undergo a rigorous series of clinical tests before being approved by the Food and Drug Administration. On average, 17.5 new chemical entities

(NCEs) received FDA approval per year between 1970 and 1986 [13]. Only about 23 percent of the new chemical entities entered into human trials emerged with marketing approval from the FDA. Counting both successes and failures, but ignoring the time value of invested funds, the average pre-clinical and clinical research and development cost of new drugs appearing on the market during the late 1970s and early 1980s was nearly $100 million (in 1987 dollars). See DiMasi *et al.* [1991].

Henry GRABOWSKI and John VERNON [1990, 1994] used detailed data on drug sales to estimate the gross profitability (before deduction of R&D costs) of new chemical entities (other than cancer drugs) approved by the FDA during the 1970s and early 1980s whose development was carried out by industrial companies in the United States. Subtracting estimated production and marketing costs from sales revenues, domestic and foreign, they obtained for each drug what are best described as Marshallian quasi-rents to R&D investment [14]. These quasi-rents were discounted at a real discount rate of 9 percent to the date at which the drugs were first marketed. The drugs were divided into deciles in descending discounted quasi-rent order, leading to the value distribution shown in Figure 6 for average quasi-rents of drugs introduced during the 1970s. A similar analysis with nearly identical results was conducted for drugs introduced between 1980 and 1984. Also estimated was the average research and development investment per approved new chemical entity, including the cost of failed experiments, brought forward at compound interest to the time of marketing – $81 million (in 1986 dollars) per new drug introduced during the 1970s. Drugs in the top decile – the so-called blockbusters – generated 55 percent of total 1970s NCE sample quasi-rents, *i.e.*, 5.6 times the average R&D costs underlying their market entry [15]. Drugs in the second decile yielded double their R&D investments, drugs in the third decile essentially broke even, and drugs in the seven lowest deciles brought in discounted quasi-rents less than their average R&D investments.

A high degree of skewness is evident in Figure 6. To permit a more detailed analysis, GRABOWSKI and VERNON supplied the quasi-rent data for individual NCEs, multiplied to maintain confidentiality by an undisclosed disguise parameter. (Multiplication by a constant does not distort the size distribution parameters in which we are interested.) Figure 7 plots on

---

13. Pharmaceutical Manufacturers Association, Statistical Fact Book (August 1988), Table 2-4. The typical new drug is protected by one product patent and sometimes by a few process patents. In 1976, U.S. pharmaceutical manufacturers obtained at least 868 patents and, allowing for incomplete sample coverage, as many as 1,000. See SCHERER (1983, p. 110). Thus, there is far from a one-to-one correspondence between new patent counts and new product counts.

14. Grabowski and Vernon assumed the same ratio of production and distribution costs relative to sales for each NCE. If the better-selling NCEs had lower variable cost ratios, the resulting quasi-rent size distribution could be biased toward concavity. LU and COMANOR [1997] found that more important therapeutic advances had higher prices and hence, all else equal, higher profit margins. However, in an analysis of 28 NCEs introduced during the 1980s, I was unable to find any systematic relationship between sales and the degree of therapeutic advance, as characterized by the U.S. Food and Drug Administration.

15. One might expect R&D costs to be higher for the most lucrative drugs, but the available evidence fails to provide support. See DiMasi *et al.* [1995], p. 169.

FIGURE 6

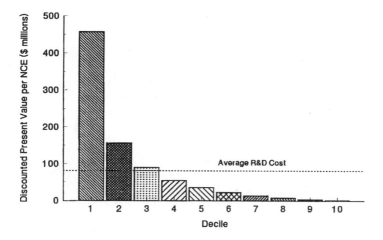

FIGURE 7

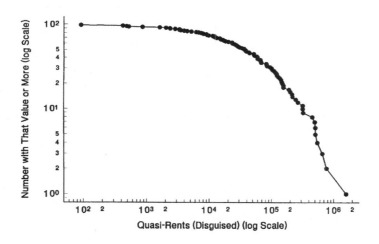

double log coordinates the data for 98 NCEs introduced during the 1970s. (Two observations with negative quasi-rents are omitted.) Figure 8 does the same for 66 NCEs introduced between 1980 and 1984. As with the quite differently constituted university patent bundle data, the distribution is much too concave to be Pareto-Levy. However, if one focuses only on

FIGURE 8

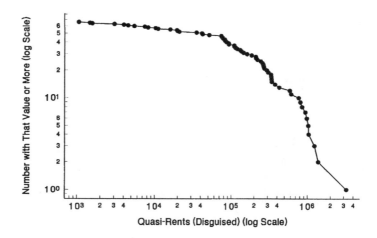

the most successful third of all the new products, a log linear regression fits tolerably well:

	1970s NCEs	1980s NCEs
Estimated slope	1.14	1.18
Standard error	(.040)	(.075)
r^2	0.964	0.926
Number of NCEs	33	22

Here, for the first time, with samples that cover almost exhaustively the relevant population of domestically developed and approved new chemical entities in their time frames, we find slope values in the tail exceeding the unit threshold below which Pareto-Levy first moments are asymptotically infinite.

Figure 9 plots the NCE data for the 1970s on log normal probability coordinates. As with the Harvard invention bundle sample, the plot deviates visibly from linearity. Its consistent downward concavity suggests more equality among the observations, and hence less skewness, than one would expect if the data conformed to a log normal process. The computation of moments for logarithms of the quasi-rent values for both the 1970s and 1980s samples (including all positive values) leads to the following coefficients:

	1970s NCEs	1980s NCEs
$\sqrt{\beta_1}$ (skewness)	−0.54	−123.16
β_2 (kurtosis)	3.27	777.31

484

FIGURE 9

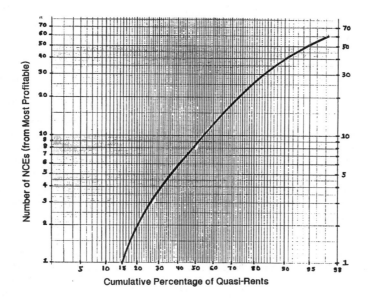

Cumulative Percentage of Quasi-Rents

The skewness coefficient for the 1970s differs from the zero value associated with log normality at the 0.05 level; the kurtosis coefficient is significantly different from 3.0 only at the 0.20 level. For the 1980s, the significance thresholds are strongly exceeded. Both distributions exhibit skewness to the *left* relative to the log normal, and the 1980s distribution is highly leptokurtic, *i.e.*, tightly bunched but with long thin tails.

As one would expect, a Bryson graph (not reproduced here, but comparable to Figure 4) of the 1970s quasi-rent data yields a plot clearly convex downward. A Bryson graph of the 1980s data, on the other hand, has two cycles of concavity followed by convexity. The most one can conlclude on this basis is that the 1980s data are ill-behaved, possibly combining two quite different distribution functions. See D'AGOSTINO and STEPHENS [1986], pp. 15-18.

4 High-Technology Venture Firm Star-tups

An institution that contributes enormously to America's prowess in high-technology fields is its venture capital industry. Hundreds of new firms are founded each year to develop and commercialize promising ideas emerging from university laboratories, independent inventors, and industrial corporations that for some reason chose not to pursue the opportunities internally. See ROBERTS [1991]. Typically, initial experiments and bench model development are supported using the technically trained entrepreneur's own funds and seed money raised from acquaintances (who as high-technology "angels" may sustain many such early investments). When this low-cost preliminary activity yields promising results, the fledgling enterprise turns to a high-technology venture fund for financial support, which ranges from a few hundred thousand to several million dollars. The venture capital fund raises money from an array of investors – in the industry's early history, from wealthy individuals, but more recently, from pension funds and university endowments – and attempts to pool its risks by investing in dozens of startup enterprises. If an individual venture succeeds in marketing one or more new products with good prospects, it "goes public" – i.e., it floats an initial public offering (IPO) of its common stock; or (somewhat more frequently) its investors sell out their shares to a well-established company. The venture fund investors then "cash in" their proceeds or reinvest them in the new publicly-traded company shares.

The first modern U.S. high-technology venture capital fund was the American Research and Development Corporation (ARDC), founded in Boston shortly after the close of the Second World War. Figures 10a and 10b, drawn from WILLMANN [1991], trace ARDC's early portfolio history. Figure 10a shows the number of individual startup companies in which ARDC invested annually (light dotted line) and the total number of companies in its portfolio (solid line). During the 1950s, its portfolio contained from 23 to 30 companies. Its investment target count rose into the mid 40s by the 1960s. Figure 10b traces the net value of ARDC's investment portfolio. During the mid-1950s, a few successes (such as High Voltage Engineering Company and Airborne Instruments Inc.) fueled an appreciable portfolio value increase. In 1966, however, the portfolio value exploded. By decomposing the portfolio into two parts – Digital Equipment Company (DEC) and more than 40 other companies – Figure 10b shows that most of the increase was attributable to ARDC's $70,000 investment (in 1957) in DEC. DEC's great success came with the introduction of the first time-sharing computer, the PDP-6, in 1964, and a powerful but inexpensive minicomputer, the PDP-8, in 1965. An initial public offering of DEC's common stock was floated on the New York Stock Exchange in 1966.

From the history of ARDC, we see considerable skewness in the returns from high-technology investments and the volatility such skewness can impart, despite venture investors' attempts to hedge against risk by forming sizeable portfolios. To determine how well the history of ARDC generalizes, two additional data sources were tapped.

One study of venture capital performance was conducted by the leading source of information on U.S. venture funds, Venture Economics, Inc. (1988, Chapter II). Venture Economics analyzed the success of 383 individual startup company investments made by 13 U.S. venture portfolios between 1969 and 1985 whose investment cycles had been largely completed by

486

FIGURE 10

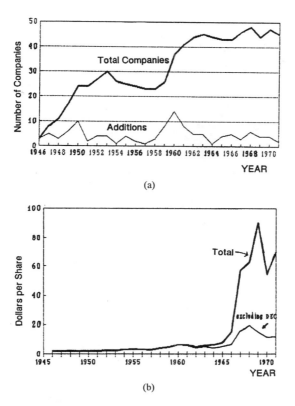

(a)

(b)

1986 [16]. Figure 11 arrays the individual investments by the multiple of terminal value relative to original investment outlays. The 26 individual startups returning ten times or more the funds' initial stakes accounted for 49 percent of total terminal portfolio values. More than a third of the ventures returned less than their original fund investments. Figure 12 plots the distribution function on double log coordinates in two ways, one (solid line) using interval average values per portfolio investment as the horizontal axis variable (and assuming "total losses" to return 10 percent of the initialinvestment); the other using the lower threshold values for the intervals. Since the average return in the highest-return interval was reported to be 21.6 times original investment values, the threshold approach suppresses important information on the distribution's upper tail. With both methods, the distribution function is concave, not linear as implied by

---

16. During the early 1980s, venture capital funds began to invest in real estate deals, leveraged buyouts, and other targets as well as high-technology startups. The fraction of the investments attributable to genuinely high-technology startups in the portfolios analyzed here was not disclosed.

FIGURE 11

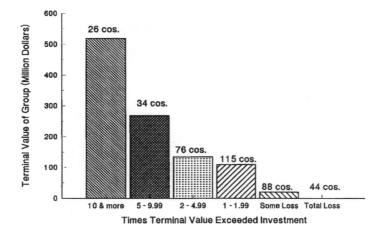

Times Terminal Value Exceeded Investment

FIGURE 12

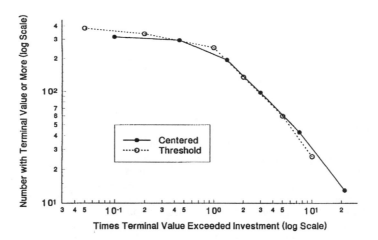

Times Terminal Value Exceeded Investment (log Scale)

the Pareto-Levy hypothesis. If a linear regression is forced upon the full centered observation data set by least squares, the implied slope value is 0.60. However, if the regression is limited to the four highest-value (*i.e.*, right-hand tail) interval means, the fitted slope coefficient is 0.974, with standard error of 0.044 and r^2 of 0.996.

Figure 13 summarizes the results of a similar study by a San Francisco venture capital house, Horsley Keogh Associates (1990). Included in the analysis were 670 distinct investments (totalling $496 million) in 460 companies made between 1972 and 1983 by 16 venture capital partnerships.

488

FIGURE 13

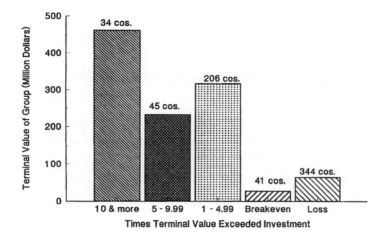

FIGURE 14

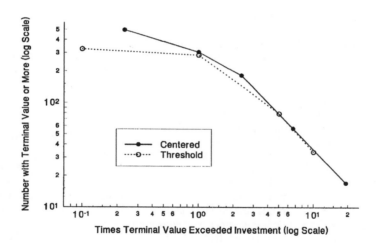

The ultimate portfolio value was calculated as of December 1988, at which time the funds had distributed to their partners $822 million and retained assets of $278 million. The 34 investments (*i.e.*, five percent of the total) that yielded ten times or more their original value contributed 42 percent of the portfolios' total terminal value. Slightly more than half of the investments entailed some loss. Figure 14 plots the distribution function on double-log coordinates, again using both mean values (solid line) and interval threshold values (dotted line). (Investments in the most lucrative interval returned on average 19.25 times their initial value.) Again we find concavity over the full range of observations, but near linearity in the right-hand tail. For all centered data points, the fitted least-squares line has an α of 0.77. However, for the four highest-value centered observations, the slope is 0.998, its standard error 0.083, and $r^2 = 0.986$.

5 Ongoing Empirical Research

To supplement the insights achieved through the studies summarized above, two more ambitious empirical research projects were in their initial stages at the time this paper was originally presented. Both remain incomplete at the time of revision. However, sufficient progress has been made to report preliminary insights.

One project, carried out by research associate Jörg Kukies, analyzes the stock price histories of 131 U.S. high-technology companies, initially backed by venture capital funds, that floated initial public stock offerings between 1983 and 1986. The 131 companies are believed to be an exhaustive sample of such IPOs in the relevant time frame. Monthly changes in their common stock values were tracked to the end of 1995 or to disappearance of the companies through merger or liquidation. The stock values for companies with a continuing presence evolve over a period of ten to twelve years in what was evidently a random walk, with frequent path crossovers and with a few big "winners" emerging among the much more numerous humdrum performances. When cross-sectional size distributions are plotted, they become increasingly skew over time, but after ten years remain concave downward on doubly logarithmic coordinates.

A second project, conducted jointly with Dietmar HARHOFF of the Center for European Economic Research in Mannheim, Germany, probes the tail of the distribution of values associated with patents applied for in 1977 and eventually issued by the German Patent Office. From that population 4,349 patents, including 1,435 patents of domestic German origin and 896 of U.S. origin, paid all maintenance fees and expired after running their full statutory 18-year term in 1995. The German maintenance fees, it is worth noting, are among the highest and most progressive in the world. Through mail and telephone surveys, rough preliminary discounted present value estimates were obtained from German and U.S. companies holding the full-term patents. Pareto plots of the survey response data showed only slight concavity relative to doubly logarithmic coordinates. The estimated slope value for the bounded German data (with 772 responses) was 0.404, with standard error 0.039 and r^2 of 0.973. For 223 U.S. patents linked to equivalent full-term German patents, the estimated slope value was 0.31, with standard error of 0.016 and r^2 of 0.984. The U.S. patents exhibit more skewness than the German sample, at least in part because they were three times filtered – once for application both in Germany and the United States, then for being issued in both jurisdictions, and then for renewal to full term in Germany. Interviews were held with 73 German companies holding patents

490

reported in the first-stage survey to have had a value in 1980 exceeding DM 5 million. More precise profitability estimates obtained through these interviews ranged from less than DM 5 million (*i.e.*, where survey responses were exaggerated) to more than DM 1 billion. The size distribution of patent values in this "tail of tails" was concave downward, rather than exhibiting the linearity on doubly logarithmic coordinates associated with a Pareto-Levy distribution.

6 Implications

It seems clear that there are important regularities in the size distribution of profit returns from technological innovation. The distributions uniformly exhibit some downward concavity on doulby logarithmic coordinates. The Pareto-Levy hypothesis is not strongly supported. However, the concavity is greater – *i.e.*, there is less skewness – for whole innovations (such as new drug chemical entities) and for the fortunes of new high-technology firms as integrated entities than for individual patents. Since new high-technology firms often hold numerous patents and since innovations are commonly fenced in by a multiplicity of patents, complementarities among individual patents would appear to eliminate some of the skewness.

The variance of returns from portfolios of inventions, both at the level of the individual firm and on a broader macroeconomic plane, depends critically on the shape of the most valuable tail of the size distribution. It is for that reason that I have reported separately log-log slope values for the right-hand tail of the distribution. In most cases the tail plots on Pareto coordinates are very close to linear, with slope values that range from 0.41 (for our survey of U.S. patents with full-term German counterparts) to unity (for high-technology venture investments) and slightly more than unity (for new drug chemical entities). When $\alpha = 1$, the Pareto distribution coincides with the Yule distribution, a variant of the log normal distribution. See IJIRI and SIMON (1977, p. 75). Simulation analyses reveal that over a plausible range of α values, it is quite difficult to distinguish between Pareto and log normal distributions on the basis of right-hand tail observations. Another simulation analysis (to be reported in a separate paper) reveals that, given the quasi-rent size distribution found for new drug chemical entities introduced during the 1970s, which closely approximates log normality, aggregated profit returns are quite unstable even when portfolios as large as those held by all innovating pharmaceutical firms together are formed.

That there are persistent regularities in the distribution of profit outcomes from innovation suggests that more or less well-defined behavioral processes generate those outcomes. Subsequent research will attempt to identify those processes.

One possibility, emphasized inter alia by EATON and KORTUM [1994], is that some Supreme Power regularly strews about the industrial landscape a distribution of raw profit potentials for technological innovation that is highly skew, just as the distribution of petroleum reservoirs within a land mass, and hence the opportunity for profiting from exploratory well drilling, is believed to be log normal. See ADELMAN (1972, p. 35). The profit opportunities from innovation might be roughly proportional to the size of markets, which, we know from the distribution of sales or value added across conventionally defined industries, is skew-distributed.

An alternative or complementary hypothesis is that the distribution of returns from innovation results from some variant of a Gibrat process, under which numerous chance events interact multiplicatively, reducing the profits actually realized from an innovative potential which may or may not be skew initially. See GIBRAT [1931]. If P_0 is the initial potential and ε_i is the i-th stochastic multiplier affecting the amount of value that can be appropriated by an innovator, the ultimate innovator's quasi-rent is:

$$(2) \qquad V = P_0\,\varepsilon_1 \,...\, \varepsilon_i \,...\, \varepsilon_n;$$

where the typical ε consists of an expected value less than unity plus an error component. The ϵ's reflect inter alia the initial probability of technical success, the time at which the innovator arrives on the market with its new product and hence the strength of first-mover advantages, the strength of the innovator's patent protection, the finesse with which initial marketing efforts are conducted (crucial e.g. in the competition between anti-ulcer drugs TAGAMET and ZANTAC), and the extent to which the market is fragmented by imitators in each subsequent year of commercial sales (which is likely to be correlated with the strength of first-mover advantages). Taking logarithms, we have:

$$(3) \qquad \log V = \log P_0 + \log \varepsilon_1 + ... + \log \varepsilon_i + ... + \log \varepsilon_n;$$

which, by the central limit theorem, is normally distributed with sufficiently large n. Thus, under the logic of Gibrat's law, a log normal distribution of V might be anticipated. The "sufficiently large n" assumption may be crucial, since patents, new drugs, and the startup phases of new high-technology ventures are bounded in time–perhaps too much so for a Gibrat process to converge on log normality.

When, contrary to the standard Gibrat model's assumptions, the initial population is not fixed and entry is concentrated in the low-value tail, a Yule distribution emerges instead of a log normal distribution. See IJIRI and SIMON [1977]. At the other extreme, long high-value tails could result from stochastic processes with path dependence, i.e., in which an early head start leads to increasing dominance over time. See e.g. DEVANY and WALLS [1996]. Month-to-month stock price movements for the 131 high-technology companies that floated initial public stock offerings are being analyzed for the deviations from a random walk that would reveal path dependence. Interviews with the holders of particularly valuable German patents will also provide evidence on the extent of path dependence.

Thus, there are plausible links between the stochastic search, experimentation, and market penetration processes associated with innovation and the kinds of profit return distributions found here. Further

492

theory-based and simulation research will attempt to identify plausible stochastic processes generating the observed profit return distributions. It is hoped that in this way a deeper understanding of the economics of technological innovation will follow.

● References

ADELMAN, Morris A. (1972). – *"The World Petroleum Market"*, Johns Hopkins University Press.

ALDRIDGE, S. (1996). – *"The Thread of Life: The Story of Genes and Genetic Engineering"*, Cambridge University Press.

D'AGOSTINO, R. B., STEPHENS, M. A. (1986). – *"Goodness-of-Fit Techniques"*, New York: Marcel Dekker.

BRYSON, M. C. (1974). – "Heavy-Tailed Distributions: Properties and Test", *Technometrics*, vol. 16, pp. 61-68.

DEVANY, A., WALLS, W. D. (1996). – "Bose-Einstein Dynamics and Adaptive Contracting in the Motion Picture Industry", *Economic Journal,* vol. 106, pp. 1493-1514.

DIMASI, J., HANSEN, R. W., GRABOWSKI, H., LASAGNA, L. (1995). – "Research and Development Costs for New Drugs by Therapeutic Category", *PharmacoEconomics*, vol. 7, pp. 152-169.

EATON, J., KORTUM, S. (1994). – "International Patenting and Technology Diffusion", *National Bureau of Economic Research working paper no. 4931*.

GIBRAT, R. (1931). – *Les Inégalités Économiques*, Paris: Recueil Sirey.

GRABOWSKI, H., VERNON, J. (1990). – "A New Look at the Returns and Risks to Pharmaceutical R&D", *Management Science*, vol. 36, pp. 804-821.

GRABOWSKI, H., VERNON, J. (1994). – "Returns on New Drug Introductions in the 1980s", *Journal of Health Economics*, vol. 13, pp. 383-406.

HANSON, N. R. (1958). – *"Patterns of Discovery"*, Yale University Press.

Horsley Keogh Associates, *Horsley Keogh Venture Study,* San Francisco: *Privately distributed.*

IJIRI, Y., SIMON, H. A. (1977). – *"Skew Distributions and the Sizes of Business Firms"*, Amsterdam: North-Holland.

LANJOUW, J. O. (1992). – "The Private Value of Patent Rights in Post WWII West Germany", *working paper, Yale University.*

LEVIN, R. C., KLEVORICK, A., NELSON R. R., WINTER, S. C. (1987). – "Appropriating the Returns from Industrial Research and Development", *Brookings Papers on Economic Activity*, no. 3, pp. 783-820.

LU, Z. J., COMANOR, W. S. (1998). – "Strategic Pricing of New Pharmaceuticals", *Review of Economics and Statistics*, vol. 80, pp. 108-118.

MANDELBROT, B. (1963). – "New Methods in Statistical Economics", *Journal of Political Economy*, vol. 71, pp. 421-440.

NORDHAUS, W. D. (1989). – "Comment", Brookings Papers on Economic Activity: Microeconomics, pp. 320-325.

PAKES, A., SCHANKERMAN, M. (1984). – "The Rate of Obsolescence of Patents, Research Gestation Lags, and the Private Rate of Return to Research Resources", in Zvi Griliches, ed., *R&D, Patents, and Productivity (University of Chicago Press)*, pp. 73-88.

Pakes, A. (1986). – "Patents as Options: Some Estimates of the Value of Holding European 1986 Patent Stocks", *Econometrica*, vol. 54, pp. 755-784.

Roberts, Edward B. (1991). – *Entrepreneurs in High Technology* (New York: Oxford University Press).

Sanders, B., Rossman, J., Harris, L. J. (1958). – "The Economic Impact of Patents", *Patent, Trademark, and Copyright Journal*, vol. 2, pp. 340-363.

Sanders, B. (1964). – "Patterns of Commercial Exploitation of Patented Inventions by Large and Small Corporations", *Patent, Trademark, and Copyright Journal*, vol. 8, pp. 51-93.

Schankerman, M., Pakes A., (1986) – "Estimates of the Value of Patent Rights in European Countries during the Post-1950 Period", *Economic Journal*, vol. 97, pp. 1-25.

Schankerman, M. (1991). – "How Valuable Is Patent Protection? Estimates by Technology Field Using Patent Renewal Data", *National Bureau of Economic Research Working Paper no. 3780.*

Scherer, F. M. (1965). – "Firm Size, Market Structure, Opportunity, and the Output of Patented Inventions", *American Economic Review*, vol. 55, pp. 1097-1123.

Scherer, F. M. (1977). – The Economic Effects of Compulsory Patent Licensing (New York University Graduate School of Business Administration, *Monograph Series in Finance and Economics*).

Scherer, F. M. (1983). – "The Propensity To Patent", *International Journal of Industrial Organization*, vol. 1, pp. 107-129.

Scherer, F. M. (1986). – "On the Current State of Knowledge in Industrial Organization", in H. W. de Jong and W. G. Shepherd, eds. *Mainstreams in Industrial Organization,* Book I (Dordrecht: Kluwer), pp. 5-22.

Venture Economics, Inc., (1988) *Venture Capital Performance* (Boston).

Willmann, H. (1991). – "Innovation in the Venture Capital Industry: A Study of American Research and Development Corporation", *term paper*, John F. Kennedy School of Government, Harvard University.

Winston-Smith S. (1996). – "The Cohen-Boyer Patent: A Case Study", *term paper*, John F. Kennedy School of Government, Harvard University.

494

Looking for International Knowledge Spillovers A Review of the Literature with Suggestions for New Approaches

Lee G. BRANSTETTER *

ABSTRACT. – This paper reviews the recent empirical literature on international knowledge spillovers. I start by summarizing the theoretical models that have highlighted the potential importance of these spillovers. Then, drawing upon the older micro productivity research tradition, I lay out a simple conceptual framework (though not a formal theoretical framework) for thinking about the various kinds of knowledge transfers that may exist, how they might be mediated, and the means by which their effects might be traced empirically. I then review some influential empirical papers, demonstrating that empirical work to date may very well not have identified the effects the authors set out to measure. Finally, I describe some promising new approaches which may allow researchers in this field to identify more precisely, both conceptually and empirically, certain kinds of international knowledge spillovers.

* L. G. BRANSTETTER: U. C. Davis, NBER. The ideas expressed in this paper owe a substantial intellectual debt to discussions with Bee-Yan Aw, Magnus Blomstrom, Akira Goto, Ann Harrison, Adam Jaffe, Wolfgang Keller, Sam Kortom, Pierre Mohnen, Manuel Trajtenberg, Daniel Trefler, Ryuhei Wakasugi, Larry Westphal, and, especially, Zvi Griliches. I also thank two anonymous referees for their insightful comments. I note that parts of this paper draw heavily from my 1996 working paper, "Are Knowledge Spillovers Intranational or International in Scope?", and my 1996 Harvard Ph.D. thesis. All mistakes, errors, and misunderstandings are my own fault.

D. Encaoua et al. (eds.), The Economics and Econometrics of Innovation, 495–518.
© 2000 *Kluwer Academic Publishers. Printed in the Netherlands.*

1 Introduction

Although the earliest models demonstrating the benefits of trade, due to David Ricardo, are based on technological differences between nations, both theoretical and empirical research in the Ricardian tradition has tended to take these differences as exogenous. Much of the work in international trade since the 1940s has been undertaken within the context of the Heckscher-Ohlin framework, in the most common version of which technology levels are assumed to be the same across countries. Even during the "Heckscher-Ohlin era", there were prominent voices within the international economics research community calling for studies of the role of technology and technological innovation in determining both the patterns of trade and the potential gains from trade, among them Raymond VERNON [1970]. Nevertheless, with a few exceptions, this extremely important nexus of questions has been all but ignored until very recently. Recent empirical tests of the Heckscher-Ohlin theory conducted by Daniel TREFLER [1993, 1995] have underscored the importance of this oversight, as he has convincingly demonstrated that the assumption of identical technology levels is one of the assumptions most strongly rejected by the data [1].

Two developments, which were more or less simultaneous, helped change this state of affairs. One was the introduction into theoretical international economics of methods of modeling imperfect competition and technological innovation. These methods were first developed in the fields of industrial organization and theory, then brought into international economics by such authors as KRUGMAN [1984, 1987], ETHIER [1982], ROMER [1990], GROSSMAN and HELPMAN [1991], and YOUNG [1991]. A reasonably complete exposition of some of the most influential of these modeling tools can be found in the book by GROSSMAN and HELPMAN [1991] although a rich literature has developed since its publication. These new models not only brought technological differences back into the core of the model, but they endogenized technological innovation, allowing the rate and direction of inventive activity to be affected by the global pattern of specialization and trade, and also allowing the pattern of trade to be, in turn, affected by the rate and direction of inventive activity, both in the global economy in aggregate and in individual countries. Bringing in technology in this fashion can affect both the nature and the degree of the gains from trade. The other development was the sudden and striking emergence of Japan, and later, other East Asian countries, as important suppliers of "high-technology" goods. This development, the political concerns it raised over "competitiveness", and the challenge it presented to the traditional view of comparative advantage as a static feature of the economy determined by

---

1. One of the other assumptions resoundingly rejected by the data is that of homotheticity of consumption across countries. The obvious "home bias" in consumption in most countries may be related to the discussion in this paper and elsewhere of "market access" informational spillovers.

496

exogenous factor endowments combined to give the new theories empirical relevance.

I lack space in this survey to do justice either to the range or to the depth of the theoretical models that have emerged thus far from this research tradition. However, I will note a few of its central conclusions, and sketch out the basic conceptual machinery that drives those conclusions. First, as was noted by ETHIER [1982], and in a dynamic context by ROMER and RIVERA-BATIZ [1991] and others, technological considerations can expand the gains from trade. Liberal trade policies provide domestic entrepreneurs with the possibility of exploiting a global market rather than merely a national one, inducing more R&D (or greater specialization) and leading to higher rates of growth and/or higher levels of welfare. By much the same logic, the negative impact of import restrictions can be magnified if they force domestic consumers or domestic producers to not only pay higher prices for the same range of consumer goods or producer intermediates, but also to have to make do with a narrower range of goods and intermediates (see ROMER [1990] and FEENSTRA [1992]). When consumer utility or producer productivity is a function of either the range of goods available or the level of quality of the available goods, the second-order effects of trade restrictions found in typical trade models can have first-order adverse welfare impact.

However, it has also been demonstrated that the gains from trade can be diminished or even overturned under some circumstances in these models [2]. Since these are also the circumstances under which technological developments can actually determine the long-run pattern of trade, they are worth closer examination.

2 Theoretical Foundations

The productivity research community has been interested in the causes, effects, and implications of R&D spillovers for a long time. A particularly detailed discussion of the issues appears in GRILICHES [1979]. "Partial equilibrium" theoretical treatments of the effects of R&D spillovers were presented by SPENCE [1984] and COHEN and LEVINTHAL [1989], among many others. However, this topic and its fundamental importance with regard to economic growth in the long run was introduced to a larger audience within economics through the "endogenous growth" and "growth and trade" literatures.

---

2. In these models, moving from autarky to free trade generates one-time welfare gains by enlarging consumption possibilities. However, if a country's comparative advantage is in a technologically stagnant sector, then it can be "trapped" by free trade into an equilibrium rate of output growth that is even lower than it would obtain under autarky. Thus, the static gains from trade can be offset by dynamic losses, see FEENSTRA [1994] and YOUNG [1991].

The theoretical contributions of GROSSMAN and HELPMAN [1990, 1991, 1995] have had a strong impact on empirical research on international R&D spillovers. Grossman and Helpman present a general equilibrium framework of two trading economies in which the rate of world economic growth is determined by the rate of innovation. R&D activity requires private investment of resources, but it also utilizes a stock of general knowledge – "the state of the art" – which is presumed to be costlessly accessible to all innovators. In turn, each innovation yields both a new product design (whose benefits the innovator can appropriate) and a unit addition to the stock of general knowledge. Over time, this foundation of knowledge grows, and this allows more innovation to occur without an increase in its resource cost. Thus, knowledge spillovers serve as "engines of endogenous growth", allowing economic growth to proceed indefinitely without diminishing returns setting in [3].

In this sort of framework, the impact of innovation on the global pattern of trade depends crucially on the assumptions one makes about the scope of knowledge spillovers. If knowledge spillovers are global in scope, then trade is still determined by the exogenous traditional forces of comparative advantage. On the other hand, if knowledge spillovers are intranational, then trade patterns can exhibit path dependence. Comparative advantage itself can become endogenous. GROSSMAN and HELPMAN [1995] describe this process with the following example: "Suppose it is country A that begins with more research experience. Then initially this country's researchers have a competitive advantage in the research lab, and they perform all of the world's R&D at time 0. But then additional knowledge accumulates in country A, while in the absence of international knowledge spillovers, the knowledge stock remains fixed in country B. So, country A's competitive lead in R&D widens and there is even greater reason for this country to conduct all the world's research in the next period. The initial lead is self-reinforcing and eventually country A comes to dominate production in the high-technology sector [4]." The presence of this mechanism means that an "accident of history" or a temporary policy that provides one country with a temporary advantage in the R&D-intensive sector "can have long-lasting implications for trade when there is a national component to the knowledge capital stock" [5].

Why might knowledge spillovers flow more easily within countries than across them? Several reasons immediately suggest themselves. First is geography – it is clearly easier for scientists and engineers to interact and

---

3. This phrase was itself coined by GROSSMAN and HELPMAN.

4. This quote and the others in this paragraph are taken from "Technology and Trade" by GROSSMAN and HELPMAN, published as Chapter 2 in the *Handbook of International Economics,* vol. 3.

5. This is particularly well-phrased. If spillovers are *purely* intranational, the effects of a temporary policy can last forever. In the case of partial international spillovers, the Grossman-Helpman framework predicts that, in the very long-run, the world economy can eventually converge to the same steady-state equilibrium that obtains in the case of complete international spillovers. However, the process of convergence could take decades (or longer), so that temporary policies can indeed have "long-lasting", but not necessarily permanent effects in the case of partial international spillovers.

observe one another if they are geographically proximate. Compounding this is the issue of language, which also acts as a barrier to the transfer of knowledge across national boundaries. More important that either of these, however, may be the limited mobility of research personnel across national boundaries, as opposed to within them. Finally, the full set of regulatory barriers that makes transnational business more complicated and costly than business within a single country may also act to inhibit the cross-border flow of knowledge [6].

It is obvious that this parameter, namely the differential impact of intranational versus international knowledge spillovers, is an extremely important one, with strong implications not only for the predictions of the theoretical model but also the traditional trade economist's policy prescription of a liberal, laissez-faire trade policy. Thus it is not surprising that these theoretical results have inspired empirical work attempting to measure international knowledge spillovers. Unfortunately, the real world is not nearly so nice, neat, and symmetrical as the theoretical world constructed by Grossman and Helpman. In looking in the data for the empirical traces of international and intranational knowledge spillovers, it is important to keep in mind what phenomena the theory focus on and how we might be ablve to focus on that same phenomena in empirical work. Given this challenge, it seems worthwhile to review the taxonomy that GRILICHES [1992] has introduced to classify knowledge spillovers.

3 A Taxonomy of Spillover Effects

A knowledge spillover occurs when firm a is able to derive economic benefit from R&D activity undertaken by firm b without sharing in the cost firm b incurred in undertaking its R&D. Using this definition, we immediately make a distinction between spillovers *per se* and technology transfer, in which the innovator sells its right to use technology to another firm or establishes a subsidiary and transfers technology to it. As long as the innovator is able to appropriate all (or even most) of the surplus from the transfer, then there is no significant "externality".

Confining our attention for the moment to cases of actual spillovers, we can easily imagine at least two types. First, there is the case where a firm produces a new or improved product, but is unable to appropriate all of the surplus from its innovation because of its inability to perfectly price discriminate and due to existing competition with suppliers of substitute goods or, perhaps, the potential entry of imitators. In this case, the firm passes along some of the surplus to the purchasers of the goods. This is

---

6. I thank an anonymous referee for encouraging me to be more explicit about the reasons why knowledge spillovers are likely to have an intranational component.

an externality, to be sure, but it is what GRILICHES [1979, 1992] has termed a "precuniary externality". Purchasers are able to obtain a better input for less than their reservation price, and this can be a substantial gain. It is not, however, the kind of knowledge spillover that powers endogenous growth in the models of Grossman and Helpman. In this case, innovation occurs in the upstream sector, but the benefits spill over downstream. There is no presumption, though, that this financial windfall will create further innovation – *i.e.*, a shift in the production possibilities frontier – of the downstream sector. At most, it may allow firms in the downstream sector to move along their existing production possibilities frontiers to a more optimal point reflecting the effective change in input prices. This is the kind of adjustment we would expect in the wake of, say, an exogenous decline in oil prices. It is not the stuff of which endogenous growth is made. Without further innovation in the upstream sector, the benefits of which "leak" downstream thanks to competition, there will be no further growth.

As GRILICHES [1992] has pointed out, this kind of spillover can be contrasted with a disembodied "knowledge spillover". In this case, the new technological knowledge embodied in new goods produced by firm a is eventually "reverse-engineering" and becomes part of a general pool of knowledge – the "state of the art". Subsequent innovators are able to build upon this foundation of general knowledge, using it as a complement to their own R&D activities. With these kinds of spillovers, innovations tend to beget subsequent innovations, which, in turn, become part of the state of the art. It is ultimately this kind of spillover that can produce both endogenous growth and endogenous changes in the pattern of comparative advantage among nations [7].

To make this point more concretely, we note that in the late 1980s, there was a vigorous debate in the United States over what the federal government should do, if anything, to assist the American semiconductor industry in coping with what then seemed to be insurmountable competition from Japanese firms. In defending the Bush Administration's laissez-faire approach, economist Michael Boskin, then Chair of the Council of Economic Advisors, made the famous quip, "It doesn't matter whether America produces semiconductor chips or potato chips". In the absence of technological externalities, Professor Boskin is probably correct. Furthermore, if technological externalities are purely pecuniary in nature, Professor Boskin may still be right. As long as American consumers of semiconductor products have free access to Japanese semiconductor products, they will receive precisely the same level of pecuniary spillover as Japanese consumers when they purchase the product [8]. However, it

---

7. In modeling this sort of spillover, Grossman and Helpman abstract from the possibility of simple imitation by assuming perfect protection of intellectual property.

8. This will not necessarily hold in all conceivable circumstances. High transport or other trade costs could create *localized* pecuniary externalities. Alternatively, an appreciation of the yen relative to the dollar could make Japanese semiconductors more expensive for American consumers.

500

may be that, in fact, innovation in the semiconductor industry has the effect of abetting innovation in the computer industry, which further begets innovation in the software industry. These are knowledge spillovers. If they are strong and if they are purely or primarily *intranational* in scope, then Professor Boskin may be wrong. Boskin's successor, Professor Laura Tyson [1993], argued strongly that these types of knowledge spillovers do emanate from the semiconductor industry into other related sectors, and justified U.S. protection of this industry by appealing to such externalities. It is important to emphasize, though, that if knowledge spillovers in the semiconductor industry are global in scope, then Professor Boskin is *still* right. If American computer manufacturers and software firms can learn from innovation in the Japanese semiconductor sector as easily as they can from innovation in the American semiconductor sector, then one cannot justify protection on the basis of these externalities.

Having distinguished these two types of knowledge spillovers, we can now consider how they might be mediated and how we might find their traces in the data. Obviously, pecuniary spillovers are mediated through actual commercial transactions – one obtains this kind of spillover by buying a new or improved good at less than the "full quality-adjusted price", (in the usage of Griliches [1992]) and the amount of spillover will be a function of the frequency and intensity of ones purchases. In linking upstream innovation to the benefits it generates downstream, it will be necessary to find or construct an "input-output" matrix or some other mapping of the pattern of input purchases across sectors. In fact, Scherer [1982] and others have made quite ambitious attempts to use such matrices to construct measures of the rate of return to R&D, taking account of the fact that much of the benefit leaks downstream.

It is doubtful, though, that the pattern of propagation of knowledge spillovers is the same as the pattern of propagation of pecuniary spillovers. Certainly, we would not expect the pattern of knowledge spillovers to be necessarily proportional to the pattern of commercial transactions between firms and sectors. On an annual basis, professors of economics generally spend far more on health care, housing services, and automobile maintenance than they do on subscriptions to economics journals. Yet, if they are at all like me, they have learned comparatively little from their doctors, landlords, or mechanics, relative to the knowledge spillovers they receive from the economic research of other scholars. To cite a more serious example from Griliches's [1992] survey, "the photographic equipment industry and the scientific instruments industry may not buy much from each other but may be, in a sense, working on similar things and hence benefiting much from each other's research". At the firm level, the most intense knowledge spillovers may be those which take place between direct competitors who buy nothing from one another [9].

---

9. This is not meant to imply that knowledge spillovers cannot occur between upstream and downstream firms or industries or that the pattern of knowledge spillovers is always orthogonal to the pattern of commercial transactions.

If knowledge spillovers are the primary phenomena of interest, and theory strongly suggests that they are, then the search for them would seem to require a measure of "proximity" in technology space [10]. In turn, obtaining a reasonable measure of proximity in technology space will require us to do empirical work at a level that is much more disaggregated then the level at which most of the empirical work on international R&D spillovers has been done, because there is enormous technological heterogeneity across and even within industries. This point can be made in a simple way with an example from my 1996 working paper: "For instance, a maker of industrial solvents is unlikely to directly benefit from the research of pharmaceuticals companies on psychoactive drugs, even though both are in the "chemical" industry... If we find no relationship between the productivity of our industrial solvent manufacturer and research and development by the pharmaceuticals manufacturer, that does not mean there are no knowledge spillovers. On the other hand, if we find a relationship, it is difficult to give it a causal interpretation. We are more likely observing common demand or input price shocks or a common time trend than actual spillovers [11]."

Distilling "real" knowledge spillover effects from potentially spurious correlation of this kind requires a measure of technological proximity by which to weight "external" R&D, domestic and foreign. Such a measure can only be obtained by using data at the level of the producer which provides a rich description of the R&D activities of individual firms and the distribution of that effort across different technological fields. Such data exist, and I will argue consistently throughout this survey that we have little chance of obtaining good estimates of knowledge spillovers without using them.

Before we leave our taxonomy of spillovers, I will touch on a completely different topic – what might be called "market access spillovers", a term taken from the survey by BLOMSTROM and KOKKO [1996] though some of these ideas have also been explored at length by James RAUCH [1996] and by AITKEN, HARRISON, and HANSON [1994]. If foreign consumers have imperfect information about the quality of indigenous producers, then welfare improving trade may not take place simply due to lack of information. This is Akerlof's "lemons problem" on a global scale [12]. Once

---

10. A referee has suggested that where both pecuniary and knowledge spillovers are present, it may be difficult to distinguish between them. This is likely to be true. One way around this problem is to rely on indices of innovation, such as patents, that are less affected by input cost shocks then revenue-based indices like TFP. Furthermore, since knowledge spillovers are likely proportionate to *technological proximity* rather than proximity in transactions space, the availability of data on technological proximity can also help researchers distinguish between the two effects.

11. Professor F.M. SCHERER and others have pointed out to me that problem is exacerbated by the way R&D data is collected in some countries. In the U.S., R&D expenditure data is collected from firms. Then, these sums are assigned to the single industry identified as its "primary" industry. For diversified firms, which do a large fraction of private sector R&D in the U.S., this can lead to severe measurement problems. GRILICHES [1992] also notes this point.

12. See AKERLOF [1970].

502

a sufficient number of purchases have taken place, especially if foreign consumers learn from watching other foreign consumers behavior, the prior expectation of the distribution of quality among foreign producers may be updated such that foreign consumers suddenly demand the products of indigenous producers. Indigenous producers (and foreign consumers) can benefit from "reputation spillovers" of this kind. Likewise, indigenous producers may learn about the feasibility of exporting to certain foreign markets (and the potential profits from doing so) by observing the export activities of other indigenous producers. If international trade and investment can be described by a search model with a reasonably high search cost, then these kinds of information spillovers may be quite important [13]. However, they are not knowledge spillovers. Furthermore, it is not clear that these information spillovers will generate anything other than one-time gains from the advent of mutually advantageous trade. They will not drive endogenous growth. Thus we will not consider them further in this survey.

4 Empirical Methods for Measuring International R&D Spillovers

Up to now, most empirical papers on international R&D spillovers have used either production functions of some kind or the dual of the production function, a cost function. Both empirical models have their pitfalls, as a generation of work within the microproductivity research community has demonstrated. Here, I only summarize the rich and eminently readable discussions found in GRILICHES [1992] and in GRILICHES and MAIRESSE [1995]. In the case of the production function, the basic method is to model output as a function of labor, physical capital, and knowledge capital such that

$$Q = C^\alpha L^\beta K^\gamma e^\varphi$$

where Q is output, C is physical capital, L is labor, K is "knowledge capital", and the φ represents a set of controls for industry and time effects [14]. It is worth pointing out that the theory of production undergirding this model is specified at the level of the *firm*. Typically, firm level data

---

13. See the paper by KINOSHITA and MODY [1996] for a development of these ideas with respect to foreign direct investment and empirical work using data on Japanese FDI in Asia.

14. This is a simple "Cobb-Douglas" production function. Of course, one can estimate more complicated functional forms, such as the translog. However, if measurement error is a substantial problem, then the interpretation of the coefficients on higher-order terms becomes especially problematic.

is hard to come by, and in the empirical literature on international R&D spillovers production functions are often run on aggregated industry or even national-level data. This presents a number of conceptual problems. It is one thing to assume that a firm maximizes output given a vector of prices. It is quite another thing to imagine that an industry or a nation undertakes a similar maximization across multiple distinct product markets. Under a number of rather stringent assumptions, of course, researchers can treat an industry or a country as a single firm, but such assumptions generally do not do justice to the observed heterogeneity of individual producers.

In any case, the production function approach generally treats knowledge capital, or R&D capital, in a way symmetric to that of physical capital [15]. Taking the logs of both sides of this equation and expressing it in difference form allows us to model output growth as a function of the growth of inputs.

$$q_{i,t} - q_{i,t-1} = \alpha \left(c_{i,t} - c_{i,t-1} \right) + \beta \left(l_{i,t} - l_{i,t-1} \right)$$
$$+ \gamma \left(k_{i,t} - k_{i,t-1} \right) + \left(\varphi_i - \varphi_i \right) + u_{i,t} - u_{i,t-1}$$

This expression is linear in the logs of the variables and has the convenient feature of differencing away "fixed effects". The coefficient on the changes in the knowledge capital stock has the interpretation of the partial effect on output holding other factors constant, which, in turn, is generally interpreted as the relationship between total factor productivity growth and knowledge capital [16].

The manner in which K is constructed will be of particular interest. If there are no R&D spillovers, of course, then K will simply be a "stock" measure constructed, via the perpetual inventory method, from past investments in R&D by only the unit of observation; typically a firm or industry. If there are only intranational R&D spillovers, we might include domestic "external" R&D investments along with "own" R&D investments in the construction of our stock measure. Since some of the external R&D is bound to be more relevant to "own" output then others, we need some weight matrix by which to focus on the relevant external R&D and screen out the rest. As we have reasoned above, the best weight matrix will be some measure of technological proximity between "own" and "other" R&D-performing units. Furthermore, as we have reasoned, this matrix will be most believable if it is constructed at or at least based on information from the firm level. If there are international R&D spillovers, then we must construct a parallel weighted sum of technologically relevant R&D conducted in other countries. Allowing the international and intranational R&D spillover terms to enter symmetrically into the production function,

---

15. This treatment has itself been criticized by a number of scholars in the micro productivity research community, including NELSON [1988], GRILICHES [1979], and KLETTE [1994].

16. An alternative frequently pursued in the literature is to calculate a "Solow residual" by subtracting from the log of output a Tornqvist index of the log of inputs. The resulting series can be interpreted as TFP, and this can then be regressed on various measures of knowledge capital.

we may have something like

$$q_{i,t} - q_{i,t-1} = \alpha\left(c_{i,t} - c_{i,t-1}\right) + \beta\left(l_{i,t} - l_{i,t-1}\right) + \phi\left(r_{i,t} - r_{i,t-1}\right)$$
$$+ \gamma\left(s_{di,t} - s_{di,t-1}\right) + \rho\left(s_{fi,t} - s_{fi,t-1}\right)$$
$$+ \left(\varphi_i - \varphi_i\right) + u_{i,t} - u_{i,t-1}$$

so that we have "own" R&D (denoted r) and two kinds of spillovers, domestic (s_d) and foreign (s_f). We can then compare their relevant impact on productivity growth by comparing the coefficients on the two spillover terms.

The construction of the "own" and external knowledge stocks presents a number of conceptual and measurement problems. Leaving aside for the moment the problem of how to construct a measure of technological proximity, we also need a measure of depreciation of knowledge capital and a sense of the lag structure of past internal and past external R&D in terms of its effect on output. There is little firm empirical evidence to guide us here, nor is there any reason to believe that these parameters should remain stable over time or across firms and industries. It is therefore likely that the knowledge stocks will be measured with considerable error.

Unfortunately, it is also true that fluctuations in output, controlling for labor and capital (hence, TFP), will be influenced by many things other than cost reducing process innovation or quality-enhancing product innovation. Demand and cost shocks will also be present, as will be shortcomings in the ability of the official price deflators to accurately measure quality change over time. Fluctuations in measured TFP will also be affected by changes in the firms' ability to appropriate the benefits from its innovations, and here the model runs into a major conceptual difficulty. The microfoundations of the neoclassical production function are derived under conditions in which the firm is a price-taker in the output market. Of course, endogenous technological change requires that firms have the incentive to undertake costly research – hence it implies the existence of at least temporary monopoly power at the firm level. If we allow output prices to differ from that which would hold under perfect competition, then we begin to move away from the theoretical microfoundations of the production function [17]. This presents a theoretical problem, and ultimately we will need an empirical model that explicitly and formally takes into account imperfect competition among firms to resolve it [18]. It also presents a practical problem, in that measured TFP varies for reasons that have like to do with innovative effort [19].

An alternative specification is to estimate a "knowledge production function" by using some measure of innovation other than output growth on the left hand side of the equation. One obvious alternative is to use counts

---

17. I wish to thank Zvi GRILICHES for raising this point.
18. Zvi GRILICHES and Tor KLETTE [1997] have done research along the lines, developing an empirical analog of the "quality ladder model".
19. For a particularly dramatic example of this, see the Bronwyn HALL's [1994] "Has the Rate of Return Declined?"

of patents as a measure of innovation. Thus, suppressing time subscripts, the regression equation becomes

$$N_i = R_i^\beta \, S_{di}^{\gamma_1} \, S_{fi}^{\gamma_2} \, \Phi_i$$

where N is the number of patents obtained by firm i, R is "own" R&D spending, S_d and S_f represent domestic and foreign spillovers, respectively, and $\Phi_i = e^{\sum \delta_c \, D_{ic}} \, e^{\varepsilon_i}$, a set of controls for industry and time effects, plus an error term.

Patent counts are less likely than deflated sales to be subject to cost and demand shocks. Unfortunately, patent counts have problems of their own as measures of innovation, not the least of which is the fact that most corporate patents are found, *ex post*, to be of little or no economic value. Some progress can be made, potentially, by weighting patent output by the subsequent citations of those patents. Bronwyn Hall is currently pursuing such research with Adam Jaffe and Manuel Trajtenberg.

A seemingly sensible alternative is to estimate a cost function rather than a production function. As GRILICHES [1992] notes, "the advantage of the cost structure approach is that it is often more flexible in functional form used and that it benefits from imposing more structure, considering the impact of R&D not only on total costs but also on the amount of labor and intermediate products used". Like its dual, the production function, it is specified at the level of the firm. Running regressions of cost functions on industry or national data will pose the same conceptual problems as does running production functions on aggregate data. However, the cost function does possess the following advantage over its dual: it can be estimated, in principle, when a firm is not a price-taker in the output market, as long as it is a price taker in the various input markets.

Although a number of different models based on the cost function have been estimated, I describe here the approach taken by Jeffrey Bernstein and a number of co-authors. I summarize his own description, using his notation [20]. Bernstein assumes a production process characterized by

$$y_t = F\left(v_t, \, K_t, \, S_{t-1}\right)$$

where y is output, v is the vector of non-capital inputs, K is the vector of capital inputs (physical capital and R&D capital), and S is the vector of spillover variables, both domestic (aggregate domestic R&D spending in all other industries) and foreign (R&D spending in the corresponding foreign industry). Spillover terms are lagged by one period, hence the different subscript.

Producers are assumed to minimize cost. The optimization problem can therefore be split into two stages. In the first stage, output quantity is given and capital stocks are fixed. The cost of non-capital inputs are minimized subject to the production function. The solution to the first stage of the problem yields the variable cost function,

$$c_t^\nu = C^\nu \left(w_t, \, y_t, \, K_t, \, S_{t-1}\right)$$

---

20. See BERNSTEIN *et al.* [1994, 1995].

where c^v is variable cost and w is the vector of non-capital input prices. C^v is assumed to be twice continuously differentiable, nondecreasing in w and y, and nonincreasing in K, concave, and homogeneous of degree one in w and convex in K. Applying Shepherd's Lemma, the demands for non-capital factors of production can be retrieved, such that

$$\nu_t = \nabla_w C^v(w_t, y_t, K_t, S_{t-1})$$

The non-capital factor demands depend on the non-capital factor prices, output quantity, the capital inputs, and the R&D spillovers. Turning to the second stage, the demands for capital inputs are found by minimizing variable plus capital cost, producing the following equilibrium conditions relating to the capital input demands

$$-\omega_t = \nabla_k C^v(w_t, y_t, K_t, S_{t-1})$$

where ω is the vector of capital input prices or rental rates. Capital input demands depend on non-capital input prices, output quantity, R&D spillovers, and capital input prices. The last two equation sets constitute the system of equations that is estimated.

There are a number of disadvantages to this approach. The most important, as noted by Griliches, is that the cost function requires the use of good input price data which varies across our units of observation and over time. This generally does not exist for R&D and physical capital even at the industry level. At the firm level, where the theory of the cost function is actually specified, this kind of data does not exist at all, nor is there generally *firm-specific* information on the costs of intermediate inputs. Furthermore, the use on the right hand side of *ex-post* output, rather than "expected output", has the tendency to produce, in GRILICHES's [1992] words "an unwarranted appearance of economies of scale and is likely to bias upward the own and outside R&D capital coefficients, especially in the absence of any other trend-like terms in the equations". This last problem is explored at some length in GRILICHES and HAUSMAN [1986].

5 A Brief Review of the Received Empirical Literature

• Estimates of Knowledge Spillovers

Certainly, the most widely cited and influential study in the literature on international R&D spillovers so far has been the work by COE and HELPMAN [1995] and the similar paper by COE, HELPMAN, and HOFFMAISTER [1995]. In both papers, the authors calculate TFP residuals for a set of countries, using aggregate data on capital and labor. These TFP residuals are then regressed on aggregate R&D spending and a weighted measure of external R&D spending, where the weights are measures of bilateral trade between the countries. This approach has been criticized on a number of grounds. First, of course, there are the conceptual problems raised with estimating what amounts to a production function with country level data. More importantly, the authors' aggregate approach allows them no way to control for technological heterogeneity across firms, industries, and countries. Thus there is no measure of technological proximity. Third, by using trade-related weights, the authors effectively impose on the data the assumption that trade is the prime vehicle through which spillovers are mediated [21]. Fourth, the authors interpret their regressions as cointegrating regressions and were unable to provide standard errors due to the problems of calculating the asymptotic properties of their estimators in a panel in which the time series data exhibit a unit root and cointegration.

These conceptual and methodological problems notwithstanding, the results Coe and Helpman presented in their 1995 *European Economic Review* article are quite striking, implying that international R&D spillovers, mediated through trade, are significant and strong. If Coe and Helpman are interpreting their results correctly, then international trade is evidently an *extremely* potent channel by which technology spills over across countries [22]. The authors have also received some econometric support from Bangtian CHEN and CHIWHA KAO [1995]. Using their previous research on cointegration in panel data, CHEN and KAO are able to place adjusted standard errors around Coe and Helpman's coefficients, confirming their main result that import-weighted "foreign" R&D spillovers are significantly correlated with domestic productivity levels.

Unfortunately, a recent paper by Wolfgang Keller (KELLER [1996]) casts doubt on the interpretation the authors give to the results in their papers. Keller's approach is very simple. Having obtained the data set used for the original Coe and Helpman paper, he first replicates their initial results. Then, using a "Monte-Carlo" approach, Keller takes the ingenious next step of creating a series of randomly generated bilateral trade relationships and uses these randomly generated trade matrices to create the trade-weighted "foreign" R&D stock. He then reruns the baseline Coe-Helpman regressions of aggregate total factor productivity growth on aggregate national and trade-weighted "foreign" R&D stocks. He replicates this experiment one thousand times for each of the main regression models estimated by Coe and Helpman. He finds that "randomly created bilateral trade shares also give rise to large estimated international R&D spillovers; often, in fact, to larger estimated

---

21. American University economist Walter PARK [1995] also uses data on OECD countries in his study of international R&D spillovers, but he first disaggregates R&D by source – public or private – then further disaggregates by sector. Park constructs a measure of technological proximity between countries based on similarity in the sectoral allocation of R&D, and uses this measure to weight "external" public and private R&D. Like Coe and Helpman, Park finds evidence of international R&D spillovers.

22. Empirical work by BERNARD and JONES [1996] casts some doubt on the view that trade is an important channel of spillovers. The authors demonstrate that the much-noted convergence in aggregate TFP levels across OECD economies is entirely a function of productivity convergence in the *service* sector. Disaggregating by industry, they show that there has been no tendency toward productivity convergence in manufacturing industries, despite the fact that most international trade takes place in manufactured goods rather than services.

spillover effects which are more precisely estimated than by employing the 'true' bilateral trade shares". As Keller himself modestly notes in the abstract to his paper. "This casts some doubt on the earlier results in the literature". Table 1 and Table 2 compare econometric results of Coe and Helpman, Chen and Kao, and Keller. Table 1 presents the Coe and Helpman "baseline" specification. Table 2 presents what is in some ways Coe and Helpman's preferred specification in that it weights "foreign" R&D stocks by the share of imports in that country's GDP. It also allows for the effect of domestic R&D stocks to be higher for the G7 countries. One can see that in all cases, randomly created trade shares lead to higher estimates of the impact of international R&D spillovers than the use of the actual shares.

TABLE 1

The Impact of Domestic and Foreign R&D Spillovers on Productivity.

Variable	Grossman and Helpman	Chen and Kao	Keller
Domestic R&D	.097	.093	0.28
	(.009)	(.051)	(.011)
Foreign R&D	.092	.100	.157
	(.016)	(.070)	(.013)

TABLE 2

The Impact of Domestic and Import-weighted Foreign R&D Spillovers on Productivity.

Variable	Grossman and Helpman	Chen and Kao	Keller
Domestic R&D	.078	.074	0.28
	(.008)	(.036)	(.011)
G7*Domestic R&D	.156	.158	
	(.015)	(.098)	
Import-weighted Foreign R&D	.294	.310	.337
	(.041)	(.145)	(.030)

Professor Jeffrey Bernstein of Carleton University in Canada has, together with various co-authors, undertaken several studies of international R&D spillovers between the U.S. and Japan and between Canada and various trading partners. These papers all share a common methodology: the "cost function" approach outlined earlier. Interpretation of his findings is clouded by the shortcomings of this approach. First of all, the cost functions are estimated using highly aggregated sectoral level data. The assumption that a firm minimizes cost is, as economic assumptions go, not too difficult to swallow. The assumption that the "chemical industry" minimizes costs across several distinct product markets is harder to defend. Furthermore, Bernstein and his co-authors lack data on R&D "prices" or capital goods prices that vary across sectors. At the aggregate level at which he undertakes his analysis, Bernstein is unable to control for technological heterogeneity within sectors. Typically, Bernstein and his co-authors find evidence of R&D spillovers, though his estimates of the elasticities of R&D spillovers vary widely across sectors and countries. Because of the fundamental differences in econometric specification, it is not really possible to compare these results to those reported in Tables 1 and 2, but some of the estimated spillover effects are quite large. For instance, Bernstein and Mohnen found that R&D spillovers from the United States accounted for more than 50% of Japanese productivity growth in the R&D-intensive sectors, whereas spillovers from Japan accounted for about 15% of US productivity growth [23].

6 New Departures

• The use of Measures of Technological Proximity at the Micro Level

One alternative approach to the problem of estimating international knowledge spillovers is to do analysis at the micro level in a way which explicitly controls for technological distance. I have undertaken precisely this approach in my 1996 working paper, "Are Knowledge Spillovers International or Intranational in Scope?" In summarizing my paper in this section, I borrow liberally from that paper.

It builds on the methodologies suggested by Zvi GRILICHES [1979] and first implemented by Adam JAFFE [1986]. Since Jaffe's paper is a familiar one, I will use his notation and follow his development of the model. The typical firm conducts R&D in a number of technological fields simultaneously. I obtain a measure of a firm's location in "technology space" by measuring the distribution of its R&D effort across various technological fields. Let a firm's R&D program be described by the vector F, where

$$(1) \qquad\qquad F_i = (f_1...f_k)$$

and each of the k elements of F represent the firm's research resources and expertise in the k-th technological area. We can infer from the number

---

23. While industry-level studies may suffer from potential problems of aggregation bias, firm-level studies will inevitably suffer from potential problems of sample selection bias. Most firm-level studies use data on larger, publicly traded firms for reasons of data availability. It is not clear that the results obtained from such studies apply to the relevant industry or the economy as a whole. So, I do not want to be excessively critical of studies done on more aggregate data. To paraphrase Zvi Griliches, in empirical work, there is also no free lunch.

510

of patents taken out in different technological areas what the distribution of R&D investment and technological expertise across different technical fields has been.

Like Jaffe, I assume that "the existence of technological spillovers implies that a firm's R&D success is affected by the research activity of its neighbors in technology space" [24]. We can measure the "technological proximity" between two firms by measuring the degree of similarity in their patent portfolios. We can state this more precisely: the "distance" in "technology space" between two firms i and j can be approximated by P_{ij} where P_{ij} is the uncentered correlation coefficient of the F vectors of the two firms, or

$$(2) \qquad P_{ij} = \frac{F_i F_j'}{[(F_i F_i')(F_j F_j')]^{1/2}}$$

Other things being equal, firm i will receive more "R&D spillovers" from firm j if firm j is doing a substantial amount of investment in new technologies. Firm i will also receive more R&D spillovers if its research program is very similar to that of firm j. Thus, the total potential pool of intranational R&D spillovers for a firm can be proxied by calculating the weighted sum of the R&D performed by all other firms with the "similarity coefficients" for each pair of firms, P_{ij}, used as weights. More simply, suppressing time subscripts here and in the equations below for expositional convenience, the intranational, or "domestic" spillover pool for the i-th is S_{di}, where S_{di} is

$$(3) \qquad S_{di} = \sum_{i \neq j} P_{ij} R_j$$

Here R_j is the R&D spending of the j-th firm (j not equal to i) and P_{ij} is the "similarity coefficient". Similar, the potential international, or "foreign", spillover pool is computed as

$$(4) \qquad S_{fi} = \sum_{i \neq j} P_{ij} R_j$$

Where R_j is the R&D of firms based in a foreign country, again weighted by the P_{ij}'s. Assume that innovation is a function of own R&D and external knowledge. Then, the "knowledge production function" for the i-th firm is

$$(5) \qquad n_{it} = \beta r_{it} + \gamma_1 s_{dit} + \gamma_2 s_{fit} + \sum_c \delta_c D_{ic} + \varepsilon_{it}$$

---

24. This quote was taken from JAFFE [1986].

Following Jaffe, all variables are expressed in logs. In (5), n_{it} is innovation, r_{it} is the firm's own R&D investment, s_{dit} is the domestic spillover pool, s_{fit} is the international spillover pool, the D's are dummy variables to control for differences in the propensity to generate new knowledge across technological fields (indicated by the subscript c), and ε is an error term [25].

I estimate a number of such knowledge production functions, using both patent counts and total factor productivity growth as indices of innovative output, with panel data on Japanese and U.S. high-technology firms. Because I have panel data, I am able to estimate both random and fixed effects versions of my knowledge production. Table 3 compares my fixed effects results to those of JAFFE [1986]. A number of differences in the results can be noted and explained. In theory, fixed effects models control for the effects of left-out variables (especially unmeasured firm-specific heterogeneity) that change slowly over time. However, this comes at the cost of throwing out the cross-sectional variance, which is typically most of the variation in a firm-level data set. Furthermore, given that both R&D and, to a much greater extent, spillovers are measured with error, fixed effects models can actually worsen the bias arising from measurement error. Nevertheless, they are useful as a strong test of the robustness of ones results.

In interpreting the results, the reader must note that, as JAFFE [1986] has pointed out, "From a purely technological point of view, R&D spillovers constitute an unambiguous positive externality. Unfortunately, we can only observe various economic manifestations of the firm's R&D success. For this reason, the positive technological externality is potentially confounded with a negative effect of other's research due to competition. It is not possible, with available data, to distinguish between these two effects...". To put it more concretely, patents are a tool of appropriation. If technological rivalry with other firms is intense enough, and the scope of intellectual property

TABLE 3

Impact of Spillovers on Innovation as Measured by Firm-Level Patenting Fixed Effects Specification.

Variable	Jaffe (U.S.)	Branstetter (U.S.)	Branstetter (Japan)
Own R&D	.398	.246	.095
	(.225)	(.091)	(0.98)
Domestic Spillovers	.179	.364	.927
	(.058)	(.532)	(.356)
Interaction Term	.020	n.a.	n.a.
	(.025)		
Foreign Spillovers	n.a.	−.657	.373
		(.402)	(.502)

25. Jaffe includes an interaction term between own and external R&D in his version of (5), reasoning that part of the effect of R&D spillovers may be to improve the productivity of a firm's own R&D.

512

rights conferred by patents is broad enough, firms may sometimes find themselves competing for a limited pool of available patents – a patent race. Because of this, if actual flows of knowledge are weak or nonexistent, and rivalry is strong, our estimates may be negative even though the underlying technological externality is positive.

Jaffe's results are presented in the second column. Unlike Jaffe, my specification of (5) does not include an interaction term between own and external R&D, but I do allow for international and well as intranational spillovers. My results for U.S. firms in the third column are not that different from Jaffe's, given that I use a much narrower cross-section of firms (209 firms to his 432) and a time period that is more than a decade later. I estimate larger intranational spillover effects, but they are estimated with less precision such that they fall below conventional significance levels; The truly new result is the estimated impact of Japanese R&D – it is not significantly different from zero, but the point estimate is negative. I see this as being consistent with anecdotal evidence that U.S. firms are not good at monitoring foreign R&D, whereas Japanese firms were extremely aggressive about patenting in the U.S. Here, a weak positive externality has been "drowned out" by a "patent race" effect. The results presented in the fourth column for Japan are quite different. First, the estimated effect of own R&D is smaller both in magnitude and in statistical significance. In my view, this is primarily a function of measurement error in the Japanese micro-level R&D data, which is more severe than that for U.S. firms. I should also note that in random effects and nonlinear specifications, the elasticity of own R&D is higher and significant. Second, the intranational spillover effect is extremely large and quite significant. Third, the estimated impact of R&D spillovers form American firms is positive, but again, it falls below conventional significance levels. The surprising conclusion that emerges is that R&D spillovers seem to be a predominantly *intranational* phenomenon. This is strikingly different from the results one gets with aggregate data, as seen in Table 2, where innovative output elasticity of "foreign R&D spillovers" is consistently estimated to be higher than that of domestic spillovers, and underscores the importance of working with data at the producer level.

In my 1996 working paper, I estimate linear, random effects, and nonlinear versions of equation 5 with patent counts as the dependent variable. In addition, I use TFP growth as an index of innovative output for both U.S. and Japanese firms. The results are qualitatively similar to those shown here [26]. In most specifications, I can formally reject the hypothesis of equality of intranational and international R&D spillovers. When that is impossible, it is generally because the impact of international R&D spillovers is not significantly different from zero.

---

26. It is interesting to note that this econometric evidence matches well with survey evidence on where Japanese managers think their "spillovers" come from. When asked in a recent survey undertaken by the Science and Technology Agency of Japan whether, in effect, foreign or domestic sources of spillovers were more important, Japanese R&D managers overwhelmingly cited domestic sources. (This information is based on personal communication with Professor Akira Goto of the Science and Technology Agency.)

• The Use of Patent Citations Data

Of course, my approach has the serious disadvantage of being able to infer the existence of spillovers only indirectly. In principle, at least, a direct measure is available – patent citations. Jaffe and Trajtenberg use this data along with a "citations function" in which the likelihood that any particular patent K granted in year T will cite some particular patent k granted in year t is assumed to be determined by the combination of an exponential process by which knowledge diffuses and a second exponential process by which knowledge becomes obsolete. This relationship is defined as

$$p(k, K) = \alpha(k, K) \exp[-\beta_1(k, K)(T - t)][1 - \exp(-\beta_2(T - t))]$$

where β_1 determines obsolescence and β_2 diffusion. In their econometric specifications, Jaffe and Trajtenberg are able to derive a nonlinear estimating equation based on this citation function which allows them to predict the probability of citations conditioning on a number of factors, including the nationality of the inventors of both patent k and patent K. Drawing upon an enormous data base of patents taken out in the U.S. by both domestic and foreign inventors and the associated data on citations, JAFFE and TRAJTENBERG [1996] have found that inventors are much more likely to cite previous patents taken out by inventors from their own country than one would expect given the distribution of scientists and research resources across countries. Furthermore, this tendency holds up even after controlling for technological field, cohort effects, and other factors. This finding suggests that R&D spillovers have a very strong "intranational" component. In related work, Francis NARIN [1995] finds similar disproportionately "intranational" citation patterns in his bibliometric study of scientific papers in the biological sciences. The implications of these findings for the global economy are far from clear, but they at least suggest that R&D spillovers may be much more of an *intranational* phenomenon than the estimates embodied in the work of Coe and Helpman suggest. Jaffe and Trajtenberg are currently working on using the direct measures of knowledge spillovers obtainable from this patent citation data base to construct technology flow matrices between industries and countries, which can then be used to measure the impact of international and intranational spillovers on output and productivity.

• From Spillovers to Transfer

Up to this point, this paper has focused on the extent to which research activity in one country contributes to innovation in another. This kind of international technological interaction generally occurs between innovating developed countries at the technological frontier. This is, or arguably should be, a parameter of great interest to policymakers in the small number of advanced countries where most of the world's new technological knowledge is developed, for innovation is the principal means by which these countries can continue to grow.

514

For the majority of humankind, however, a far more important potential source of growth is not the development of new technologies but the implementation of existing technologies that have already been developed abroad. This is a different kind of phenomenon, and it probably requires a different conceptual framework [27]. Unfortunately, the "new departures" I have outlined here will be of little use in the context of examining technology transfer between developed and developing countries since there is little or no observable "innovation" by third world producers (*i.e.*, no independent patenting by the recipients of the transfer). As a result, I will have to leave consideration of this very important issue for another time.

7 Conclusion

I began this survey by reviewing the theoretical models that have highlighted the importance of international knowledge spillovers. I then pointed out that the knowledge spillovers highlighted in the theoretical literature can be distinguished conceptually, and possibly empirically, from "pecuniary spillovers". I further reasoned that identifying the traces of knowledge spillovers in the data requires a measure of technological proximity between firms. Given the enormous technological heterogeneity within, say, 3-digit industries, obtaining such a measure requires that researchers undertake their analyses at a very disaggregated level. I have argued that the most appropriate level of aggregation is the micro level [28].

From there, I reviewed some well-known empirical studies, pointing out various weaknesses in each, including the failure to control for technological proximity. Finally, I reviewed two alternative approaches to the measurement of knowledge spillovers. I pointed out, though, that these methodologies will be of limited usefulness in exploring the important question of how and to what extent first-world technology is being transferred to developing countries.

Theorists have shown that the presence of knowledge spillovers may matter a lot for trade theory and the traditional policy prescriptions that have flowed form it. Ultimately, though, the significance of these theories will be, and rightly should be, determined by empirical evidence. This survey shows that confronting these theories with data is not easy, and that we have made limited progress so far. However, I also hope that I have demonstrated that there are data and modeling tools at hand which may allow us to push forward. It is my hope that at least some readers will be persuaded to contribute to this effort. Grossman and Helpman and others have raised some very important questions. Now, we need answers.

---

27. Grossman and Helpman give this sort of technology transfer entirely separate treatment in their landmark book (GROSSMAN and HELPMAN [1991]).
28. I acknowledge again, however, the "sample selection" issues that are likely to arise with the use of micro-level data.

● References

AITKEN, BRIAN, HANSON, G., HARRISON, A. (1994). – "Spillovers, Foreign Investment, and Export Behavior", *NBER Working Paper No. 4967.*

AKERLOF, G. (1970). – "The Market for 'Lemons': Quality Uncertainty and the Market Mechanism", *Quarterly Journal of Economics,* 84(3).

ANDREW, B., JONES, C. (1996). – "Comparing Apples to Oranges: Productivity Convergence Across Countries and Industries", *American Economic Review,* December 1996.

BERNSTEIN, J., MOHNEN, P. (1994). – "International R&D Spillovers Between U.S. and Japanese R&D Intensive Sectors", *National Bureau of Economic Research Working Paper 4682.*

BERNSTEIN, J., YAN, X. (1995). – "International R&D Spillovers Between Canadian and Japanese Industries", *NBER Working Paper 5401.*

BLOMSTROM, M., KOKKO, A. (1996). – "Multinational Corporations and Spillovers", *National Bureau of Economic Research Working Paper.*

BLUNDELL, R., GRIFFITH, R., VAN REENAN, J. (1994). – "Dynamic Count Data Models of Technological Innovation", *mimeo,* ESRC Center for Microeconomic Analysis of Fiscal Policy.

CABALLERO, R., JAFFE, A. (1994). – "How High Are the Giants' Shoulders?" in *1994 Macroeconomics Annual,* National Bureau of Economic Research.

BANGTIAN, C., KAO, Ch. (1995). – "International R&D Spillovers Revisited: An Application of Panel Data with Cointegration", Department of Economics and Center for Policy Research, Syracuse University, *mimeo.*

COE, D., HELPMAN, E. (1995). – "International R&D Spillovers", *European Economic Review,* 39(5).

COE, D., HELPMAN, E., HOFFMAISTER, A. (1995). – "North-South R&D Spillovers", *NBER Working Paper.*

COHEN, W., LEVINTHAL, D. (1989). – "Innovation and Learning: The Two Faces of R&D", *The Economic Journal, No. 99.*

ETHIER, W. (1982). – "National and International Returns to Scale in the Modern Theory of International Trade", *American Economic Review,* 72, pp. 389-405.

FEENSTRA, R. (1992). – "How Costly is Protectionism?" *Journal of Economic Perspectives,* Vol. 6, No. 6.

FEENSTRA, R. (1996). – "Trade and Uneven Growth", *Journal of Development Economics,* February.

GOTO, A. (1993). – *Nihon no Gijutsu Kakushin to Sangyo Soshiki* (Japan's Technological Progress and Industrial Organization), Tokyo: University of Tokyo Press.

GRILICHES, Z. ed. (1984). – *R&D, Patents, and Productivity,* Chicago: University of Chicago Press.

GRILICHES, Z. (1979). – "Issues in Assessing the Contribution of R&D to Productivity Growth", *Bell Journal of Economics,* 10 (1), pp. 92-116.

GRILICHES, Z. (1992). – "The Search for R&D Spillovers", *Scandinavian Journal of Economics,* 94, Supplement, pp. 29-47.

GRILICHES, Z., HAUSMAN, J. (1986). – "Errors in Variables in Panel Data", *Journal of Econometrics,* 41 (1), pp. 93-118.

GRILICHES, Z., MAIRESSE, J. (1995). – "Production Functions – the Search for Identification", *NBER Working Paper.*

GRILICHES, Z., KLETTE, T. (1997). – "Empirical Patterns of Firm Growth and R&D Investment: A Quality Ladder Model Interpretation", *NBER Working paper #5945.*

GROSSMAN, G., HELPMAN, El. (1990). – "Comparative Advantage and Long-Run Growth", *American Economic Review,* vol. 80, No. 4.

516

GROSSMAN, G., HELPMAN, El. (1991). – Innovation and Growth in the Global Economy, Cambridge: *The MIT Press.*

GROSSMAN, G., HELPMAN, El. (1995). – "Technology and Trade", in *Handbook of International Economics,* vol. 3, edited by Gene Grossman and Kenneth Rogoff.

HALL, B., GRILICHES, Z., HAUSMAN, J. (1986). – "Patents and R&D – Is There a Lag?" *International Economic Review,* 27, pp. 265-283.

HALL, B. (1993). – "Has the Rate of Return Declined?" *The Brookings Papers on Economic Activity,* vol. 2: Microeconomics.

HAUSMAN, J., HALL, B., GRILICHES, Z. (1984). – "Econometric Models for Count Data with an Application to the Patents-R&D Rerlationship", *Econometrica,* 52, 4.

FUMIO, H., INOUYE, T. (1991). – "The Relationship Between Firm Growth and Q with Multiple Capital Goods: Theory and Evidence from Panel Data on Japanese Firm", *Econometrica,* 59(3).

ELHANAN, H., KRUGMAN, P. (1985). – *Market Structure and Foreign Trade: Increasing Returns Imperfect Competition, and the International Economy,* (Cambridge, MIT Press).

ELHANAN, H., KRUGMAN, P. (1989). – *Trade Policy and Market Structure,* (Cambridge, MIT Press).

IRWIN, D., KLENOW, P. (1994). – "Learning by Doing Spillovers in the Semiconductor Industry", *Journal of Political Economy,* 102 (6).

JAFFE, A (1986). – "Technological Opportunity and Spillover of R&D: Evidence from Firms' Patents, Profits, and Market Value", *American Economic Review,* 76, pp. 984-1001.

JAFFE, A., TRAJTENBERG, M., HENDERSON, R. (1993). – "Geographic Localization of Knowledge Spilloversas Evidenced by Patent Citations", *Quarterly Journal of Economics,* 108 (3).

JAFFE, A., TRAJTENBERG, M. (1996). – "Flows of Knowledge Spillovers", working paper presented at the Strasbourg Conference on the Economics and Econometrics of Innovation.

JONES, C. (1995). – "R&D-Based Models of Economic Growth", *Journal of Political Economy,* vol. 103, No. 4.

KELLER, W. (1995). – "International R&D Spillover and Intersectoral Trade Flows: Do They Match?", *Yale University manuscript.*

KELLER, W. (1996). – "Absorptive Capacity", *Journal of Development Economics.*

KELLER, W. (1996). – "Are International R&D Spillovers Trade-related? Analyzing Spillovers among Randomly Matched Trade Partners", *working paper,* UW-Madison, Department of Economics.

YUKO, K., MODY, As. (1996). – "Private and Public Information for Foreign Investment Decision", *Working paper.*

KLETTE, Tor Jacob (1994). – "R&D, Scope Economies, and Company Structure: A 'Not-so-Fixed-Effect' Model of Plant Performance", *Statistics Norway Research Department mimeo.*

KRUGMAN, P. (1984). – "Import Protection as Export Promotion: International Competition in the Presence of Oligopoly and Economies of Scale", in Henryk Kierzhowski, ed., *Monopolistic Competition and Foreign Trade,* (Clarendon Press).

KRUGMAN, P. (1987). – "The Narrow Moving Band, the Dutch Disease, and the Competitive COnsequences of Mrs. Thatcher: Notes on Trade in the Presence of Dynamics Scale Economies", *Journal of Development Economics,* 27, pp. 41-55.

KRUGMAN, P. (1990). – *The Age of Diminished Expectations,* (Cambridge, The MIT Press).

KRUGMAN, P. (1992). – *Rethinking International Trade,* (Cambridge, The MIT Press).

KRUGMAN, P. ed. (1986). – *Strategic Trade Policy and the New International Economics*, (Cambridge, The MIT Press).

KEUN, K., SCHERER, F. M. (1992). – "Reactions to High-Tech Import Competition", *The Review of Economics and Statistics*, pp. 202-212.

LEVIN, R. D. *et al.* (1987). – "Appropriating the Returns from Industrial Research and Development", *Brooking Papers on Economic Activity*, Vol. 3, pp. 783-820

LIEBERMAN, M. (1984). – "The Learning Curve and Pricing in the Chemical Processing Industries", *Rand Journal of Economics*.

MANSFIELD, E. (1985). – "How Rapidly Does New Industrial Technology Leak Out?" *Journal of Industrial Economics*, 34, pp. 217-223.

MONTALVO, J., YAFEH, Y. (1994). – "A Micro-Econometric Analysis of Technology Transfer: The Case of Licensing Agreements of Japanese Firms", *International Journal of Industrial Organization*, Vol. 12, No. 2.

NADIRI, M. I. (1993). – "Innovations and Technological Spillovers", *NBER Working Paper No. 4423*.

NELSON, R. (1988). – "Modelling the Connections in the Cross Section Between Technical Progress and R&D Intensity", *Rand Journal of Economics*, 19, pp. 478-85.

HIROYUKI, O. (1983). – "R&D Expenditures, Royalty Payments, and Sales Growth in Japanese Manufacturing Corporations", *The Journal of Industrial Economics*, Vol. XXXII, No. 1.

PARK, W. (1995). – "International R&D Spillovers and OECD Economic Growth", *Economic Inquiry*, Vol. 23, No. 4.

RAUCH, J. (1995). – "Search Costs in International Trade", *NBER Working Paper*.

RIVERA-BATIZ, L., ROMER, P. (1991). – "Economic Integration and Endogenous Growth", *Quarterly Journal of Economics*, Vol. 56, pp. 531-555.

ROMER, P. (1990). – "Endogenous Technical Change", *Journal of Political Economy*, 98, S71-S102.

SCHERER, F. M. (1982). – "Interindustry Technology Flows and Productivity Growth", *Review of Economics and Statistics*, LXIV, pp. 627-634.

Science and Technology Agency, Government of Japan (1991), *Gijutsu Yoran (Technology Indicators)*.

SPENCE, A. Michael (1984). – "Cost Reduction, Competition, and Industry Performance", *Econometrica*, 50, pp. 483-499.

TEECE, D. (1976). – *The Multinational Corporation and the Resource Cost of Technology Transfer*, (Cambridge, MA, Ballinger Publishing Company).

TREFLER, D. (1993). – "International Factor Price Differences: Leontief Was Right!", *Journal of Political Economy*, vol. 101, No. 6.

TREFLER, D. (1995). – "The Case of the Mising Trade and Other Mysteries", *American Economic Review*,

TYSON, Laura D'Andrea (1993). – *Who's Bashing Whom?: Trade Conflict in High-Technology Industries*, Washington: Institute for International Economics.

VERNON, R. ed. (1970). – *The Technology Factor in International Trade*, NBER, distributed by Columbia University Press.

WAKASUGI, R. (1986). – *Gijutsu Kakushin to Kenkyu Kaihatsu no Keizai Bunseki: Nihon no Kigyo Kodo to Sangyo Seisaku* (The Economic Analysis of Research and Development and Technological Progress: Japanese Firm Activity and Industrial Policy), Tokyo: Toyo Keizai Shimposha.

YOUNG, A. (1991). – "Learning by Doing and the Dynamic Effects of International Trade", *Quarterly Journal of Economics*, 106, pp. 369-406.

518

Factor Intensities, Rates of Return, and International R&D Spillovers: The Case of Canadian and U.S. Industries

Jeffrey I. BERNSTEIN *

ABSTRACT. – This paper estimates the effects of both intranational and international spillovers on production cost, and factor intensities (including R&D intensity) for eleven manufacturing industries in the U.S., and Canada. In addition, social rates of return to R&D capital are calculated, and decomposed into private rates of return, and the extra-returns due to intranational and international spillovers.

International spillovers are usually cost reducing, and increase R&D and physical capital intensities. International spillovers are generally labor and intermediate input intensity reducing. In Canada, international spillover effects are more elastic than domestic spillover elasticities. In the U.S. the same relationship exists, but is not as pronounced.

Social rates of return to R&D capital are substantially above the private rates in both Canada and U.S. In Canada, international spillovers generally account for a greater percentage of the social returns relative to the domestic spillovers. In the U.S. the converse occurs. Canadian social rates are from two and a half to twelve times greater than private returns, while U.S. social returns are from three and a half to ten times greater than the private rates.

* J. I. BERNSTEIN: Carleton University, and The National Bureau of Economic Research. I would like to thank Xiaoyi Yan, and Lin Bian for their research assistance. Brian Erard, Steven Globerman, Zvi Griliches, Jacques Mairesse, Ross Preston, Somshwar Rao, and two anonymous referees provided valuable comments and suggestions. Funding for this study was provided by Industry Canada.

D. Encaoua et al. (eds.), The Economics and Econometrics of Innovation, 519–542.

1 Introduction

Until recently, economic analysis paid little attention to the significance of R&D. Theories of growth, production, and investment treated technological change as an exogenous process. The view has now shifted towards an emphasis on R&D investment and the resulting innovations that respond to incentives as sources of technological progress.

There is a public good aspect to R&D capital accumulation. The benefits from R&D cannot be completely appropriated by R&D performers and, inevitably, there are spillovers. There are numerous transmission channels associated with R&D spillovers. Examples relate to physical capital, and intermediate input acquisition, labor mobility, licensing agreements, and joint ventures. Spillovers (positive ones at least) imply that R&D performers have not been adequately compensated for their efforts. When R&D is performed not only investors benefit, but benefits are spilled over to other users inside and outside the performing industry. Indeed, R&D spillovers spur the diffusion of new knowledge, while simultaneously creating disincentives to undertake R&D investment. A number of recent empirical papers have shown that domestic R&D spillovers are important means of knowledge transmission (see GRILICHES [1991], and NADIRI [1993] for surveys).

In a world with international trade, foreign direct investment, and the international exchange of information, a country's stock of knowledge depends on its own R&D investment, as well as the R&D efforts of other countries. R&D spillovers extend beyond national boundaries. The purpose of this paper is to investigate the effects of both intranational and international spillovers between Canadian and U.S. industries on costs of production, and factor intensities, and to determine the relative contribution of domestic and foreign spillovers to the social rates of return to R&D capital. The focus of international spillovers between Canada and the U.S. arises because of the importance of international trade and foreign direct investment links between the two countries.

This paper is organized into five sections. Section 2 contains the estimation model. Section 3 relates to the intranational and international spillovers elasticities of production cost and factor intensities. Social rates of returns, and the contributions of domestic and foreign spillovers are discussed in section 4. The last section is the conclusion.

2 Estimation Model of Spillovers

This section develops a model of production with intranational and international spillovers for Canadian and U.S. industries. This model can be used, in part, to determine intranational and international spillover effects on production cost, and factor intensities.

520

We specify a variable cost function, or more precisely an average variable cost function. An average variable cost function leads to a model specification in terms of factor intensities. This feature implies that, irrespective of the degree of returns to scale, the same set of equations are estimated (apart from any parameter restrictions arising from constant returns to scale). The average variable cost function is denoted as [1],

$$
(1) \qquad c_t^v / y_t = \left(\sum_{i=1}^{2} \beta_i\, w_{it} + 0.5 \sum_{i=1}^{2} \sum_{j=1}^{2} \beta_{ij}\, w_{it}\, w_{jt}\, W_t^{-1} \right.
$$

$$
\left. + \sum_{i=1}^{2} \sum_{j=1}^{2} \phi_{ij}\, w_{it}\, S_{jt-1} + \sum_{i=1}^{2} \phi_i\, w_{it}\, t \right) y_t^{\eta-1}
$$

$$
+ \left[\sum_{i=1}^{2} \alpha_i\, k_{it} + 0.5 \sum_{i=1}^{2} \sum_{j=1}^{2} \alpha_{ij}\, k_{it}\, k_{jt} / y_t^{\eta-1} \right.
$$

$$
\left. + \sum_{i=1}^{2} \sum_{j=1}^{2} \psi_{ij}\, k_{it}\, S_{jt-1} + \sum_{i=1}^{2} \psi_i\, k_{it}\, t \right] W_t
$$

where the parameters to be estimated are given by β_i, β_{ij}, ϕ_{ij}, ϕ_i, α_i, α_{ij}, ψ_{ij}, ψ_i, i, $j = 1, 2$ and η is the inverse of the degree of returns to scale. The noncapital factor prices are denoted as w_i, $i = 1$ is the labor price, and $i = 2$ is the price of intermediate inputs. R&D spillovers are denoted by S_{1t} as the intranational (or domestic) spillover, and S_{2t} as the international (or foreign) spillover. Capital intensities are $k_i = K_i/y$, where K_i is the capital input, $i = 1$ is physical capital, $i = 2$ is R&D capital, y is output, and t is the time trend, representing non-spillover exogenous technological efficiency effects. $W = \Sigma_{i=1}^{2} a_i\, w_i$, where a_i, $i = 1, 2$ are fixed coefficients. W can be defined as a Laspeyres index of non-capital input prices. By defining W in this manner we do not have to normalize the cost function by any one noncapital input price, but rather by a weighted average of both prices [2].

In the literature, international R&D spillovers are measured in a number of ways. COE and HELPMAN [1995] use trade flows as carriers of international R&D spillovers, EATON and KORTUM [1996], and BRANSTETTER [1996] rely on foreign patenting, whereas LICHTENBERG and VAN POTTELSBERGHE de la POTTERIE [1996] consider both trade and foreign direct investment. Trade or foreign investment linkages can bias the effects of international spillovers. KELLER [1996] shows that randomly generated trade shares lead to international spillover effects on productivity growth that are higher than those estimated using actual trade shares. Implicit in the use of patent weights is the assumption that the value of patents are assumed to be invariant across producers, within and between countries, and over time. Moreover, international transactions do not have to occur in order for spillovers to flow between nations.

---

1. See DIEWERT [1982] for the properties of cost functions.

2. The attractive feature of this average variable cost function is that the curvature conditions can be imposed on the function. See DIEWERT and WALES [1987, 1988] for this discussion.

In this paper, we do not need to hypothesize any specific transmission channel. Spillovers between the U.S., and Canada arise from the stocks of R&D capital defined at an aggregate industrial level in each country. The stock of R&D capital in one country can affect production cost, and factor intensities in the other country, because spillovers occur within the context of a bilateral model of production and investment (see JORGENSON and NISHIMIZU [1978], and JORGENSON, SAKURAMOTO, YOSHIOKA, and KURODA [1990] for this class of model in the absence of R&D spillovers). The significance of this approach is that transmission channels are not specified independently of production (including R&D) decisions, and that all production decisions are modeled simultaneously.

The domestic spillover is the sum of one period lagged R&D capital stocks of all domestic industries other than the one under consideration [3]. Spillovers are estimated for industries defined at the two-digit Standard Industrial Classification (SIC) level. This means that domestic spillovers are also interindustry spillovers. The foreign spillover is the lagged R&D stock of the corresponding industry in the foreign country. International spillovers are intraindustry. Spillovers that operate across national boundaries and between industries are assumed to be indirectly captured through the domestic spillovers, which are themselves influenced by foreign R&D capital stocks.

Most existing studies of international R&D spillovers estimate simple Cobb-Douglas production functions where domestic and foreign R&D enter as separate inputs. The assumed functional form implies that factor intensities are independent of any spillovers. However, theoretically, GROSSMAN and HELPMAN [1991] have shown that spillovers affect factor intensities. In this paper a flexible functional form is specified for the cost function, which permits the estimation of factor intensity effects of international spillovers.

Using the average variable cost function, and Shephard's Lemma (see DIEWERT [1982]), noncapital input intensities, are given by,

$$
\begin{aligned}
(2) \quad \vartheta_{it} = &\left(\beta_i + \sum_{j=1}^{2} \beta_{ij}\, w_{jt}\, W_t^{-1} - 0.5 \sum_{h=1}^{2}\sum_{j=1}^{2} \beta_{hj}\, w_{ht}\, w_{jt}\, W_t^{-2}\, a_i \right. \\
&+ \sum_{j=1}^{2} \phi_{ij} S_{jt-1} + \phi_i t \bigg) y_t^{\eta-1} + \left(\sum_{j=1}^{2} \alpha_j k_{jt} + 0.5 \sum_{h=1}^{2}\sum_{j=1}^{2} \alpha_{hj} k_{ht} k_{jt} / y_t^{\eta-1} \right. \\
&+ \sum_{h=1}^{2}\sum_{j=1}^{2} \psi_{hj} k_{ht} S_{jt-1} + \sum_{h=1}^{2} \psi_h k_{ht} t \bigg) a_i, \qquad i = 1, 2,
\end{aligned}
$$

---

3. For any one producer, the accumulation of undepreciated R&D investment by other producers is the source of R&D spillovers. Spillovers emanate from the stocks of R&D capital. Thus it is not surprising that the use of one or two year lags on the stocks in defining spillovers does not affect the results.

where noncapital input intensities are $\vartheta_i = \nu_i/y$, $i = 1$, 2, and ν_1, is labor input, and ν_2 is intermediate input. The intensities associated with labor and intermediate inputs depend on their factor prices, output quantity, physical and R&D capital intensities, and R&D spillovers.

Based on the average variable cost function, and cost minimization, the demands for the physical and R&D capital inputs, in intensive form are [4],

$$(3) \qquad k_{it} = (\alpha_{jj} A_{it} - \alpha_{ij} A_{jt})/\mathcal{A}, \qquad i \neq j, \quad i, j = 1, 2$$

where $A_{it} = (-\alpha_i - \Sigma_{j=1}^2 \psi_{ij} S_{jt-1} - \psi_i t - \omega_{it} W_t^{-1}) y_t^{\eta-1}$, $i = 1$, 2, and $\mathcal{A} = (\alpha_{11} \alpha_{22} - \alpha_{12}^2)$, ω_i is the factor price of the i-th capital input. The physical and R&D capital intensities depend on labor and intermediate input prices, the input prices of physical and R&D capital, output quantity, and the R&D spillovers. Equation sets (2), and (3) define the model that is to be estimated [5].

The model is estimated for each of eleven manufacturing industries. The industries are defined at the two-digit SIC level, and are; chemical products, electrical products, food and beverage, fabricated metals, nonelectrical machinery, nonmetallic mineral products, paper and allied products, petroleum products, primary metals, rubber and plastics, and transportation equipment. For each industry, Canadian and U.S. data are pooled. Thus the model is in the class of bilateral production models (see JORGENSON and KURODA [1990], JORGENSON and NISHIMIZU [1978]). The sample period is 1962-1989. The variables used in the models are defined in the Data Appendix. The estimator of equation sets (2), and (3) is nonlinear maximum likelihood. From the tables in the Estimation Results Appendix, we see that the correlation coefficients between the actual and fitted values of the endogenous variables are high. The model fits the data quite well [6].

3 Spillover Elasticities

The purpose of this section is to present and discuss the effects of domestic and foreign spillovers on average variable cost of production, and

---

4. The capital input demands are derived from the minimization of total cost, which is $c^v + \Sigma_k \omega_k K_k$, where c^v is given by equation (1) after multiplying both sides of (1) by y. Solving the first order conditions for the capital inputs leads to equation (3).

5. Because our interest lies in the measurement of long-run spillover elasticities, along with the determination of long-run social rates of return to R&D capital, we abstract from the dynamics arising from adjustment costs.

6. In the estimation we impose the restriction that the variable cost function must be concave in the noncapital input prices. Thus $\beta_{ii} = -b_{ii}^2$. In addition, with the matrix of β_{ij} parameters defined as B, the vector of β_i parameters defined as β, and the vector of coefficients a_i defined as a, we note that $(B + 2a\beta^T)$ parameters are identified. Thus for identification, we introduce two restrictions, $\beta_{ii} + \beta_{ij} = 0$, $i \neq j$, $i, j, = 1, 2$. In addition, there are at least 27 observations times 4 equations minus 22 parameters or 86 degrees of freedom for each of the eleven industry models that are estimated.

factor intensities (including R&D intensity). The spillover elasticities are determined by differentiating equaitons (1), (2), and (3) with respect to S_1 and S_2. First, in terms of the capital intensities, from equation (3),

$$(4) \quad ek_c S_j = S_j y^{\eta-1}(\alpha_{12}\psi_{dj} - \alpha_{dd}\psi_{cj})/Ak_c \quad j=1, 2, \ c \neq d, \ c, \ d = 1, 2$$

where, $ek_c S_j$ is the j-th spillover elasticity of the c-th capital intensity.

Second, turning to the noncapital input intensities,

$$(5) \quad e\vartheta_i S_h = \left[[\phi_{ih} y^{\eta-1}/a_i + (\psi_{hh}k_h + \psi_{gh}k_g)] + (ek_1 S_h)(k_1/S_h) \right.$$
$$\left(\alpha_1 + \sum_{j=1}^{2} \alpha_{1j}k_j y^{\eta-1} + \sum_{j=1}^{2} \psi_{1j}S_j + \psi_1 t \right) + (ek_2 S_h)(k_2/S_h)$$
$$\left. \left(\alpha_2 + \sum_{j=1}^{2} \alpha_{j2}k_j y^{\eta-1} + \sum_{j=1}^{2} \psi_{2j}S_j + \psi_2 t \right) \right] a_i S_h/\vartheta_i,$$
$$i = 1, 2 \ g \neq h, \ g, \ h = 1, 2$$

where, $e\vartheta_i S_h$ is the h-th spillover elasticity of the i-th noncapital input intensity. There are two effects of the spillovers on the noncapital intensities. The first is the direct effect (denoted by the terms in the first set of square brackets) arising from the fact that noncapital input prices interact with the spillovers. The second effect is the indirect effect that arises because the noncapital input intensities are affected by the capital intensities. The latter intensities are directly affected by the spillovers.

The last set of elasticities shows the effects of the spillovers on average variable cost. They are,

$$(6) \quad ec_y^v S_h = \left[[(\phi_{1h}w_1 + \phi_{2h}w_2)y^{\eta-1}/W + \psi_{hh}k_h + \psi_{gh}k_g] \right.$$
$$+ (ek_1 S_h)(k_1/S_h)\left(\alpha_1 + \sum_{j=1}^{2} \alpha_{1j}k_j y^{\eta-1} + \sum_{j=1}^{2} \psi_{1j}S_j + \psi_1 t \right)$$
$$+ (ek_2 S_h)(k_2/S_h)\left(\alpha_2 + \sum_{j=1}^{2} \alpha_{j2}k_j y^{\eta-1} \right.$$
$$\left. \left. + \sum_{j=1}^{2} \psi_{2j}S_j + \psi_2 t \right) \right] W S_h/(c^v/y), \quad g \neq h, \quad g, h = 1, 2$$

where, $ec_y^v S_h$ is the h-th spillover elasticity of average cost. There are also two effects of the spillovers on average variable cost. The first is the direct effect, (denoted by the terms inside the first set of square brackets) and the second is the indirect effect which operates through the capital intensities.

The direct effect of spillovers on average variable cost represents changes in the non-capital input intensities; namely labor and intermediate inputs,

524

when capital intensities do not change. R&D spillovers can decrease non-capital intensities and thereby decrease variable cost [7].

The sum of the direct and indirect spillover effects can be variable cost-increasing. Recall that the indirect effect relates to changes in capital intensities. Thus it is possible for a spillover to directly reduce variable cost, and also decrease capital intensities. Lower capital intensities imply higher variable cost. The latter effect can more than offset the direct cost-reducing effect [8].

Tables 1 and 2 show the sample mean and standard deviation of the annual spillover elasticities relating to factor intensities, and variable cost (both the direct and combined direct and indirect elasticities of variable cost).

From table 1, domestic or intranational spillovers reduce average variable cost for six U.S. industries. They are chemical products, non-electrical and allied products, primary metals, rubber and plastics. The effects are inelastic, and the elasticities range from a low of 0.002 for non-electrical machinery to a high of 0.69 for transportation equipment. In Canada, domestic spillovers reduce average variable cost in five industries. These industries are, electrical products, food and beverage, petroleum products, rubber and plastics and transportation equipment. The range of variable cost reductions is wider in Canada relative to the U.S., and except for rubber and plastics, and transportation equipment, there is little overlap in the industry groupings between the two countries. This result suggests that domestic spillover effects are different in the two countries.

TABLE 1

Domestic Spillover Elasticities: Mean Values of Annual Elasticities
(standard deviations of annual elasticities in parentheses)

	United States					
Industry	Labor Intensity	Interm. Input Intensity	Phy. Cap. Intensity	R&D Cap. Intensity	Avg. Var. Cost	Dir. Avg. Var. Cost
Chemical Products	−0.0059	−0.0168	0.0015	0.0006	−0.0116	−0.0110
	(0.0011)	(0.0050)	(0.0002)	(0.0001)	(0.0022)	(0.0020)
Electrical Products	0.1107	0.2238	−0.2584	0.2221	0.1597	0.1681
	(0.0390)	(0.0152)	(0.0537)	(0.0172)	(0.0297)	(0.0348)
Food & Beverage	0.0519	0.1192	−0.0107	−0.0319	0.1004	0.0993
	(0.0053)	(0.0176)	(0.0015)	(0.0040)	(0.0117)	(0.0117)

---

7. Spillovers could also increase product demand, and thereby revenue. This could result in a greater demand for non-capital inputs, and higher variable cost. Although product demand is not modeled, by conditioning on output, parameter estimates capture output increases over time (including those arising from spillovers). In this situation revenue increases more than offset any rise in cost.

8. Another way spillovers can be cost increasing is if they lead to future cost reductions. Thus, in present value terms spillovers are cost-reducing, but at any point in time, they can directly lead to cost increases.

TABLE 1 (continued)

United States						
Industry	Labor Intensity	Interm. Input Intensity	Phy. Cap. Intensity	R&D Cap. Intensity	Avg. Var. Cost	Dir. Avg. Var. Cost
Fabricated Metals	0.0117	0.0180	-0.2631	0.3691	0.0150	-0.0102
	(0.0126)	(0.0196)	(0.0577)	(0.0379)	(0.0162)	(0.0252)
Non-electrical Machinery	-0.0016	-0.0028	0.0039	0.0009	-0.0022	-0.0016
	(0.0013)	(0.0017)	(0.0008)	(0.0002)	(0.0015)	(0.0014)
Non-metallic Minerals	0.0673	0.1086	0.1947	0.1396	0.0874	0.0232
	(0.0063)	(0.0109)	(0.0458)	(0.0859)	(0.0073)	(0.0078)
Paper & Allied Products	-0.0261	-0.0558	-0.0234	-0.3432	-0.0428	-0.0509
	(0.0046)	(0.0125)	(0.0039)	(0.0889)	(0.0075)	(0.0093)
Petroleum Products	0.0173	0.0242	0.0138	-0.2771	0.0236	0.0176
	(0.0015)	(0.0016)	(0.0035)	(0.0453)	(0.0016)	(0.0019)
Primary Metals	-0.1580	-0.3011	0.0114	-0.3976	-0.2434	-0.2467
	(0.0484)	(0.1234)	(0.0018)	(0.0934)	(0.0911)	(0.0909)
Rubber & Plastics	-0.0172	-0.0331	0.2450	0.0959	-0.0261	-0.0189
	(0.0051)	(0.0162)	(0.1401)	(0.0075)	(0.0105)	(0.0103)
Transportation Equipment	-0.4552	-0.8696	-0.5342	0.3355	-0.6925	-0.6869
	(0.1440)	(0.4225)	(0.1128)	(0.0230)	(0.2634)	(0.2721)

Canada						
Industry	Labor Intensity	Interm. Input Intensity	Phy. Cap. Intensity	R&D Cap. Intensity	Avg. Var. Cost	Dir. Avg. Var. Cost
Chemical Products	0.0188	0.0338	-0.0136	-0.2159	0.0303	0.0266
	(0.0088)	(0.0139)	(0.0015)	(0.0226)	(0.0126)	(0.0129)
Electrical Products	-0.0272	-0.0378	0.1220	-0.3524	-0.0336	-0.0410
	(0.0160)	(0.0110)	(0.0321)	(0.1843)	(0.0090)	(0.0104)
Food & Beverage	-0.0010	-0.0017	-0.0125	0.2426	-0.0016	-0.0014
	(0.0004)	(0.0007)	(0.0020)	(0.0199)	(0.0006)	(0.0006)
Fabricated Metals	0.0227	0.0205	-0.0579	0.4881	0.0212	0.0195
	(0.0062)	(0.0032)	(0.0094)	(0.2181)	(0.0042)	(0.0041)
Non-electrical Machinery	0.0539	0.0701	0.0694	0.7311	0.0647	0.0655
	(0.0828)	(0.1198)	(0.0170)	(0.0262)	(0.1068)	(0.1069)
Non-metallic Minerals	0.0379	0.0437	0.0556	0.1519	0.0418	0.0363
	(0.0131)	(0.0109)	(0.0060)	(0.0478)	(0.0116)	(0.0112)
Paper & Allied Products	0.0409	0.0612	-0.3214	0.1164	0.0554	0.0422
	(0.0318)	(0.0358)	(0.0400)	(0.0371)	(0.0346)	(0.0354)
Petroleum Products	-0.0093	-0.0116	-0.0137	0.3217	-0.0115	-0.0086
	(0.0015)	(0.0022)	(0.0025)	(0.0413)	(0.0022)	(0.0030)
Primary Metals	0.0266	0.0347	-0.0681	-0.0492	0.0328	0.0306
	(0.0083)	(0.0052)	(0.0072)	(0.0045)	(0.0058)	(0.0058)
Rubber & Plastics	1.1677	1.1952	-0.1557	-0.2996	-1.1743	-1.1330
	(0.9799)	(1.1588)	(0.0275)	(0.0453)	(1.1273)	(1.0963)
Transportation Equipment	-0.0600	-0.0819	-0.1825	-1.8678	-0.0769	-0.0597
	(0.0364)	(0.0337)	(0.0225)	(0.5542)	(0.0346)	(0.0339)

TABLE 2

International Spillower Elasticities: Mean Values of Annual Elasticities
(standard deviations of annual elasticities in parentheses)

	United States					
Industry	Labor Intensity	Interm. Input Intensity	Phy. Cap. Intensity	R&D Cap. Intensity	Avg. Var. Cost	Dir. Avg. Var. Cost
Chemical Products	0.1446	0.3994	−0.1176	0.0156	0.2790	0.2438
	(0.0272)	(0.0459)	(0.0199)	(0.0024)	(0.0078)	(0.0145)
Electrical Products	−0.0798	−0.1404	0.1365	−0.1266	−0.1072	−0.1132
	(0.0707)	(0.0830)	(0.0512)	(0.0721)	(0.0782)	(0.0842)
Food & Beverage	−0.2828	−0.6680	0.0516	0.2463	−0.5550	−0.5488
	(0.1318)	(0.3526)	(0.0157)	(0.0799)	(0.2731)	(0.2704)
Fabricated Metals	−0.0316	−0.0482	0.0539	0.0288	−0.0404	−0.0345
	(0.0181)	(0.0273)	(0.0244)	(0.0152)	(0.0228)	(0.0208)
Non-electrical Machinery	−0.1432	−0.2145	0.7234	0.2263	−0.1807	−0.0640
	(0.1859)	(0.2761)	(0.0936)	(0.0899)	(0.2299)	(0.1843)
Non-metallic Minerals	−0.0219	−0.0353	0.0407	0.2085	−0.0284	0.0198
	(0.0107)	(0.0183)	(0.0140)	(0.1310)	(0.0143)	(0.0115)
Paper & Allied Products	−0.1497	−0.3149	0.2585	0.5366	−0.2429	−0.1978
	(0.0230)	(0.0383)	(0.0276)	(0.1029)	(0.0220)	(0.0133)
Petroleum Products	−0.1528	−0.2181	0.1791	0.0067	−0.2125	−0.1885
	(0.0572)	(0.0937)	(0.0266)	(0.0025)	(0.0915)	(0.0987)
Primary Metals	0.0381	0.0692	−0.0082	0.0786	0.0568	0.0566
	(0.0070)	(0.0087)	(0.0016)	(0.0103)	(0.0073)	(0.0074)
Rubber & Plastics	−0.0469	−0.0607	−1.5544	−0.0845	−0.0560	−0.0911
	(0.0830)	(0.1218)	(1.6098)	(0.0374)	(0.1058)	(0.1232)
Transportation Equipment	0.2451	0.4346	0.0784	−0.1128	0.3556	0.3432
	(0.0498)	(0.0938)	(0.0086)	(0.0274)	(0.0362)	(0.0369)

	Canada					
Industry	Labor Intensity	Interm. Input Intensity	Phy. Cap. Intensity	R&D Cap. Intensity	Avg. Var. Cost	Dir. Avg. Var. Cost
Chemical Products	−0.0434	−0.0778	0.0266	0.5385	−0.0696	−0.0611
	(0.0252)	(0.0415)	(0.0047)	(0.0525)	(0.0375)	(0.0376)
Electrical Products	−0.6640	−0.7987	0.3576	0.6264	−0.7351	−0.6874
	(0.5593)	(0.2050)	(0.0568)	(0.0242)	(0.2741)	(0.2623)
Food & Beverage	−0.7540	−1.2567	0.9681	0.3153	−1.1489	−1.1321
	(0.4035)	(0.7425)	(0.0078)	(0.0296)	(0.6529)	(0.6486)
Fabricated Metals	−0.4810	−0.4275	1.2628	2.8523	−0.4455	−0.3929
	(0.1879)	(0.1273)	(0.0651)	(0.9532)	(0.1469)	(0.1443)
Non-electrical Machinery	−0.1426	−0.2123	0.1320	0.1399	−0.1879	−0.1774
	(0.0756)	(0.0904)	(0.0428)	(0.0169)	(0.0857)	(0.0837)
Non-metallic Minerals	−0.4673	−0.5334	0.5831	0.2105	−0.5111	−0.4371
	(0.2035)	(0.1864)	(0.0505)	(0.0468)	(0.1916)	(0.1799)
Paper & Allied Products	−0.0420	−0.0524	0.2228	0.8684	−0.0495	−0.0448
	(0.0677)	(0.0879)	(0.0605)	(0.4925)	(0.0818)	(0.0806)
Petroleum Products	−0.3220	−0.4077	1.0786	−0.4325	−0.4038	−0.3588
	(0.1098)	(0.1578)	(0.0744)	(0.0542)	(0.1562)	(0.1662)
Primary Metals	−0.1980	−0.2556	0.2757	0.2940	−0.2422	−0.2326
	(0.0760)	(0.0590)	(0.0266)	(0.0319)	(0.0621)	(0.0615)

TABLE 2 (continued)

Industry	Labor Intensity	Interm. Input Intensity	Phy. Cap. Intensity	R&D Cap. Intensity	Avg. Var. Cost	Dir. Avg. Var. Cost
			Canada			
Rubber & Plastics	1.0078	1.7086	−0.3075	−0.5507	1.2793	1.1992
	(0.8769)	(1.5140)	(0.1028)	(0.1797)	(0.4928)	(0.4546)
Transportation Equipment	−0.3435	−0.4947	2.4249	1.7695	0.4281	0.3887
	(0.1262)	(0.0847)	(0.2127)	(0.6727)	(0.1009)	(0.0947)

The elasticities of international spillovers on average variable cost point out that foreign spillovers also operates differently in the two countries. U.S. R&D capital generates relatively more elastic effects in the corresponding Canadian industry, compared to the effects of international spillovers from Canada. In addition, in Canada, international spillover elasticities of average variable cost tend to be more elastic relative to intranational spillovers. The same result is observed for the U.S., but it is not as robust. However, the relative magnitude of international spillover elasticities in Canada could reflect differences in the size of the R&D capital stocks in the two countries, and the fact that international spillovers are also intraindustry. In the U.S. situation, the result shows that intraindustry/international spillovers dominate interindustry/intranational spillovers, even though Canadian R&D capital stocks (the source of international spillovers) are much smaller than the interindustry sum of U.S. R&D capital stocks (the source of domestic spillovers).

International spillovers generally reduce average variable cost. In Canada, spillovers from U.S. R&D capital reduce average variable cost in nine of elevent industries. Cost increases occur in only rubber and plastics and transportation equipment. In the U.S., foreign spillovers from Canada reduce average variable cost in eight industries. Cost increases arise in chemical products, primary metals, and transportation equipment. Thus transportation equipment is the only industry common to both countries that exhibits increasing cost. This result could arise from the special bilateral relationship between the two countries, known as the North American Auto Pact.

The spillover elasticities on R&D intensity generally show that there is a complementary relationship between R&D intensity and the international spillover in each country. Increases in the foreign spillover increase R&D intensity in eight U.S. industries, and nine Canadian industries. The increases in R&D intensity are in the range from 0.01 percent for petroleum products to 0.54 percent for paper and allied products in the U.S., and from 0.14 percent for nonelectrical machinery to 2.85 percent for fabricated metal products in Canada.

With respect to domestic spillovers, the number of industries that exhibit a complementary relationship between R&D intensity and the spillover are seven in the U.S. and six in Canada. The Canadian range is from 0.24 percent for food and beverage to 0.73 percent for nonelectrical machinery.

The U.S. range is from 0.001 percent for chemical products to 0.37 percent for fabricated metal products. In Canada, foreign spillover effects on R&D intensity are relatively more elastic than domestic spillover effects. In addition, in the U.S., about half the industries display a similar type of behavior. This result is, perhaps, not so surprising given the fact that international spillovers are intraindustry, while intranational spillovers are interindustry.

The last set of spillover elasticities relates to the non-R&D capital intensities. International spillovers increase physical capital intensity in eight U.S. industries, and ten Canadian industries. However, Canadian domestic spillovers are generally substitutable for physical capital, or, in other words, physical capital reducing. This result occurs in eight industries. In the U.S., domestic spillovers increase physical capital intensity in six of the eleven industries. Labor and intermediate input elasticities always respond in the same direction to either intranational or international spillovers. International spillovers are usually noncapital input intensity reducing in both countries (eight industries in the U.S., and ten in Canada). The effects of domestic spillovers in the U.S. on labor and intermediate input intensities is mixed. However, in Canada, unlike international spillovers, domestic spillovers generally reduce noncapital intensities.

The results relating to domestic spillovers, which are interindustry, are consistent with BERNSTEIN [1988] for Canada, and BERNSTEIN and NADIRI [1988] for the U.S. The international spillover results are the first estimates of spillover elasticities linking Canadian and U.S. industries. The Canadian findings are consistent with MOHNEN [1990], where Canadian manufacturing R&D, and physical capital are complementary to the aggregate international spillover from five OECD countries. There are few studies that investigate the effects of international spillovers on factor intensities, or factor demands of U.S. industries. Most studies just consider the productivity effects of international spillovers (see the survey by NADIRI [1993]). It is interesting to note that O'SULLIVAN and ROGER [1991] find no evidence of aggregate international spillovers from developed nations to the U.S. BERNSTEIN and MOHNEN [1997] find no evidence of Japanese spillovers to the U.S. Clearly, the significant spillovers from Canadian to U.S. industries found in this paper, highlight the importance of distinguishing among nations, and industries as sources of R&D spillovers to the U.S.

4 Private and Social Rates of Return

An analysis of R&D spillovers from the vantage point of spillover sources relates to the private and social rates of return. The social rate of return to R&D capital consists of the private return plus the extra-private return due to the spillover. These latter returns are calculated by considering a situation where the spillovers are internalized. In this regard, define joint costs to be,

$$(7) \qquad \Omega_\tau = \sum_{j=1}^{2} \sum_{i=1}^{11} (C^{\nu ij} (w_\tau^{ij}, y_\tau^{ij}, K_\tau^{ij}, S_{\tau-1}^{ij}, t^{ij}) + \omega_\tau^{ij\tau} K_\tau^{ij})$$

The superscript j refers to the country, and superscript i refers to the industry.

Consider the right side of equation (7), evaluated at the equilibrium factor intensities for each country. In equilibrium, the cost for each producer is at a minimum. However, joint cost is not minimized relative to the case where the spillovers are internalized. With the internalization of the R&D spillovers, there is additional cost variability from each of the R&D capital stocks. Using the average variable cost function, equation (1), differentiate equation (7) with respect to R&D capital. The joint domestic cost effect per dollar of R&D investment, from an increase in the R&D capital from the f-th industry in the j-th country is,

$$(8) \qquad d_{2t}^{fj} = \sum_{\substack{i=1 \\ i \neq f}}^{11} \left[\sum_{g=1}^{2} \phi_{g1}^{ij} w_{gt}^{ij} (y_t^{ij})^{\eta^{ij}-1} + \sum_{h=1}^{2} k_{ht}^{ij} \psi_{h1}^{ij} W_t^{ij} \right] y_t^{ij} / q_{2t}^{fj},$$

$$f = 1, ..., 11, \ j = 1, 2$$

where q_2 is the price of R&D investment.

Next the joint foreign cost effect per dollar of R&D investment is

$$(9) \qquad i_{2t}^{fj} = \left[\sum_{g=1}^{2} \phi_{g1}^{fk} w_{gt}^{fk} (y_t^{fk})^{\eta^{fk}-1} + \sum_{h=1}^{2} k_{ht}^{fk} \psi_{h1}^{fk} W_t^{fk} \right] y_t^{fk} / q_{2t}^{fj},$$

$$f = 1, ..., 11, \ j \neq k, \ j, k = 1, 2.$$

Equations (8), and (9) define the domestic and foreign wedges between the social and private rates of return to R&D capital that arise from the R&D capital of the f-th industry in the j-th country.

The private rate of return to R&D capital in long-run equilibrium is the marginal cost reduction per dollar of R&D investment. This return is defined gross of depreciation and before tax. The private return is the before tax rental rate deflated by the price of R&D investment. Defining ρ_{2t}^{fj} to be the private rate of return to R&D capital for industry f in country j, then the social rate of return to R&D capital is [9],

$$(10) \qquad \gamma_{2t}^{fj} = \rho_{2t}^{fj} + d_{2t}^{fj} + i_{2t}^{fj}.$$

The social rates of return to R&D capital for the U.S., and Canada are presented in tables 3, and 4, respectively. The private rate of return averages

---

9. The private rate of return can be derived from equation (1). Indeed, $\rho_{2t}^{fj} = (\partial c_t^{\nu fj} / \partial k_{2t}^{fj}) / q_{2t}^{fj}$.

among the U.S. industries to be 16.4 percent, and for the Canadian industries the rate averages 12.8 percent. These are before tax gross of depreciation, purchasing power adjusted (Canada to U.S.), nominal rates of return. The returns from the intranational and international spillovers are presented in the first and second columns of tables 3, and 4. These columns define the domestic and foreign spillover wedges between the private and social rates of return to R&D capital.

From table 3, in the U.S. the extra-private returns that arise from the domestic spillovers are generally more important than the returns obtained from the externalities sent to Canada. We find in two U.S. industries that the foreign-based spillover returns substantially exceed the domestic-based returns. These are primary metals and transportation equipment. In three industries the returns from domestic and foreign spillovers are about the same. These industries are food and beverage, fabricated metals, and non-metallic minerals. In the remaining six industries the domestic spillover returns are vastly greater than the international returns, and in one industry (rubber and plastics) the return from the international spillover is negative. This result occurs when the direct cost effect of the spillover is cost increasing. However, even in the rubber and plastics industry, the sum of the intranational and international spillover returns is positive.

From table 4, the spillover returns for Canadian industries show that for eight of the eleven industries, the returns from international spillovers

TABLE 3

Rates of Return

Industry	United States (mean percent)		
	Spillover Return		Social Rate of Return
	Domestic	Foreign	
Chemical Products	80.550	1.635	98.244
Electrical Products	75.723	6.535	95.555
Food & Beverage	80.625	84.663	183.134
Fabricated Metals	63.047	77.854	157.266
Non-electrical Machinery	63.759	2.504	85.334
Non-metallic Minerals	63.981	50.841	132.144
Paper & Allied Products	66.470	14.236	99.223
Petroleum Products	103.837	52.703	174.518
Primary Metals	39.495	54.738	111.212
Rubber & Plastics	34.495	−2.661	43.876
Transportation Equipment	15.784	58.002	88.459

TABLE 4

Rates of Return

Industry	Canada (mean percent)		
	Spillover Return		Social Rate of Return
	Domestic	Foreign	
Chemical Products	43.204	−7.450	48.483
Electrical Products	57.012	101.357	158.369
Food & Beverage	20.961	110.936	144.626
Fabricated Metals	40.052	101.024	153.805
Non-electrical Machinery	38.317	110.848	161.895
Non-metallic Minerals	20.753	77.812	111.294
Paper & Allied Products	21.630	92.060	126.419
Petroleum Products	18.908	94.421	126.059
Primary Metals	45.768	−6.350	52.151
Rubber & Plastics	49.479	92.517	154.879
Transportation Equipment	30.079	−11.136	31.673

dominate the returns from the domestic externalities. In fact, in the three industries where domestic returns are more important, the returns from international spillovers are negative. These three industries are chemical products, primary metals, and transportation equipment. Nevertheless, these negative returns are more than offset by the positive domestic-based returns.

The social rates of return to R&D capital in the U.S. and Canada are found in the last column of tables 3 and 4 respectively. It is important to note that these returns are purchasing power parity-based. Canadian data is purchasing power parity adjusted to the U.S. data. Hence these returns are comparable across countries. In each country, the social returns greatly exceed the private rates of return. In Canada, the social returns two and a half to twelve and a half times the private rates of return. In the U.S. the social returns are from three and a half to ten times the private rates of return.

With respect to the ranking of social returns in the two countries, the ordering of the industries differ. There is no uniform ranking across countries because the magnitude of international spillover returns of the U.S. relative to the international spillover returns to Canada, differ across industries. Although international spillovers are intraindustry, a high international spillover return in a U.S. industry (relative to other U.S. industries), does not imply a high international spillover return in the same Canadian industry (relative to other Canadian industries). Five of the eleven industries are roughly in (or close to) the same position in Canada and the U.S.

These industries are food and beverage, fabricated metals, paper and allied products, and chemical products. Three industries that are near the top of the Canadian ranking are close to the bottom of the U.S. ranking. These industries are non-electrical machinery, electrical products, and rubber and plastics. In addition, three industries ranked near the bottom in Canada are close to the top in the U.S. The three are; petroleum products, non-metallic minerals, and primary metals. We see that the rates of return to R&D capital in Canada vary from around 32 percent to 162 percent and in the U.S. the returns range from 44 percent to 183 percent.

Clearly, there are large social returns to investing in R&D capital, and a major portion of these returns are international in nature. Large differentials between private and social returns are found in many studies (see GRILICHES [1991], and NADIRI [1993]). Social rates of return can exceed private rates from 9 percent to 160 percent. The vast majority of these studies relate to domestic spillovers. However, the large productivity gains associated with international spillovers (see COE and HELPMAN [1995]) imply that international spillovers cause social returns to be far in excess of private returns. The large social returns, estimated in this paper, imply that at existing levels of R&D capital, there is substantial underinvestment in R&D. Moreover, this underinvestment arises from both intranational and international spillovers.

5 Conclusion

International (but intraindustry) spillovers between Canadian and U.S. industries generally exert greater influence on production cost, and factor intensities relative to domestic (but interindustry) spillovers. This effect is not as pronounced in the U.S., as it is in Canada. In addition, spillovers emanating from the U.S. generate greater effects than spillovers from Canada to the U.S.

International spillovers tend to reduce cost and increase both R&D and physical capital intensities. This conclusion is found for both countries. In addition, in the U.S., and Canada, international spillovers reduce labor and intermediate input intensities.

Due to significant domestic and international spillovers, social rates of return to R&D capital are substantially above the private rates in both Canada and the U.S. In Canada, international spillovers generally account for a greater percentage of the social returns relative to the domestic spillovers. In the U.S. the converse is true. Canadian social rates of return (nominal, before tax, gross of depreciation) range from a low of 32 percent in transportation equipment to a high of 162 percent in non-electrical machinery. Social rates are from two and a half to twelve times greater than private returns. In the U.S. social returns are from three and a half to ten times greater than private rates. The social rates range from a low of 44 percent for rubber and plastics to a high of 183 percent for the food and beverage industry.

These high social returns mean that at current R&D levels, there is substantial underinvestment in R&D. This underinvestment arises from both intranational and international spillovers. Indeed, we can interpret these returns such that for a $100 increase in industrial R&D capital, increases in Canadian industrial output range from $32 to $162, and increases in U.S. industrial output range from $44 to $183. Our findings point to an important set of relationships between the two economies that are not reflected in international trade, and foreign investment, but in international knowledge diffusion.

534

APPENDIX 1

Data

The non-R&D data is described in detail in DENNY et al. [1992]. The quantity of output is measured in millions of 1986 dollars. The price of output is a price index which is obtained by dividing current dollar gross output by 1986 dollar gross output. The price is indexed to 1.00 in 1986. The quantity of labor is labor compensation in millions of 1986 dollars. The price of labor is current dollar labor compensation divided by 1986 dollar labor compensation and is indexed to 1.00 in 1986. The quantity of intermediate inputs is obtained by netting value added from gross output, and its price is obtained in the same manner as the price of output.

Both physical and R&D capital stocks are measured in 1986 millions of dollars. In constructing R&D capital we assumed a 10 percent depreciation rate. Recent work by NADIRI and PRUCHA [1993], has estimated rates of depreciation that are close to 10 percent. In addition, to deflate Canadian R&D expenditures, we used the price indexes from BERNSTEIN [1992] for the period 1964-1987, and extrapolated back to 1962 and forward to 1989 using the percentage change in the gross domestic product deflator. To deflate U.S. R&D expenditures, the R&D price index was obtained from JANKOWSKI [1993], for the period from 1969 to 1988, and we extrapolated back to 1962 and forward to 1989 using the percentage change in the U.S. gross domestic product deflator.

The rental rates (that is the factor prices) of physical and R&D capital are obtained as follows. The rental rate of physical capital is before-tax and is defined as,

$$\omega_k = q_k \left(r + \delta_\kappa \right) \left(1 - itc_k - u_c z \right)/(1 - u_c)$$

where q_k is the acquisition price of capital, r is the interest rate on long-term government bonds, δ_k is physical capital depreciation rate, itc_k is the investment tax credit rate, u_c is the corporate income tax rate and z is the present value of capital cost allowances.

The present value of capital cost allowances (z) is calculated using the declining balance method. The sum is calculated under two regimes, distinguished by whether the half-year rule is in effect or not. In addition, capital cost allowances are different for buildings and engineering construction and for machinery and equipment. For buildings and engineering construction, the discounted sum of capital cost allowances, z_b, outside the half-year rule is,

$$z_b = cca_b \left(1 - itc_b \right) \left(1 + r \right)/(r + cca_b)$$

where cca_b is capital cost allowances and the subscript b refers to building and engineering construction. Inside the half-year rule the present value of capital cost allowances is,

$$z_b = cca_b \left(1 - itc_b \right)/2 + \left(1 - cca_b/2 \right) \left(cca_b \left(1 - itc_b \right)/(r + cca_b) \right).$$

The present value of cost allowances for machinery and equipment, z_m, outside the half-year rule is,

$$z_m = \sum_{t=0}^{T} cca_m \left(1 - itc_m\right)/(1+r)^t,$$

where t represents time, T represent number of years and the subscript, m, stands for machinery and equipment. Inside the half-year rule the discounted sum is,

$$z_m = \sum_{t=0}^{T-1} cca_m \left(1 - itc_m\right)/(1+r)^t + cca_m \left(1 - itc_m\right)\left(1 + 1/(1+r)^T\right)/2$$

The aggregate z is an index of z_b and z_m, where the weights are the shares of the acquisition values of the capital stocks.

The before-tax rental rate on R&D capital is defined as:

$$w_r = q_r \left(r + \delta_r\right)\left(\left(1 - u_c\right)\left(1 - itc_r\right) - u_c\, d\right)/(1 - u_c)$$

where q_r is the R&D investment price, $\delta_r = 0.1$ is the R&D capital depreciation rate, itc_r is the R&D investment tax credit, d is the present value of incremental R&D investment allowances.

The present value of incremental investment allowances at time t is:

$$d = iia_r \left(1 - \sum_{t=1}^{3} 1/(3(1+r)^t)\right)$$

where iia_r is the incremental investment allowance rate. If the current R&D investment expenditures exceed an average of R&D expenditures in the past three years, then a tax reduction is allowed on the R&D expenditures in period t at the rate iia_r.

Estimation Results

The estimation results are presented in the following tables. We performed likelihood ratio tests to see if the set of spillover parameters should be included in the industry models. In each case we could reject the hypothesis of no spillovers. In addition, we set $\alpha_{12} = \lambda (\alpha_{11} \alpha_{22})^{.5}$, so that for convexity of the variable cost function in the capital inputs, $\lambda^2 < 1$; and $\alpha_{ii} > 0$. These conditions are satisfied for each industry. In the tables when no estimate is presented for the inverse of the degree of returns to scale, η, it means that $\eta = 1$. For each industry, intranational and international spillover parameters, first order parameters, and the degree of returns to scale can differ between the two countries.

Estimation Results

Para-meters	Chemical Products		Electrical Products		Food & Beverage		Fabricated Metals	
	Estimate	Standard Error	Estimate	Standard Error	Estimate	Standard Error	Estimate	Standard Error
$\beta 1U$	0.8736	0.3367	1.0090	0.4980	0.5737	0.1358	0.4562	0.2064
$\beta 1C$	0.4112	0.0801	0.6934	0.2427	0.3462	0.0504	1.4656	0.4471
b11	0.5088	0.1228	0.6758	0.1428	0.2336	0.1355	0.5310	0.1579
$\alpha 1U$	-2.4615	0.9350	-3.1741	0.7118	-10.9893	2.6222	2.2709	0.8048
$\alpha 1C$	-2.8447	0.5856	-4.4627	0.7524			1.4702	0.4291
$\alpha 2U$	-8.6792	3.2739	-1.5072	0.6059	-6.6427	3.4459	-1.5023	0.5840
$\alpha 2C$	1.0830	0.8833	-0.6714	1.0417	-0.8258	0.3115	2.8132	0.9571
$\alpha 11$	2.3466	0.8739	13.8208	6.1451	27.8762	6.7870	3.7694	1.2285
$\alpha 22$	0.8754	0.5129	3.0489	1.3092			42.7053	13.1159
λ	-0.0333	0.0175	0.2151	0.1991	0.0055	0.0030	-0.0416	0.0305
$\psi 11U$	-0.0780	0.0248	0.0002	0.0001	-0.0002	0.0001	-0.0001	0.0001
$\psi 11C$	-0.9867	0.2841	0.0002	0.0001			0.0004	0.0002
$\psi 22U$	-0.0011	0.0011	0.00001	0.00001	-0.0003	0.0001	-0.0006	0.0004
$\psi 22C$	-0.0001	0.0001	0.00004	0.00002	-0.0005	0.0002	-0.0004	0.0003
$\psi 12U$	0.0006	0.0001	-0.00006	0.00007	0.0080	0.0033	0.0003	0.0001
$\psi 12C$	0.00001	0.00002	-0.00001	0.000007	0.0079	0.0024	-0.0001	0.0001
$\psi 21U$			-0.15515	0.43834	-0.0007	0.0006	-0.0003	0.0004
$\psi 21C$	0.0001	0.0001	0.91369	0.93690	-0.0010	0.0008	-0.0002	0.0002

Estimation Results

$\beta 2U$	2.3395	0.9454	1.30880	0.70022	0.7738	0.3765	3.2386	1.3326
$\beta 2C$	1.5168	0.3706	1.47590	0.56923	1.19124	0.2917	2.7701	0.6649
ηU	0.8660	0.0441					0.9186	0.0043
ηC							0.8515	0.0035
Log of the Likelihood Function	362.584		312.771		598.044		493.312	

Correlation Coefficient of Actual and Fitted Values								
Labor Intensity	0.96		0.99		0.99		0.99	
Inter. Input Intensity	0.91		0.96		0.69		0.90	
Phy. Capital Intensity	0.99		0.99		0.99		0.99	
R&D Capital Intensity	0.99		0.99		0.99		0.99	
Variable Cost	0.99		0.99		0.93		0.99	

Estimation Results

Para-meters	Non-electrical Machinery		Non-metallic Minerals		Paper & Allied Products		Petroleum Products	
	Estimate	Standard Error	Estimate	Standard Error	Estimate	Standard Error	Estimate	Standard Error
$\beta 1U$	0.2601	0.5696	0.4248	0.0588	0.5513	0.0871	0.0687	0.0110
$\beta 1C$	0.6692	0.1155	0.5269	0.0674	0.2533	0.0552	0.0040	0.0016
b11	0.0814	0.0261	0.5012	0.1067	0.0652	0.0693	0.0071	0.0032
$\alpha 1U$	-2.1437	0.8233			-1.9984	0.8735		
$\alpha 1C$	-1.0311	0.7092	-1.4751	0.2332	-0.7864	0.4281	-5.2793	2.6110
$\alpha 2U$	5.0248	0.2010	0.5345	0.1820	-1.7339	0.4611	-0.3812	0.1400
$\alpha 2C$	0.0717	0.0539	0.2971	0.1591	-1.9544	0.6282	-0.8440	0.3271
$\alpha 11$	6.3299	0.7410	0.6615	0.3639	1.7158	0.0554	53.5902	41.2804
$\alpha 22$	40.4963	17.1125	3.1060	1.8736	8.7641	3.6680	27.4732	20.3332

λ	-0.0231	0.0251	0.1095	0.1027	-0.0739	0.0419	0.0820	0.0499
$\psi 11U$					0.0002	0.0001		
$\psi 11C$	0.0001	0.0001	0.00003	0.00002	0.0004	0.0002	-0.0005	0.0003
$\psi 22U$	0.0003	0.0002	0.00004	0.00001	0.0001	0.0001	-0.0001	0.0002
$\psi 22C$	0.0001	0.0001	0.00003	0.00001	0.0008	0.0013	-0.00001	0.00004
$\psi 12U$			-0.00005	0.00008	-0.0003	0.0002	-0.0003	0.0003
$\psi 12C$	0.000005	0.000004	-0.00010	0.00006	-0.0001	0.0001	-0.0001	0.0001
$\psi 21U$			-0.00005	0.00003	0.0005	0.0004	-0.0002	0.0003
$\psi 21C$	-0.0001	0.0002	-0.00003	0.00002	0.0010	0.0006	-0.0003	0.0002
$\beta 2U$	0.8477	0.3945	2.8504	0.9938	1.2621	0.5334	0.3931	0.1451
$\beta 2C$	0.5731	0.1962	1.1533	0.2366	0.8791	0.1181	0.0684	0.0421
ηU			0.7604	0.0399				
ηC	1.0580	0.03916	0.8225	0.0561				
Log of the Likelihood Function	336.759		278.195		466.837		490.220	

Correlation Coefficient of Actual and Fitted Values								
Labor Intensity	0.99		0.99		0.97		0.99	
Inter. Input Intensity	0.97		0.85		0.91		0.87	
Phy. Capital Intensity	0.93		0.99		0.99		0.99	
R&D Capital Intensity	0.99		0.85		0.99		0.98	
Variable Cost	0.99		0.99		0.99		0.95	

Estimation Results

Parameters	Primary Metals		Rubber & Plastics		Transportation Equipment	
	Estimate	Standard Error	Estimate	Standard Error	Estimate	Standard Error
$\beta 1U$	1.8890	0.5663	2.5331	0.1624	0.1469	0.0873
$\beta 1C$	2.4714	0.8031	0.8218	0.4371	0.2142	0.0331

Estimation Results

b11	1.7766	0.4147	0.6113	0.3552	−0.6477	0.2611
$\alpha 1U$					−4.4481	1.9007
$\alpha 1C$	−0.9501	0.4998	−4.6145	2.6622	−2.1744	1.6539
$\alpha 2U$	−0.7763	0.4312	−1.7203	0.7238	2.4533	1.0441
$\alpha 2C$	−1.1361	0.7233	−1.0008	0.7507	0.7815	0.3255
$\alpha 11$	0.5983	0.3269	18.1376	6.4237	13.8021	12.0915
$\alpha 22$	0.1130	0.0920	23.3702	9.3721	39.3561	29.9807
λ	0.2257	0.8318	−0.0252	0.0186	−0.0660	0.0417
$\psi 11U$	0.0006	0.0002	−0.0003	0.0002	−0.0003	0.0001
$\psi 11C$	0.0006	0.0003	−0.0001	0.0001	0.0002	0.0002
$\psi 22U$	−0.0002	0.0001	0.0005	0.0002	−0.0002	0.0002
$\psi 22C$	−0.0004	0.0002	−0.0004	0.0003	−0.00001	0.00001
$\psi 12U$	0.0002	0.0003	0.0002	0.0001	−0.00003	0.00001
$\psi 12C$	0.0001	0.0002	0.0002	0.0001	−0.000008	0.000004
$\psi 21U$	0.0004	0.0002			−0.0001	0.0001
$\psi 21C$	0.0006	0.0004	−0.0002	0.0001	−0.00004	0.00003
$\beta 2U$	9.3310	3.2077	0.6721	0.4732	1.1121	0.4388
$\beta 2C$	13.8166	10.2944	0.4316	0.2155	0.3962	0.1343
ηU	0.8144	0.0529				
ηC	0.7710	0.0540			1.0998	0.0771
Log of the Likelihood Function	422.552		184.225		316.660	

Correlation Coefficient of Actual and Fitted Values		
Labor Intensity	0.99	0.96	0.98
Inter. Input Intensity	0.86	0.97	0.97
Phy. Capital Intensity	0.96	0.76	0.98
R&D Capital Intensity	0.93	0.99	0.98
Variable Cost	0.97	0.99	0.99

• References

BERNSTEIN, J. I., MOHNEN, P. (1977). – "International R&D Spillovers Between U.S. and Japanese R&D Intensive Sectors", forthcoming *Journal of International Economics.*

BERNSTEIN, J. I. (1992). – "Price Indexes for Canadian Industrial Research and Development Expenditures, Statistics Canada, Services, Science and Technology Division *Working Paper No. 92-01.*

BERNSTEIN, J. I. (1988). – "Costs of Production, Intra-and Inter-Industry R&D Spillovers: Canadian Evidence", *Canadian Journal of Economics,* 21, pp. 324-347.

BERNSTEIN, J. I., NADIRI, M. I. (1988). – "Interindustry R&D Spillovers, Rates of Return, and Production in High-Tech Industries", *American Economic Review, Papers and Proceedings* 78, pp. 429-434.

BRANSTETTER, L. (1996). – "Are Knowledge Spillovers International or Intranational in Scope?, Microeconomic Evidence from the U.S. and Japan". Paper presented at the International Conference on Economics and Econometrics of Innovation, Strasbourg.

COE, D. T., HELPMAN, E. (1995). – International R&D Spillovers", *European Economic Review,* 39, pp. 859-887.

DENNY, M., BERNSTEIN, J., FUSS, M., NAKAMURA, S., WAVERMAN, L. (1992). – "Productivity in Manufacturing Industries, Canada, Japan, and the United States, 1953-1986, Was the 'Productivity Slowdown' reversed?", *Canadian Journal of Economics,* 25, pp. 584-603.

DIEWERT, W. E., WALES, T. J. (1988). – "A Normalized Quadratic Semiflexible Function Form", *Journal of Econometrics, 37,* pp. 327-342.

DIEWERT, W. E., WALES T. J. (1987). – "Flexible Functional Forms and Global Curvature Conditions", *Econometrics, 55,* pp. 43-68.

DIEWERT, W. E. (1982). – "Duality Approaches to Microeconomic Theory", in K. Arrow and M. Intrilligator, Eds., *Handbook of Mathematical Economics,* Vol. 2; Elsevier Science Publishers, Amsterdam, The Netherlands.

EATON, J., KORTUM, S. (1996). – "Trade in Ideas: Patenting and Productivity in the OECD", *Journal of International Economics, forthcoming.*

GRILICHES, Z. (1991). – "The Search for R&D Spillovers", *Scandinavian Journal of Economics, Supplement,* 94, pp. 29-47.

GROSSMAN, G. M., HELPMAN, E. (1991). – *Innovation and Growth in the Global Economy, MIT press,* Cambridge, Massachusetts.

JANKOWSKI, J. (1993). – "Do we Need a Price Index for Industrial R&D?", *Research Policy,* 22, pp. 195-205.

JORGENSON, D. W., KURODA M. (1990). – "Productivity and International Competitiveness in Japan and the United States 1960-1985", in C. Hulten, Ed., *Productivity Growth in Japan and the United States,* University of Chicago Press, Chicago.

JORGENSON, D. W., SAKURAMOTO, H., YOSHIOKA, K., KURODA, M. (1990). – "Bilateral Models of Production for Japanese and U.S. Industries", in C. Hulten, Ed., *Productivity Growth in Japan and the United States,* University of Chicago press, Chicago.

JORGENSON, D. W., NISHIMIZU, M. (1978). – U.S. and Japanese economic growth 1952-1974, an international comparison, *Economic Journal,* 88, pp. 707-726.

KELLER, W. (1996). – Are International R&D Spillovers Trade-Related? Analysing Spillovers Among Randomly Matched Trade Partners", *SSRI Working Paper,* 96-07.

LICHTENBERG, F., VAN POTTELSBERGHE DE LA POTTERIE, B. (1996). – "International R&D Spillovers: a Re-Examination, *NBER Working Paper no. 5668.*

MOHNEN, P. (1990). – "Relationship between R&D and Productivity Growth in Canada and other Major Industrialized Countries", University of Quebec in Montreal.

NADIRI, M. I. (1993). – "Innovations and Technological Spillovers", *NBER Working Paper no. 4423.*

NADIRI, M. I., PRUCHA, I. (1993). – "Estimation of the Depreciation Rate of Physical and R&D Capital in the U.S. Total Manufacturing Sector", *NBER Working Paper no. 4591.*

O'SULLIVAN, L., ROGER, W. (1991). – "An Econometric Investigation of the Interrelationship of R&D Expenditures and Technical Progress", *Commission of the European Communities.*

542

Exploring the Spillover Impact on Productivity of World-Wide Manufacturing Firms

Henri CAPRON, Michele CINCERA *

ABSTRACT. – This paper analyzes the relationship between R&D activity, spillovers and productivity at the firm level. Particular attention is put on the formalization of technological spillovers. The analysis is based upon a new dataset composed of 625 worldwide R&D-intensive manufacturing firms whose information has been collected for the period 1987-1994. Given the panel data structure of the sample, ad hoc econometric techniques which deal with both firm's unobserved heterogeneity and weak exogeneity of the right hand-side variables are implemented. The empirical results suggest that spillover effects influence significantly firm's productivity. Nevertheless the effects differ substantially among the pillars of the Triad. The United States are mainly sensitive to their national stock of spillovers while Japan appears to draw from the international stock. On its side, Europe shows a tendency to internalize spillovers.

* H. CAPRON: Université libre de Bruxelles; M. CINCERA: Université libre de Bruxelles. We wish to thank Bronwyn H. Hall, Jacques Mairesse, Pierre Mohnen, Bruno Van Pottelsberghe and two anonymous referees for helpful comments and suggestions. Thanks also to participants of the 10th International ADRES Conference on "The Economics and Econometrics of Innovation", the ESEM96 and seminars at ULB and CREST-INSEE for useful discussions. Financial support of ULB is gratefully acknowledged. Remaining errors are solely ours.

D. Encaoua et al. (eds.), The Economics and Econometrics of Innovation, 543–565.

1 Introduction

The purpose of this paper is to measure the impact of technological activity of firms on their economic performance as measured by output. More specifically, the stress is put on technological spillovers [1] which are often described as a main source of technology-push. These determinants are quantified from a new database composed of 625 worldwide R&D-intensive firms over the period 1987-1994. So, our main objective is to deal with the measurement of technological spillovers at the micro level on the basis of a new dataset gathering information from large companies representative of industrialized countries. To this end, Jaffe's methodology (1986, 1988), which associates econometrics and data analysis, has been adopted. The main contributions of the paper are the enlargement of the analysis to the international dimension and the extension of the appropriability hypothesis in the construction of spillovers to take into account the geographical origin of firms in addition to their technological proximity.

In the second section, we focus the attention on the alternative ways to appreciate the impact of technological spillovers on firms' technological activity with reference to the main approaches proposed in the literature. In the following section, we discuss the methodological framework necessary to characterize and to differentiate the technological determinants. A particular attention is paid to the way in which firms are classified into technological clusters. In the fourth section, we describe the international R&D database. Then, the econometric models to be estimated by panel data methods are presented and the empirical alternative results obtained from the sample discussed. We conclude by underlining the main observations resulting from the econometric analysis as well as some points deserving further research.

2 Measuring Technological Spillovers

The economics of innovation has for a long time emphasized the role played by exogenous technological factors, often designated as "technology push forces". Among these factors, one can distinguish technological opportunity and technological spillovers.

Technological opportunity can be defined as the difficulties or the costs linked with the innovation activity in a given area of technology. These costs may vary according to technological classes given that the characteristics

---

1. See GRILICHES [1992] and MOHNEN [1996] for a review of the empirical literature.

intrinsic to technology, on the one hand, and the available stock of scientific knowledge at a certain point of time, on the other hand, differ among fields of technological specialization. These differences are assumed to be reflected by technological opportunities which vary from a technological class to another and which makes the technological activity of a given firm more profitable in some fields.

As stressed by GRILICHES [1992], there is often a confusion about the two distinct notions of technological spillovers. The first kind of spillovers is related to new products and processes which embody technological change and are bought by other firms at less then their "full quality adjusted" prices. The second kind of technological spillovers can be defined as the potential benefits of the research activity of other firms for a given firm. These spillovers exist because of the "non rival and partially excludable" property of technology. A distinction can be made between the spillovers coming from the firm's industry and those which arise from other industries. According to the firm's country, a similar distinction can be made between the national and the international nature of these spillovers. The technological opportunity, as well as the technological spillovers, affect the costs of innovation. If the appropriability of knowledge is imperfect and if many firms are involved in similar technological activities, then the costs of innovation for a given firm are likely to be affected by these activities. For instance, if the technological spillovers and the firm's own R&D are complementary, then an increase of these spillovers should lead the firm to intensify its R&D effort.

Several approaches have been proposed in the literature in order to formalize technological spillovers. MOHNEN [1996] distinguishes five approaches that may be listed into two categories according to whether the R&D stocks of all other firms or industrial sectors are weighted or not. We are here only concerned with the second category in which the R&D stocks are weighted according to the technological linkage or proximity between firms or industrial sectors. This proximity can be alternatively calculated on the basis of the matrix of intermediate input purchases, patents or innovation flows [2] as well as on the basis of the firms' positions in the technological space. This last approach was developed by JAFFE (1986, 1988). The firm's position in the technological space is characterized by the distribution of its patents over patent classes. This way of formalizing technological spillovers suffers from the limits of the use of patents as indicators of the output of the innovation activity [3].

The firm's position in the technological space, as well as the distinction between a global and a local stock of technological spillovers are the key points of this approach which has been adopted in the present paper. Thanks to the international dimension of our database, Jaffe's methodology has been extended by considering the technological proximity among firms

2. See TERLECKIJ [1974, 1980], SCHERER [1982] and ROBSON et al. [1988] for more details about these approaches.

3. For the relevance of patent statistics as an indicator of the technological output, see GRILICHES [1990] for instance.

as well as the geographic one. Hence, it is interesting to separate the national stock of spillovers from its international counterpart. Such an exercise should improve our understanding of how and to what extent R&D spillovers generated in one country affect the economic performances of other economies.

3 Locating Firms in the Technological Space

3.1. Technological Proximities and Total, Local and National Technological Spillovers

Locating firms into the technological space allows one to formalize the technological spillovers. Indeed, this way of formalizing spillovers is closely related to the notion of technological proximity: the closer two firms are in the technological space, the more the research activity of one firm is supposed to be affected by the technological spillovers generated by the research activities of the second firm. Hence, it is assumed that each firm faces a potential 'stock' of spillovers, which is a weighted sum of the technological activities undertaken by all other firms. In order to measure the technological closeness between firm i and j, Jaffe used the 'angular separation' between them, *i.e.* he computed the uncentered correlation between their respective vectors of technological position, $T_i = (t_{i1}, ..., t_{iK})$ and $T_j = (t_{j1}, ..., t_{jK})$:

$$
(1) \qquad P_{ij} = \frac{\sum\limits_{k=1}^{K} T_{ik} T_{jk}}{\sqrt{\sum\limits_{k=1}^{K} T_{ik}^2 \sum\limits_{k=1}^{K} T_{jk}^2}}
$$

This measure of closeness takes values between one and zero according to the common degree of research interest of both firms. In order to measure the distribution of the firm's research interests through the different technological areas, we use the patent distribution over 50 technological sectors according to the International Patent Classification (IPC). The patent distribution relies on the whole number of patent applications [4] filed to the European Patent Office during the period 1978-1994.

---

4. The patents considered here are those classified by date of application rather then by date of issue as is it the case in Jaffe's study. According to JAFFE [1986], patents classified by date of application are preferable because they reflect the moment when a firm makes out itself to have generated an innovation and because of the existence of long lags in a patent's application process.

546

In the following example, we observe that Solvay and Du Pont de Nemours are closer to each other than to Renault or Honda. This is quite normal given the nature of the research activities of these firms.

Example of Technological Proximity between Firms.

FIRM	NPA[a]	SOLVAY	DU PONT	RENAULT	HONDA
SOLVAY	284	1			
DU PONT DE NEMOURS	4412	.785	1		
RENAULT	636	.021	.058	1	
HONDA	618	.044	.063	.946	1

a: # of patent applications field to the European Patent Office during the period 1978-1994.

It should be observed that this measure is purely directional, *i.e.* it does not depend on the technological vector's length. Once the measure of closeness between firms i and j is calculated, the potential stock of technological spillovers of the ith firm can be evaluated as follows:

$$(2) \qquad\qquad S_i = \sum_{\substack{j \\ j \neq i}} P_{ij} K_j$$

where:

$$S_i = \text{stock of spillovers of firm } i,$$
$$K_j = \text{R\&D capital stock of firm } j.$$

This index of technological distance relies on the strong assumption that the appropriability conditions of knowledge are the same for all firms (JAFFE, 1988) [5]. Another drawback of this method is that firms which encounter a rather diversified technological activity will benefit to a lesser extent from the stock of spillovers. Indeed, the more the firm's R&D activities are diversified, the more its patent distribution over technological classes is uniform and the more the index of technological closeness is likely to be close to zero. A firm which is technologically diversified will be located in the central region of the technological space so that it will not be close to any firm. An alternative standpoint is to say that firms are aware of the research activities undertaken by only a few technologically similar firms. In that sense, even if all stocks of technological spillovers are relevant, they will probably not be taken into account completely due to imperfect information about the content of R&D realized by rivals. In order to examine this possibility, Jaffe divided the potential stock of spillovers into two distinct components obtained by applying a clustering method: a local stock which

---

5. According to SPENCE [1984], an imperfect appropriation can be defined as the proportion Φ of the output of each firm's technological activity that is disclosed. If $\Phi = 0$, then appropriability is perfect, if $\Phi = 1$, then R&D is a pure public good.

corresponds to the sum of R&D stocks of firms belonging to a same cluster of technological activities and an external stock which is computed from the other firms. Thanks to the international dimension of our sample, Jaffe's methodology has been extended by distinguishing, besides the local and external stocks, national stocks [6] from international ones. In this way, we will be able to appreciate to what extent geographical and cultural contiguity matters. Furthermore, in order to consider the technological as well as the geographical closeness, the potential stock of spillovers was dissociated into four components: the local national stock, the local international stock, the non-local or external national and international stocks.

3.2. **Firm's Attribution to Technological Clusters**

This section discusses the procedure which allows one to group the firms into homogeneous categories or clusters on the basis of their technological 'nearness'. Because of this closeness, firms belonging to a same cluster are assumed to face the same state of technological opportunity. Among the several techniques available to combine firms into clusters, the K-means clustering method is one of the most commonly used [7]. In the present paper, we experimented this technique as well as two others: the K-Means clustering with 'strong centers' and the agglomerative hierarchical clustering methods [8]. The algorithm, which has been used to combine firms into clusters, works on the factorial coordinates of a preliminary principal components analysis. The advantage of this method is that it uses an Euclidean distance between firms, which permits considering an objective criterion in order to evaluate the quality of the firms' partition. This distance is used for measuring how far apart two firms are in the factorial space. Besides the benefit of the orthogonality of factorial axes, another advantage of this method is that it does not take into account the last factorial axes which often carry random components. Given the nature of our data, the analysis of binary correspondence of the contingency table, *i.e.* the table of the firm's patent distribution across 50 IPC classes, has been performed to compute the factorial axes.

A common difficulty to all clustering techniques is to fix the number of clusters present in the data. Different procedures for determining the 'optimal' number of clusters have been proposed in the literature [9]. In this study, the three experimented clustering techniques are based on Ward's aggregation criterion. This criterion allows one to measure the quality of the firm's partition into technological clusters by considering the within and the without cluster inertia. The within cluster inertia represents the mean of the squared distances between the firms' cluster and its center of gravity, while the without cluster inertia consists in the mean of the squared

---

6. In this paper, we consider alternatively Europe and the European countries as specific geographic regions.

7. Jaffe [1986] derived a modified version of this method which allows him to take the multinomial structure of the firm's patent distribution into account.

8. See Lebart, Morineau and Fenélon [1979] for a description of these methods.

9. For an examination of some of these procedures, see Milligan and Cooper [1985].

distances between all cluster centers of gravity and that of the whole data sample. Ward's criterion for forming the clusters consists of maximizing the ratio between these two inertia in order to get the most homogenous and the most distant possible clusters. It should be noticed that such a ratio does not permit one to compare two partitions with a different number of clusters. Actually, the partition into $k+1$ clusters will always have a higher ratio of inertia than a partition into k clusters. Ultimately, the best possible partition would be the one which has as many clusters as the number of firms. In this case the ratio of inertia is equal to zero given that each firm is blended with its cluster center. To choose the number of clusters, a two step procedure has been applied. In a first step, the agglomerative hierarchical and the K-Mean with Strong Centers clustering methods have been identified as the best candidates as far as the measure of inertia is concerned. In a second step, we experimented different stocks of local spillovers constructed from different partitions into k clusters according to the agglomerative hierarchical method for k equal 15 to 29. These stocks have been systematically tested in the productivity regression model. The local stock based on k equal to 18 has appeared the most satisfactory both in terms of the regression's overall fit and the estimated standard error associated to the local stock coefficient. For these reasons, we decided to retain the partition with 18 clusters, against 21 clusters in Jaffe's analysis.

4 Data, Total Factor Productivity and Econometric Models for Panel Data

4.1. Data and Variables

The R&D database has been constructed with the view of setting up a representative sample of the largest firms at the international level that reported R&D expenditure during the last 10 years. The database consists of a balanced panel of 673 firms over the period 1987 to 1994. This dataset has been extracted from the *Worldscope* database which provides information on financial profiles for companies around the world [10]. For each firm, information is available for net sales, number of employees, capital stock, annual R&D expenditure and major industry group according to the Standard Industrial Classification (SIC-2 digits) [11]. The European Patent Office (EPO)

---

10. The *Worlsdcope* database is produced by Worldscope/Disclosure partners.

11. More details regarding this information is provided in the Worldscope data definitions guide (1994).

is the second source of information. This office supplies the firm's patent applications across technological classes according to the International Patent Classification (IPC) for the whole period from 1978 to 1994.

A major task in constructing the sample has been the matching of patents to firms. In a first step, patents were assigned to firms on the basis of their generic names [12]. Second, many large firms have several R&D performing subsidiaries and it is not obvious to link the patents applied by these subsidiaries to the parent company [13]. Thanks to the software provided in the EPO database, it has been possible to minimize these issues to a great extent. Indeed, by choosing one or more criteria (such as firm's name or parts of it, country codes,...), the software retrieves all documents meeting these criteria. For instance, searching for the word 'Du Pont' gave 4599 patent documents (from 1978 up to 1994). Examining more in details the firm's full names reported in these documents, it appeared that 4191 patents were assigned to 'E.I. Du Pont De Nemours and Company' while 221 documents were attributed to foreign subsidiaries of the US parent company and 120 to 'Du Pont Merck Pharmaceutical Company'. Hence, 4412 patents have been retained for Du Pont de Nemours. This procedure has been repeated for each firm of the sample: for about four fifths of the sample there was only one firm's name in the retrieved documents. For the rest, firm's names which could be identified without any doubts as subsidiaries have been included in the matching process of generic names.

In order to allow for comparison, all variables have been converted to constant 1990 dollars. R&D expenditures have been deflated using the GDP deflators of respective countries, while the deflator of physical capital has been used for the capital stock [14]. Also, due the presence of outliers [15], a cleaning procedure has been applied to this subset of firms (for details, see annex 1) in order to reject firms whose variables displayed very high and often irrelevant variations. The final sample retained for estimations includes 625 firms. A substantial number of firms in the sample have more than one product line at the SIC two digit level. Furthermore, these firms are multinational so that a large amount of their sales is performed outside the domestic market. Since these firms are 'multiproducts' and have subsidiaries in several countries, the use of domestic output prices indexes at the 2 digit industry level for each country did not seem to be a relevant

---

12. For instance, Honda has been used for Honda Motor Co. LTD and Honda Giken Kogyo Kabushiki Kaisha.

13. Ideally, one has to have a 'mapping' of the main firms to their subsidiaries. However it is not easy at all to construct an accurate mapping since by essence it changes over time.

14. The capital stock measures correspond to the net property, plant and equipment of firms. 'Net' means that accumulated reserves for depreciation, depletion and amortization are not included. Information on capital annual expenditures is available as well. Hence it may have been possible to construct a capital stock according to the perpetual inventory method. However, this approach requires to know the rates of depreciation of physical capital which vary across firms and over time. Since this information is unavailable and capital expenditures are missing for some firms and years, this approach has not been considered.

15. Mainly due to the process of mergers and acquisitions of firms over time. Indeed, 419 firms in our sample acquired at least one company during the period investigated.

approach to deflate net sales [16]. Instead, thanks to the availability of the shares of sales performed in the home country [17] and abroad, a more general price index has been performed according to the following formula:

$$(3) \quad WPI_i = d_i\, PI_i + (1 - d_i) \sum_{j \neq i}^{n} w_j\, PI_j \quad \text{and} \quad w_j = \frac{VA_j}{\sum\limits_{j \neq i}^{n} VA_j}$$

where WPI_i is the weighted manufacturing price index used to deflate net sales of firm i,

d_i is the share of sales of firm i performed in its home country,

PI_i is the price index of added value for the whole manufacturing sector in firm's i home country,

$j = 1, ..., n$ and n is the number of countries considered in this study,

w_j is the share of added value of country j with respect to the sum of added value of the $(n - 1)$ countries.

Some variables have been constructed for the purpose of the analysis. The stock of R&D capital has been built on the basis of the permanent inventory method with a depreciation rate equal to 15 percent and an initial stock of R&D capital calculated by assuming a growth rate of R&D expenditure equal to 5 percent. The IPC classification allows one to identify the technological classes of patent applications. The IPC at the two digit level is composed of 118 technological classes. In order to ease the calculations, these 118 classes were grouped into 50 broader classes. On this basis, a table of contingency, *i.e.* a table reporting the distribution of the firms' patents across the 50 IPC classes, has been constructed. This table was used for computing the index of technological closeness [18] and consequently the stocks of spillovers.

The first column in Table 1 gives a view of the geographical and sectorial composition of the sample. With sixty per cent of firms, the United-States are largely over-represented in the sample. If we have a look at the sectorial distribution of firms, we observe that the weight of American firms is particularly important in some sectors: computer & office equipment, professional goods and software. European firms account for only sixteen percent while Japanese firms cover twenty one per cent of the sample. So, a main drawback of the sample is the under-representativeness of European firms. This is mainly a consequence of the miss of data availability for

---

16. It should be noticed that the Worldscope data are based on firm's consolidated accounts unless specified. This raises the question of the comparability of data. Due to the diversity of accounting practices across countries, it is not obvious how subsidiaries or affiliates should be aggregated. In order to aggregate data in the most possible accurate way, the terminology used in reported accounting information has been redefined in a generic standard way by the Worldscope analysts.

17. For instance, for the Swedish firms of the sample, the average share of sales performed by these firms in Sweden is 13.7% while for the Japanese firms this figure is 79.6%.

18. It might be objected that the measure of technological proximities that we get using European patents applied by non-European firms may be quite distorted or incomplete. Indeed it can be expected that the propensity of European firms to patent in Europe differs from that of U.S. firms and Japanese firms and that this propensity varies across fields for firms based in different continents. Yet in the absence of a "global" patent office, we have no choice but to use national or regional patent data.

these firms for the first years covered by the sample. Indeed, despite the availability of data for a larger sample of European firms for a shorter period, the panel so built allows to optimize jointly the number of firms as well as the number of periods.

TABLE 1

Sectorial and Geographical Characteristics of Variables
(average over the period 1987-1994)

	Number of firms				Sales [b]	Employ-ment [c]	Physical capital [b]	R&D capital [b]	R&D [b]	Spill-overs [b]	R&D inten-sity [d]
	RW [a]	EU	JP	US							
Aircraft	0	5	2	10	5897	46	1355	1879	302	130589	5.1
Chemicals	0	15	25	37	3034	16	1123	776	127	83415	4.2
Computer	0	3	6	35	5598	32	1498	2275	426	106502	7.6
Construction	0	2	5	2	9003	65	1696	3162	619	78252	6.9
Drugs	3	13	19	19	3474	19	1198	1362	281	114782	8.1
Electrical	0	1	7	15	3993	26	1120	608	113	96669	2.8
Electronics	2	9	15	52	3003	22	798	1108	218	134997	7.3
Fabricated metal	1	4	6	16	2046	12	650	172	34	68370	1.7
Food	0	5	2	12	5564	38	1669	394	74	39326	1.3
Instruments	0	7	5	55	1452	11	430	495	94	109744	6.4
Machinery	0	9	11	38	2211	14	560	358	60	73479	2.7
Mining	1	4	0	11	20614	40	1248	1598	255	106463	1.2
Motor vehicles	0	11	6	14	15528	83	4156	3318	673	114262	4.3
Paper	0	1	2	16	2330	13	1632	153	27	54551	1.1
Primary metal	5	8	11	12	3383	15	1843	274	53	84054	1.6
Rubber	0	2	4	6	1500	12	542	227	39	76222	2.6
Software	0	0	0	14	519	3	101	232	62	99824	11.9
Stone	0	2	4	4	2200	16	1048	323	58	85220	2.6
Textiles	0	0	3	4	1364	5	398	100	22	69395	1.6
Wood	1	0	0	6	1533	13	486	87	17	24470	1.1
Average					4198	23	1477	979	187	98618	4.5
Rest of the world [a]	13				2113	12	1342	444	90	80712	4.3
Europe		101			7373	53	2404	1959	375	104076	5.1
Japan			133		3444	13	1023	808	157	111562	4.5
United-States				378	3687	20	1394	796	151	93221	4.1

a: Australia and Canada, b: Millions US dollars 1990, c: in thousands, d: %.

The next column in Table 1 shows the characteristics of the sample. The R&D intensity of industries goes from 1.1 percent in the wood and paper industries to 11.9 percent in the software industry. Regarding the R&D intensity of the different geographical areas, European and Japanese firms included in the sample are more R&D intensive than US ones, which is a consequence of the higher number of US firms. Table 2 gives a view of the representativeness of the sample comparatively to the business enterprise R&D expenditures of the different geographical areas. These percentages have to be interpreted cautiously as the data come from different sources. Nevertheless, these percentages show that despite only 625 firms are retained in this analysis they account for around 32 to 53 percent of the R&D outlays realized in the three main geographical areas.

TABLE 2

Representativeness of the Sample: R&D Realized by Firms as a Percentage of Business Enterprise R&D [a].

	1987	1988	1989	1990	1991	1992
Rest of the world	17.5	16.9	16.6	20.7	18.3	18.3
Europe	40.1	43.0	43.4	44.7	46.2	47.6
Japan	34.8	33.6	33.7	32.2	34.2	37.5
United-States	46.4	48.8	51.7	52.6	52.8	53.4

a: OECD's ANBERD database.

4.2. The Productivity Equation

The R&D activity implemented by firms is expected to stimulate their productivity. Besides the impact of the firm's own R&D capital as well as the influence of labor and of physical capital stock on productivity, it is worth examining to what extent the spillover stocks improve firm's productivity. In order to answer this question, the Cobb-Douglas production function framework is used. Formally, we have:

$$(4) \quad \ln S_{it} = \alpha_i + \lambda_t + \beta_1 \ln L_{it} + \beta_2 \ln C_{it} + \beta_3 \ln K_{it} + \gamma \ln X_{it} + \varepsilon_{it}$$

where ln is the natural logarithm,
L_{it} is the employment of firm i at time t ($i = 1$ to 625, $t = 1$ to 8),
K_{it} is the stock of R&D capital,
S_{it} is the net sales,
C_{it} is the stock of physical capital,
α_i is the firm's specific effect,
λ_t is a set of time dummies,
X_{it} is a vector of spillover components,
γ is its associated vector of parameters and
ε_{it} is the disturbance term.

Four alternative specifications of X_{it} have been considered:

– Specification I: Impact of the total stock of spillovers

$$(5) \qquad\qquad \gamma \ln X_{it} = \gamma_T \ln TS_{it},$$

where TS is the total stock of spillovers.

– Specification II: Differentiated impact of the local and external stocks of spillovers

(6) $$\gamma \ln X_{it} = \gamma_L \ln LS_{it} + \gamma_E \ln ES_{it},$$

where LS, ES are the local and external stocks of spillovers respectively.

– Specification III: Differentiated impact of the national and international spillover stocks

(7) $$\gamma \ln X_{it} = \gamma_N \ln NS_{it} + \gamma_I \ln IS_{it},$$

where NS, IS are the national and international spillover stocks respectively.

– Specification IV: Totally differentiated impact of the spillover stocks

(8) $$\gamma \ln X_{it} = \gamma_{LN} \ln LNS_{it} + \gamma_{LI} \ln LIS_{it} + \gamma_{EN} \ln ENS_{it} + \gamma_{EI} \ln EIS_{it},$$

where LNS, LIS, ENS, EIS are the local national, local international, external national and external international spillover stocks respectively.

The R&D stock represents the firm's research activity. As GRILICHES and MAIRESSE [1984] pointed out, the omission of materials as a production factor in the equation above can lead to misspecifications and hence biases in the estimated coefficients. In order to avoid this issue, it is possible to use the added value instead of the sales. Some authors tested whether the use of sales versus added value give different results. The conclusion of GRILICHES and MAIRESSE [1984], CUNÉO and MAIRESSE [1984] and MAIRESSE and HALL [1996] is that the use of sales or added value as a dependent variable leads to similar results. On the other hand, SCHANKERMANN [1981] and HALL and MAIRESSE [1995] indicate that the estimated R&D elasticities are sensitive to the double-counting between R&D and capital expenditures as well as between total employees and the workers allocated to R&D activities. According to these authors, correcting for double-counting tends to slightly increase the R&D elasticity. Consequently, our results should be interpreted cautiously as materials are not included in the model and the R&D estimated coefficients are a measure of the 'excess' R&D elasticity of output.

4.3. Econometric Panel Data Models

To estimate the equations specified above, we used standard panel data estimation procedures which allows one to take into account firm's unobserved over time fixed effects. These effects take into account permanent differences among firms. For instance the ability of engineers to discover new inventions is a typical unobserved variable of firms. Actually, these unobservables are likely to be 'transmitted' to the R&D decision since firms facing higher abilities will generally invest more in research activities. Hence neglecting these effects as it is the case in cross-section estimates may lead to some omitted variable biases. In the context of panel data, it is possible to get around this issue by appropriate transformations of data in order to 'eliminate' unobserved fixed effects.

554

The fixed effects can be removed through the so-called within transformation which can be estimated consistently by OLS provided that the α_i are fixed over time and the regressors are strictly exogeneous[19]. Unfortunately, the strict exogeneity condition is a hypothesis which is hard to maintain in the productivity framework. According to GRILICHES [1995] for instance, when we want to measure the elasticities of the right hand side variables in the equation above, it is not clear to what extent the explanatory variables depend on past, current or future values of the dependent variables or inversely. In other words, does R&D for instance causes output or is it output which causes R&D? A solution to this simultaneity problem is to use an instrumental variable approach, but quoting MAIRESSE and HALL [1996], applying this approach to the within transformation often invalidate the estimates because the only available instruments are generally lagged values of explanatory variables and in short panels, these variables are likely to be correlated with the disturbances, once the firms means have been removed. Another way to eliminate the unobserved fixed effects consists of first-differencing the productivity equation. An advantage of this transformation is that it does not longer require the strict exogeneity of regressors. However due to possible measurement errors in all the variables, this approach leads generally to estimates which are more biased towards zero than does the within correction (GRILICHES and HAUSMAN [1986]).

In order to allow for all effects to be present, i.e. correlated fixed effects and simultaneity, we performed our estimates using the same methodology as MAIRESSE and HALL [1996][20]. The methodology departs by assuming the presence of correlated fixed effects with regressors in the productivity equation (so that this equation has to be first-differenced) and by assuming that only lag 2 or higher values of regressors are available as instruments (because later values are correlated with the error term). These assumptions imply the following set of orthogonality conditions between instruments and the error term:

(9) $E[X_{is} \Delta \varepsilon_{it}] = 0$ where $i = 1, ..., N$; $s = 1, ..., t-2$ and $t = 3, ..., T$.

These moment conditions are then estimated by means of the General Method of Moments. Relaxing the assumption of lag 2 or higher values of regressors as valid instruments, implies additional moment conditions. Testing the validity of these additional conditions allows one to determine if the regressors are lag 2, lag 1, weakly or strongly exogeneous. Furthermore, if the fixed effects are not correlated with the regressors, then it is appropriate to estimate the productivity equation in level. Here again, considering this equation in level rather in first-differences implies additional moment conditions whose validity can be tested in order to answer the question of correlated fixed effects.

---

19. Substracting individual means from equation above eliminates the fixed effects (provided that they are constant over time) but contaminates the ε_{it}'s with the disturbances from the other years, $\varepsilon_{i1}, ..., \varepsilon_{iT}$. Hence strict exogeneity of the regressors is required, i.e. $E[x_{is} \varepsilon_{it}] = 0$, $\forall s = 1, ..., T$ and $\forall t = 1, ..., T$.

20. This methodology is based on that of ARELLANO and BOND [1991] and KEANE and RUNKLE [1992].

It should be noticed that though this GMM framework seems quite attractive in terms of the modelling possibilities it contains and the weak distributional assumptions it relies on, it nevertheless rests on an instrumental variable approach and as pointed out by GRILICHES and MAIRESSE [1995], the past levels as instruments for current growth rates of regressors such as R&D capital are likely to be quite poor and possess little resolving power.

5 Empirical Results

Estimates of the productivity equation are given in Table 3. We observe that the alternative estimation methods lead to different results, particularly for the spillover variables and GMM estimates. The coefficients obtained for the employment and the physical capital are significant. Yet, their values are inferior to those obtained in some studies, what can be explained by the fact that we use sales instead of added value. While materials were not introduced in the equation due to data unavailability, the coefficients are comparable to those obtained by studies using sales. If we suppose constant return to scale for traditional production factors, the elasticity for materials should be expected to be about .3 to .4.

Regarding the R&D capital elasticities, the estimates give coefficients whose values are globally higher than the measures reported in the literature, what can be explained by the high proportion of R&D-intensive companies in our sample. Indeed, a split of data into two subsamples has given R&D elasticities which are respectively .43 and .44 for high R&D-intensive firms against .12 and .22 respectively for other firms. The GMM estimates are comparable to within and first difference ones in two specifications. Discrepancies among GMM results can be explained by the different sets of instruments used to implement this procedure.

The total spillover stock elasticities are significant and higher than the own R&D elasticities. The distinction between the local and external components exhibits a higher elasticity of output with respect to the external spillover stock. This observation seems to indicate that the inter-industry spillover effects are relatively more important than the intra-industry ones, as far as we consider that there is a close relationship between industries and technological classes.

The breakdown of spillovers between their national [21] and international components puts forward the importance of foreign R&D activities. At the opposite, the national stock gives ambiguous and scattered results. The negative coefficients obtained for within and first difference estimates are astonishing. Yet, this result is not confirmed by the GMM estimate. When

---

21. When the measure of national stocks of European countries is based on the European entity instead of individual countries the estimates are to a large extent similar to the ones reported here.

TABLE 3

Productivity Estimates.

dependent Variable: ln S				sample: 625 firms × 8 years	
WITHIN Level est. s.e. [a]		OLS F.D. est. s.e.		GMM-IV F.D. est. s.e.	
lnL	.50 (0.16)*	ΔlnL	.41 (.029)*	ΔlnL	.53 (.069)*
lnC	.21 (.013)*	ΔlnC	.17 (.022)*	ΔlnC	.07 (.061)
lnK	.24 (.015)*	ΔlnK	.32 (.043)*	ΔlnK	.13 (.048)*
lnTS	1.11 (.151)*	ΔlnTS	.94 (.277)*	ΔlnTS	.80 (.302)*
R_a^2 .993		R_a^2 .358		X^2 [d.f.] [b] Sim. [c]:	130.3 [76] +L1
lnL	.49 (.016)*	ΔlnL	.40 (.029)*	ΔlnL	.41 (.018)*
lnC	.21 (.013)*	ΔlnC	.17 (.022)*	ΔlnC	.15 (.012)*
lnK	.24 (.015)*	ΔlnK	.32 (.043)*	ΔlnK	.25 (.017)*
lnLS	.25 (.042)*	ΔlnLS	.24 (.067)*	ΔlnLS	.26 (.049)*
lnES	.59 (.125)*	ΔlnES	.60 (.228)*	ΔlnES	.37 (.155)*
R_a^2 .993		R_a^2 .359		X^2 [d.f.] Sim. :	300.3 [195] S
lnL	.50 (.016)*	ΔlnL	.41 (.029)*	ΔlnL	.56 (.095)*
lnC	.22 (.013)*	ΔlnC	.17 (.022)*	ΔlnC	.08 (.094)
lnK	.25 (.015)*	ΔlnK	.33 (.042)*	ΔlnK	.22 (.080)*
lnNS	−.31 (.050)*	ΔlnNS	−.19 (.106)**	ΔlnNS	.13 (.209)
lnIS	1.03 (.122)*	ΔlnIS	.65 (.209)*	ΔlnIS	.99 (.530)**
R_a^2 .993		R_a^2 .359		X^2 [d.f.] Sim. :	108.0 [45] +L3
lnL	.50 (.016)*	ΔlnL	.41 (.029)*	ΔlnL	.82 (.088)*
lnC	.22 (.013)*	ΔlnC	.17 (.022)*	ΔlnC	.01 (.083)
lnK	.24 (.015)*	ΔlnK	.32 (.043)*	ΔlnK	.26 (.073)
lnLNS	−.06 (.025)*	ΔlnLNS	−.01 (.045)	ΔlnLNS	−.04 (.094)
lnLIS	.19 (.035)*	ΔlnLIS	.15 (.060)*	ΔlnLIS	.15 (.131)
lnENS	−.41 (.046)*	ΔlnENS	−.26 (.096)*	ΔlnENS	−.21 (.175)
lnEIS	.68 (.097)*	ΔlnEIS	.46 (.185)*	ΔlnEIS	1.3 (.442)*
R_a^2 .993		R_a^2 .359		X^2 [d.f.] Sim. :	143.4 [63] +L3

a: heteroskedastic-consistent standard errors in brackets, * (**) = statistically significant at the 5 (10)% level; b: overidentification test; c: predeterminancy of X_{it}: $W(S)$ = weak (strong) exogeneity, $+L3 = \text{lag } 3$ and lower values of X_{it} as instruments

the spillover stock is completely disaggregated, the local national stock has no effect, what is not the case for the other components. Yet, only the international stocks influence positively the output while the external stock has a negative impact. There is no rational explanation for this unexpected effect and, consequently, it is worth turning to alternative specifications in order to see if such a result holds. Although it might be argued that it is a consequence of multicollinearity among the different stocks, their correlation coefficients are weak as can be seen from annex 2.

TABLE 4

Productivity Estimates: Opportunity Effects.

dependent Variable: Δln S			First differences
est. s.e. [a]	est. s.e.	est. s.e.	est. s.e.
ΔlnL .40 (0.29)*	.40 (.029)*	.41 (.028)*	.40 (.027)*
ΔlnC .17 (.022)*	.17 (.022)*	.17 (.021)*	.17 (.021)*
ΔlnK .32 (.043)*	.32 (.044)*	.32 (.041)*	.31 (.041)*
ΔlnTS .79 (.298)*	.57 (.367)	.63 (.275)*	.27 (.369)
X^2 stat. [d.f.] on: ind. effects	technol. effects	geogr. effects	all effects
60.9 [18]*	51.1 [17]*	228.6 [15]*	291.5 [50]*
R_a^2 .364	.363	389	392
ΔlnL .40 (.028)*	.40 (.028)*	.41 (.027)*	.40 (.027)*
ΔlnC .17 (.022)*	.17 (.022)*	.17 (.021)*	.17 (.021)*
ΔlnK .32 (.043)*	.31 (.043)*	.32 (.040)*	.32 (.041)*
ΔlnLNS −.01 (.048)	−.05 (.051)	.05 (.042)	.06 (.049)
ΔlnLIS .15 (.065)*	.09 (.100)	.08 (.059)	.02 (.099)
ΔlnENS −.28 (.102)*	−.28 (.104)*	.11 (0.91)	.05 (.099)
ΔlnEIS .20 (.184)	.29 (.214)	−.08 (.183)	−.38 (.210)**
X^2 stat. [d.f.] on: ind. effects	technol. effects	geogr. effects	all effects
61.7 [18]*	59.2 [17]*	240.5 [15]*	305.1 [50]*
R_a^2 .365	.365	.388	.393

a: heteroskedastic-consistent standard errors in brackets, * (**) = statistically significant at the 5 (10)% level.

In order to appreciate to what extent the introduction of opportunity effects influences the impact of spillovers, alternative results are reported in Table 4. It appears that, despite a diminution of its value, the elasticity of the total spillover stock remains significant when the sectorial and geographical dummies are introduced. On the other hand, the taking into account of technological opportunities destroys the significativeness of spillovers. The results obtained when we consider the different components of spillovers lead to temper this observation. Indeed, technological dummies as well as sectorial and geographical ones seem to contribute to the deterioration of results. A negative effect predominates when some significant coefficients are obtained. Regarding the coefficients obtained for the external national spillover stock, we observe that it remains significantly negative when sectorial and technological dummies are introduced and turns to be insignificant when geographical dummies are considered. Consequently, it can be suspected that the negativity of this coefficient is linked to a geographical specificity.

To verify this observation, we report in Table 5 the results obtained for the regressions realized for each geographical area. A first observation is that the coefficients obtained for the explanatory variables are significantly different among the three areas. The elasticities for the labor and the physical capital are similar in Europe and the United-States and significantly different in Japan. Regarding the own R&D stocks, the results are more

558

TABLE 5

Productivity Estimates by Geographic Area.

dependent Variable: ln S					
WITHIN Level est. s.e. [a]		OLS F.D. est. s.e.		GMM-IV F.D. est. s.e.	
US sample 3024 (2646) obs.					
lnL	.66 (0.30)*	ΔlnL	.47 (.031)*	ΔlnL	.51 (.012)*
lnC	.11 (.027)*	ΔlnC	.13 (.025)*	ΔlnC	.10 (.001)*
lnK	.18 (.024)*	ΔlnK	.28 (.039)*	ΔlnK	.25 (.013)*
lnNS	.69 (.179)*	ΔlnNS	.59 (.202)*	ΔlnNS	.56 (.075)*
lnIS	−.02 (.155)	ΔlnIS	−.43 (.273)	ΔlnIS	−.35 (.122)*
R_a^2 .995		R_a^2 .468		X^2 [d.f.] [b] Sim. [c]:	239.8 [195] S
JP sample 1064 (931) obs.					
lnL	.23 (.053)*	ΔlnL	.11 (.040)*	ΔlnL	.09 (.001)*
lnC	.28 (.033)*	ΔlnC	.18 (.035)*	ΔlnC	.12 (.001)*
lnK	.07 (.040)**	ΔlnK	.28 (.114)*	ΔlnK	.10 (.001)*
lnNS	−.17 (.149)	ΔlnLS	−.23 (.403)	ΔlnNS	.28 (.028)*
lnIS	.91 (.307)*	ΔlnIS	1.46 (.621)*	ΔlnIS	.97 (.065)*
R_a^2 .992		R_a^2 .221		X^2 [d.f.] Sim. :	122.9 [120] W
EU sample 808 (707) obs.					
lnL	.63 (.052)*	ΔlnL	.53 (.066)*	ΔlnL	.56 (.001)*
lnC	.18 (.035)*	ΔlnC	.09 (.040)*	ΔlnC	.11 (.001)*
lnK	.04 (.053)	ΔlnK	.22 (.105)*	ΔlnK	.15 (.001)*
lnNS	.13 (.140)	ΔlnNS	.13 (.281)	ΔlnNS	.12 (.032)*
lnIS	.32 (.269)	ΔlnIS	.06 (.565)	ΔlnIS	−.12 (.030)*
R_a^2 .996		R_a^2 .417		X^2 [d.f.] Sim. :	97.4 [95] +L1

a: heteroskedastic-consistent standard errors in brackets (except for JP and EU GMM estimates),
* (**) = statistically significant at the 5 (10)% level; b: overidentification test; c: predeterminancy of X_{it}: W (S) = weak (strong) exogeneity, $+L3$ = lag 3 and lower values of X_{it} as instruments. For the GMM estimates, the variance-covariance matrix of orthogonality conditions has been held fixed across all tests and is based on the estimates of the corresponding specification in first differences and with lag 2 instruments.

controversial. The first-difference estimates are similar while the within estimates are significantly different and the GMM estimates are in an intermediary position.

Turning to the effects of spillovers, it appears that their influences are drastically different for each geographical area. In the United-States, the national stock affects significantly the output which it is not the case for the international stock. An opposite observation emerges for Japan which appears to benefit from the international stock. So, Japan seems to depend, to a large extent, on technologies developed outside while American firms are mainly turned to their domestic technologies. Interestingly, BERNSTEIN and MOHNEN [1995] in their study of the effects of international R&D spillovers on productivity growth of R&D intensive sectors, find that international spillovers exist from the U.S. to Japan, but not in the converse direction. BRANSTETTER [1996] too, reports some evidence that Japanese firms benefit positively from R&D undertaken by U.S. firms while no effect of Japanese R&D on U.S. firms' output growth is found. As far as Europe is concerned, no consistent effect is obtained for this continent. Consequently, the receptivity of European firms to new technologies can be questioned. These empirical observations are, to a large extent, in accordance with the positioning often emphasized for the three geographical areas. As a technological leader, the United-States is principally concerned by its own technological development. On its side, Japan has demonstrated that it was highly successful in implementing technologies developed outside, particularly in the United-States. The weakness of European countries in fast growing technological fields, their higher specialisation in slow growing or declining activities and a more defensive and/or passive behaviour regarding R&D intensive activities induce a lesser sensitiveness to spillovers. Consequently, the lesser R&D intensity of European countries combined to a weaker propensity to internalize technological spillovers might jeopardize its long term competitiveness.

To complete the analysis, we have used a similar approach to the one developed by JAFFE. Table 6 compares Jaffe's results [1988] with the ones obtained from our sample. It should be noticed that first, the productivity equation used by Jaffe directly estimates a rate of return to R&D rather than an elasticity. Second, in the preceding tables, the impacts of the local and external components of spillovers are estimated separately, while Jaffe quantifies the impact of the total stock and tries to find out if there is a significant premium for the local stock [22]. Finally, because of data availability, Jaffe estimated long differences between average years 1976-1978 and 1971-1973. Consequently, we have also calculated long differences between average years 1987-1989 and 1992-1994.

When industry effects are not taken into account, the spillover coefficients are not significant in the international sample as well as in the US sample. The return to R&D is similar to the measure obtained by Jaffe. The labor elasticity is also comparable to Jaffe's result, the main difference is observed for the capital stock elasticity in the international sample which is triple of the estimate obtained in the US sample and by Jaffe. The introduction of industry effects does not change drastically the value of estimates except for the spillover variables which turn to be significant. The coefficients are higher than the ones obtained by Jaffe and give evidence that there is a

---

22. Actually, Jaffe's specification is based on a perfect substituability hypothesis among the spillover stocks, while a unitary one is assumed in our previous specification. Alternatively, we have tried to estimate the value of the elasticity of substitution from a CES production function. Yet, the test has been unfortunately inconclusive.

560

TABLE 6

Productivity Estimates: Comparison with Jaffe [1988].

dependent Variable: ln S					long differences
international sample (1993-1988) 625 obs		US sample (1993-1988) 378 obs		Jaffe sample (1977-1972) 434 obs	
est. s.e. [a]	est. s.e.	est. s.e.	est. s.e.	est. s.e.	est. s.e.
ΔlnL .55 (.129)*	.52 (.142)*	.76 (.050)*	.76 (.050)*	.72 (.047)*	.69 (.038)*
ΔlnC .31 (.133)*	.34 (.144)*	.12 (.054)*	.14 (.052)*	.04 (.045)*	.13 (.047)*
RD/S 1.7 (.575)*	1.8 (.761)*	1.2 (.437)*	1.1 (.641)**	1.9 (.410)*	1.5 (.0460)*
ΔlnLS −.14 (.178)	.28 (.131)*	.10 (.071)	.38 (.386)*	.04 (.049)	.10 (.051)**
Δln(ES/LS) −.0045 (.006)	.0100 (.005)**	.0029 (.005)	.0179 (.007)*	.0003 (.001)	.0004 (.0003)
X^2 stat. [d.f.] on industry effects	39.8 [19]*		41.5 [19]*		6.2 [19]*
R_a^2 .683	.693	.783	.795	.618	.742

a: heteroskedastic-consistent standard errors in brackets, * (**) = statistically significant at the 5 (10)% level.

premium effect for external stock relatively to the local stock. The estimates for our sub-sample of US firms are remarkably close to the ones reported by Jaffe. The only important difference is about the local spillover component which is somewhat high in our sample. So, it seems that US firms have become closer technologically [23] and hence may benefit more from R&D performed by technological neighbors. The estimated coefficient associated to the R&D intensity variable implies a somewhat lower annual excess rate of returns of .23 against .34 in Jaffe's study. This result suggests that for the US firms the impact of own R&D has decreased over time.

5 Conclusion

The purpose of the paper has been to assess the importance of the main determinants of technological activity of international firms on productivity. Among the main determinants, the firms' own R&D capital as well as the technological spillovers were considered. Technological spillovers have been formalized by weighting the firms' R&D stocks according to their proximity into the technological space on the basis of the patent distribution of firms across technological classes. The new constructed dataset which

---

23. An alternative explanation may be found in the fact that we use European patents for US firms.

enlarges Jaffe's study to the international scope is representative of a main part of R&D expenditures in industrialized countries. In order to provide a distinction between local and external components of the total spillover pool, three clustering procedures have been investigated. National and international spillover stocks have also been constructed on the basis of the geographic location of firms. Despite these improvements, such an approach has some limitations which are difficult to overcome. The main drawbacks of this methodology are the difficulty to take into account firms which do not apply for any patents as well as the risk of erroneous technological location for firms which applied for a small number of patents. These problems have really been encountered in the empirical analysis.

The estimates obtained have been performed by using ad hoc panel data estimation methods which control for specific hypotheses typically associated with this kind of data, namely, correlated firms' unobserved fixed effects with regressors and weakly exogenous explanatory variables. However the GMM techniques which seem to promise so much in theory has delivered less than might be hoped in the way of useful results. On the whole, results for traditional production factors appeared to be consistent with the findings of previous related studies. Some evidence about the effects of technological spillovers on productivity has also been found. The results lead one to conclude that the sensitivity of firms to spillovers differs significantly among the three geographical areas. Indeed, the United States, Japan and Europe seem to adopt very differentiated behaviors. While US firms are mainly concerned with their national spillover stock, Japanese ones are more receptive to the international stock and European ones do not seem to particularly benefit from both sources of spillovers. Furthermore, our results confirm to a large extent those obtained by Jaffe, our elasticity of productivity with respect to spillovers is higher and we cannot exclude that the external stock benefit from a premium effect.

In our opinion, the measure of technological spillovers is facing with lots of methodological problems. If the concept of technological space is very attractive, its measure is not direct and the choice of a distance metric can affect the nature of results. In a same vein, there is also the question of heterogeneity in technological space. Moreover, given the positioning of firms into the technological space, to what extent two firms benefit from spillovers from each other given the possible existence of asymmetrical information flows? The timing of spillover effects should also be considered. How much time take the spillovers to concretize in new products and processes and as a result in productivity? Because of lags in the diffusion of knowledge, spillover effects are probably not immediate. This last point is perhaps the main explanation why empirical studies encounter lots of difficulties to measure the real impact of spillovers.

So far, we do not have clear answers to these questions and there are consequently still lots of bottlenecks to overcome in the burgeoning literature on the relationship between productivity growth and technological spillovers.

ANNEX 1

The balanced panel of 673 firms from 1987 to 1994 was cleaned according to similar criterions as those used by HALL and MAIRESSE [1995], what led to remove 48 observations (7.1%):

a) Any observations for which R&D intensity was less than 0.2% or greater than 50% were removed. This eliminated 6 firms.

b) Any observations for which net sales per worker, capital stock per worker and R&D capital per worker was outside of three times the interdecile range above or below the median were removed This eliminated 15 firms.

c) Any observations for which the growth rate of net sales was less than minus 90% or greater than 300% or for which the growth rate of labor, capital and R&D stocks was less than minus 60% or greater than 240% were removed. This eliminated 27 firms.

ANNEX 2

Correlation Matrix of Spillover Components

	ΔTS	ΔLS	ΔES	ΔNS	ΔIS	ΔLNS	ΔLIS	ΔENS
ΔLS	.49							
ΔES	.79	.10						
ΔNS	.50	.29	.40					
ΔIS	.88	.29	.71	.27				
ΔLNS	.28	.61	.07	.38	.09			
ΔLIS	.43	.43	.19	.16	.42	.02		
ΔENS	.44	.11	.51	.74	.27	−.01	.18	
ΔEIS	.68	.05	.88	.23	.74	.04	.09	.29

● References

ARELLANO, M., BOND, S. (1991). – "Some Tests of Specification for Panel Data: Monte Carlo Evidence and an Application to Employment Equations", *Review of Economic Studies*, 58, pp. 277-298.

BERNSTEIN, J. I., MOHNEN, P. (1995). – "International R&D Spillovers between US and Japanese R&D Intensive Sectors", revision of *Working Paper 4682*, National Bureau of Economic Research, Cambridge.

BRANSTETTER, L. (1996). – "Are Knowledge Spillovers International or Intranational in Scope? Microeconometric Evidence from the U.S. and Japan", *Working Paper 5800*, National Bureau of Economic Research, Cambridge.

CUNÉO, P., MAIRESSE, J. (1984). – "Productivity and R&D at the Firm Level in French Manufacturing?", in Z. Griliches (ed.), *R&D, Patents and Productivity*, Chicago: University of Chicago, pp. 375-392.

GRILICHES, Z., (1979). – "Issues in Assessing the Contribution of R&D to Productivity Growth", *Bell Journal of Economics*, 10, pp. 92-116.

GRILICHES, Z. (1990). – "Patent Statistics as Economic Indicators: A Survey", *Journal of Economic Literature*, 28, pp. 1661-1707.

GRILICHES, Z. (1992). – "The Search for R&D Spillovers", *Scandinavian Journal of Economics*, 94, pp. 29-48.

GRILICHES, Z., LICHTENBERG, F. (1984). – "R&D and Productivity at the Industry Level: Is There Still a Relationship", in Z. Griliches (ed.), *R&D, Patents and Productivity*, Chicago: *University of Chicago*, pp. 462-501.

GRILICHES, Z., MAIRESSE, J. (1984). – "Productivity and R&D at the Firm Level", in Z. Griliches (ed.), *R&D, Patents and Productivity, Chicago: University of Chicago*, pp. 339-368.

GRILICHES, Z., MAIRESSE, J. (1995). – "Production Functions: The Search for Identification", *Working Paper 5067*, National Bureau of Economic Research, Cambridge.

HALL, B. H., MAIRESSE, J. (1995). – "Exploring the Relationship between R&D and Productivity in French Manufacturing Firms", *Journal of Econometrics*, 65, pp. 263-93.

JAFFE, A. B. (1986). – "Technological Opportunity and Spillovers of R&D", *American Economic Review*, 76, pp. 984-1001.

JAFFE, A. B. (1988). – "R&D Intensity and Productivity Growth", *Review of Economics and Statistics*, 70, pp. 431-437.

KEANE, M., RUNKLE, D. (1992). – "On the Estimation of Panel Data Models with Serial Correlation When Instruments Are Not Strictly Exogenous", *Journal of Business and Economic Statistics*, 10, pp. 1-9.

LEBART, L., MORINEAU, A., FENÉLON, J. P. (1979). – *Traitement des données statistiques*, Dunod.

MAIRESSE, J., HALL, B. H. (1996). – "Estimating the Productivity of Research and Development: An Exploration of GMM Methods Using Data on French and United States Manufacturing Firms", *Working Paper 5501*, National Bureau of Economic Research, Cambridge.

MAIRESSE, J., SASSENOU, M. (1991). – "Recherche-Développement et Productivité: Un Panorama des Etudes Econométriques sur Données d'Entreprises", *STI Revue*, pp. 9-45.

MILLIGAN, G., COOPER, M. (1985). – "An Examination of Procedures for Determining the Number of Clusters in a data set", *Psychometrika*, 50, pp. 159-179.

MOHNEN, P. (1996). – "R&D Externalities and Productivity Growth ", *STI review*, pp. 39-66.

ROBSON, M., TOWSEND, J., PAVITT, K. (1988). – "Sectoral Patterns and Use of Innovations in the UK: 1945-1983", *Research Policy*, 17, pp. 1-14.

SCHANKERMAN, M. (1981). – "The Effects of Double-Counting and Expensing on the Measured Returns to R&D", *Review of Economics and Statistics*, 63, pp. 454-458.

SCHERER, F. M. (1982). – "Demand-Pull and Technological Innovation: Schmookler Revisited", *Journal of Industrial Economics*, 30, pp. 225-238.

SPENCE, A. M. (1984). – "Cost Reduction, Competition, and Industry Performance", *Econometrica*, 52, pp. 101-122.

TERLECKYJ, N. (1974). – "Effects of R&D on the Productivity Growth of Industries: An Exploratory Study", National Planning Association, Washington, D.C.

TERLECKYJ, N. (1980). – "Direct and Indirect Effects of Industrial Research and Development on the Productivity Growth of Industries", in J.N. Kendrick and B.N. Vacara (eds.), *New developments in Productivity Measurement and Analysis*, University of Chicago Press, Chicago.

Innovation Spillovers and Technology Policy

Y. KATSOULACOS, D. ULPH *

ABSTRACT. – We examine a model of R&D competition and cooperation in the presence of spillovers. However, unlike virtually all the literature, we treat these spillovers as endogenous and under the control of firms. We show that it is then essential to make a number of distinctions that are ignored in the literature. In particular we need to distinguish between the amount of R&D that firms do and the amount of spillover they generate; between *information sharing* and *research coordination*; between each of the latter and cooperation; between *substitute* and *complementary* research paths; between firms being located in the same industry or in different industries. These distinctions matter because, as we show, *coordination* can arise without *cooperation* (different industries, complementary research, research design) while *cooperation* need not induce *information sharing* (same industry, substitute research, information sharing). In many cases, however, allowing cooperation is sufficient to induce full *information sharing/research coordination*, in which case the justification, if any, for a technology policy that takes the form of an R&D subsidy lies in encouraging firms to undertake more R&D. Our analysis suggests that cooperative arrangements between firms may often produce too little R&D, and therefore that R&D subsidies can be justified – but not to correct information problems, but other market failures in the amount of R&D firms choose to do.

* Y. KATSOULACOS: Athens University of Economics and Business, CEPR; D. ULPH: University College London, CEPR. We are grateful to CEPR for a research grant under their Competition and Markets Programme which enabled us to collaborate. Earlier versions of this paper were presented at seminars at CREST-ENSAE, OECD, INSEAD, University of Leuven, WZB Berlin and at the French Economic Association Conference in Nantes (June 1995), and we would like to thank seminar participants for their comments. We would particularly like to acknowledge the many useful comments we received from Raymond De Bondt, David Encaoua, Bruno Jullien, Patrick Rey and two anonymous referees.

D. Encaoua et al. (eds.), The Economics and Econometrics of Innovation, 567–585.

1 Introduction

In this paper we develop a model of oligopolistic R&D rivalry and cooperation in the presence of R&D spillovers. However, in contrast to virtually all the existing literature our focus is on the case where firms choose their spillover parameters **endogenously**. Now as soon as we allow this possibility, it turns out to be critical to make a number of distinctions that are typically not made in the literature.

We usually think of spillovers as arising through one firm's acquiring information about the research discoveries of the other. There are two factors that will bear on the extent of this spillover: the amount of information acquired (quantity of information), and the usefulness of that information to the acquiring firm (quality of information). In principle both of these facets of the spillover are under the firms' control, so when, as here, we think of these spillovers being endogenously determined by firms, we need to be clear about what is being chosen. We will show that this matters by focussing on two polar cases. The first is that of a pure **information sharing** spillover where it is the quantity of information that passes between firms that is being chosen, implicitly assuming that it is useful and that there is no scope for choosing the research design. The second is that where firm's choose their **research design** in order to control the quality of information acquired by the other firm. In this case we implicitly assume that firms have no control over the quantity of information that passes between them.

Second we show that it matters whether the spillover arises between firms that are operating in the **same industry** or in **different industries** since this will crucially affect the private incentives to give potentially beneficial spillovers to another firm. If firms operate in completely separate industries then each has nothing to lose from having the other firm benefit from a spilloer from itself, whereas if they are in the same industry then, if one firm alone has made a discovery, it can be damaging to have its rival receive a beneficial spillover.

Third it is important to distinguish between the case where the research that is being undertaken by one firm is a **substitute** or a **complement** for that undertaken by the other. Again this affects our understanding of the incentives to create spillovers. In the **substitute** case firms are essentially undertaking the same research, and will consequently make the same discovery. Thus if *both* firms make a discovery then neither can benefit from any spillover, though one firm can benefit from the other's when it has not itself discovered. When research is **complementary**, then one firm's discovery can be of benefit to the other, and is indeed likely to be most beneficial whern they have both made a discovery. Notice that this distinction relates to the previous one in that if firms are operating in completely different industries they will not be undertaking substitute research whilst if they are operating in the same industry they may be undertaking substitute or complementary research.

Finally it is important to distinguish between **cooperation** and **information sharing/coordinating research design**. Just because firms

568

choose to cooperate (maximise joint profits) it does not necessarily mean that they will choose to share information or coordinate research design – and we will show that there are cases where indeed cooperation does not induce information sharing/research coordination. Equally, the fact that firms choose not to cooperate does not mean that they will not share information or coordinate their research, and again we will show that full research coordination can arise even when firms do not cooperate.

One important motivation for studying a model with endogenous spillovers is to provide a framework for examining **technology policies** that take the form of subsidies to information-sharing (or result-sharing) research joint-ventures (RJVs) – a type of policy that is particularly common in the EU Commission. Notice that there are two parts to the policy: the allowance of cooperative arrangements between firms, and the subsidy to R&D. In order to examine the rationale for such a policy we need to understand what incentives firms may or may not have to share information or coordinate research design in the absence of any policy.

Now in recent years there has been a growing interest among economists in the potential role of research joint ventures (RJVs) in allowing firms to internalise R&D spillovers, coordinate their research activities, and achieve higher R&D output (see, for example, KATZ [1986]; D'ASPREMONT et al. [1988]; KATZ and ORDOVER [1990]; SUZUMURA [1992]; BEATH and ULPH [1989]; MOTTA [1992a, 1992b]; KESTELOOT and DE BONDT [1993]. In this literature spillovers are typically modelled as follows. Assuming a duopoly producing a homogeneous product, the unit cost of firm i is taken to depend on its own R&D, x_i, and the R&D of its rival, x_j, via an exogenously given spillover parameter δ. Thus if the unit cost of firm i is c_i, then $c_i = A - x_i - \delta x_j$, $A > 0$, $0 < \delta \leq 1$. Within this framework an RJV is thought of as involving the firms in setting their R&D levels cooperatively to maximise joint profits. In some formulations (for example, D'ASPREMONT et al. [1988]) it is assumed that the same spillover parameter applies to the RJV as in the non-cooperative equilibrium, while in others (for example, BEATH and ULPH [1989], MOTTA [1992b] and CREPON et al. [1992]) it is assumed that the RJV can automatically achieve full information-sharing/research design coordination ($\delta = 1$). Notice that this also means setting cooperatively the total spillovers δx so, even though cooperation is modelled as being on R&D investment levels (and not on the spillover parameter), RJVs do serve as a spillover internalisation device.

By treating spillovers exogenously these models conflate the decision to invest in R&D with that on information sharing/research design and they also conflate the latter decision with that of cooperation. The first conflation means that these models cannot deal with the fact that we have to deal potentially **with two distinct market failures**: that associated with the R&D investment levels and that associated with the level of information revelation.

To analyse what happens when we endogenise the spillover parameter, we are going to follow the existing literature by focusing on the case where there are just two firms that might potentially form an RJV but allow these firms to be located either in the **same** industry, or in **different** industries and to pursue either **complementary** or **substitute** research. We examine three types of equilibria. In the **non-cooperative equilibrium** firms choose their R&D and spillover parameters independently. In the **cooperative equilibrium** firms choose their R&D and spillover parameters to maximise joint profits, but there is no subsidy to R&D. Third we consider the **social optimum**. Here a social planner chooses the R&D levels and spillover parameters to maximise social surplus. We can thus explore what market failures arise in terms of both the amount of R&D that is undertaken and in the extent of information sharing/research design coordination; We can examine how far these would be corrected by simply allowing cooperative arrangements without any subsidy.

We show the following:

• When firms operate in the *same industry* pursuing *substitute research*, then, when the spillover takes the form of *information sharing* the *non-cooperative* equilibrium involves no information sharing. When firms cooperate they may still decide not to share information. **Thus cooperation need not involve any information sharing.** When the *cooperative equilibrium* does indeed entail no information sharing then cooperation involves less R&D spending than in the non-cooperative equilibrium. The *social optimum* requires full information sharing. When the *cooperative equilibrium* produces full information sharing then it typically does not produce enough R&D so an R&D subsidy is justified, but not to correct any market failure on information sharing. However, when the *cooperative equilibrium* produces no information sharing, then an R&D subsidy may not be able to produce the social optimum, since the subsidy required to induce full information sharing may be larger than that required to correct the R&D failure.

When firms operate in the *same industry* but pursue *complementary* research paths then much the same qualitative conclusions go through as in the above case (so this latter case is not examined in the paper). Thus the fact that research paths are complementary is not in itself sufficient to induce full information sharing under cooperation.

• When firms operate in different industries, pursuing complementary research, and the spillover takes the form of *research design coordination*, then the non-cooperative equilibrium produces full coordination. **Thus full coordination can arise without cooperation.** (Though not discussed here it can be shown that the same result holds with information sharing spillovers). *Cooperation* produces full research design coordination (and full information sharing), and a higher level of R&D spending than under *non-cooperation*. However, it we compare the *cooperative equilibrium* to the *social optimum*, then, while cooperation produces the optimal degree of coordination, in a wide class of cases the level of R&D spending will be too low, so there could be some justification for an R&D subsidy.

The structure of the paper is as follows: in Section 2 we set out the generic model that we use in the rest of the paper. The bulk of the analysis comes in Sections 3 and 4 where we focus on two opposing cases. Section 3 considers the case where the firms operate in the *same industry* pursuing *substitute research* and there are *information sharing* spillovers while Section 4 considers the polar opposite case where firms are in *independent industries* pursuing *complementary research* and the spillover takes the form of *research design* coordination. Section 5 concludes.

2 The Generic R&D Model

2.1. Types of Spillover, Types of Equilibria and order of decisions

As noted in the introduction, we will distinguish between spillovers that arise from *information sharing* and those from *research design coordination*. However, the distinction really only matters in the *non-cooperative equilibrium*. To see this let us consider each of the three types of equilibrium in turn.

• *Non-cooperative*

Here the two firms choose their levels of R&D and their spillover parameters independently. This is modelled as a two-stage decision process, and, as de FRAJA [1991] has noted, the order in which the decisions get taken can matter. It is this ordering of decisions which reflects the distinction between the two types of spillover.

When the spillover takes the form of *information sharing,* then, since firms can only share information once they have made a discovery, it is natural to think of their first deciding how much R&D to do and then, once they have made a discovery, choosing how much information about this discovery to reveal. So here the R&D is chosen first and then the spillover parameter.

When the spillover is controlled through the choice of *research design* then clearly this has to get determined before deciding how intensively to pursue the research, so here the spillover parameter is chosen first, and then decisions are taken about the amount of R&D.

• *Fully Cooperative in Absence of Subsidy*

Here there is no R&D subsidy, but firms privately decide to cooperate and choose both R&D and spillovers to maximise joint profits. The assumption is that by cooperating firms can enter into some binding agreement on both R&D and the spillover parameter and therefore, in reaching the agreement, these two variables are chosen simultaneously. Hence the previous distinction is no longer applicable.

• Social Optimum

Here if a social planner can exercise control over the R&D levels and the degree of spillover, it is natural to think of these as being chosen simultaneously to maximise total surplus. Once again the distinction between the nature of the spillover is no longer applicable.

So let $\delta = (\delta_1, \delta_2)$ be the spillovers. Then, generally, we will indicate the profit of firm i as follows:

$\pi_i^t(\delta)$-profits of i if both firms discover;

$\pi_i^w(\delta)$-profits of i if it alone discovers;
$\pi_i^\ell(\delta)$-profits of i if the other firm alone discovers;
π_i^0-profits of i if neither firm discovers.

2.2. The R&D Process

We model R&D as a stochastic process. The amount of R&D chosen by each firm simply determines the probability that it will make a discovery, which is independent of that of the other firm, so there is a chance that both will discover, that each alone will discover, and that neither will discover. This is true whether firms operate in a cooperative or non-cooperative environment. To set out the R&D model in more detail, we concentrate now on the non-cooperative equilibrium.

When firms act non-cooperatively they each choose their R&D taking as given the spillover parameters, and hence the profits that they will make contingent on the various possibilities that one and/or the other makes a discovery. This is because either spillovers have been chosen in the previous period (as in the case of research design) or, when spillovers will be chosen in the next period (as with information sharing) their value will be 0 or 1 independently of R&D (as we show below).

Throughout the analysis we will use the probability of discovery as the choice variable and model the R&D technology through a cost function, $c(p)$ giving the amount a firm has to spend on R&D to achieve a probability p. We assume

$$c(0) = 0, \quad c'(0) = 0;$$
$$\forall p, \quad 0 < p < 1, \quad c'(p) > 0; \quad c''(p) > 0$$
$$c(p), \quad c'(p) \to \infty \quad \text{as } p \to 1$$

where the first part of the assumption guarantees that as long as the innovation is profitable a firm will choose to spend a positive amount on R&D, while the latter part guarantees that no firm would end up innovating for sure [1].

The archetypal non-cooperative model is therefore that in which the objective function of firm 1 is:

(1)

$$V_1 = p_1 p_2 \pi_1^t + p_1 (1-p_2) \pi_1^w + p_2 (1-p_1) \pi_1^\ell + (1-p_1)(1-p_2) \pi_1^0 - c(p_1)$$

The profits that appear in this expression will depend on the spillover parameters chosen by each of the two firms. There is an analogous function for firm 2.

---

1. A functional form that satisfies all these conditions is:
$$c(p) = -\log(1-p) - p, \quad \text{so } c'(p) = \frac{p}{1-p}, \quad c''(p) = \frac{1}{(1-p)^2}$$

Let

(2) $\quad A = (\pi_1^t - \pi_1^\ell); \ \ B = (\pi_1^w - \pi_1^0); \ \ C = (\pi_2^t - \pi_2^\ell); \ \ D = (\pi_2^w - \pi_2^0)$

Then the first-order conditions for each of the two firms are:

(3) $$Ap_2 + B(1 - p_2) = c'(p_1)$$

(4) $$Cp_1 + D(1 - p_1) = c'(p_2)$$

A and C are the *competitive threats* of the two firms – that is they show the increase in profits a firm will obtain if the other firm has already innovated. They determine the best response R&D choice by each firm when the other firm's probability of discovery is 1. B and D are the *profit incentives*–that is they show the increase in profits that a firm will obtain if the other firm has not innovated. They determine the best response choice of R&D by each firm when the other firm's probability of discovery is zero [2]. Each firm's optimal p is a strictly increasing (decreasing) function of the other firm's if its *competitive threat* is greater (less) than its *profit incentive*. It is straightforward to show that given our assumptions on $c(p)$ the model has a unique stable solution.

Having set out the basics of the model, we now analyse in detail the outcomes in each of two basic cases.

3 Same Industry, Substitute Research, Information Sharing Spillover

3.1. Basic Constructs for the Same Industry/Substitute Research Case

As already mentioned we assume symmetry [3] between firms (so whenever it is convenient we drop subscripts). The basic constructs for the individual firms can be expressed through the following assumptions on their profit functions:

Assumption 1: Profits if both firms discover are independent of spillovers, and equal to π^t, reflecting the fact that since the discoveries are effectively

---

2. See, for example, BEATH, KATSOULACOS and ULPH [1991, 1992] for a more detailed discussion of the role these two incentives play in the theory of strategic R&D competition.

3. As mentioned by one of the referee's in general we need not expect symmetric outcomes even when firms cooperate.

identical, in this case each firm neither gains nor loses from any spillover. Of course, profits each firm makes if no one discovers are also independent of spillovers and equal to π^0.

Assumption 2: Profits from winning, $\pi^w(\delta)$ are strictly decreasing in δ whilst profit from losing, $\pi^\ell(\delta)$, are strictly increasing in δ.

Assumption 3: We assume that

$$(5) \qquad\qquad \pi^w(0) > \pi^t > \pi^0 > \pi^\ell(0)$$

Notice the following:

• The innovation is profitable in that if both firms discover their profits (π^t) will be higher than in the initial position when neither has discovered.

• Each firm's profits are greatest if it alone is the sole innovator and it gives no spillover to its rival, since then the innovator can increase its market share while the other firm loses market share and so finds their profits below those it makes if neither innovates (Assumption 3).

However, precisely because each firm is engaged in identical research and produces a homogeneous product, any spillover from the successful innovator to the rival enables the rival to close the gap on the innovator, thus reducing the profits of the innovating firm and increasing those of the non-innovating firm (Assumption 2). Indeed, we would expect that in the limit, as the spillover tends to 1, each firm's profits will tend to those it would have made had both firms succeeded in making a discovery. Thus in this case the model contrasts with the *independent industry/complementary research* case (examined below) where we must allow for the possibility that a non-innovating firm may not gain anything from the information gleaned from its rival, and certainly would not gain as much from the innovation as the innovating firm.

For society we assume that:

Assumption 4: Analogously with profits, S^t, the total surplus in the industry if both firms innovate and S^0, the total surplus in the industry if neither firm innovates, are independent of spillovers.

Assumption 5: The total surplus in the industry if a single firm innovates and gives a spillover δ to its rival, $S^s(\delta)$, is strictly increasing in δ.

Assumption 6: We assume

$$(6) \qquad \begin{aligned} & S^t > S^0; \quad S^t > S^s(0); \\ & S^t > 2\pi^t; \quad S^0 > 2\pi^0; \quad S^s(0) > \pi^w(0) + \pi^\ell(0) \end{aligned}$$

Hence total surplus is higher when both firms innovate than is the case either in the absence of any innovation, or in the case where one firm alone innovates (and there is no spillover). Also total surplus always exceeds total profits.

3.2. Non-Cooperative Equilibrium

Since we are dealing with a case where the spillover takes the form of *information sharing*, the non-cooperative equilibrium takes the form of a two-stage game in which firms first choose their R&D and then, when they have made a discovery, decide how much of the information they have discovered to reveal. In the case where one firm alone makes a discovery, it is clear from the specification of profits that since the discovering firm's profits are strictly decreasing in its own spillover, it will choose to reveal nothing. In the case where both firms make a discovery, since they have both discovered effectively the same thing, they have nothing to gain or lose from any information revelation so we can take the spillover parameter to be zero. Thus we have:

Result 1: The non-cooperative equilibrium spillover parameters will be zero whenever firms compete in the same market engage in substitute research and the spillover takes the firms of information sharing.

Let us therefore turn to the first stage of the game – the choice of R&D. It is easy to check that when the spillover parameters are both zero the competitive threats facing the two firms are $A = C = \pi^t - \pi^\ell (0)$, while the *profit incentives* are $B = D = \pi^w (0) - \pi^0$. Therefore the symmetric non-cooperative equilibrium value of p is given by

$$p \left[\pi^t - \pi^\ell (0) \right] + (1 - p) \left[\pi^w (0) - \pi^0 \right] = c' (p)$$

For later purposes, it helps to write this as

(7) $$\left[\pi^w (0) - \pi^0 \right] + p \left[\pi^t + \pi^0 - \pi^w (0) - \pi^\ell (0) \right] = c' (p)$$

It is important to note that the *competitive threat* can be greater or less than the *profit incentive* so the two firms' R&D levels can be strategic complements or strategic substitutes.

3.3. The Cooperative Equilibrium

Here p and δ are chosen to maximise expected profits per firm, *i.e.* so as to maximise

(8) $$V (p, \delta) = p^2 \pi^t + p (1 - p) \left[\pi^w (\delta) + \pi^\ell (\delta) \right] + (1 - p)^2 \pi^0 - c (p)$$

We can see immediately that:

Result 2: If total industry profit when just one firm innovates (the term in square brackets) is increasing in δ then the cooperative equilibrium value of $\delta = 1$ [4].

---

4. This would certainly be the case if $\pi^w (\delta)$ and $\pi^\ell (\delta)$ are linear functions of δ, specifically if $\pi^w (\delta) = \delta \pi^t + (1 - \delta) \pi^w (0)$, and $\pi^\ell (\delta) = \delta \pi^t + (1 - \delta) \pi^\ell (0)$, and
$$2 \pi^t > \pi^w (0) + \pi^\ell (0)$$
so that industry profits are greater when both firms have the new technology than when only one alone has it. We should stress here that this linearity assumption is not necessary and can be replaced by assumptions of convexity or monotonicity (that will hold in a very wide class of cases) without changing any of the results or insights of the paper (so, essentially, all we are missing is the case where profit takes an interior maximum).

The cooperative equilibrium value of p if Result 2 holds is given by:

$$(9) \qquad\qquad 2(1-p)(\pi^t - \pi^0) = c'(p)$$

Result 3: In the opposite case, that is, where total industry profit is decreasing in δ then the cooperative equilibrium value of $\delta = 0$, and the cooperative equilibrium value of p is given by:

$$(10) \quad (\pi^w(0) + \pi^\ell(0) - 2\pi^0) + 2p[\pi^t + \pi^0 - (\pi^w(0) + \pi^\ell(0))] = c'(p)$$

Result 3 illustrates a case where cooperation does not lead to any information revelation. This substantiates the point made in the introduction that when we endogenise spillovers we have to be very careful to distinguish between these two notions [5].

To undertake a comparison of the cooperative and the non-cooperative equilibria, it is useful to begin with this latter case, for then there is no information revelation in either equilibrium, and the only difference is in the R&D levels. Notice that since, by assumption, $\pi^\ell(0) < \pi^0$, the first term on the LHS of (10) is smaller than the corresponding term on the LHS of (7). Given this and the fact that the second constant term on the LHS of equation (11) is negative and twice the value of the same term in equation (7) clearly implies that:

Result 4: In the present case of same industry, substitute research and information sharing spillovers, if industry profits when just one firm innovates are decreasing in δ, cooperation will result in firms investing less in R&D than when acting independently [6].

In the opposite case where total profits are increasing in δ when one firm innovates, under cooperation firms will choose maximum information revelation ($\delta = 1$). In this case, comparing equations (7) to (9) we see that:

Result 5: When total industry profits are increasing in δ when one firm innovates, the probability of discovery can be greater, equal or smaller when

---

5. When firms engage in **complementary research** then because once again an innovating firm's profits will be a decreasing function of its own spillover, in the non-cooperative equilibrium each firm wil set its (information sharing) spillover to zero. However because now (with complementary research) firms have more to gain from sharing information if they **both** innovate it is more likely that under cooperation $\delta = 1$. That is, under cooperation δ will be certainly unity if the condition in Result 2 above holds, but it may also be unity even if this condition does not hold. To see this, note that, with complementary research, π^t will be an increasing function of δ. Thus $V(p, \delta)$–equation (8)–may be then increasing in δ (and we may get $\delta = 1$) **even if** the term in square brackets (*i.e.* total profit) is decreasing in δ.

6. This result is consistent with that by D'ASPREMONT and JACQUEMIN [1988]. In ttheir model if the exogenous spillover parameter is small (less than 0.5) cooperation results in a decrease in R&D. Here, on the other hand, with linear profit functions, **for as long as** $2\pi^t < \pi^w(0) + \pi^\ell(0)$ **firms will choose not to reveal any information under a cooperative agreement** ($\delta = 0$) **and will choose to invest less on R&D than they would have done independently.**

576

firms cooperate relative to its value when they act independently [7].

3.4. The Social Optimum

The problem is to choose p and δ to maximise total expected surplus in the industry where this is given by:

$$(11) \qquad \overline{W}(p, \delta) = p^2 S^t + 2p(1-p) S^s(\delta) + (1-p)^2 S^0 - 2c(p)$$

where $S^s(\delta)$ has been defined above as the social surplus when a single firm innovates and the degree of information revelation is δ. Given that $S^t > S^s(0)$, $S^s(\delta)$ is strictly increasing in δ and so therefore is expected social surplus. Thus:

Result 6: It is socially optimal to engage in maximum information revelation (the socially optimal value of $\delta = 1$).

With $\delta = 1$, from (11), the socially optimal value of p is defined by the first-order condition:

$$(12) \qquad (1-p)(S^t - S^0) = c'(p)$$

where we have used the fact that $S^s(1) = S^t$ [8].

There are clearly two distinct distortions that the market may produce that may justify policy intervention. First the market may under cooperation generate less than optimal information revelation (a value of δ that is less than unity). Secondly, even when there is maximum information revelation under cooperation, the amount of R&D and hence probability of success may be less than at the socially optimal level.

Consider first the case where total industry profit when one firm innovates is increasing in δ so under cooperation firms will choose maximum information revelation ($\delta = 1$) and the only market distortion can come from suboptimal p. In this case equilibrium p is given by (9) which can be rewritten in the presence of a subsidy as

$$(13) \qquad 2(1-p)(\pi^t - \pi^0) = c'(p)(1-s)$$

---

7. Also note that in the latter case where $\delta = 1$ under cooperation each firm gets π' either when both discover or one discovers. In the first event that occurs with probability p^2 there is needless duplication. The second event occurs with probability $2p(1-p)$. Thus the probability of discovery is $2p - p^2 = p(2-p)$. The R&D cost is $2c(p)$. The total R&D cost of getting the same probability with just one active R&D laboratory is $c(p(2-p))$. So when $c(p(2-p)) > 2c(p)$ it is better to have two active R&D laboratories whilst in the reverse case it is better to have one active R&D laboratory. If $c(p) = -p - \log(1-p)$ then $c(p(2-p)) > 2c(p)$ and we can assume that both firms will have active R&D laboratories. If however $c(p) = p^2$ then $c[p(2-p)] < 2c(p)$ if $p > 2 - \sqrt{2}$ and so for large p it is best to have only one R&D laboratory active. We will assume that $c(p) = -p - \log(1-p)$ so it is optimal to have two laboratories active.

8. There is again the issue of whether to have 1 or 2 R&D laboratories and the same conditions govern this as for private firms, so given above cost function it is optimal to have two laboratories.

Comparing (13) to (12) we see that with $s = 0$ optimum p will be greater (equal, smaller) than equilibrium p if $S^t - S^0$ is greater (equal, smaller) than $2(\pi' - \pi^0)$. So we have:

Result 7: If total industry profit when one firm innovates in increasing in δ, in the linear demand case where $S^t - S^0 = 4(\pi' - \pi^0)$ the social optimum is greater than the equilibrium value of p and the optimum subsidy is positive–indeed it should be 50%.

On the other hand, if total industry profit is decreasing in δ then the cooperative equilibrium value of $\delta = 0$, and the cooperative equilibrium value of p is given by (10). So the market is now generating the wrong amount of information revelation and, as a comparison of (10) and (12) shows, the cooperative equilibrium value of p will in general be different from the optimum value of p, $\hat{p}$, though, at this level of generality it is impossible to say whether p is greater than or less than $\hat{p}$. That is, there are now two market failures, and as intuition also suggests, it may not be possible to correct them and achieve the optimum outcome with the single instrument of an R&D subsidy [9].

4 Independent Industry, Complementary Research, Research Design Spillover

In this section we consider a case when the spillover arises through *research design coordination*. As we pointed out in section 2, in this case in the non-cooperative equilibrium, we think of the spillover being chosen first and the R&D level second.

In the case where firms are undertaking substitute research, the research design is essentially fixed, and the only form of spillover is *information sharing* so we will focus our attention in this section on the case where firms are undertaking complementary research. Further we will assume that firms operate in different industries.

4.1. Basic Constructs for the Independent Industry/ Complementary Research Case

To start with we will make the following assumptions about the firms' profit functions:

Assumption 7: Profits π^w of either firm if it alone innovates and profits π^0 of either firm if neither firm innovates are independent of spillovers.

Assumption 8: Profits $\pi^t(\delta)$ of firm i if both innovate and it gets spillover δ from the other firm are strictly increasing in δ. Profits $\pi^\ell(\delta)$ of firm i if the other firm alone innovates and it again gets spillover δ from the other firm are non-decreasing in δ.

Assumption 9: We assume that

$$(14) \qquad \pi^t(1) > \pi^w > \pi^\ell(1) \geq \pi^0$$

These assumptions capture the following features.

• If a single firm innovates it gains nothing from the rival firm's R&D (since it has not innovated) but loses nothing by revealing information to its rival (since the other firm is in a different industry).

• If a firm fails to innovate then, precisely because the research is on different lines, the non-innovating firm may gain nothing from the discovery of the rival firm – even if the spillover is 1. However although we also allow the possibility that the non-innovating firm will gain something from the spillover from the innovator, we assume that even when the spillover is 1 the non-innovating firm will not gain as much from the discovery as the innovating firm, thus reflecting the idea that the discovery is best suited to the firm making the discovery.

Indeed although we allow the possibility that a firm might gain from the other firm's spillover, even if it itself has not discovered, we want to assume that:

Assumption 10:

$$(15) \qquad \pi^t(1) - \pi^w > \pi^\ell(1) - \pi^0$$

so that what each firm gains from the other firm's innovation is greatest when that firm has itself innovated.

• If both firms innovate, then each can gain from any spillover from the rival firm. In terms of social welfare we assume that:

Assumption 11: The total surplus arising in a *single* industry in which the firm is the sole innovator, S^w, and the total surplus arising in *each* industry i if neither firm innovates, S^0, are independent of spillovers.

Assumption 12: The total surplus in industry i it if fails to innovate but it receives a spillover δ from a successful discovery in industry j, $S^\ell(\delta)$, is increasing in δ. The total surplus arising in industry i if *both* industries innovate, and there is a spillover δ from a successful discovery in industry j, $S^t(\delta)$, is strictly increasing in δ.

Assumption 13: We assume

$$(16) \qquad S^t(1) > S^w > S^\ell(1) \geq S^0$$

and that

$$(17) \qquad S^t(1) > \pi^t(1); \quad S^w > \pi^w; \quad S^\ell(1) > \pi^\ell(1); \quad S^0 > \pi^0.$$

Thus society's ranking of the various outcomes in any industry simply reflects the degree of innovation that accrues there and therefore generates the same ranking as industry profits. In particular this means that the final inequality in (16) is strict if and only if that in (14) is strict. As is usual social surplus in any industry always exceeds industry profits.

4.2. The Non-Cooperative Equilibrium

Consider then a two-stage non-cooperative equilibrium, in which the two firms in the different industries first choose the spillover, and then their level of R&D.

We solve backwards, and analyse first the R&D decisions. On doing the substitutions of the profit expressions into (2) we find that in this case the competitive threats and profit incentives are defined by:

$$(18) \qquad A = \delta_2 \left[\pi^t (1) - \pi^\ell (1) \right] + (1 - \delta_2) \left[\pi^w - \pi^0 \right]; \quad B = \left[\pi^w - \pi^0 \right]$$

and

$$(19) \qquad C = \delta_1 \left[\pi^t (1) - \pi^\ell (1) \right] + (1 - \delta_1) \left[\pi^w - \pi^0 \right]; \quad D = \left[\pi^w - \pi^0 \right]$$

Thus in determining the relative magnitudes of the *competitive threats* and *profit incentives* everything just depends on the relative magnitudes of the two terms in square brackets that appear in the *competitive threats*. Now we can re-write these as

$$\pi^t - \pi^\ell = (\pi^t - \pi^w) + (\pi^w - \pi^\ell); \quad \pi^w - \pi^0 = (\pi^t - \pi^0) + (\pi^w - \pi^t)$$

The second term on the RHS of these expressions is identical, so the only difference lies in the first terms which measure the value to a firm of the other firm's discovery if (i) it itself has discovered, or (ii) is has not discovered. In (15) we have assumed that the former is greater than the latter, so that, as long as there are any spillovers at all, $A - B > 0$ and $C - D > 0$, the *competitive threat* is greater than the *profit incentive*. Thus, in the present case the reaction functions are upward sloping – R&D expeditures are strategic complements (BULOW et al., [1985]).

4.3. The Incentive to Coordinate in the Non-Cooperative Equilibrium

Having determined the optimal R&D decisions of firms, conditional on spillovers, we now have to work out the spillover they will choose – *i.e.* their incentive to coordinate. Let $V_i(\delta_1, \delta_2)$ be the expected value of profits of firm i with the equilibrium choices of R&D conditional on the chosen levels of spillovers.

Thus, for firm 1 we have

$$(20) \qquad \begin{aligned} V_1(\delta_1, \delta_2) = & p_1 p_2 \left[\delta_2 \pi^t (1) + (1 - \delta_2) \pi^w \right] + p_1 (1 - p_2) \pi^w \\ & + (1 - p_1) p_2 \left[\delta_2 \pi^\ell (1) + (1 - \delta_2) \pi^0 \right] \\ & + (1 - p_1)(1 - p_2) \pi^0 - c(p_1) \end{aligned}$$

580

The incentive for *research coordination* in the stage 1 decision is determined by the sign of $\frac{\partial V_i}{\partial \delta_i}$. Using the envelope theorem we have:

$$(21) \qquad \frac{\partial V_1}{\partial \delta_1} = \delta_2 \left[p_1 \left(\pi_1^t (1) - \pi_1^w \right) + (1 - p_1) \left(\pi_1^\ell (1) - \pi_1^0 \right) \right] \frac{\partial p_2}{\partial \delta_1}.$$

Thus, because each firm's profits are independent of their own spillower parameter, the only effect of firm 1's increasing its spillower paramater can come from the effect that this can have in inducing firm 2 to change the amount of R&D it does – and this will only affect firm 1 if it receives a positive spillover from firm 2. The term in square brackets is unambiguously positive showing that, provided there is any spillover from firm 2, firm 1 gains if firm 2 does more R&D. Moreover an increase in disclosure by firm 1 will raise the competitive threat of firm 2 and so, given that R&D expenditures are strategic complements, this will lead to an increase in its equilibrium R&D level. That is, $\partial p_2 / \partial \delta_1 > 0$ and hence,

$$(22) \qquad \frac{\partial V_1}{\partial \delta_1} \gtreqqless 0 \quad \text{as} \quad \delta_2 \gtreqqless 0$$

Notice also that

$$(23) \qquad \frac{\partial V_1}{\partial \delta_2} = \delta_2 \left[p_1 \left(\pi_1^t (1) - \pi_1^w \right) + (1 - p_1) \left(\pi_1^\ell (1) - \pi_1^0 \right) \right] \frac{\partial p_2}{\partial \delta_2}$$
$$+ p_1 p_2 \left\{ \left[\pi^t (1) - \pi^w \right] + (1 - p_1) p_2 \left[\pi^\ell (1) - \pi^0 \right] \right\}$$

Thus an increase in firm 2's spillover has two effects on firm 1's profits. There is the direct effect – the term in curly brackets, which is positive – and there is the indirect effect brought about by the stimulus this gives to firm 2's R&D. As above this is positive if firm 2's spillover is positive. Hence

$$(24) \qquad \frac{\partial V_1}{\partial \delta_2} > 0$$

So we can see that there are two Nash equilibria – $(0, 0)$ and $(1, 1)$, though notice that if one firm's spillover is zero, the other firm is indifferent as to which spillover to choose, so there is no guarantee that it would choose also 0. Thus $(1, 1)$ is the only stable equilibrium, and, given (22) and (24) Pareto dominates $(0, 0)$. Thus the natural equilibrium to select here is $(1, 1)$ and so, as our intuition would suggest, firms would be independently willing to go for as much coordination as possible, that is, the non-cooperative equilibrium spillover parameters are both 1. Thus:

Result 8: When firms operate in distinct industries pursuing complementary research and the spillover takes the form of research design coordination then full coordination will be achieved without any cooperation.

4.4. The Complete Non-Cooperative Equilibrium

Knowing that the spillover parameters of both firms will be 1, we can now return to the R&D decision. Setting the spillover parameters means that the *competitive threats* and *profit incentives* of the two firms are identical, and so too is the equilibrium probability of success. If we substitute (18) into (3), then the equilibrium is characterised by

$$[\pi^t(1) - \pi^\ell(1)]\, p + [\pi^w - \pi^0]\,(1-p) = c'(p)$$

i.e.

(25) $[\pi^w - \pi^0] + [\pi^t(1) + \pi^0 - \pi^w - \pi^\ell(1)]\, p = c'(p)$

Given our assumptions (especially (15)) both the constant and the coefficient on p on the LHS of (25) are positive.

It is worth noting here that the non-cooperative equilibrium value of p determined by (25) is larger than that where the spillover comes from information sharing (a case we examine in the Appendix). In this latter case firms set $\delta = 0$. That is:

Result 9: The fact that under *research design coordination* firms choose to fully coordinate their R&D gives them a greater incentive to do R&D than in the *information sharing* case where firms do not share any information in the non-cooperative equilibrium.

4.5. The Cooperative Equilibrium

In the absence of any R&D subsidy, the two firms would choose p and δ to maximise expected joint profits, or alternatively (given symmetry), expected profit per firm. Formally then the problem is to

(26)
$$\text{MAX}\,\overline{V}(p, \delta) \equiv p^2\, \pi^t(\delta) + p\,(1-p)\,[\pi^w + \pi^\ell(\delta)] + (1-p)^2\, \pi^0 - c(p)$$

Since both $\pi^t(\delta)$ and $\pi^\ell(\delta)$ are non-decreasing in δ while the former is strictly increasing, it immediately follows that:

Result 10: The cooperative equilibrium value of $\delta = 1$. Thus cooperation achieves maximum research design coordination.

Choosing p to maximise expected profits gives

(27) $[(\pi^w - \pi^0) + (\pi^\ell(1) - \pi^0)] + 2\,p\,[\pi^t(1) + \pi^0 - \pi^\ell(1) - \pi^w] = c'(p)$

If we compare (27) with (25) then we see that the constant term on the LHS of (27) is at least as great as that on the LHS of (25), while, given the assumption expressed by (15), the coefficient on p in (25) and (27) is positive. Hence we have:

Result 11: The cooperative level of R&D spending is certainly greater than that in the non-cooperative equilibrium when firms are in distinct industries engage in complementary research and spillovers take the form of research design coordination.

582

4.6. The Social Optimum

The problem here is to choose p and δ to maximise total expected surplus in both industries, or, given symmetry, expected surplus per industry. Formally the problem is to choose p and δ to maximise

$$\overline{W}(p, \delta) \equiv p^2 S^t(\delta) + p(1-p)[S^w + S^\ell(\delta)] + (1-p)^2 S^0 - c(p).$$

Since both $S^t(\,.\,)$ and $S^\ell(\,.\,)$ are strictly increasing in δ it follows that:

Result 12: The social optimum will require $\delta = 1$, that is, full research design coordination. The optimum value of p will therefore satisfy

$$(28) \qquad [S^w + S^\ell(1) - 2S^0] + 2p[S^t(1) + S^0 - S^\ell(1) - S^w = c'(p)$$

Since the cooperative equilibrium and the social optimum involve maximising the total payoff to R&D from both firms it is not surprising that (28) and (27) are formally equivalent with profits just being replaced by social surplus. Although surplus always exceeds profits it is less clear how the surplus differences that appear in (28) compare with the profit differences that appear in (27). However we can prove that [9]:

Result 13: There will be a very wide range of cases consisting of perturbations around the linear case under which the optimum value of p exceeds that under cooperation and then the optimal subsidy is positive. Note however that the subsidy is not inducing firms to reveal more information than they would have done autonomously – it does not correct a distortion in the degree of spillover – but induces firms to undertake the right amount of R&D investment.

---

9. If we let $S^w + S^\ell(1) - 2S^0 \equiv k_1 \Psi$, where $\Psi \equiv \pi^w + \pi^\ell(1) - 2\pi^0$ and $S^t(1) - S^0 \equiv k_2 \Omega$, where $\Omega = \pi'(1) - \pi^0$ then (27) and (28) can be re-written as:

$$(27') \qquad\qquad\qquad \Psi + 2p[\Omega - \Psi] = c'(p)$$

and

$$(28') \qquad\qquad\qquad k_1 \Psi + 2p[k_2 \Omega - k_1 \Psi] = c'(p)$$

If $k_2 \geq k_1 > 1$ then the optimum value of p is unambiguously greater than the cooperative equilibrium. One case where this is definitely true is the following. If the two firms are monopolists in their individual industries, if the demand curves are linear, and marginal costs are constant, then we know that the deadweight loss from monopoly is half monopoly profits, so that $k_1 = k_2 = 1.5$. Indeed, in this case the optimal subsidy to R&D would be 33%.
To see this, notice that when $k_1 = k_2 = 1.5$ we can re-write (28') as $\Psi + 2p[\Omega - \Psi] = \frac{2}{3} c'(p)$. If we compare this with the formula in (27') for the R&D chosen in a cooperative equilibrium we see that this indeed determines the amount of R&D that would be chosen cooperatively if R&D was subsidised by 1/3.

5 Conclusions

We have shown that when we endogenise spillovers in models of R&D competition and cooperation, then it is essential to make a number of distinctions that are often ignored in the literature. In particular we need to distinguish between the amount of R&D that firms do and the amount of spillover they generate; between *information sharing* and *research coordination*; between each of the latter and cooperation; between *substitute* and *complementary* research paths; between firms being located in the same industry or in different industries.

These distinctions matter because, as we have shown, *coordination of the spillovers* can arise without *cooperation* (as in the case of different industries, complementary research, research design) while *cooperation* need not induce *information sharing* (as in same industry, substitute research, information sharing). In many cases, however, allowing cooperation is sufficient to induce full *information sharing/research coordination,* in which case the justification, if any, for the subsidy lies in encouraging firms to undertake more R&D. Indeed our analysis suggests that cooperative arrangements between firms may often produce too little R&D.

There is still much work that requires to be done on the issues raised in this paper. For example, we have considered cooperative arrangements whereby firms cooperate on both R&D and the spillovers. Yet the idea of information-sharing RJVs seems to be limited to cooperation on the spillovers alone. So we need to analyse how such partially cooperative arrangements might operate, and what the rationale might be for limiting firms to cooperation in this dimension alone.

● References

BEATH, J., KATSOULACOS, Y., ULPH, D. (1988). – "R&D Rivalry Versus R&D Cooperation Under Uncertainty", *Recherches Économiques de Louvain*, 54, pp. 373-384.

BEATH, J., KATSOULACOS, Y., ULPH, D. (1989). – "Strategic R&D Policy", *Economic Journal* (Supplement), 99, pp. 74-83.

BEATH, J., KATSOULACOS, Y., ULPH, D. (1991). – "Strategic Innovation", in M. BACHARACH, M. DEMPSTER and J. ENOS (Eds), *Mathematical Models of Economics*, (Oxford: Oxford University Press).

BEATH, J., KATSOULACOS, Y., ULPH, D. (1992). – "Game-Theoretic Approaches" in P. STONEMAN (Ed.), *Handbook of the Economics of Innovation and Technological Change* (Oxford; Basil Blackwell, forthcoming).

BEATH, J., ULPH, D. (1989). – "Cooperative and Non-cooperative R&D in Duopoly with Spillovers: A Comment", *Discussion Paper N° 89/235*, University of Bristol, Department of Economics, Bristol.

BULOW, J., GEANAKOPLOS, J., KLEMPERER, P. (1985). – "Multimarket Oligopoly: Strategic Substitutes and Complements", *Journal of Political Economy*, 93, pp. 488-511.

CRÉPON, B., DUGUET, E., ENCAOUA, D., MOHNEN, P. (1992). – "Cooperative, Non-cooperative R&D and Optimal patent lile", *INSEE Discussion Paper 9208*.

D'ASPREMONT, C., JACQUEMIN, A. (1988). – "Cooperative and Non-cooperative R&D in a Duopoly with Spillovers", *American Economic Review,* 78, pp. 1133-1137.

DE FRAJA, G. (1991). – "Strategic Spillovers in Patent Races", *mimeo* (University of Bristol).

JACQUEMIN, A. (1988). – "Cooperative Agreements in R&D and European Antitrust Policy", *European Economic Review*, 32, pp. 551-60.

JACQUEMIN, A., SOETE, L. (1994). – "Cooperation in R&D, Efficiency and European Policy", *mimeo*.

KATZ, M. (1986). – "An Analysis of Cooperative Research and Development", *RAND Journal of Economics*, 17 (Winter), pp. 527-43.

KATZ, M., ORDOVER, J. (1990). – "R&D Cooperation and Competition", *Brookings Papers, Microeconomics,* pp. 137-203.

KESTELLOOT, K., DE BONDT, R. (1993). – "Demand-Creating R&D in a Symmetric Oligopoly", *Economics of Innovation and New Technology*, Vol. 2, pp. 171-183.

MOTTA, M. (1992a). – "Cooperative R&D and Vertical Product Differentiation", *International Journal of Industrial Organization*, 10, pp. 643-61.

MOTTA, M. (1992b). – "National R&D Cooperation: a Special Type of Strategic Policy", *mimeo*, CORE, Louvain-la-Neuve.

SUZUMURA, K. (1992). – "Cooperative and Non-cooperative R&D in an Oligopoly with Spillovers", *American Economic Review*.

ULPH, D. (1990). – "Technology Policy in the Completed European Market", *Discussion Paper N° 90/264* (University of Bristol, Department of Economics).

Index of names

Abel, A. 422, 432
Acs, Z.J. 178, 186, 199, 202, 222
Adams, J.D. 103-107, 109, 130, 140, 189, 199, 383, 396
Adelman, M.A. 492-493
Aghion, P. 3, 26, 31, 34-35, 52, 56, 81, 84-85, 93, 98-99,103
Aitken, B. 502, 516
Akerlof, G. 502, 516
Albach, H. 400, 433
Aldridge, S. 480, 493
Allison, P. 144-145, 175
Anant, T.C.A. 81
Andrew, B. 516
Aoki, R. 215, 222
Archibugi, D. 180, 199
Arellano, M. 185, 196, 412, 415, 417-420, 432, 555, 564
Armstrong, J. 178, 193, 199
Arora, A. 6, 141, 145, 169, 175
Arrow, K.J. 1, 26, 57, 81, 268, 304
Arundel, A. 268, 304
Atkeson, A. 33, 52
Audretsch, D.B. 178, 186, 193, 199, 202, 222, 401, 432
Auerbach, A.J. 403, 432

Bagwell, K. 244, 266
Bailey, M. 368, 396
Baltagi, B.H. 134, 140
Baltensperger, E. 402, 432
Barlet, C. 2, 19, 435
Barro, R.J. 3, 26
Bean, C.R. 84, 103, 412-413, 432
Beath, J. 569, 573, 584
Bebchuk, L. 205, 222
Beck, R. 268, 304
Beise, M. 337
Bernstein, J.I. 23, 400, 432, 506, 509-510, 516, 519-520, 529, 535, 541, 560, 564
Besanko, D. 402, 432
Bessen, S. 360, 365
Bester, H. 402, 432, 458, 471
Bhagat, S. 202, 222
Bhattacharya, S. 404, 432
Blanchard, O. 422, 432
Blomstrom, M. 502, 516
Blundell, R.W. 289, 304, 384, 396, 420, 432, 516
Bond, S.R. 17-18, 26, 376-385,396, 411-415, 417-420, 422-423, 425, 428, 432, 555, 564
Bound, J. 317, 336, 374, 396
Bover, O. 420, 432
Brander, J. 458, 471
Branstetter, L. 21-22, 495, 521, 541, 560, 564

Bresnahan, T.F. 4, 26
Brickley, J.A. 202, 222
Bryson, M.C. 479, 491, 493
Bulow, J. 580, 584
Bussy, J.C. 238, 304

Caballero, R. 85-87, 516
Cameron, C. 13, 26, 319, 331-332, 336
Campbell, D. 368, 396
Capron, H. 23, 543
Carl, D. 358
Cerisier, F. 5, 83
Chang, H.F. 226-227,240
Chen, B. 508-509, 516
Cheng, L. 32, 52
Chernoff, H. 331, 336
Chiesa, G. 404, 432
Chirinko, R. 423, 433
Choi, J.P. 12, 26, 215, 222
Chou, C.F. 5, 26, 59, 81, 360, 365
Church, J. 360, 365
Cincera, M. 23, 543
Clemenz, G. 402, 433
Coe, D.T. 22, 26, 507-509, 514, 516, 521, 533, 541
Cohen, W.M. 2, 26, 199, 214, 222, 268, 273, 289, 304, 308, 314, 336, 374, 396, 408, 433, 445, 456, 497, 516
Coles, J.L. 202, 222
Comanor,W.S. 482, 493
Cooper, M. 548, 565
Cooter, R. 203, 222
Corneo, G. 465, 471
Costa-Cabral, C. 19, 457
Crampes, C. 12, 243, 269, 304
Crépon, B. 13, 26, 271-273, 279, 289, 303-304, 309, 318, 324-325, 336, 444, 456, 585
Cummings, C. 336, 396
Cunéo, P. 554, 564

D'Agostino, R.B. 479, 491, 493
D'Aspremont, C. 24, 26, 358, 576, 585
D'Autume, A. 85,103
Darby, M. 178, 193, 199
Dasgupta, P. 2, 26, 143, 175-176, 439, 456
David, P.A. 4, 8, 14, 27, 32-34, 52, 141-145, 154, 175
Davis, S.J. 6, 27
De Bondt, R. 569, 585
De Brock, L. 268, 304
De Fraja, G. 571, 585
De Vany, A. 492-493
Deneckere, R. 358, 465, 471
Denicolo 228, 238, 240
Denny, M. 535, 541

Index of subjects

absorptive capacities 168
academic research sector 145; science 143
accelerator model 399, 401, 411-417
acceptance in the marketplace 436
accounting information 270; practices 551
accounts 551
additive separability 430
adjudication 210
adjustment 523; costs 404-397, 413, 375; convex 370; processes 417
administrative centralization 178, 193-195, 198-199
adoption effects 360
advance of knowledge 178
advanced degrees 106, 108, 135, 137-139
adverse effect of stimulating entry 247; selection 402; - game 247
advertising expenditures 244
aggregate production level 364; publications 146, 164, 167-168, 173; research productivity 143, 167
aggregation 237; level 515, 522
agriculture 107, 126-134, 137-138
air transport technology 188
Airborne Instruments inc. 486
aircraft 245, 273-274
Amemiya's method 276
American Research and Development Corporation (ARDC) 486
amount of funding 152
analytical chemistry 187
angular separation 546
antihistamine 437
application costs 157, 161, 163; form 148
appropriability 284, 369, 393; conditions 283; hypothesis 544; mechanism 327; of knowledge conditions 547; - imperfect 545
appropriation 268; imperfect 547; strategy 267
aquaculture 187
Arellano-Bover estimator 420
Arguments against patenting 246; to promote patents 247
articulability of research outcomes 194-195, 197, 199
artificial intelligence 188, 194
Association of University Technology Managers 477
asymmetric information 202-197, 244-245, 248-249, 399, 402, 404, 421, 562
asymptotic least squares 267, 276, 280
asymptotically infinite moments 473, 481, 484
AT&T 341
auction 225, 227-229, 342; all-pay 225, 229; efficient 230; theory 228
audit 424

Austria 181
autocorrelation 372, 375, 382
autoregressive error term 384

backward induction 250, 580
balance sheet data 425
balanced growth path 91
bankruptcy 253
banks 400, 404, 423
bargaining Nash solution 206; power 98, 269; - relative 88; pre-trial 203, 222; process 86
basic genetic vectors 480; metals 271, 273-274, 373, 395; research 106, 109, 130, 133, 137-138; science 132; scientific knowledge 439
Bayh-Dole Act 477
BEA university deflator 108
Belgium 181
Bellman equation 372, 428
best response function 462-464
between group 133-134
Beveridge relation 92, 94
bibliometric indicators 180
bibliometry 514
bid 229
bidding behaviour 231; function 232
bio-instrumentation 141, 146, 160, 165
biochemistry 182-183
biology 107, 126, 128-134, 137-140, 514
biomedical 154; sciences 182, 184
biotechnology 141, 146, 193, 202, 208, 211, 219, 480
Biotechnology and Bio-instrumentation 141-142, 145-148, 154
Bonn database 401
borrower 400, 402; quality 402
borrowing constraint 429
Boskin 500-493
breadth requirement 253, 262
breakthrough 41; persistence in major 393; process 449, 453
Bryson graph 479, 485
budget allocation 156-157; asked 149, 155, 157, 161-163, 165; equations 159-160; granted 149, 155, 157, 161-163
building and engineering construction 535
Bundesanzeiger 407, 424
burden of proof reversals 221
Bureau of Economic Analysis (BEA) 108
Bush 500

call options 403
Canada 519-520, 522-523, 525, 528-535
canonical models 56-57
capital 379, 503-498, 535, 556, 558; accumulation 367, 371, 375, 393; cost 403; -

593

extrapolation 474, 535

fabricated metals 273-274
face-to-face collaboration 194; interaction 193
factor analysis 312; intensities 519-522, 525,
533; equilibrium – 530; prices 521; -
Laspeyres index 521
factorial coordinates 548
Federal Court filings 208
Federal Court of Appeals 218
Federal Judicial Center 208, 222
federal R&D 131-133
feedback mechanism 368, 383; positive 154
field of science 107-108, 145; boundaries 109;
effects 194
financial accounts data 416; institutions 404;
hierarchy 404; pecking order 403;
performance 407-408; statements 426
financing constraints 213, 399-394, 404-397,
413-414, 416, 420-423, 427, 429-430;
external 213; hierarchies 402; systems 423
Finland 181
firm characteristics 311, 314, 317, 327-328,
410; effects 411; size 307, 311, 317, 323, 325,
328, 405-398, 410, 435, 443; value 202, 211
first differences 384-385, 555-556, 559
first mover advantage 492
five-points scale 283, 312, 421
fixed costs 324; effects 131, 143, 377-378, 382-
384, 392, 394, 408, 504, 512, 554-555, 562;
correlated - 555
flexible functional form 522
follower 256
food and beverage 523, 525, 531, 533-534
Food and Drug Administration 481-482
foreign demand 308; direct investment 202,
220, 503, 520-521; investment 203; markets
273, 312; mother company 317
foundations 147
France 56-57, 145, 178-181, 245, 267, 272,
274, 309, 312, 318, 324-325, 435, 453
Frascati criteria 297; definitions 310, 425
Fraunhofer Institute 179
free-trade equilibrium price 463; level 457-459,
462, 465, 467-470
French Ministry of Industry Innovation Survey
435, 454; NAP classifcation 297, 300, 446;
survey on appropriation (EFAT) 267, 270-
271, 278, 281, 296-297;
full-term expiration 473-474, 490; cohort 475
functional form 443
fundamental stocks of knowledge 189
funding agency 144, 146, 153; decision 162;
level 155-156; institutional mechanisms 173

gains from innovation 449
game: Bertrand 465; Cournot-style 342;
investment and production 249; price setting
459, 465; sequential move – 459; structure

342; three-stage 465; two-stage 212, 245, 249,
457-458, 460, 575
GATT 209
GAUSS 385
General Purpose Technology (GPT) 32-34, 36-
45, 47-52
Generalized Method of Moments (GMM) 384,
412, 418, 420, 555-556, 559, 562
genetic engineering 145-147, 179
geographic 499, 544, 546, 548, 551, 560, 562;
centralization 194, 197-199; concentration
179, 193-195, 197; dummies 558;
organization 193
geography 498
geology 182, 184
German corporate law 408, 49
Germany 145, 178-181, 216, 218-219, 308,
311-312, 317-318, 329, 399, 401, 406-399,
413, 416, 421-424, 473; East- 317, 327, 329
goodness of fit 444
goods: compatible 339; identical 340; inherent
value 344
government requirements on testing 238;
research labs 312
graduate teaching 108, 126-127, 136, 139;
students 136-137, 139
graduation rates 191
grants 155
Greece 180-181
group effects 130
growth 220, 368; and trade 497; endogenous
497, 500; engines of – 498; of R&D input
108; of research output 108; rate 92, 98, 109; -
of number of existing journals 146; optimal
70; revenue 410

harmonized questionnaire 329
head start 492
health 178
heterogeneity 186, 190, 309, 323, 370, 374,
446, 562; unobserved 152, 154, 163, 173,
194, 315, 320-321, 411, 543
heteroskedasticity 320, 333
high tech angels 486; companies 207, 490;
fields 485; firms 512; goods 453, 456;
industries 405, 408; startups 487; venture
capital investments 475, 486
higher quality faculty 130
hiring constraints 161; delay 88, 94; process 86,
88; rule 101
historians of science 143
history of game 249
horticulture 188
hospital research labs 147
households 56 59
human capital 84, 404, 413; resources 173;
trials 482
hurdle model 307, 309, 319-321, 323, 325, 327-
328
hydrobiology 187

Harvard 477-480; invention bundle sample 484
Heckman-Mills procedure 159-160
Hecksher-Ohlin framework 496
Helpman-Trajtenberg model 34-35, 37, 39
Herfindahl index 300-293; inverse 195, 197; of
  industrial concentration 271, 281, 301; of
  market concentration 348-349
High Voltage Engineering Company 486
Honda 547, 550
Horsley Keogh Associates 488, 493

identification 160-161, 381, 385, 523; exclusion
  restrictions 161-162, 281; through functional
  form 161-162
imaging 188
imitation 45, 268, 273-274, 308, 310, 314, 368;
  blocking 475; competitive 475; cost 268, 282;
  lag 268, 282; non infringing 283; product 435,
  448, 449, 451, 455
impact factors 146, 148
impatience 65
imperfect competition 84, 99, 379; information
  243; matching 83-84, 86-87, 100
Impetus Consultants 180
implicit functions theorem 94, 102; subsidy to
  R&D investment 219
implicitly funded research 106
import 457; quantitative restraints 457; quota
  459; restrictions 497; substitution argument
  470
improvement 283; process 445, 449; product
  435, 445, 449, 451, 453, 455; therapeutic 437
Inada conditions 92
incentives 457; to innovate 268-269; to patent
  296
incomplete contracts 402
incumbent 243, 245-246, 249-254, 256-261,
  269, 347
individual effects 108; investigators 143
indivisibilities of research equipment 194
induction 475
industrial applications 269; chemicals and
  pharmaceuticals 389; development 178;
  innovation 106; output 534; organization 400,
  496; policy 56; solvents 502; transferability of
  research 147, 160-163, 167, 169
industry dummies 377, 425, 440, 445; effects
  281-282, 284, 289, 292, 503; manufacturing
  519, 523; productivity growth 189; structure
  227-228
inequality: output 348; price 348
inertia effect 437, 455
infant industry argument 458-459, 470-471
informal communication 155, 161
information accuracy 205; acquired 260, 568;
  advantage 244; cascade 40; disclosure 243;
  incomplete 260; private 244; quality 568;
  quantity 568; revelation 576-579; sharing 567,

569, 571, 582, 584; - coordination 569-570; -
  spillover 568, 573, 576, 578; - subsidy to 569;
  sources 325; technical 248
infrastructure 109, 155, 165-166; effect 166;
  legal 221
infringement 248, 253, 258, 260, 282, 292
initial public offering (IPO) 486, 490
innate research capabilities 171, 173
innovation activities 310, 329; content of
  exports 441; cost 268; - reducing 457-458;
  determinants 267; five types 439-441, 443-
  444, 447-449; flows 545; function 296;
  incremental 310, 324; intensity 450;
  knowledge-driven 437; market-driven 437;
  non-patentable 324; outputs 454; policy 405;
  process 269, 312, 319, 329, 369, 381, 435,
  437, 440, 448-449, 451; - opportunities 380;
  product 271, 312, 319, 369, 380-381, 435-
  437, 440, 448, 455; production function 289;
  profiles 448; profitable 392; rate 59, 85; ratio
  448; survey 329, 421; - postal 421
Innovation Survey in French manufacturing
  firms 438-439, 445
innovative content 435; effort 505;
  opportunities 388; potential 437, 439; strategy
  437
innovator 368, 574
input: intermediate 520, 523-524, 533, 535,
  545; intensity 519, 522-523; - output matrix
  501; price data 507
Institut für Angewandte Sozialforschung (infas)
  329
Institute for Scientific Information (ISI) 108-
  109, 127, 154, 337
institutions of scientific research 143
Instituto de Linguistica Teorica e
  Computational (ILTEC) 179
instrument development 163
instrumental variables 141, 144, 164, 384, 412,
  555; alternative sets 384; choice 415; in
  differences 385, 389; in growth rates 387; in
  levels 385, 387, 389; validity 412, 418
instruments 271, 273-274
insurance policy 202
intangible assets 400
Intel 209
intellectual property: protection 225-228, 237-
  238, 500; - optimal extent of coverage 226; -
  system 232, 237; rights (IPRs) 108, 208, 214,
  238, 314, 512; - enforcement 201-194, 221; -
  imperfection 230, 233; - incentives 220; -
  litigation 214-215, 219; - strength 220-221; -
  system 215
Intellectual Property Reserve Corporation 202
Inter-university Consortium for Political and
  Social Research 208
interaction term 512-513

Luxembourg 180

M-estimation 280-281
machinery 408; and equipment 536
macro level 220
maintenance fees 474
managers 401-394, 422, 429
Mannheim Innovation Panel 307, 311, 327,
  329, 424-426
manufacturers 190-191, 198
marginal costs of application 317; product of
  budget 164-165; knowledge capital 393;
  publications 168; research efforts 154;
  research inputs 146; utility 70; value of equity
  403; value of firm 403; worker 88
market capitalization 401; coverage 344-345,
  349-350; competition 339, 460, 462, 464;
  demand 437; domestic 438, 455; dominance
  357; failure associated with level of:
  information revelation 569, 578; - R&D
  investment 569, 578; foreign 455, 503; game
  462, 464; global 497; home 314; impetus 439;
  information 244; novelties 312; power 292,
  37, 3760; penetration processes 492;
  profitability 243, 245, 247, 249, 256; - index
  251; pull 435, 439, 446-448; risk 317; share
  271, 281, 283, 289, 292, 296, 300-293, 350,
  574; size 361, 492; structure 346, 359; value
  61-62, 69, 245; world 312
marketing 248, 282; effort 492
markup on marginal costs 56, 379, 381, 385
Marshallian quasi rents to R&D investment 482
matching function 87
materials 379, 395, 556; technology 182
Mathematica 349
Mathematical Reviews 109
mathematical sciences 126-127
mathematics 107, 109, 126, 128-134, 137-138,
  140, 187; applications 109
Matthew effect 144
maximum legal duration 245
maximum likelihood 276, 278, 280, 319, 435,
  444, 523
McFadden R-square 444
measurement 171; errors 139, 410, 503, 512-
  513, 555; problems 502, 505
mechanical engineering 182, 184
medicine 107, 126, 128-134, 137-138, 140, 182,
  184, 196
Merck 550
mergers and acquisitionsn 550
metal products 373, 389, 395; fabricated 523,
  528, 531, 533
methodology 196-197, 199
metrology 189
metropolitan area 165
Mezzogiorno 147, 161-162
micro foundations 505

microbiology 187
microelectronics 182, 185
Microsoft 341
mineral products 373
minimum distance 280
missing data 147
mixed strategy 259, 261, 464-465
mobility of research personnel 498
molecular biology 145-147
Monopolies and Mergers Commission (MMC)
  238, 241
monopolistic competition 85-86 90; varieties 63
monopoly 67, 75, 250, 251-254, 268; absolute
  226; constrained 465-466; copyright 226;
  local 460; power 98, 226, 292, 340, 348;
  temporary − 505; rent 357; rights 268;
  temporary 268; welfare losses 238
moral hazard 202
motor vehicles 273-274
motors and generators 245
move: endogeneity 465; sequence 464;
  simultaneous 465
moving average 412, 418
multi player research competition 227
multicolliinearity 557
multinationals 327, 550
multiple equilibria 100
multiproduct firm 550
multisectoral model 83, 85, 100

national labs 191; public organizations 180,
  191; R&D budgets 142, 191
National Science Board 106, 140, 200, 308
National Science Foundation 108, 142
natural sciences 127, 173
needless duplication 577
negotiations 269
net present value 371
network 339; benefits 343; externality 340-341,
  344, 346-349, 352-354, 357, 359-360;
  marginal − 347; goods 339, 352, 360; pure
  340, 344; industries 341, 357; size 361-362
new drug 238; economics of science 145;
  processes 193, 310, 545; product ratio (NPR)
  436, 438-443, 445, 448-449, 451; export -
  438, 441, 443, 449, 451, 455; total sales - 441,
  445, 451, 455; products 55, 310, 545
New York Stock Exchange 486
NIW 308, 337
non-contingent behavior 258; ergodic 154;
  parametric chi-square test of association 181,
  185; patenting strategy 268-269; profit
  research institutions 147
non electrical and allied products 523;
  machinery 271, 523, 528, 533
non metallic minerals 523, 531, 533; products
  273-274

pseudo distribution 279; maximum likelihood 276, 279-280
public domain 59, 62; funding 141-142, 173; organizations 192; research agencies 155; - centers 179, 191, 198-199; - institutions 161; resource allocation 142, 173; sector 106; - employment 191; service 133; support for scientific research 142
publications 132, 141, 144, 146, 148, 154, 167, 192, 195, 198; equation 159-160, 165; output 149, 154, 156-157 161; past 149, 164, 167, 171; production of 157
publicly traded firms 400, 510
pulp and paper 245
purchasing power parity 532
pure strategies 355

qualitative variables 454
quality 160-161, 171, 340, 345, 437, 458, 497; adjusted publications 141, 167; change 505; differences 340; enhancing product innovation 505; ladder 505; measure 148, 157; of university 131; product 380
quantity rationing equilibrium 402
quasi linear preferences 468

R&D accumulation 367, 379; activities 400, 404, 424, 500; - foreign 556; budgets 143; capital 369, 375, 377, 379-380, 393, 504, 506-499, 528, 535; - accumulation: public good aspect 520; - intensity 523; - stock 376, 392, 522, 528, 535, 547, 550; - foreign 522; competition 567, 584; - strategic 573; cooperation 273, 325, 567-568, 584; cost 255, 577; - minimizing level 466; - reducing 457, 462; decentralization 178-179; decisions: optimal 580; deflator 107-109; departments 317; effort 308, 327, 368, 383, 404; - innovative opportunities 382; relative - 381; elasticity 289; employees 424; expenditures 106, 108, 126-128, 140, 178, 202, 213, 221, 307-308, 316, 324, 327, 329, 404, 406, 408, 411-412, 414, 424-426, 454, 458-459, 470, 535, 549-551, 553, 562; - aggregate domestic 506-499; cooperative level - 582; extramural - 396; intramural - 396; - growth rate 376; residual - 255; strategic complements - 580-581; external 502, 513; firm's own department 312; foreign: monitoring 513; formal, informal 41, 382; inputs 271; - needless duplication 268; intensity 373-374, 377, 390, 408, 424, 519, 533, 552; - ranks 374-376; intensive firms 384; investment 178, 203, 367-371, 381-382, 393-394, 399, 408, 458, 467, 511; - cost 372; - empirical patterns 393; external - 504; - joint foreign cost effect per dollar 530; optimal - 369, 372; own - 504; undepreciated - 522; lab 577; levels: strategic complements 575; strategic substitutes 575; managers 245, 270, 421; optimal level 466;

organizations 180, 185-186; overinvestment 316; personnel 317, 408, 425; potency 385, 388; price 509, 535; productivity 65, 307, 315, 325; programs 194, 219, 317; - centralized 177; - organization 178, 193; projects 194; publicly funded - 177-178; rate of return 501; rivalry 309, 328; oligopolistic - 568; statistics 106, 317; stock 551; - foreign 509; strategic value 458, 466; subsidy 567, 578; success 512; tacitness 177-178, 193; timing pattern 386; to sales ratio 273; underinvestment 533-534
random effects 512-513
randomness in innovation process 392
rate: dismissal 99; innovation 85, 498; of return 393, 519; private 519, 529-530, 532; extra- due to spillovers 519, 531; - to knowledge capital 367, 370; - to R&D capital 532-533, 560; - social 519-520; - to R&D investment 369, 390-391, 393-394; - private 377, 392; social 529-530, 532-534
rationing behavior 404; rule 464;
reaction function 460; upward sloping 580
real business cycle 573
reasons to patent 281
Recombinant Capital 211
reduced form 136, 149, 162-164, 276, 280-281, 289, 413
reduction of variety 360
Refac Corporation 202
reference firm 379, 381
relative domestic production cost 459
Renault 547
renewal fee 243-245, 249, 252, 254-256, 260, 473
rentability condition 93; of R&D investments 62, 69
rental 395; rate 535; before tax - on R&D capital 536
representative agent 55, 91; consumer 251; household 60, 71
Republic of Science 173
reputation 141, 143-144, 154, 171, 173, 205, 210; capital 152-153
research activities 554; applied 133; arbitrage equation 38; budgets 144; collaborations 148; coordination 567, 584; costs 166; design 567, 568; - coordination 568-571, 578, 581-582; - maximum 582, 583; - spillover 578; effort 155, 157-158, 283; externalities 107, 128; grants 144; groups 141-143, 145, 147, 163; input 107; joint venture (RJV) 569; - information sharing 584; labs 145, 147, 498; output 106, 144, 155, 107, 126-128, 131, 137, 139; - intergenerational 135; path: complementary 567-568, 570-571, 574, 576, 578, 581-582; substitute 567-568, 573, 576, 578; planned 158; productivity 105, 141, 143; program 108, 129, 164, 227, 229; proposals 149; sector 100; spillovers 105; units 155

Research and Technological Development Database (RTD) 178-179, 189, 193-196, 199; Projects 194-195; Programs 194-195; number of projects 195, 198; program funding 195, 198; Publications 194-195; Results 194-195, 197

Researchers: evaluating 273; rewarding 273

reserve 225, 229

resource allocation 144, 164; optimal 167

response bias 329-330

retaliation 460

returns to: past performance 167, 169; scale 307, 521, 537; constant - 61, 87, 91, 94, 105, 107, 127, 139-140, 289, 385, 413, 416, 521; decreasing - 105, 107, 127-128, 131, 139-140, 289, 416; - increasing 127

reunification 407

reverse engineering 500

Ricardo 496

right-hand tail 475, 477, 480, 487

risk 169, 308, 437; hedging 474, 486; idiosyncratic 406; neutrality 232, 429; of imitation 245; pooling 475; product market 436

risky debt 403; projects 404

rival award 220

rivalry 446, 513

robotics 189

robustness 162, 302, 370, 392, 512, 528; to distributional assumptions 279

Romania 180

Roper Corp. v Systems Inc. 209

rounding errors 424

royalties 209, 229, 268, 473, 477, 479-480

rubber and plastics 273, 523, 525, 528, 531, 533-534

sales 281, 289, 292, 299, 312, 339-340, 344, 347, 372, 380 408, 414, 425, 435, 438, 549-551, 556; domestic 438; drug 482; foreign 438; total 448

sample split 414, 416, 420

SAS-IML 279

saving rate 52

scale effect 98

Schumpeter 51

Schumpeterian growth model 35, 99-92; hypotheses 308; process 83-85, 100

Science and Engineering Indicators 178

Science and Technology Agency of Japan 513, 518

Science Citation Index 108, 146, 148, 154

sciences 106

scientific base 437, 439; expertise 186; fields 177, 181, 185, 191-192, 199; infrastructure 325; institutions 312, 325; instrument industry 501; - prototypes 147; knowledge stock 545; papers 106-99, 514; sources 317

search 315; costs 503; model 503

secrecy 57, 62, 74-75, 214, 268, 314, 404, 408

sector: downstream 500-493; dummies 327, 448; high-tech 325, 327; low-tech 327; upstream 500-493

seemingly unrelated regressions (SUR) 135, 137

selection 145-146, 152, 157, 162, 271, 302, 386, 408, 426, 440; bias 141, 173, 222, 510; correction 159-160; criteria 156; effects 166; equation 161, 169; issues 515; probability 171

semiconductor 245; industry 500-493; physics 187

senior scientists 143

sequence of price choices 465

sequential game 243, 256

serial correlation 418; second order 420

service activities 132-133; companies 191, 198

settlement 203-198, 209

share of new products 435

shareholder 401-395; wealth 202

Shepard's lemma 507, 522

ships, aircraft and rail 273

signal 244, 256, 261, 269, 402; game 247

signalling 205, 246-248, 260; value 408

similarity coefficients 511

simulation 71-74, 203, 215-216, 218, 235, 474, 491, 493, 508

simultaneity 283, 327, 555

Single European Act 194

size distribution 473-474; effect 283, 289, 445, 448, 455; of inventive step 227

skewness 484, 490-492; in distribution of 408; budget asked 149; budget granted 149; elasticity of output w.r.t. budget 164, 167; firm size 440; individal research productivity 144; patent application numbers 310; patent value 216; profits from innovation 473-474; publications 145, 149, 169, 171, 173; R&D intensities 374, 391; rates of return 392; returns from high-tech investments 486; royalties 477

skill 196-197, 199; differentials 47; mismatch 100; premium 49; shortage 50; speed of acquisition 48; update 100

slack resources 403

Slovenia 180

small firms 213, 219, 308, 310, 317, 328, 401, 405, 414, 416, 420-422

social learning 34, 40, 43, 45-47; optimum 570-571, 577, 583; planner 70, 570; surplus 480, 570-571, 574, 577, 579-580, 583; welfare 55, 69, 226, 228, 232-233, 244, 251, 268, 364, 579; - function 232, 238, 251

sociologists 143, 145; of science 173

software 225, 238, 341, 360; industry 501

soil science 188

Solow residual 381, 504

340; patent protection 215-216, 308; patents 392
variance to mean ratio 320
variety model 59
venture capital 211, 485, 488; funds 486-487, 490
Venture Economics, Inc. 211, 486, 494
vertically differentiated goods 274
vintage 220
voluntary export restraints (VERs) 460, 470

wage inequality 47; setting 89-90, 94, 100-93
Wall Street Journal 202
Wang Laboratories 209
weaving 229
weighted data 329-330
weights: patent 521; output by citations 506; matrix 504; trade related 508
welfare 468-470; analysis 140, 269, 459; domestic 457, 459, 468, 470; total (TW) 468-469; loss 296
willingness to avoid trial 296; enforce patents 201, 221; patent 321; pay 343-344, 346, 361, 363
win rate 209-210
winner's relative return 228
winning type 230
within estimator 134, 556, 559; group 133-134; transformation 555
working papers 148
world-wide manufacturing firms 543-544
Worldscope/Disclosure partners 549
Worldscope database 549, 551

Yale survey 268-269
young faculty 130; talent 169

Zantac 492
Zentrum für Europäische Wirtschaftsforschung (ZEW) 337, 311, 329, 490
Zentrum Mikroelektronik Dresden 180
zoology 182, 185